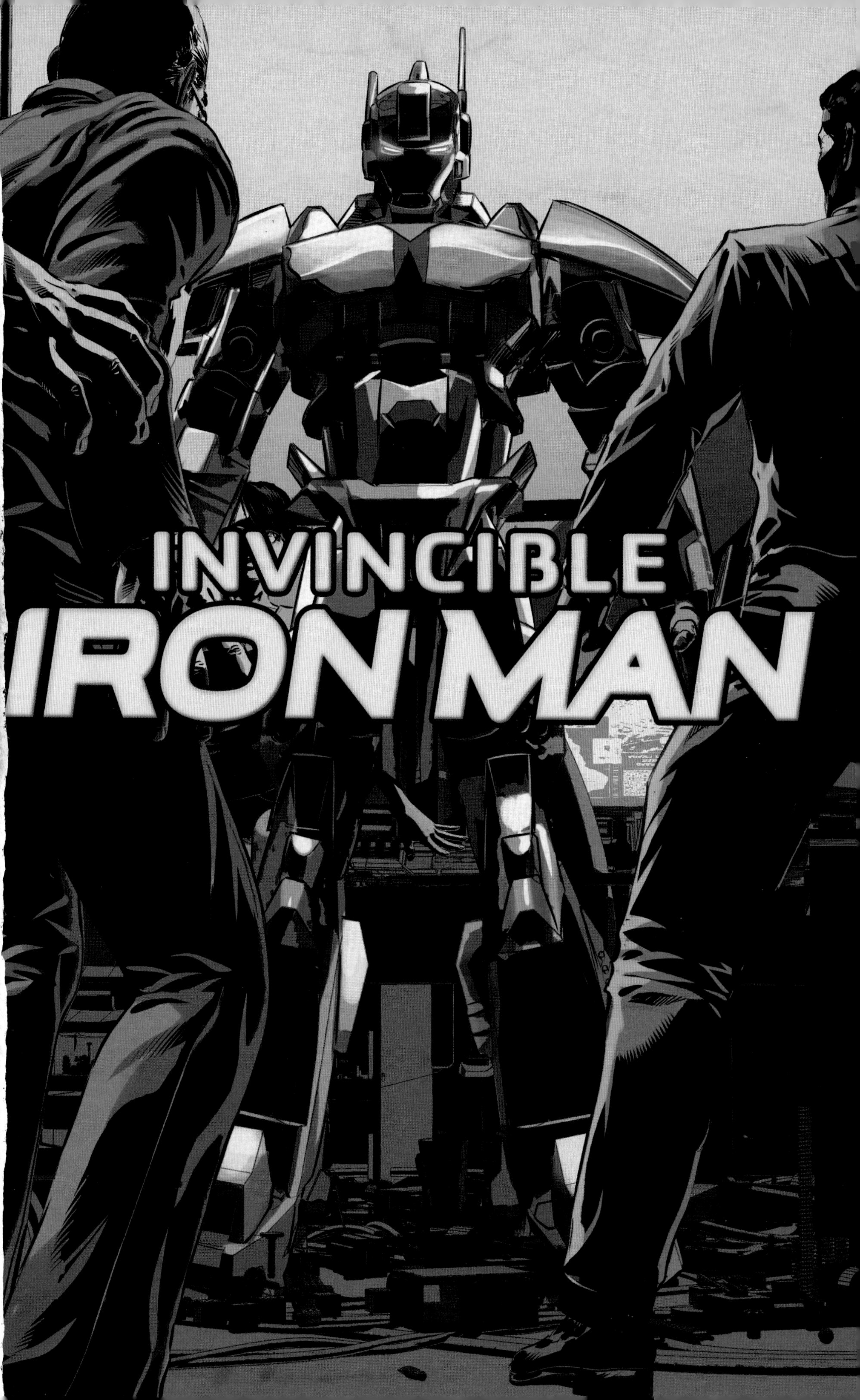
INVINCIBLE
IRON MAN

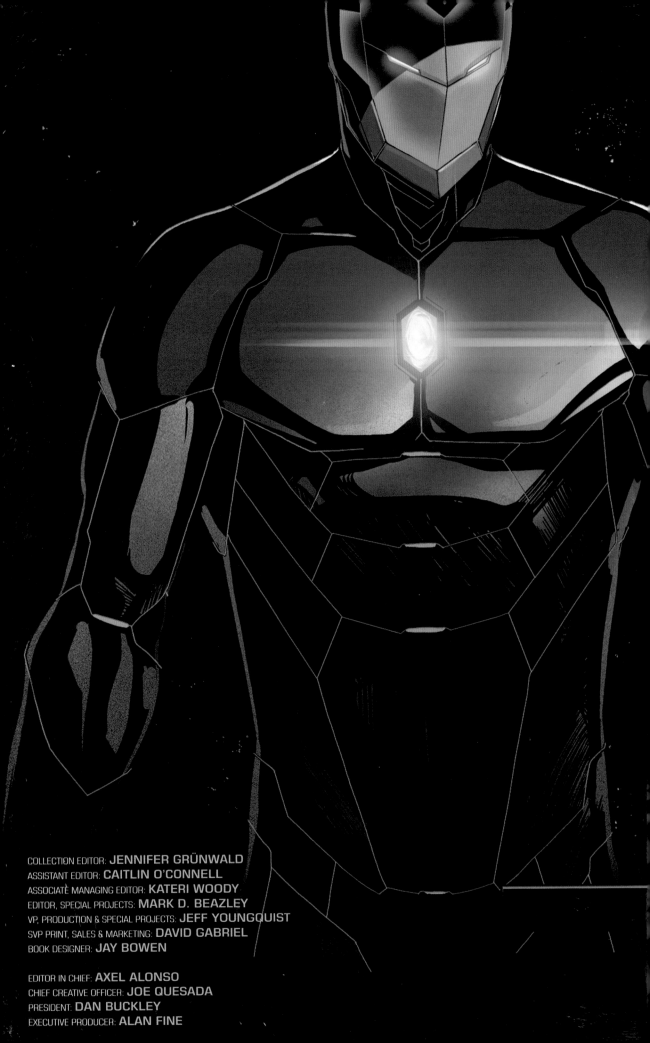

COLLECTION EDITOR: **JENNIFER GRÜNWALD**
ASSISTANT EDITOR: **CAITLIN O'CONNELL**
ASSOCIATE MANAGING EDITOR: **KATERI WOODY**
EDITOR, SPECIAL PROJECTS: **MARK D. BEAZLEY**
VP, PRODUCTION & SPECIAL PROJECTS: **JEFF YOUNGQUIST**
SVP PRINT, SALES & MARKETING: **DAVID GABRIEL**
BOOK DESIGNER: **JAY BOWEN**

EDITOR IN CHIEF: **AXEL ALONSO**
CHIEF CREATIVE OFFICER: **JOE QUESADA**
PRESIDENT: **DAN BUCKLEY**
EXECUTIVE PRODUCER: **ALAN FINE**

INVINCIBLE IRON MAN

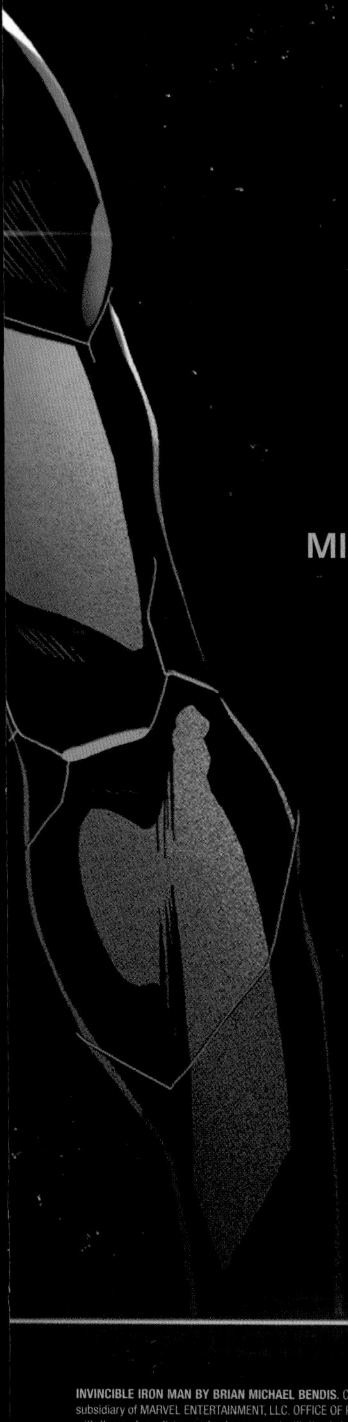

BRIAN MICHAEL BENDIS
WRITER

ISSUES #1-5

DAVID MARQUEZ
ARTIST

JUSTIN PONSOR
COLOR ARTIST

DAVID MARQUEZ & JUSTIN PONSOR
COVER ART

ISSUES #6-14

MIKE DEODATO JR.
ARTIST

FRANK MARTIN
COLOR ARTIST

MIKE DEODATO JR. & FRANK MARTIN (#6, #8-9, #12-13),
MIKE DEODATO JR. & DEAN WHITE (#7),
MIKE DEODATO JR. & RAIN BEREDO (#11),
KATE NIEMCZYK (#10)
AND DALE KEOWN & JASON KEITH (#14)
COVER ART

VC'S CLAYTON COWLES
LETTERER

ALANNA SMITH
ASSISTANT EDITOR

TOM BREVOORT
WITH KATIE KUBERT
EDITORS

IRON MAN CREATED BY STAN LEE,
LARRY LIEBER, DON HECK & JACK KIRBY

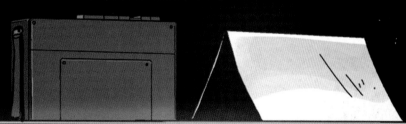

INVINCIBLE IRON MAN BY BRIAN MICHAEL BENDIS. Contains material originally published in magazine form as INVINCIBLE IRON MAN #1-14. First printing 2018. ISBN# 978-1-302-90448-7. Published by MARVEL WORLDWIDE, INC., a subsidiary of MARVEL ENTERTAINMENT, LLC. OFFICE OF PUBLICATION: 135 West 50th Street, New York, NY 10020. Copyright © 2018 MARVEL No similarity between any of the names, characters, persons, and/or institutions in this magazine with those of any living or dead person or institution is intended, and any such similarity which may exist is purely coincidental. Printed in China. DAN BUCKLEY, President, Marvel Entertainment; JOE QUESADA, Chief Creative Officer; TOM BREVOORT, SVP of Publishing; DAVID BOGART, SVP of Business Affairs & Operations, Publishing & Partnership; C.B. CEBULSKI, VP of Brand Management & Development, Asia; DAVID GABRIEL, SVP of Sales & Marketing, Publishing; JEFF YOUNGQUIST, VP of Production & Special Projects; DAN CARR, Executive Director of Publishing Technology; ALEX MORALES, Director of Publishing Operations; SUSAN CRESPI, Production Manager; STAN LEE, Chairman Emeritus. For information regarding advertising in Marvel Comics or on Marvel.com, please contact Vit DeBellis, Integrated Sales Manager, at vdebellis@marvel.com. For Marvel subscription inquiries, please call 888-511-5480. Manufactured between 10/6/2017 and 12/18/2017 by R.R. DONNELLEY ASIA PRINTING SOLUTIONS, CHINA.

10 9 8 7 6 5 4 3 2 1

#1

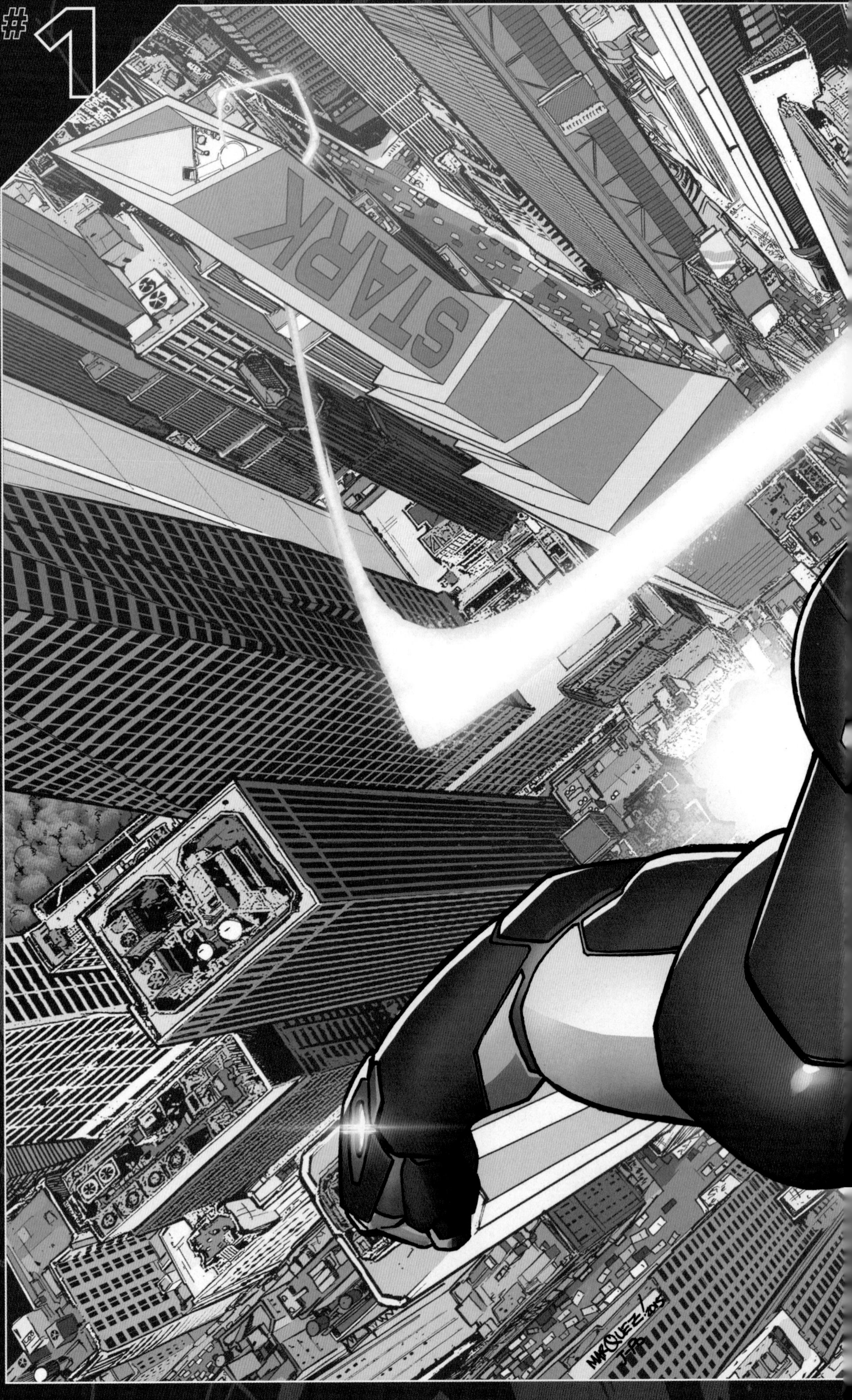
STARK

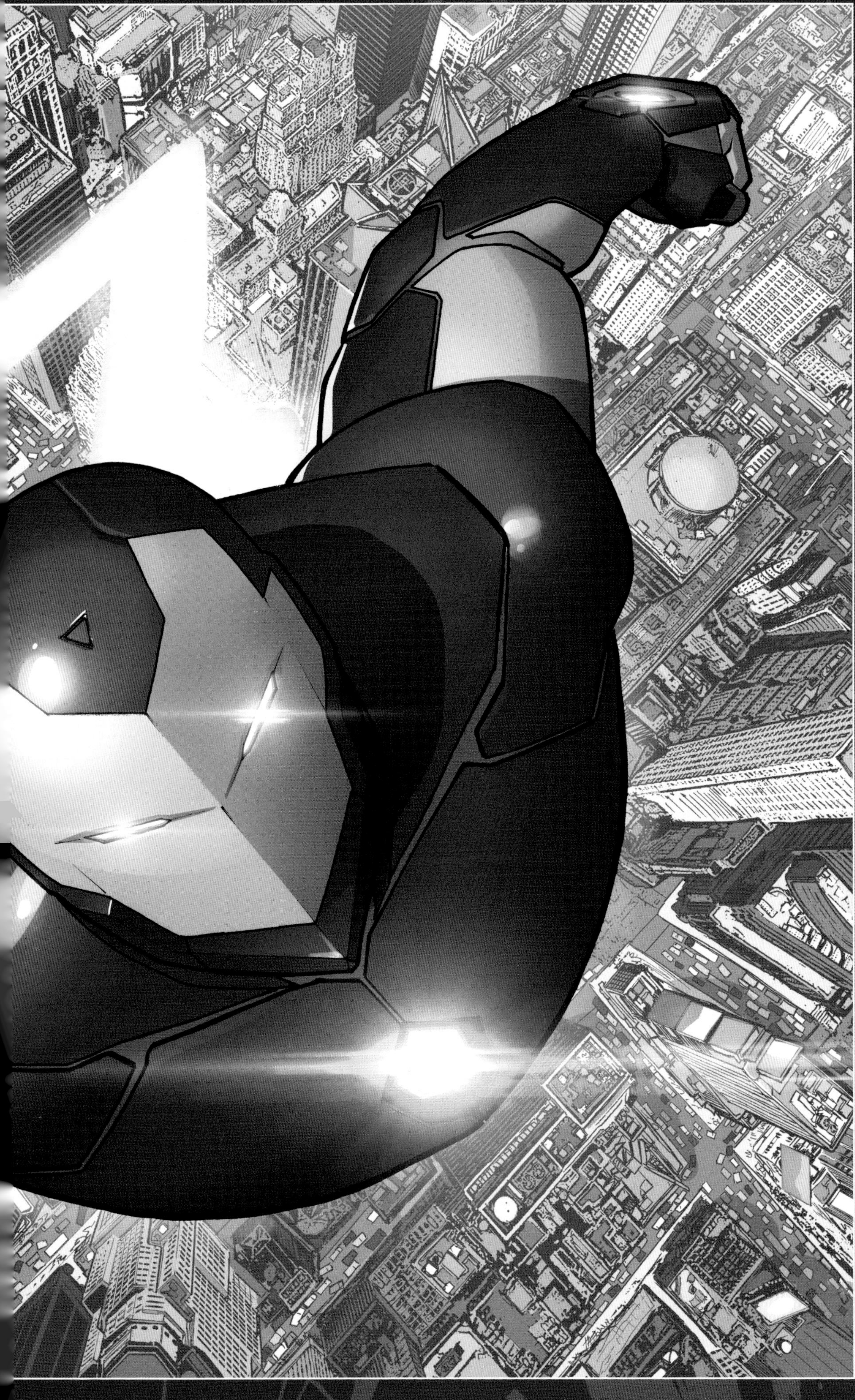

INVINCIBLE
IRON MAN

ANOTHER STARK INNOVATION

Billionaire playboy and genius industrialist Tony Stark was kidnapped during a routine weapons test. His captors attempted to force him to build a weapon of mass destruction. Instead he created a powered suit of armor that saved his life. From that day on, he used the suit to protect the world as the invincible Avenger IRON MAN.

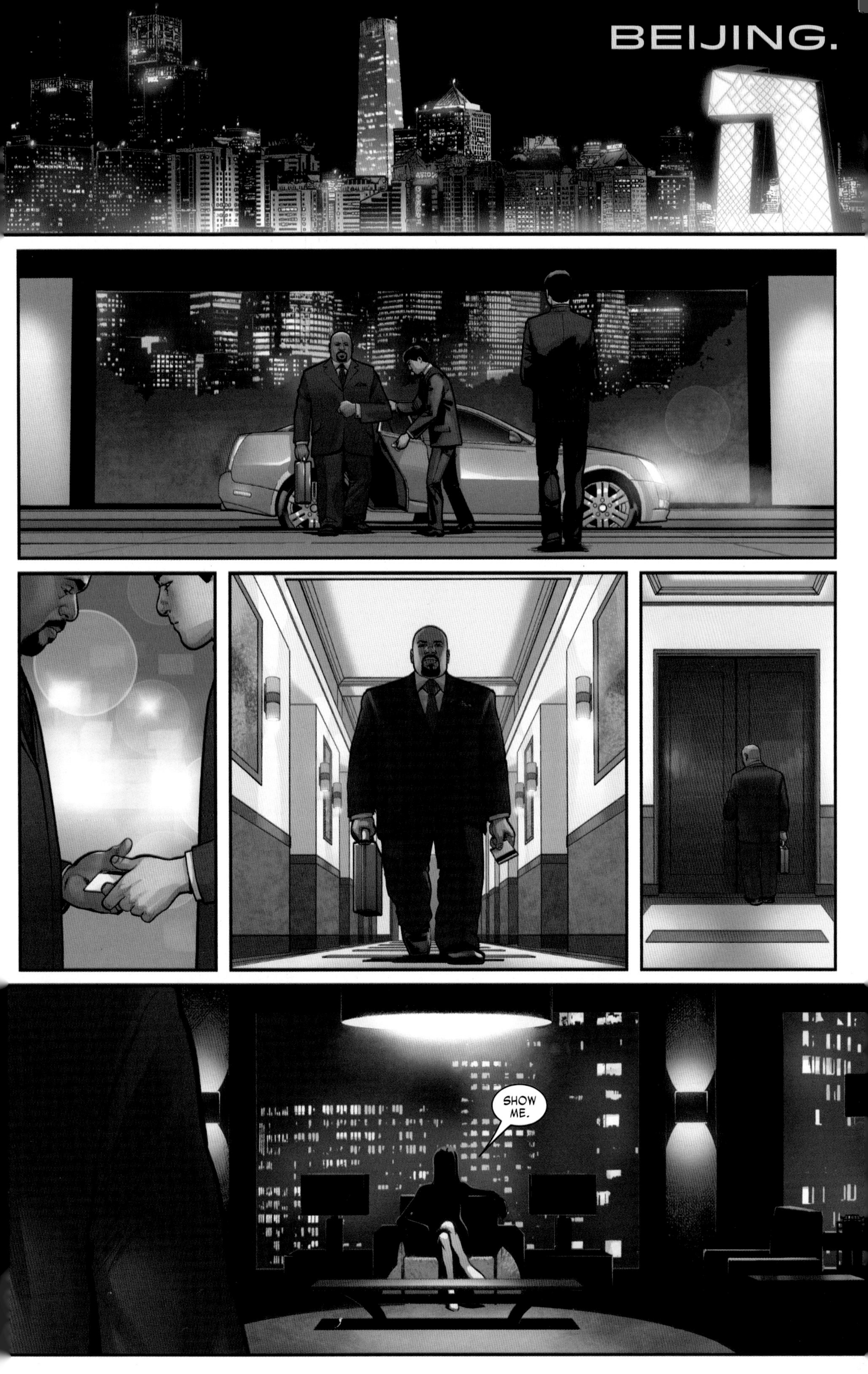
BEIJING.
SHOW ME.

HERE.

THAT'S IT?

ALL OF IT.

WHY DID YOU DO THIS?

WHY?

I WANT TO KNOW.

BECAUSE A.I.M. IS A BUNCH OF WACKADOOS AND I'VE WASTED HALF MY LIFE THERE.

AND I JUST WANT A BUYOUT BIG ENOUGH TO DISAPPEAR...

...IN STYLE.

I DESERVE THAT MUCH.

IS IT REAL?

OH, IT'S REAL.

BECAUSE IF IT'S NOT...

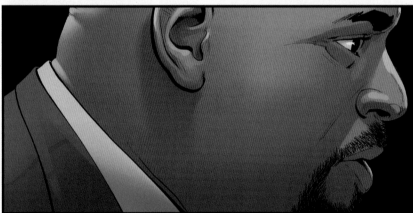

YOU'LL FIND ME AND KILL ME.

YES.

BELIEVE ME, I KNOW.

OPEN IT.

SEE FOR YOURSELF.

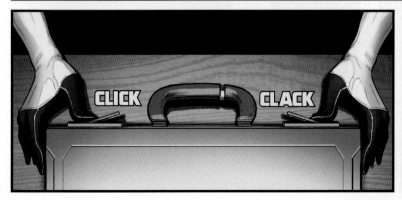

CLICK

CLACK

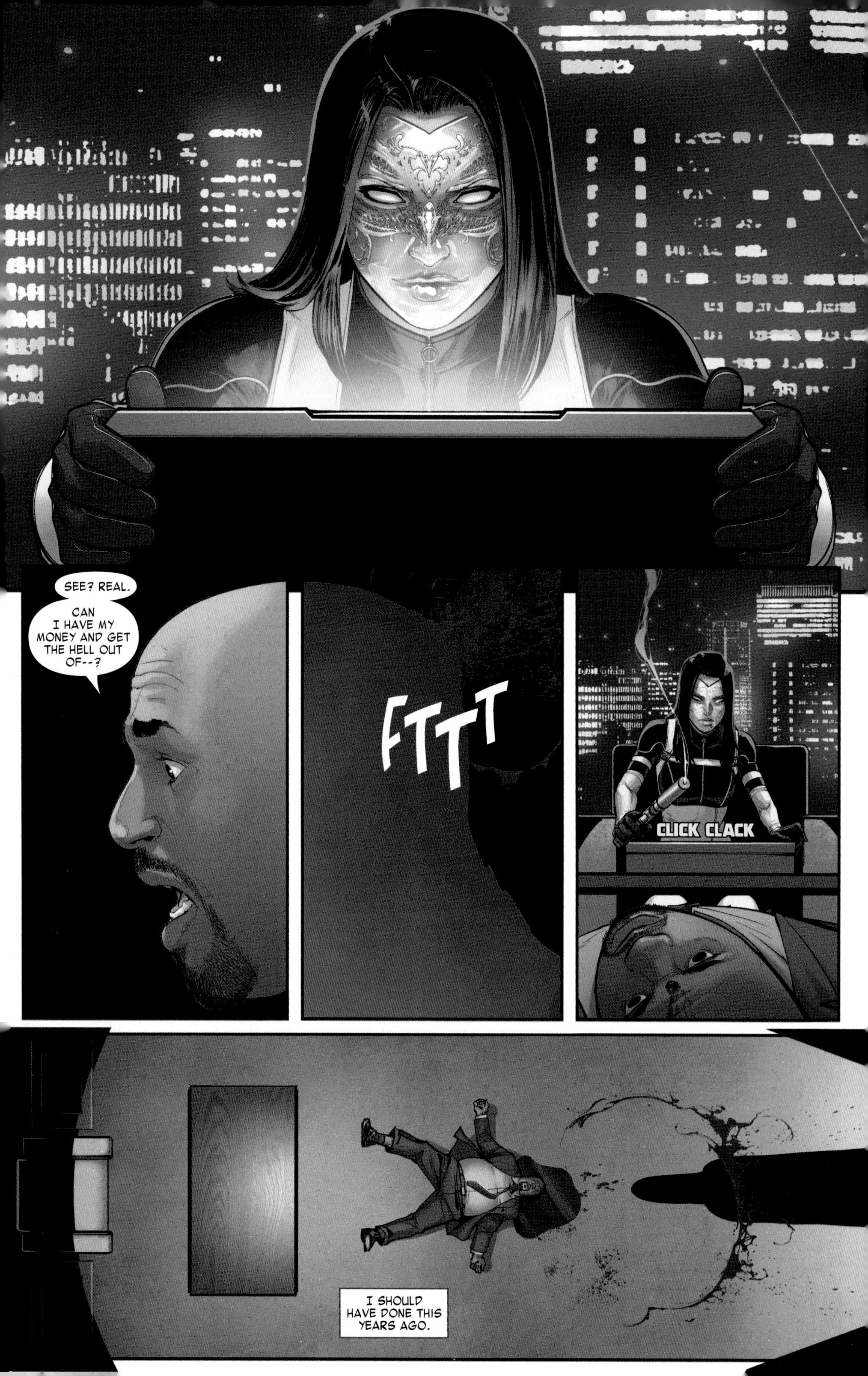
SEE? REAL.
CAN I HAVE MY MONEY AND GET THE HELL OUT OF--?
FTTT
CLICK CLACK
I SHOULD HAVE DONE THIS YEARS AGO.

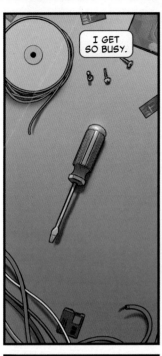

I GET SO BUSY.

SAVING THE WORLD.

AVENGING. GUARDING.

PUTTING OUT FIRES.

(METAPHORICAL AND REAL ACTUAL FIRES.)

REELING FROM THE FACT THAT MY PARENTS AREN'T REALLY MY PARENTS.

THEN COMPLETELY NOT DEALING WITH THE FACT THAT MY PARENTS AREN'T REALLY MY PARENTS ON ANY LEVEL.

SOME 15-YEAR-OLD AT M.I.T. REVERSE ENGINEERS IT ON A DARE AND POSTS IT ONLINE.

(DICK.)

I'M SUPPOSED TO BE SO AHEAD OF THE CURVE NO ONE ELSE CAN EVEN SEE THE CURVE.

BUT IT'S MY FAULT.

I PROMISED MYSELF I WOULD SPEND SOME SHOP TIME EVERY WEEK.

BUT I NEED THIS TIME FOR ME AND I NEED IT FOR HIM.

MY ARMOR NEEDS TO GROW AND EVOLVE. IT NEEDS TO SURPRISE EVERYONE AND AT THE SAME TIME BE THAT THING EVERYONE CAN COUNT ON.

IT'S ALL MY METAPHORS.

I'M OUT THERE-- GIVING THE PEOPLE WHAT THEY WANT.

TONY STARK
YESTERDAY'S FUTURE
Is the Iron Age over?

(OR WHAT THEY THINK THEY WANT...)

SAVING THE WORLD, PUNCHING THE BAD GUY... AND BEFORE I KNOW IT THIS ONCE-GROUNDBREAKING-PIECE-OF-TECH SUIT THAT DEFINES ME IS OLD HAT.

IT'S CLICHÉ.

I PROMISED.

FIRST OF ALL, I'M A BETTER PERSON TO BE AROUND WHEN I SPEND A LITTLE TIME IN MY CHURCH.

THIS IS MY MEDITATION.

THIS IS ALONE TIME WITH MY FAVORITE PERSON. ME.

(IF ONLY THAT WERE TRUE.)

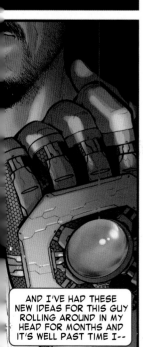

AND I'VE HAD THESE NEW IDEAS FOR THIS GUY ROLLING AROUND IN MY HEAD FOR MONTHS AND IT'S WELL PAST TIME I--

OH...

I--I THINK I DID IT.

THIS--THIS WILL WORK, WON'T IT?

DAMN.

I WOULD TOTALLY KISS ME RIGHT NOW IF NOT FOR MY FEAR OF BEARD BURN.

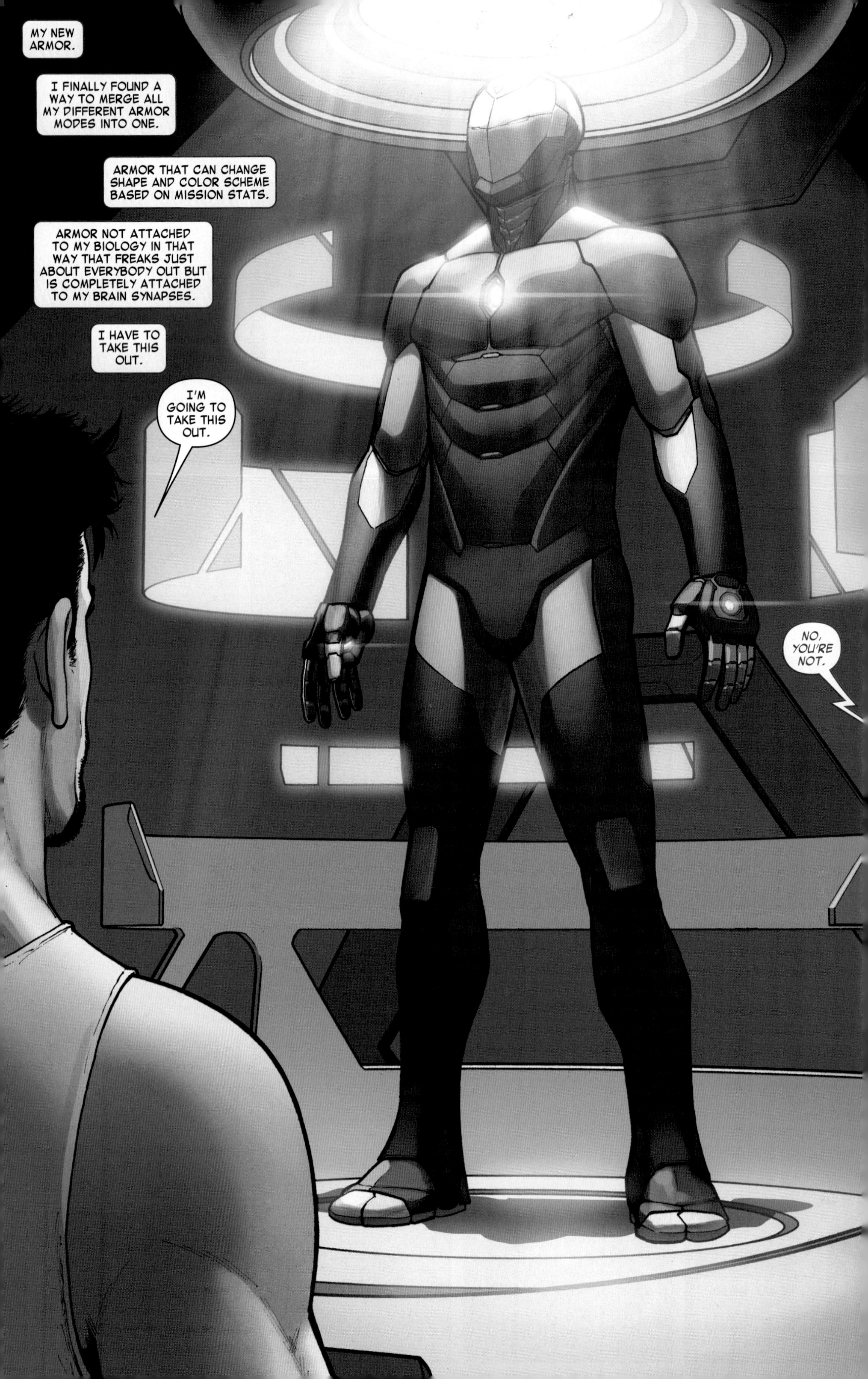
MY NEW ARMOR.
I FINALLY FOUND A WAY TO MERGE ALL MY DIFFERENT ARMOR MODES INTO ONE.
ARMOR THAT CAN CHANGE SHAPE AND COLOR SCHEME BASED ON MISSION STATS.
ARMOR NOT ATTACHED TO MY BIOLOGY IN THAT WAY THAT FREAKS JUST ABOUT EVERYBODY OUT BUT IS COMPLETELY ATTACHED TO MY BRAIN SYNAPSES.
I HAVE TO TAKE THIS OUT.
I'M GOING TO TAKE THIS OUT.
NO, YOU'RE NOT.

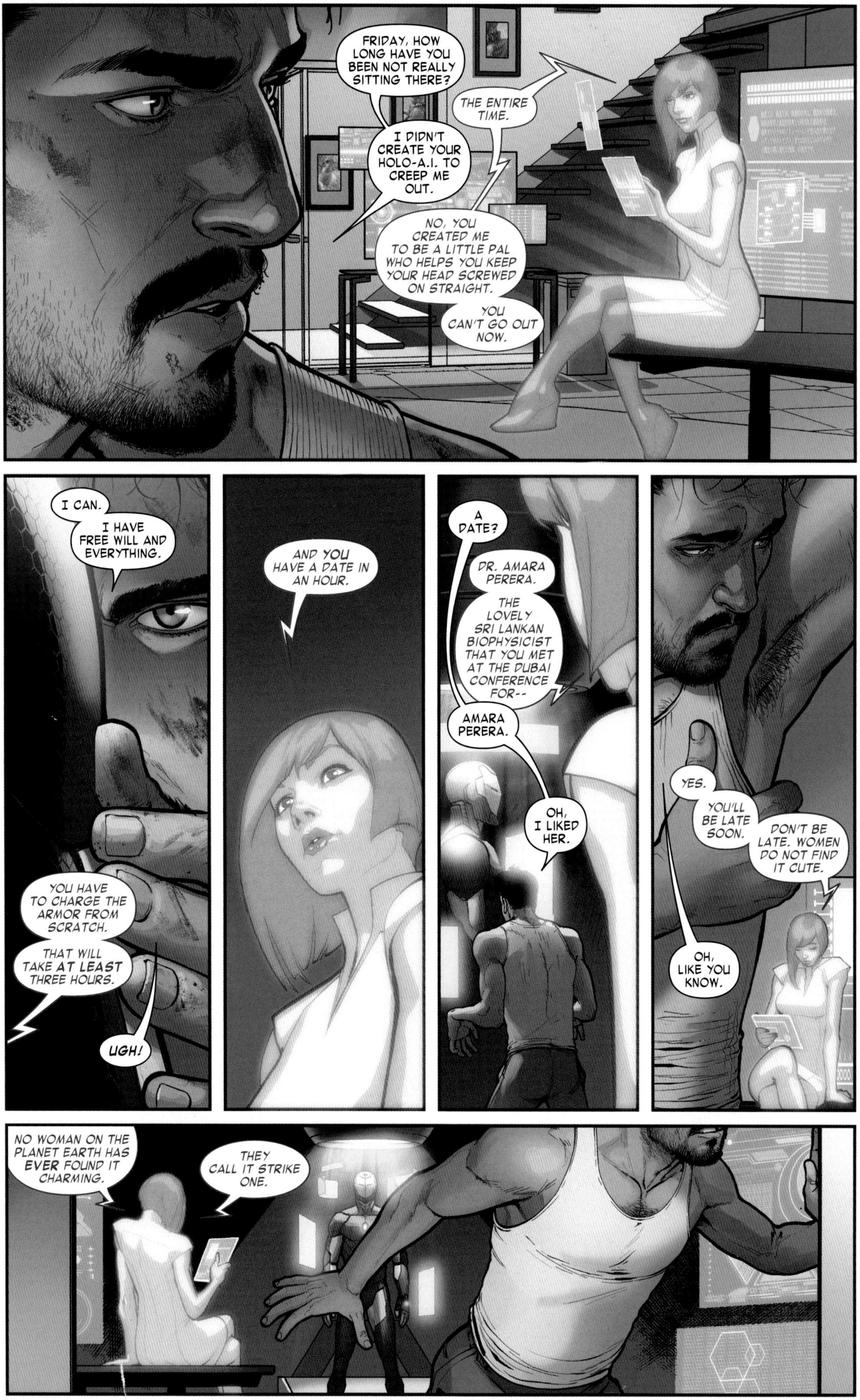

FRIDAY, HOW LONG HAVE YOU BEEN NOT REALLY SITTING THERE?
THE ENTIRE TIME.
I DIDN'T CREATE YOUR HOLO-A.I. TO CREEP ME OUT.
NO, YOU CREATED ME TO BE A LITTLE PAL WHO HELPS YOU KEEP YOUR HEAD SCREWED ON STRAIGHT.
YOU CAN'T GO OUT NOW.
I CAN.
I HAVE FREE WILL AND EVERYTHING.
YOU HAVE TO CHARGE THE ARMOR FROM SCRATCH.
THAT WILL TAKE AT LEAST THREE HOURS.
UGH!
AND YOU HAVE A DATE IN AN HOUR.
A DATE?
DR. AMARA PERERA.
THE LOVELY SRI LANKAN BIOPHYSICIST THAT YOU MET AT THE DUBAI CONFERENCE FOR--
AMARA PERERA.
OH, I LIKED HER.
YES.
YOU'LL BE LATE SOON.
DON'T BE LATE. WOMEN DO NOT FIND IT CUTE.
OH, LIKE YOU KNOW.
NO WOMAN ON THE PLANET EARTH HAS EVER FOUND IT CHARMING.
THEY CALL IT STRIKE ONE.

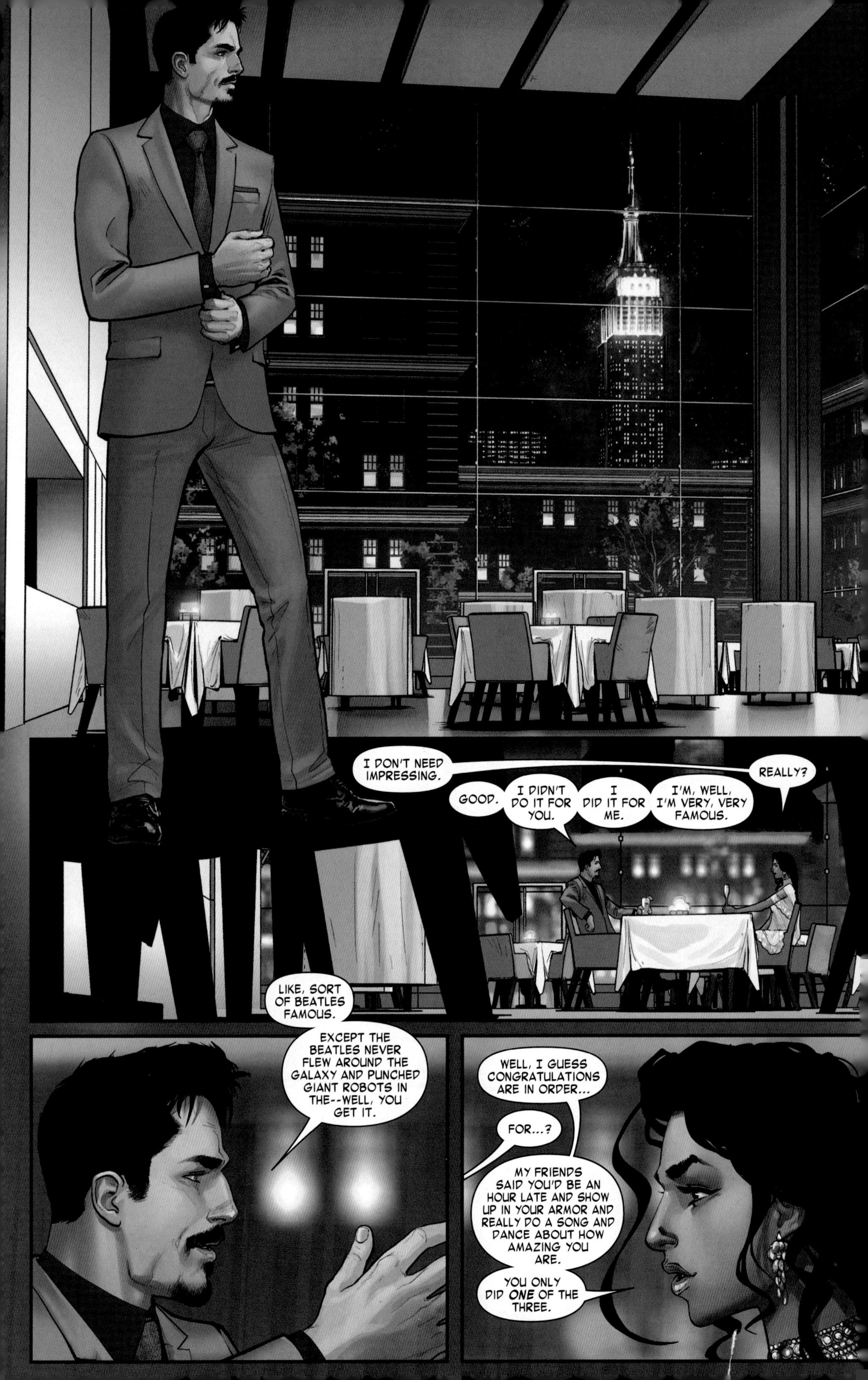
I DON'T NEED IMPRESSING.
GOOD.
I DIDN'T DO IT FOR YOU.
I DID IT FOR ME.
I'M, WELL, I'M VERY, VERY FAMOUS.
REALLY?
LIKE, SORT OF BEATLES FAMOUS.
EXCEPT THE BEATLES NEVER FLEW AROUND THE GALAXY AND PUNCHED GIANT ROBOTS IN THE--WELL, YOU GET IT.
WELL, I GUESS CONGRATULATIONS ARE IN ORDER...
FOR...?
MY FRIENDS SAID YOU'D BE AN HOUR LATE AND SHOW UP IN YOUR ARMOR AND REALLY DO A SONG AND DANCE ABOUT HOW AMAZING YOU ARE.
YOU ONLY DID ONE OF THE THREE.

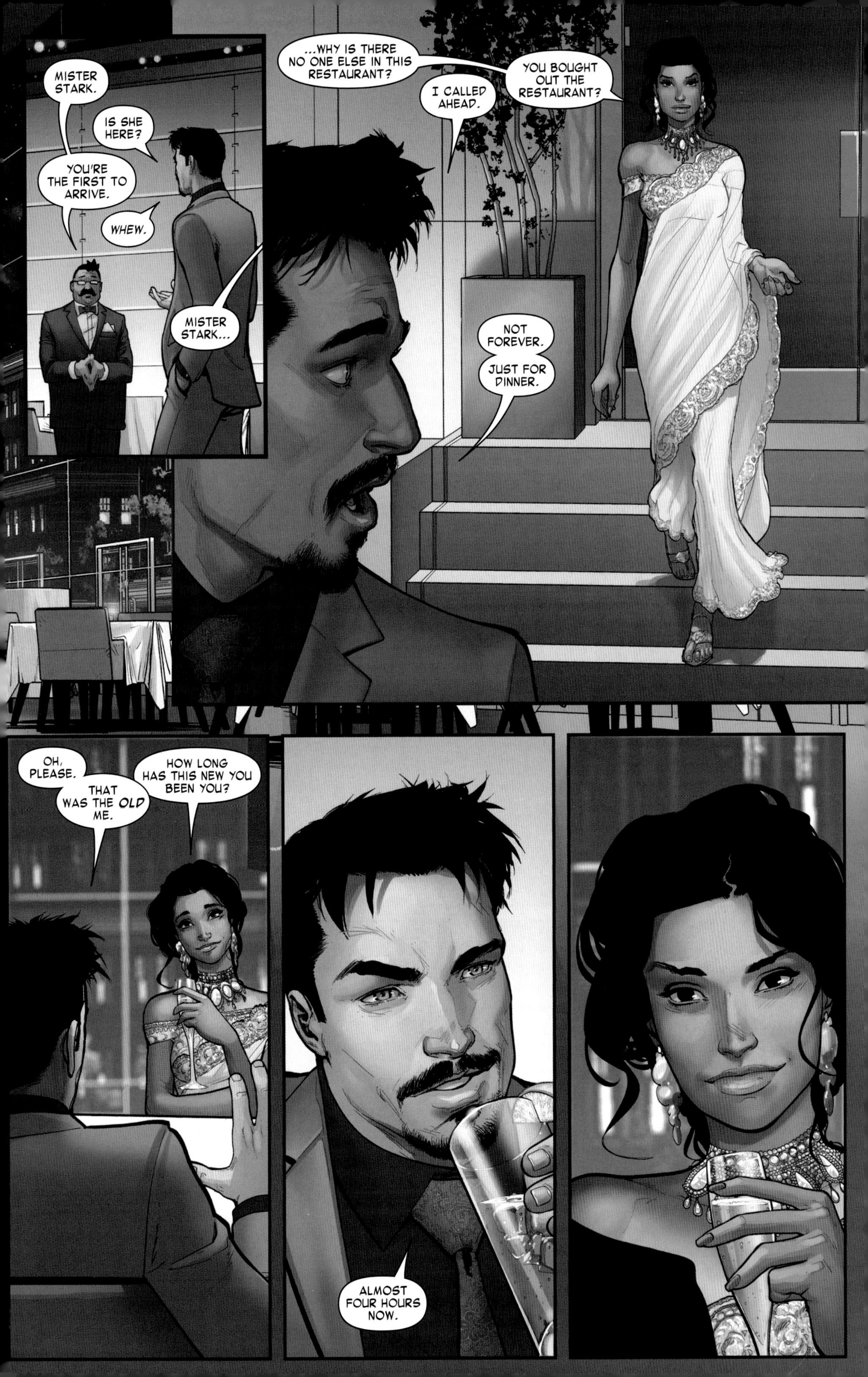

MISTER STARK.
IS SHE HERE?
YOU'RE THE FIRST TO ARRIVE.
WHEW.
MISTER STARK...
...WHY IS THERE NO ONE ELSE IN THIS RESTAURANT?
YOU BOUGHT OUT THE RESTAURANT?
I CALLED AHEAD.
NOT FOREVER.
JUST FOR DINNER.
OH, PLEASE.
THAT WAS THE *OLD* ME.
HOW LONG HAS THIS NEW YOU BEEN YOU?
ALMOST FOUR HOURS NOW.

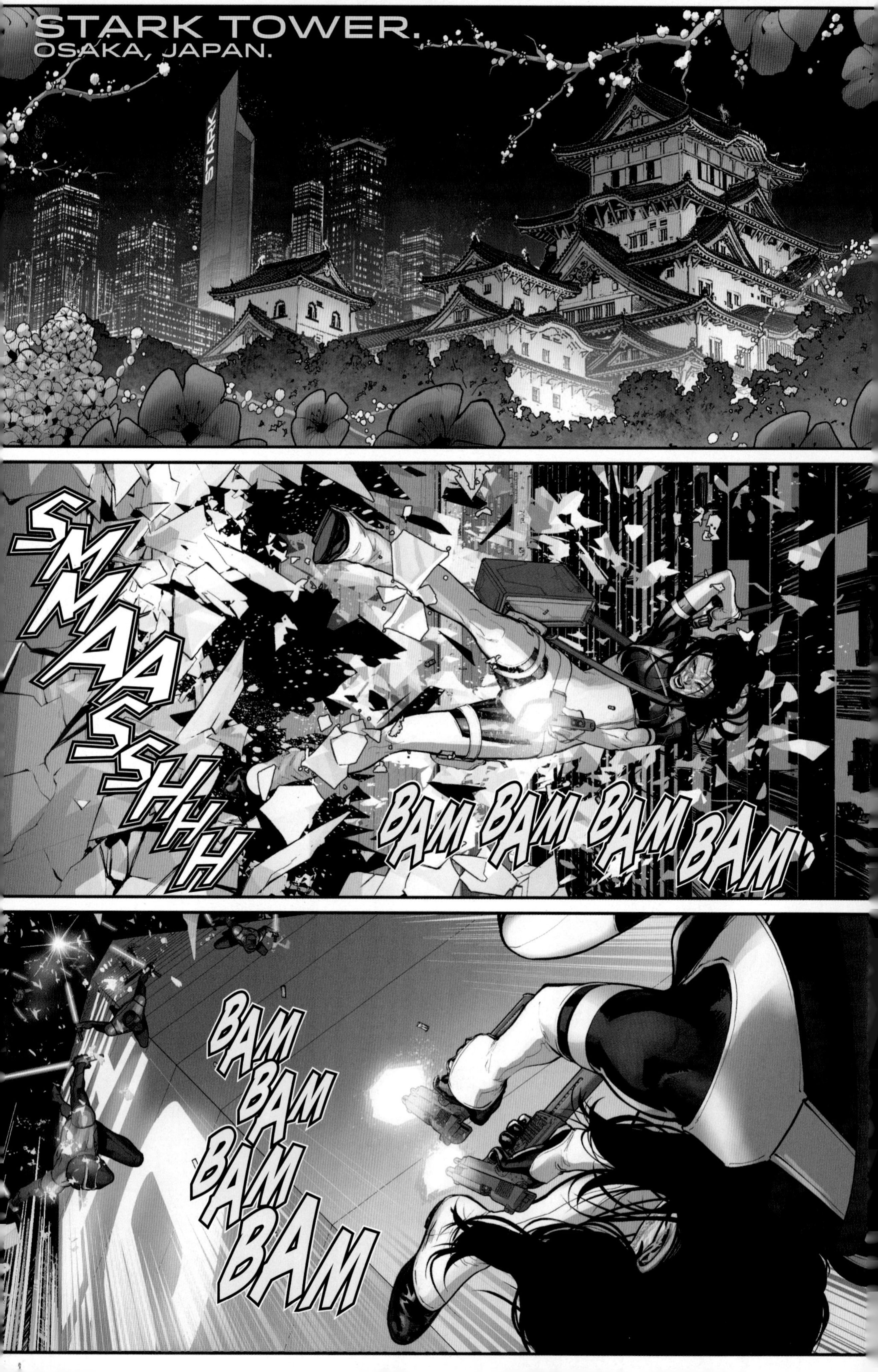
STARK TOWER.
OSAKA, JAPAN.
STARK
SMMAASSHHH
BAM BAM BAM BAM
BAM BAM BAM BAM

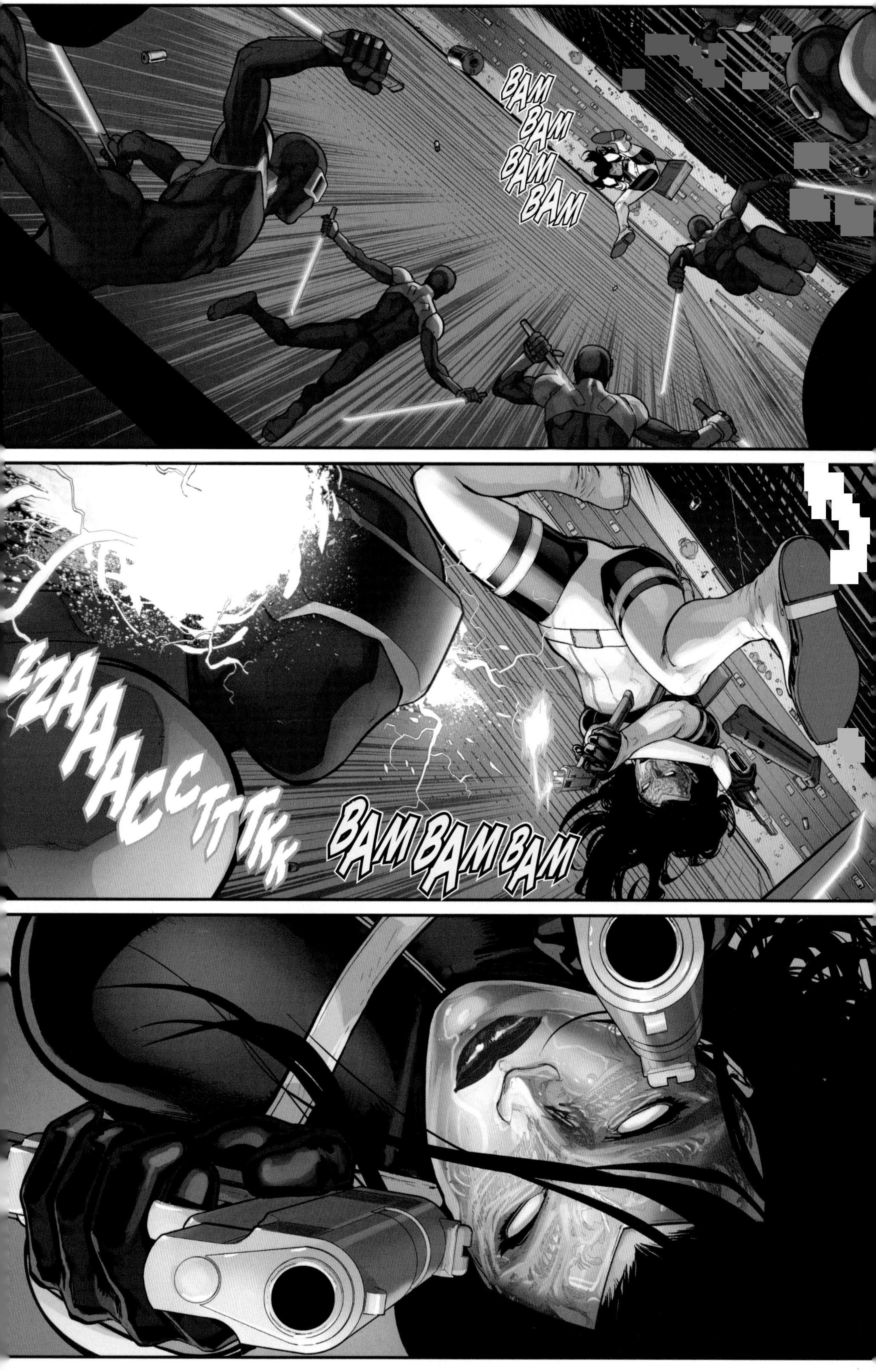
BAM BAM BAM BAM
ZZAAACCTTTKK
BAM BAM BAM

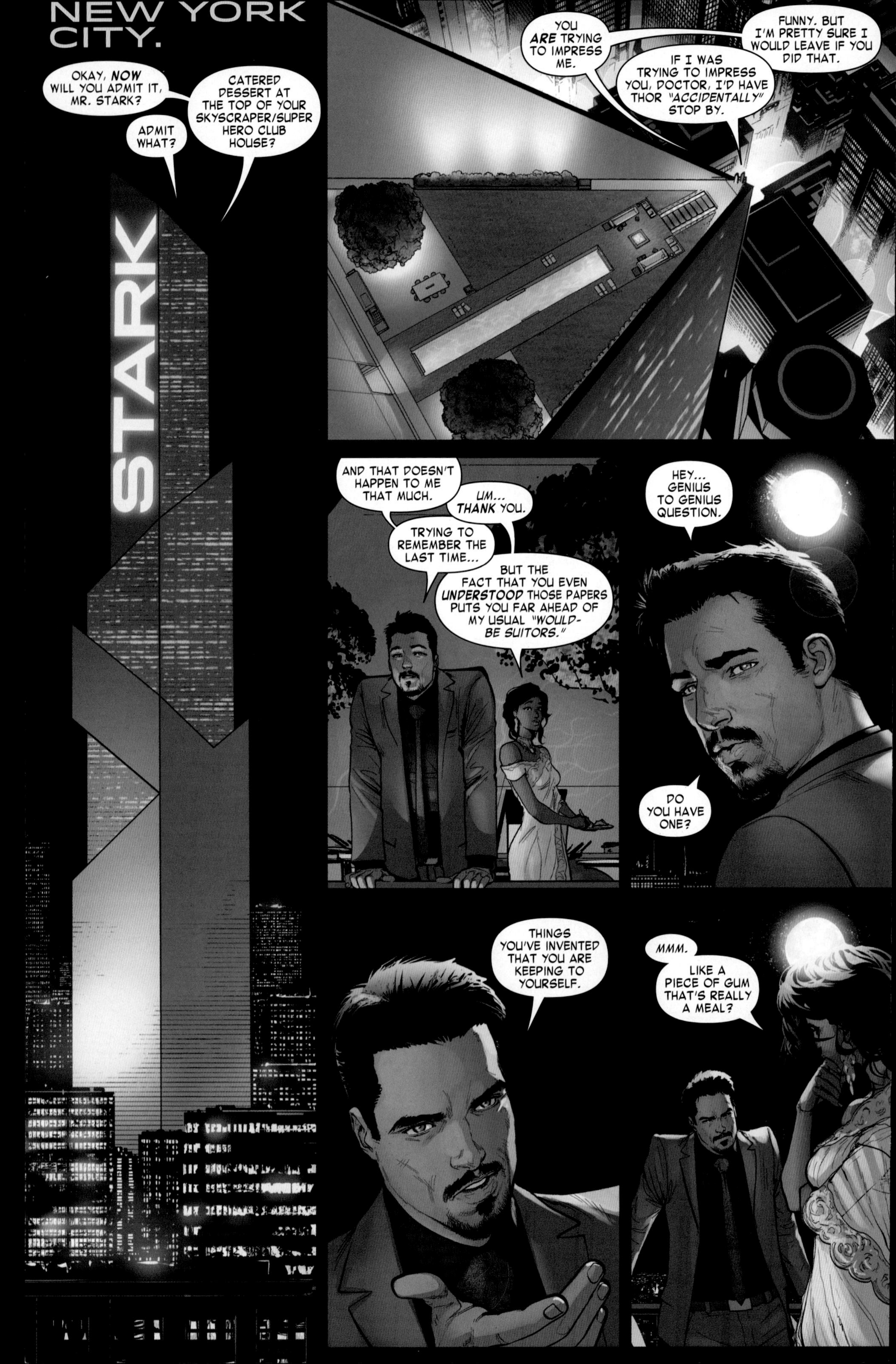
NEW YORK CITY.
OKAY, NOW WILL YOU ADMIT IT, MR. STARK?
ADMIT WHAT?
CATERED DESSERT AT THE TOP OF YOUR SKYSCRAPER/SUPER HERO CLUB HOUSE?
STARK
YOU ARE TRYING TO IMPRESS ME.
IF I WAS TRYING TO IMPRESS YOU, DOCTOR, I'D HAVE THOR "ACCIDENTALLY" STOP BY.
FUNNY. BUT I'M PRETTY SURE I WOULD LEAVE IF YOU DID THAT.
AND THAT DOESN'T HAPPEN TO ME THAT MUCH.
UM... THANK YOU.
TRYING TO REMEMBER THE LAST TIME...
BUT THE FACT THAT YOU EVEN UNDERSTOOD THOSE PAPERS PUTS YOU FAR AHEAD OF MY USUAL "WOULD-BE SUITORS."
HEY... GENIUS TO GENIUS QUESTION.
DO YOU HAVE ONE?
THINGS YOU'VE INVENTED THAT YOU ARE KEEPING TO YOURSELF.
MMM.
LIKE A PIECE OF GUM THAT'S REALLY A MEAL?

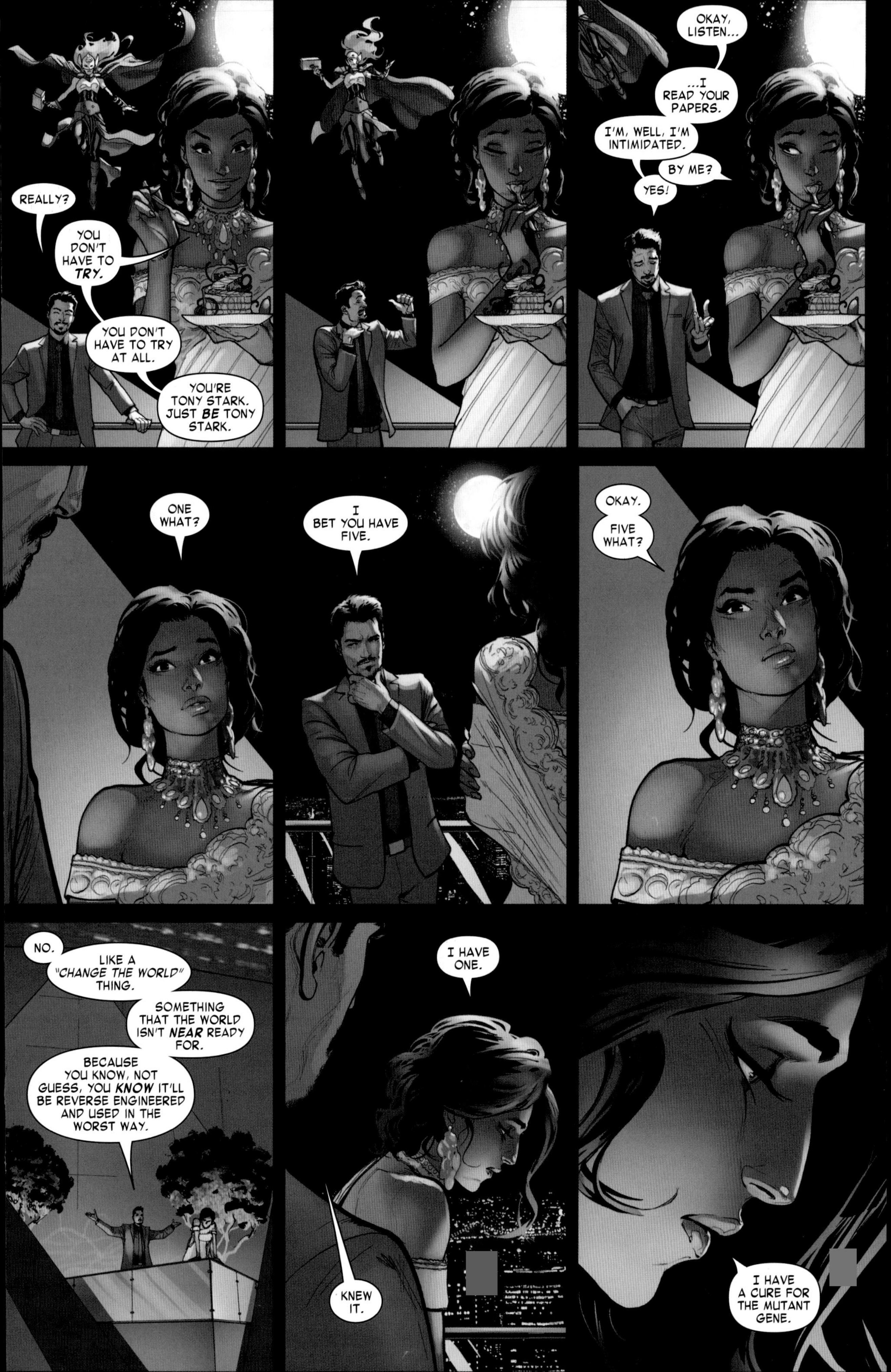
REALLY?
YOU DON'T HAVE TO TRY.
YOU DON'T HAVE TO TRY AT ALL.
YOU'RE TONY STARK. JUST BE TONY STARK.
OKAY, LISTEN...
...I READ YOUR PAPERS.
I'M, WELL, I'M INTIMIDATED.
BY ME?
YES!
ONE WHAT?
I BET YOU HAVE FIVE.
OKAY.
FIVE WHAT?
NO.
LIKE A "CHANGE THE WORLD" THING.
SOMETHING THAT THE WORLD ISN'T NEAR READY FOR.
BECAUSE YOU KNOW, NOT GUESS, YOU KNOW IT'LL BE REVERSE ENGINEERED AND USED IN THE WORST WAY.
I HAVE ONE.
KNEW IT.
I HAVE A CURE FOR THE MUTANT GENE.

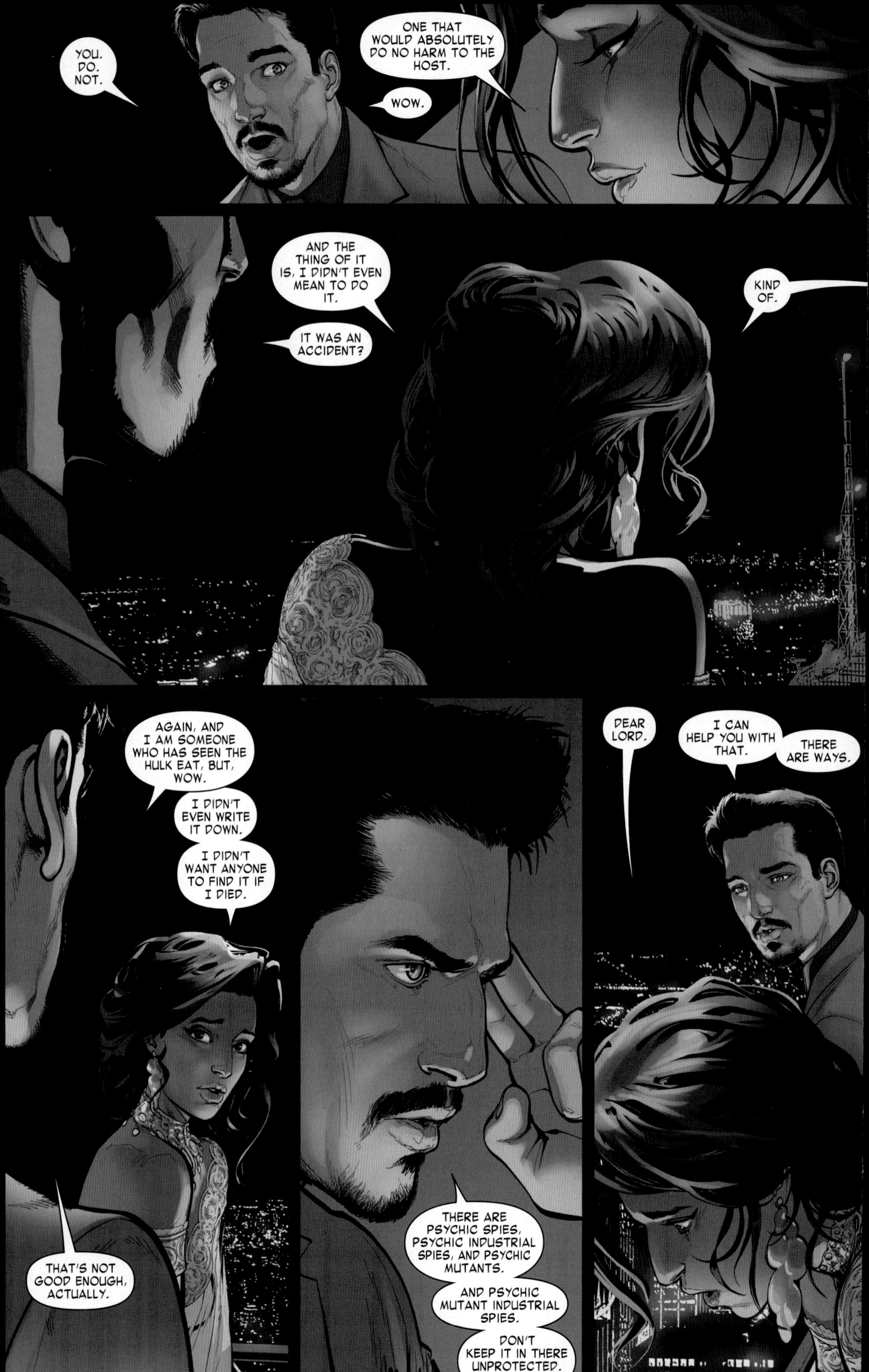
YOU. DO. NOT.
ONE THAT WOULD ABSOLUTELY DO NO HARM TO THE HOST.
WOW.
AND THE THING OF IT IS, I DIDN'T EVEN MEAN TO DO IT.
IT WAS AN ACCIDENT?
KIND OF.
AGAIN, AND I AM SOMEONE WHO HAS SEEN THE HULK EAT, BUT, WOW.
I DIDN'T EVEN WRITE IT DOWN.
I DIDN'T WANT ANYONE TO FIND IT IF I DIED.
THAT'S NOT GOOD ENOUGH, ACTUALLY.
THERE ARE PSYCHIC SPIES, PSYCHIC INDUSTRIAL SPIES, AND PSYCHIC MUTANTS.
AND PSYCHIC MUTANT INDUSTRIAL SPIES.
DON'T KEEP IT IN THERE UNPROTECTED.
DEAR LORD.
I CAN HELP YOU WITH THAT.
THERE ARE WAYS.

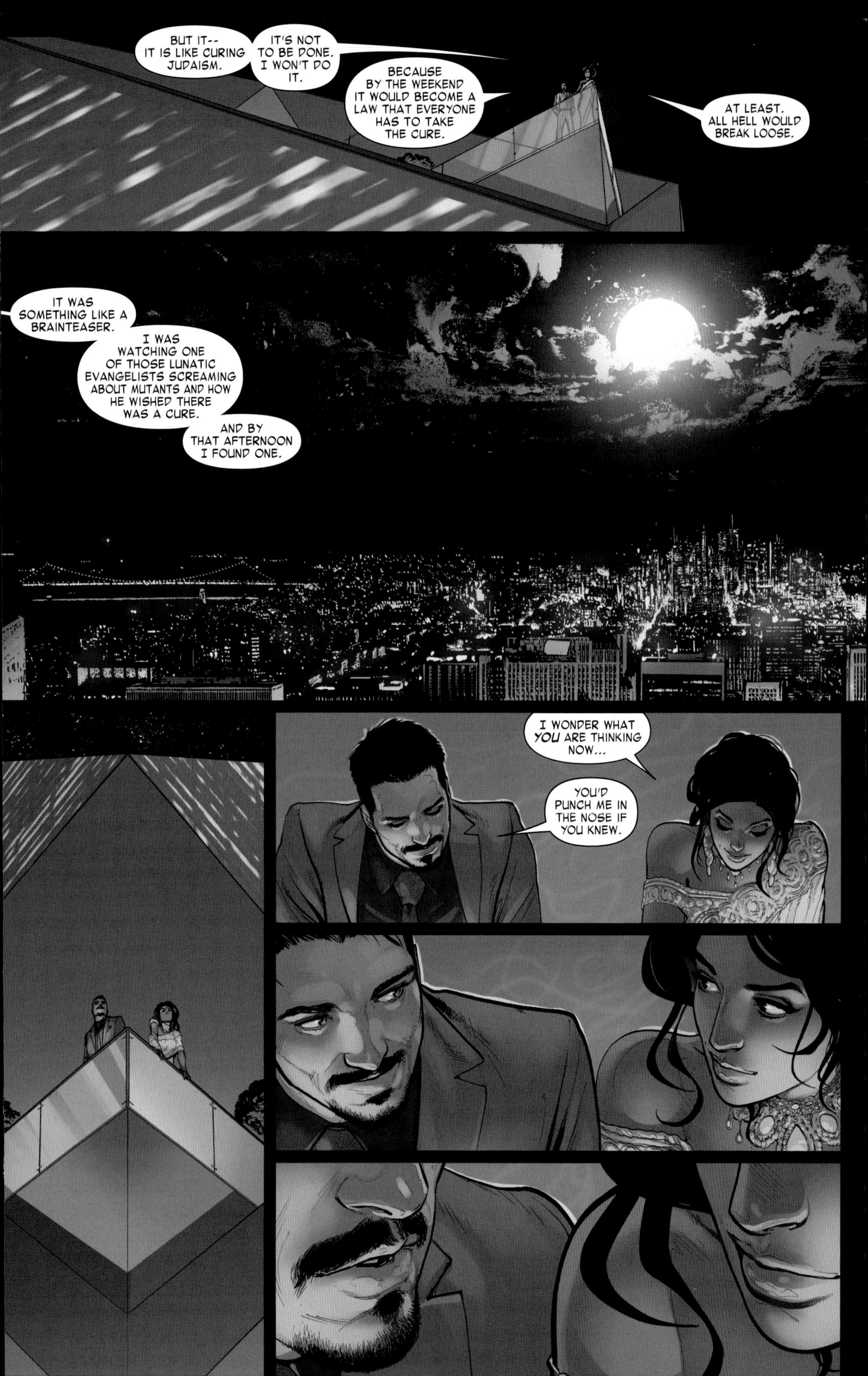
BUT IT-- IT IS LIKE CURING JUDAISM.
IT'S NOT TO BE DONE. I WON'T DO IT.
BECAUSE BY THE WEEKEND IT WOULD BECOME A LAW THAT EVERYONE HAS TO TAKE THE CURE.
AT LEAST. ALL HELL WOULD BREAK LOOSE.
IT WAS SOMETHING LIKE A BRAINTEASER.
I WAS WATCHING ONE OF THOSE LUNATIC EVANGELISTS SCREAMING ABOUT MUTANTS AND HOW HE WISHED THERE WAS A CURE.
AND BY THAT AFTERNOON I FOUND ONE.
I WONDER WHAT YOU ARE THINKING NOW...
YOU'D PUNCH ME IN THE NOSE IF YOU KNEW.

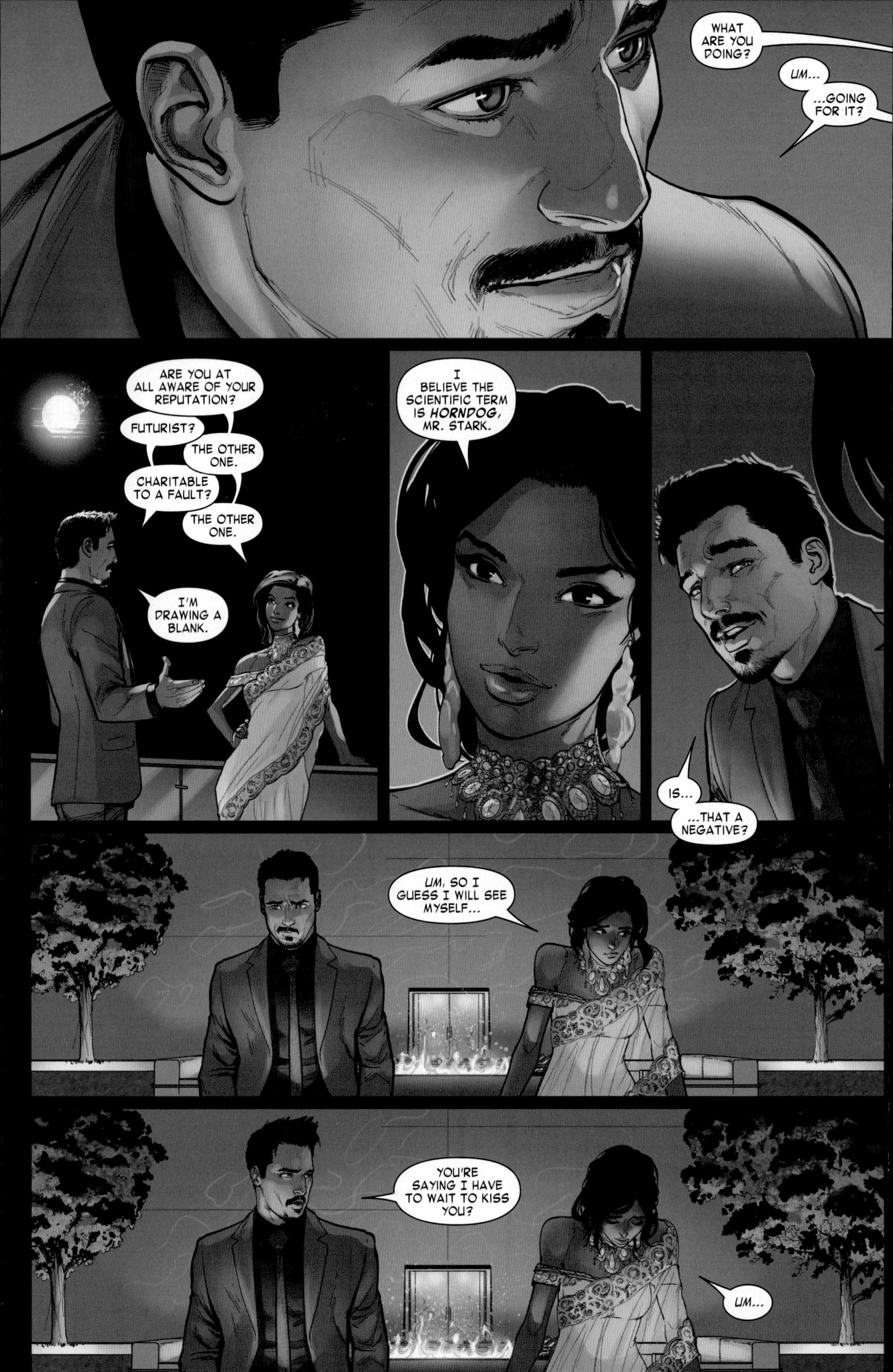

WHAT ARE YOU DOING?
UM...
...GOING FOR IT?
ARE YOU AT ALL AWARE OF YOUR REPUTATION?
FUTURIST?
THE OTHER ONE.
CHARITABLE TO A FAULT?
THE OTHER ONE.
I'M DRAWING A BLANK.
I BELIEVE THE SCIENTIFIC TERM IS HORNDOG, MR. STARK.
IS...
...THAT A NEGATIVE?
UM, SO I GUESS I WILL SEE MYSELF...
YOU'RE SAYING I HAVE TO WAIT TO KISS YOU?
UM...

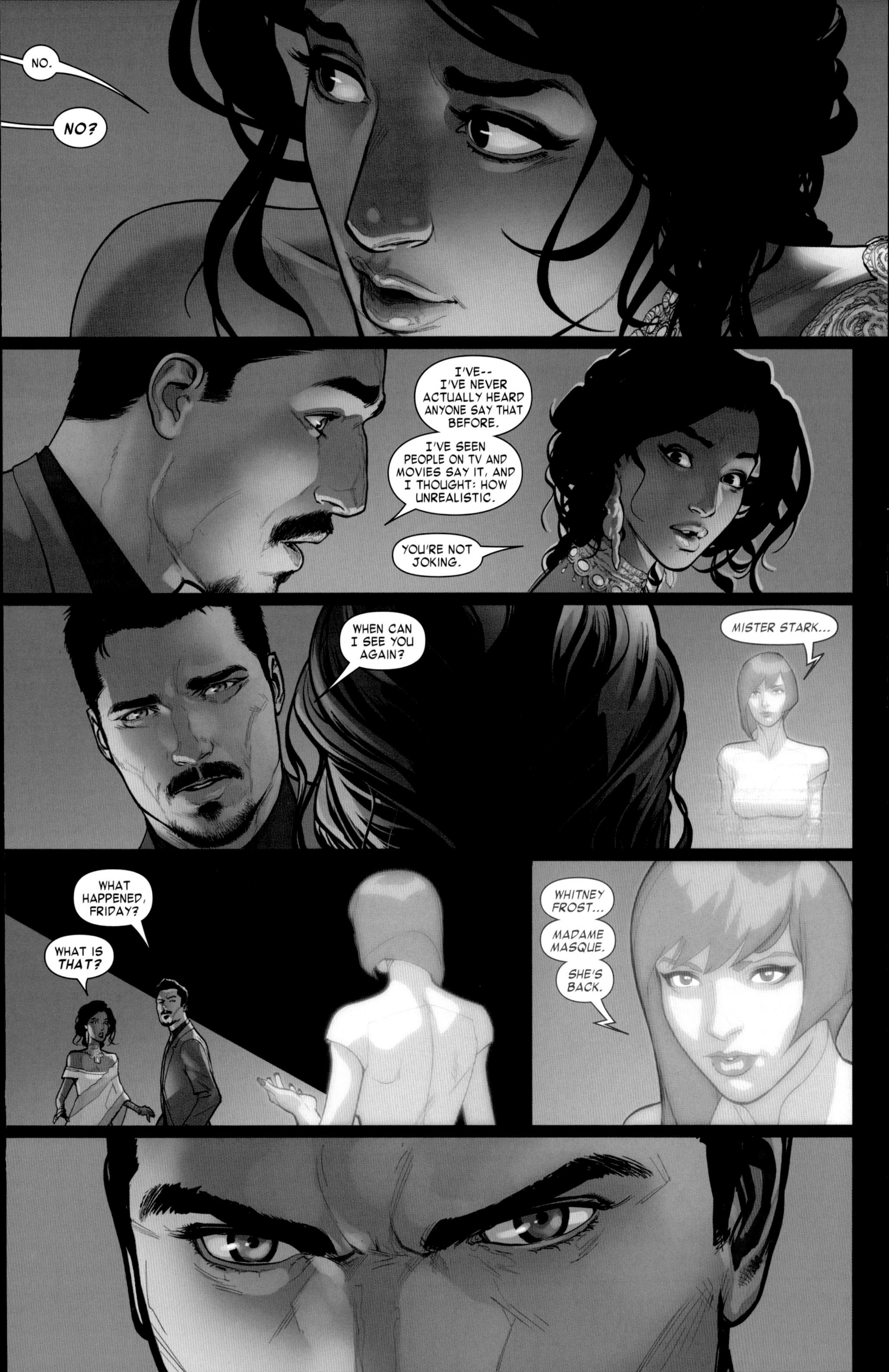
NO.
NO?
I'VE-- I'VE NEVER ACTUALLY HEARD ANYONE SAY THAT BEFORE.
I'VE SEEN PEOPLE ON TV AND MOVIES SAY IT, AND I THOUGHT: HOW UNREALISTIC.
YOU'RE NOT JOKING.
WHEN CAN I SEE YOU AGAIN?
MISTER STARK...
WHAT HAPPENED, FRIDAY?
WHAT IS THAT?
WHITNEY FROST...
MADAME MASQUE.
SHE'S BACK.

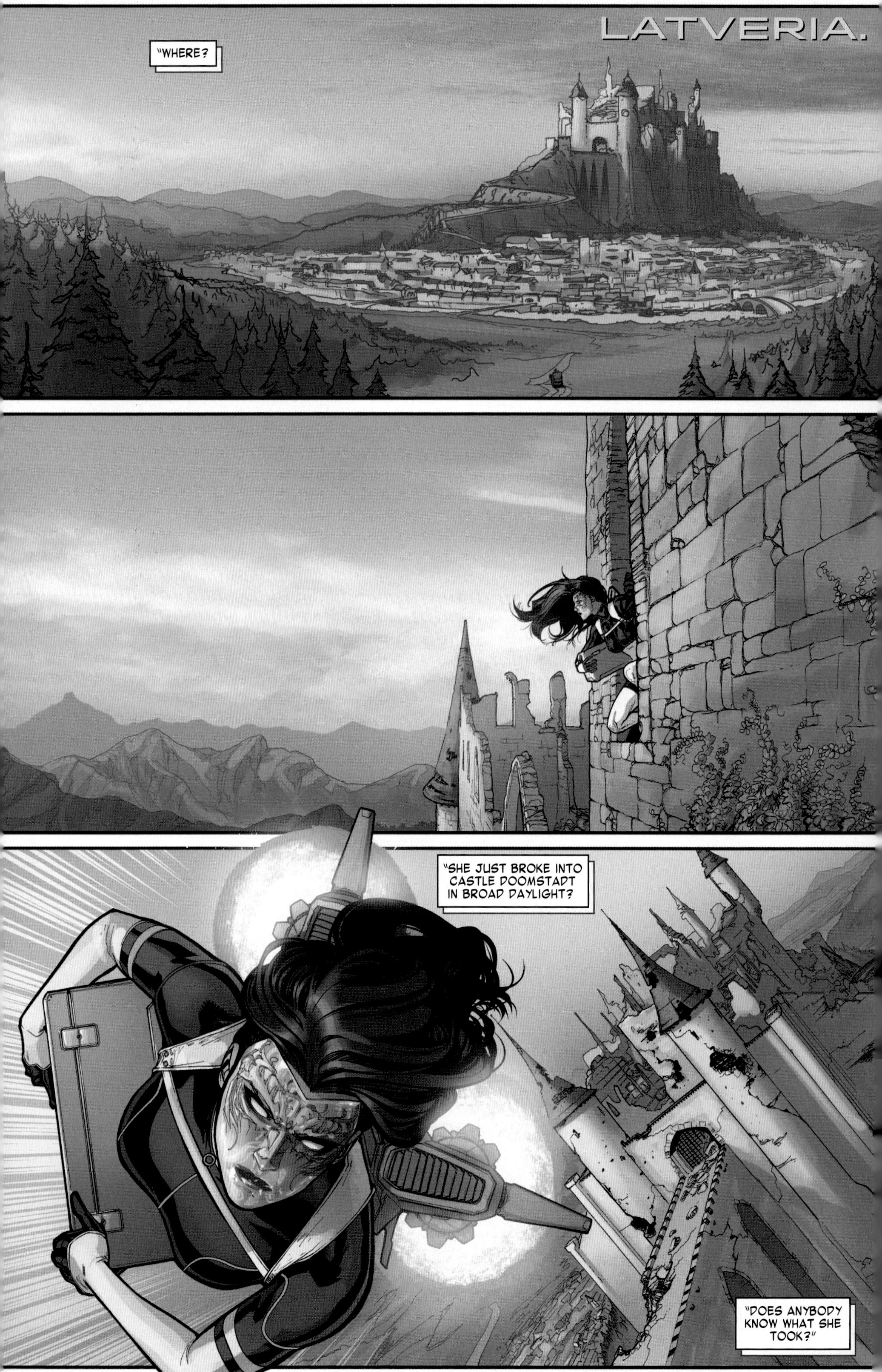
LATVERIA.
"WHERE?
"SHE JUST BROKE INTO CASTLE DOOMSTADT IN BROAD DAYLIGHT?
"DOES ANYBODY KNOW WHAT SHE TOOK?"

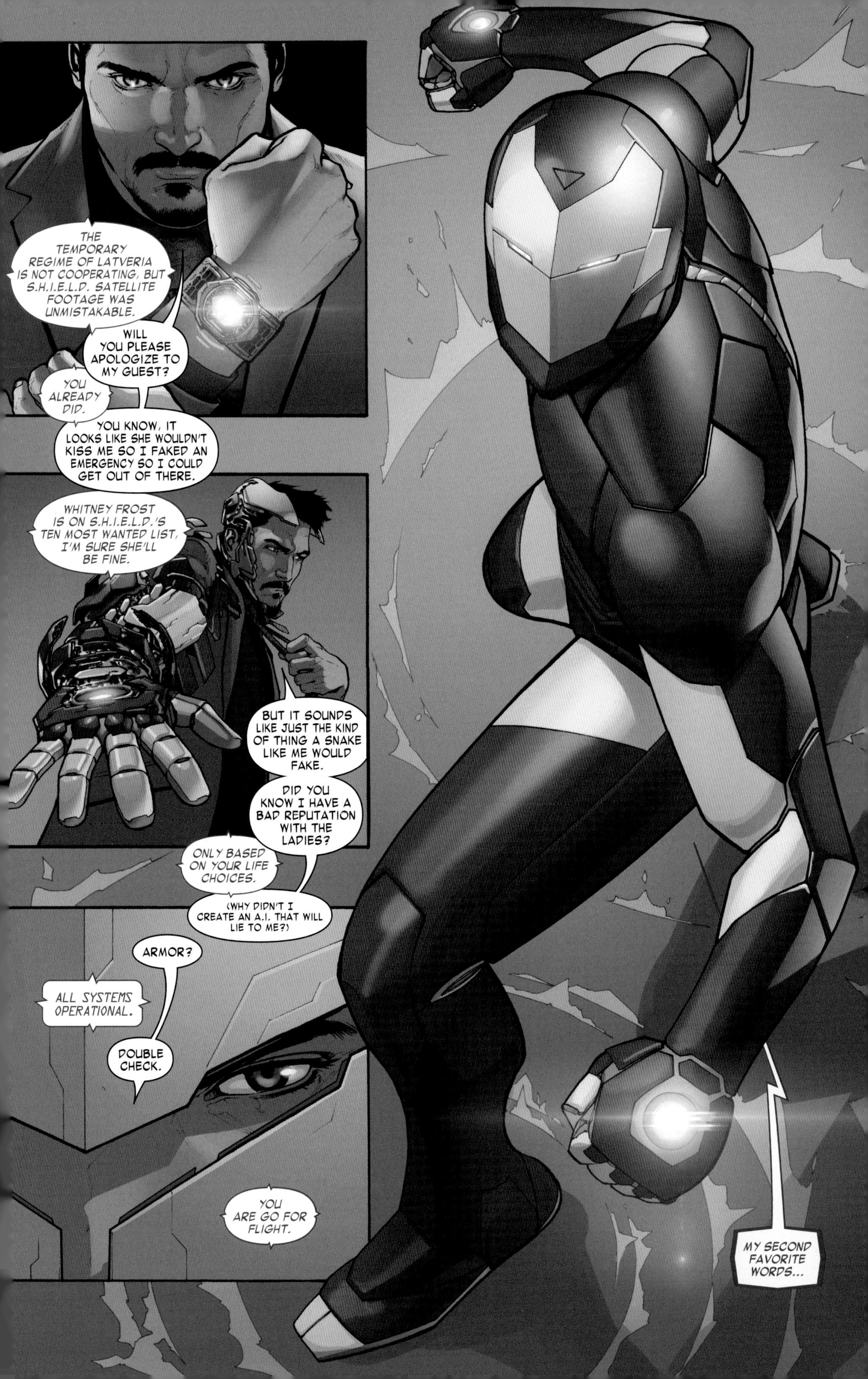
THE TEMPORARY REGIME OF LATVERIA IS NOT COOPERATING, BUT S.H.I.E.L.D. SATELLITE FOOTAGE WAS UNMISTAKABLE.
WILL YOU PLEASE APOLOGIZE TO MY GUEST?
YOU ALREADY DID.
YOU KNOW, IT LOOKS LIKE SHE WOULDN'T KISS ME SO I FAKED AN EMERGENCY SO I COULD GET OUT OF THERE.
WHITNEY FROST IS ON S.H.I.E.L.D.'S TEN MOST WANTED LIST, I'M SURE SHE'LL BE FINE.
BUT IT SOUNDS LIKE JUST THE KIND OF THING A SNAKE LIKE ME WOULD FAKE.
DID YOU KNOW I HAVE A BAD REPUTATION WITH THE LADIES?
ONLY BASED ON YOUR LIFE CHOICES.
(WHY DIDN'T I CREATE AN A.I. THAT WILL LIE TO ME?)
ARMOR?
ALL SYSTEMS OPERATIONAL.
DOUBLE CHECK.
YOU ARE GO FOR FLIGHT.
MY SECOND FAVORITE WORDS...

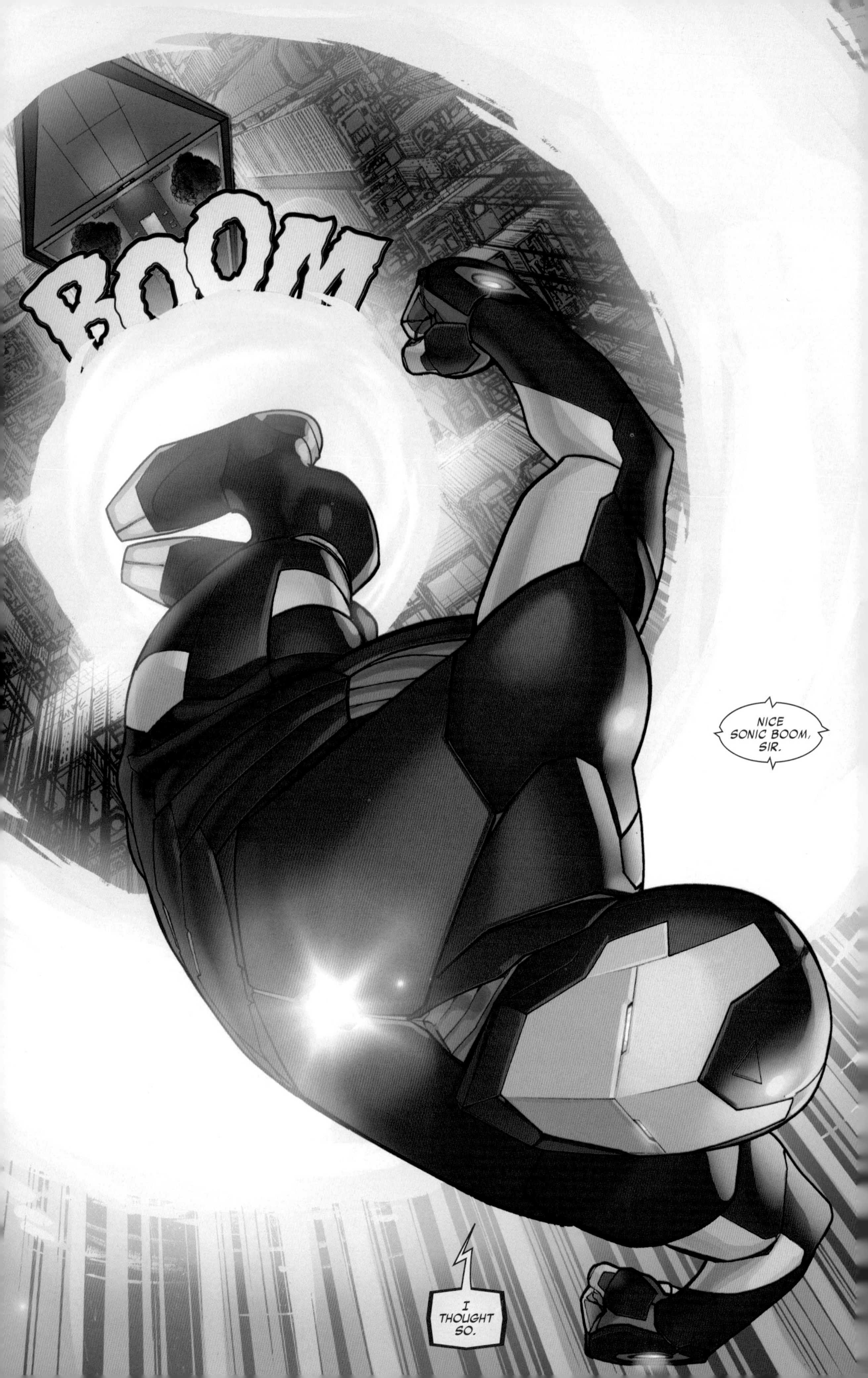
BOOM
NICE SONIC BOOM, SIR.
I THOUGHT SO.

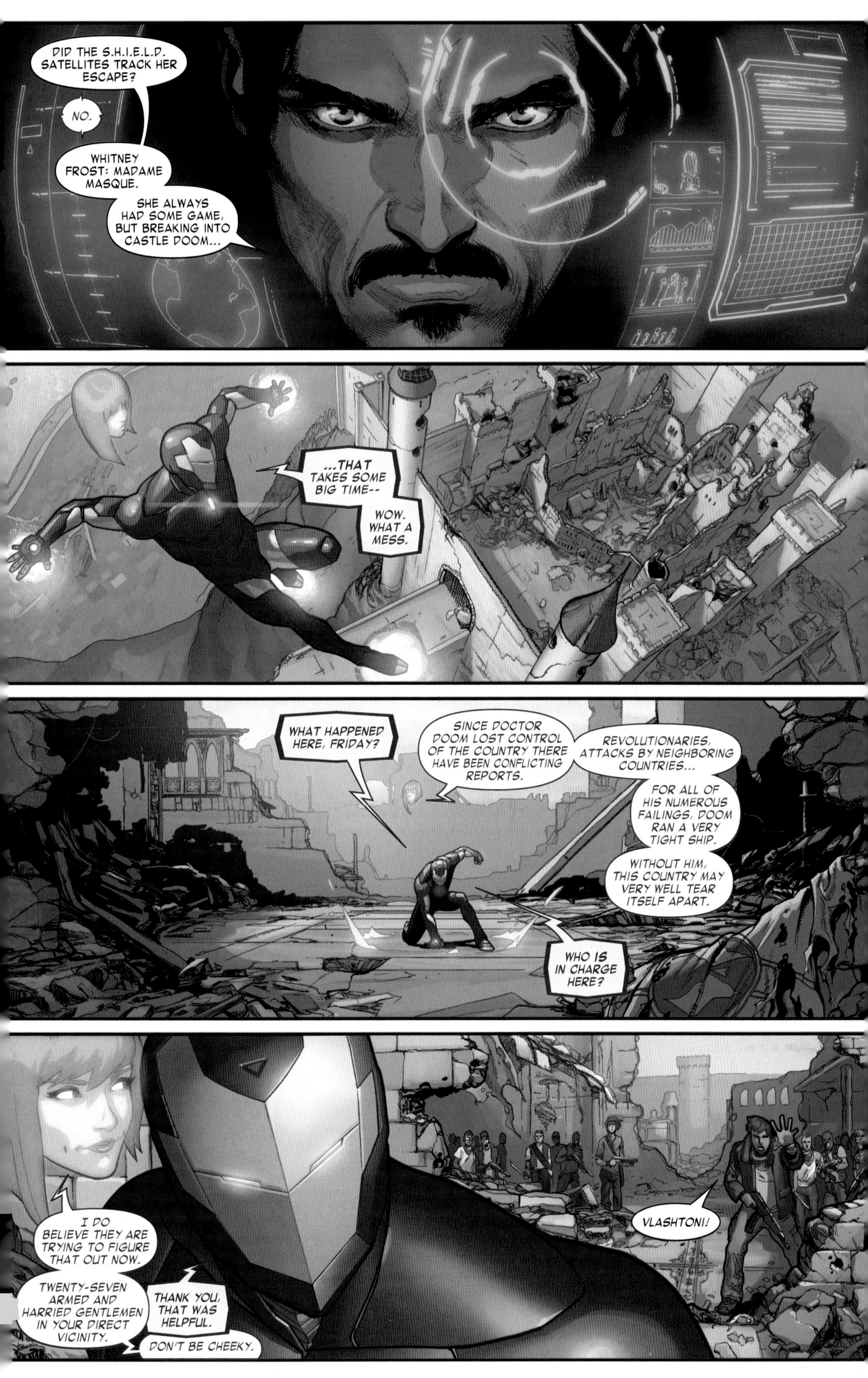
DID THE S.H.I.E.L.D. SATELLITES TRACK HER ESCAPE?
NO.
WHITNEY FROST: MADAME MASQUE.
SHE ALWAYS HAD SOME GAME, BUT BREAKING INTO CASTLE DOOM...
...THAT TAKES SOME BIG TIME--
WOW. WHAT A MESS.
WHAT HAPPENED HERE, FRIDAY?
SINCE DOCTOR DOOM LOST CONTROL OF THE COUNTRY THERE HAVE BEEN CONFLICTING REPORTS.
REVOLUTIONARIES, ATTACKS BY NEIGHBORING COUNTRIES...
FOR ALL OF HIS NUMEROUS FAILINGS, DOOM RAN A VERY TIGHT SHIP.
WITHOUT HIM, THIS COUNTRY MAY VERY WELL TEAR ITSELF APART.
WHO IS IN CHARGE HERE?
I DO BELIEVE THEY ARE TRYING TO FIGURE THAT OUT NOW.
TWENTY-SEVEN ARMED AND HARRIED GENTLEMEN IN YOUR DIRECT VICINITY.
THANK YOU, THAT WAS HELPFUL.
DON'T BE CHEEKY.
VLASHTONI!

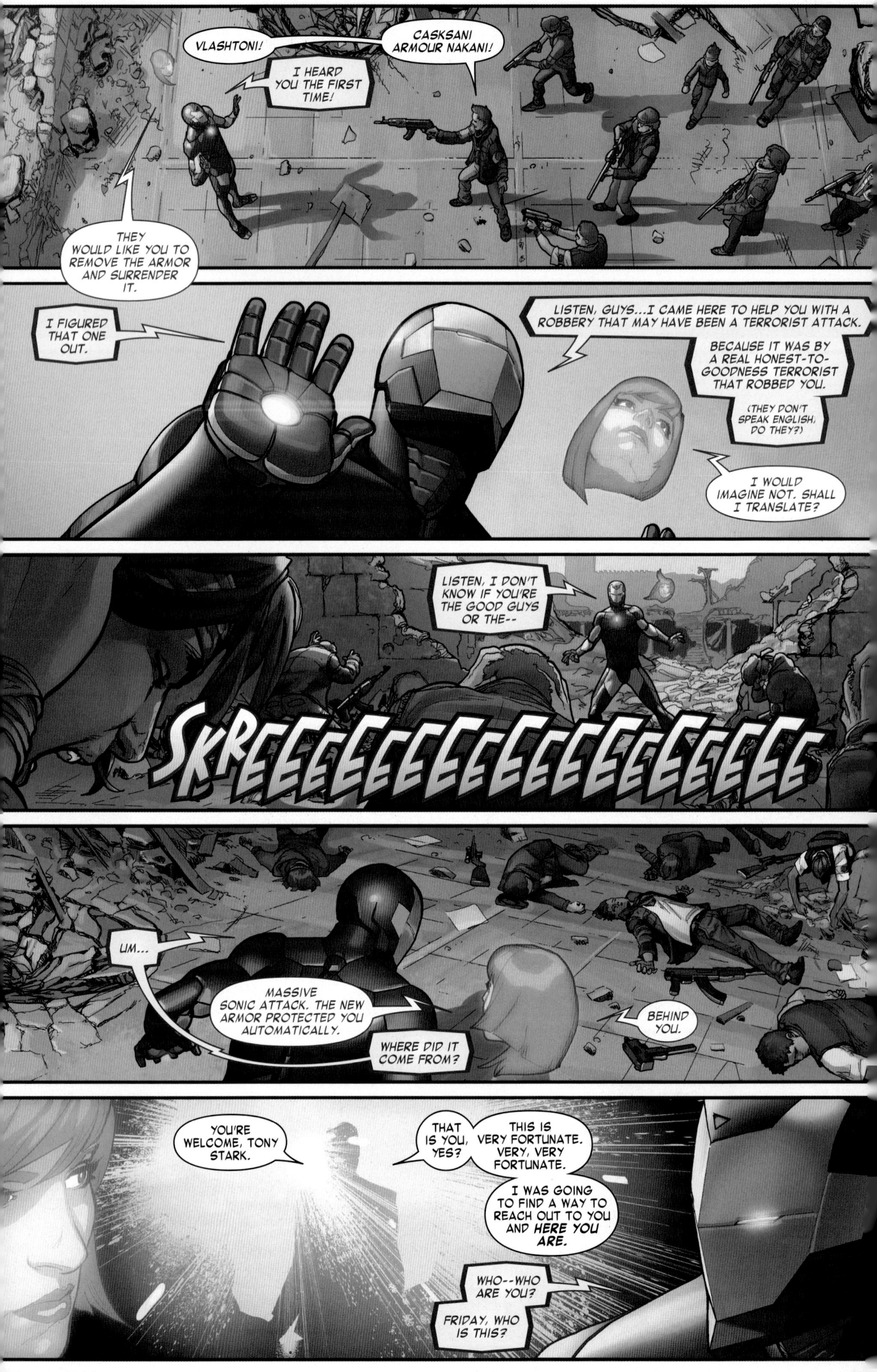
VLASHTONI!
CASKSANI ARMOUR NAKANI!
I HEARD YOU THE FIRST TIME!
THEY WOULD LIKE YOU TO REMOVE THE ARMOR AND SURRENDER IT.
I FIGURED THAT ONE OUT.
LISTEN, GUYS...I CAME HERE TO HELP YOU WITH A ROBBERY THAT MAY HAVE BEEN A TERRORIST ATTACK.
BECAUSE IT WAS BY A REAL HONEST-TO-GOODNESS TERRORIST THAT ROBBED YOU.
(THEY DON'T SPEAK ENGLISH, DO THEY?)
I WOULD IMAGINE NOT. SHALL I TRANSLATE?
LISTEN, I DON'T KNOW IF YOU'RE THE GOOD GUYS OR THE--
SKREEEEEEEEEEEEEEEEEEEEE
UM...
MASSIVE SONIC ATTACK. THE NEW ARMOR PROTECTED YOU AUTOMATICALLY.
WHERE DID IT COME FROM?
BEHIND YOU.
YOU'RE WELCOME, TONY STARK.
THAT IS YOU, YES?
THIS IS VERY FORTUNATE. VERY, VERY FORTUNATE.
I WAS GOING TO FIND A WAY TO REACH OUT TO YOU AND HERE YOU ARE.
WHO--WHO ARE YOU?
FRIDAY, WHO IS THIS?

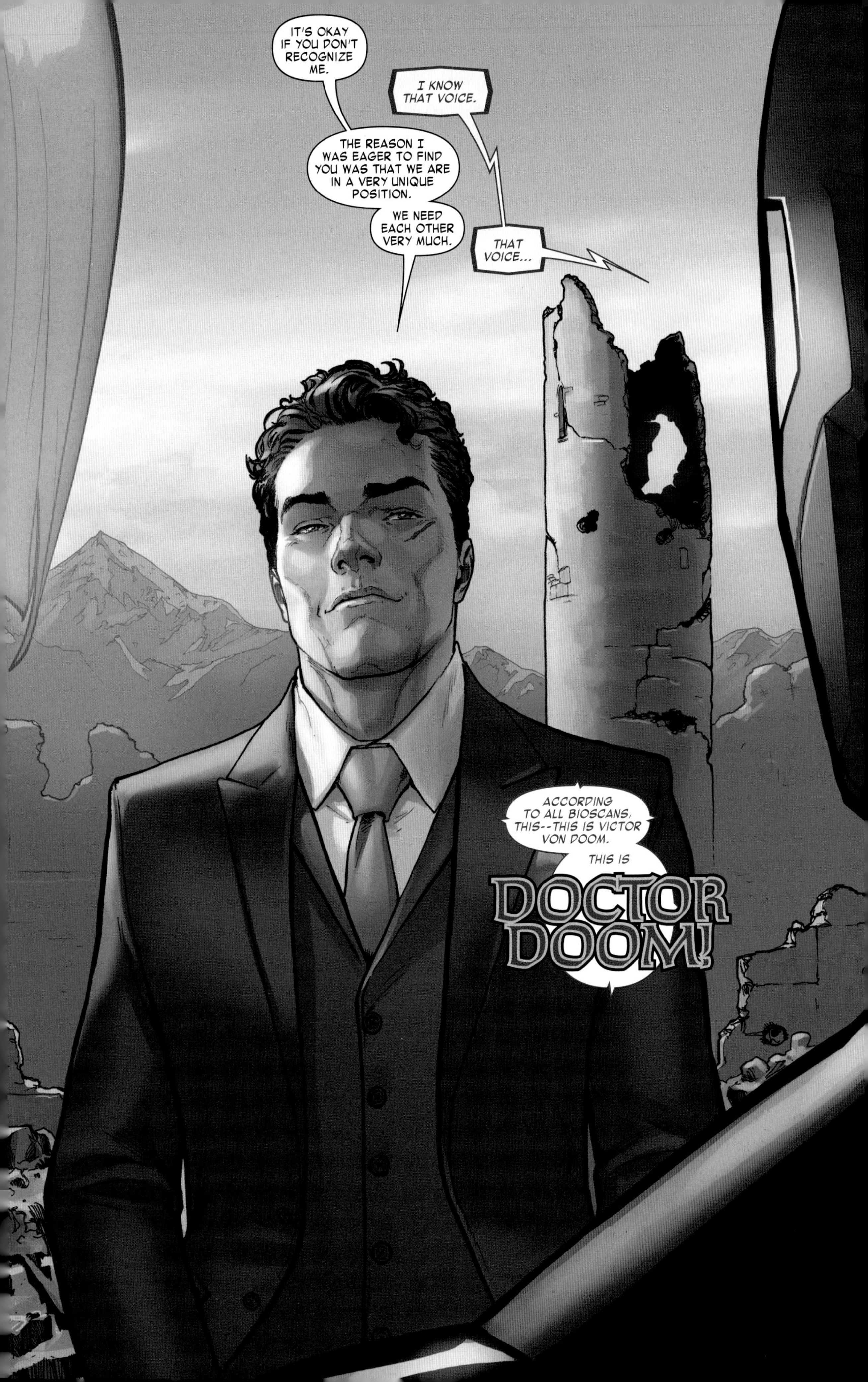
IT'S OKAY IF YOU DON'T RECOGNIZE ME.
I KNOW THAT VOICE.
THE REASON I WAS EAGER TO FIND YOU WAS THAT WE ARE IN A VERY UNIQUE POSITION.
WE NEED EACH OTHER VERY MUCH.
THAT VOICE...
ACCORDING TO ALL BIOSCANS, THIS--THIS IS VICTOR VON DOOM.
THIS IS
DOCTOR DOOM!

#2

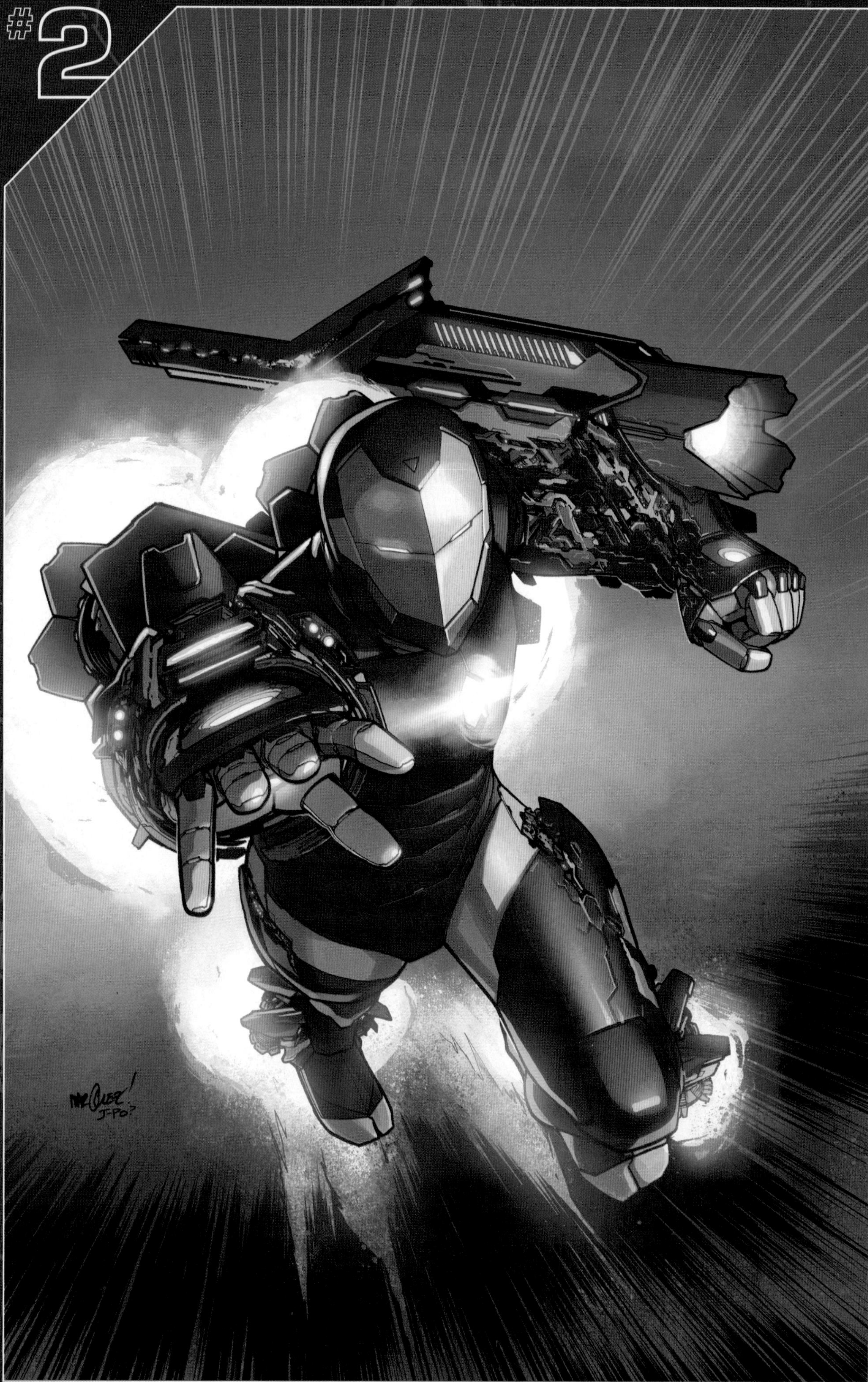

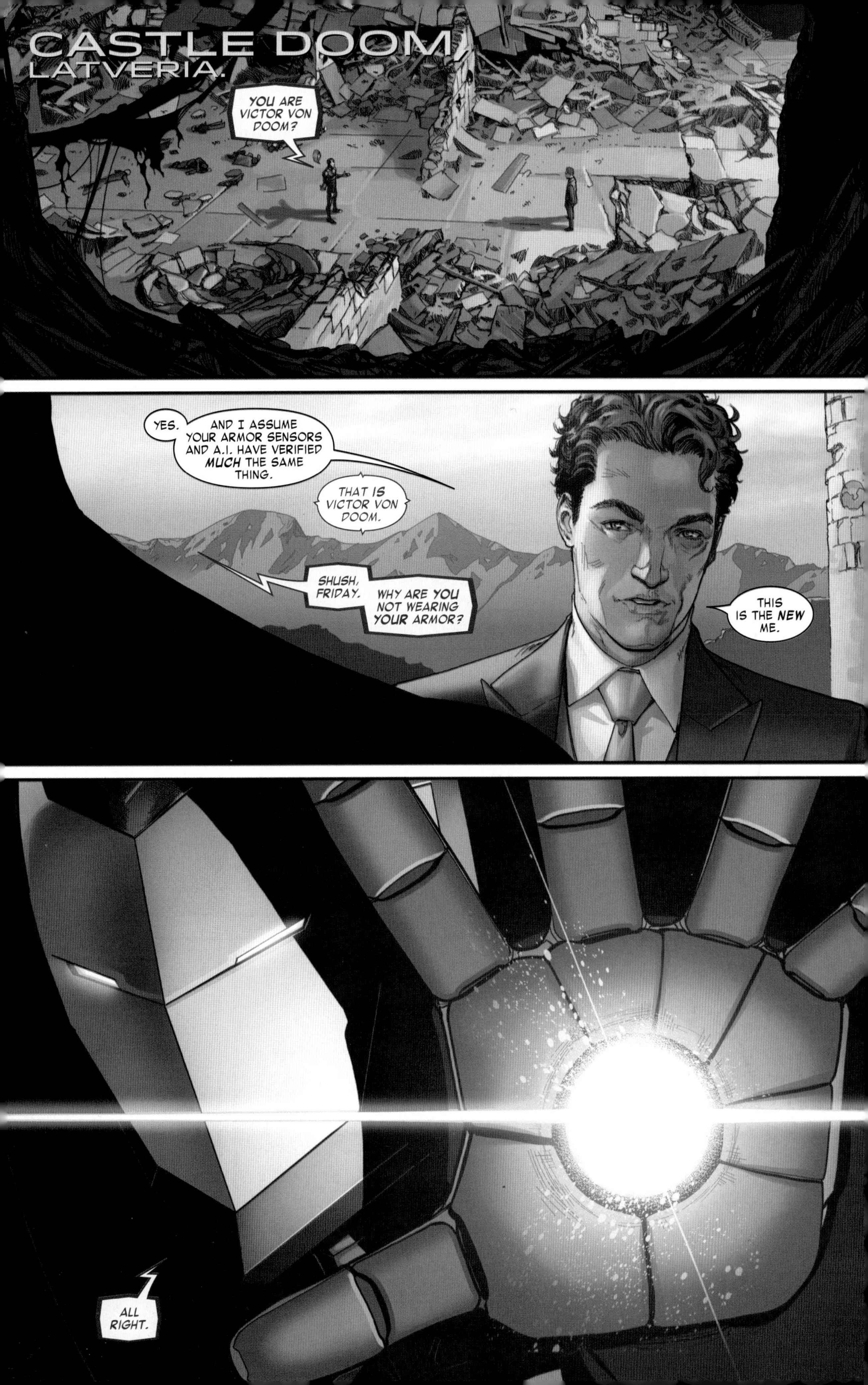
CASTLE DOOM, LATVERIA.
YOU ARE VICTOR VON DOOM?
YES.
AND I ASSUME YOUR ARMOR SENSORS AND A.I. HAVE VERIFIED MUCH THE SAME THING.
THAT IS VICTOR VON DOOM.
SHUSH, FRIDAY.
WHY ARE YOU NOT WEARING YOUR ARMOR?
THIS IS THE NEW ME.
ALL RIGHT.

HE'S BLOCKING YOU USING A COMBINED MYSTICAL SPELL DEFENSE.

ARE YOU FINISHED?

HE REALLY IS VICTOR VON DOOM.

I'M NOT SURE WHAT TO DO HERE, FRIDAY...

VICTOR VON DOOM, THE MOST DANGEROUS MAN ON THE PLANET, IS JUST STANDING HERE SMILING AT ME.

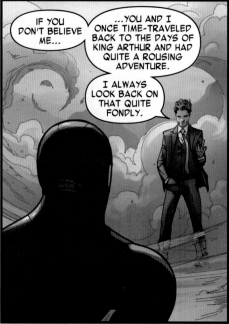

IF YOU DON'T BELIEVE ME...

...YOU AND I ONCE TIME-TRAVELED BACK TO THE DAYS OF KING ARTHUR AND HAD QUITE A ROUSING ADVENTURE.

I ALWAYS LOOK BACK ON THAT QUITE FONDLY.

YOU TRIED TO MURDER ME AND LEAVE ME THERE.

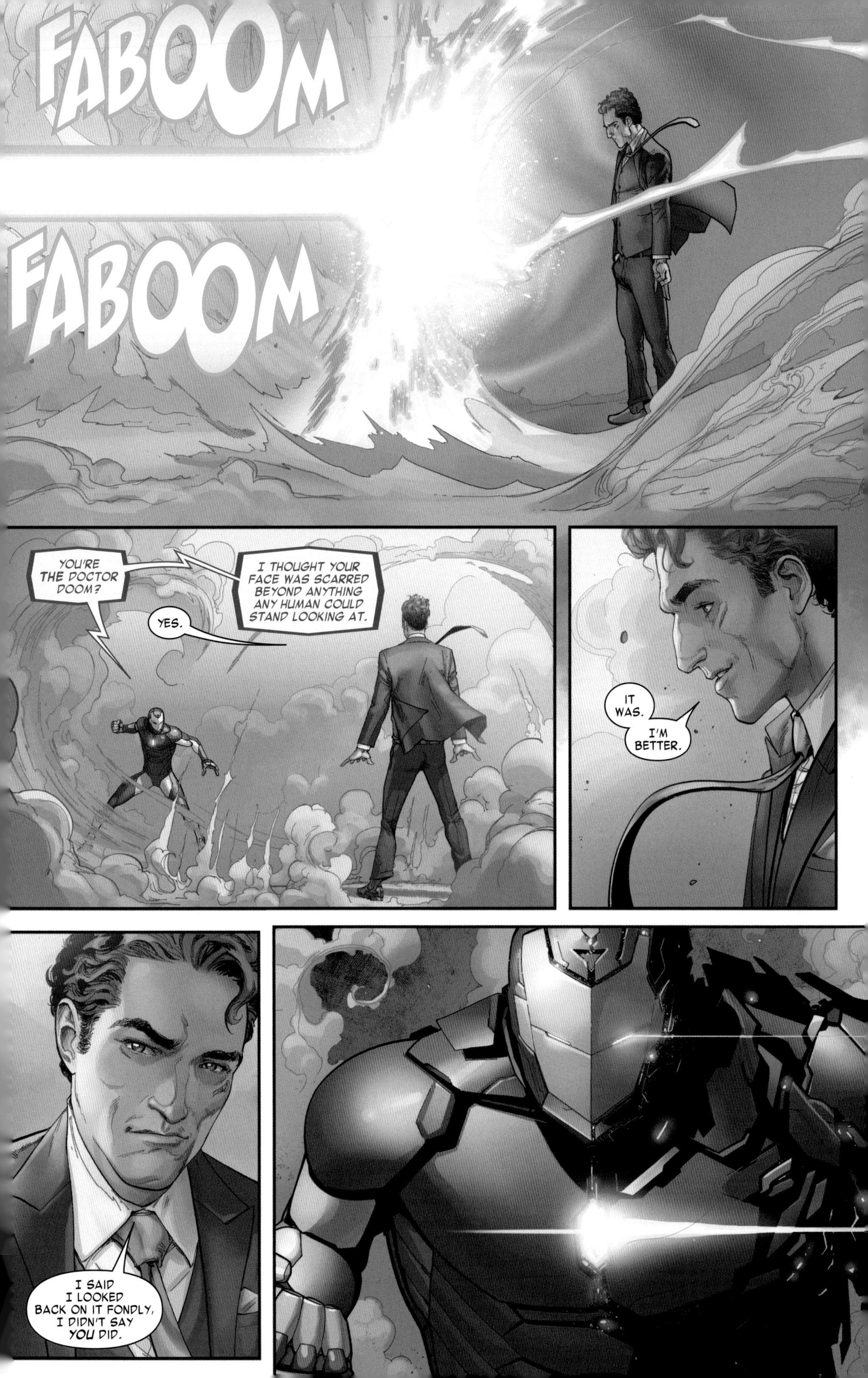
FABOOM
FABOOM
YOU'RE THE DOCTOR DOOM?
YES.
I THOUGHT YOUR FACE WAS SCARRED BEYOND ANYTHING ANY HUMAN COULD STAND LOOKING AT.
IT WAS.
I'M BETTER.
I SAID I LOOKED BACK ON IT FONDLY, I DIDN'T SAY YOU DID.

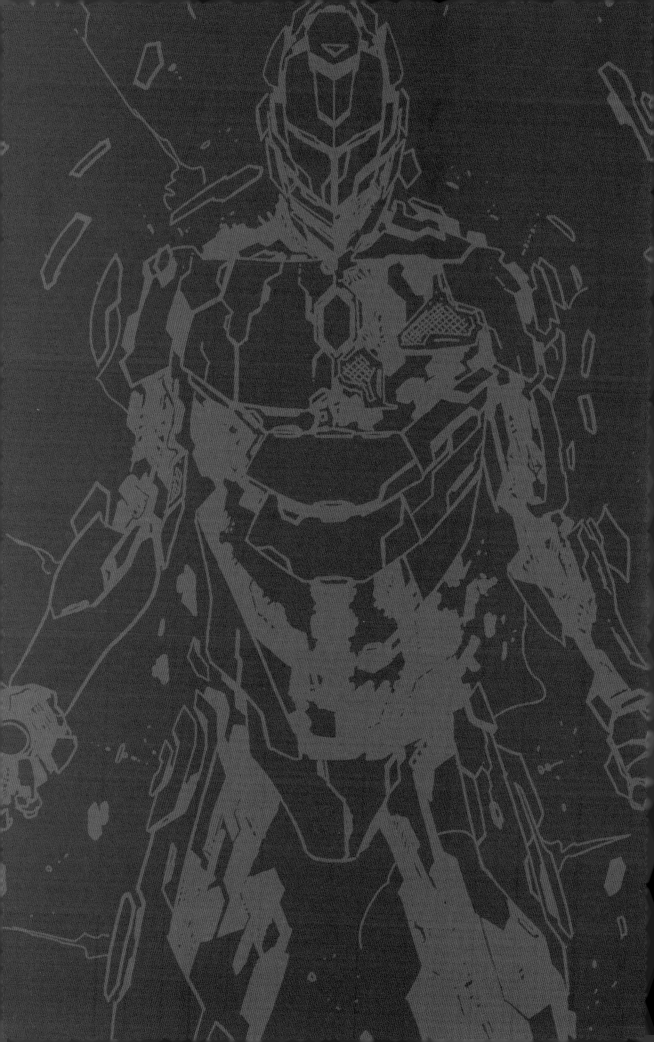

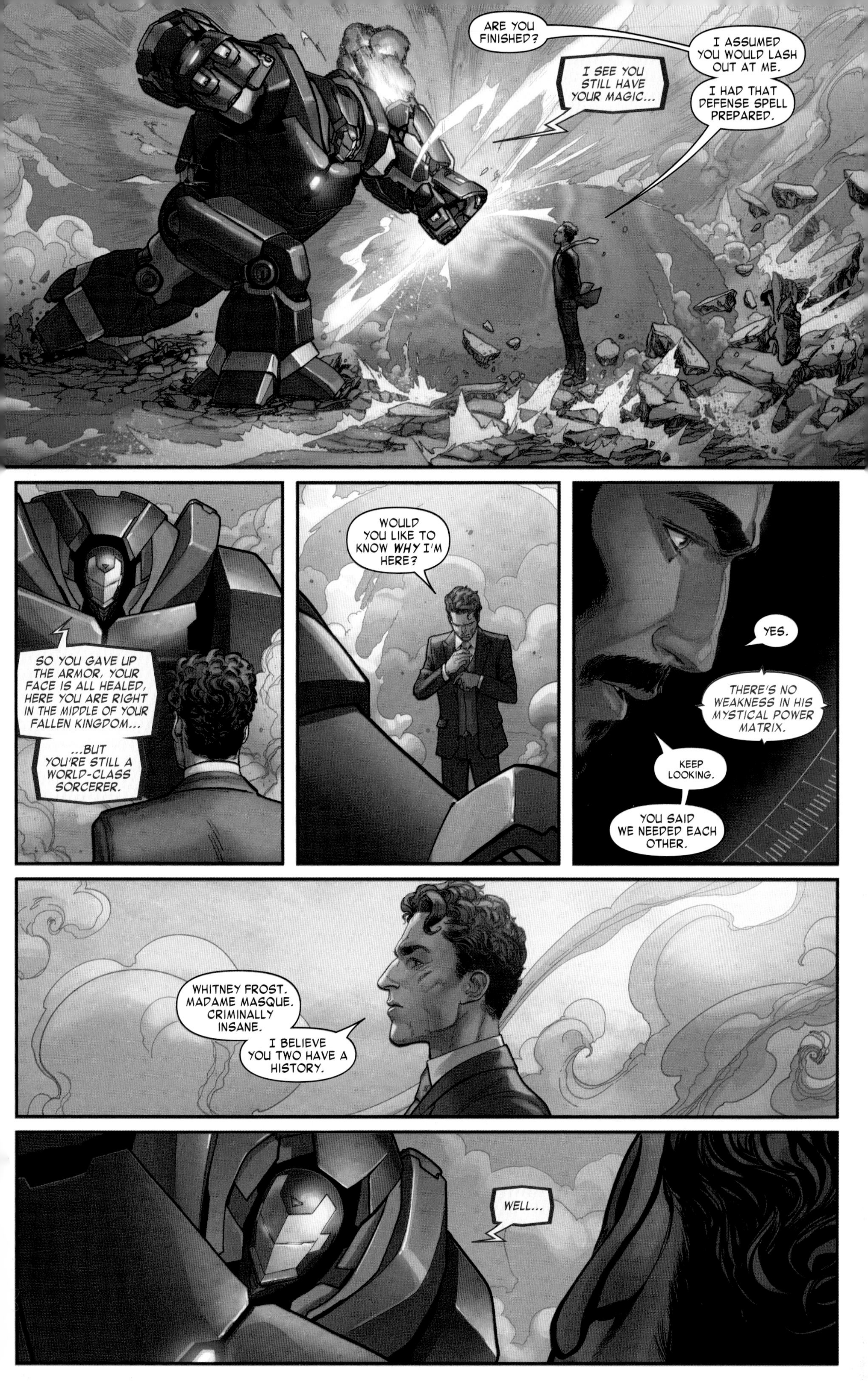
ARE YOU FINISHED?
I SEE YOU STILL HAVE YOUR MAGIC...
I ASSUMED YOU WOULD LASH OUT AT ME.
I HAD THAT DEFENSE SPELL PREPARED.
SO YOU GAVE UP THE ARMOR, YOUR FACE IS ALL HEALED, HERE YOU ARE RIGHT IN THE MIDDLE OF YOUR FALLEN KINGDOM...
...BUT YOU'RE STILL A WORLD-CLASS SORCERER.
WOULD YOU LIKE TO KNOW *WHY* I'M HERE?
YES.
THERE'S NO WEAKNESS IN HIS MYSTICAL POWER MATRIX.
KEEP LOOKING.
YOU SAID WE NEEDED EACH OTHER.
WHITNEY FROST. MADAME MASQUE. CRIMINALLY INSANE.
I BELIEVE YOU TWO HAVE A HISTORY.
WELL...

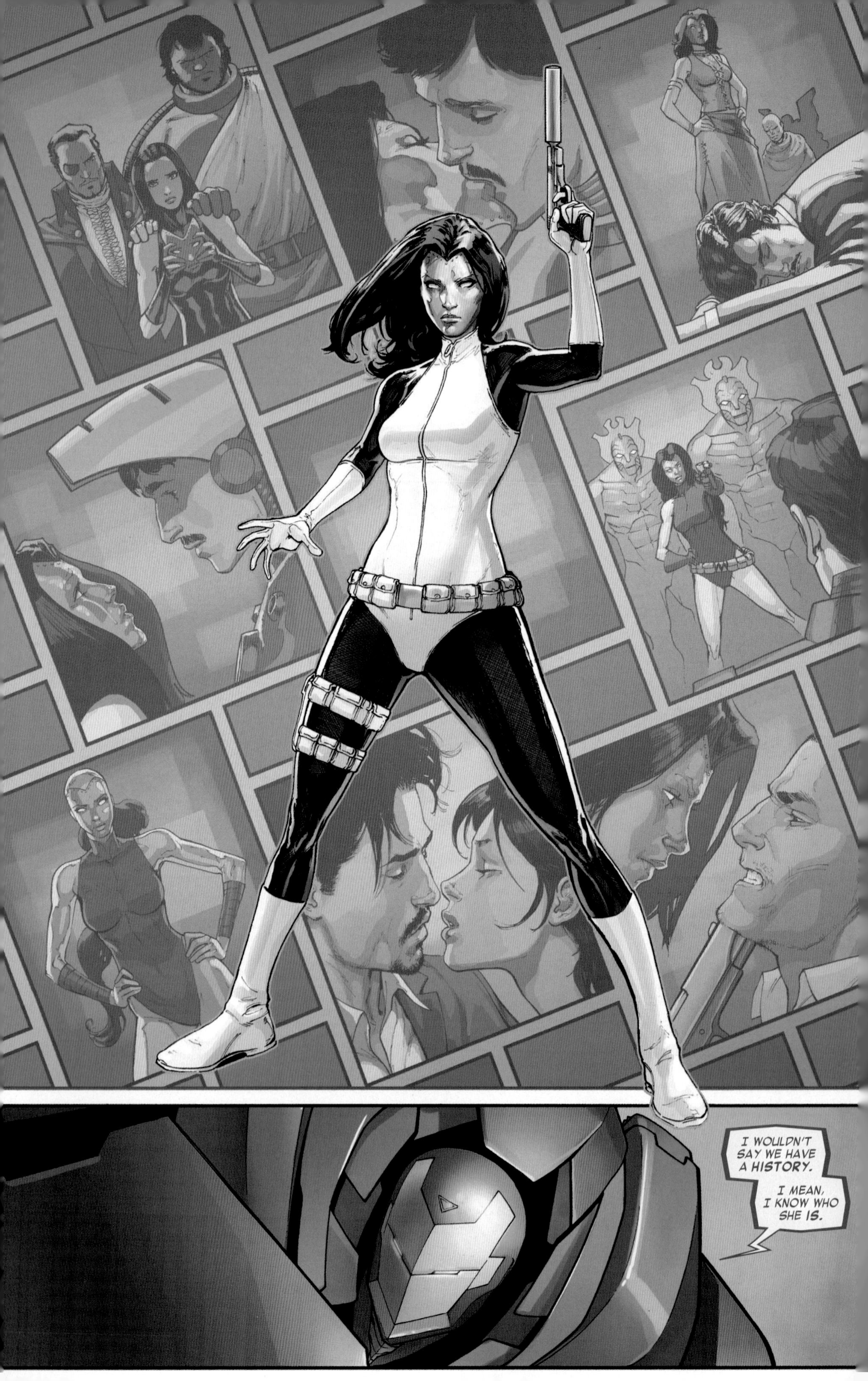
I WOULDN'T SAY WE HAVE A HISTORY.
I MEAN, I KNOW WHO SHE IS.

UH-HUH.

REGARDLESS, SHE HAS EMBARKED ON A VERY DANGEROUS TREASURE HUNT.

ACCUMULATING POWERFUL ITEMS AROUND THE WORLD.

ITEMS THAT YOU DON'T WANT SOMEONE LIKE *HER* HAVING THEIR HANDS ON.

LIKE WHAT?

INFINITY STONES? COSMIC CUBES?

WEB-SHOOTERS?

I'D BE A *LITTLE* SURPRISED.

I DON'T THINK IT WOULD BE A SURPRISE FOR YOU TO FIND OUT THAT THIS PLANET LIVES ON A CROSSROADS OF INTER-DIMENSIONAL COSMIC ENERGIES--

DON'T BE COY.

THIS PLANET HAS SURVIVED *ALL* TYPES OF INCURSIONS AND DIMENSIONAL RIFTS.

AND WHEN THINGS LIKE THAT OCCUR, ITEMS THAT *DO NOT* FOLLOW THE RULES OF OUR PHYSICS OR OUR BIOLOGY TEND TO FALL THROUGH THE CRACKS.

THINGS LAND ON THIS PLANET THAT JUST DON'T BELONG HERE.

THIS WAY...

AAAAAAND?

AND THESE ITEMS CERTAINLY DON'T BELONG IN THE HANDS OF A WOMAN LIKE WHITNEY FROST.

SHE'S A SICK WOMAN.

WHAT WAS SHE DOING HERE?

WHAT WERE YOU HIDING?

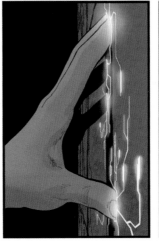

DOOM, I'M TELLING YOU, MY ARMOR KNOWS WHERE I AM. IF I DISAPPEAR, THE AVENGERS KNOW TO--

I KNOW.

IF I WANTED TO KILL YOU, YOU'D BE DEAD.

I WANT YOU TO SEE THIS...

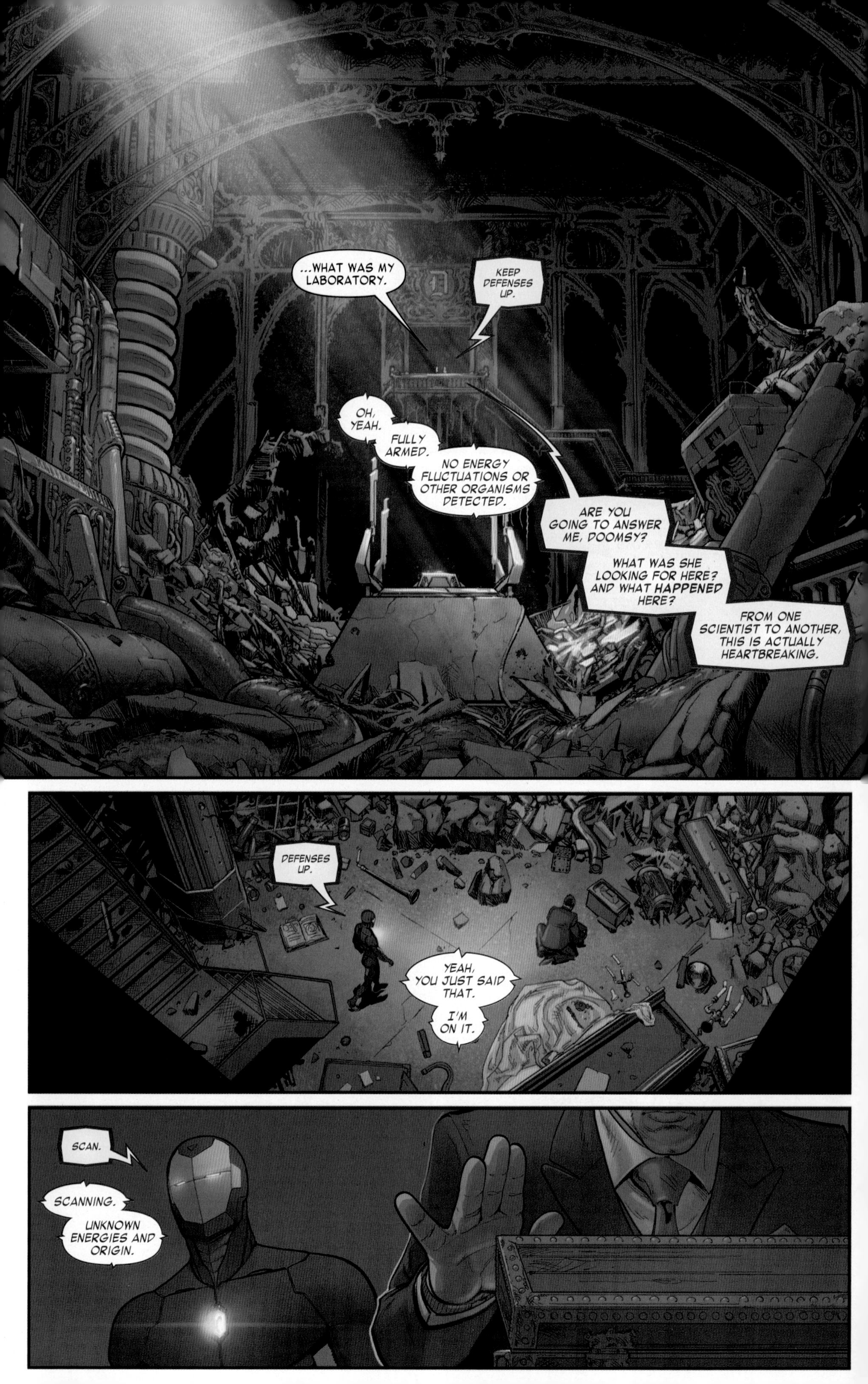
...WHAT WAS MY LABORATORY.
KEEP DEFENSES UP.
OH, YEAH.
FULLY ARMED.
NO ENERGY FLUCTUATIONS OR OTHER ORGANISMS DETECTED.
ARE YOU GOING TO ANSWER ME, DOOMSY?
WHAT WAS SHE LOOKING FOR HERE? AND WHAT HAPPENED HERE?
FROM ONE SCIENTIST TO ANOTHER, THIS IS ACTUALLY HEARTBREAKING.
DEFENSES UP.
YEAH, YOU JUST SAID THAT.
I'M ON IT.
SCAN.
SCANNING.
UNKNOWN ENERGIES AND ORIGIN.

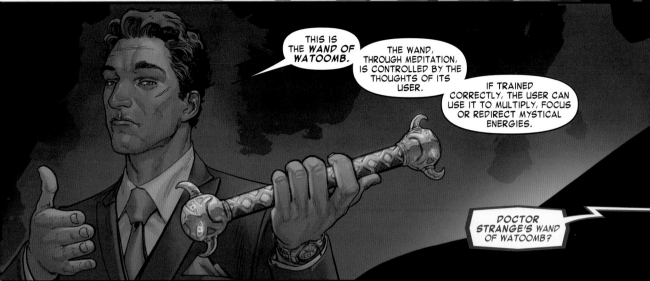

THIS IS THE *WAND OF WATOOMB.*

THE WAND, THROUGH MEDITATION, IS CONTROLLED BY THE THOUGHTS OF ITS USER.

IF TRAINED CORRECTLY, THE USER CAN USE IT TO MULTIPLY, FOCUS OR REDIRECT MYSTICAL ENERGIES.

DOCTOR STRANGE'S WAND OF WATOOMB?

NO. THIS ONE WAS MINE.

THERE'S ANOTHER ONE?

YES. YOU'RE LOOKING AT IT.

THERE MAY BE FIVE MORE ACROSS THE DIFFERENT DIMENSIONS.

THIS ONE WAS MINE.

HOW DO YOU HAVE IT?

I JUST TOLD YOU.

IT SLIPPED THROUGH THE CRACKS OF THE WORLD.

YES.

TAKE IT.

WHY?

BECAUSE IT IS BETTER OFF IN YOUR HANDS THAN IN HERS.

OR MINE.

CALL IT A SIGN OF GOOD FAITH.

OKAY, HOLD ON... STOP.

WHAT IS THIS?

YOU AND I, FROM NOW ON, ARE GOING TO HELP EACH OTHER.

AND THE ONLY WAY I THINK THIS WILL WORK IS IF YOU LEARN TO *TRUST* ME.

I'LL NEVER TRUST YOU.

YOU'LL **LEARN** TO.

UM, TONY, BECAUSE YOU PROGRAMMED ME TO SAY IT THIS WAY, I HAVE TO SAY:

WE HAVE COMPANY.

OKAY, THERE'S LITERALLY PEOPLE STORMING THE CASTLE OUTSIDE.

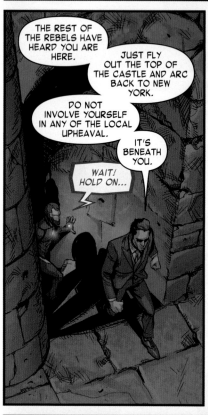

THE REST OF THE REBELS HAVE HEARD YOU ARE HERE.

JUST FLY OUT THE TOP OF THE CASTLE AND ARC BACK TO NEW YORK.

DO NOT INVOLVE YOURSELF IN ANY OF THE LOCAL UPHEAVAL.

IT'S BENEATH YOU.

WAIT! HOLD ON...

IS THIS ACTUALLY A-- WHAT ARE YOU UP TO HERE?

I KNOW THE HOLE I HAVE DUG FOR MYSELF.

I KNOW IT WON'T BE EASY.

OH, MAN, ARE YOU SAYING YOU'VE TURNED OVER A NEW LEAF?

YOU SHOULD GO.

I WISH YOU COULD SEE HOW MUCH I'M LAUGHING AT YOU **AND** ROLLING MY EYES SIMULTANEOUSLY.

THE IRONY IS: THESE REBELS ARE PUNISHING THE PEOPLE OF THIS COUNTRY.

WHEN I WAS THEIR LEADER, THESE PEOPLE LIVED HEALTHY LIVES.

OH, DAMN...

I LEFT THE MEDAL OF FREEDOM I GOT YOU IN MY OTHER ARMOR.

TRACK THE ENERGY SIGNATURES FROM THIS CASTLE AND YOU WILL BE ABLE TO TRIANGULATE WHERE MADAME MASQUE HAS BEEN AND WHAT SHE HAS TAKEN.

WHAT DID SHE TAKE WHEN SHE WAS HERE?

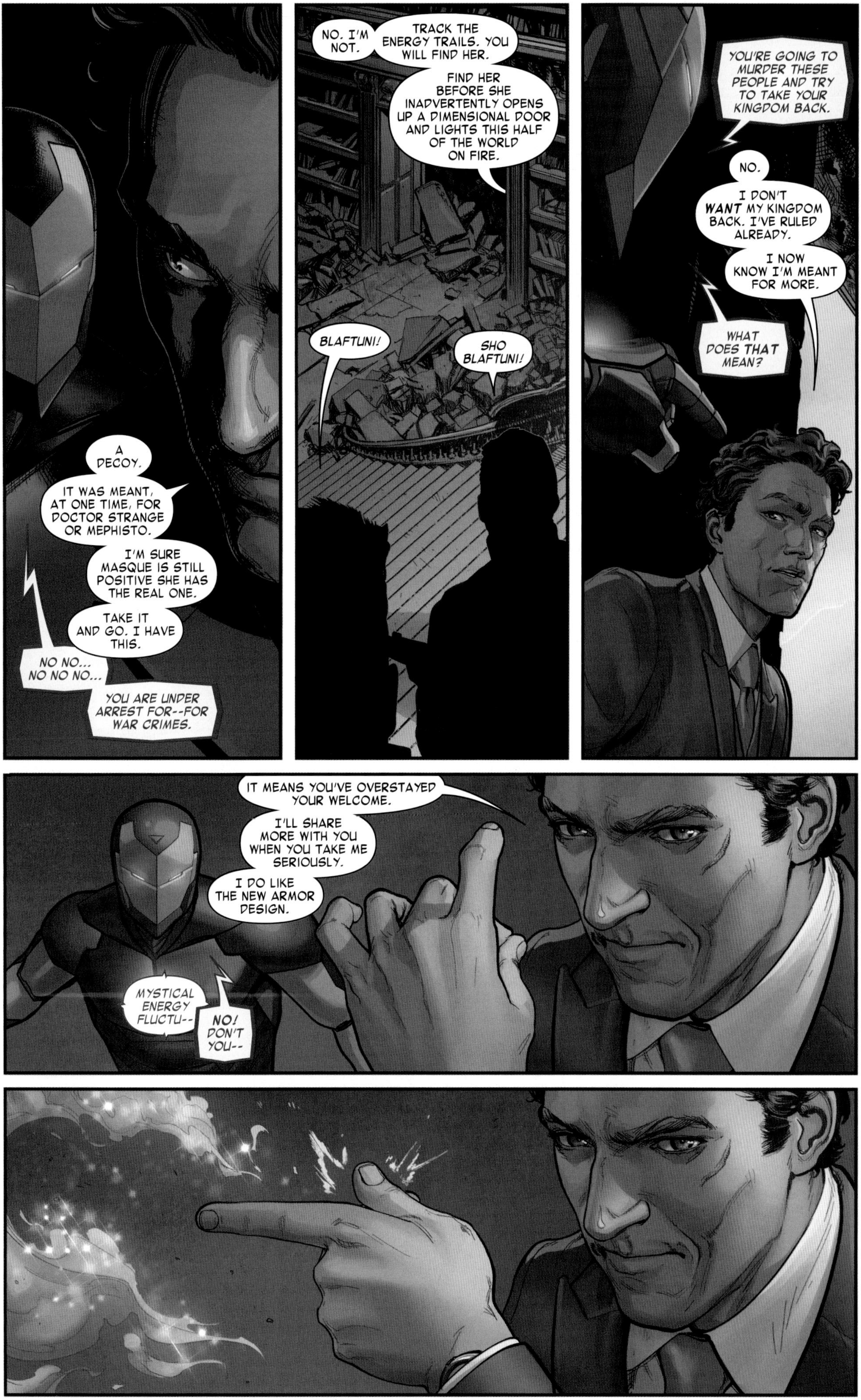
A DECOY.
IT WAS MEANT, AT ONE TIME, FOR DOCTOR STRANGE OR MEPHISTO.
I'M SURE MASQUE IS STILL POSITIVE SHE HAS THE REAL ONE.
TAKE IT AND GO. I HAVE THIS.
NO NO... NO NO NO...
YOU ARE UNDER ARREST FOR--FOR WAR CRIMES.
NO. I'M NOT.
TRACK THE ENERGY TRAILS. YOU WILL FIND HER.
FIND HER BEFORE SHE INADVERTENTLY OPENS UP A DIMENSIONAL DOOR AND LIGHTS THIS HALF OF THE WORLD ON FIRE.
BLAFTUNI!
SHO BLAFTUNI!
YOU'RE GOING TO MURDER THESE PEOPLE AND TRY TO TAKE YOUR KINGDOM BACK.
NO.
I DON'T WANT MY KINGDOM BACK. I'VE RULED ALREADY.
I NOW KNOW I'M MEANT FOR MORE.
WHAT DOES THAT MEAN?
IT MEANS YOU'VE OVERSTAYED YOUR WELCOME.
I'LL SHARE MORE WITH YOU WHEN YOU TAKE ME SERIOUSLY.
I DO LIKE THE NEW ARMOR DESIGN.
MYSTICAL ENERGY FLUCTU--
NO! DON'T YOU--

ARE WE DEAD?

PLEASE TELL ME THIS ISN'T HELL.

RECALIBRATING SYSTEM.

WRONG ANSWER.

DUDE!

IT'S FRICKIN' *IRON MAN!*

I LIKED IT BETTER WHEN HE HAD A NOSE ON HIS MASK.

(IT WAS MORE PERSONABLE.)

OH, YOU'RE INSANE.

HEY! IF HE'S IN SOME KIND OF SPACE-ALIEN FIGHT, WE NEED TO GET THE HELL *OUT* OF HERE!

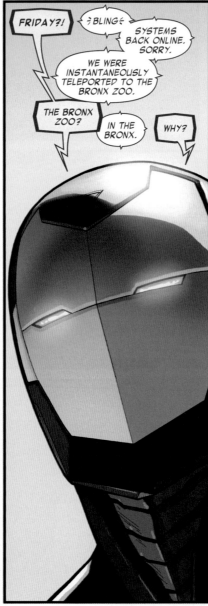

FRIDAY?!

⸮BLING⸮

SYSTEMS BACK ONLINE. SORRY.

WE WERE INSTANTANEOUSLY TELEPORTED TO THE BRONX ZOO.

THE BRONX ZOO?

IN THE BRONX.

WHY?

BECAUSE DOOM IS JUST... ODD?

PLOT A COURSE BACK TO LATVERIA.

NO.

NO?

NO, THANK YOU?

LISTEN, ACCORDING TO NEW HACKED SATELLITE FOOTAGE, THAT FIGHT IS OVER AND DOOM IS GONE.

HOW ABOUT INSTEAD I TRACK THE ENERGY TRAIL DOOM POINTED OUT COULD LEAD US TO MADAME MASQUE?

OR YOU COULD DO THAT!

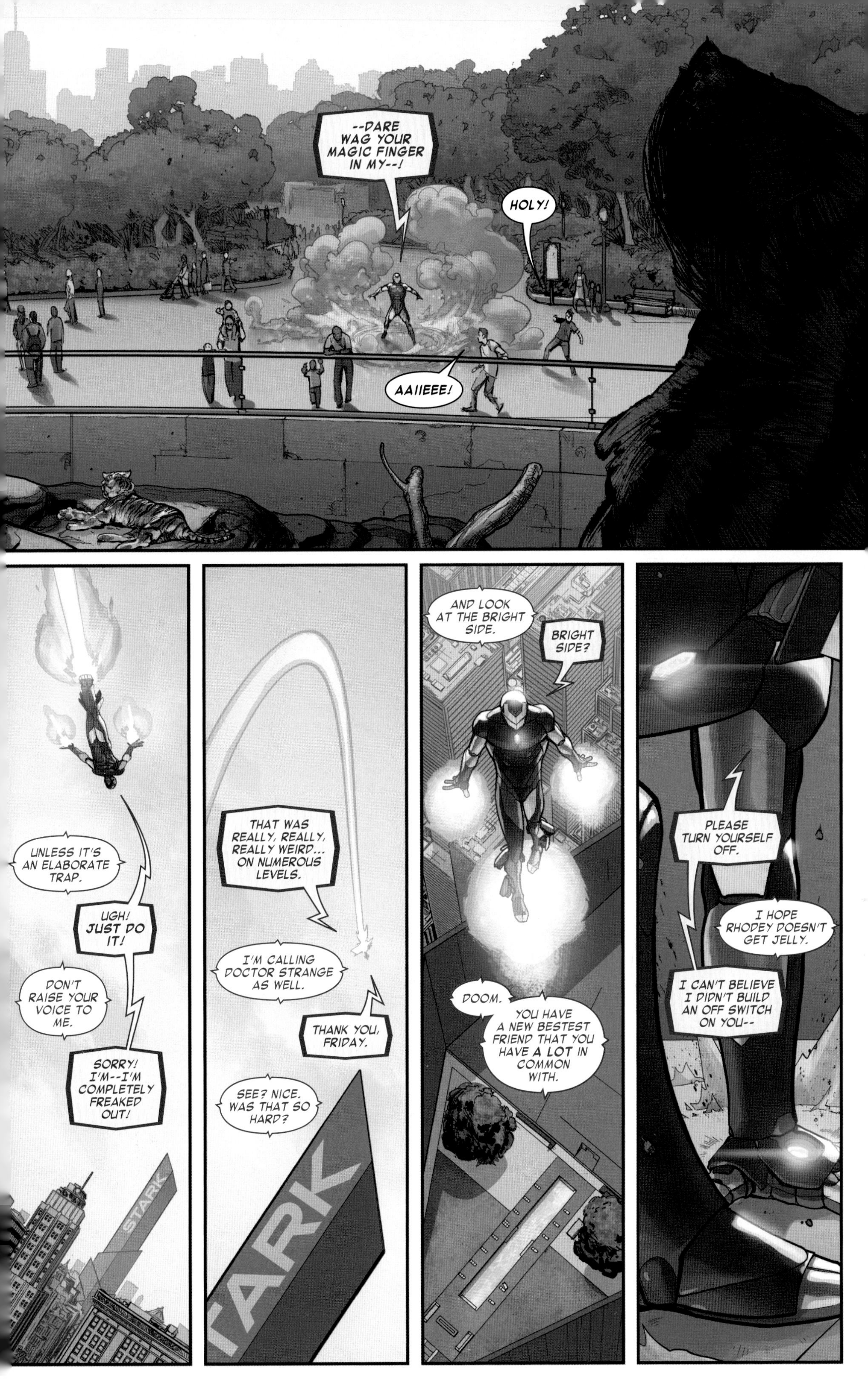
--DARE WAG YOUR MAGIC FINGER IN MY--!
HOLY!
AAIIEEE!
UNLESS IT'S AN ELABORATE TRAP.
UGH! JUST DO IT!
DON'T RAISE YOUR VOICE TO ME.
SORRY! I'M--I'M COMPLETELY FREAKED OUT!
STARK
THAT WAS REALLY, REALLY, REALLY WEIRD... ON NUMEROUS LEVELS.
I'M CALLING DOCTOR STRANGE AS WELL.
THANK YOU, FRIDAY.
SEE? NICE. WAS THAT SO HARD?
STARK
AND LOOK AT THE BRIGHT SIDE.
BRIGHT SIDE?
DOOM.
YOU HAVE A NEW BESTEST FRIEND THAT YOU HAVE A LOT IN COMMON WITH.
PLEASE TURN YOURSELF OFF.
I HOPE RHODEY DOESN'T GET JELLY.
I CAN'T BELIEVE I DIDN'T BUILD AN OFF SWITCH ON YOU--

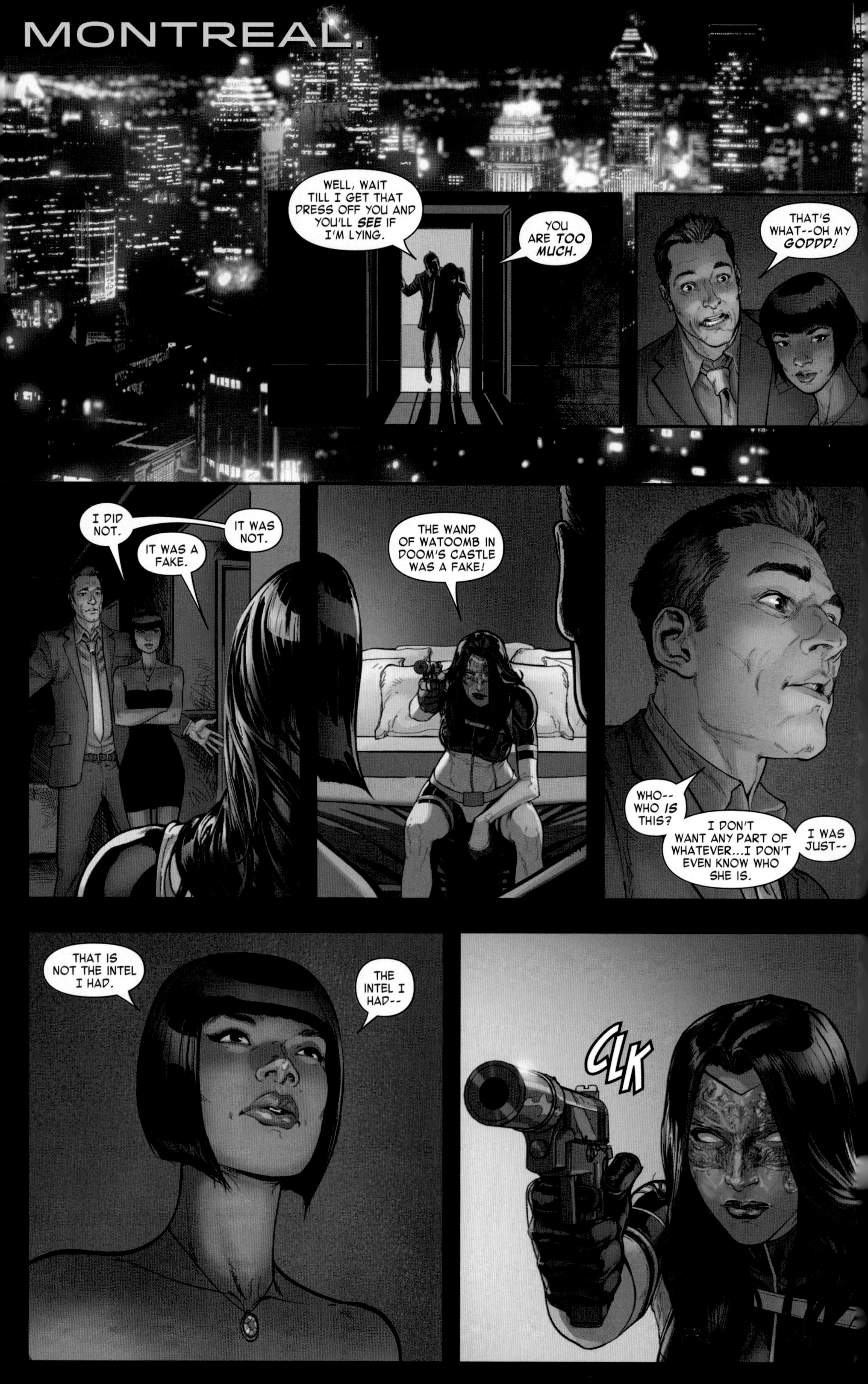
MONTREAL.
WELL, WAIT TILL I GET THAT DRESS OFF YOU AND YOU'LL SEE IF I'M LYING.
YOU ARE TOO MUCH.
THAT'S WHAT--OH MY GODDD!
I DID NOT.
IT WAS NOT.
IT WAS A FAKE.
THE WAND OF WATOOMB IN DOOM'S CASTLE WAS A FAKE!
WHO-- WHO IS THIS?
I DON'T WANT ANY PART OF WHATEVER...I DON'T EVEN KNOW WHO SHE IS.
I WAS JUST--
THAT IS NOT THE INTEL I HAD.
THE INTEL I HAD--
CLK

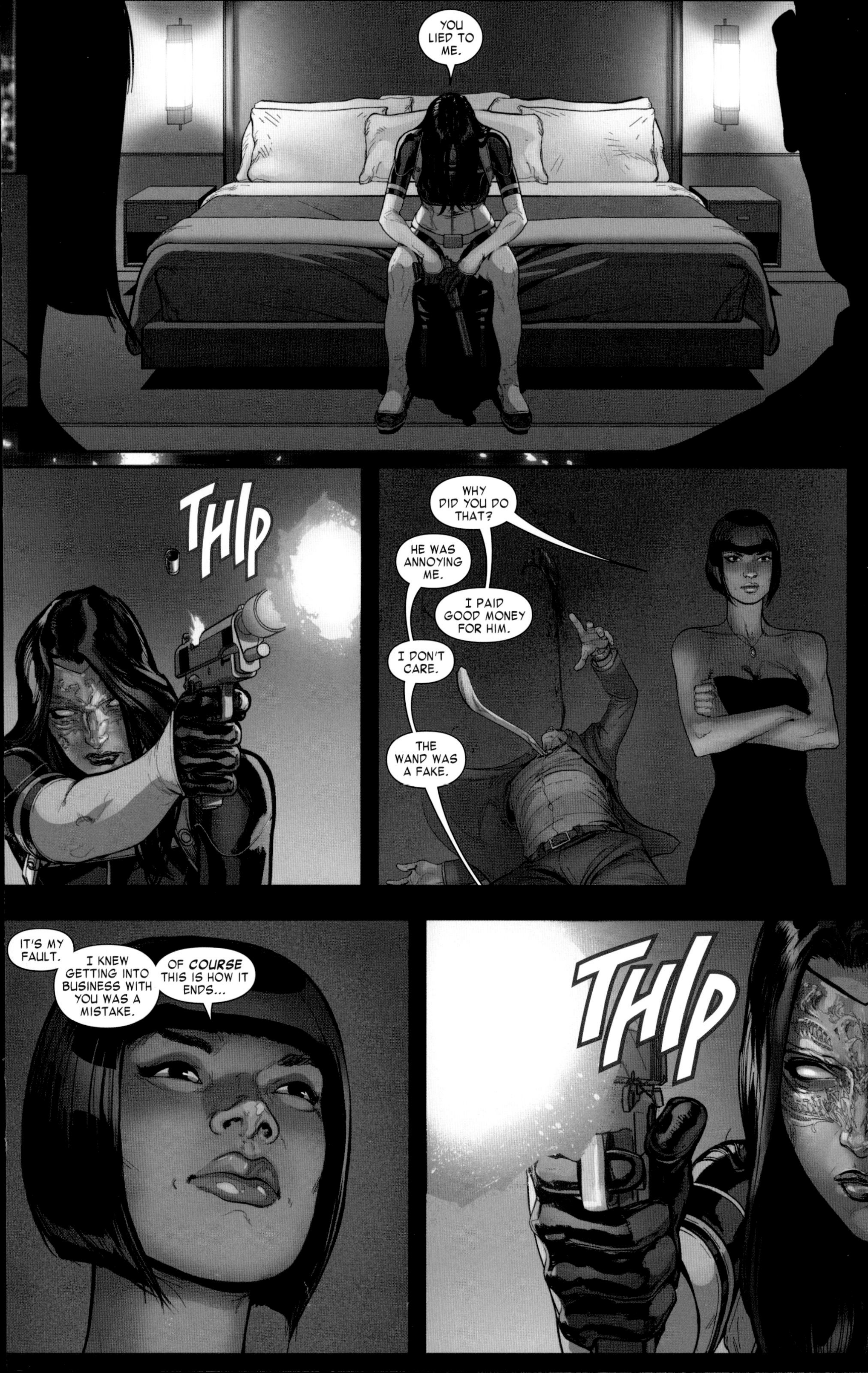

YOU LIED TO ME.
THIP
WHY DID YOU DO THAT?
HE WAS ANNOYING ME.
I PAID GOOD MONEY FOR HIM.
I DON'T CARE.
THE WAND WAS A FAKE.
IT'S MY FAULT.
I KNEW GETTING INTO BUSINESS WITH YOU WAS A MISTAKE.
OF COURSE THIS IS HOW IT ENDS...
THIP

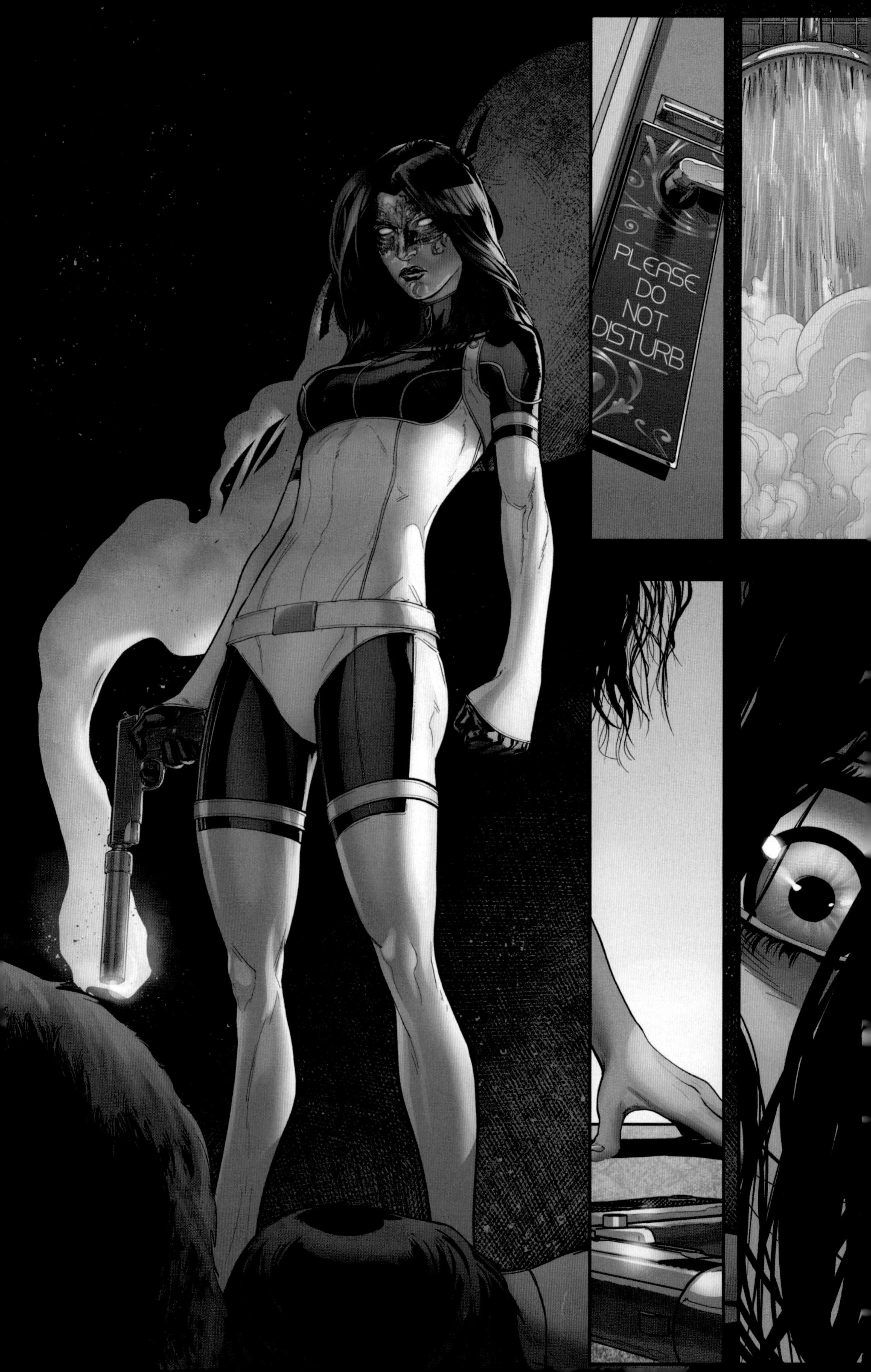

PLEASE DO NOT DISTURB

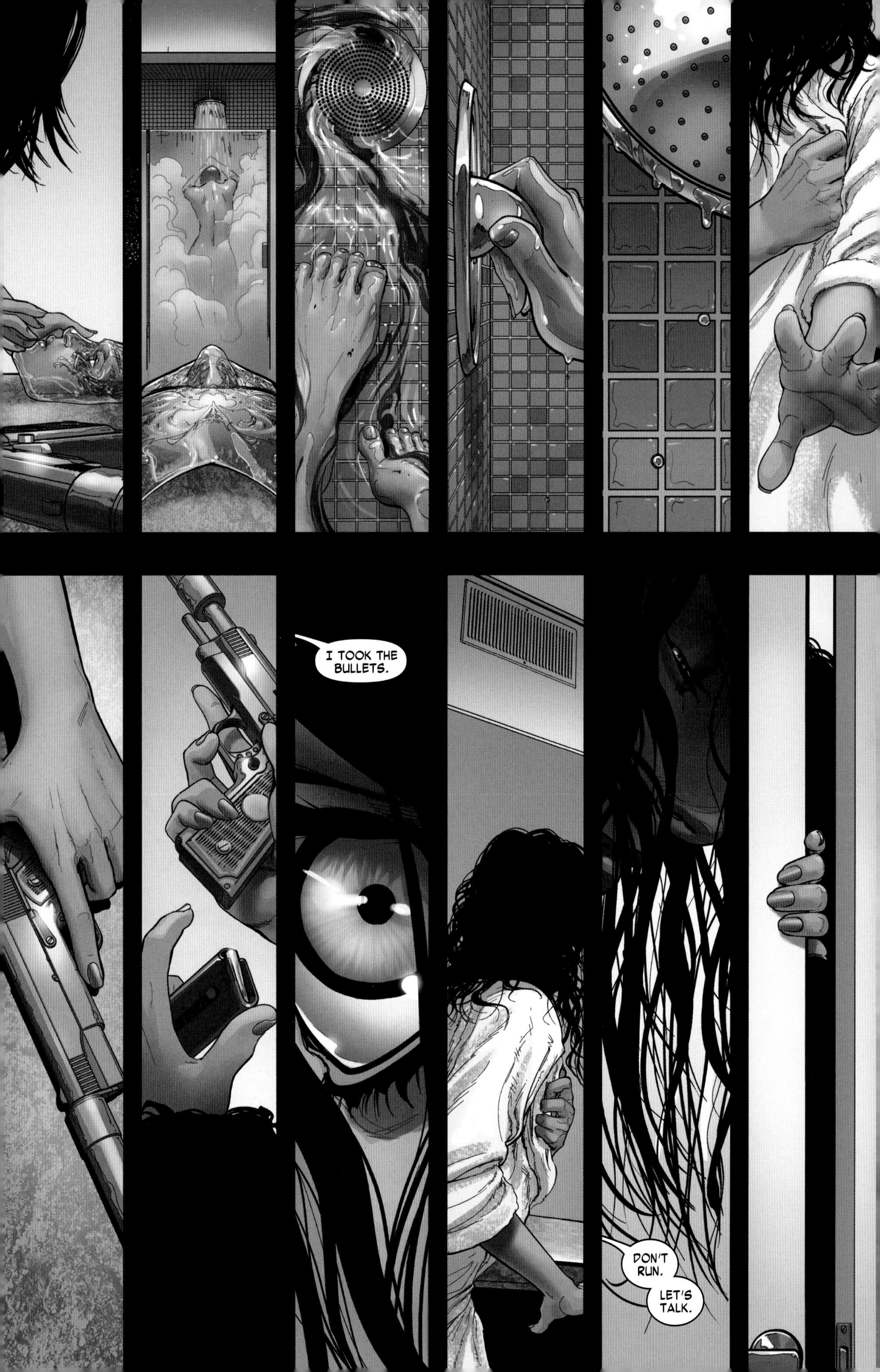
I TOOK THE BULLETS.
DON'T RUN.
LET'S TALK.

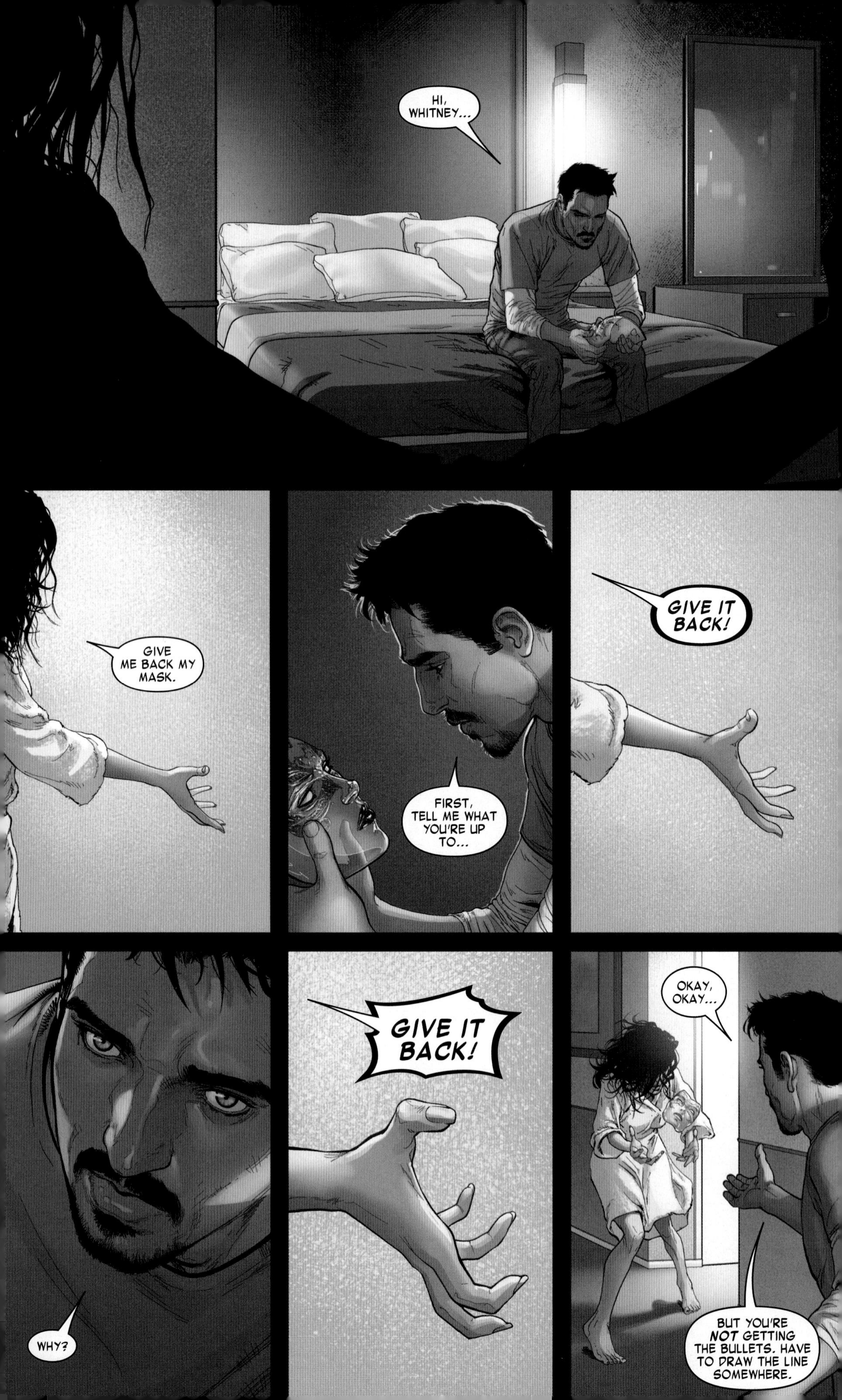
HI, WHITNEY...
GIVE ME BACK MY MASK.
FIRST, TELL ME WHAT YOU'RE UP TO...
GIVE IT BACK!
WHY?
GIVE IT BACK!
OKAY, OKAY...
BUT YOU'RE NOT GETTING THE BULLETS. HAVE TO DRAW THE LINE SOMEWHERE.

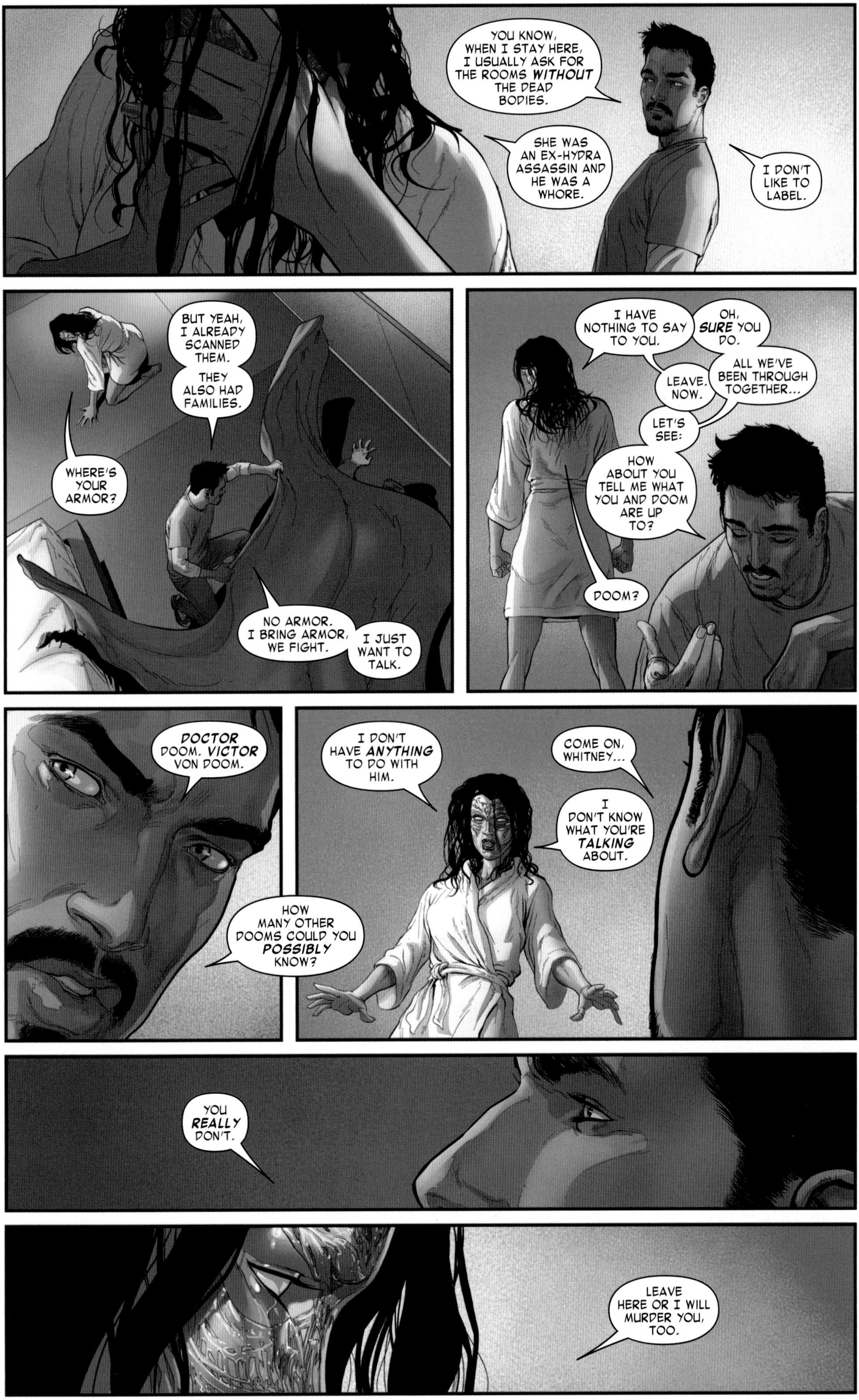

YOU KNOW, WHEN I STAY HERE, I USUALLY ASK FOR THE ROOMS WITHOUT THE DEAD BODIES.
SHE WAS AN EX-HYDRA ASSASSIN AND HE WAS A WHORE.
I DON'T LIKE TO LABEL.
BUT YEAH, I ALREADY SCANNED THEM.
THEY ALSO HAD FAMILIES.
WHERE'S YOUR ARMOR?
NO ARMOR. I BRING ARMOR, WE FIGHT.
I JUST WANT TO TALK.
I HAVE NOTHING TO SAY TO YOU.
OH, SURE YOU DO.
LEAVE. NOW.
ALL WE'VE BEEN THROUGH TOGETHER...
LET'S SEE:
HOW ABOUT YOU TELL ME WHAT YOU AND DOOM ARE UP TO?
DOOM?
DOCTOR DOOM. VICTOR VON DOOM.
HOW MANY OTHER DOOMS COULD YOU POSSIBLY KNOW?
I DON'T HAVE ANYTHING TO DO WITH HIM.
COME ON, WHITNEY...
I DON'T KNOW WHAT YOU'RE TALKING ABOUT.
YOU REALLY DON'T.
LEAVE HERE OR I WILL MURDER YOU, TOO.

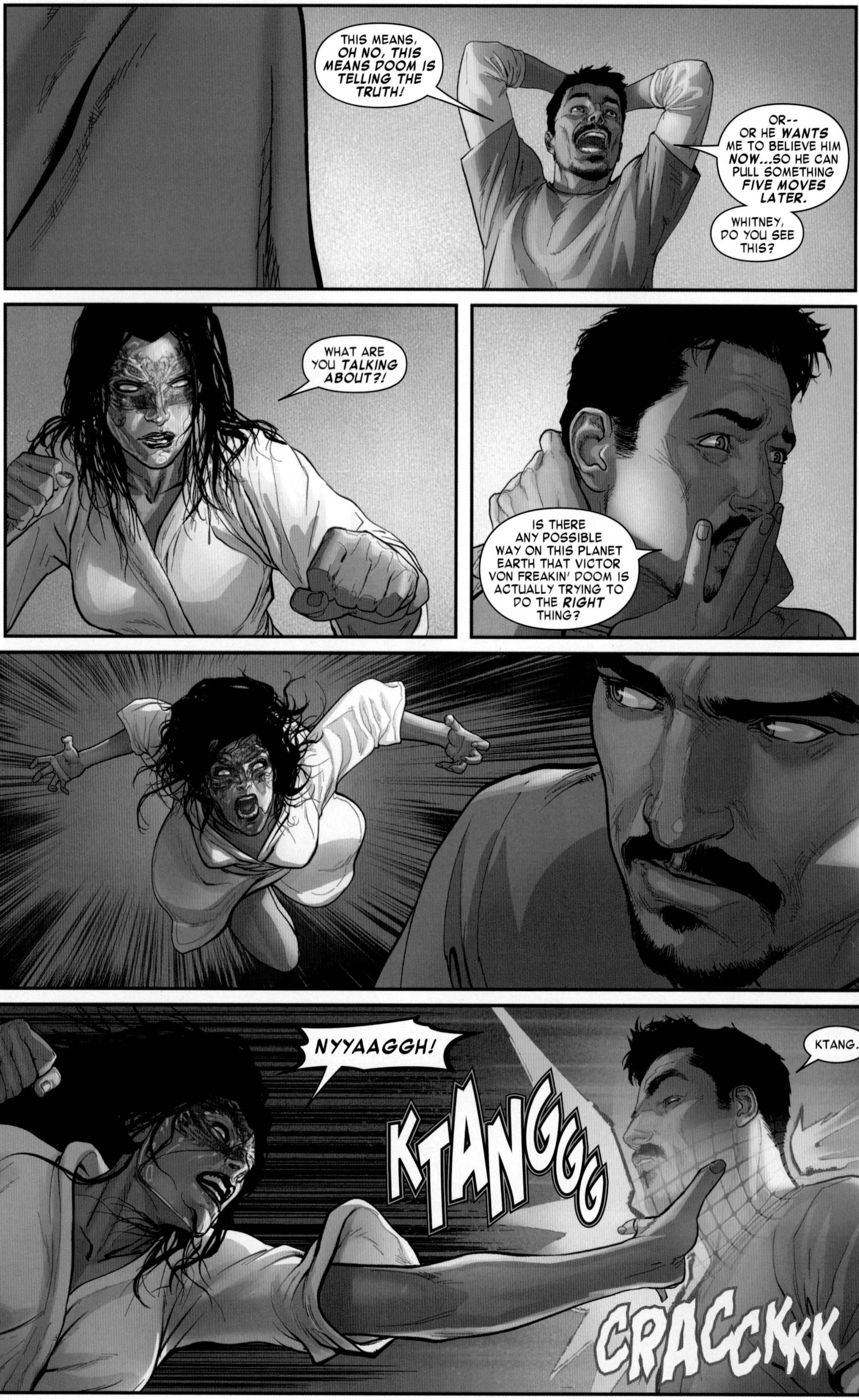
THIS MEANS, OH NO, THIS MEANS DOOM IS TELLING THE TRUTH!
OR-- OR HE WANTS ME TO BELIEVE HIM NOW...SO HE CAN PULL SOMETHING FIVE MOVES LATER.
WHITNEY, DO YOU SEE THIS?
WHAT ARE YOU TALKING ABOUT?!
IS THERE ANY POSSIBLE WAY ON THIS PLANET EARTH THAT VICTOR VON FREAKIN' DOOM IS ACTUALLY TRYING TO DO THE RIGHT THING?
NYYAAGGH!
KTANGGG
KTANG.
CRACCKKK

STEALTH MODE. STANDARD ON ALL THE NEW MODELS. IT'S ALL THE RAGE WITH US A-LIST-TOP-TIER-ARMOR-WEARING SUPER HEROES.

MMRRR!

I KNOW. YOUR HAND'S BROKEN IN THREE PLACES.

WHITNEY, FOR OLD TIMES' SAKE, SHUT IT DOWN.

YOU NEED HELP. BADLY. YOU'RE UNDER ARREST. NO REASON THIS CAN'T BE CIVIL.

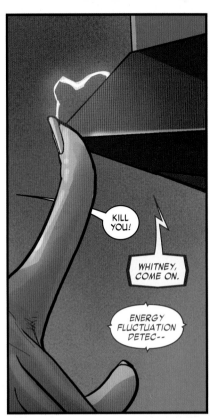

KILL YOU!

WHITNEY, COME ON.

ENERGY FLUCTUATION DETEC--

WHAT ARE YOU-- AAGH!

DIE!

FZZTTKK

DIE!

#3

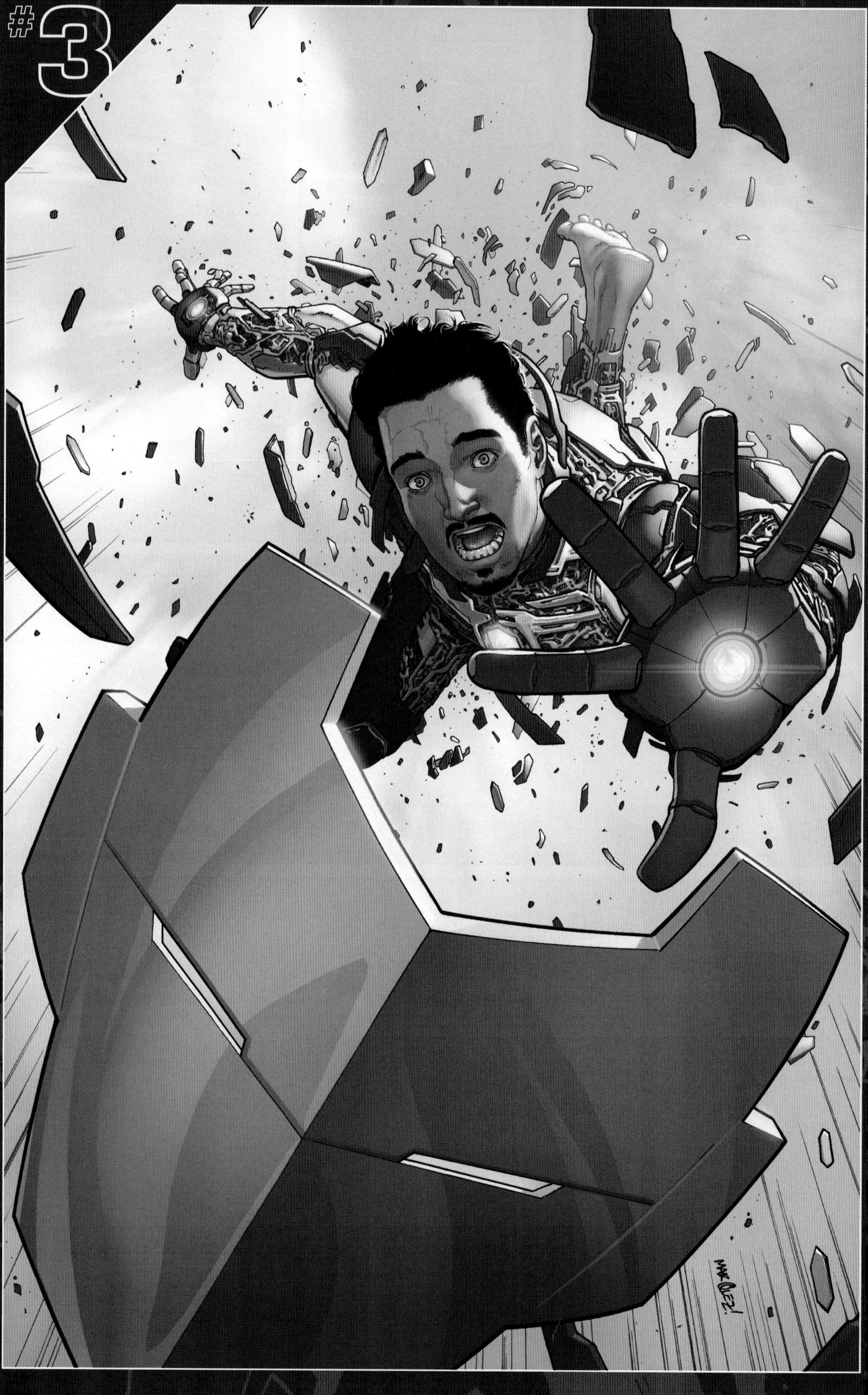

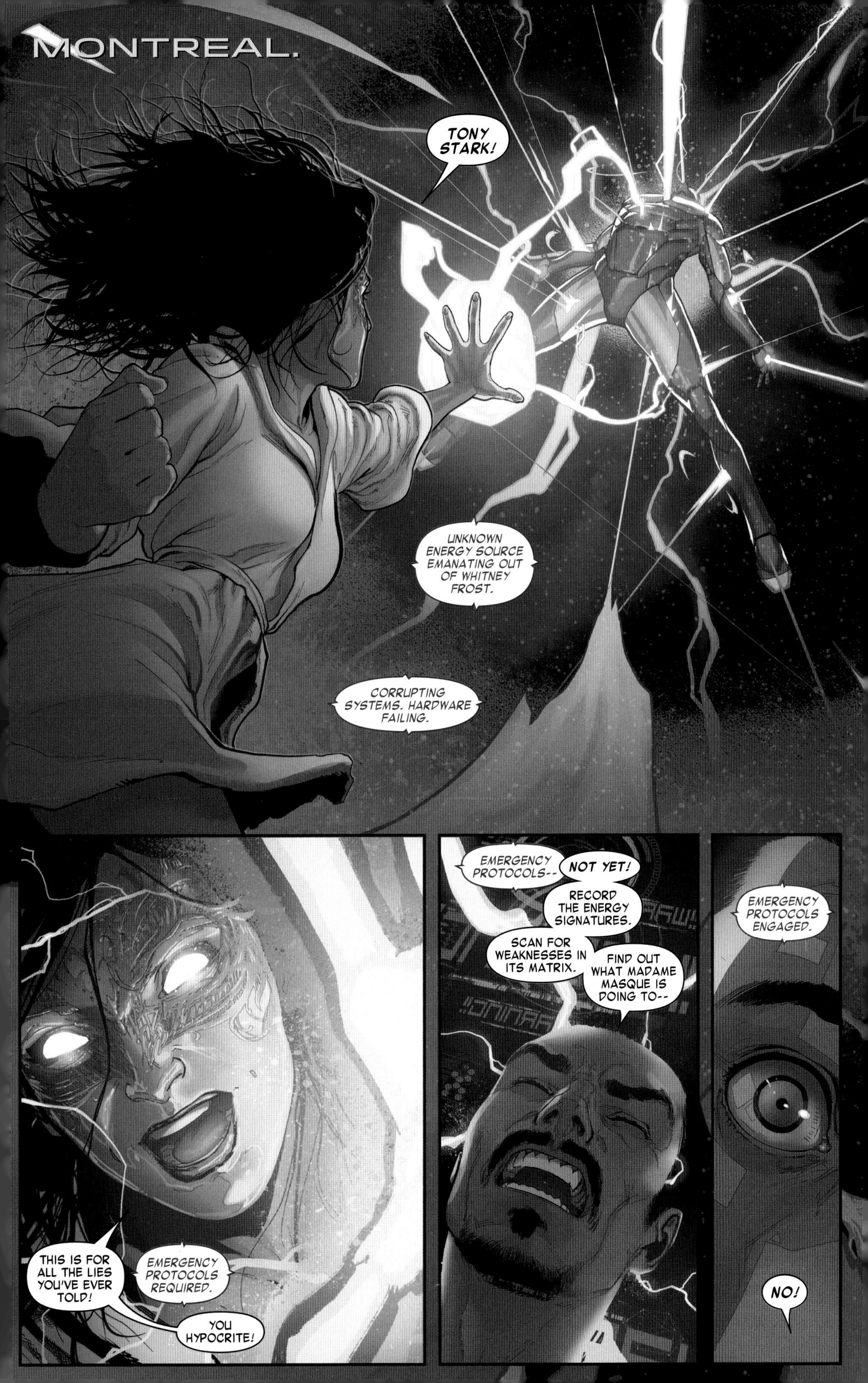
MONTREAL.
TONY STARK!
UNKNOWN ENERGY SOURCE EMANATING OUT OF WHITNEY FROST.
CORRUPTING SYSTEMS. HARDWARE FAILING.
THIS IS FOR ALL THE LIES YOU'VE EVER TOLD!
EMERGENCY PROTOCOLS REQUIRED.
YOU HYPOCRITE!
EMERGENCY PROTOCOLS--
NOT YET!
RECORD THE ENERGY SIGNATURES.
SCAN FOR WEAKNESSES IN ITS MATRIX.
FIND OUT WHAT MADAME MASQUE IS DOING TO--
EMERGENCY PROTOCOLS ENGAGED.
NO!

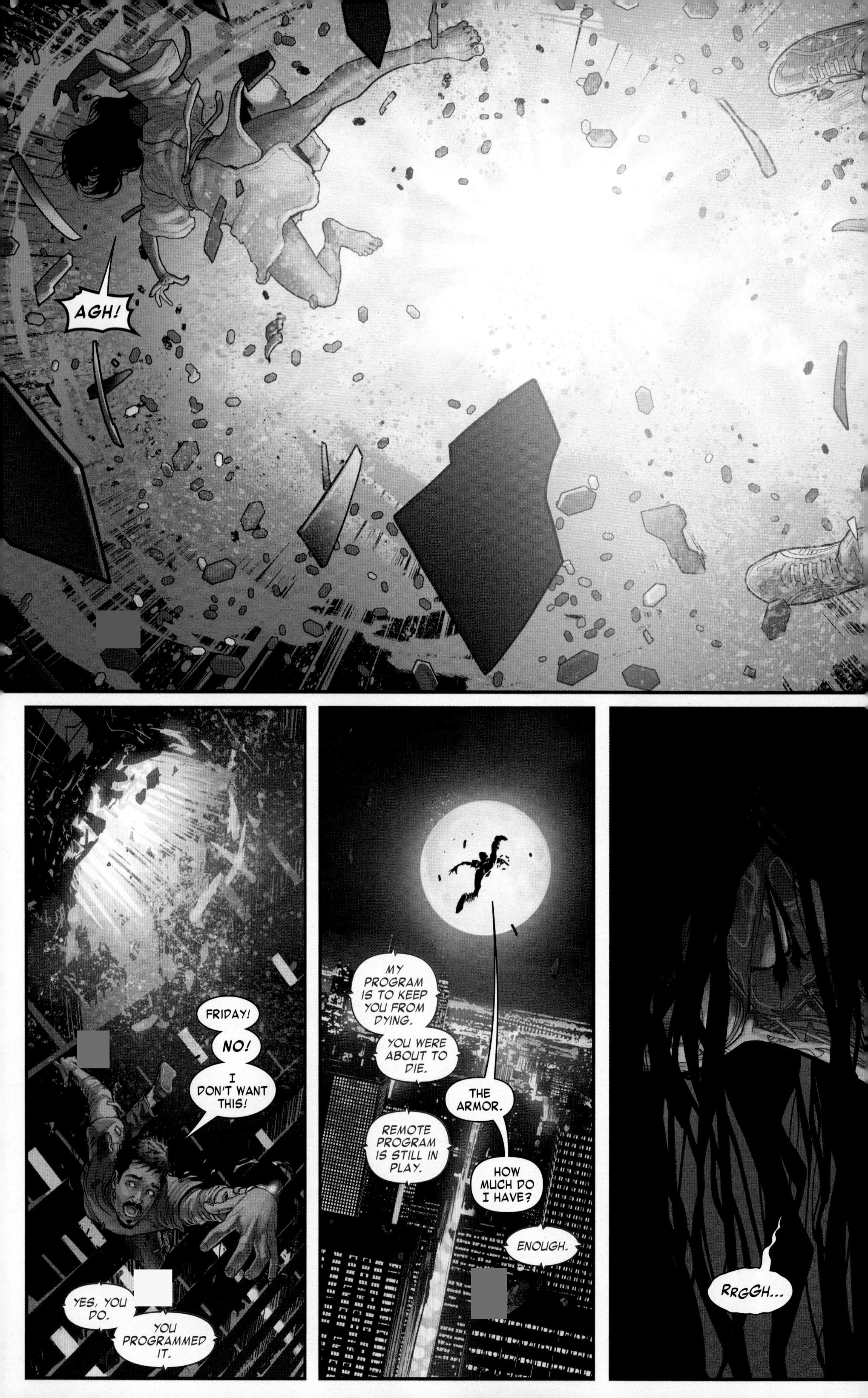
AGH!
FRIDAY!
NO!
I DON'T WANT THIS!
YES, YOU DO.
YOU PROGRAMMED IT.
MY PROGRAM IS TO KEEP YOU FROM DYING.
YOU WERE ABOUT TO DIE.
THE ARMOR.
REMOTE PROGRAM IS STILL IN PLAY.
HOW MUCH DO I HAVE?
ENOUGH.
RRGGH...

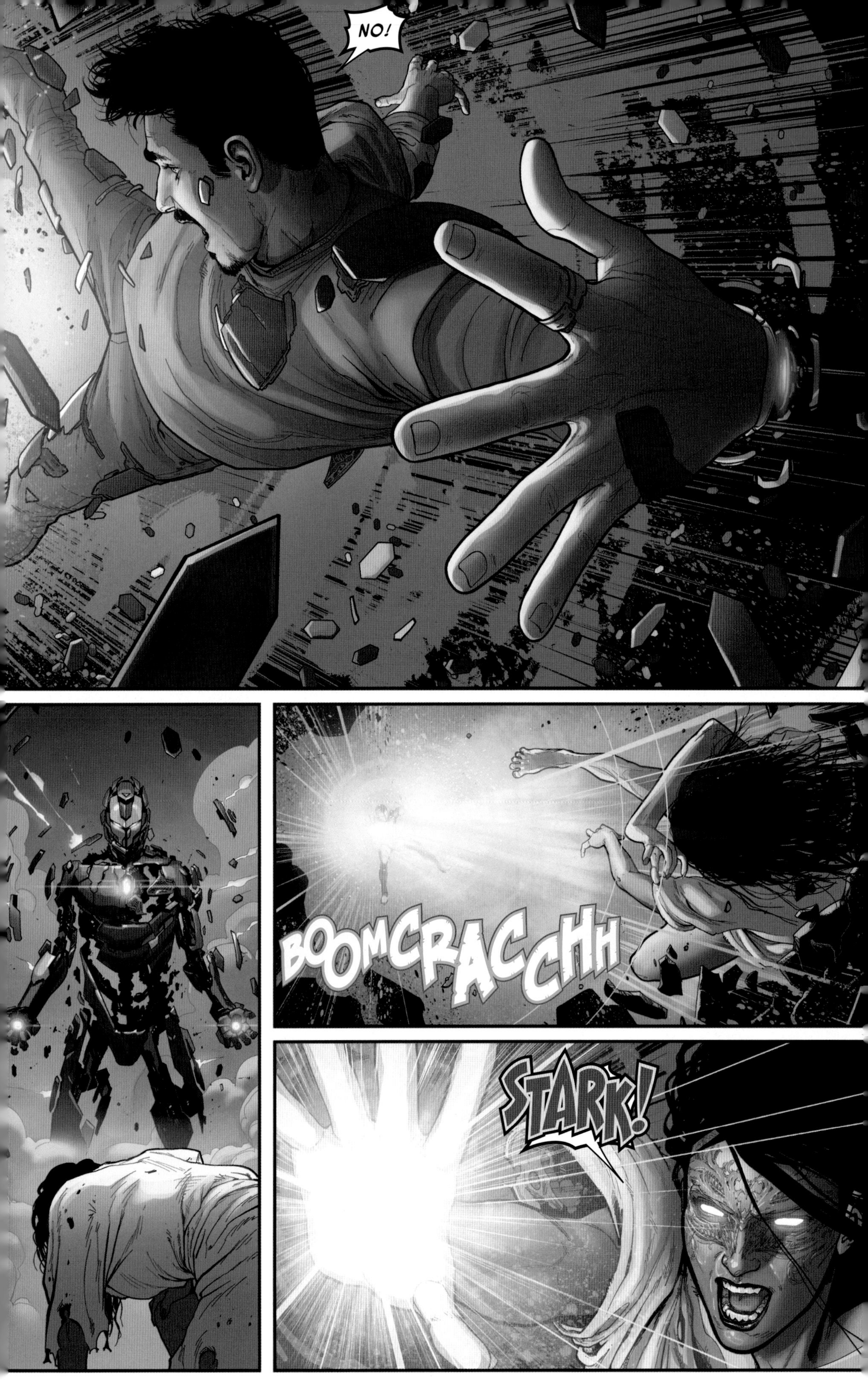
NO!
BOOMCRACCHH
STARK!

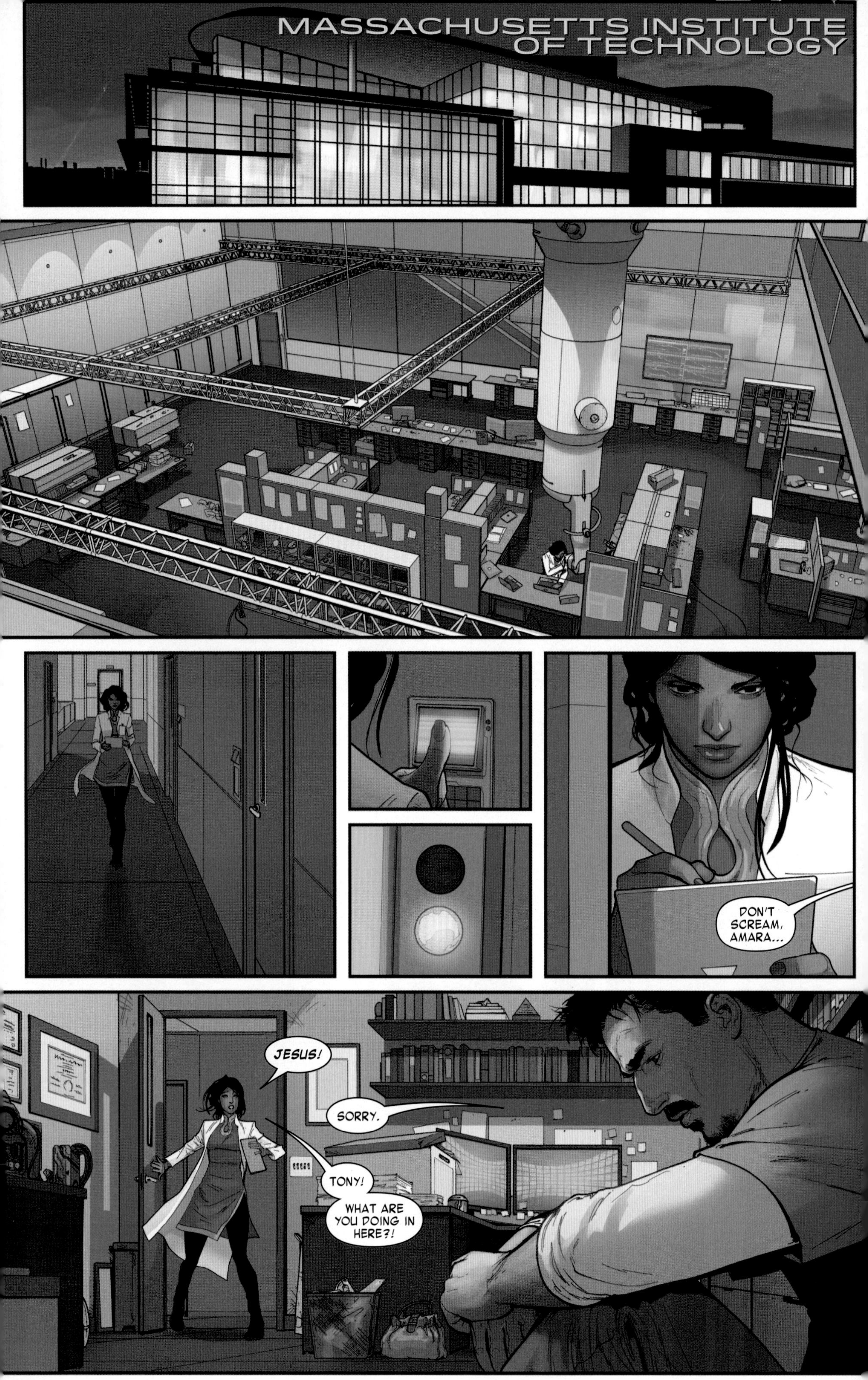
MASSACHUSETTS INSTITUTE OF TECHNOLOGY
DON'T SCREAM, AMARA...
JESUS!
SORRY.
TONY!
WHAT ARE YOU DOING IN HERE?!

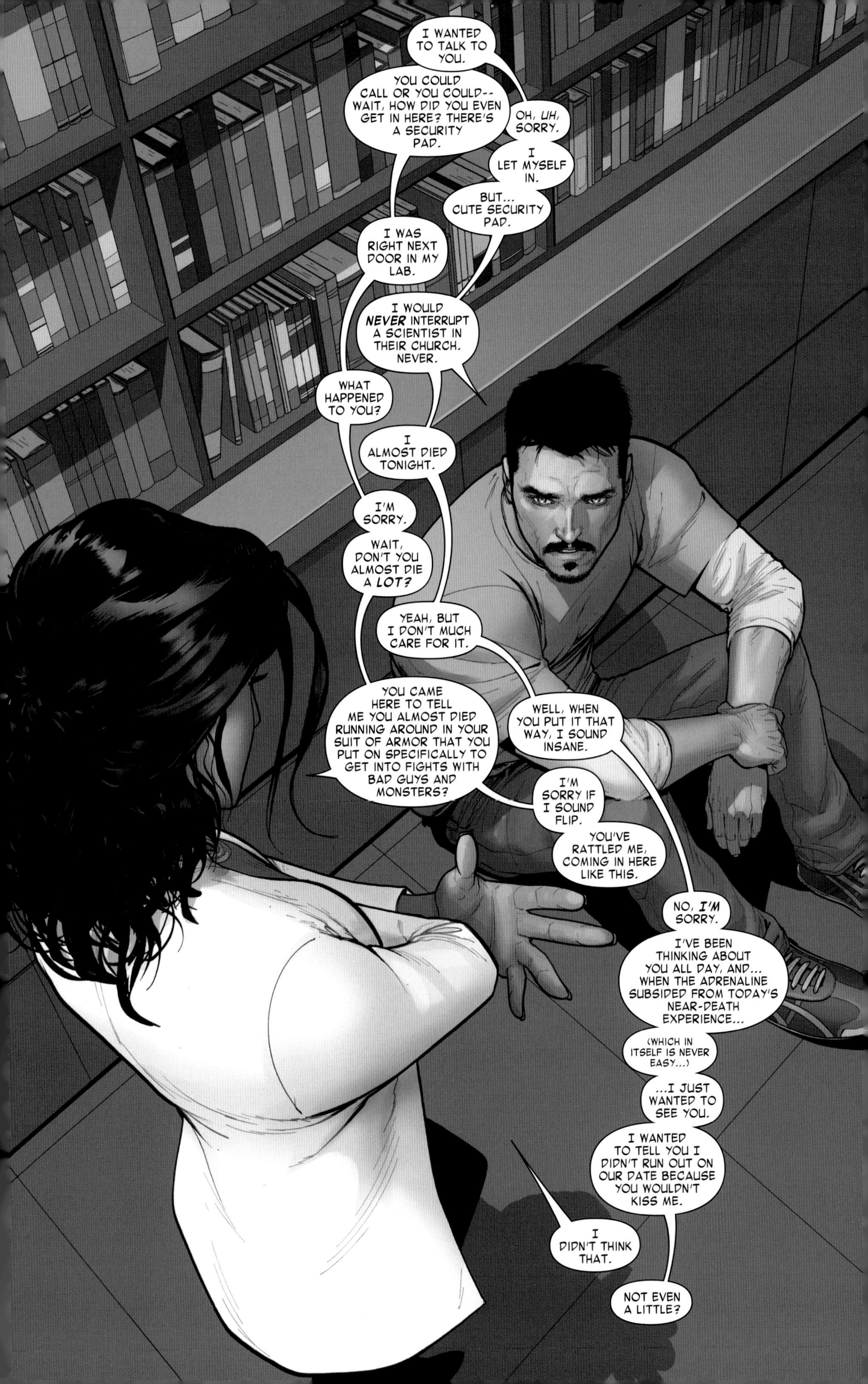
I WANTED TO TALK TO YOU.
YOU COULD CALL OR YOU COULD-- WAIT, HOW DID YOU EVEN GET IN HERE? THERE'S A SECURITY PAD.
OH, UH, SORRY.
I LET MYSELF IN.
BUT... CUTE SECURITY PAD.
I WAS RIGHT NEXT DOOR IN MY LAB.
I WOULD NEVER INTERRUPT A SCIENTIST IN THEIR CHURCH. NEVER.
WHAT HAPPENED TO YOU?
I ALMOST DIED TONIGHT.
I'M SORRY.
WAIT, DON'T YOU ALMOST DIE A LOT?
YEAH, BUT I DON'T MUCH CARE FOR IT.
YOU CAME HERE TO TELL ME YOU ALMOST DIED RUNNING AROUND IN YOUR SUIT OF ARMOR THAT YOU PUT ON SPECIFICALLY TO GET INTO FIGHTS WITH BAD GUYS AND MONSTERS?
WELL, WHEN YOU PUT IT THAT WAY, I SOUND INSANE.
I'M SORRY IF I SOUND FLIP.
YOU'VE RATTLED ME, COMING IN HERE LIKE THIS.
NO, I'M SORRY.
I'VE BEEN THINKING ABOUT YOU ALL DAY, AND... WHEN THE ADRENALINE SUBSIDED FROM TODAY'S NEAR-DEATH EXPERIENCE...
(WHICH IN ITSELF IS NEVER EASY...)
...I JUST WANTED TO SEE YOU.
I WANTED TO TELL YOU I DIDN'T RUN OUT ON OUR DATE BECAUSE YOU WOULDN'T KISS ME.
I DIDN'T THINK THAT.
NOT EVEN A LITTLE?

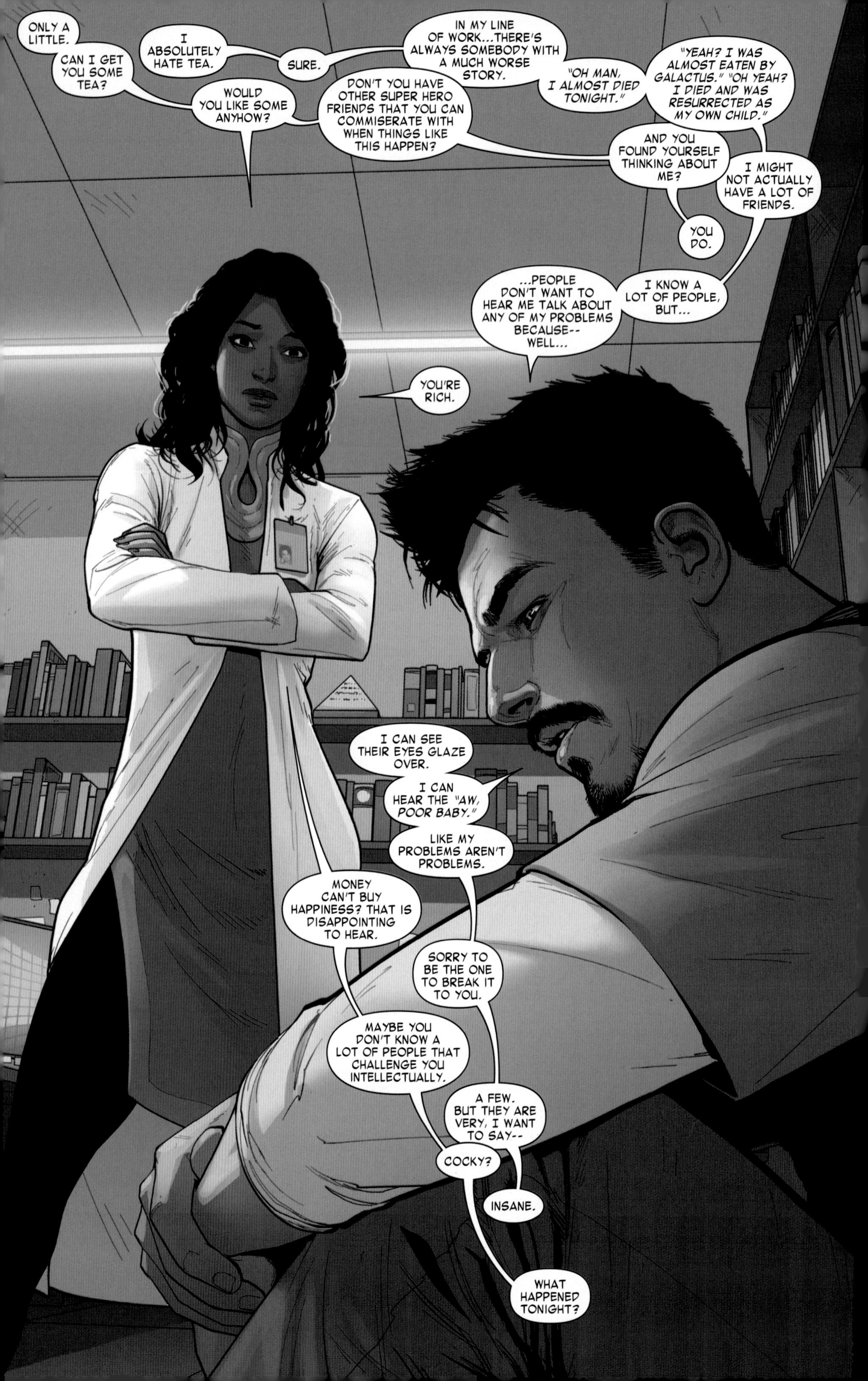
ONLY A LITTLE.
CAN I GET YOU SOME TEA?
I ABSOLUTELY HATE TEA.
WOULD YOU LIKE SOME ANYHOW?
SURE.
IN MY LINE OF WORK...THERE'S ALWAYS SOMEBODY WITH A MUCH WORSE STORY.
DON'T YOU HAVE OTHER SUPER HERO FRIENDS THAT YOU CAN COMMISERATE WITH WHEN THINGS LIKE THIS HAPPEN?
"OH MAN, I ALMOST DIED TONIGHT."
"YEAH? I WAS ALMOST EATEN BY GALACTUS." "OH YEAH? I DIED AND WAS RESURRECTED AS MY OWN CHILD."
AND YOU FOUND YOURSELF THINKING ABOUT ME?
I MIGHT NOT ACTUALLY HAVE A LOT OF FRIENDS.
YOU DO.
I KNOW A LOT OF PEOPLE, BUT...
...PEOPLE DON'T WANT TO HEAR ME TALK ABOUT ANY OF MY PROBLEMS BECAUSE-- WELL...
YOU'RE RICH.
I CAN SEE THEIR EYES GLAZE OVER.
I CAN HEAR THE "AW, POOR BABY."
LIKE MY PROBLEMS AREN'T PROBLEMS.
MONEY CAN'T BUY HAPPINESS? THAT IS DISAPPOINTING TO HEAR.
SORRY TO BE THE ONE TO BREAK IT TO YOU.
MAYBE YOU DON'T KNOW A LOT OF PEOPLE THAT CHALLENGE YOU INTELLECTUALLY.
A FEW. BUT THEY ARE VERY, I WANT TO SAY--
COCKY?
INSANE.
WHAT HAPPENED TONIGHT?

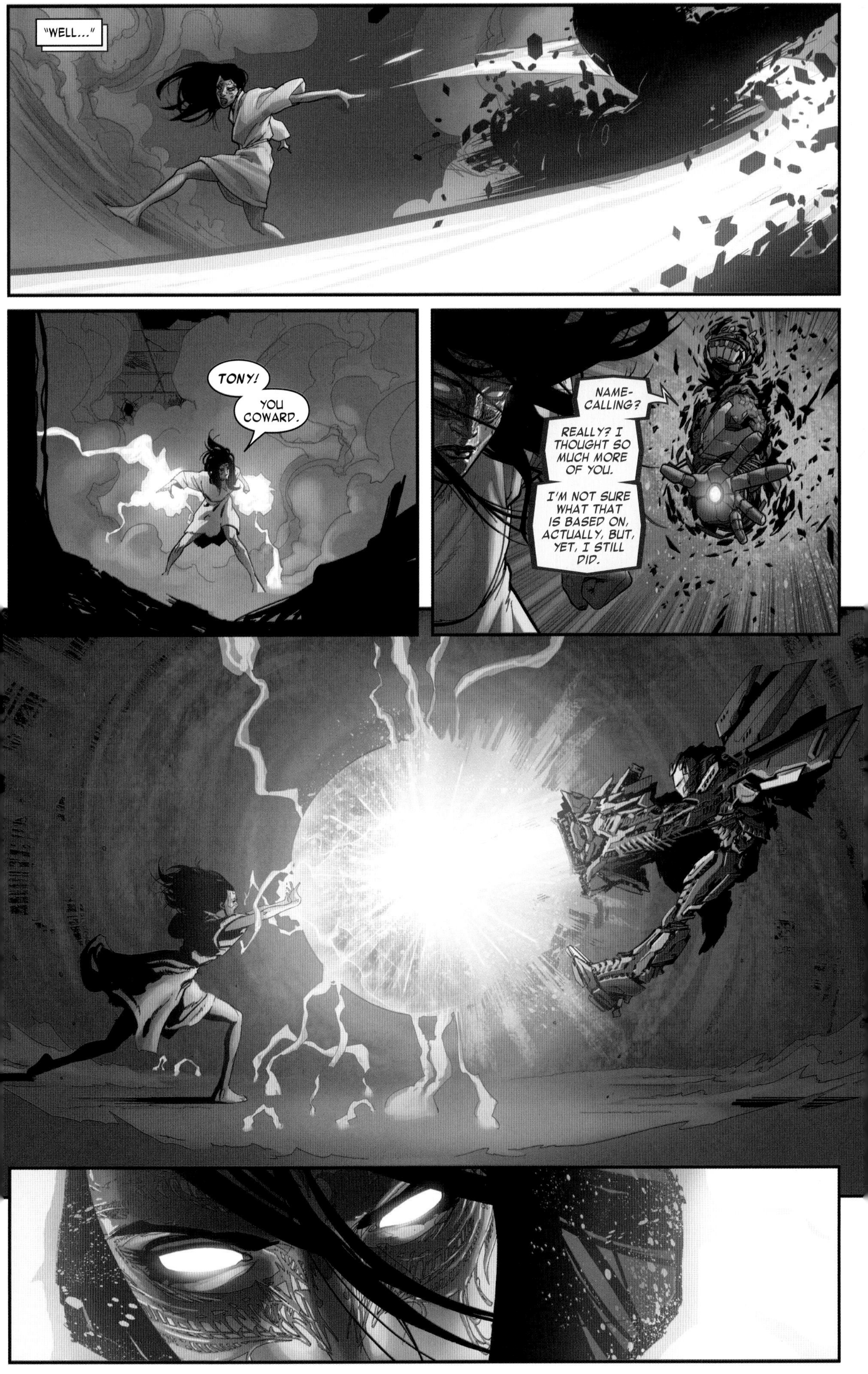
"WELL..."
TONY!
YOU COWARD.
NAME-CALLING?
REALLY? I THOUGHT SO MUCH MORE OF YOU.
I'M NOT SURE WHAT THAT IS BASED ON, ACTUALLY, BUT, YET, I STILL DID.

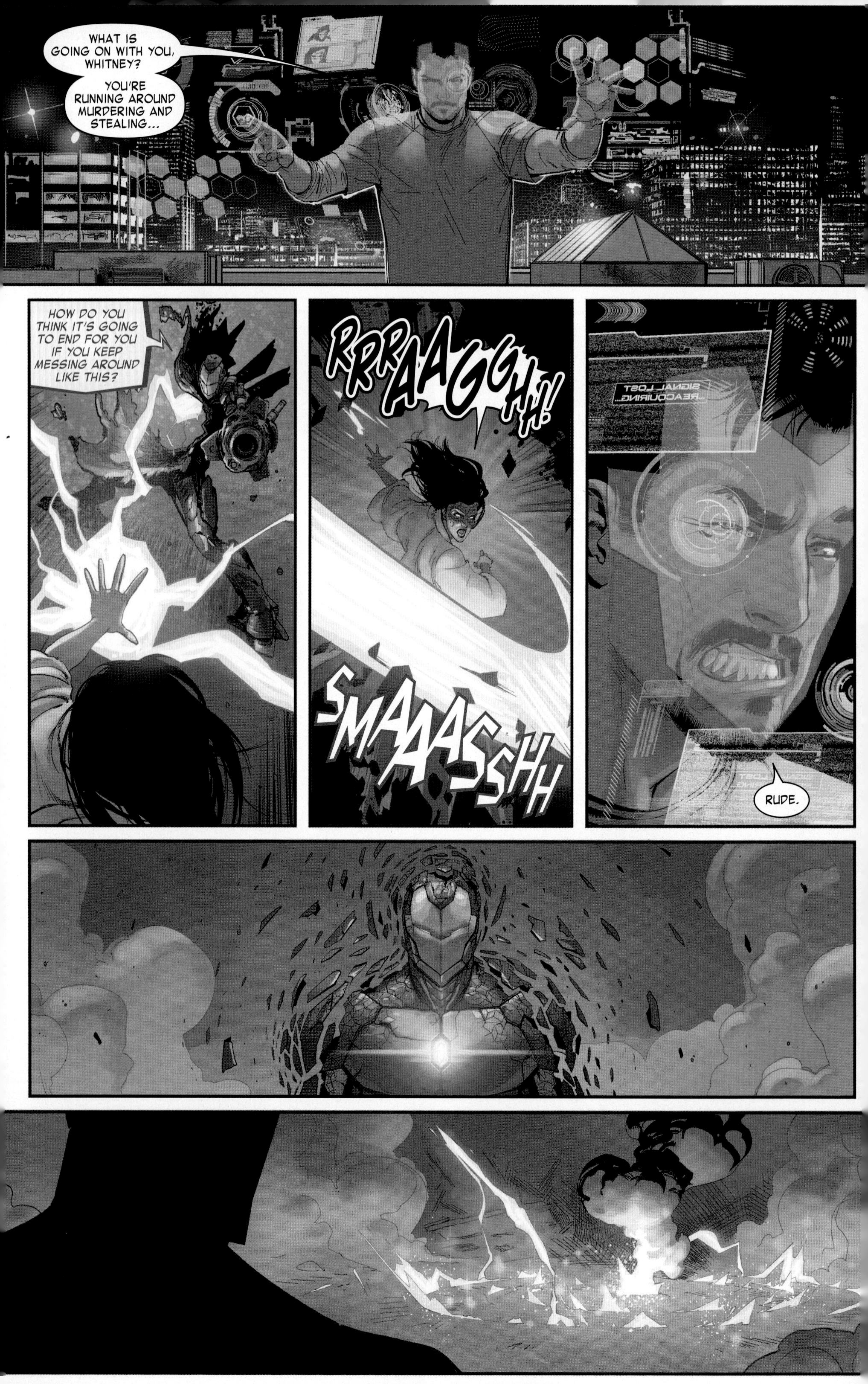
WHAT IS GOING ON WITH YOU, WHITNEY?
YOU'RE RUNNING AROUND MURDERING AND STEALING...
HOW DO YOU THINK IT'S GOING TO END FOR YOU IF YOU KEEP MESSING AROUND LIKE THIS?
RRRAAGGHH!
SMAAASSHH
SIGNAL LOST ...REACQUIRING...
RUDE.

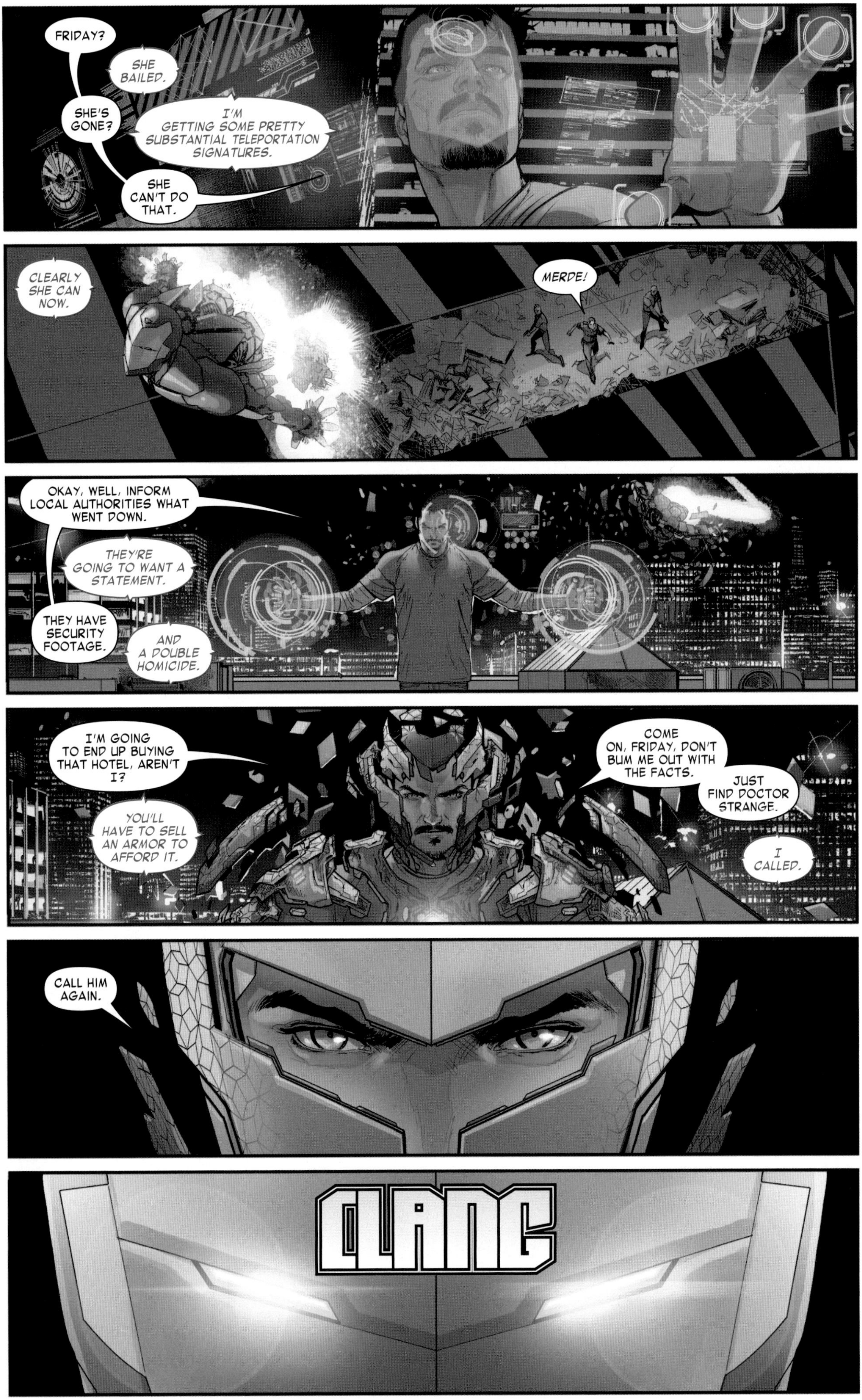

FRIDAY?
SHE BAILED.
SHE'S GONE?
I'M GETTING SOME PRETTY SUBSTANTIAL TELEPORTATION SIGNATURES.
SHE CAN'T DO THAT.
CLEARLY SHE CAN NOW.
MERDE!
OKAY, WELL, INFORM LOCAL AUTHORITIES WHAT WENT DOWN.
THEY'RE GOING TO WANT A STATEMENT.
THEY HAVE SECURITY FOOTAGE.
AND A DOUBLE HOMICIDE.
I'M GOING TO END UP BUYING THAT HOTEL, AREN'T I?
YOU'LL HAVE TO SELL AN ARMOR TO AFFORD IT.
COME ON, FRIDAY, DON'T BUM ME OUT WITH THE FACTS.
JUST FIND DOCTOR STRANGE.
I CALLED.
CALL HIM AGAIN.
CLANG

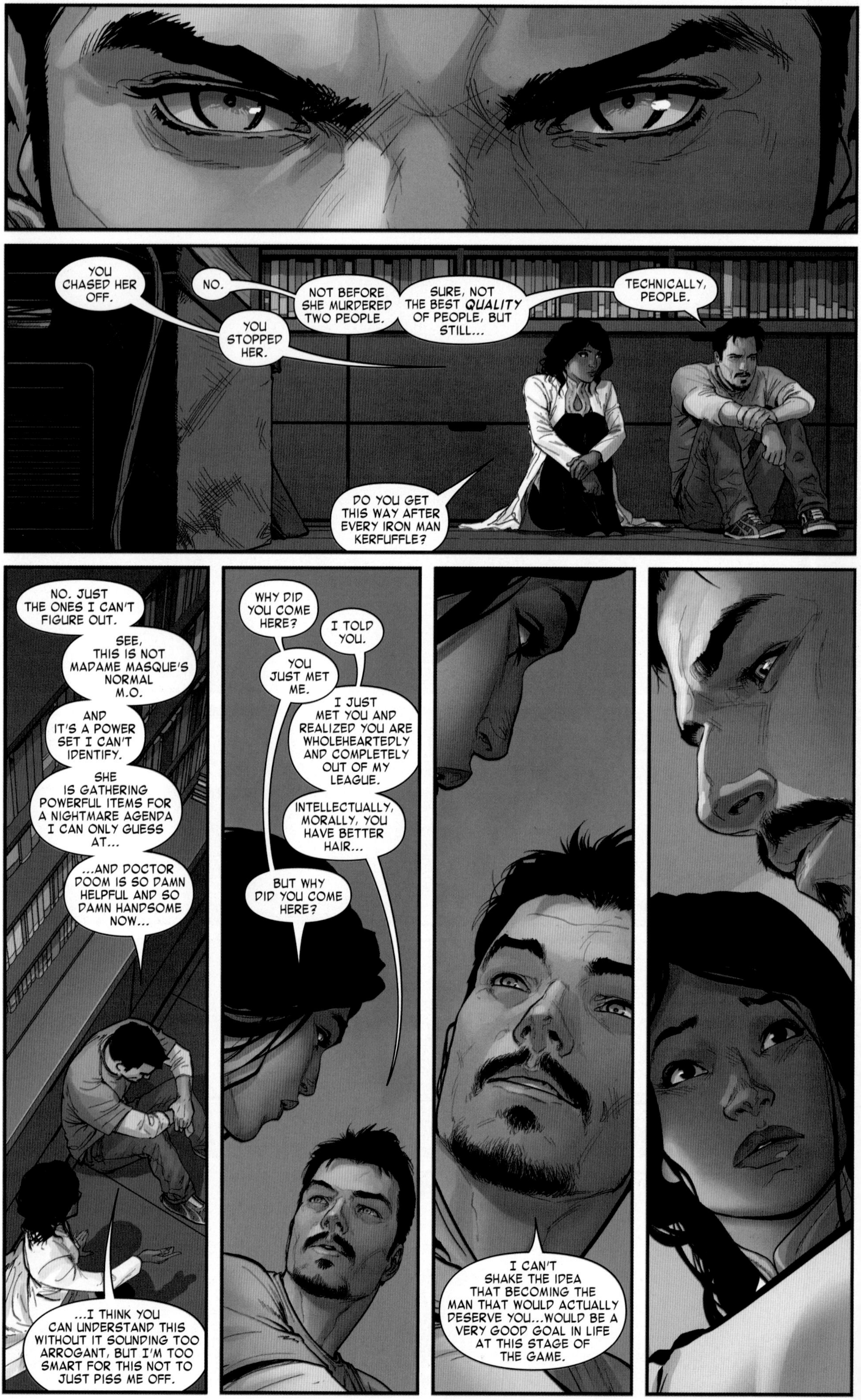

YOU CHASED HER OFF.
NO.
YOU STOPPED HER.
NOT BEFORE SHE MURDERED TWO PEOPLE.
SURE, NOT THE BEST QUALITY OF PEOPLE, BUT STILL...
TECHNICALLY, PEOPLE.
DO YOU GET THIS WAY AFTER EVERY IRON MAN KERFUFFLE?
NO. JUST THE ONES I CAN'T FIGURE OUT.
SEE, THIS IS NOT MADAME MASQUE'S NORMAL M.O.
AND IT'S A POWER SET I CAN'T IDENTIFY.
SHE IS GATHERING POWERFUL ITEMS FOR A NIGHTMARE AGENDA I CAN ONLY GUESS AT...
...AND DOCTOR DOOM IS SO DAMN HELPFUL AND SO DAMN HANDSOME NOW...
...I THINK YOU CAN UNDERSTAND THIS WITHOUT IT SOUNDING TOO ARROGANT, BUT I'M TOO SMART FOR THIS NOT TO JUST PISS ME OFF.
WHY DID YOU COME HERE?
I TOLD YOU.
YOU JUST MET ME.
I JUST MET YOU AND REALIZED YOU ARE WHOLEHEARTEDLY AND COMPLETELY OUT OF MY LEAGUE.
INTELLECTUALLY, MORALLY, YOU HAVE BETTER HAIR...
BUT WHY DID YOU COME HERE?
I CAN'T SHAKE THE IDEA THAT BECOMING THE MAN THAT WOULD ACTUALLY DESERVE YOU...WOULD BE A VERY GOOD GOAL IN LIFE AT THIS STAGE OF THE GAME.

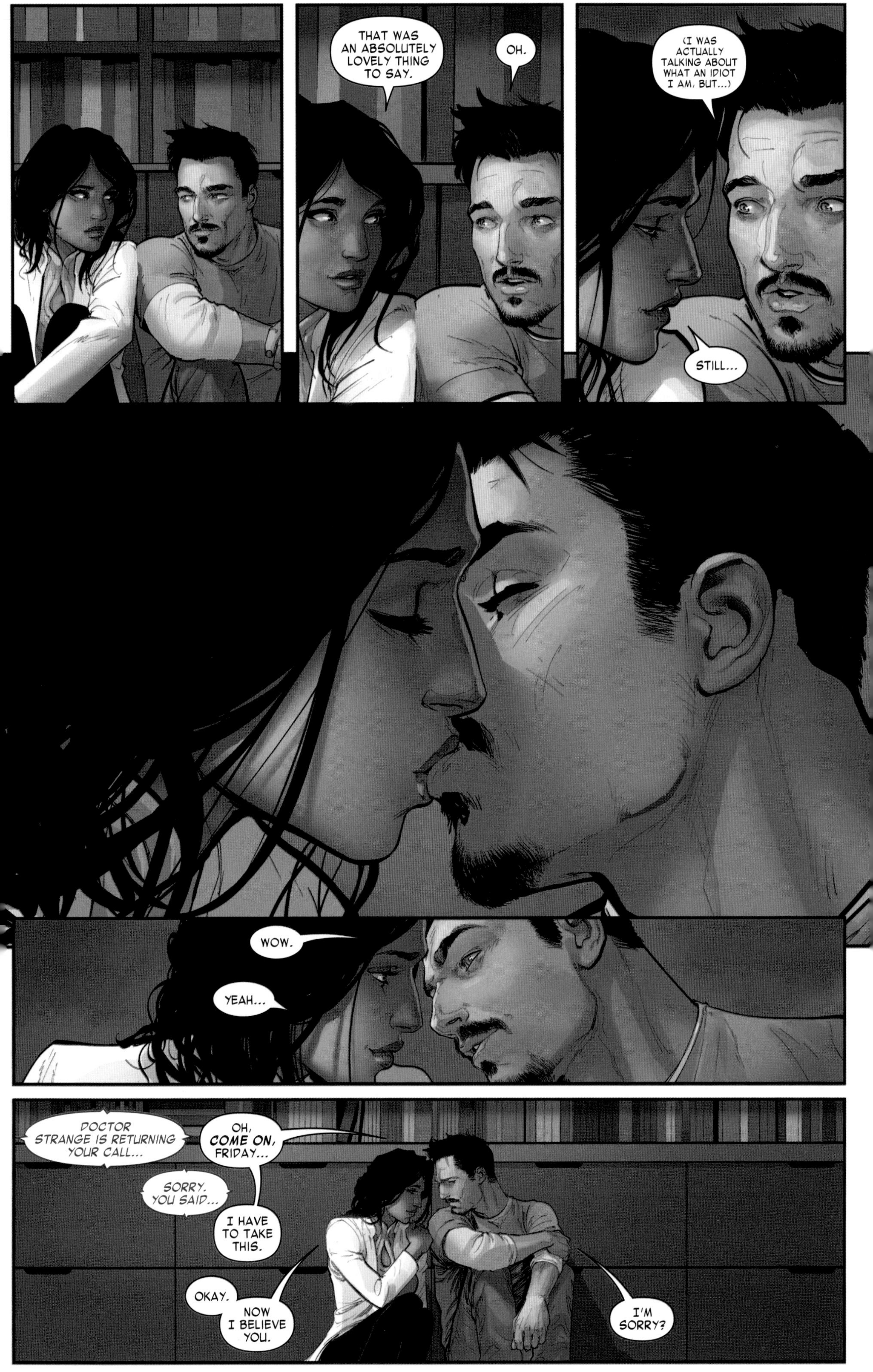
THAT WAS AN ABSOLUTELY LOVELY THING TO SAY.
OH.
(I WAS ACTUALLY TALKING ABOUT WHAT AN IDIOT I AM, BUT...)
STILL...
WOW.
YEAH...
DOCTOR STRANGE IS RETURNING YOUR CALL...
OH, COME ON, FRIDAY...
SORRY. YOU SAID...
I HAVE TO TAKE THIS.
OKAY.
NOW I BELIEVE YOU.
I'M SORRY?

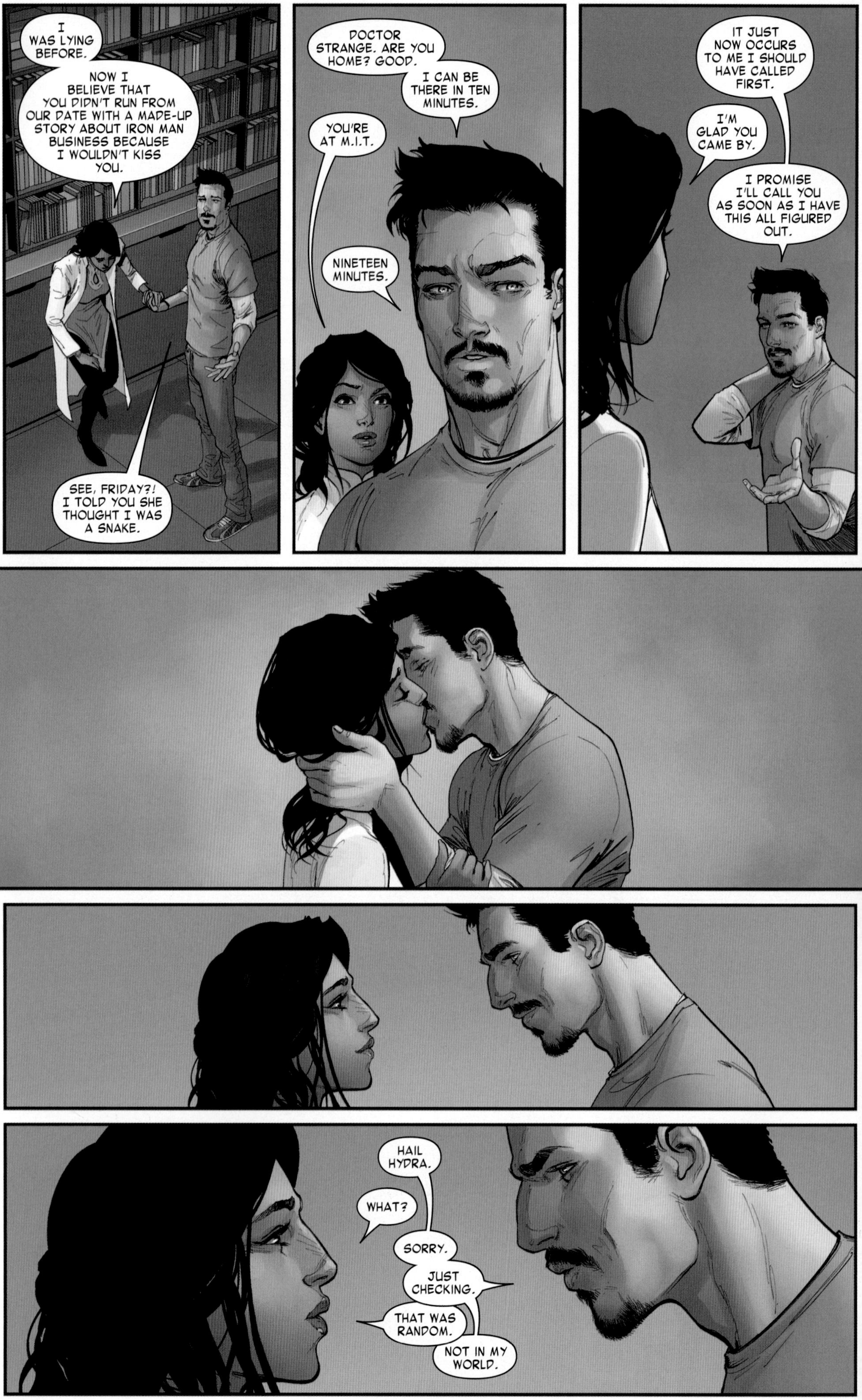
I WAS LYING BEFORE.
NOW I BELIEVE THAT YOU DIDN'T RUN FROM OUR DATE WITH A MADE-UP STORY ABOUT IRON MAN BUSINESS BECAUSE I WOULDN'T KISS YOU.
SEE, FRIDAY?! I TOLD YOU SHE THOUGHT I WAS A SNAKE.
DOCTOR STRANGE. ARE YOU HOME? GOOD.
I CAN BE THERE IN TEN MINUTES.
YOU'RE AT M.I.T.
NINETEEN MINUTES.
IT JUST NOW OCCURS TO ME I SHOULD HAVE CALLED FIRST.
I'M GLAD YOU CAME BY.
I PROMISE I'LL CALL YOU AS SOON AS I HAVE THIS ALL FIGURED OUT.
HAIL HYDRA.
WHAT?
SORRY.
JUST CHECKING.
THAT WAS RANDOM.
NOT IN MY WORLD.

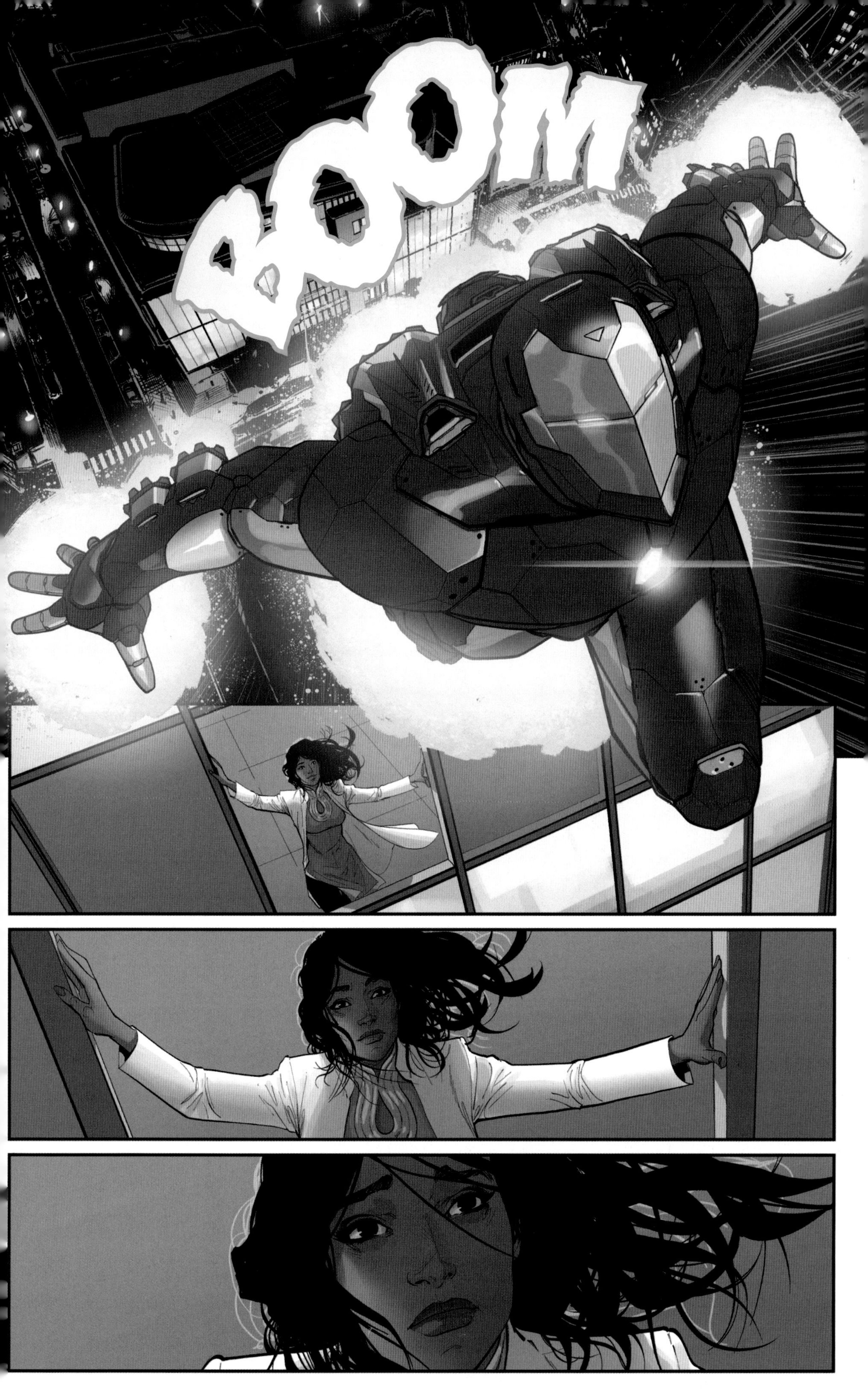
BOOM

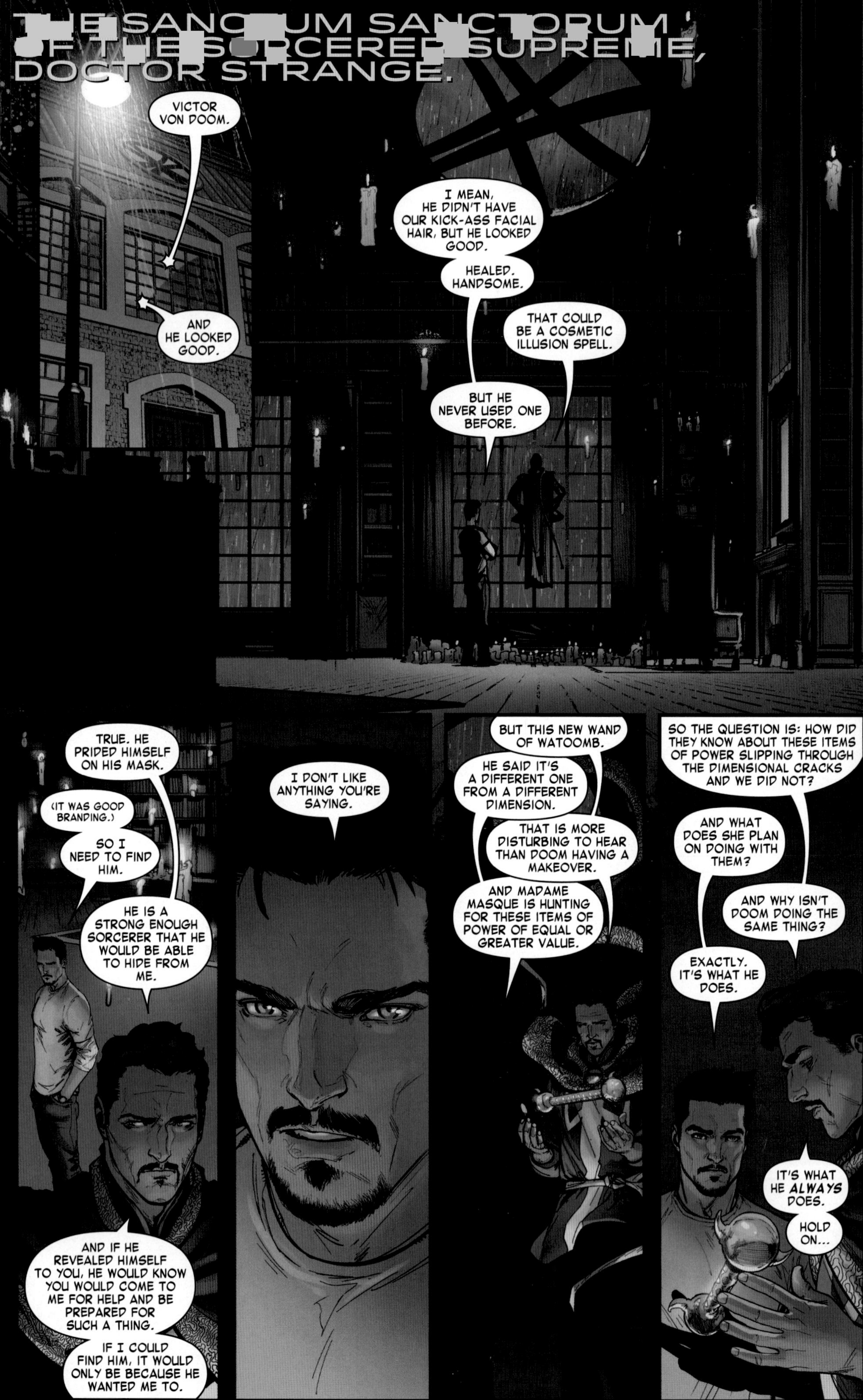
THE SANCTUM SANCTORUM OF THE SORCERER SUPREME, DOCTOR STRANGE.
VICTOR VON DOOM.
AND HE LOOKED GOOD.
I MEAN, HE DIDN'T HAVE OUR KICK-ASS FACIAL HAIR, BUT HE LOOKED GOOD.
HEALED. HANDSOME.
THAT COULD BE A COSMETIC ILLUSION SPELL.
BUT HE NEVER USED ONE BEFORE.
TRUE. HE PRIDED HIMSELF ON HIS MASK.
(IT WAS GOOD BRANDING.)
SO I NEED TO FIND HIM.
HE IS A STRONG ENOUGH SORCERER THAT HE WOULD BE ABLE TO HIDE FROM ME.
AND IF HE REVEALED HIMSELF TO YOU, HE WOULD KNOW YOU WOULD COME TO ME FOR HELP AND BE PREPARED FOR SUCH A THING.
IF I COULD FIND HIM, IT WOULD ONLY BE BECAUSE HE WANTED ME TO.
I DON'T LIKE ANYTHING YOU'RE SAYING.
BUT THIS NEW WAND OF WATOOMB.
HE SAID IT'S A DIFFERENT ONE FROM A DIFFERENT DIMENSION.
THAT IS MORE DISTURBING TO HEAR THAN DOOM HAVING A MAKEOVER.
AND MADAME MASQUE IS HUNTING FOR THESE ITEMS OF POWER OF EQUAL OR GREATER VALUE.
SO THE QUESTION IS: HOW DID THEY KNOW ABOUT THESE ITEMS OF POWER SLIPPING THROUGH THE DIMENSIONAL CRACKS AND WE DID NOT?
AND WHAT DOES SHE PLAN ON DOING WITH THEM?
AND WHY ISN'T DOOM DOING THE SAME THING?
EXACTLY. IT'S WHAT HE DOES.
IT'S WHAT HE *ALWAYS* DOES.
HOLD ON...

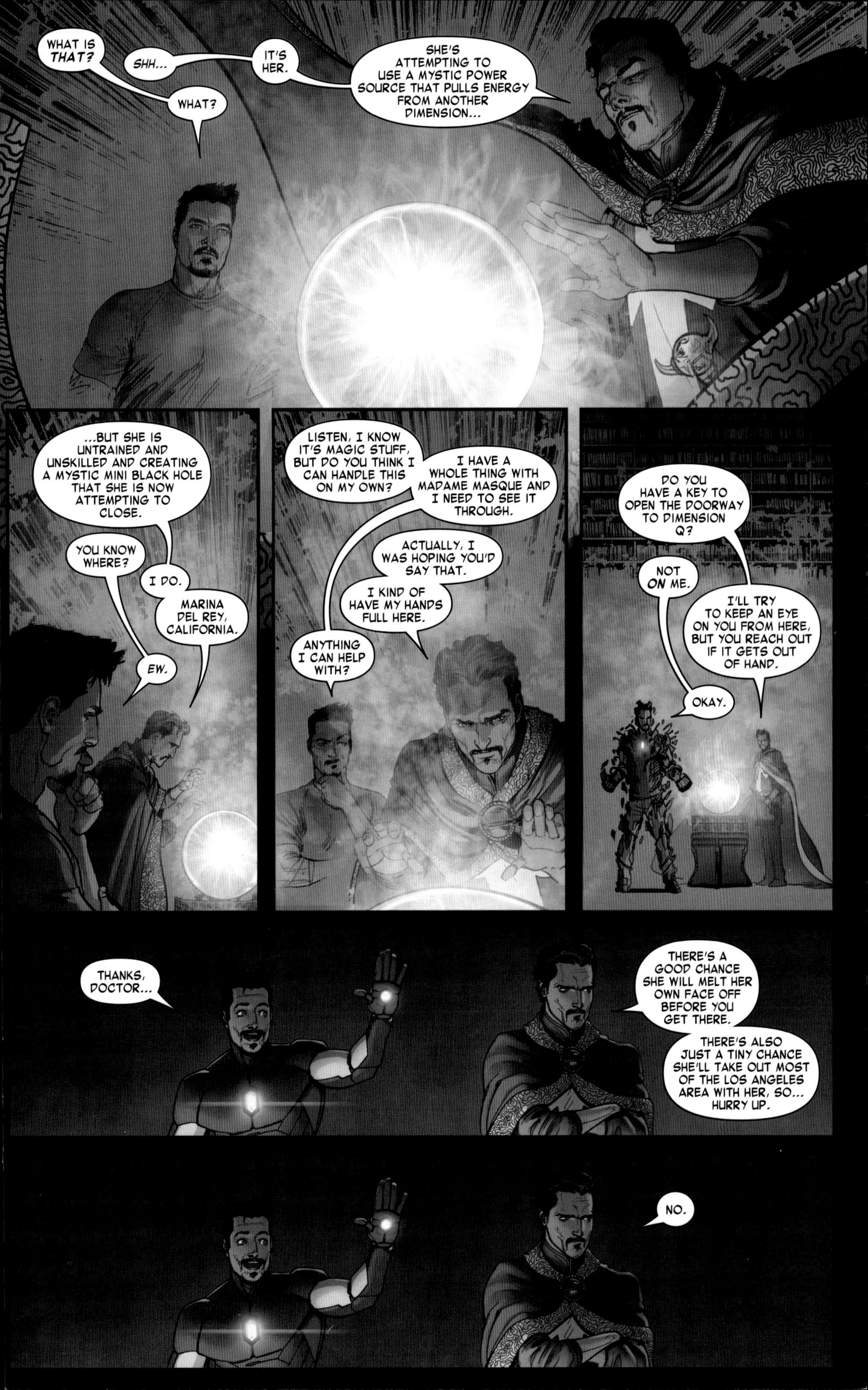
WHAT IS THAT?
SHH...
IT'S HER.
WHAT?
SHE'S ATTEMPTING TO USE A MYSTIC POWER SOURCE THAT PULLS ENERGY FROM ANOTHER DIMENSION...
...BUT SHE IS UNTRAINED AND UNSKILLED AND CREATING A MYSTIC MINI BLACK HOLE THAT SHE IS NOW ATTEMPTING TO CLOSE.
YOU KNOW WHERE?
I DO.
MARINA DEL REY, CALIFORNIA.
EW.
LISTEN, I KNOW IT'S MAGIC STUFF, BUT DO YOU THINK I CAN HANDLE THIS ON MY OWN?
I HAVE A WHOLE THING WITH MADAME MASQUE AND I NEED TO SEE IT THROUGH.
ACTUALLY, I WAS HOPING YOU'D SAY THAT.
I KIND OF HAVE MY HANDS FULL HERE.
ANYTHING I CAN HELP WITH?
DO YOU HAVE A KEY TO OPEN THE DOORWAY TO DIMENSION Q?
NOT ON ME.
I'LL TRY TO KEEP AN EYE ON YOU FROM HERE, BUT YOU REACH OUT IF IT GETS OUT OF HAND.
OKAY.
THANKS, DOCTOR...
THERE'S A GOOD CHANCE SHE WILL MELT HER OWN FACE OFF BEFORE YOU GET THERE.
THERE'S ALSO JUST A TINY CHANCE SHE'LL TAKE OUT MOST OF THE LOS ANGELES AREA WITH HER, SO... HURRY UP.
NO.

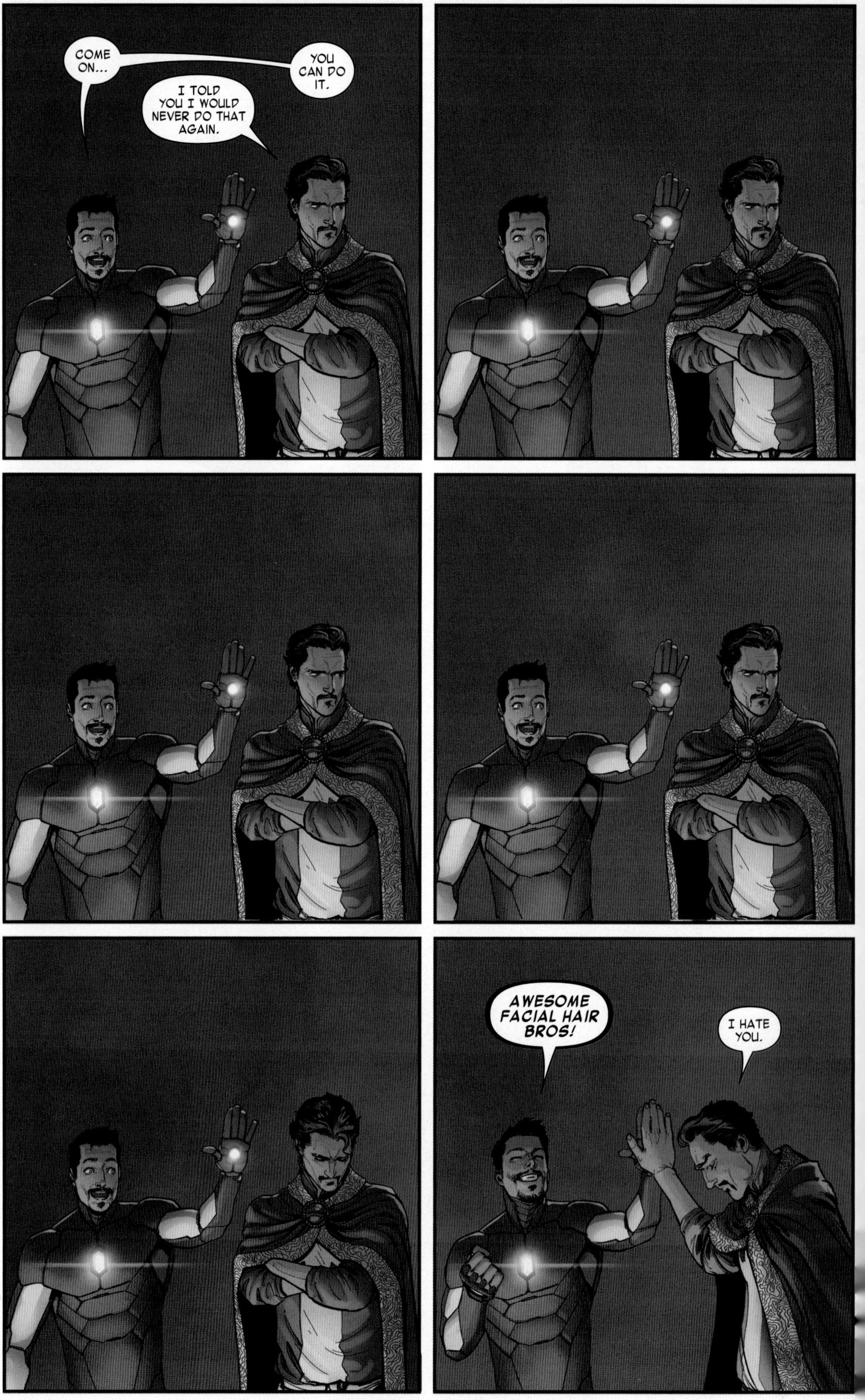
COME ON...
YOU CAN DO IT.
I TOLD YOU I WOULD NEVER DO THAT AGAIN.
AWESOME FACIAL HAIR BROS!
I HATE YOU.

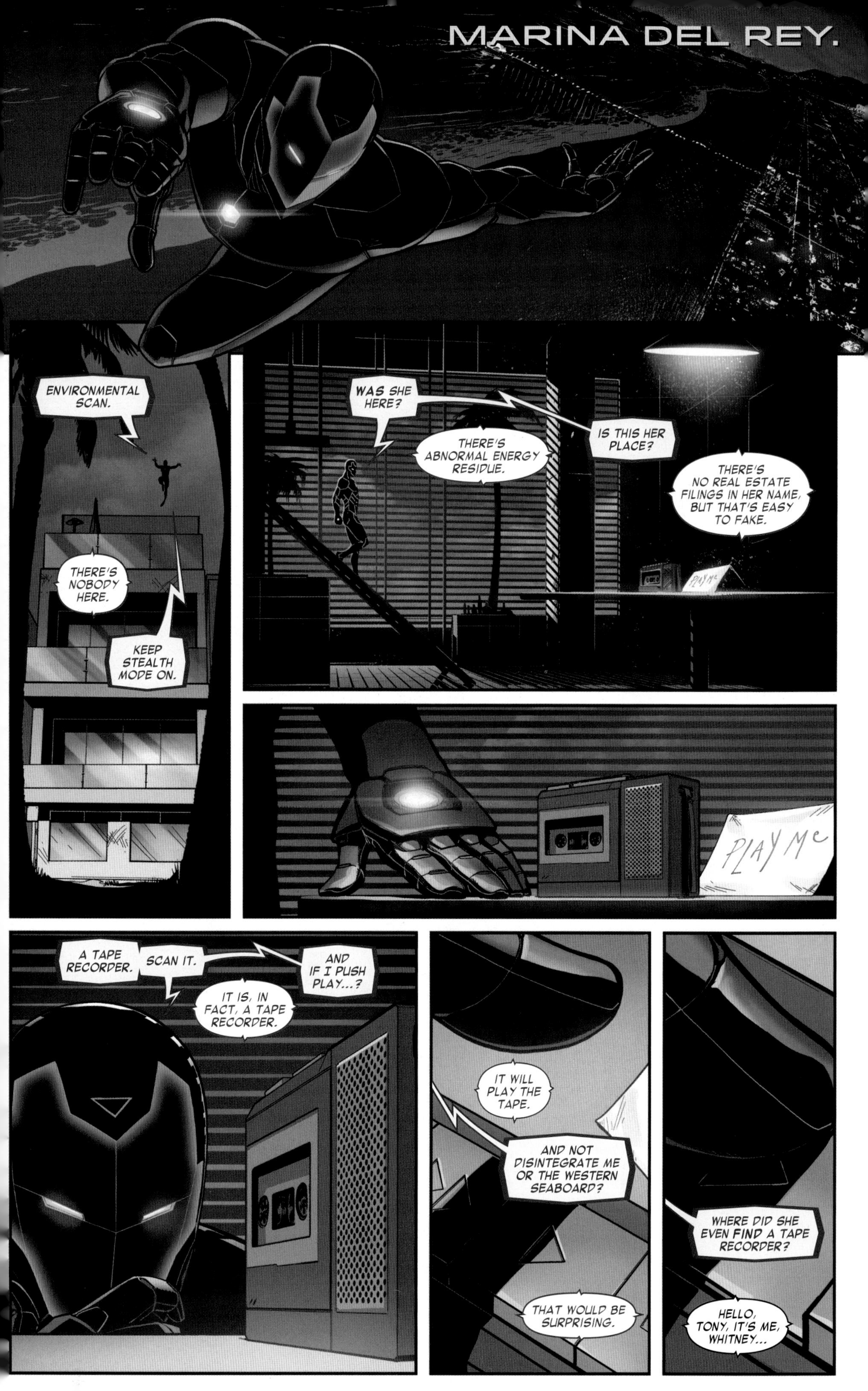
MARINA DEL REY.
ENVIRONMENTAL SCAN.
THERE'S NOBODY HERE.
KEEP STEALTH MODE ON.
WAS SHE HERE?
THERE'S ABNORMAL ENERGY RESIDUE.
IS THIS HER PLACE?
THERE'S NO REAL ESTATE FILINGS IN HER NAME, BUT THAT'S EASY TO FAKE.
PLAY ME
A TAPE RECORDER.
SCAN IT.
IT IS, IN FACT, A TAPE RECORDER.
AND IF I PUSH PLAY...?
IT WILL PLAY THE TAPE.
AND NOT DISINTEGRATE ME OR THE WESTERN SEABOARD?
THAT WOULD BE SURPRISING.
WHERE DID SHE EVEN FIND A TAPE RECORDER?
HELLO, TONY, IT'S ME, WHITNEY...

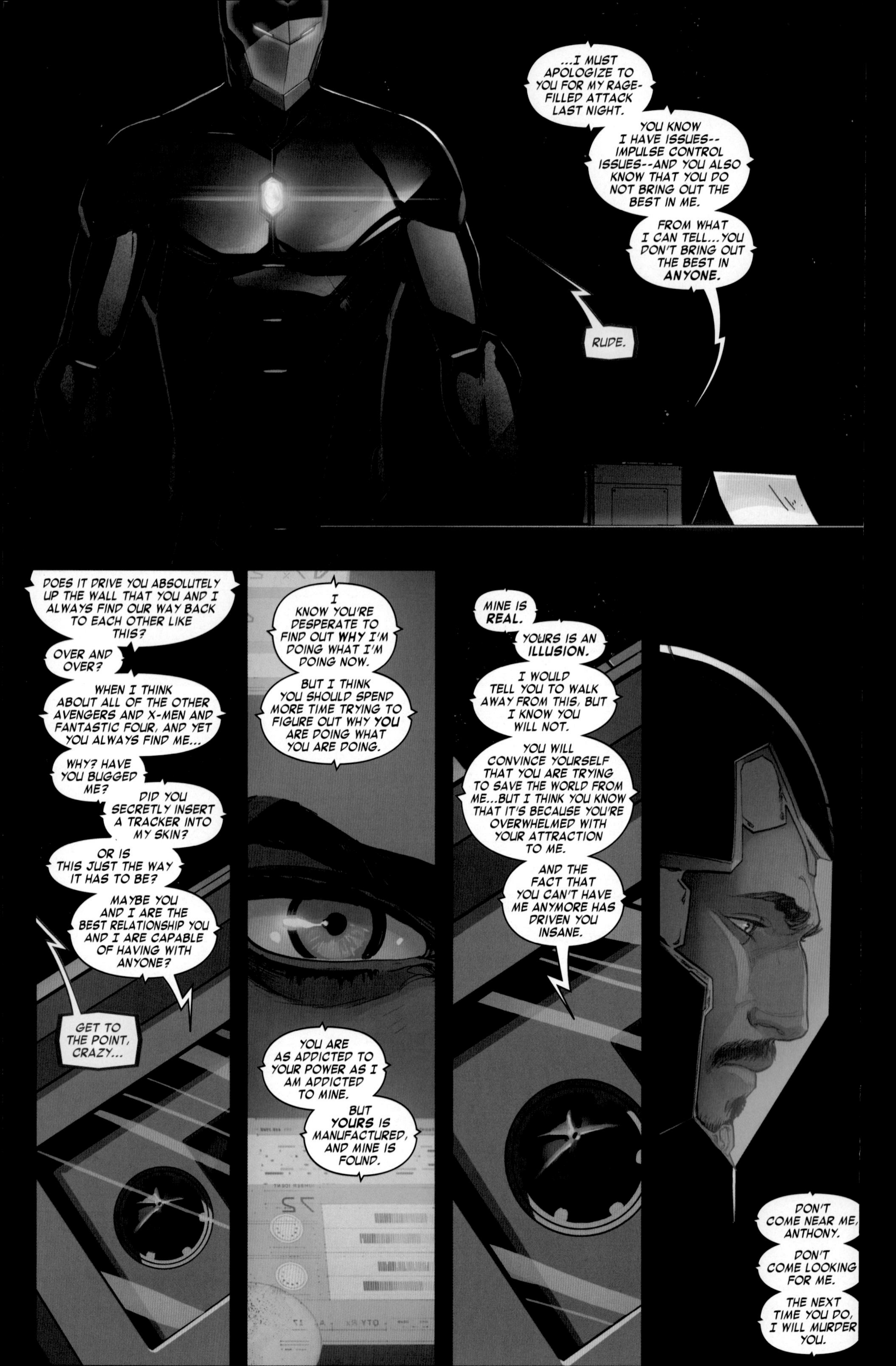
...I MUST APOLOGIZE TO YOU FOR MY RAGE-FILLED ATTACK LAST NIGHT.
YOU KNOW I HAVE ISSUES-- IMPULSE CONTROL ISSUES--AND YOU ALSO KNOW THAT YOU DO NOT BRING OUT THE BEST IN ME.
FROM WHAT I CAN TELL...YOU DON'T BRING OUT THE BEST IN ANYONE.
RUDE.
DOES IT DRIVE YOU ABSOLUTELY UP THE WALL THAT YOU AND I ALWAYS FIND OUR WAY BACK TO EACH OTHER LIKE THIS?
OVER AND OVER?
WHEN I THINK ABOUT ALL OF THE OTHER AVENGERS AND X-MEN AND FANTASTIC FOUR, AND YET YOU ALWAYS FIND ME...
WHY? HAVE YOU BUGGED ME?
DID YOU SECRETLY INSERT A TRACKER INTO MY SKIN?
OR IS THIS JUST THE WAY IT HAS TO BE?
MAYBE YOU AND I ARE THE BEST RELATIONSHIP YOU AND I ARE CAPABLE OF HAVING WITH ANYONE?
GET TO THE POINT, CRAZY...
I KNOW YOU'RE DESPERATE TO FIND OUT WHY I'M DOING WHAT I'M DOING NOW.
BUT I THINK YOU SHOULD SPEND MORE TIME TRYING TO FIGURE OUT WHY YOU ARE DOING WHAT YOU ARE DOING.
YOU ARE AS ADDICTED TO YOUR POWER AS I AM ADDICTED TO MINE.
BUT YOURS IS MANUFACTURED, AND MINE IS FOUND.
MINE IS REAL.
YOURS IS AN ILLUSION.
I WOULD TELL YOU TO WALK AWAY FROM THIS, BUT I KNOW YOU WILL NOT.
YOU WILL CONVINCE YOURSELF THAT YOU ARE TRYING TO SAVE THE WORLD FROM ME...BUT I THINK YOU KNOW THAT IT'S BECAUSE YOU'RE OVERWHELMED WITH YOUR ATTRACTION TO ME.
AND THE FACT THAT YOU CAN'T HAVE ME ANYMORE HAS DRIVEN YOU INSANE.
DON'T COME NEAR ME, ANTHONY.
DON'T COME LOOKING FOR ME.
THE NEXT TIME YOU DO, I WILL MURDER YOU.

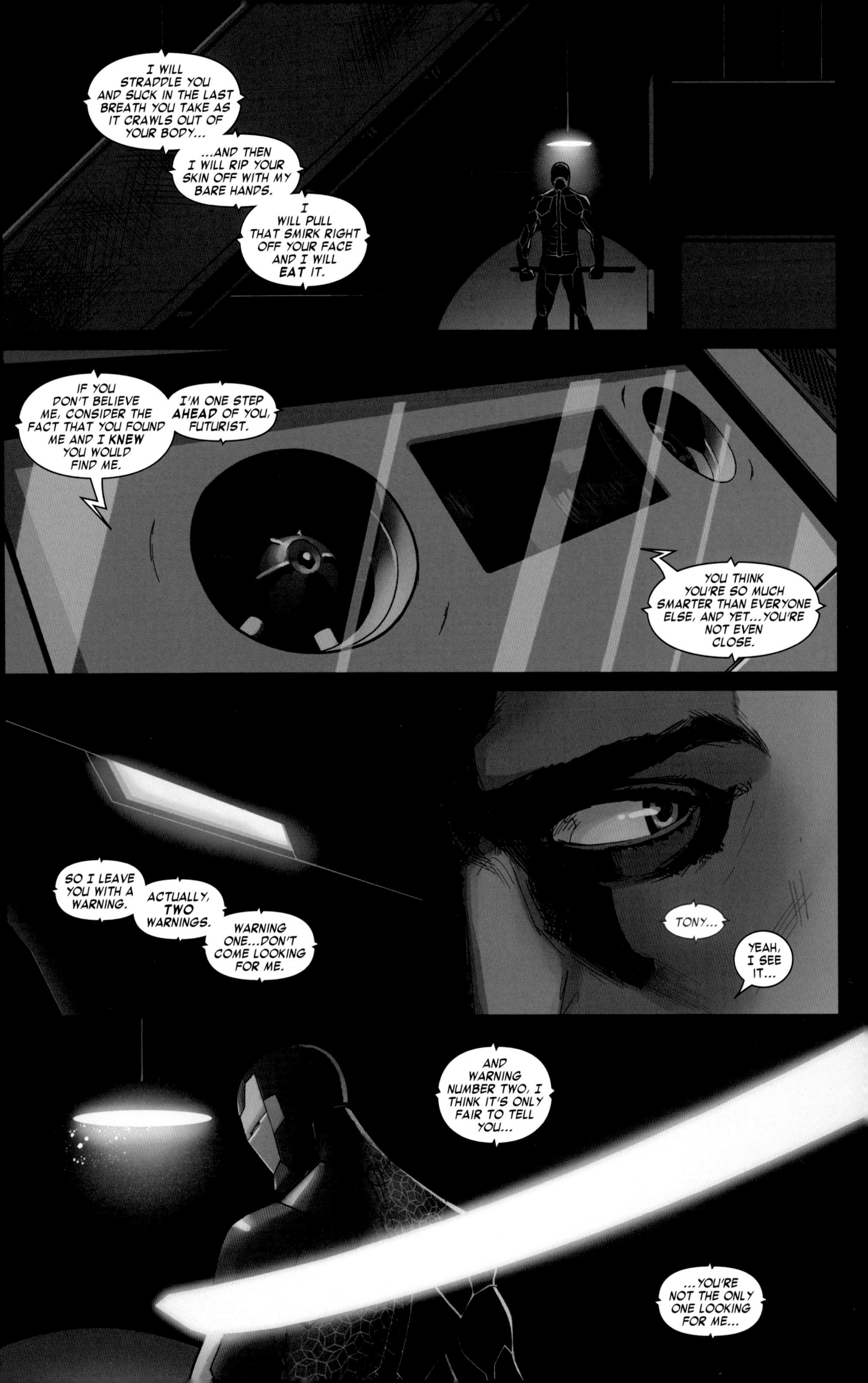

I WILL STRADDLE YOU AND SUCK IN THE LAST BREATH YOU TAKE AS IT CRAWLS OUT OF YOUR BODY...
...AND THEN I WILL RIP YOUR SKIN OFF WITH MY BARE HANDS.
I WILL PULL THAT SMIRK RIGHT OFF YOUR FACE AND I WILL EAT IT.
IF YOU DON'T BELIEVE ME, CONSIDER THE FACT THAT YOU FOUND ME AND I KNEW YOU WOULD FIND ME.
I'M ONE STEP AHEAD OF YOU, FUTURIST.
YOU THINK YOU'RE SO MUCH SMARTER THAN EVERYONE ELSE, AND YET...YOU'RE NOT EVEN CLOSE.
SO I LEAVE YOU WITH A WARNING.
ACTUALLY, TWO WARNINGS.
WARNING ONE...DON'T COME LOOKING FOR ME.
TONY...
YEAH, I SEE IT...
AND WARNING NUMBER TWO, I THINK IT'S ONLY FAIR TO TELL YOU...
...YOU'RE NOT THE ONLY ONE LOOKING FOR ME...

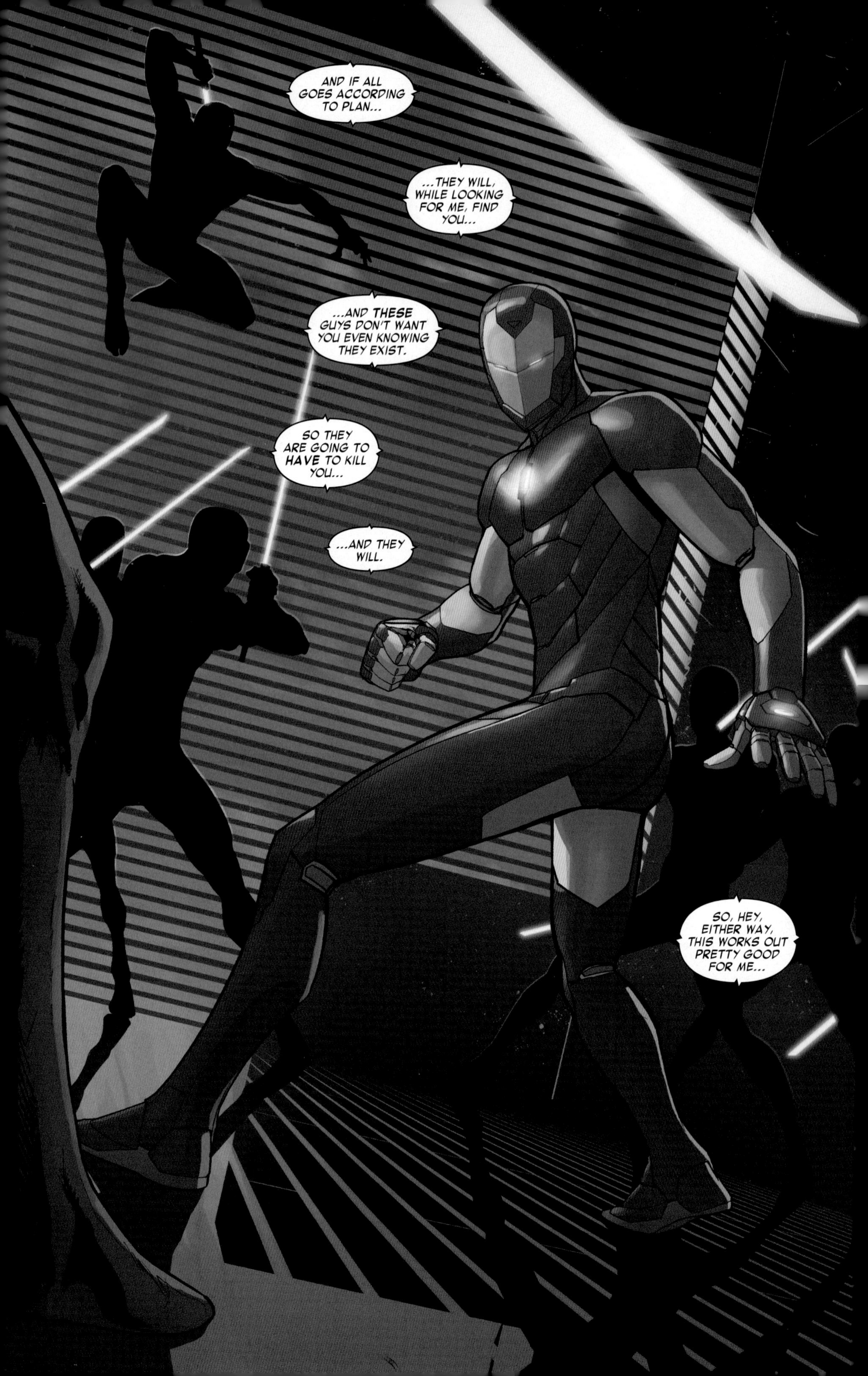
AND IF ALL GOES ACCORDING TO PLAN...
...THEY WILL, WHILE LOOKING FOR ME, FIND YOU...
...AND THESE GUYS DON'T WANT YOU EVEN KNOWING THEY EXIST.
SO THEY ARE GOING TO HAVE TO KILL YOU...
...AND THEY WILL.
SO, HEY, EITHER WAY, THIS WORKS OUT PRETTY GOOD FOR ME...

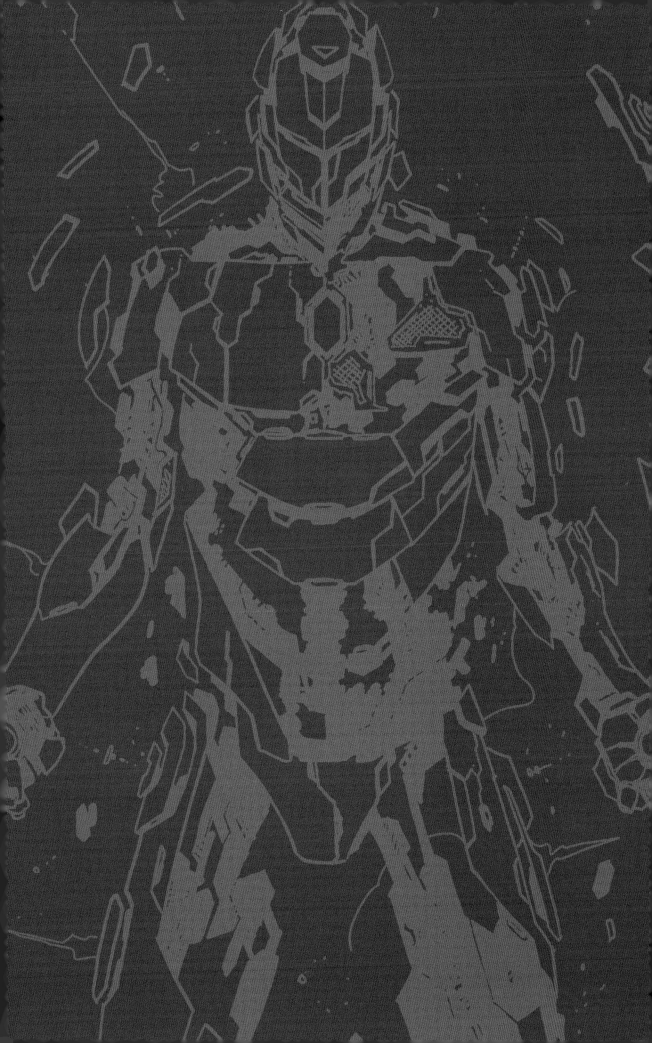

#4

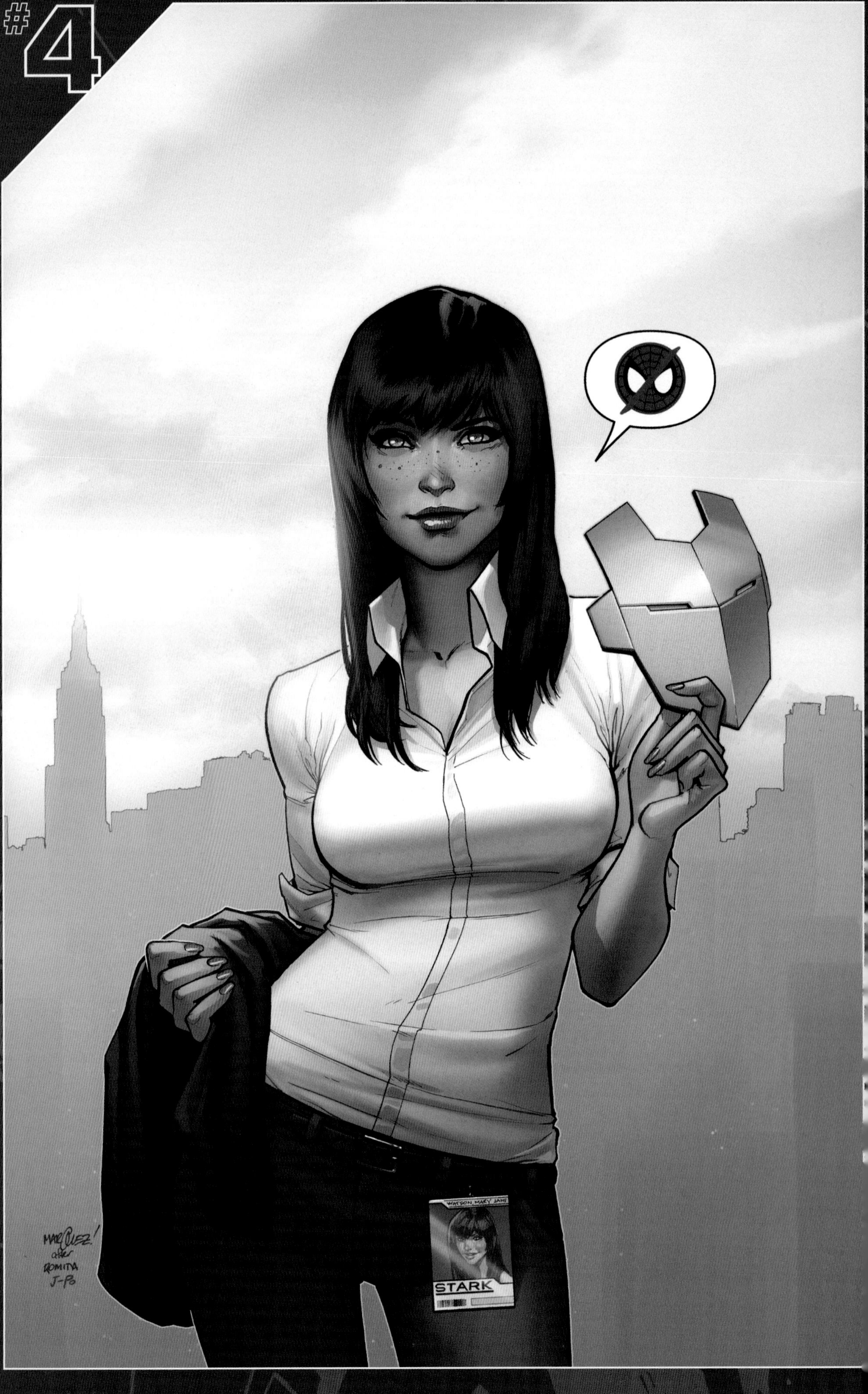
WATSON, MARY JANE
STARK
MARQUEZ! after ROMITA J-Ro

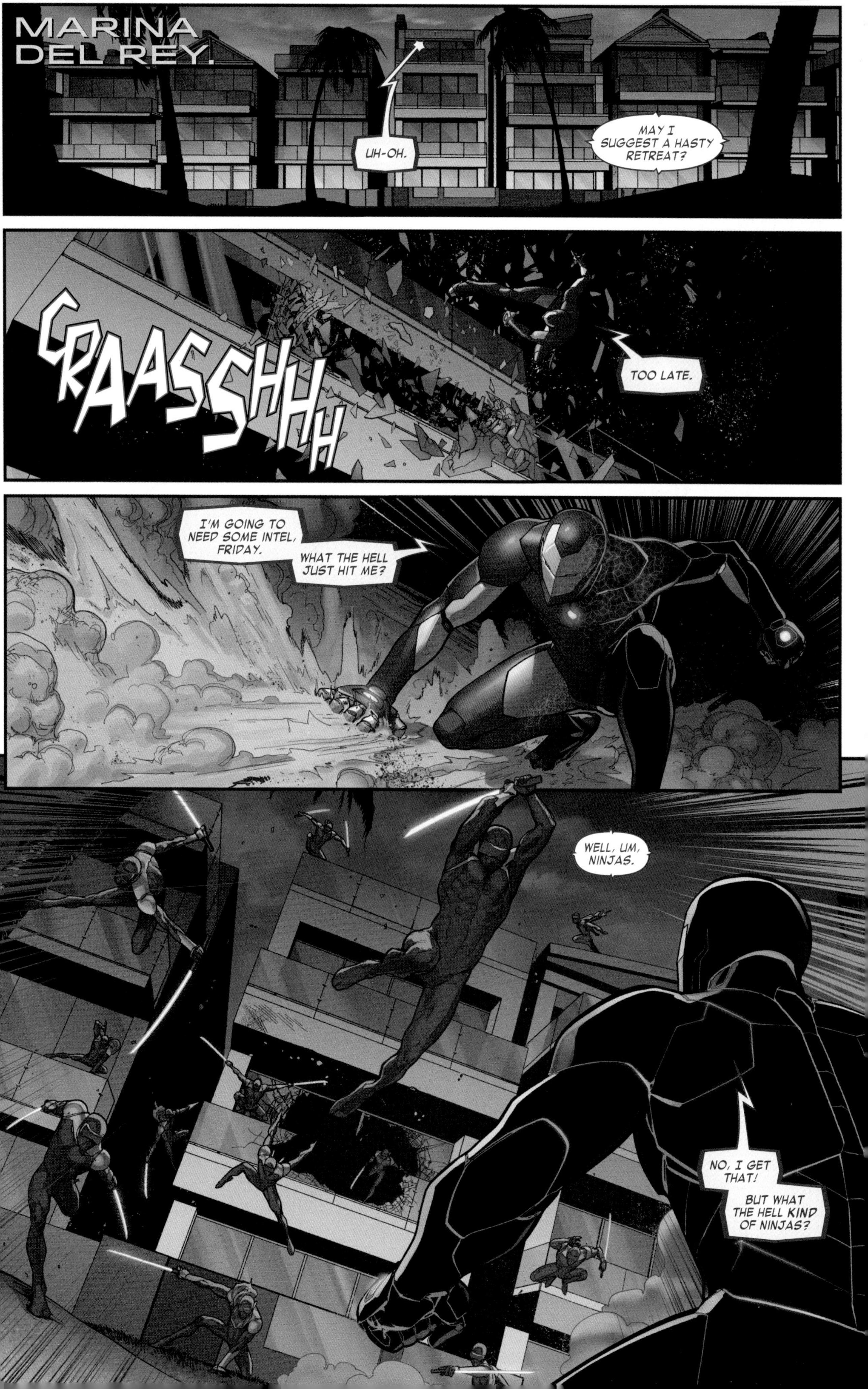
MARINA DEL REY.
UH-OH.
MAY I SUGGEST A HASTY RETREAT?
CRAASSHHH
TOO LATE.
I'M GOING TO NEED SOME INTEL, FRIDAY.
WHAT THE HELL JUST HIT ME?
WELL, UM, NINJAS.
NO, I GET THAT!
BUT WHAT THE HELL KIND OF NINJAS?

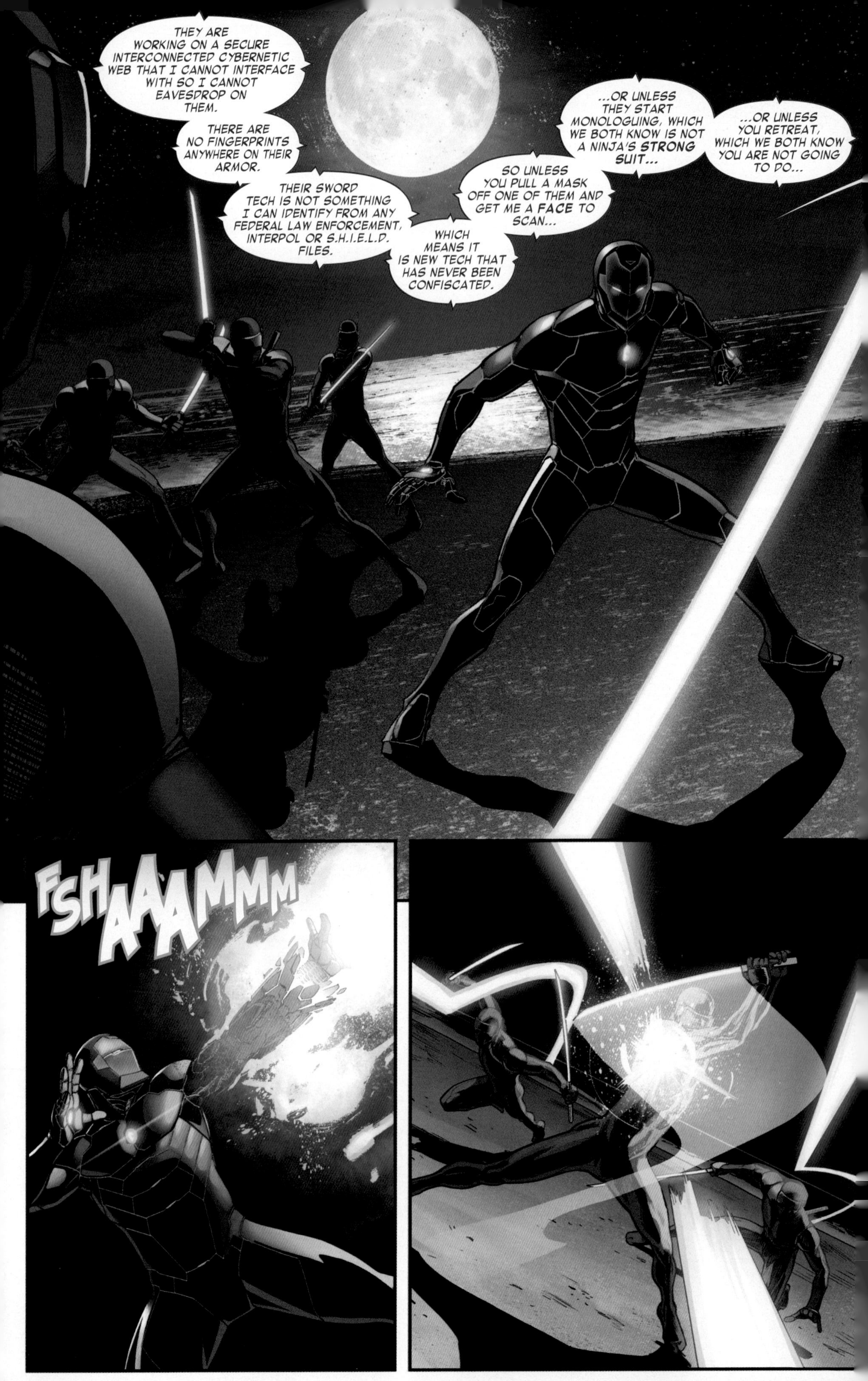
THEY ARE WORKING ON A SECURE INTERCONNECTED CYBERNETIC WEB THAT I CANNOT INTERFACE WITH SO I CANNOT EAVESDROP ON THEM.
THERE ARE NO FINGERPRINTS ANYWHERE ON THEIR ARMOR.
THEIR SWORD TECH IS NOT SOMETHING I CAN IDENTIFY FROM ANY FEDERAL LAW ENFORCEMENT, INTERPOL OR S.H.I.E.L.D. FILES.
WHICH MEANS IT IS NEW TECH THAT HAS NEVER BEEN CONFISCATED.
SO UNLESS YOU PULL A MASK OFF ONE OF THEM AND GET ME A FACE TO SCAN...
...OR UNLESS THEY START MONOLOGUING, WHICH WE BOTH KNOW IS NOT A NINJA'S STRONG SUIT...
...OR UNLESS YOU RETREAT, WHICH WE BOTH KNOW YOU ARE NOT GOING TO DO...
FSHAAAMMMM

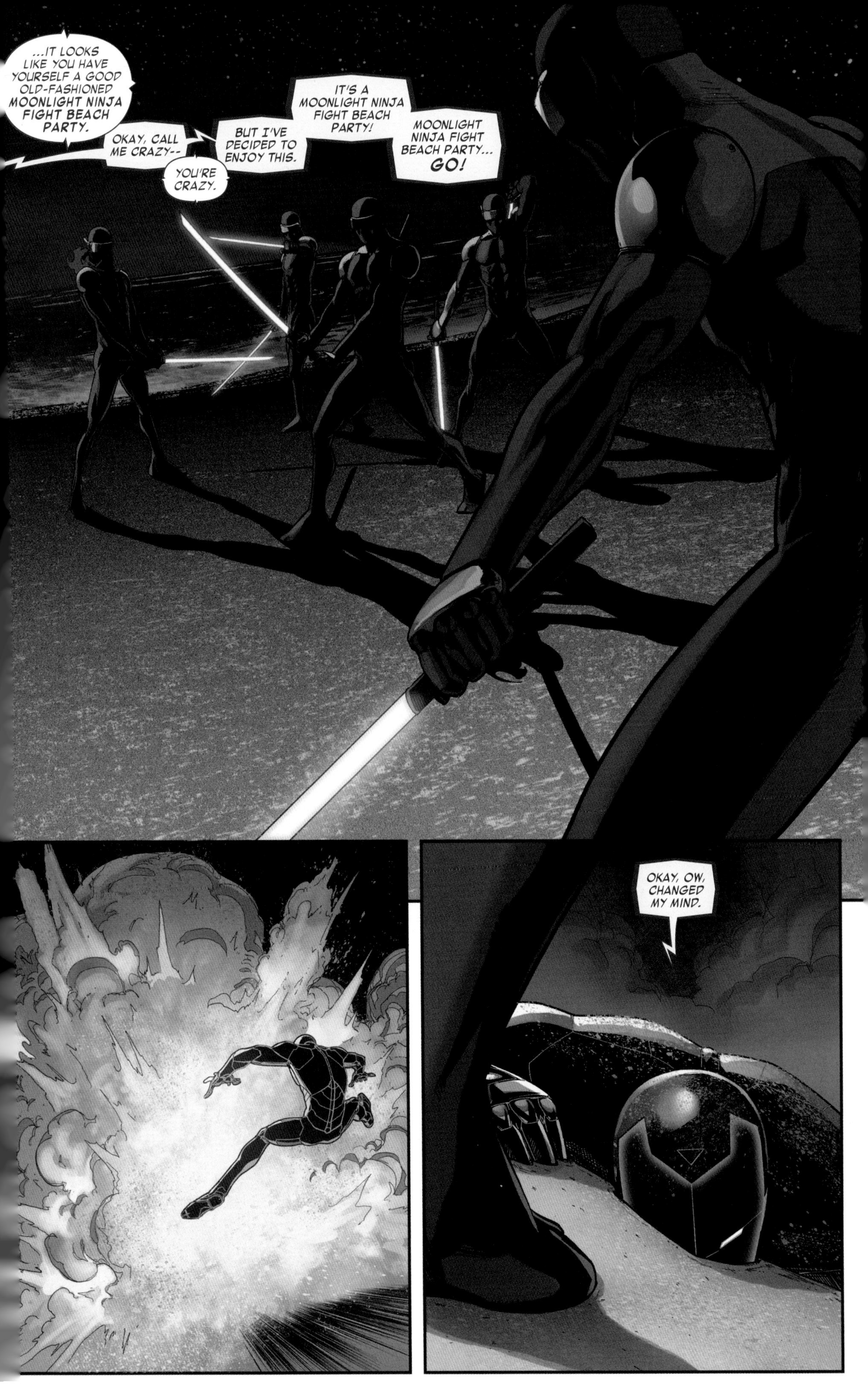
...IT LOOKS LIKE YOU HAVE YOURSELF A GOOD OLD-FASHIONED MOONLIGHT NINJA FIGHT BEACH PARTY.
OKAY, CALL ME CRAZY--
YOU'RE CRAZY.
BUT I'VE DECIDED TO ENJOY THIS.
IT'S A MOONLIGHT NINJA FIGHT BEACH PARTY!
MOONLIGHT NINJA FIGHT BEACH PARTY... GO!
OKAY, OW, CHANGED MY MIND.

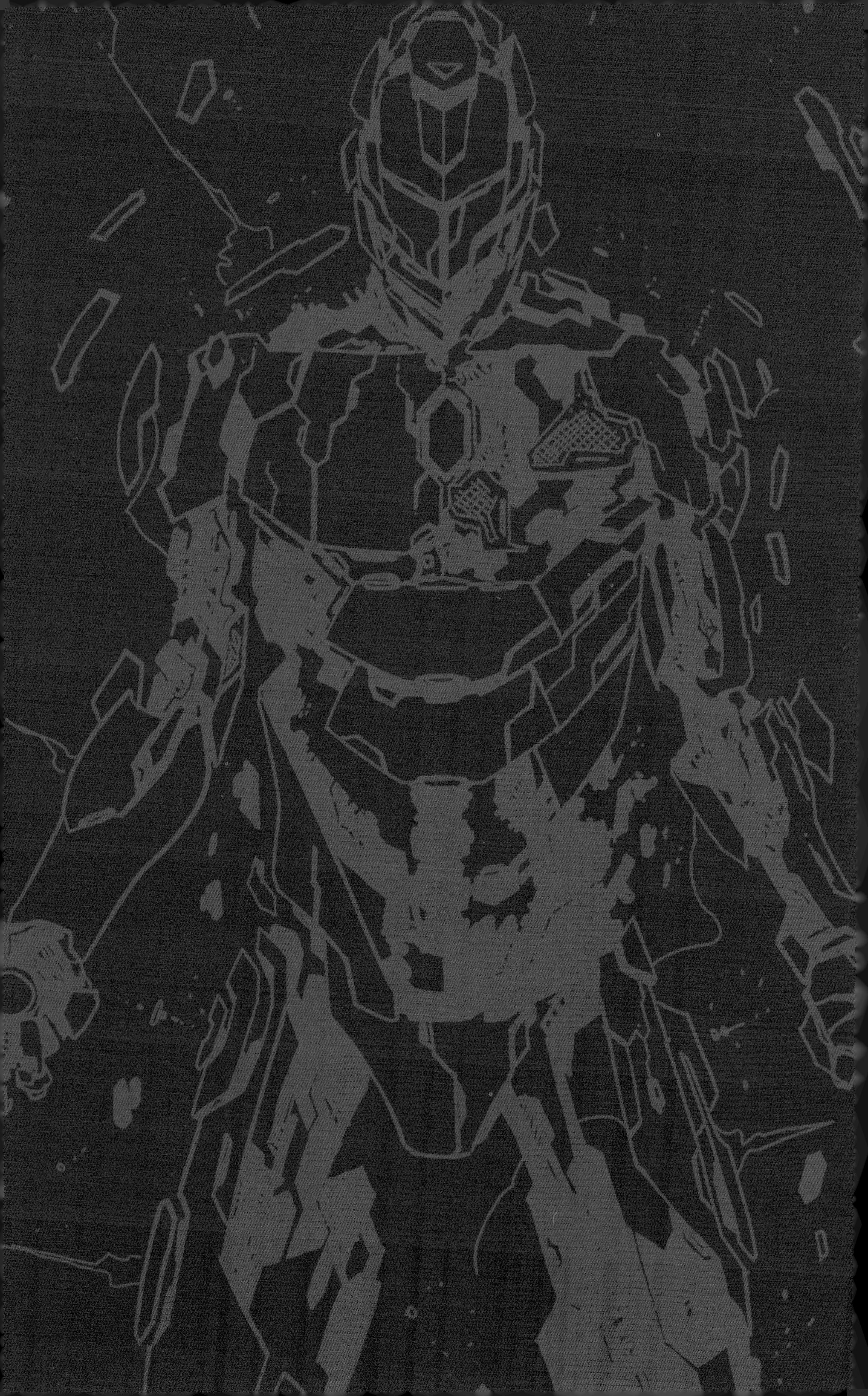

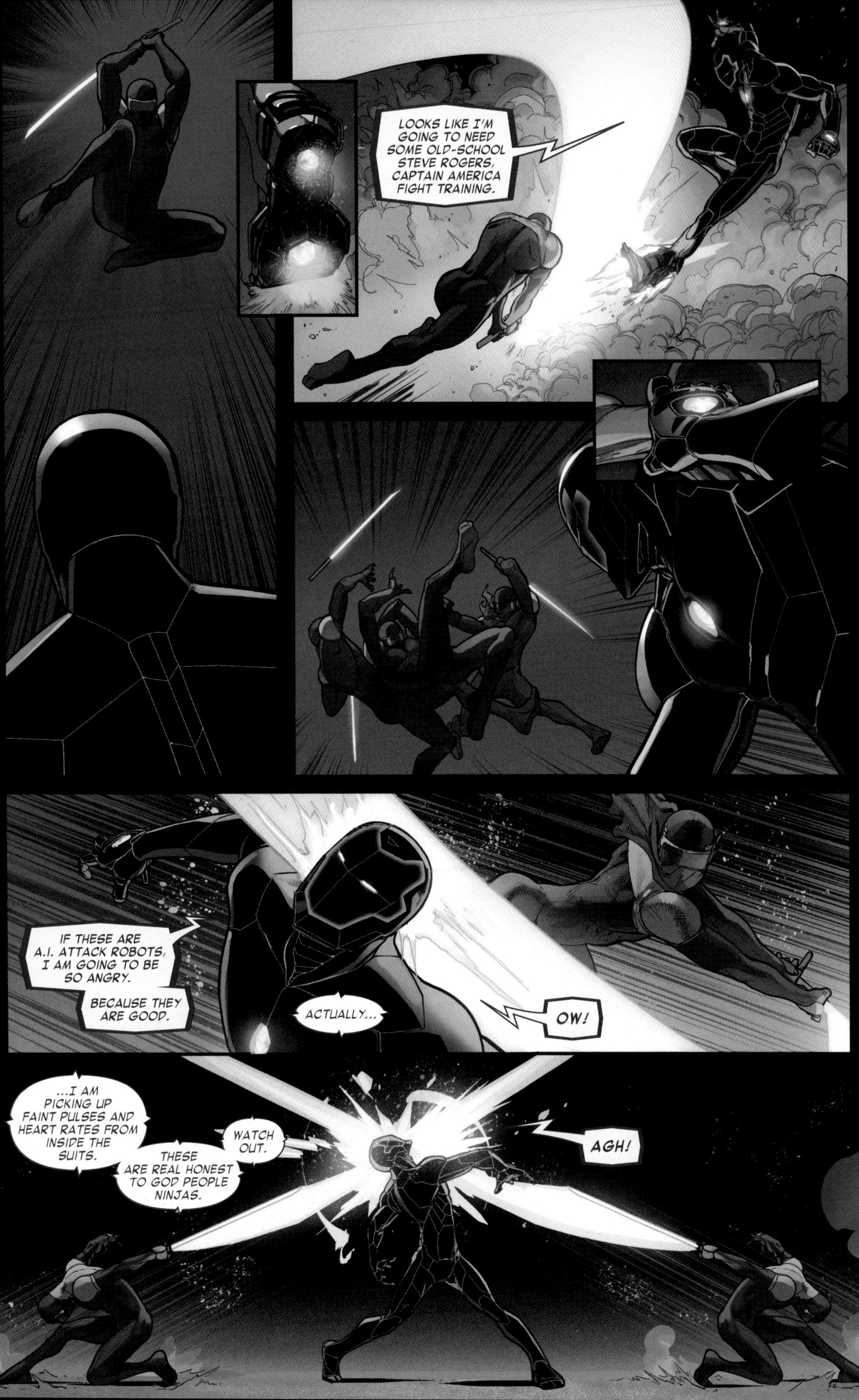
LOOKS LIKE I'M GOING TO NEED SOME OLD-SCHOOL STEVE ROGERS, CAPTAIN AMERICA FIGHT TRAINING.
IF THESE ARE A.I. ATTACK ROBOTS, I AM GOING TO BE SO ANGRY.
BECAUSE THEY ARE GOOD.
ACTUALLY...
OW!
...I AM PICKING UP FAINT PULSES AND HEART RATES FROM INSIDE THE SUITS.
THESE ARE REAL HONEST TO GOD PEOPLE NINJAS.
WATCH OUT.
AGH!

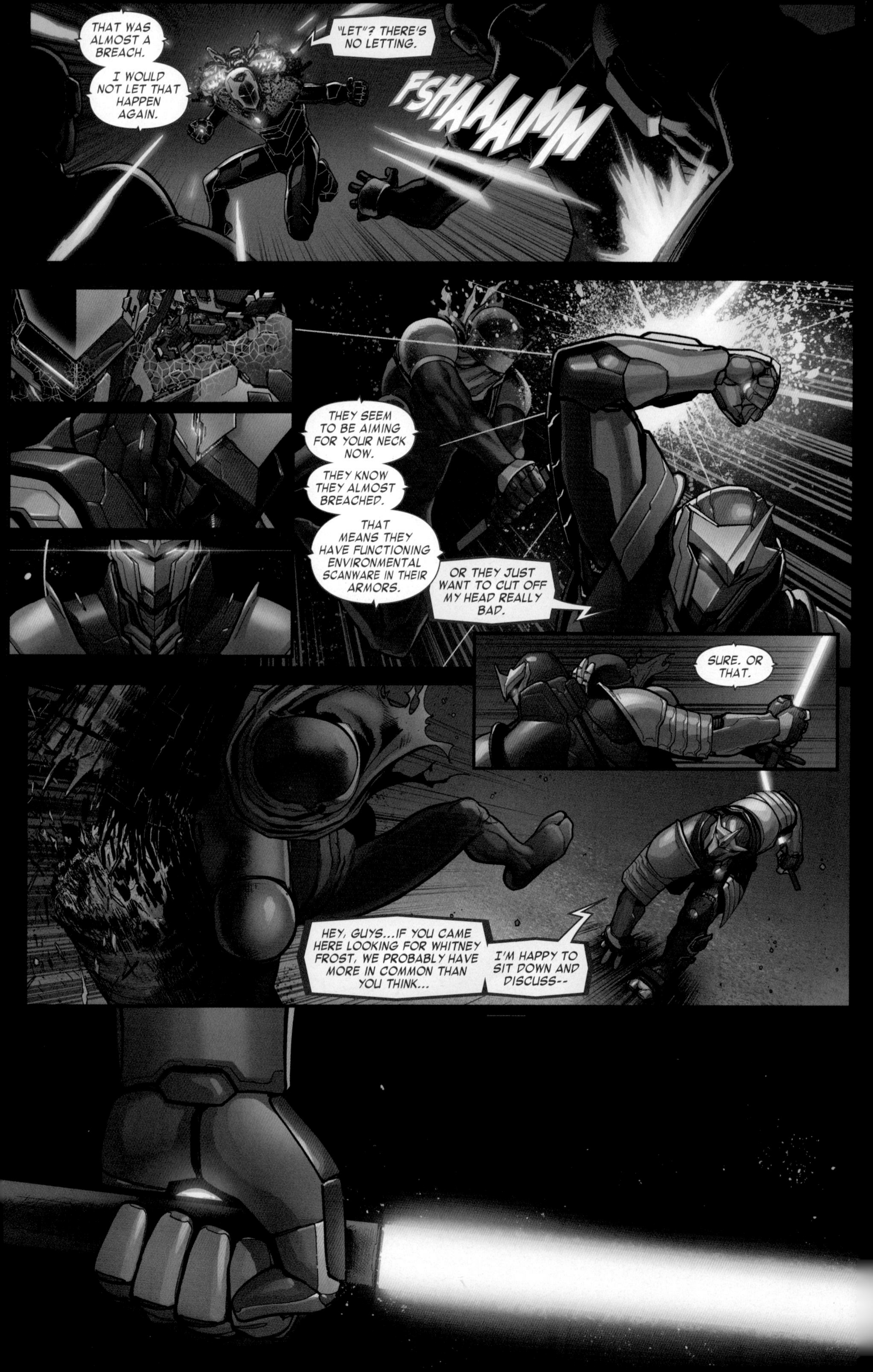

THAT WAS ALMOST A BREACH.
I WOULD NOT LET THAT HAPPEN AGAIN.
"LET"? THERE'S NO LETTING.
FSHAAAAMM
THEY SEEM TO BE AIMING FOR YOUR NECK NOW.
THEY KNOW THEY ALMOST BREACHED.
THAT MEANS THEY HAVE FUNCTIONING ENVIRONMENTAL SCANWARE IN THEIR ARMORS.
OR THEY JUST WANT TO CUT OFF MY HEAD REALLY BAD.
SURE. OR THAT.
HEY, GUYS...IF YOU CAME HERE LOOKING FOR WHITNEY FROST, WE PROBABLY HAVE MORE IN COMMON THAN YOU THINK...
I'M HAPPY TO SIT DOWN AND DISCUSS--

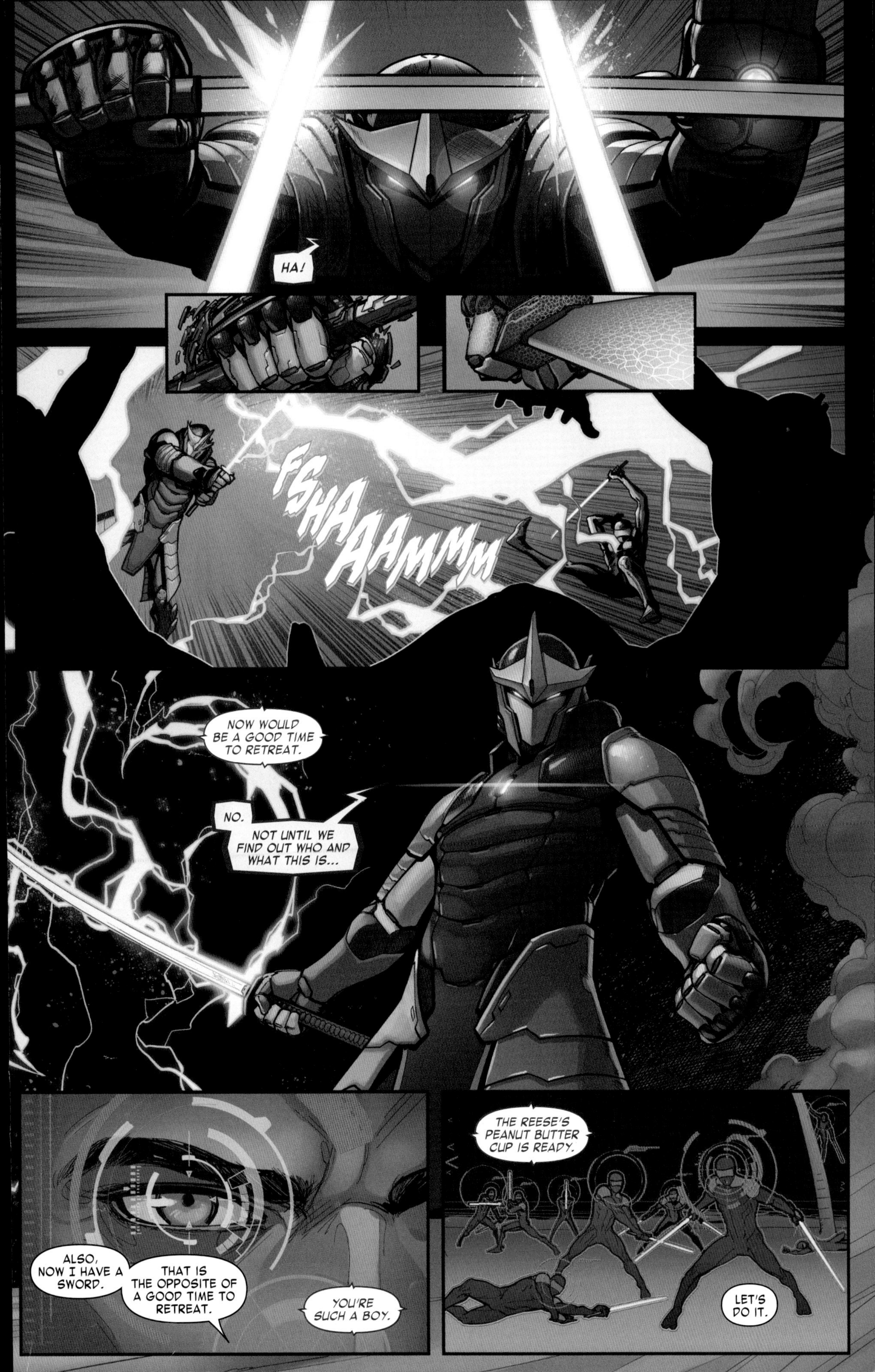
HA!
FSHAAAMMM
NOW WOULD BE A GOOD TIME TO RETREAT.
NO.
NOT UNTIL WE FIND OUT WHO AND WHAT THIS IS...
ALSO, NOW I HAVE A SWORD.
THAT IS THE OPPOSITE OF A GOOD TIME TO RETREAT.
YOU'RE SUCH A BOY.
THE REESE'S PEANUT BUTTER CUP IS READY.
LET'S DO IT.

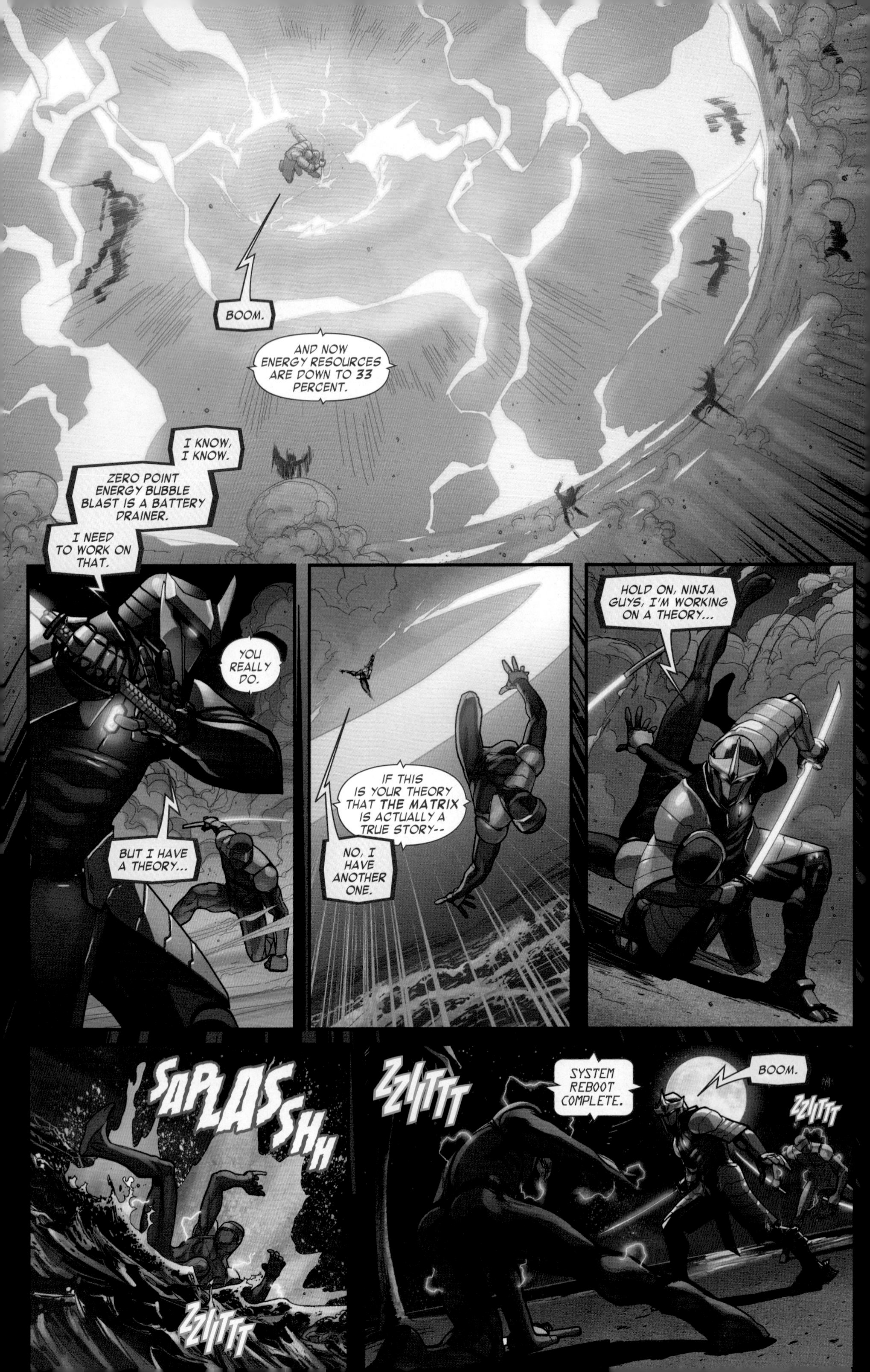
BOOM.
AND NOW ENERGY RESOURCES ARE DOWN TO 33 PERCENT.
I KNOW, I KNOW.
ZERO POINT ENERGY BUBBLE BLAST IS A BATTERY DRAINER.
I NEED TO WORK ON THAT.
YOU REALLY DO.
BUT I HAVE A THEORY...
IF THIS IS YOUR THEORY THAT THE MATRIX IS ACTUALLY A TRUE STORY--
NO, I HAVE ANOTHER ONE.
HOLD ON, NINJA GUYS, I'M WORKING ON A THEORY...
SAPLASSHH
ZZIITTT
ZZIITTT
SYSTEM REBOOT COMPLETE.
BOOM.
ZZIITTT

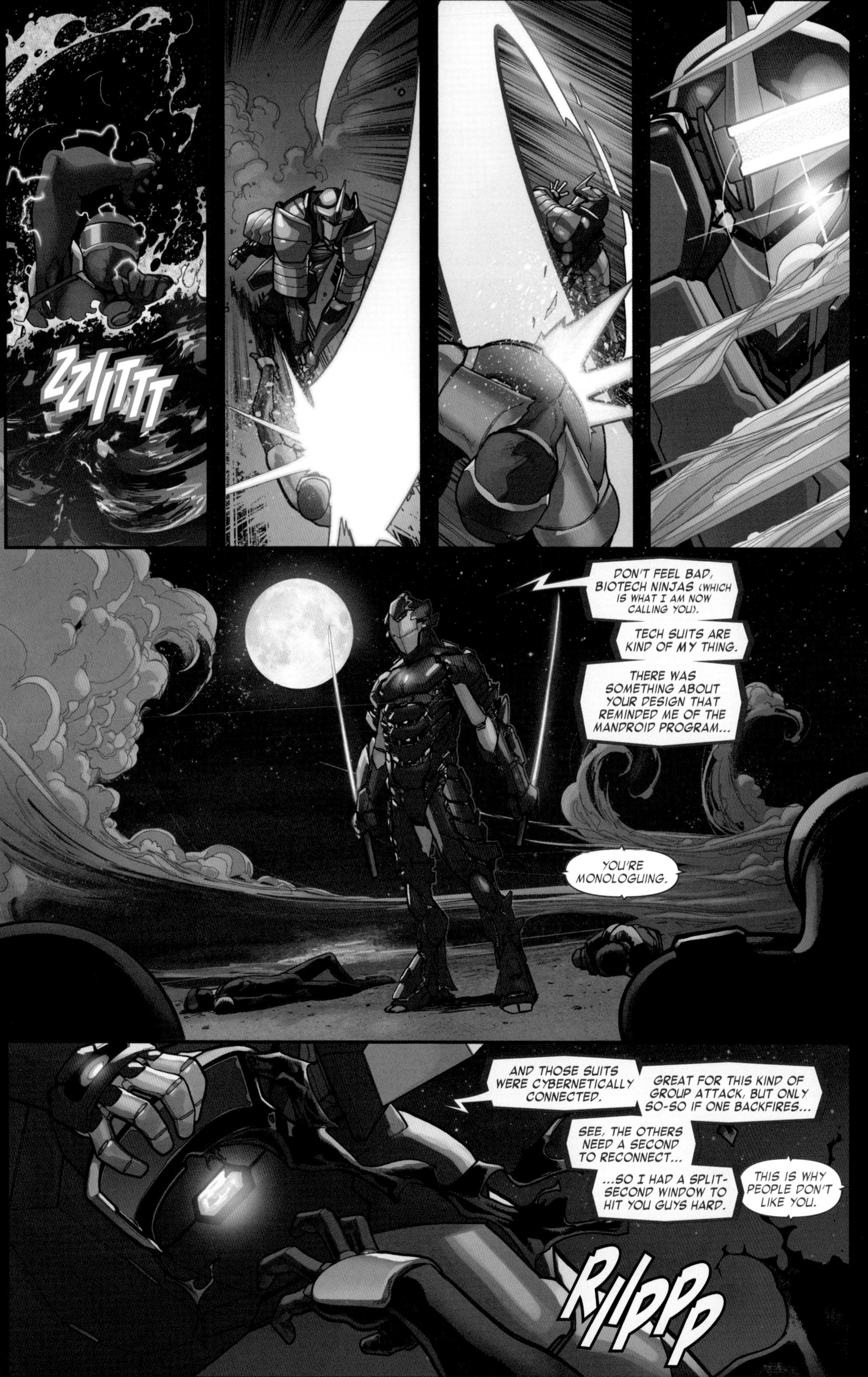
ZZIITTTT
DON'T FEEL BAD, BIOTECH NINJAS (WHICH IS WHAT I AM NOW CALLING YOU).
TECH SUITS ARE KIND OF MY THING.
THERE WAS SOMETHING ABOUT YOUR DESIGN THAT REMINDED ME OF THE MANDROID PROGRAM...
YOU'RE MONOLOGUING.
AND THOSE SUITS WERE CYBERNETICALLY CONNECTED.
GREAT FOR THIS KIND OF GROUP ATTACK, BUT ONLY SO-SO IF ONE BACKFIRES...
SEE, THE OTHERS NEED A SECOND TO RECONNECT...
...SO I HAD A SPLIT-SECOND WINDOW TO HIT YOU GUYS HARD.
THIS IS WHY PEOPLE DON'T LIKE YOU.
RIIPPP

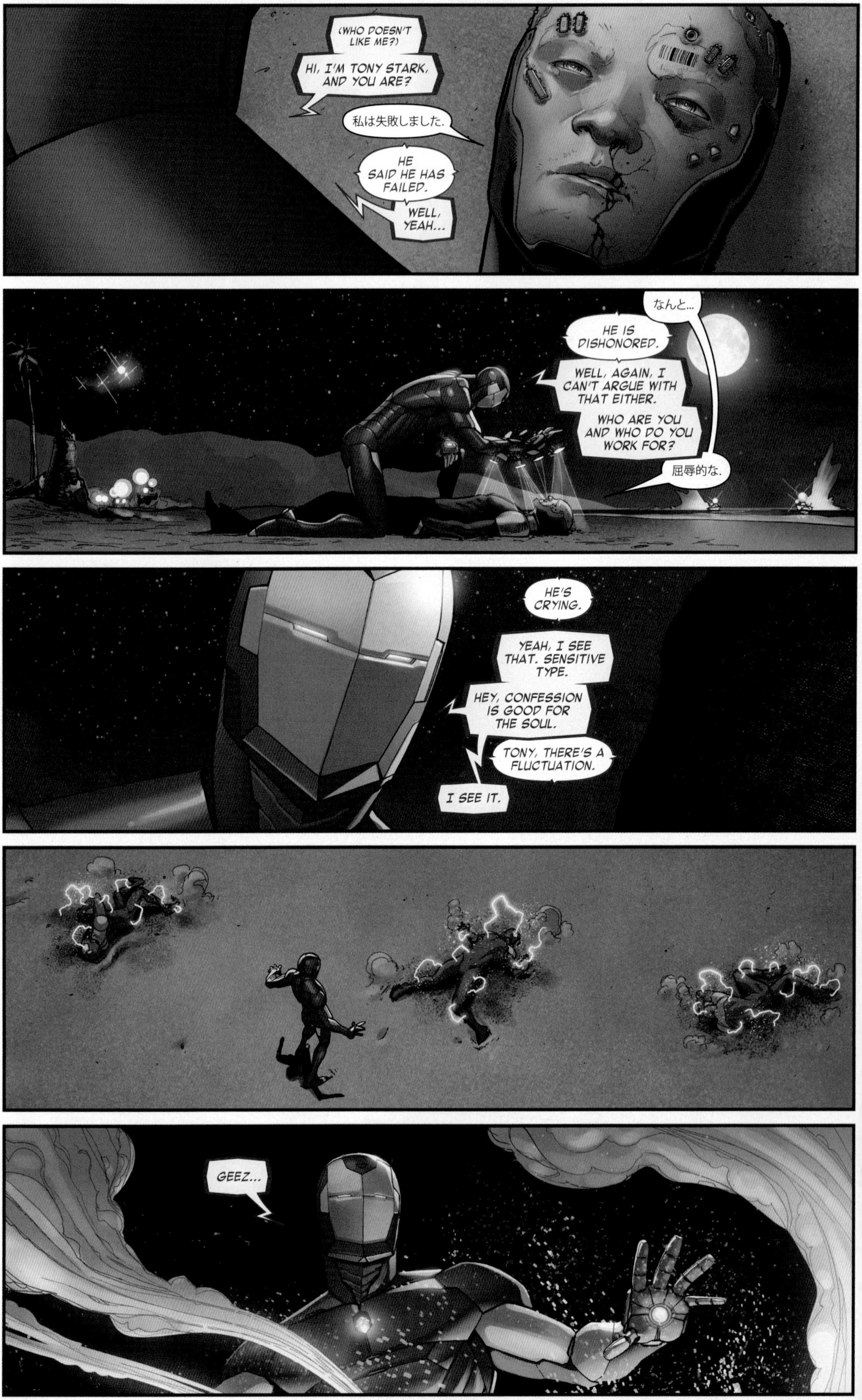
(WHO DOESN'T LIKE ME?)
HI, I'M TONY STARK, AND YOU ARE?
私は失敗しました.
HE SAID HE HAS FAILED.
WELL, YEAH...
なんと...
HE IS DISHONORED.
WELL, AGAIN, I CAN'T ARGUE WITH THAT EITHER.
WHO ARE YOU AND WHO DO YOU WORK FOR?
屈辱的な.
HE'S CRYING.
YEAH, I SEE THAT. SENSITIVE TYPE.
HEY, CONFESSION IS GOOD FOR THE SOUL.
TONY, THERE'S A FLUCTUATION.
I SEE IT.
GEEZ...

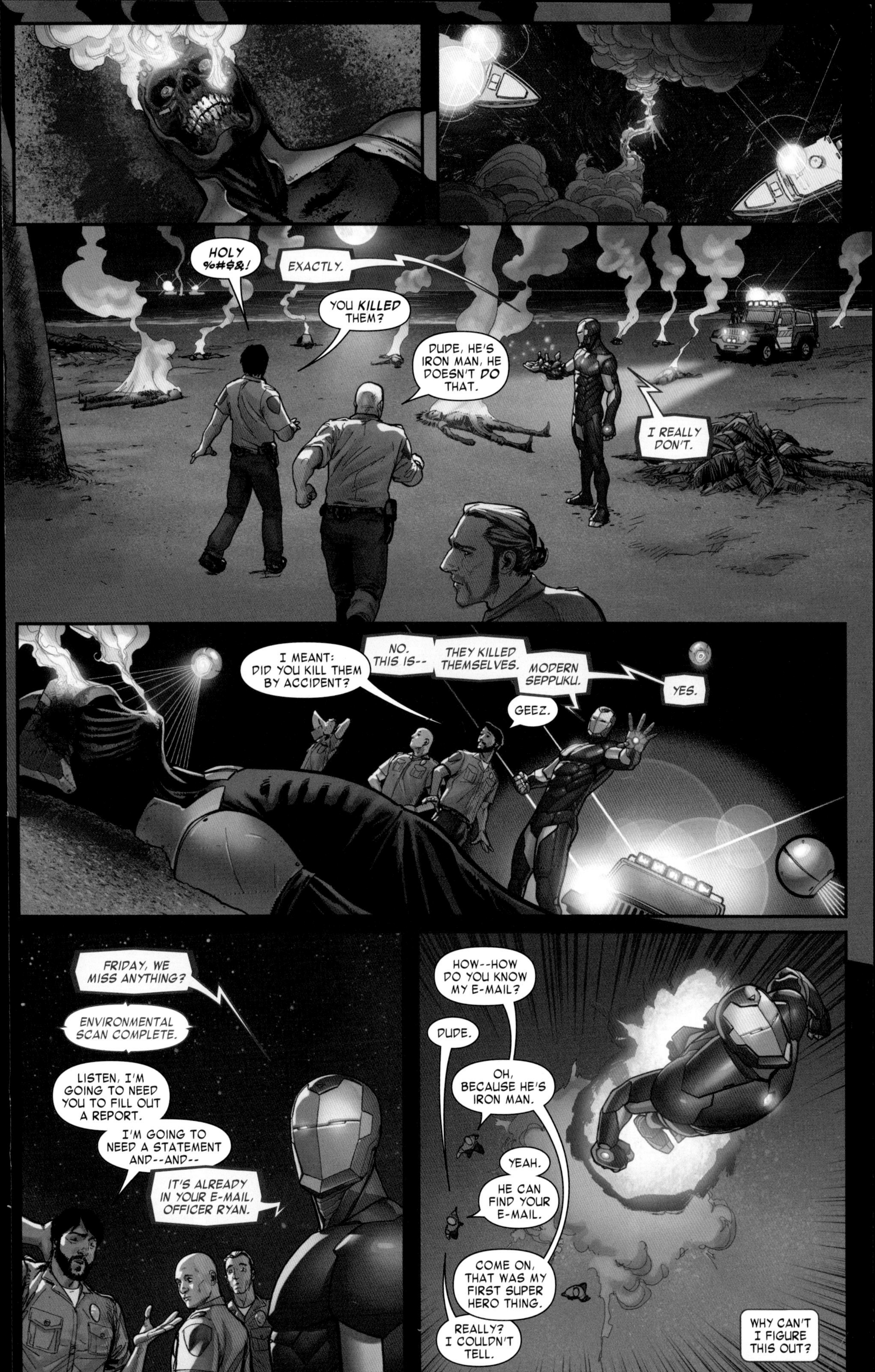

HOLY %#$&!
EXACTLY.
YOU KILLED THEM?
DUDE, HE'S IRON MAN, HE DOESN'T DO THAT.
I REALLY DON'T.
I MEANT: DID YOU KILL THEM BY ACCIDENT?
NO. THIS IS--
THEY KILLED THEMSELVES.
MODERN SEPPUKU.
GEEZ.
YES.
FRIDAY, WE MISS ANYTHING?
ENVIRONMENTAL SCAN COMPLETE.
LISTEN, I'M GOING TO NEED YOU TO FILL OUT A REPORT.
I'M GOING TO NEED A STATEMENT AND--AND--
IT'S ALREADY IN YOUR E-MAIL, OFFICER RYAN.
HOW--HOW DO YOU KNOW MY E-MAIL?
DUDE.
OH, BECAUSE HE'S IRON MAN.
YEAH.
HE CAN FIND YOUR E-MAIL.
COME ON, THAT WAS MY FIRST SUPER HERO THING.
REALLY? I COULDN'T TELL.
WHY CAN'T I FIGURE THIS OUT?

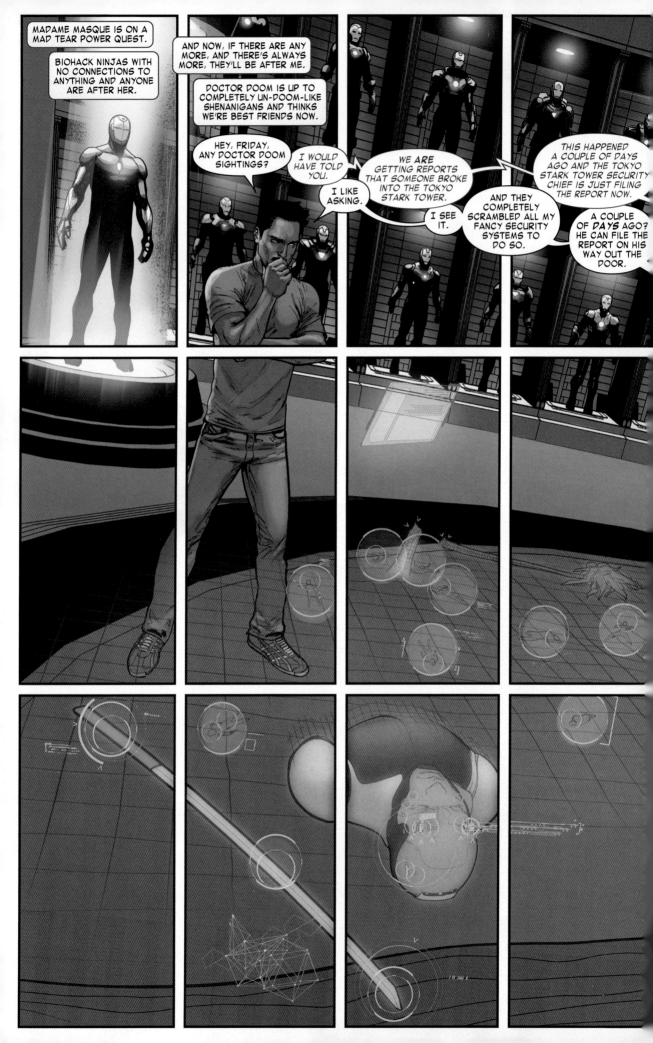

MADAME MASQUE IS ON A MAD TEAR POWER QUEST.

BIOHACK NINJAS WITH NO CONNECTIONS TO ANYTHING AND ANYONE ARE AFTER HER.

AND NOW, IF THERE ARE ANY MORE, AND THERE'S ALWAYS MORE, THEY'LL BE AFTER ME.

DOCTOR DOOM IS UP TO COMPLETELY UN-DOOM-LIKE SHENANIGANS AND THINKS WE'RE BEST FRIENDS NOW.

HEY, FRIDAY, ANY DOCTOR DOOM SIGHTINGS?

I WOULD HAVE TOLD YOU.

I LIKE ASKING.

I SEE IT.

WE *ARE* GETTING REPORTS THAT SOMEONE BROKE INTO THE TOKYO STARK TOWER.

AND THEY COMPLETELY SCRAMBLED ALL MY FANCY SECURITY SYSTEMS TO DO SO.

THIS HAPPENED A COUPLE OF DAYS AGO AND THE TOKYO STARK TOWER SECURITY CHIEF IS JUST FILING THE REPORT NOW.

A COUPLE OF *DAYS* AGO? HE CAN FILE THE REPORT ON HIS WAY OUT THE DOOR.

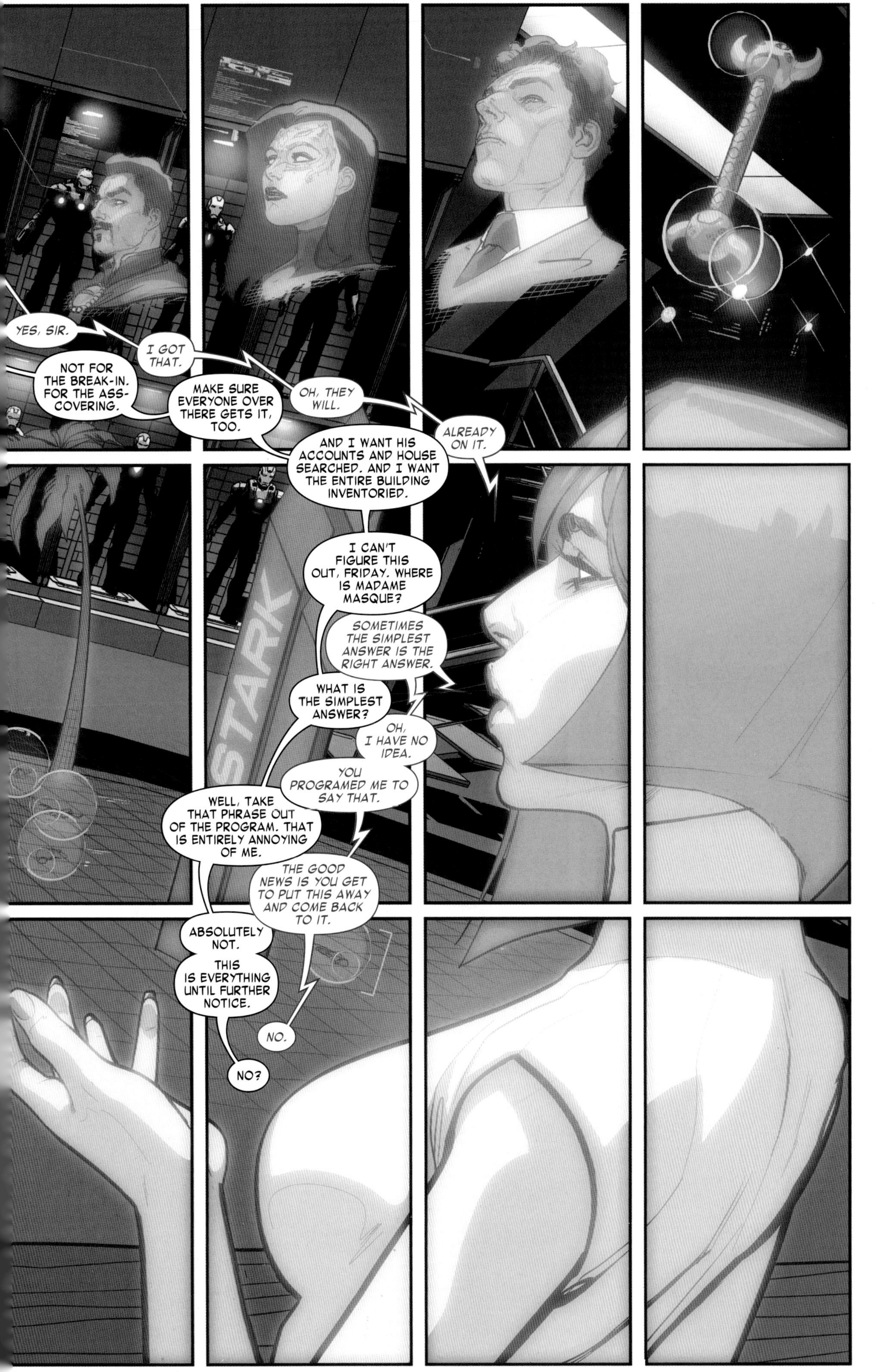
YES, SIR.
I GOT THAT.
NOT FOR THE BREAK-IN. FOR THE ASS-COVERING.
MAKE SURE EVERYONE OVER THERE GETS IT, TOO.
OH, THEY WILL.
AND I WANT HIS ACCOUNTS AND HOUSE SEARCHED. AND I WANT THE ENTIRE BUILDING INVENTORIED.
ALREADY ON IT.
I CAN'T FIGURE THIS OUT, FRIDAY. WHERE IS MADAME MASQUE?
SOMETIMES THE SIMPLEST ANSWER IS THE RIGHT ANSWER.
WHAT IS THE SIMPLEST ANSWER?
OH, I HAVE NO IDEA.
YOU PROGRAMED ME TO SAY THAT.
WELL, TAKE THAT PHRASE OUT OF THE PROGRAM. THAT IS ENTIRELY ANNOYING OF ME.
THE GOOD NEWS IS YOU GET TO PUT THIS AWAY AND COME BACK TO IT.
ABSOLUTELY NOT.
THIS IS EVERYTHING UNTIL FURTHER NOTICE.
NO.
NO?
STARK

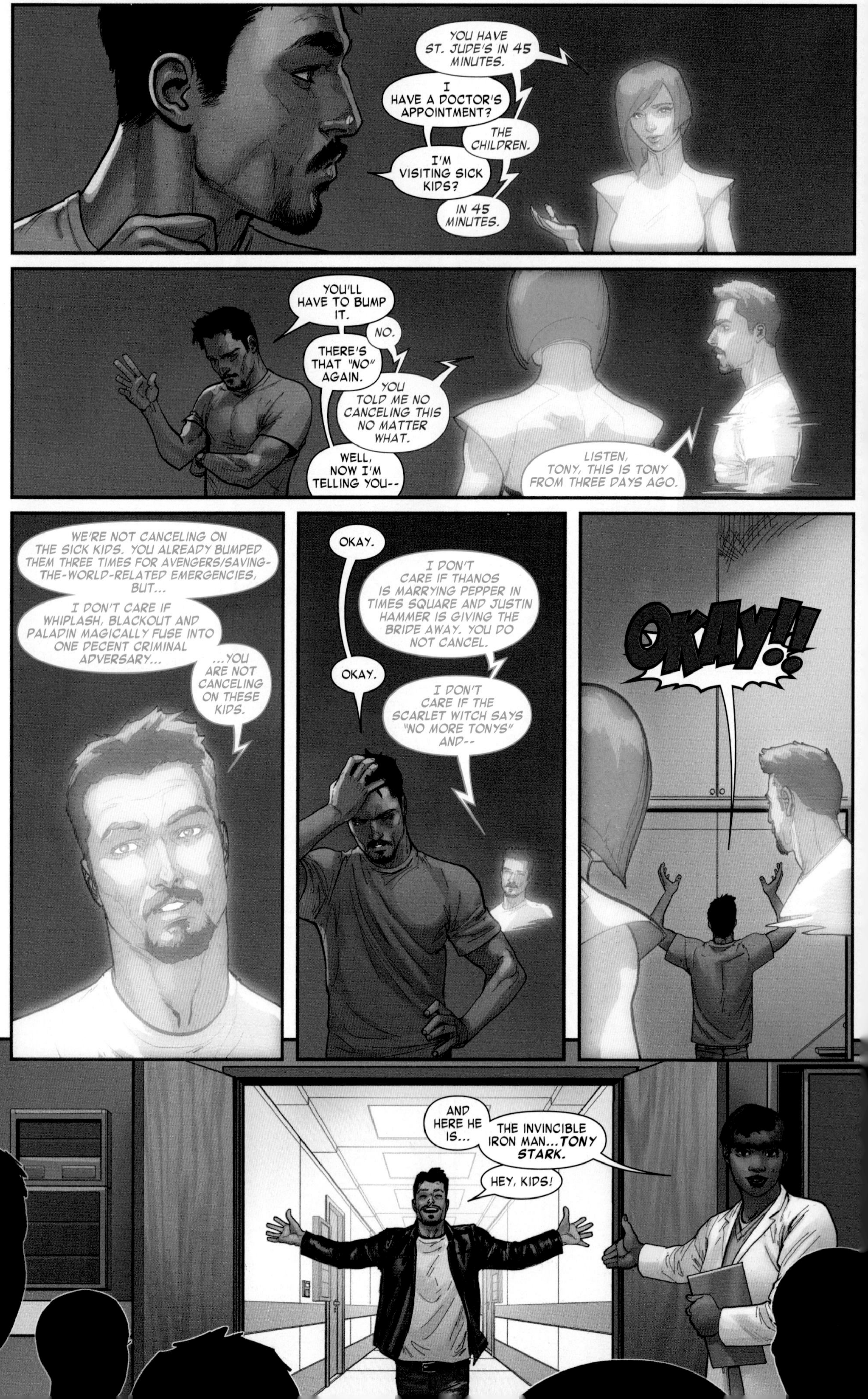

YOU HAVE ST. JUDE'S IN 45 MINUTES.
I HAVE A DOCTOR'S APPOINTMENT?
THE CHILDREN.
I'M VISITING SICK KIDS?
IN 45 MINUTES.
YOU'LL HAVE TO BUMP IT.
NO.
THERE'S THAT "NO" AGAIN.
YOU TOLD ME NO CANCELING THIS NO MATTER WHAT.
WELL, NOW I'M TELLING YOU--
LISTEN, TONY, THIS IS TONY FROM THREE DAYS AGO.
WE'RE NOT CANCELING ON THE SICK KIDS. YOU ALREADY BUMPED THEM THREE TIMES FOR AVENGERS/SAVING-THE-WORLD-RELATED EMERGENCIES, BUT...
I DON'T CARE IF WHIPLASH, BLACKOUT AND PALADIN MAGICALLY FUSE INTO ONE DECENT CRIMINAL ADVERSARY...
...YOU ARE NOT CANCELING ON THESE KIDS.
OKAY.
I DON'T CARE IF THANOS IS MARRYING PEPPER IN TIMES SQUARE AND JUSTIN HAMMER IS GIVING THE BRIDE AWAY. YOU DO NOT CANCEL.
OKAY.
I DON'T CARE IF THE SCARLET WITCH SAYS "NO MORE TONYS" AND--
OKAY!!
AND HERE HE IS...
THE INVINCIBLE IRON MAN...TONY STARK.
HEY, KIDS!

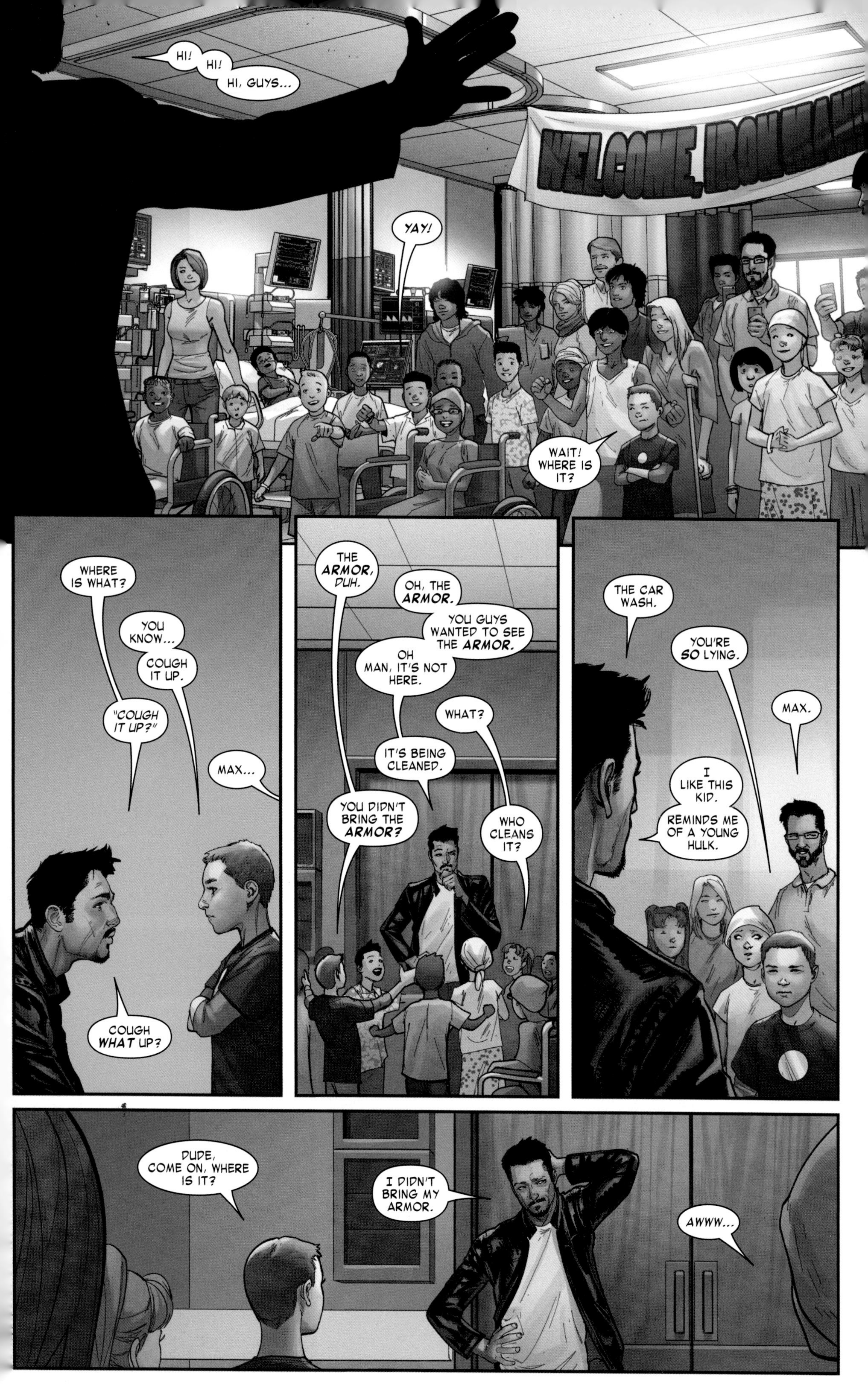
HI!
HI!
HI, GUYS...
WELCOME, IRON MAN
YAY!
WAIT! WHERE IS IT?
WHERE IS WHAT?
YOU KNOW...
COUGH IT UP.
"COUGH IT UP?"
MAX...
COUGH WHAT UP?
THE ARMOR, DUH.
OH, THE ARMOR.
YOU GUYS WANTED TO SEE THE ARMOR.
OH MAN, IT'S NOT HERE.
WHAT?
IT'S BEING CLEANED.
YOU DIDN'T BRING THE ARMOR?
WHO CLEANS IT?
THE CAR WASH.
YOU'RE SO LYING.
MAX.
I LIKE THIS KID.
REMINDS ME OF A YOUNG HULK.
DUDE, COME ON, WHERE IS IT?
I DIDN'T BRING MY ARMOR.
AWWW...

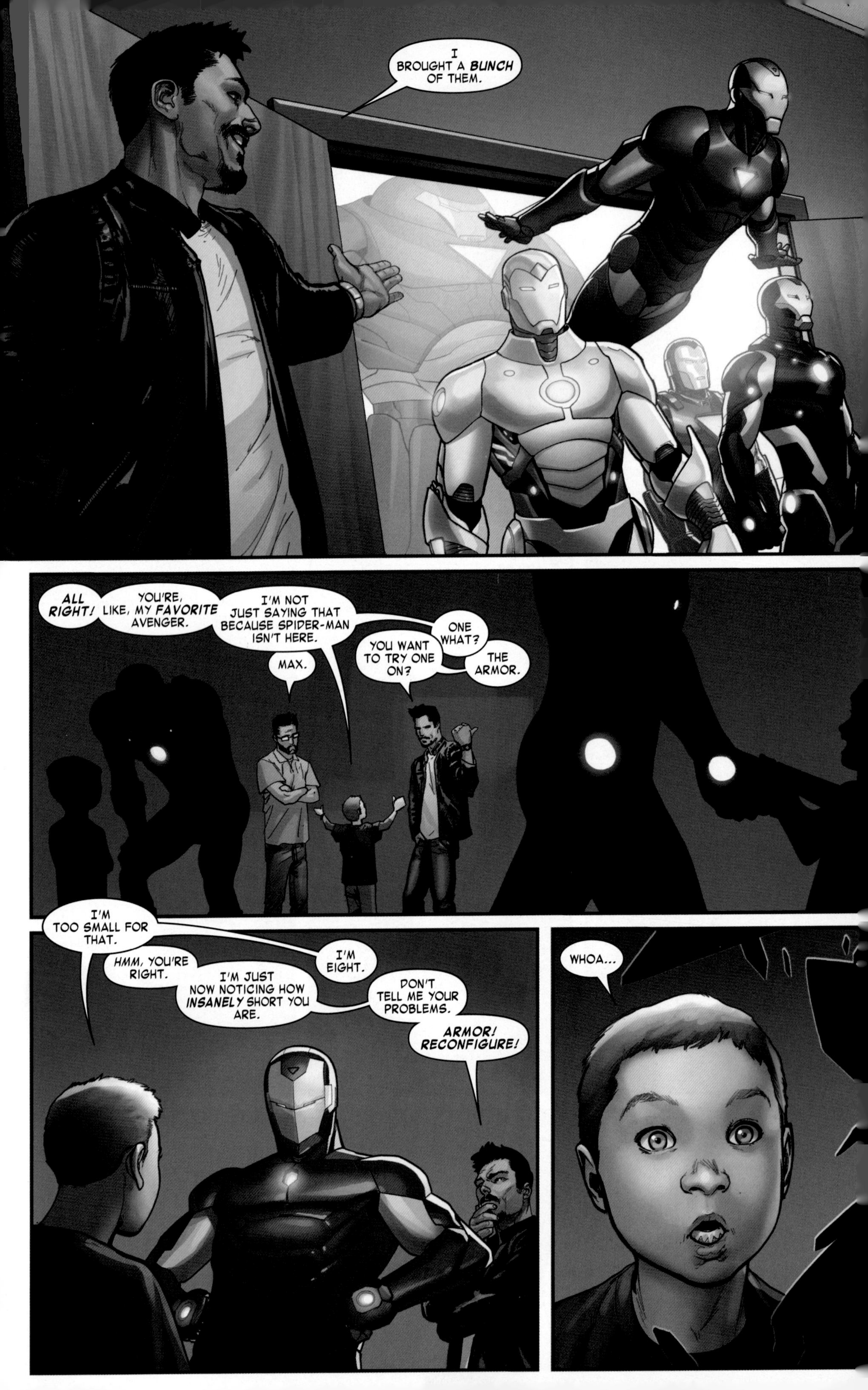
I BROUGHT A BUNCH OF THEM.
ALL RIGHT!
YOU'RE, LIKE, MY FAVORITE AVENGER.
I'M NOT JUST SAYING THAT BECAUSE SPIDER-MAN ISN'T HERE.
MAX.
YOU WANT TO TRY ONE ON?
ONE WHAT?
THE ARMOR.
I'M TOO SMALL FOR THAT.
HMM, YOU'RE RIGHT.
I'M JUST NOW NOTICING HOW INSANELY SHORT YOU ARE.
I'M EIGHT.
DON'T TELL ME YOUR PROBLEMS.
ARMOR! RECONFIGURE!
WHOA...

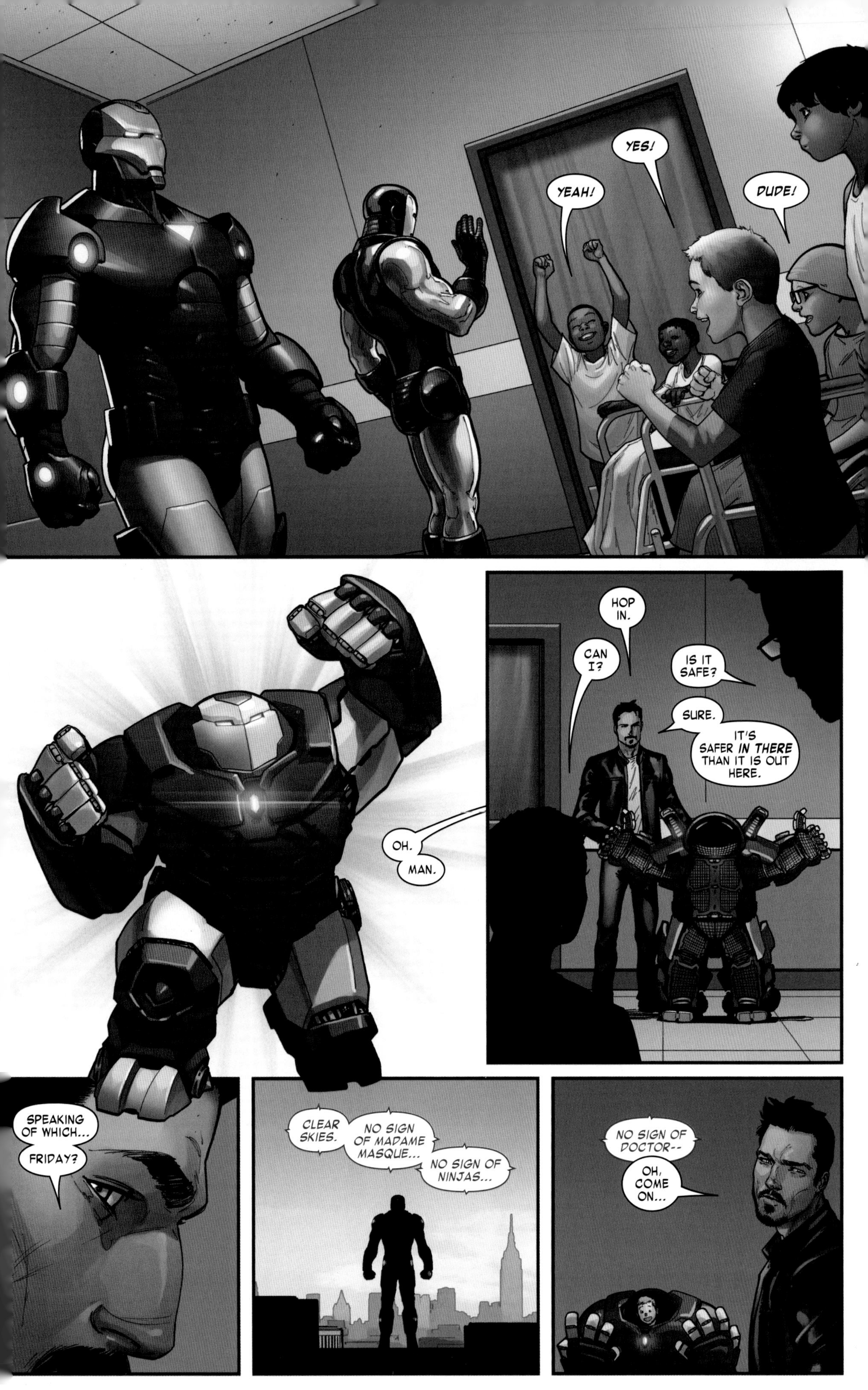
YEAH!
YES!
DUDE!
HOP IN.
CAN I?
IS IT SAFE?
SURE.
IT'S SAFER IN THERE THAN IT IS OUT HERE.
OH.
MAN.
SPEAKING OF WHICH...
FRIDAY?
CLEAR SKIES.
NO SIGN OF MADAME MASQUE...
NO SIGN OF NINJAS...
NO SIGN OF DOCTOR--
OH, COME ON...

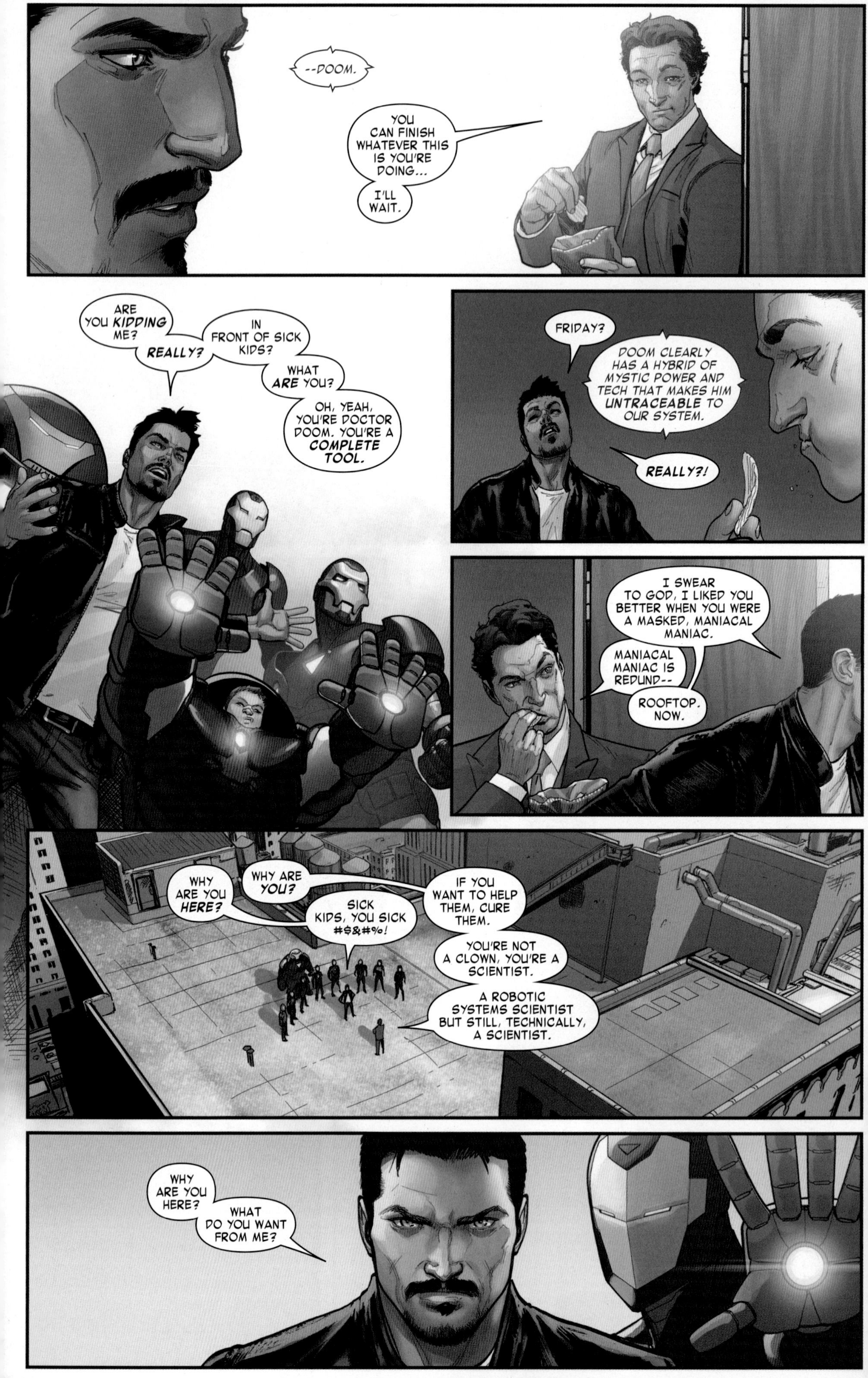
--DOOM.
YOU CAN FINISH WHATEVER THIS IS YOU'RE DOING...
I'LL WAIT.
ARE YOU KIDDING ME?
REALLY?
IN FRONT OF SICK KIDS?
WHAT ARE YOU?
OH, YEAH, YOU'RE DOCTOR DOOM. YOU'RE A COMPLETE TOOL.
FRIDAY?
DOOM CLEARLY HAS A HYBRID OF MYSTIC POWER AND TECH THAT MAKES HIM UNTRACEABLE TO OUR SYSTEM.
REALLY?!
I SWEAR TO GOD, I LIKED YOU BETTER WHEN YOU WERE A MASKED, MANIACAL MANIAC.
MANIACAL MANIAC IS REDUND--
ROOFTOP. NOW.
WHY ARE YOU HERE?
WHY ARE YOU?
SICK KIDS, YOU SICK #$&#%!
IF YOU WANT TO HELP THEM, CURE THEM.
YOU'RE NOT A CLOWN, YOU'RE A SCIENTIST.
A ROBOTIC SYSTEMS SCIENTIST BUT STILL, TECHNICALLY, A SCIENTIST.
WHY ARE YOU HERE?
WHAT DO YOU WANT FROM ME?

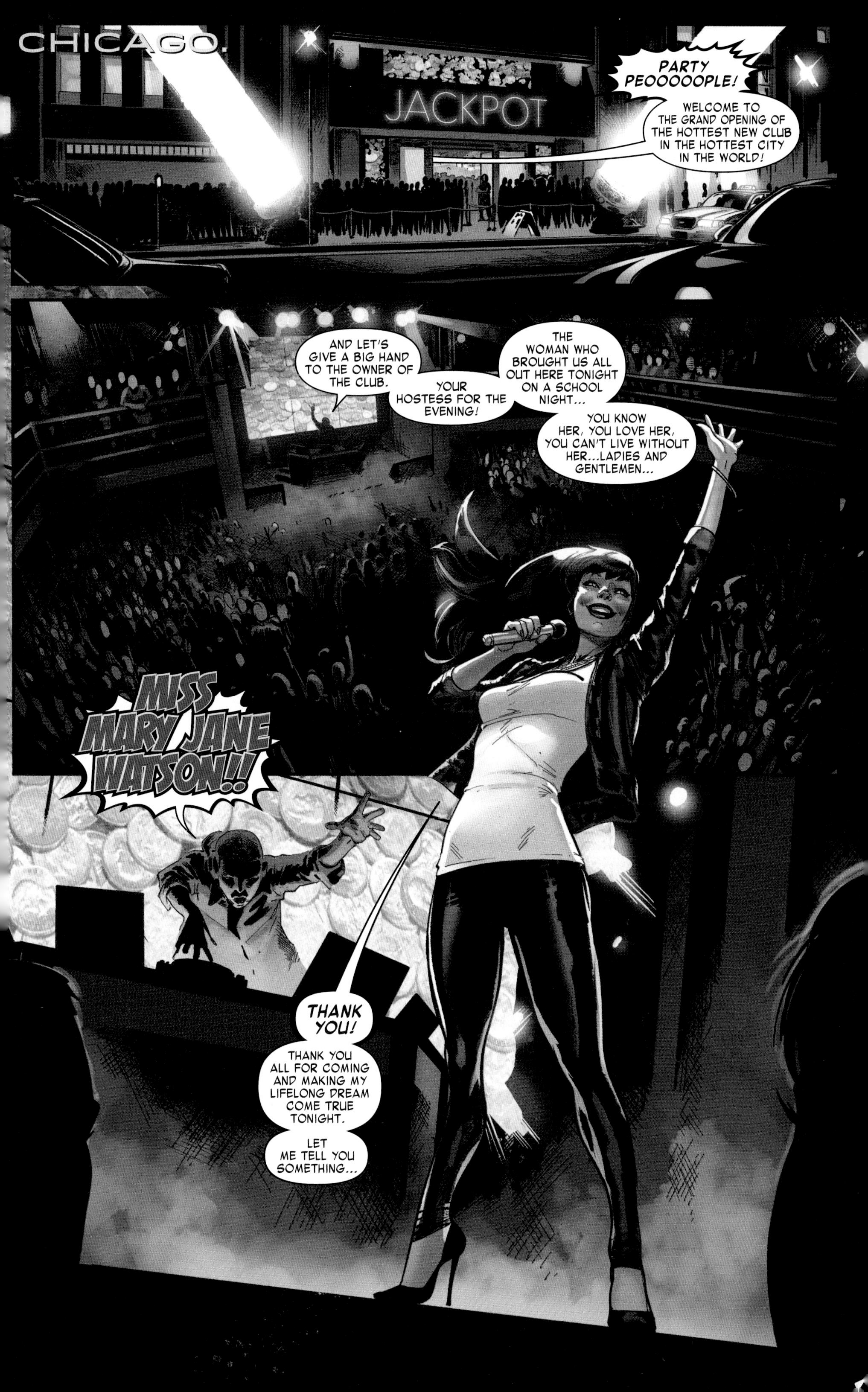
CHICAGO.
JACKPOT
PARTY PEOOOOOPLE!
WELCOME TO THE GRAND OPENING OF THE HOTTEST NEW CLUB IN THE HOTTEST CITY IN THE WORLD!
AND LET'S GIVE A BIG HAND TO THE OWNER OF THE CLUB.
YOUR HOSTESS FOR THE EVENING!
THE WOMAN WHO BROUGHT US ALL OUT HERE TONIGHT ON A SCHOOL NIGHT...
YOU KNOW HER, YOU LOVE HER, YOU CAN'T LIVE WITHOUT HER...LADIES AND GENTLEMEN...
MISS MARY JANE WATSON!!
THANK YOU!
THANK YOU ALL FOR COMING AND MAKING MY LIFELONG DREAM COME TRUE TONIGHT.
LET ME TELL YOU SOMETHING...

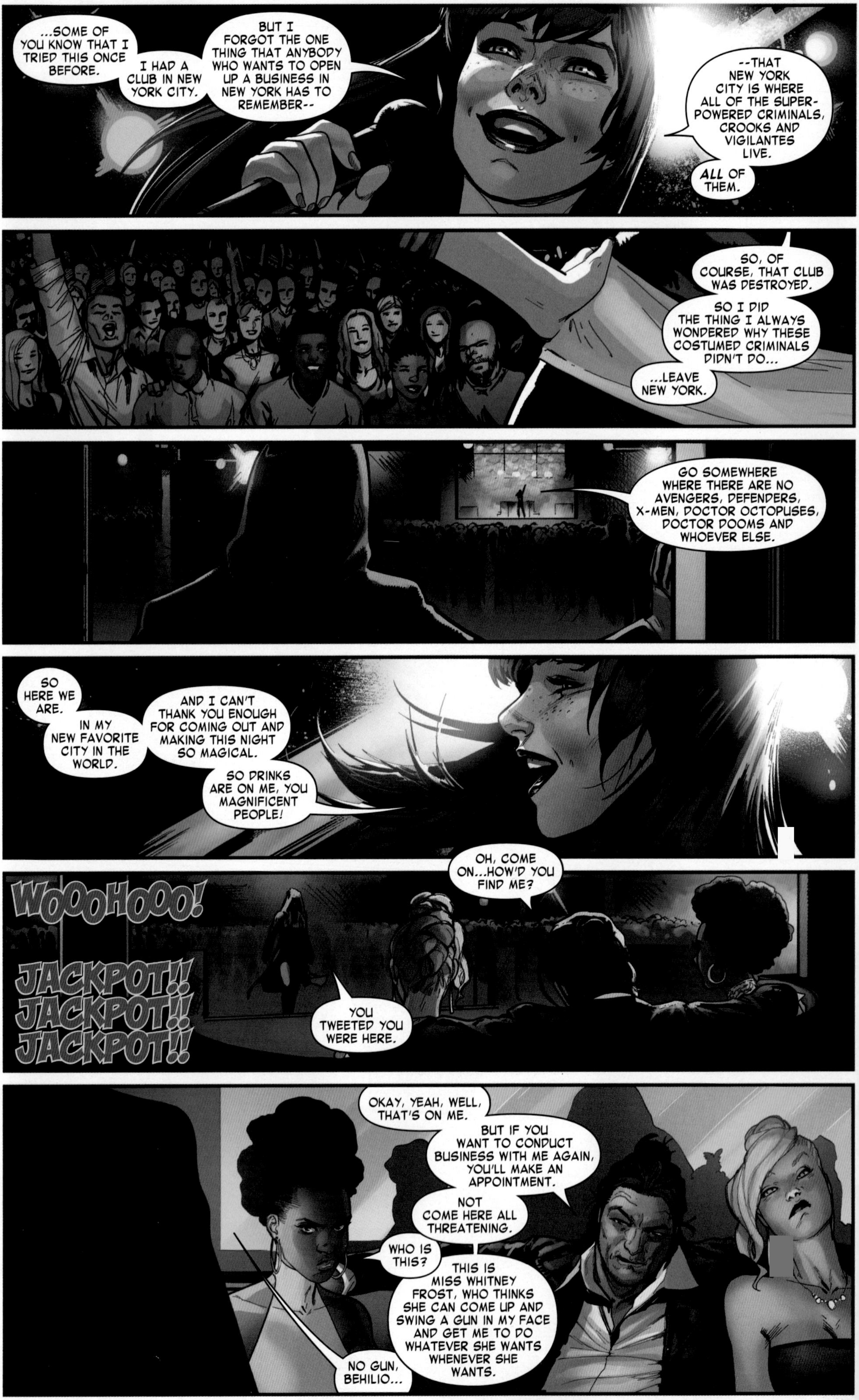
...SOME OF YOU KNOW THAT I TRIED THIS ONCE BEFORE.
I HAD A CLUB IN NEW YORK CITY.
BUT I FORGOT THE ONE THING THAT ANYBODY WHO WANTS TO OPEN UP A BUSINESS IN NEW YORK HAS TO REMEMBER--
--THAT NEW YORK CITY IS WHERE ALL OF THE SUPER-POWERED CRIMINALS, CROOKS AND VIGILANTES LIVE.
ALL OF THEM.
SO, OF COURSE, THAT CLUB WAS DESTROYED.
SO I DID THE THING I ALWAYS WONDERED WHY THESE COSTUMED CRIMINALS DIDN'T DO...
...LEAVE NEW YORK.
GO SOMEWHERE WHERE THERE ARE NO AVENGERS, DEFENDERS, X-MEN, DOCTOR OCTOPUSES, DOCTOR DOOMS AND WHOEVER ELSE.
SO HERE WE ARE.
IN MY NEW FAVORITE CITY IN THE WORLD.
AND I CAN'T THANK YOU ENOUGH FOR COMING OUT AND MAKING THIS NIGHT SO MAGICAL.
SO DRINKS ARE ON ME, YOU MAGNIFICENT PEOPLE!
WOOOHOOO!
JACKPOT!! JACKPOT!! JACKPOT!!
OH, COME ON...HOW'D YOU FIND ME?
YOU TWEETED YOU WERE HERE.
OKAY, YEAH, WELL, THAT'S ON ME.
BUT IF YOU WANT TO CONDUCT BUSINESS WITH ME AGAIN, YOU'LL MAKE AN APPOINTMENT.
NOT COME HERE ALL THREATENING.
WHO IS THIS?
THIS IS MISS WHITNEY FROST, WHO THINKS SHE CAN COME UP AND SWING A GUN IN MY FACE AND GET ME TO DO WHATEVER SHE WANTS WHENEVER SHE WANTS.
NO GUN, BEHILIO...

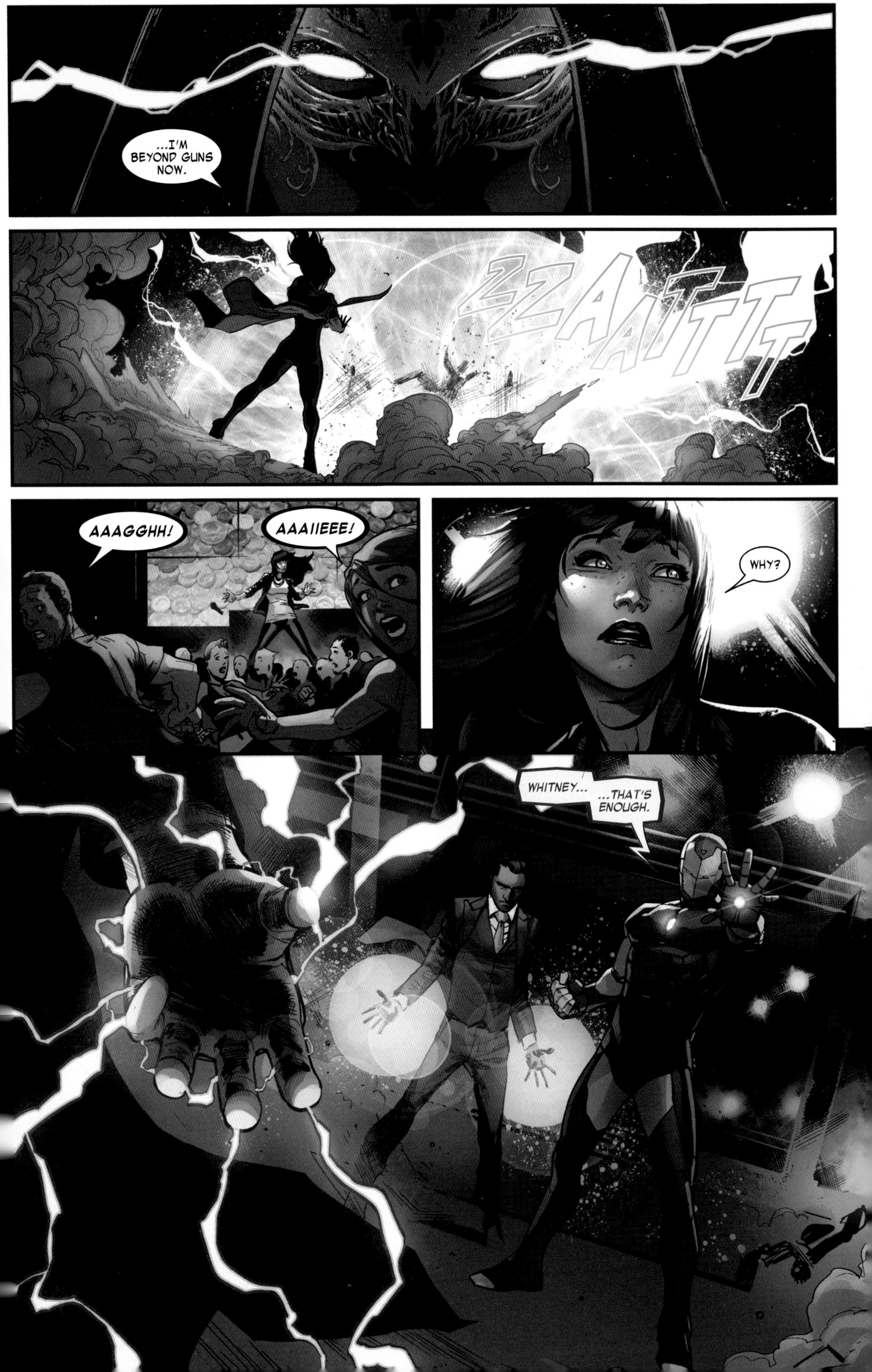

...I'M BEYOND GUNS NOW.
ZZAAATTTT
AAAGGHH!
AAAIIEEE!
WHY?
WHITNEY...
...THAT'S ENOUGH.

#5

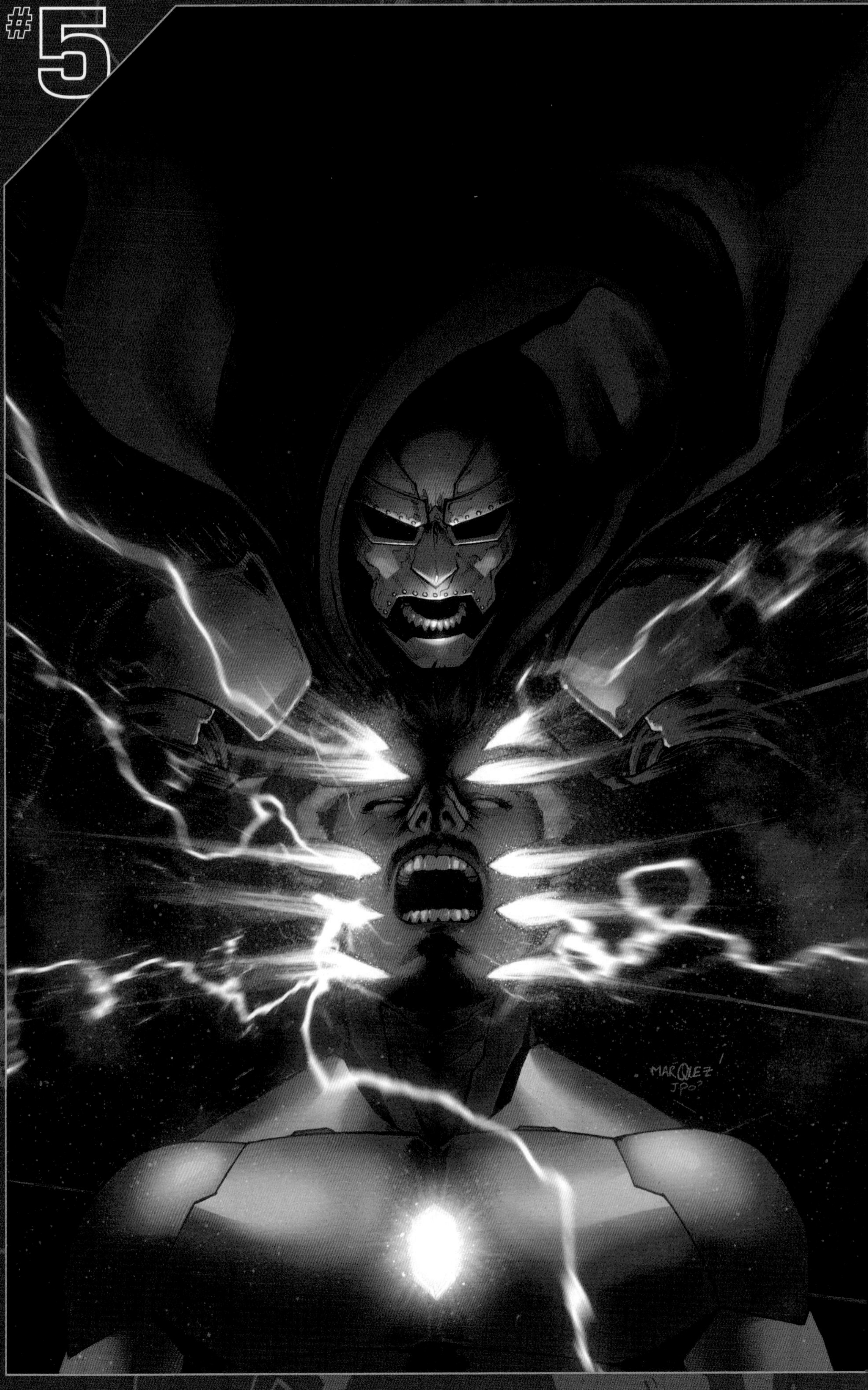
MARQUEZ
JPO

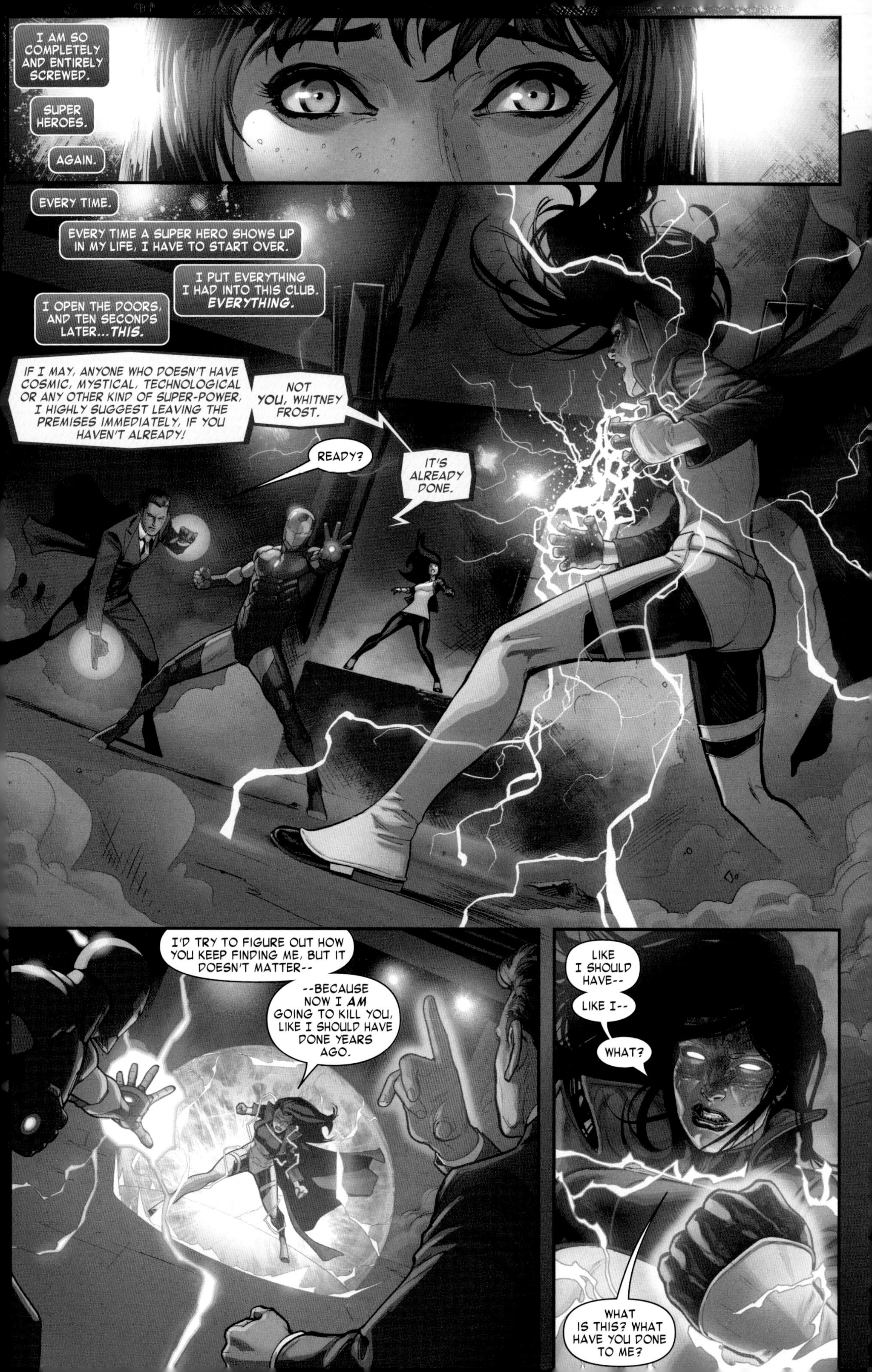
I AM SO COMPLETELY AND ENTIRELY SCREWED.
SUPER HEROES.
AGAIN.
EVERY TIME.
EVERY TIME A SUPER HERO SHOWS UP IN MY LIFE, I HAVE TO START OVER.
I PUT EVERYTHING I HAD INTO THIS CLUB. EVERYTHING.
I OPEN THE DOORS, AND TEN SECONDS LATER...THIS.
IF I MAY, ANYONE WHO DOESN'T HAVE COSMIC, MYSTICAL, TECHNOLOGICAL OR ANY OTHER KIND OF SUPER-POWER, I HIGHLY SUGGEST LEAVING THE PREMISES IMMEDIATELY, IF YOU HAVEN'T ALREADY!
NOT YOU, WHITNEY FROST.
READY?
IT'S ALREADY DONE.
I'D TRY TO FIGURE OUT HOW YOU KEEP FINDING ME, BUT IT DOESN'T MATTER--
--BECAUSE NOW I AM GOING TO KILL YOU, LIKE I SHOULD HAVE DONE YEARS AGO.
LIKE I SHOULD HAVE--
LIKE I--
WHAT?
WHAT IS THIS? WHAT HAVE YOU DONE TO ME?

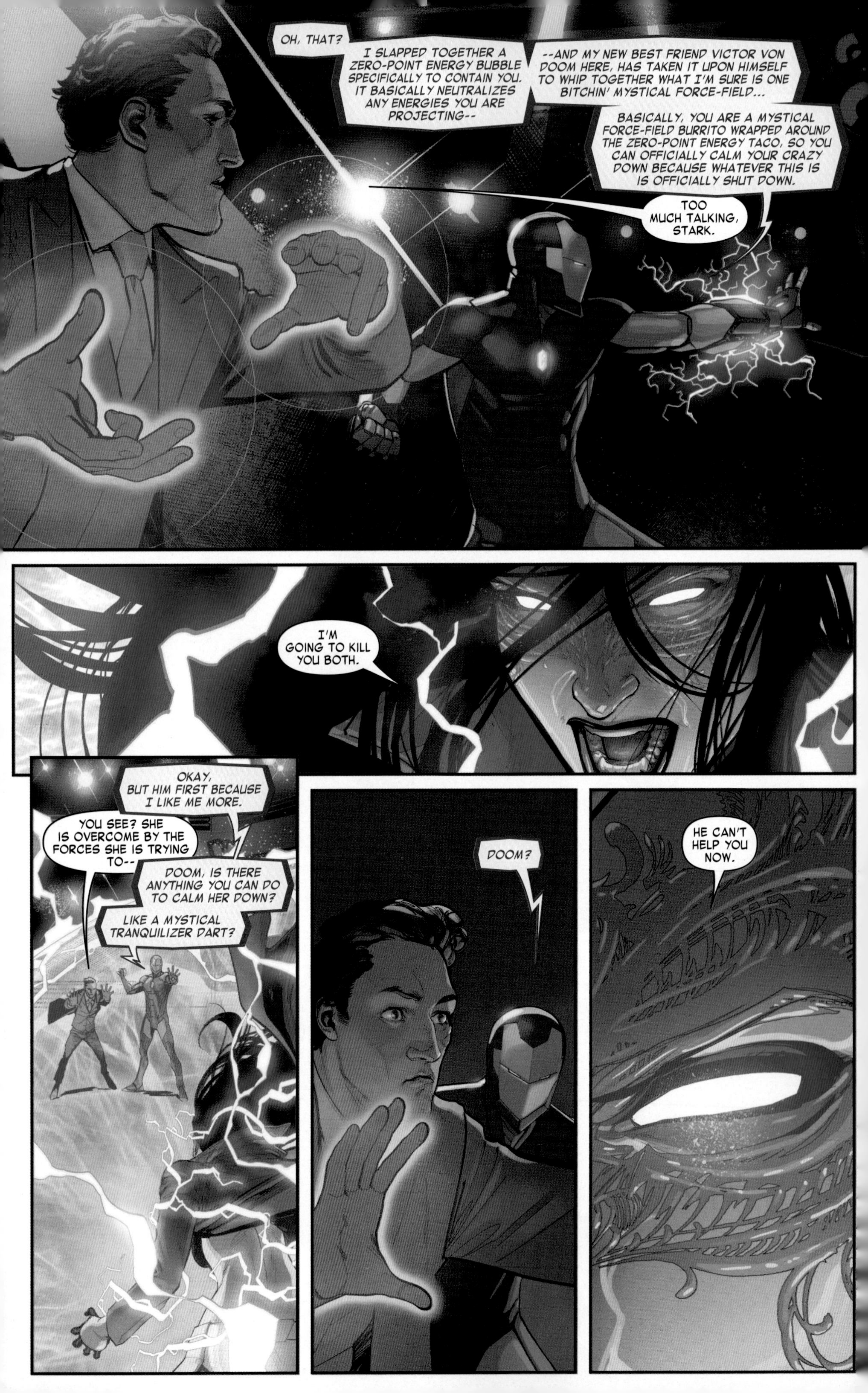
OH, THAT?
I SLAPPED TOGETHER A ZERO-POINT ENERGY BUBBLE SPECIFICALLY TO CONTAIN YOU. IT BASICALLY NEUTRALIZES ANY ENERGIES YOU ARE PROJECTING--
--AND MY NEW BEST FRIEND VICTOR VON DOOM HERE, HAS TAKEN IT UPON HIMSELF TO WHIP TOGETHER WHAT I'M SURE IS ONE BITCHIN' MYSTICAL FORCE-FIELD...
BASICALLY, YOU ARE A MYSTICAL FORCE-FIELD BURRITO WRAPPED AROUND THE ZERO-POINT ENERGY TACO, SO YOU CAN OFFICIALLY CALM YOUR CRAZY DOWN BECAUSE WHATEVER THIS IS IS OFFICIALLY SHUT DOWN.
TOO MUCH TALKING, STARK.
I'M GOING TO KILL YOU BOTH.
OKAY, BUT HIM FIRST BECAUSE I LIKE ME MORE.
YOU SEE? SHE IS OVERCOME BY THE FORCES SHE IS TRYING TO--
DOOM, IS THERE ANYTHING YOU CAN DO TO CALM HER DOWN?
LIKE A MYSTICAL TRANQUILIZER DART?
DOOM?
HE CAN'T HELP YOU NOW.

VICTOR VON DOOM?

I KNOW, RIGHT?

LIFE IS FUNNY THAT WAY.

SHE IS ATTEMPTING TO BREACH THE ARMOR WITH AN ENERGY MATRIX THAT I AM UNFAMILIAR WITH...

...WHICH MEANS IT IS MOST PROBABLY MYSTICAL IN NATURE.

YES, FRIDAY, I--

WE HAVE TO ASSUME THAT SHE HAS TAKEN HOLD OF DOCTOR DOOM AND IS ATTEMPTING TO DO THE SAME TO YOU.

YEAH...

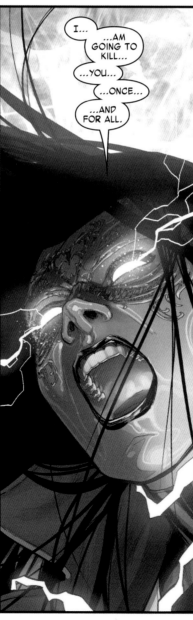

I...

...AM GOING TO KILL...

...YOU...

...ONCE...

...AND FOR ALL.

FRIDAY?

FORCES UNKNOWN. SYSTEMS FAILING.

FORCES?

GORGONZOLA.

UH-OH.

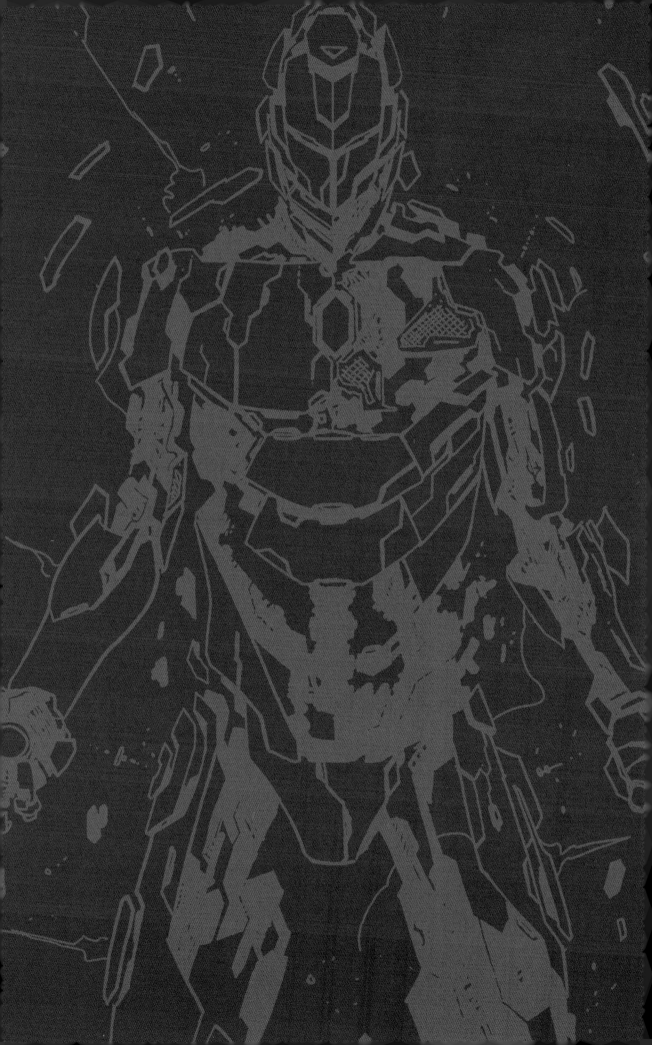

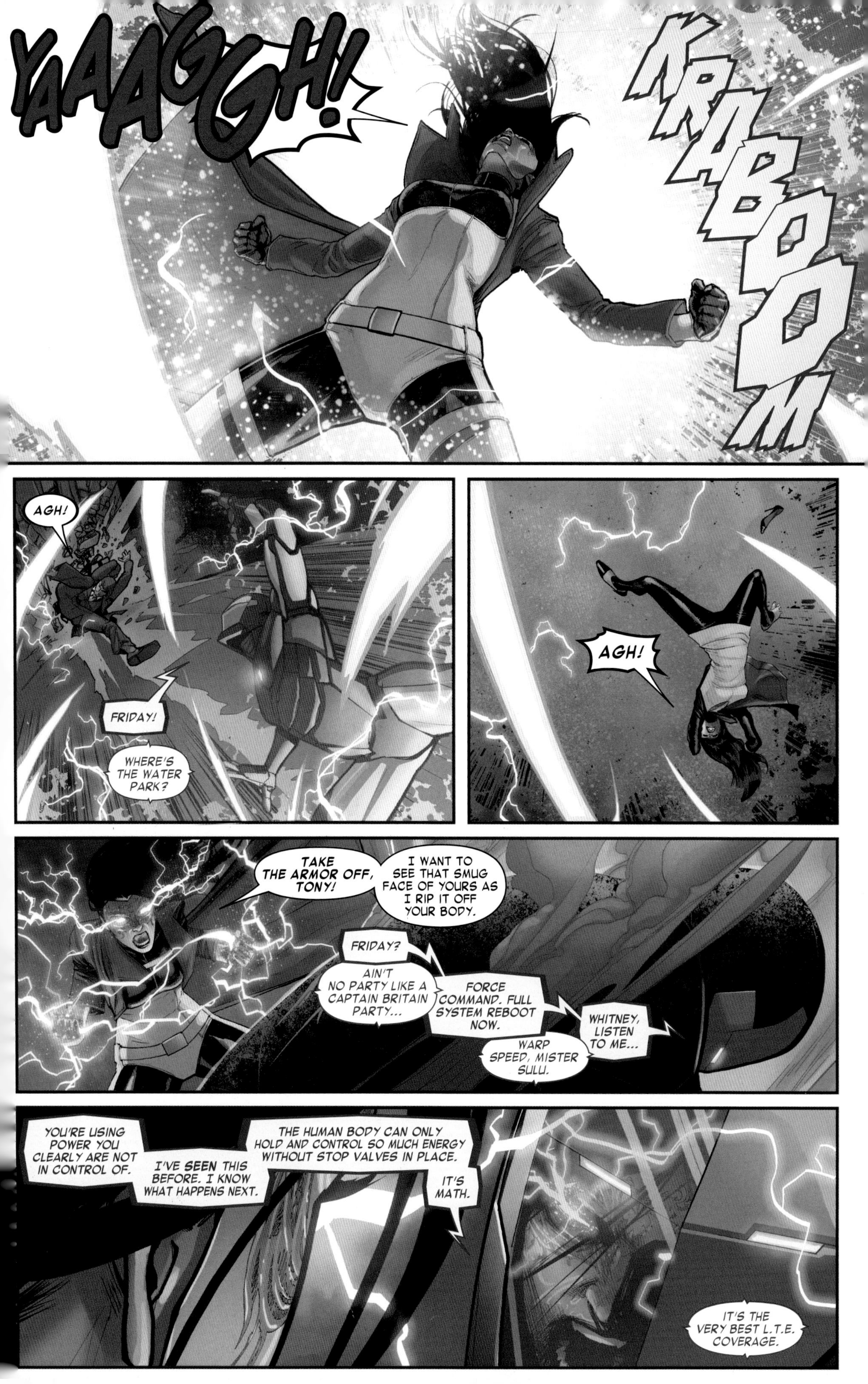
YAAAGGH!
KRABOOM
AGH!
FRIDAY!
WHERE'S THE WATER PARK?
AGH!
TAKE THE ARMOR OFF, TONY!
I WANT TO SEE THAT SMUG FACE OF YOURS AS I RIP IT OFF YOUR BODY.
FRIDAY?
AIN'T NO PARTY LIKE A CAPTAIN BRITAIN PARTY...
FORCE COMMAND. FULL SYSTEM REBOOT NOW.
WHITNEY, LISTEN TO ME...
WARP SPEED, MISTER SULU.
YOU'RE USING POWER YOU CLEARLY ARE NOT IN CONTROL OF.
I'VE SEEN THIS BEFORE. I KNOW WHAT HAPPENS NEXT.
THE HUMAN BODY CAN ONLY HOLD AND CONTROL SO MUCH ENERGY WITHOUT STOP VALVES IN PLACE.
IT'S MATH.
IT'S THE VERY BEST L.T.E. COVERAGE.

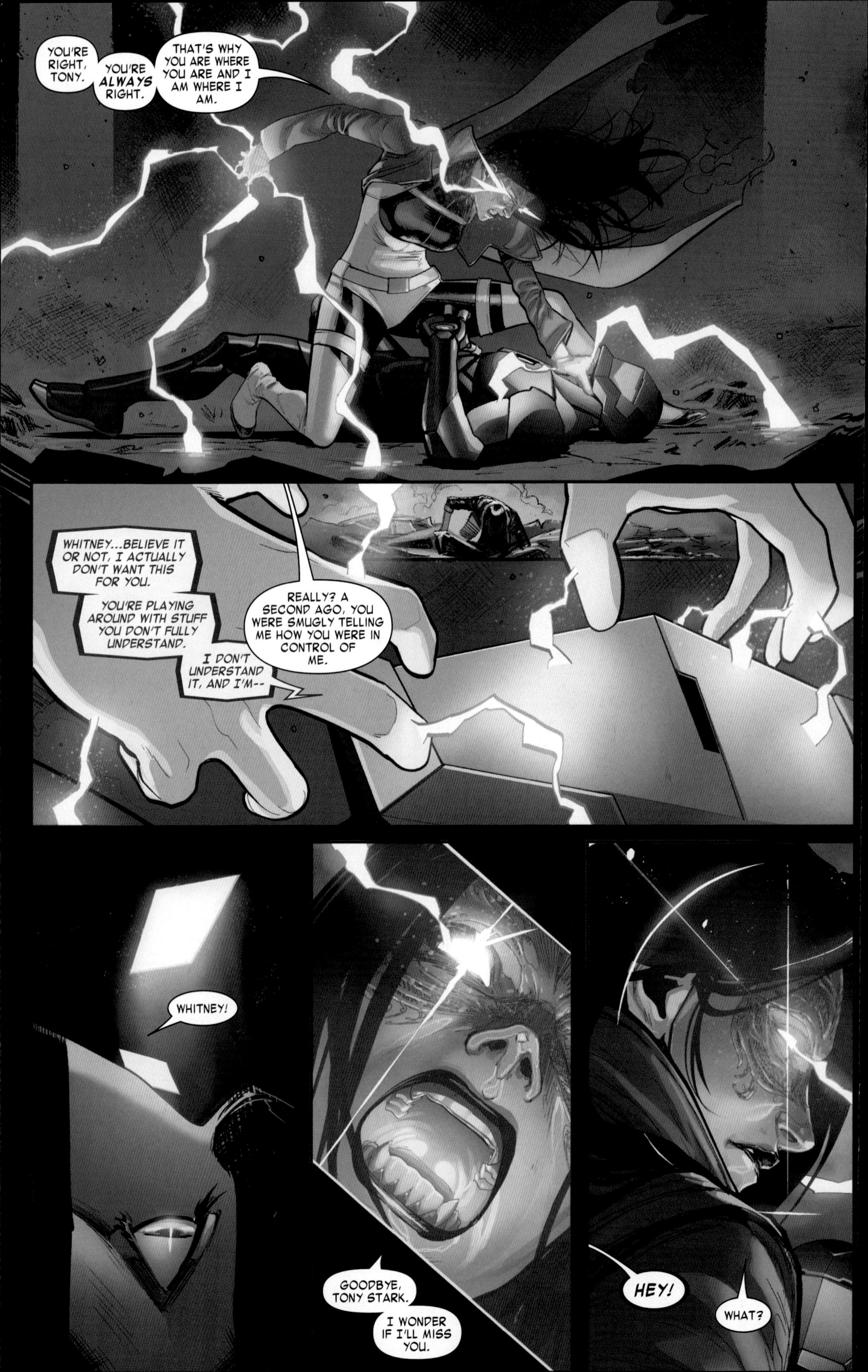

YOU'RE RIGHT, TONY.
YOU'RE *ALWAYS* RIGHT.
THAT'S WHY YOU ARE WHERE YOU ARE AND I AM WHERE I AM.
WHITNEY...BELIEVE IT OR NOT, I ACTUALLY DON'T WANT THIS FOR YOU.
YOU'RE PLAYING AROUND WITH STUFF YOU DON'T FULLY UNDERSTAND.
I DON'T UNDERSTAND IT, AND I'M--
REALLY? A SECOND AGO, YOU WERE SMUGLY TELLING ME HOW YOU WERE IN CONTROL OF ME.
WHITNEY!
GOODBYE, TONY STARK.
I WONDER IF I'LL MISS YOU.
HEY!
WHAT?

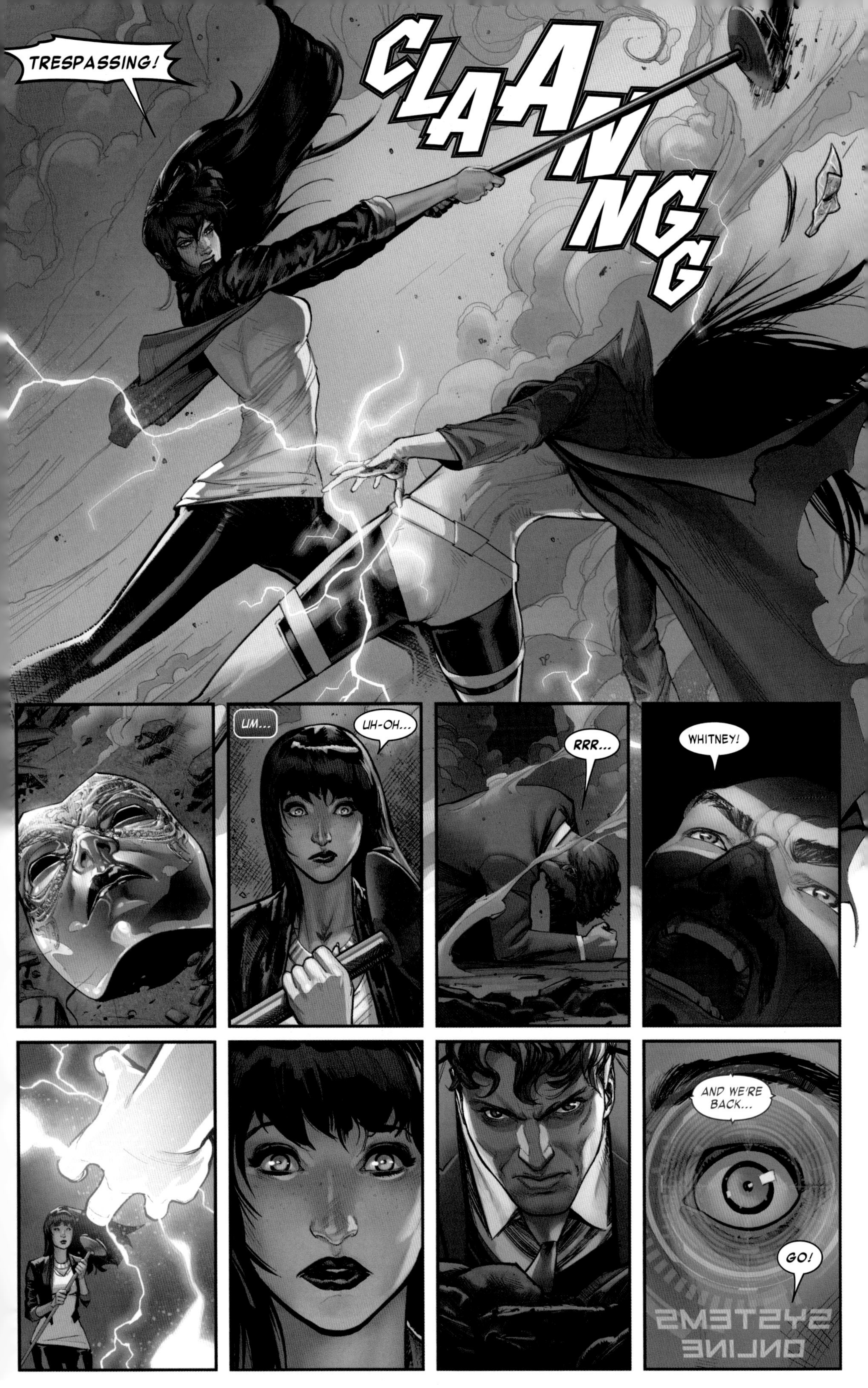
TRESPASSING!
CLAANNGG
UM...
UH-OH...
RRR...
WHITNEY!
AND WE'RE BACK...
GO!
SYSTEMS ONLINE

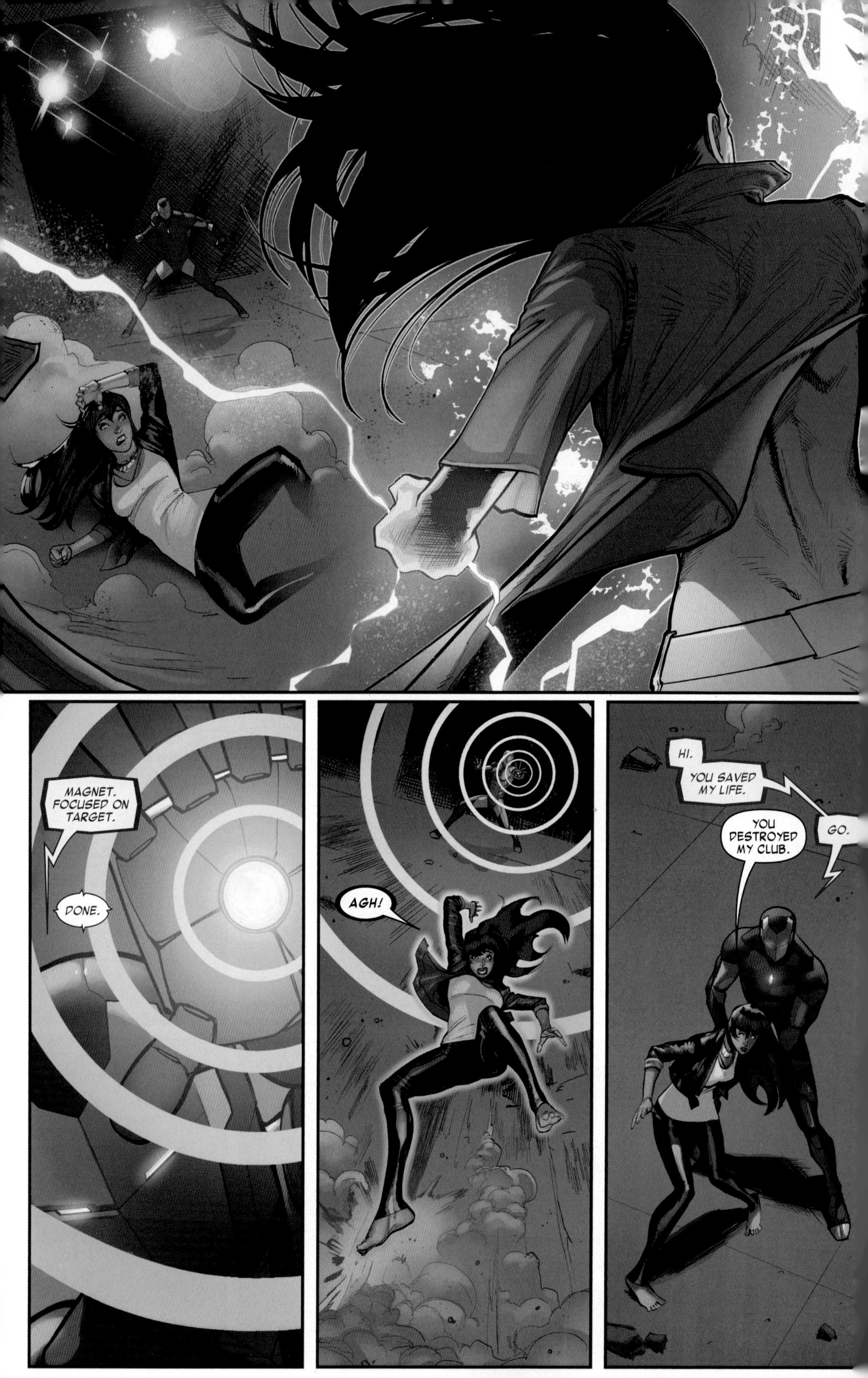
MAGNET. FOCUSED ON TARGET.
DONE.
AGH!
HI.
YOU SAVED MY LIFE.
YOU DESTROYED MY CLUB.
GO.

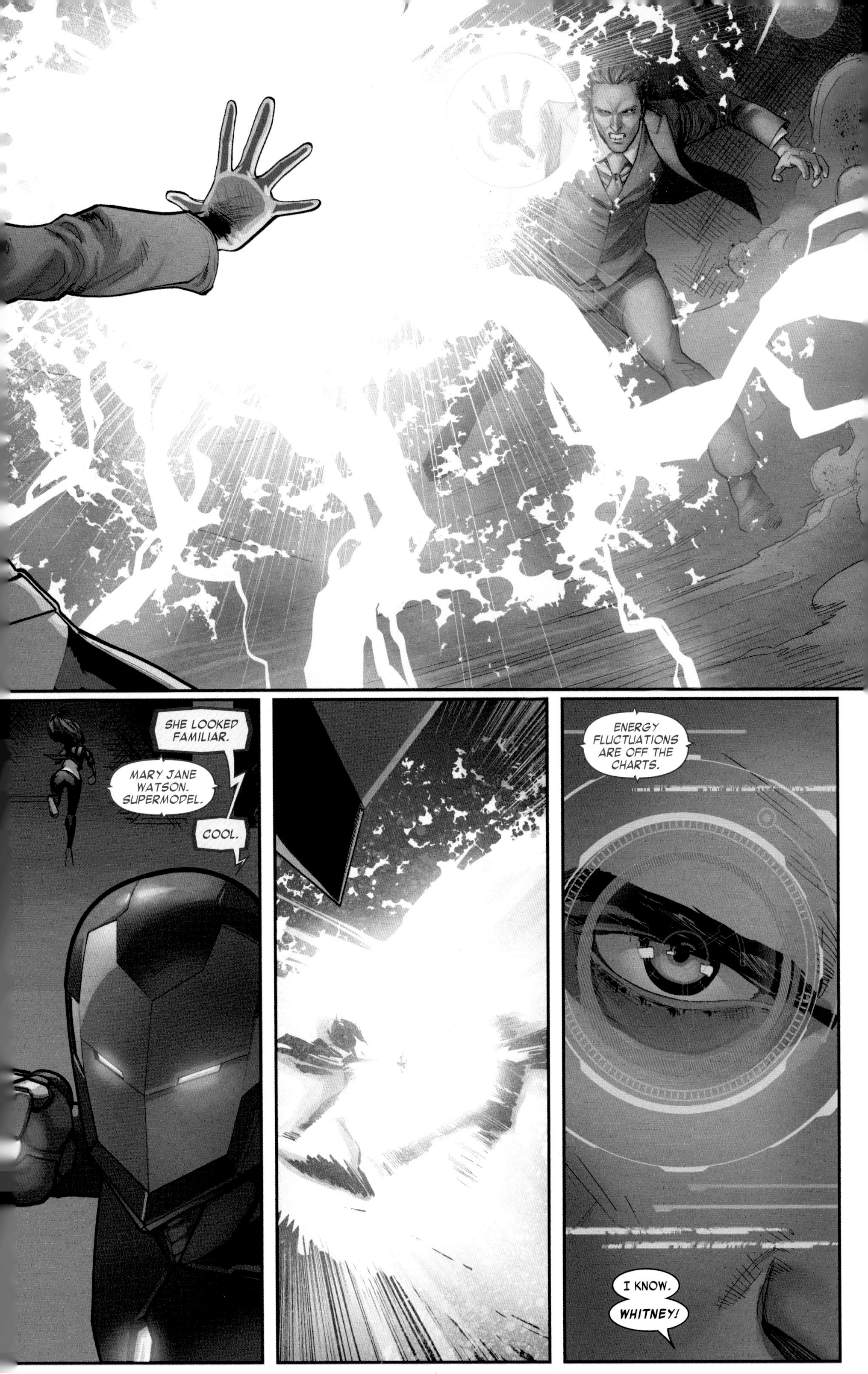
SHE LOOKED FAMILIAR.
MARY JANE WATSON. SUPERMODEL.
COOL.
ENERGY FLUCTUATIONS ARE OFF THE CHARTS.
I KNOW.
WHITNEY!

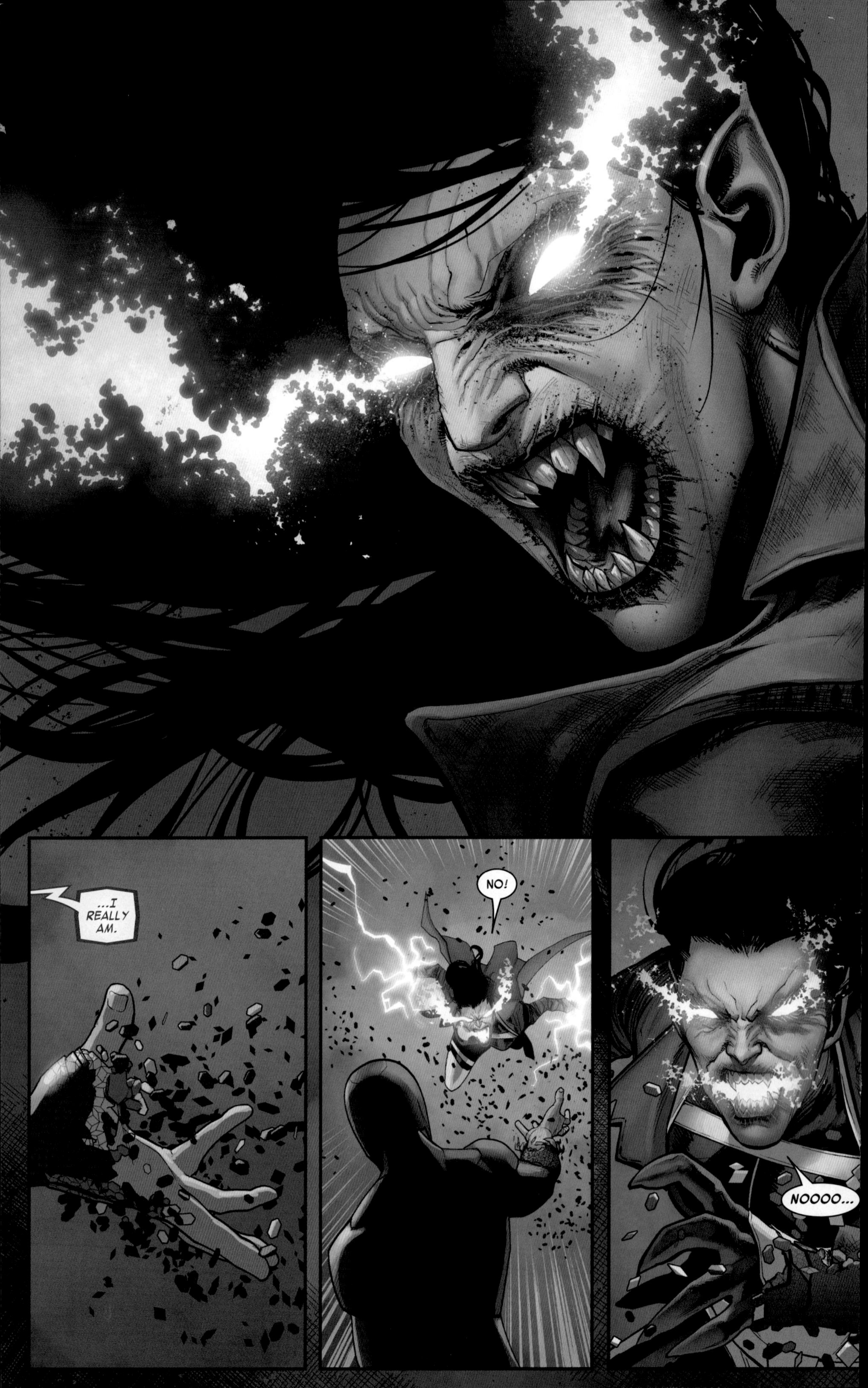
...I REALLY AM.
NO!
NOOOO...

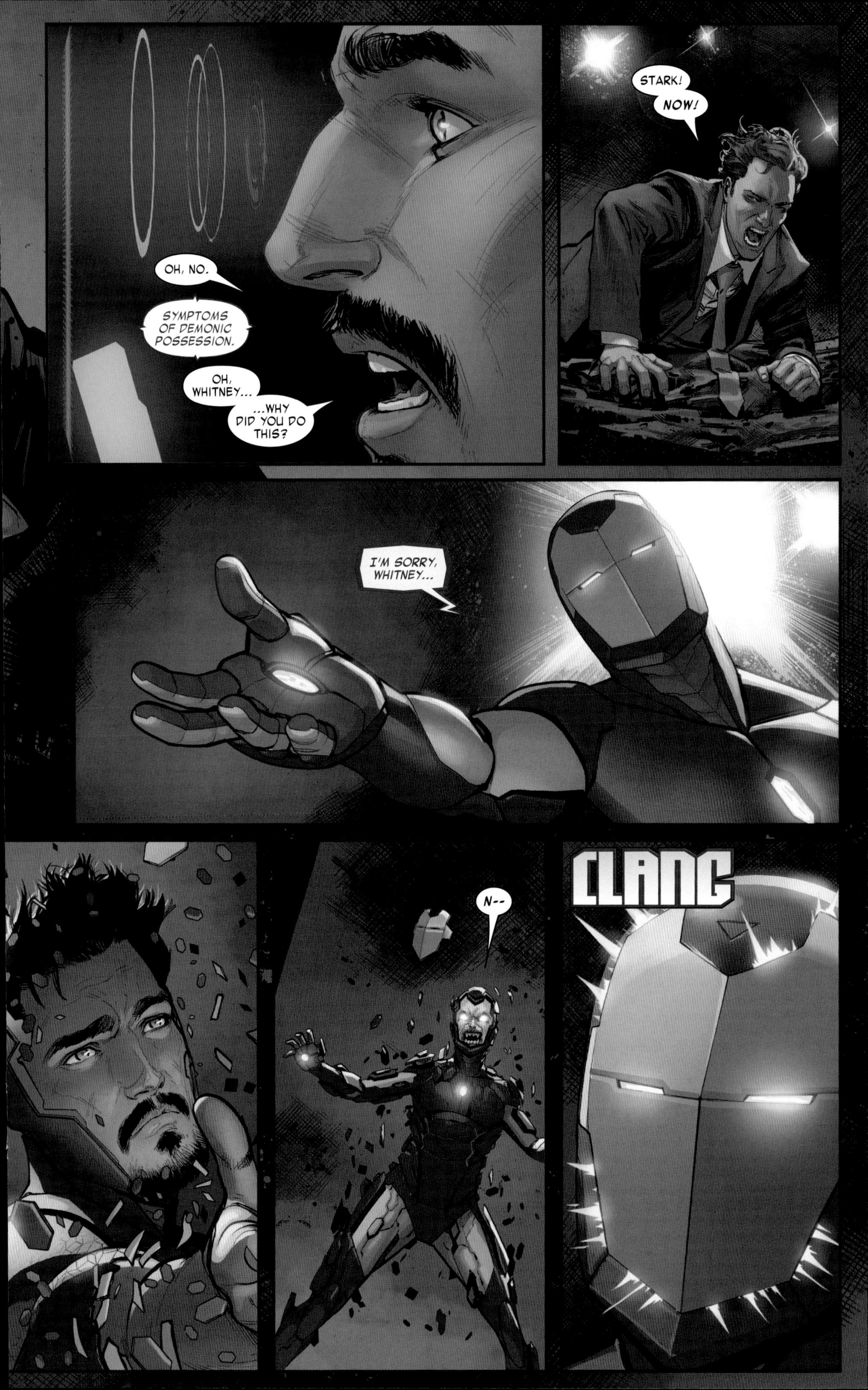
OH, NO.
SYMPTOMS OF DEMONIC POSSESSION.
OH, WHITNEY...
...WHY DID YOU DO THIS?
STARK!
NOW!
I'M SORRY, WHITNEY...
N--
CLANG

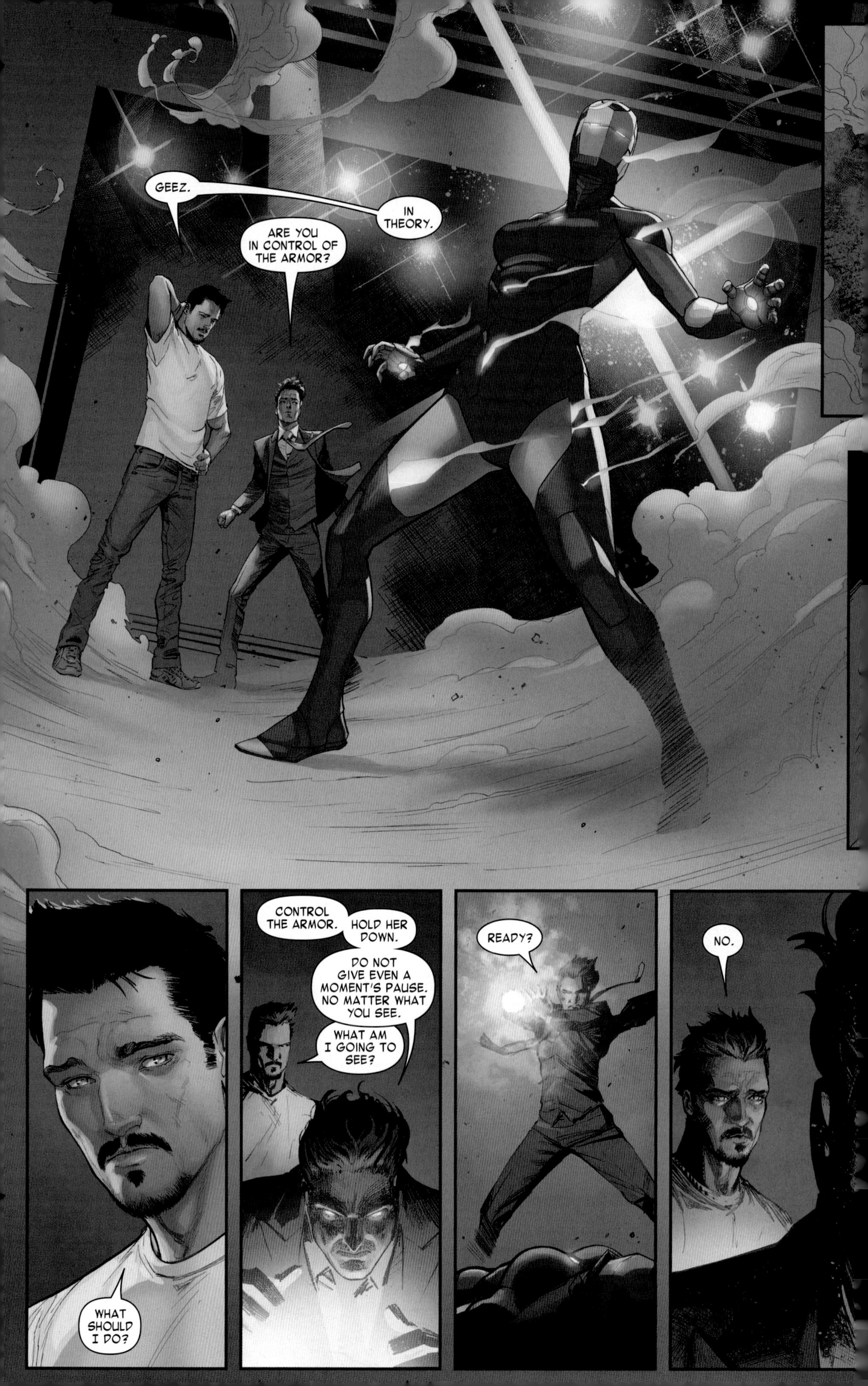
GEEZ.
ARE YOU IN CONTROL OF THE ARMOR?
IN THEORY.
WHAT SHOULD I DO?
CONTROL THE ARMOR.
HOLD HER DOWN.
DO NOT GIVE EVEN A MOMENT'S PAUSE. NO MATTER WHAT YOU SEE.
WHAT AM I GOING TO SEE?
READY?
NO.

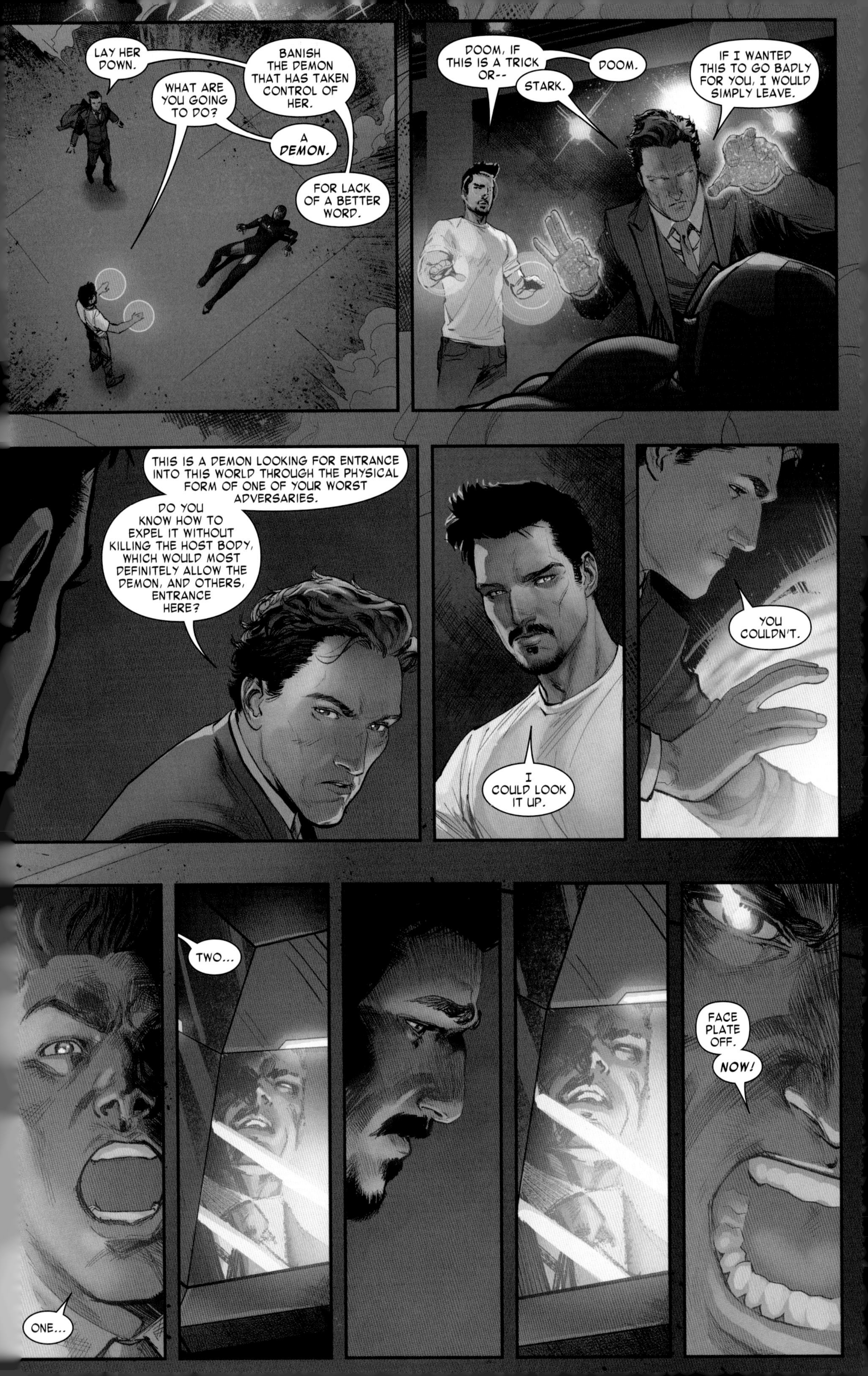

LAY HER DOWN.
BANISH THE DEMON THAT HAS TAKEN CONTROL OF HER.
WHAT ARE YOU GOING TO DO?
A *DEMON.*
FOR LACK OF A BETTER WORD.
DOOM, IF THIS IS A TRICK OR--
DOOM.
STARK.
IF I WANTED THIS TO GO BADLY FOR YOU, I WOULD SIMPLY LEAVE.
THIS IS A DEMON LOOKING FOR ENTRANCE INTO THIS WORLD THROUGH THE PHYSICAL FORM OF ONE OF YOUR WORST ADVERSARIES.
DO YOU KNOW HOW TO EXPEL IT WITHOUT KILLING THE HOST BODY, WHICH WOULD MOST DEFINITELY ALLOW THE DEMON, AND OTHERS, ENTRANCE HERE?
I COULD LOOK IT UP.
YOU COULDN'T.
ONE...
TWO...
FACE PLATE OFF.
NOW!

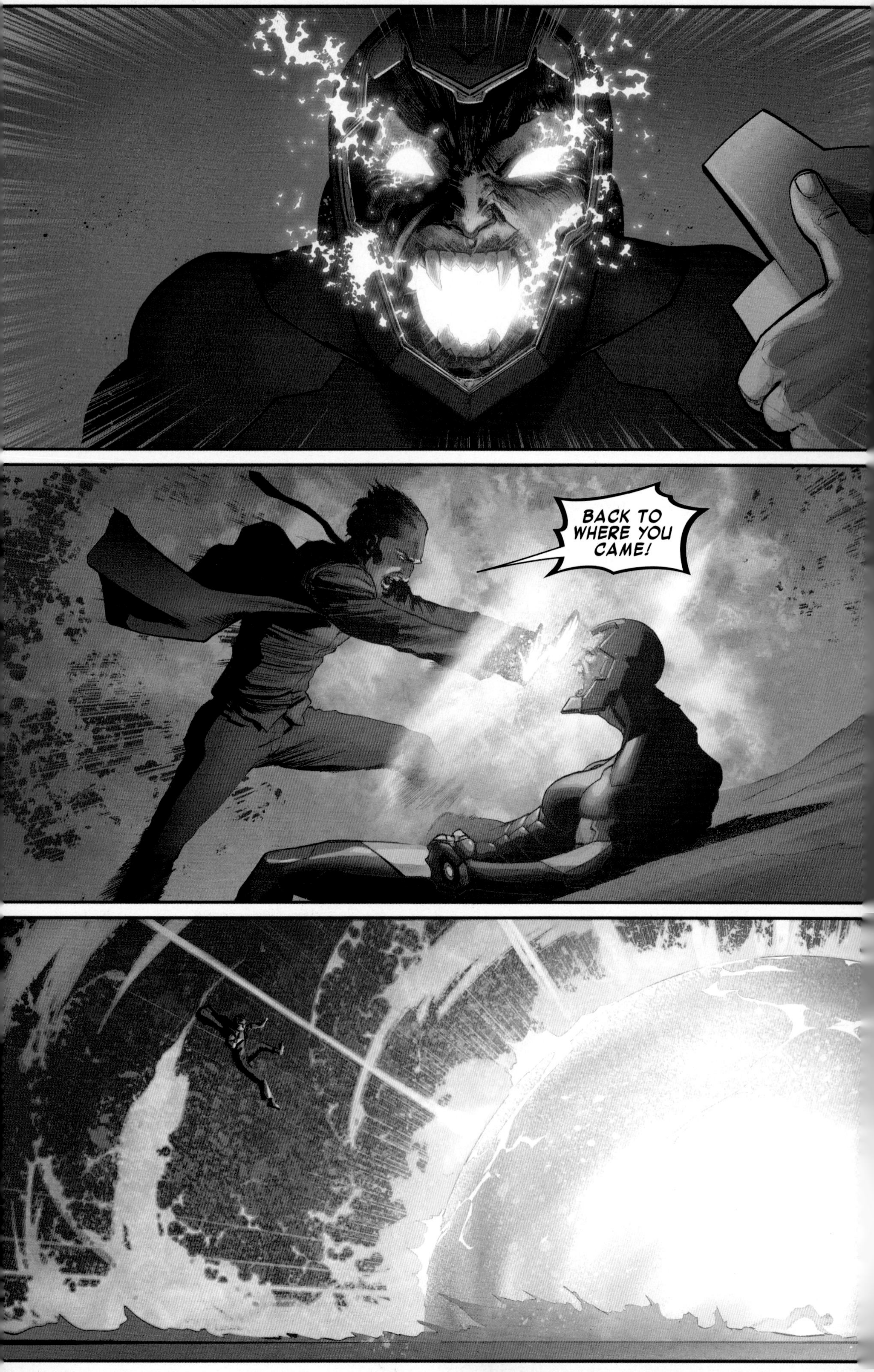
BACK TO WHERE YOU CAME!

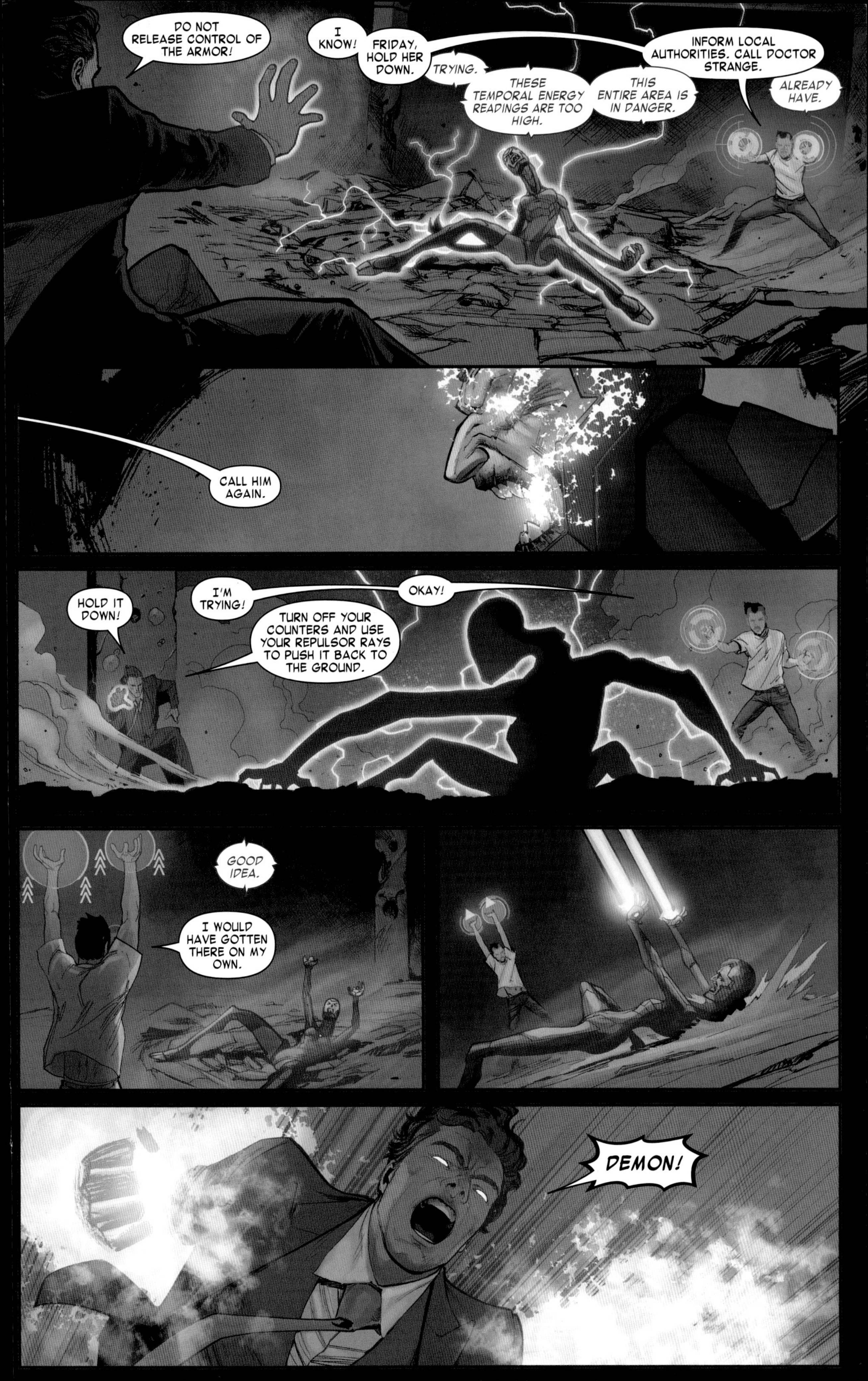
DO NOT RELEASE CONTROL OF THE ARMOR!
I KNOW!
FRIDAY, HOLD HER DOWN.
TRYING.
THESE TEMPORAL ENERGY READINGS ARE TOO HIGH.
THIS ENTIRE AREA IS IN DANGER.
INFORM LOCAL AUTHORITIES. CALL DOCTOR STRANGE.
ALREADY HAVE.
CALL HIM AGAIN.
HOLD IT DOWN!
I'M TRYING!
OKAY!
TURN OFF YOUR COUNTERS AND USE YOUR REPULSOR RAYS TO PUSH IT BACK TO THE GROUND.
GOOD IDEA.
I WOULD HAVE GOTTEN THERE ON MY OWN.
DEMON!

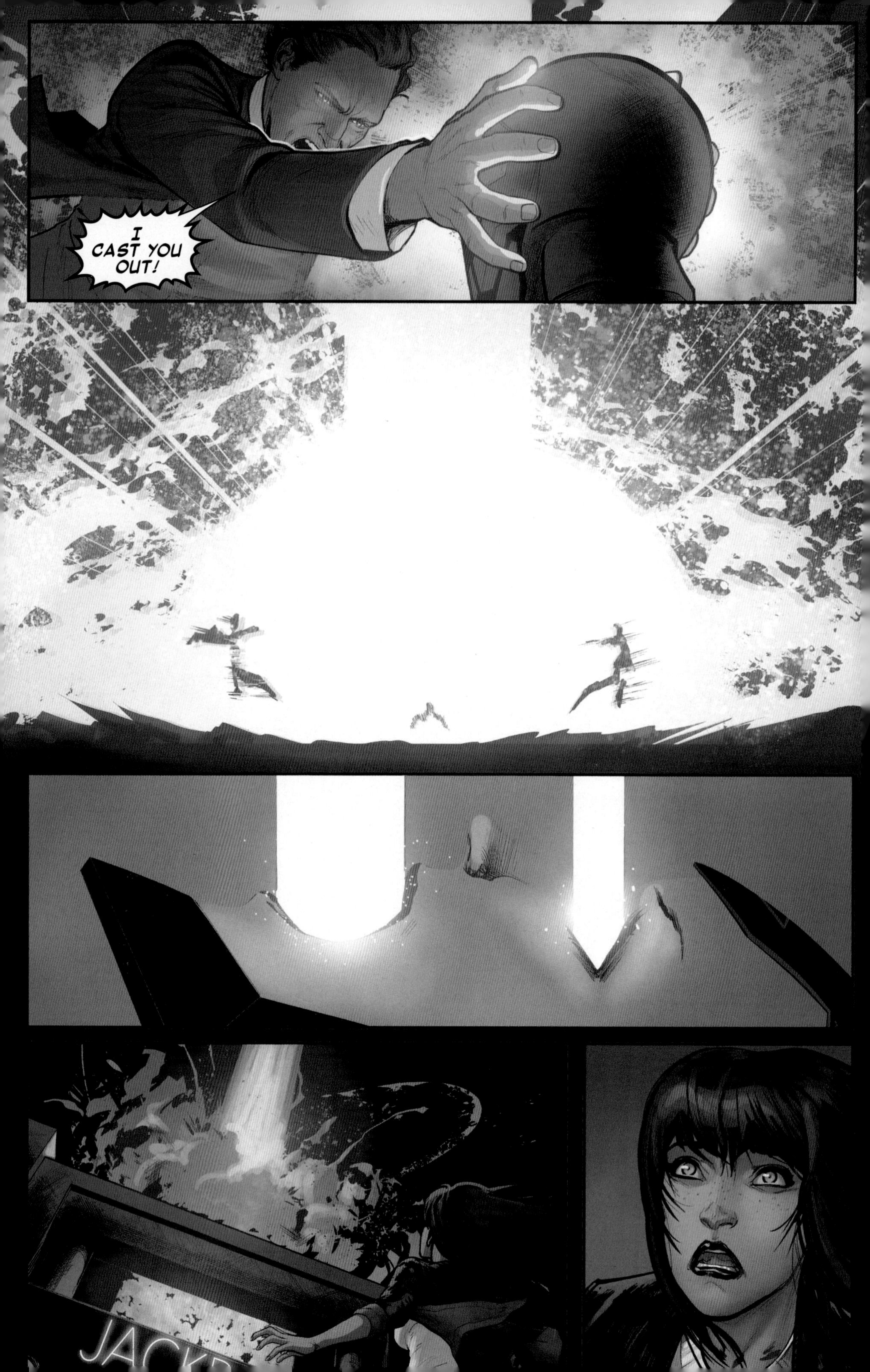
I CAST YOU OUT!
JACK

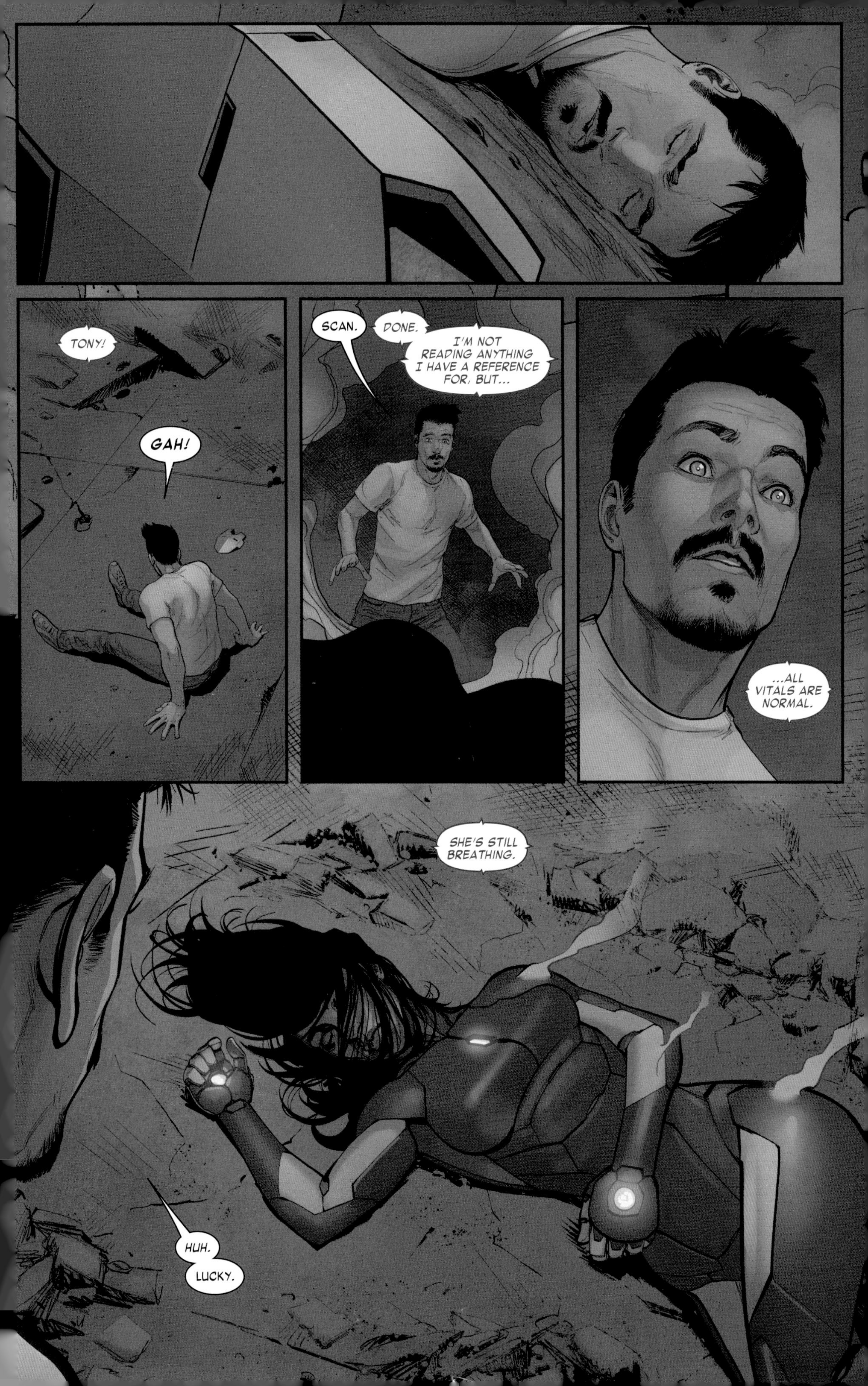
TONY!
GAH!
SCAN.
DONE.
I'M NOT READING ANYTHING I HAVE A REFERENCE FOR, BUT...
...ALL VITALS ARE NORMAL.
SHE'S STILL BREATHING.
HUH.
LUCKY.

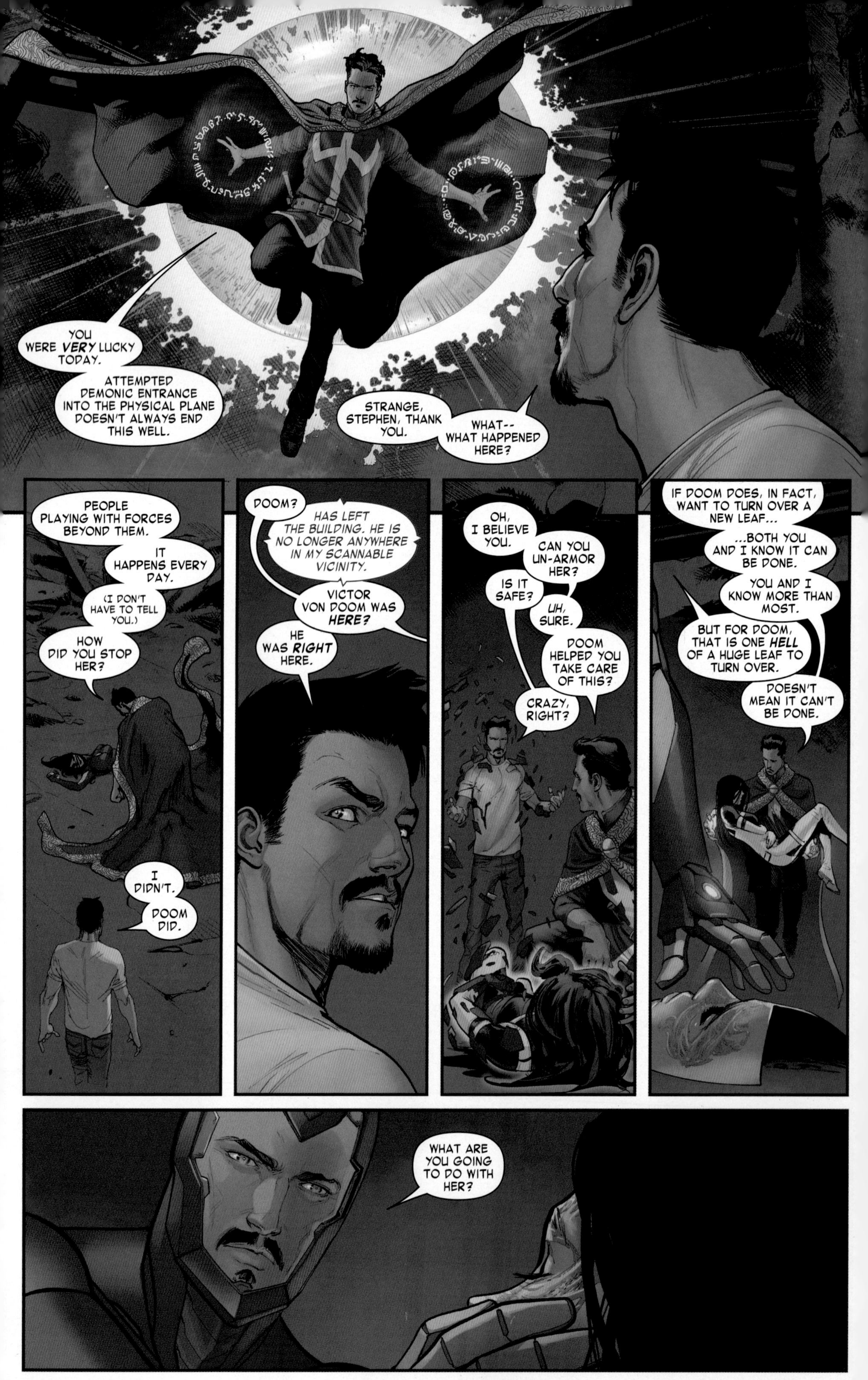
YOU WERE VERY LUCKY TODAY.
ATTEMPTED DEMONIC ENTRANCE INTO THE PHYSICAL PLANE DOESN'T ALWAYS END THIS WELL.
STRANGE, STEPHEN, THANK YOU.
WHAT-- WHAT HAPPENED HERE?
PEOPLE PLAYING WITH FORCES BEYOND THEM.
IT HAPPENS EVERY DAY.
(I DON'T HAVE TO TELL YOU.)
HOW DID YOU STOP HER?
I DIDN'T.
DOOM DID.
DOOM?
HAS LEFT THE BUILDING. HE IS NO LONGER ANYWHERE IN MY SCANNABLE VICINITY.
VICTOR VON DOOM WAS HERE?
HE WAS RIGHT HERE.
OH, I BELIEVE YOU.
CAN YOU UN-ARMOR HER?
IS IT SAFE?
UH, SURE.
DOOM HELPED YOU TAKE CARE OF THIS?
CRAZY, RIGHT?
IF DOOM DOES, IN FACT, WANT TO TURN OVER A NEW LEAF...
...BOTH YOU AND I KNOW IT CAN BE DONE.
YOU AND I KNOW MORE THAN MOST.
BUT FOR DOOM, THAT IS ONE HELL OF A HUGE LEAF TO TURN OVER.
DOESN'T MEAN IT CAN'T BE DONE.
WHAT ARE YOU GOING TO DO WITH HER?

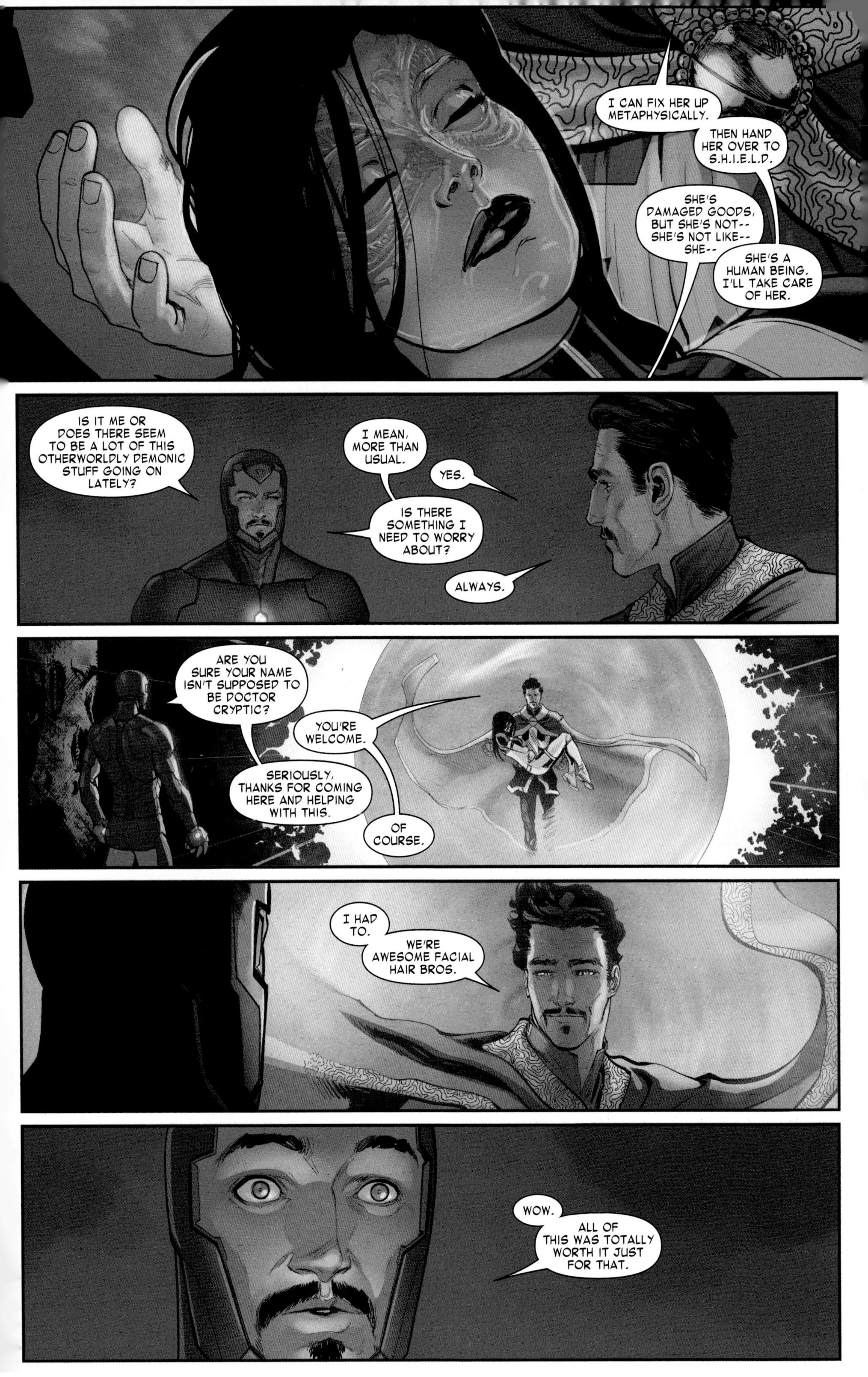
I CAN FIX HER UP METAPHYSICALLY.
THEN HAND HER OVER TO S.H.I.E.L.D.
SHE'S DAMAGED GOODS, BUT SHE'S NOT-- SHE'S NOT LIKE-- SHE--
SHE'S A HUMAN BEING. I'LL TAKE CARE OF HER.
IS IT ME OR DOES THERE SEEM TO BE A LOT OF THIS OTHERWORLDLY DEMONIC STUFF GOING ON LATELY?
I MEAN, MORE THAN USUAL.
YES.
IS THERE SOMETHING I NEED TO WORRY ABOUT?
ALWAYS.
ARE YOU SURE YOUR NAME ISN'T SUPPOSED TO BE DOCTOR CRYPTIC?
YOU'RE WELCOME.
SERIOUSLY, THANKS FOR COMING HERE AND HELPING WITH THIS.
OF COURSE.
I HAD TO.
WE'RE AWESOME FACIAL HAIR BROS.
WOW.
ALL OF THIS WAS TOTALLY WORTH IT JUST FOR THAT.

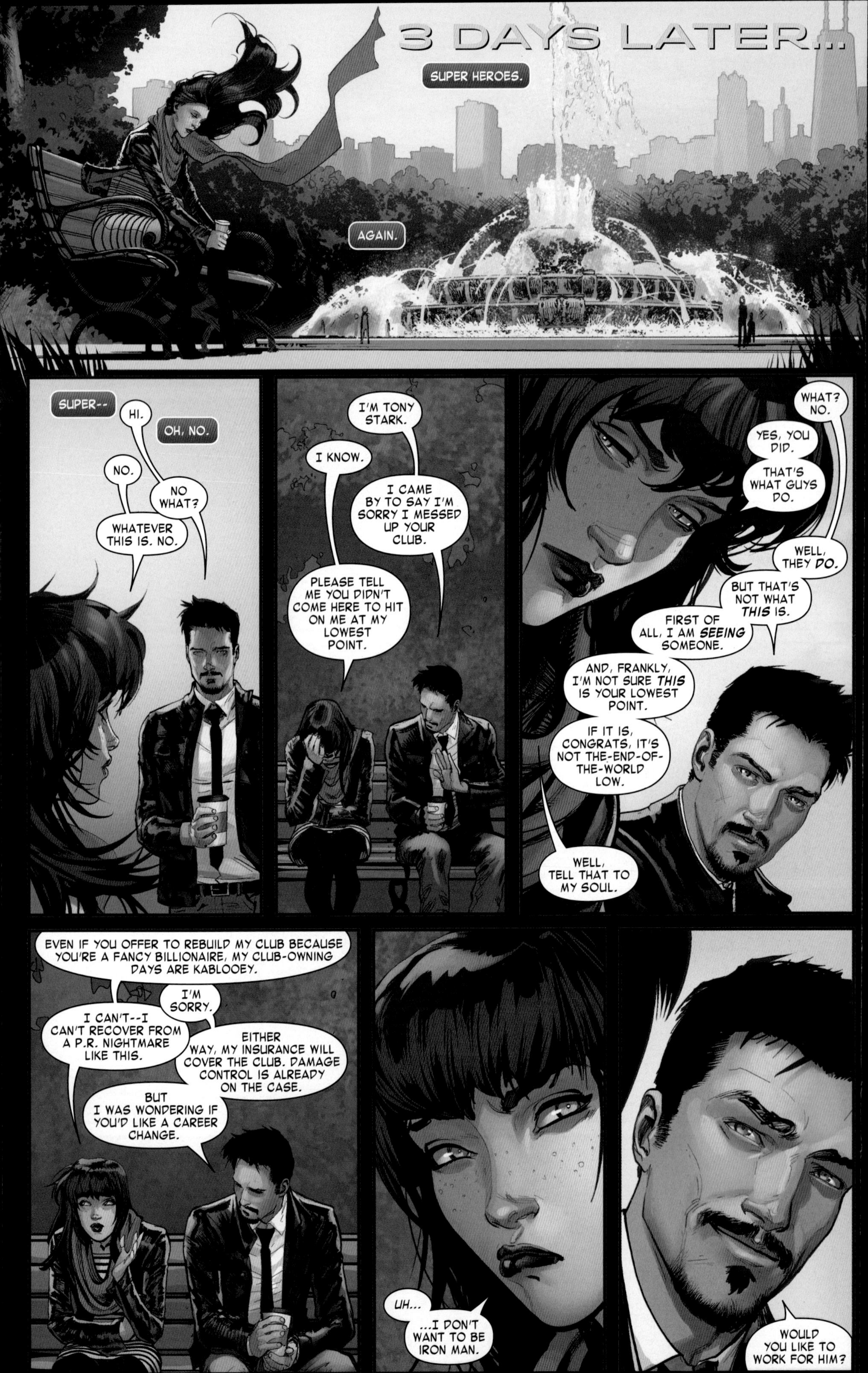
3 DAYS LATER...
SUPER HEROES.
AGAIN.
SUPER--
HI.
OH, NO.
NO.
NO WHAT?
WHATEVER THIS IS. NO.
I'M TONY STARK.
I KNOW.
I CAME BY TO SAY I'M SORRY I MESSED UP YOUR CLUB.
PLEASE TELL ME YOU DIDN'T COME HERE TO HIT ON ME AT MY LOWEST POINT.
WHAT? NO.
YES, YOU DID.
THAT'S WHAT GUYS DO.
WELL, THEY DO.
BUT THAT'S NOT WHAT THIS IS.
FIRST OF ALL, I AM SEEING SOMEONE.
AND, FRANKLY, I'M NOT SURE THIS IS YOUR LOWEST POINT.
IF IT IS, CONGRATS, IT'S NOT THE-END-OF-THE-WORLD LOW.
WELL, TELL THAT TO MY SOUL.
EVEN IF YOU OFFER TO REBUILD MY CLUB BECAUSE YOU'RE A FANCY BILLIONAIRE, MY CLUB-OWNING DAYS ARE KABLOOEY.
I'M SORRY.
I CAN'T--I CAN'T RECOVER FROM A P.R. NIGHTMARE LIKE THIS.
EITHER WAY, MY INSURANCE WILL COVER THE CLUB. DAMAGE CONTROL IS ALREADY ON THE CASE.
BUT I WAS WONDERING IF YOU'D LIKE A CAREER CHANGE.
UH...
...I DON'T WANT TO BE IRON MAN.
WOULD YOU LIKE TO WORK FOR HIM?

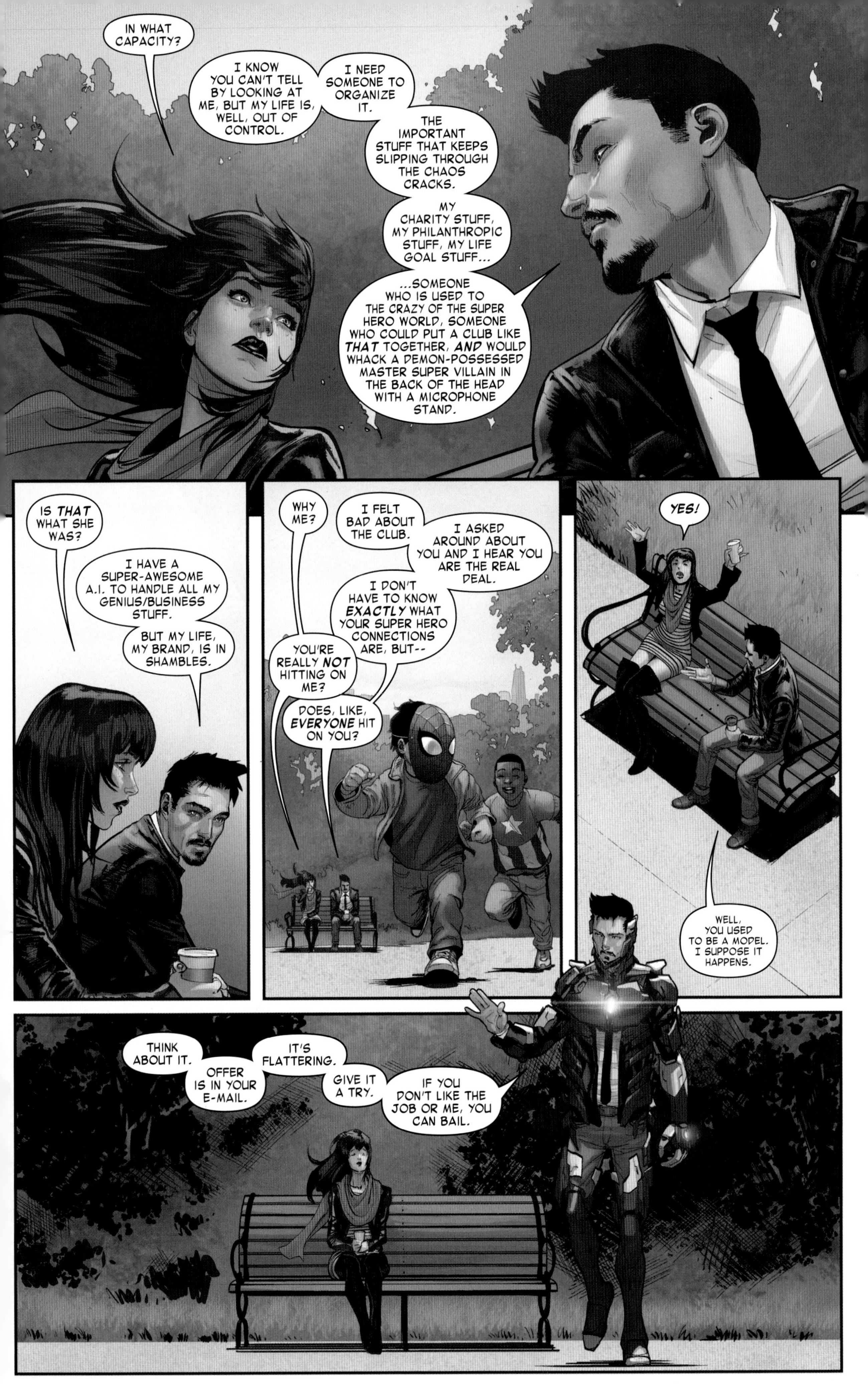
IN WHAT CAPACITY?
I KNOW YOU CAN'T TELL BY LOOKING AT ME, BUT MY LIFE IS, WELL, OUT OF CONTROL.
I NEED SOMEONE TO ORGANIZE IT.
THE IMPORTANT STUFF THAT KEEPS SLIPPING THROUGH THE CHAOS CRACKS.
MY CHARITY STUFF, MY PHILANTHROPIC STUFF, MY LIFE GOAL STUFF...
...SOMEONE WHO IS USED TO THE CRAZY OF THE SUPER HERO WORLD, SOMEONE WHO COULD PUT A CLUB LIKE THAT TOGETHER, AND WOULD WHACK A DEMON-POSSESSED MASTER SUPER VILLAIN IN THE BACK OF THE HEAD WITH A MICROPHONE STAND.
IS THAT WHAT SHE WAS?
I HAVE A SUPER-AWESOME A.I. TO HANDLE ALL MY GENIUS/BUSINESS STUFF.
BUT MY LIFE, MY BRAND, IS IN SHAMBLES.
WHY ME?
I FELT BAD ABOUT THE CLUB.
I ASKED AROUND ABOUT YOU AND I HEAR YOU ARE THE REAL DEAL.
I DON'T HAVE TO KNOW EXACTLY WHAT YOUR SUPER HERO CONNECTIONS ARE, BUT--
YOU'RE REALLY NOT HITTING ON ME?
DOES, LIKE, EVERYONE HIT ON YOU?
YES!
WELL, YOU USED TO BE A MODEL. I SUPPOSE IT HAPPENS.
THINK ABOUT IT.
OFFER IS IN YOUR E-MAIL.
IT'S FLATTERING.
GIVE IT A TRY.
IF YOU DON'T LIKE THE JOB OR ME, YOU CAN BAIL.

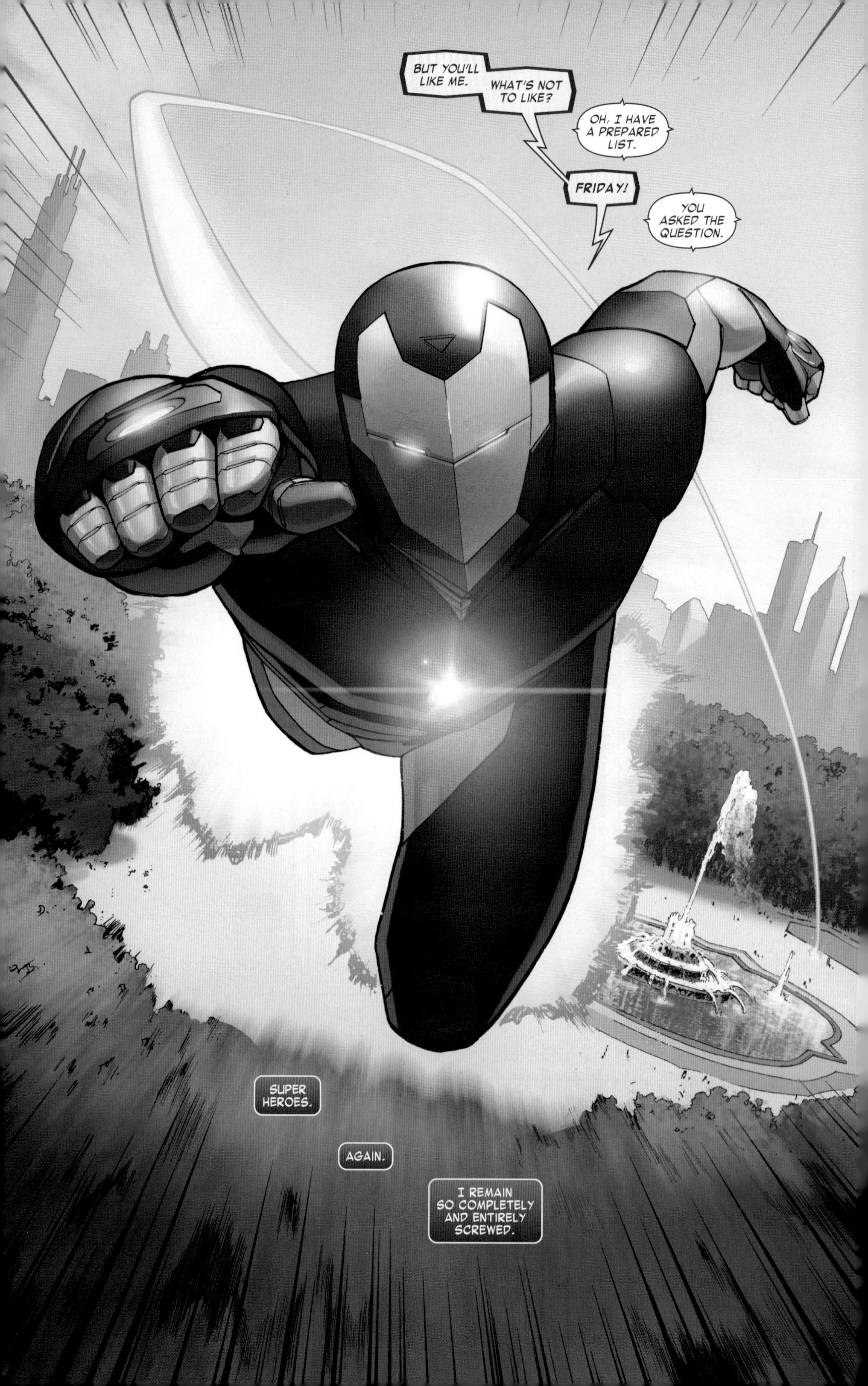
BUT YOU'LL LIKE ME.
WHAT'S NOT TO LIKE?
OH, I HAVE A PREPARED LIST.
FRIDAY!
YOU ASKED THE QUESTION.
SUPER HEROES.
AGAIN.
I REMAIN SO COMPLETELY AND ENTIRELY SCREWED.

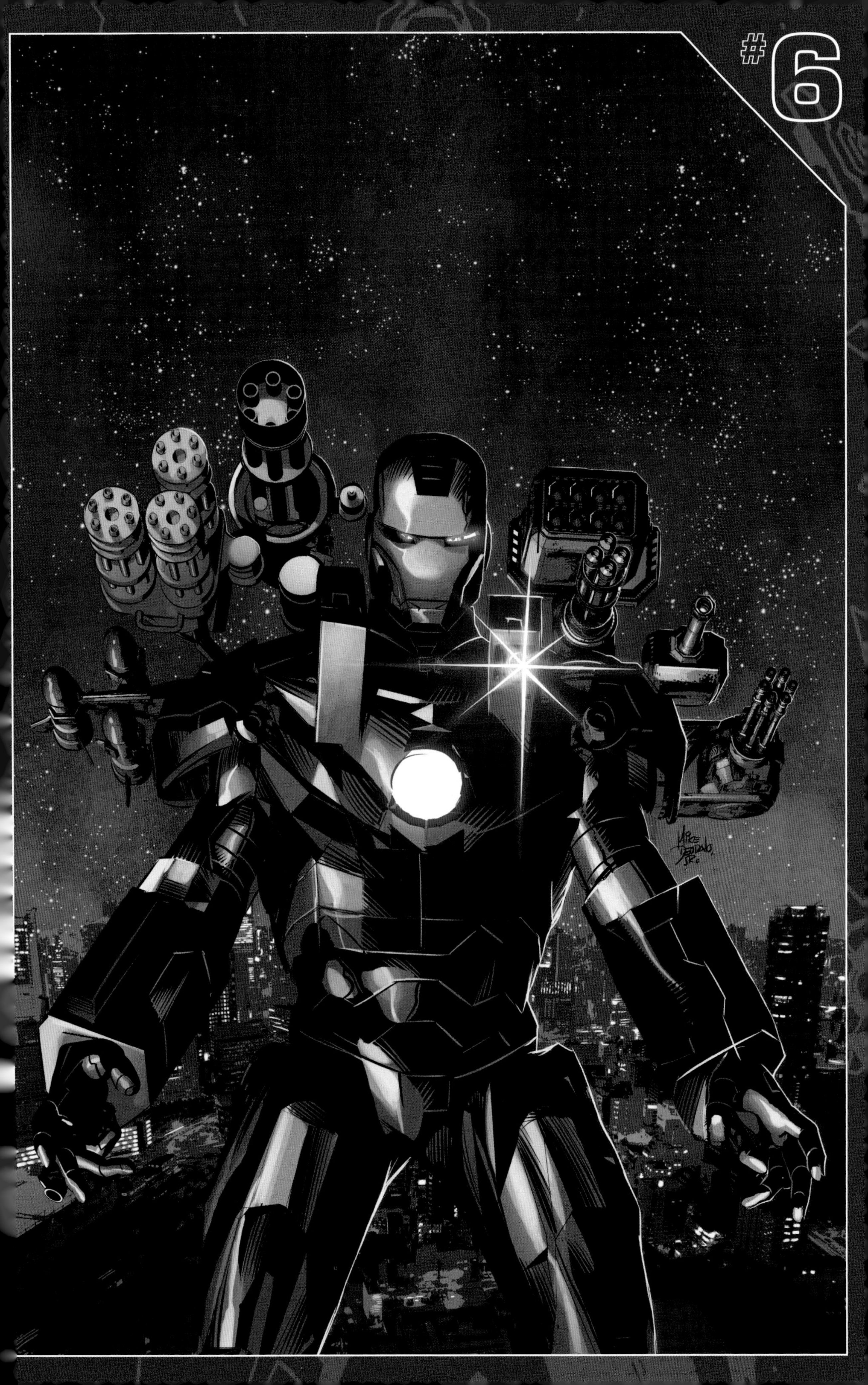
#6

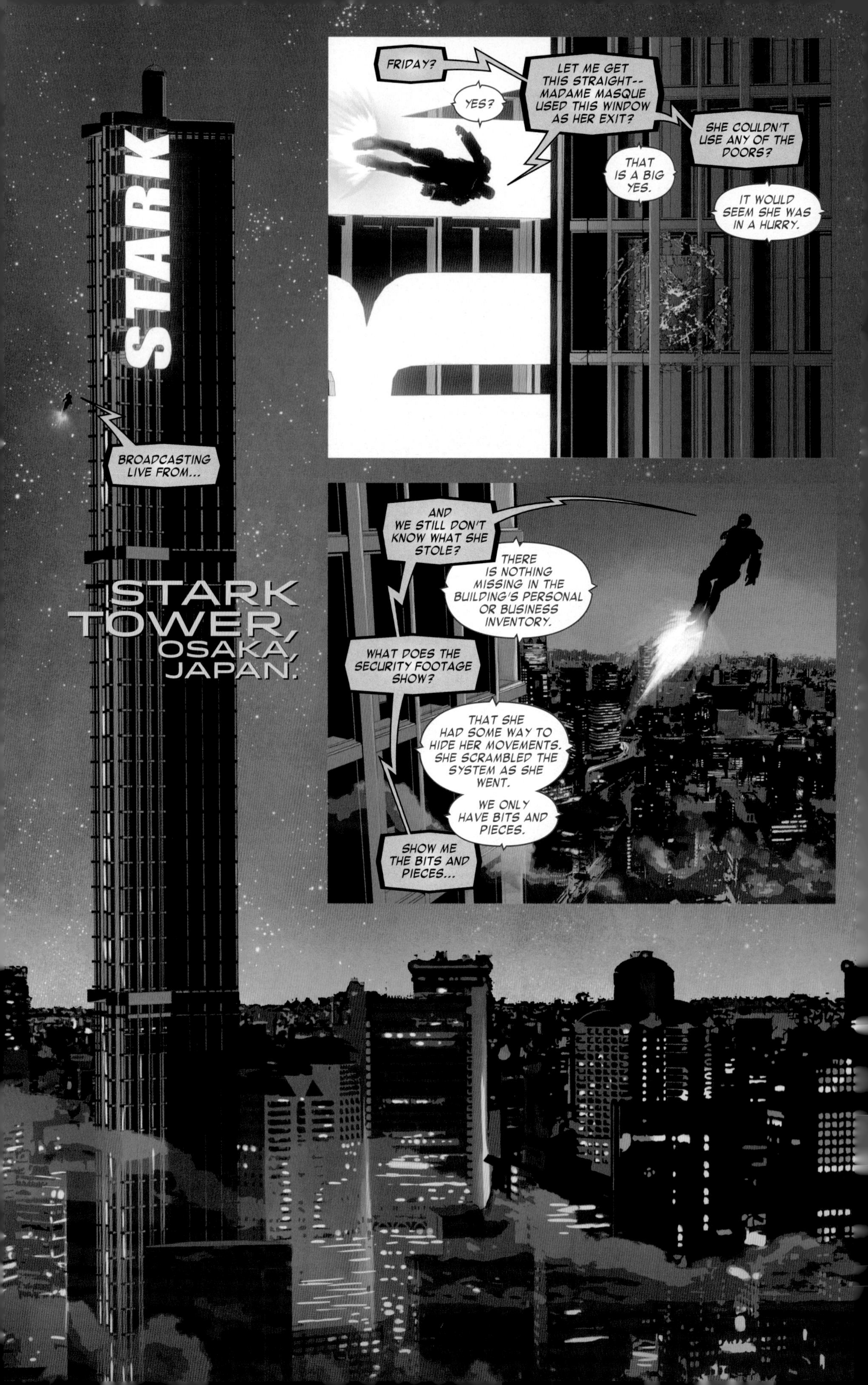
BROADCASTING LIVE FROM...
STARK TOWER, OSAKA, JAPAN.
STARK
FRIDAY?
YES?
LET ME GET THIS STRAIGHT-- MADAME MASQUE USED THIS WINDOW AS HER EXIT?
THAT IS A BIG YES.
SHE COULDN'T USE ANY OF THE DOORS?
IT WOULD SEEM SHE WAS IN A HURRY.
AND WE STILL DON'T KNOW WHAT SHE STOLE?
THERE IS NOTHING MISSING IN THE BUILDING'S PERSONAL OR BUSINESS INVENTORY.
WHAT DOES THE SECURITY FOOTAGE SHOW?
THAT SHE HAD SOME WAY TO HIDE HER MOVEMENTS. SHE SCRAMBLED THE SYSTEM AS SHE WENT.
WE ONLY HAVE BITS AND PIECES.
SHOW ME THE BITS AND PIECES...

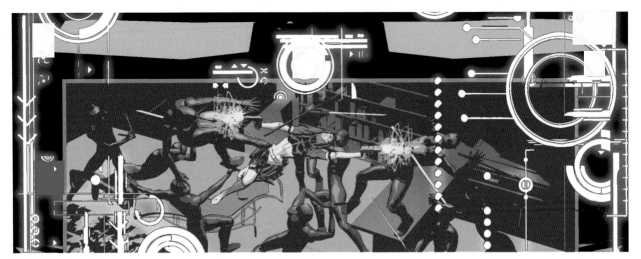

THAT'S IT?

THAT'S IT.

I'M GOING INSIDE.

YOU SCANNING THE ROOM FOR ME, FRIDAY?

FULL ENVIRONMENTAL SCAN.

I'M PICKING UP VERY THIN TRACES OF ENERGY SIGNATURE RESIDUE THAT MATCHES THE BIOHACK NINJAS FROM THE BEACH ATTACK THE OTHER NIGHT.

CAN YOU TRACE IT?

NOT ENOUGH TO TRACE.

I COULD MATCH IT IF I EVER CAME ACROSS IT AGAIN.

AND THERE WERE HOW MANY OF THESE--?

<WHO ARE YOU?>*

*TRANSLATED FROM JAPANESE.

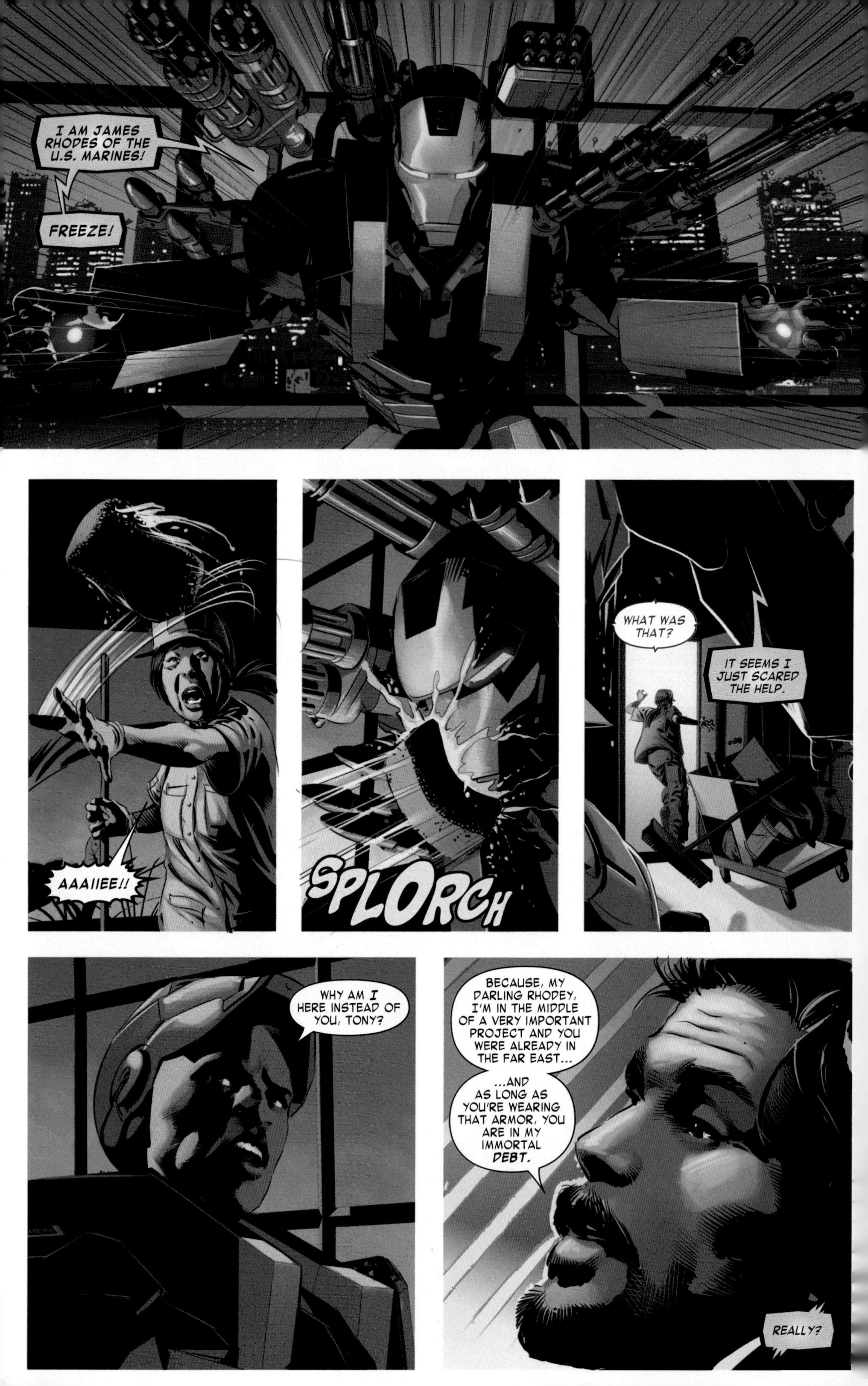
I AM JAMES RHODES OF THE U.S. MARINES!
FREEZE!
AAAIIEE!!
SPLORCH
WHAT WAS THAT?
IT SEEMS I JUST SCARED THE HELP.
WHY AM I HERE INSTEAD OF YOU, TONY?
BECAUSE, MY DARLING RHODEY, I'M IN THE MIDDLE OF A VERY IMPORTANT PROJECT AND YOU WERE ALREADY IN THE FAR EAST...
...AND AS LONG AS YOU'RE WEARING THAT ARMOR, YOU ARE IN MY IMMORTAL DEBT.
REALLY?

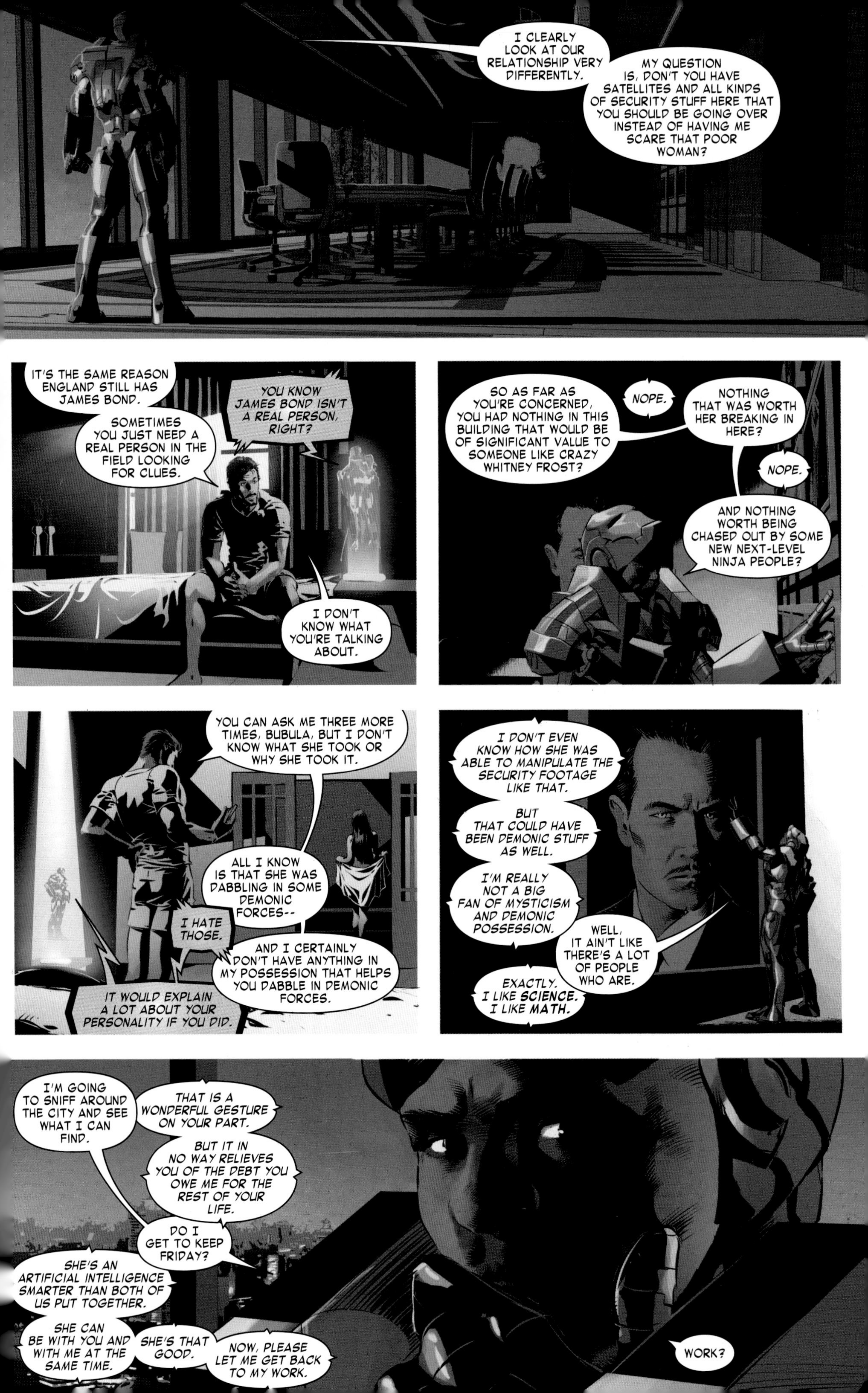

I CLEARLY LOOK AT OUR RELATIONSHIP VERY DIFFERENTLY.
MY QUESTION IS, DON'T YOU HAVE SATELLITES AND ALL KINDS OF SECURITY STUFF HERE THAT YOU SHOULD BE GOING OVER INSTEAD OF HAVING ME SCARE THAT POOR WOMAN?
IT'S THE SAME REASON ENGLAND STILL HAS JAMES BOND.
SOMETIMES YOU JUST NEED A REAL PERSON IN THE FIELD LOOKING FOR CLUES.
YOU KNOW JAMES BOND ISN'T A REAL PERSON, RIGHT?
I DON'T KNOW WHAT YOU'RE TALKING ABOUT.
SO AS FAR AS YOU'RE CONCERNED, YOU HAD NOTHING IN THIS BUILDING THAT WOULD BE OF SIGNIFICANT VALUE TO SOMEONE LIKE CRAZY WHITNEY FROST?
NOPE.
NOTHING THAT WAS WORTH HER BREAKING IN HERE?
NOPE.
AND NOTHING WORTH BEING CHASED OUT BY SOME NEW NEXT-LEVEL NINJA PEOPLE?
YOU CAN ASK ME THREE MORE TIMES, BUBULA, BUT I DON'T KNOW WHAT SHE TOOK OR WHY SHE TOOK IT.
ALL I KNOW IS THAT SHE WAS DABBLING IN SOME DEMONIC FORCES--
I HATE THOSE.
AND I CERTAINLY DON'T HAVE ANYTHING IN MY POSSESSION THAT HELPS YOU DABBLE IN DEMONIC FORCES.
IT WOULD EXPLAIN A LOT ABOUT YOUR PERSONALITY IF YOU DID.
I DON'T EVEN KNOW HOW SHE WAS ABLE TO MANIPULATE THE SECURITY FOOTAGE LIKE THAT.
BUT THAT COULD HAVE BEEN DEMONIC STUFF AS WELL.
I'M REALLY NOT A BIG FAN OF MYSTICISM AND DEMONIC POSSESSION.
WELL, IT AIN'T LIKE THERE'S A LOT OF PEOPLE WHO ARE.
EXACTLY. I LIKE SCIENCE. I LIKE MATH.
I'M GOING TO SNIFF AROUND THE CITY AND SEE WHAT I CAN FIND.
THAT IS A WONDERFUL GESTURE ON YOUR PART.
BUT IT IN NO WAY RELIEVES YOU OF THE DEBT YOU OWE ME FOR THE REST OF YOUR LIFE.
DO I GET TO KEEP FRIDAY?
SHE'S AN ARTIFICIAL INTELLIGENCE SMARTER THAN BOTH OF US PUT TOGETHER.
SHE CAN BE WITH YOU AND WITH ME AT THE SAME TIME.
SHE'S THAT GOOD.
NOW, PLEASE LET ME GET BACK TO MY WORK.
WORK?

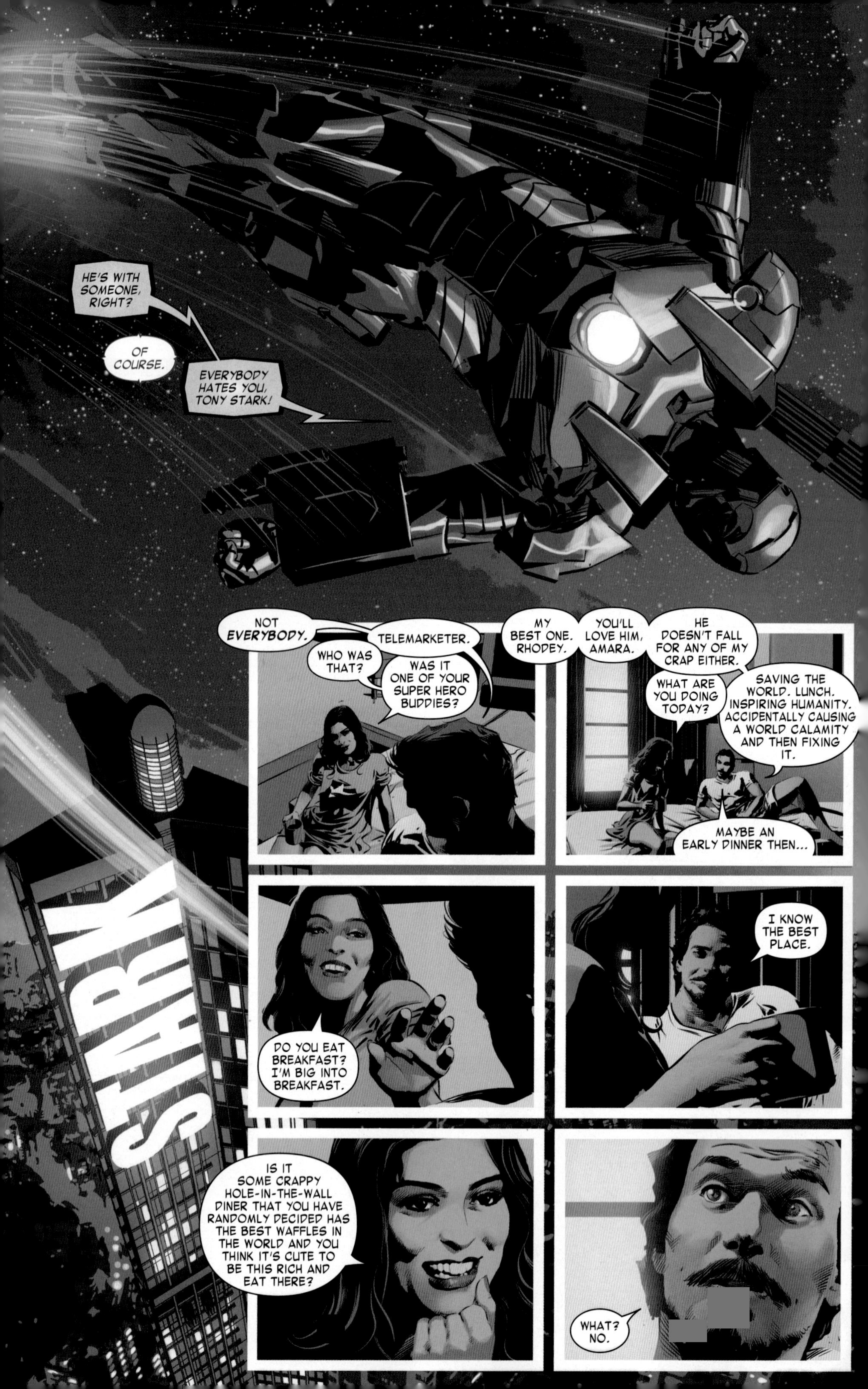
HE'S WITH SOMEONE, RIGHT?
OF COURSE.
EVERYBODY HATES YOU, TONY STARK!
STARK
NOT *EVERYBODY*.
WHO WAS THAT?
TELEMARKETER.
WAS IT ONE OF YOUR SUPER HERO BUDDIES?
MY BEST ONE. RHODEY.
YOU'LL LOVE HIM, AMARA.
HE DOESN'T FALL FOR ANY OF MY CRAP EITHER.
WHAT ARE YOU DOING TODAY?
SAVING THE WORLD. LUNCH. INSPIRING HUMANITY. ACCIDENTALLY CAUSING A WORLD CALAMITY AND THEN FIXING IT.
MAYBE AN EARLY DINNER THEN...
DO YOU EAT BREAKFAST? I'M BIG INTO BREAKFAST.
I KNOW THE BEST PLACE.
IS IT SOME CRAPPY HOLE-IN-THE-WALL DINER THAT YOU HAVE RANDOMLY DECIDED HAS THE BEST WAFFLES IN THE WORLD AND YOU THINK IT'S CUTE TO BE THIS RICH AND EAT THERE?
WHAT? NO.

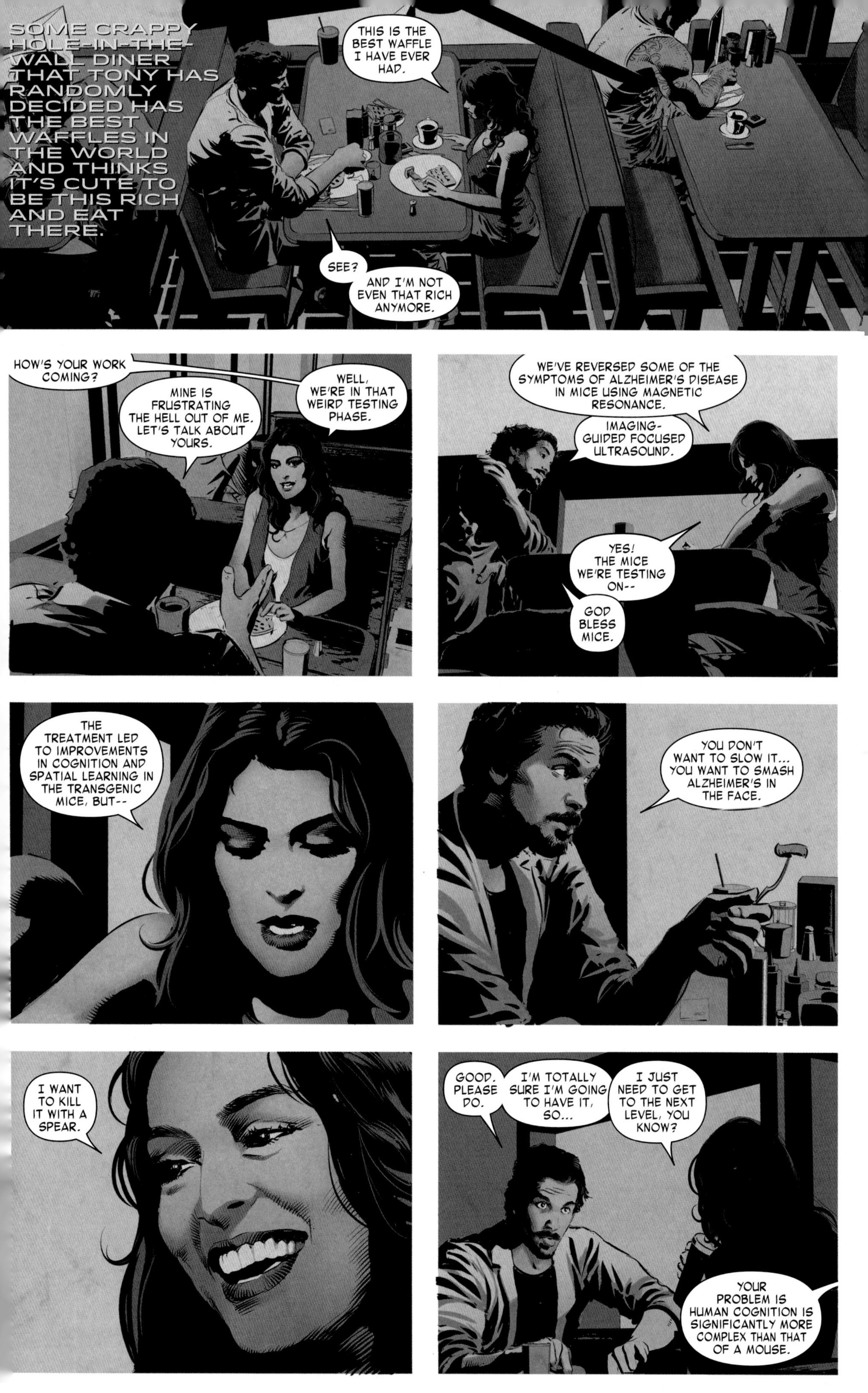
SOME CRAPPY HOLE-IN-THE-WALL DINER THAT TONY HAS RANDOMLY DECIDED HAS THE BEST WAFFLES IN THE WORLD AND THINKS IT'S CUTE TO BE THIS RICH AND EAT THERE.
THIS IS THE BEST WAFFLE I HAVE EVER HAD.
SEE?
AND I'M NOT EVEN THAT RICH ANYMORE.
HOW'S YOUR WORK COMING?
MINE IS FRUSTRATING THE HELL OUT OF ME. LET'S TALK ABOUT YOURS.
WELL, WE'RE IN THAT WEIRD TESTING PHASE.
WE'VE REVERSED SOME OF THE SYMPTOMS OF ALZHEIMER'S DISEASE IN MICE USING MAGNETIC RESONANCE.
IMAGING-GUIDED FOCUSED ULTRASOUND.
YES! THE MICE WE'RE TESTING ON--
GOD BLESS MICE.
THE TREATMENT LED TO IMPROVEMENTS IN COGNITION AND SPATIAL LEARNING IN THE TRANSGENIC MICE, BUT--
YOU DON'T WANT TO SLOW IT... YOU WANT TO SMASH ALZHEIMER'S IN THE FACE.
I WANT TO KILL IT WITH A SPEAR.
GOOD. PLEASE DO.
I'M TOTALLY SURE I'M GOING TO HAVE IT, SO...
I JUST NEED TO GET TO THE NEXT LEVEL, YOU KNOW?
YOUR PROBLEM IS HUMAN COGNITION IS SIGNIFICANTLY MORE COMPLEX THAN THAT OF A MOUSE.

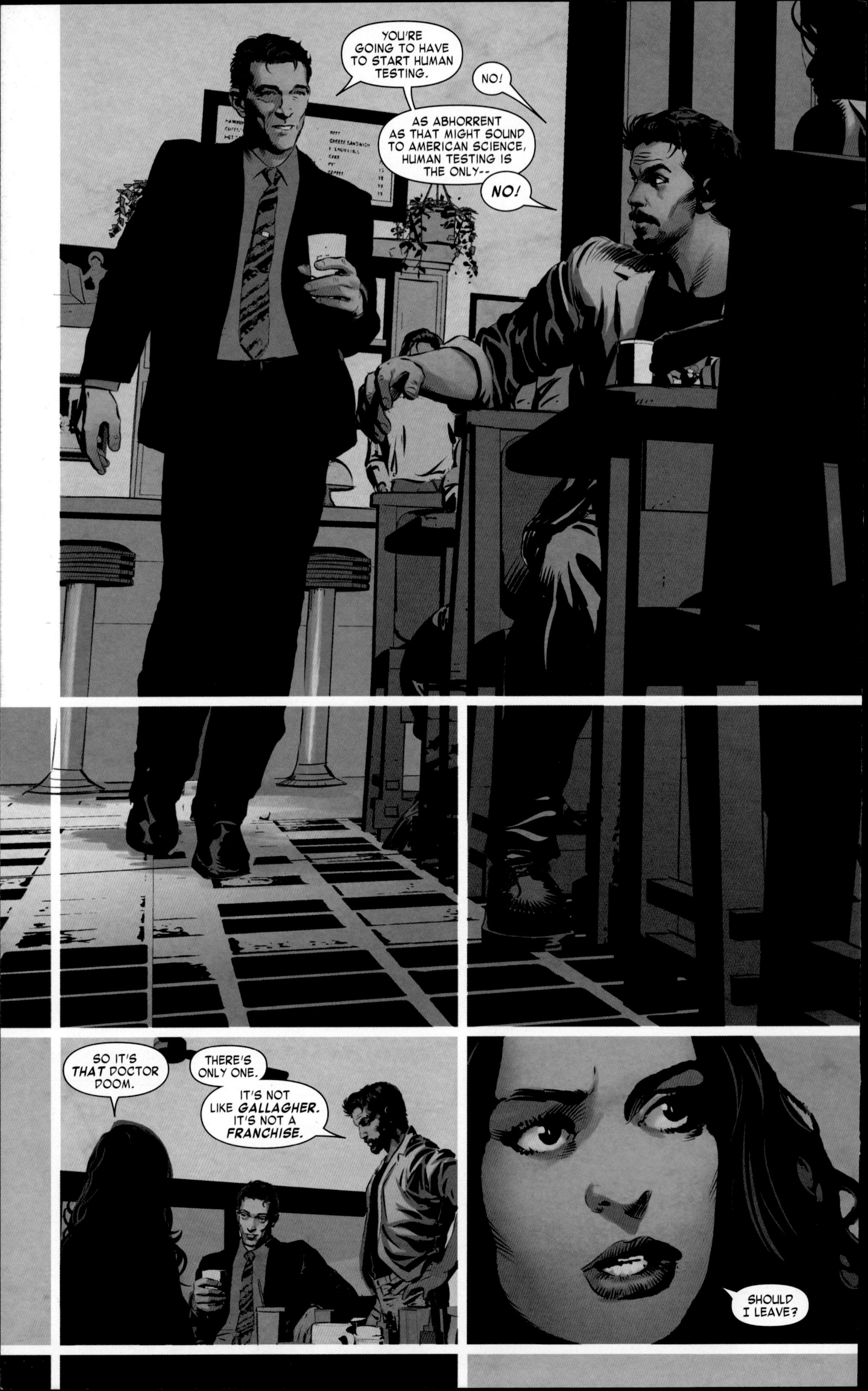
YOU'RE GOING TO HAVE TO START HUMAN TESTING.
NO!
AS ABHORRENT AS THAT MIGHT SOUND TO AMERICAN SCIENCE, HUMAN TESTING IS THE ONLY--
NO!
SO IT'S THAT DOCTOR DOOM.
THERE'S ONLY ONE.
IT'S NOT LIKE GALLAGHER. IT'S NOT A FRANCHISE.
SHOULD I LEAVE?

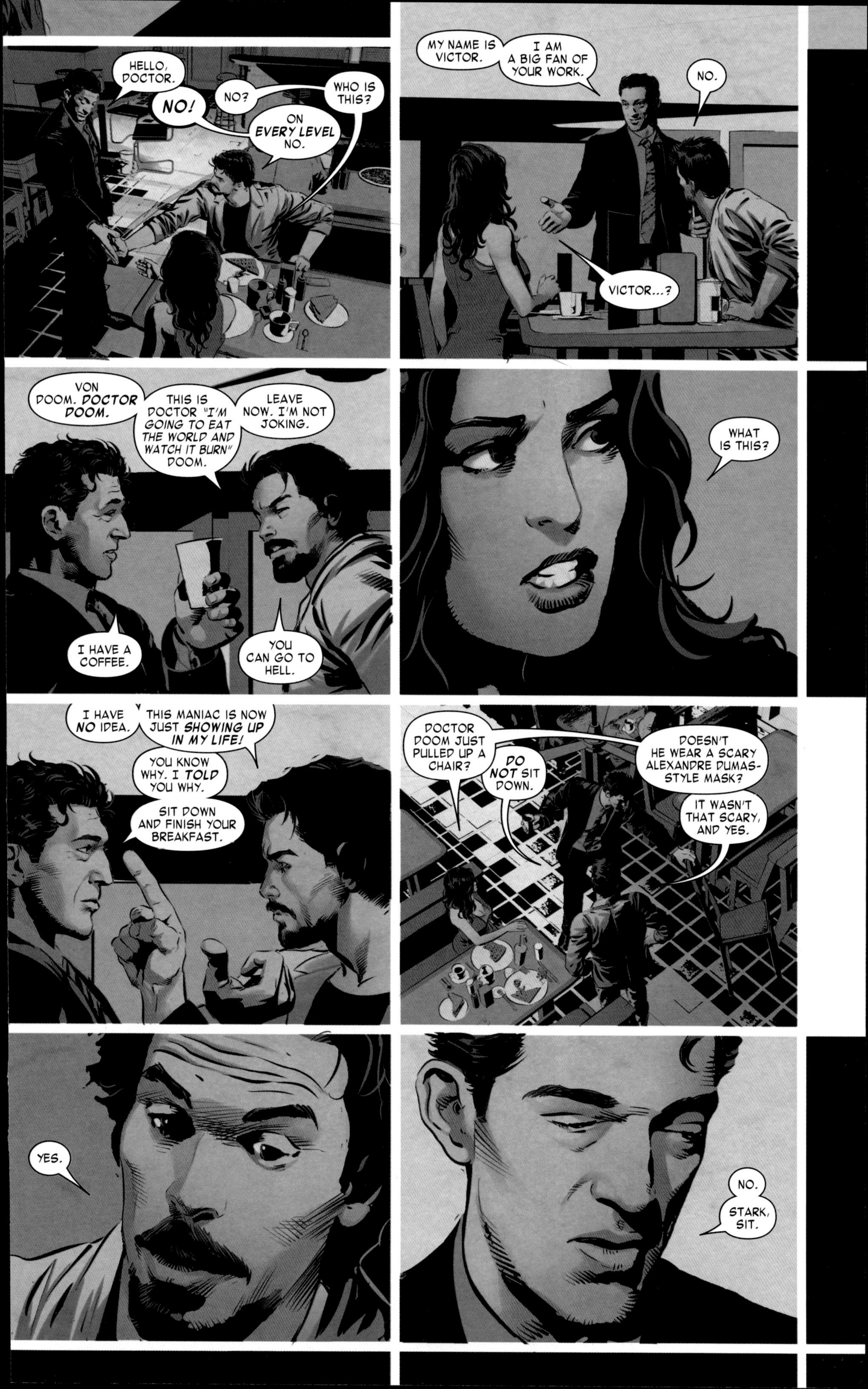

HELLO, DOCTOR.
NO!
NO?
WHO IS THIS?
ON EVERY LEVEL NO.
MY NAME IS VICTOR.
I AM A BIG FAN OF YOUR WORK.
NO.
VICTOR...?
VON DOOM. DOCTOR DOOM.
THIS IS DOCTOR "I'M GOING TO EAT THE WORLD AND WATCH IT BURN" DOOM.
LEAVE NOW. I'M NOT JOKING.
I HAVE A COFFEE.
YOU CAN GO TO HELL.
WHAT IS THIS?
I HAVE NO IDEA.
THIS MANIAC IS NOW JUST SHOWING UP IN MY LIFE!
YOU KNOW WHY. I TOLD YOU WHY.
SIT DOWN AND FINISH YOUR BREAKFAST.
DOCTOR DOOM JUST PULLED UP A CHAIR?
DO NOT SIT DOWN.
DOESN'T HE WEAR A SCARY ALEXANDRE DUMAS-STYLE MASK?
IT WASN'T THAT SCARY, AND YES.
YES.
NO.
STARK, SIT.

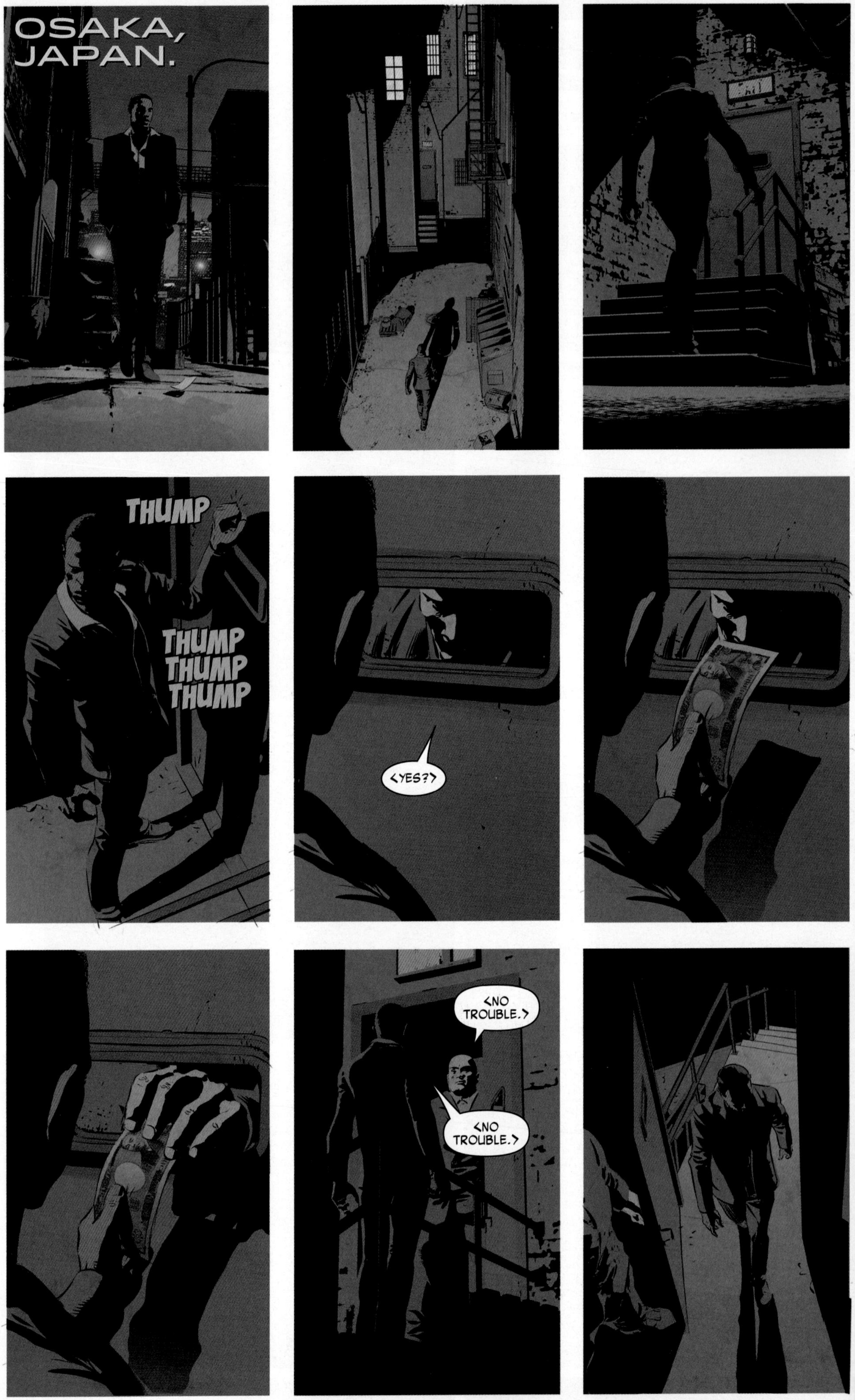
OSAKA, JAPAN.
THUMP
THUMP THUMP THUMP
<YES?>
<NO TROUBLE.>
<NO TROUBLE.>

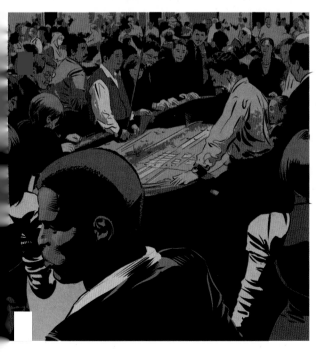

YOU SHOULDN'T BE HERE, COLONEL RHODES.

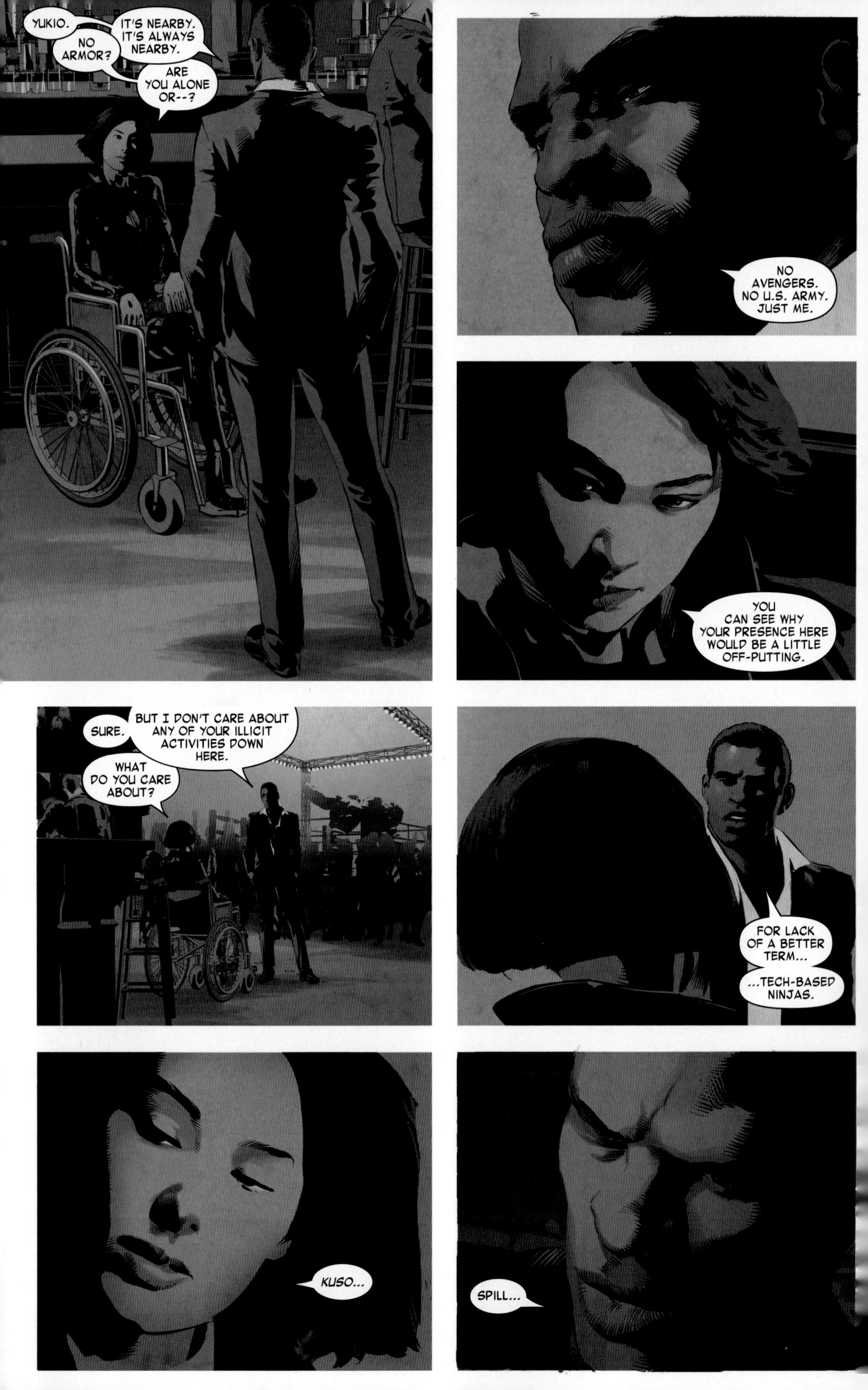
YUKIO.
IT'S NEARBY. IT'S ALWAYS NEARBY.
NO ARMOR?
ARE YOU ALONE OR--?
NO AVENGERS. NO U.S. ARMY. JUST ME.
YOU CAN SEE WHY YOUR PRESENCE HERE WOULD BE A LITTLE OFF-PUTTING.
SURE.
BUT I DON'T CARE ABOUT ANY OF YOUR ILLICIT ACTIVITIES DOWN HERE.
WHAT DO YOU CARE ABOUT?
FOR LACK OF A BETTER TERM...
...TECH-BASED NINJAS.
KUSO...
SPILL...

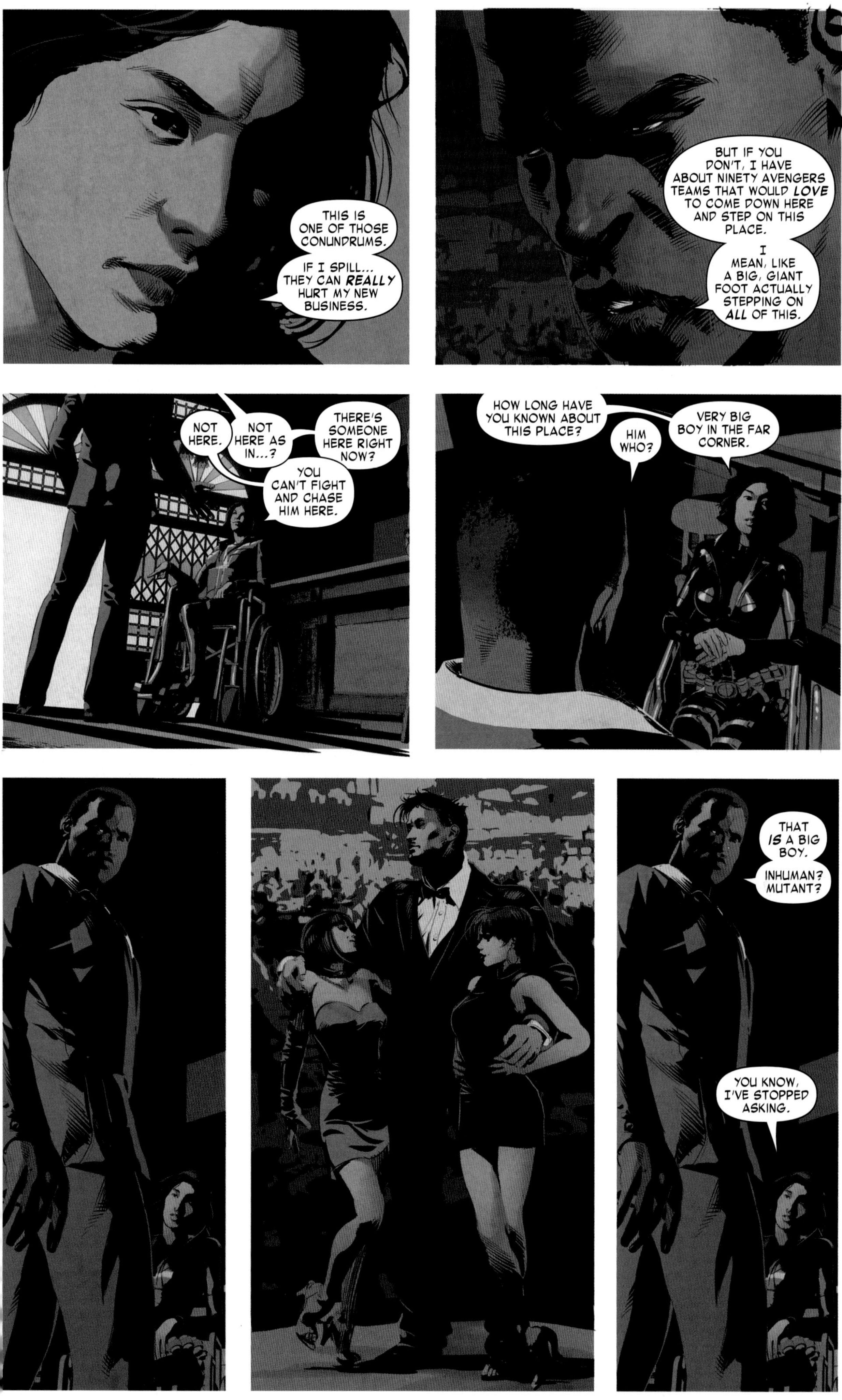
THIS IS ONE OF THOSE CONUNDRUMS.
IF I SPILL... THEY CAN REALLY HURT MY NEW BUSINESS.
BUT IF YOU DON'T, I HAVE ABOUT NINETY AVENGERS TEAMS THAT WOULD LOVE TO COME DOWN HERE AND STEP ON THIS PLACE.
I MEAN, LIKE A BIG, GIANT FOOT ACTUALLY STEPPING ON ALL OF THIS.
THERE'S SOMEONE HERE RIGHT NOW?
NOT HERE AS IN...?
NOT HERE.
YOU CAN'T FIGHT AND CHASE HIM HERE.
HOW LONG HAVE YOU KNOWN ABOUT THIS PLACE?
VERY BIG BOY IN THE FAR CORNER.
HIM WHO?
THAT IS A BIG BOY.
INHUMAN? MUTANT?
YOU KNOW, I'VE STOPPED ASKING.

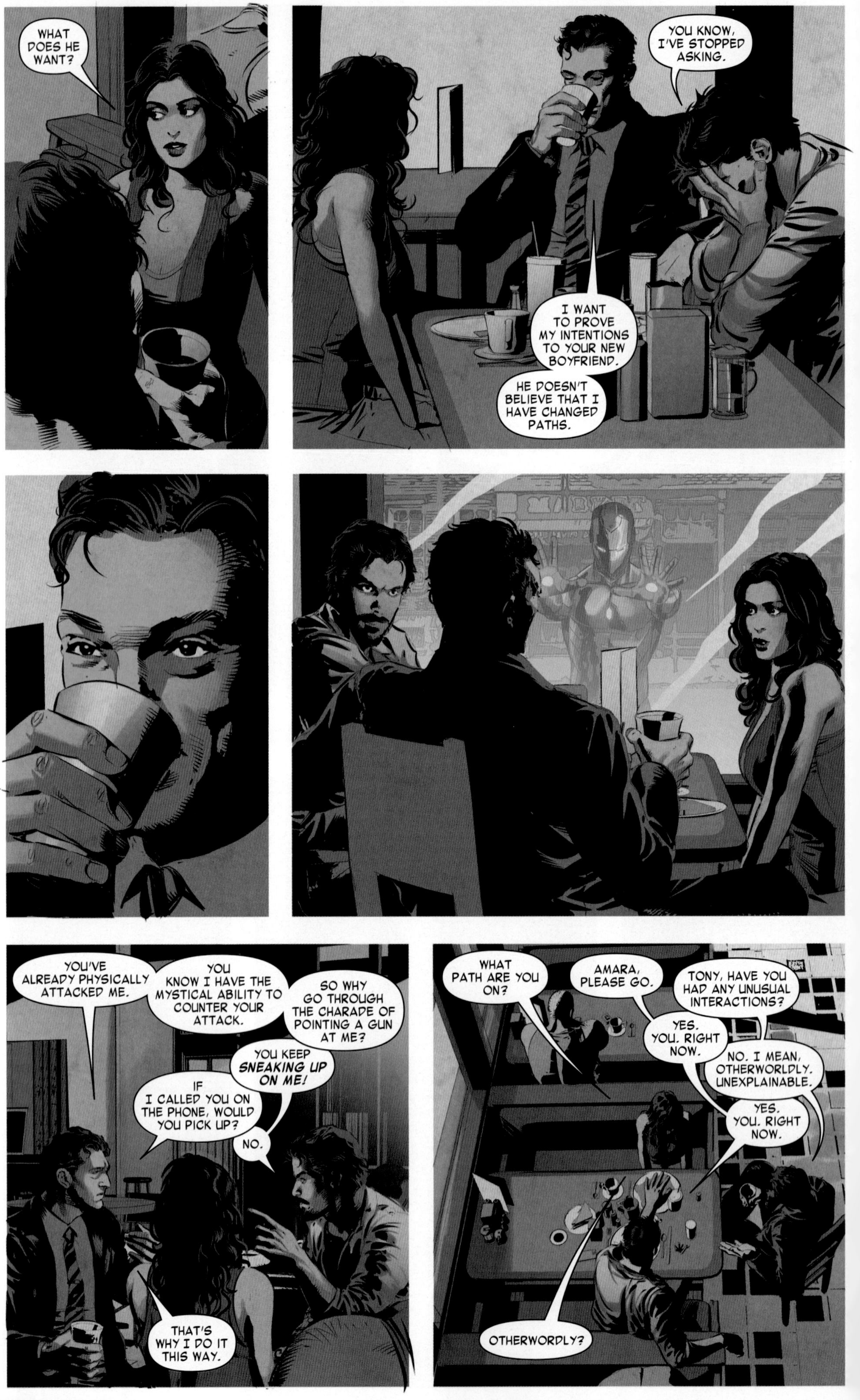
WHAT DOES HE WANT?
YOU KNOW, I'VE STOPPED ASKING.
I WANT TO PROVE MY INTENTIONS TO YOUR NEW BOYFRIEND.
HE DOESN'T BELIEVE THAT I HAVE CHANGED PATHS.
YOU'VE ALREADY PHYSICALLY ATTACKED ME.
YOU KNOW I HAVE THE MYSTICAL ABILITY TO COUNTER YOUR ATTACK.
SO WHY GO THROUGH THE CHARADE OF POINTING A GUN AT ME?
YOU KEEP *SNEAKING UP ON ME!*
IF I CALLED YOU ON THE PHONE, WOULD YOU PICK UP?
NO.
THAT'S WHY I DO IT THIS WAY.
WHAT PATH ARE YOU ON?
AMARA, PLEASE GO.
TONY, HAVE YOU HAD ANY UNUSUAL INTERACTIONS?
YES. YOU. RIGHT NOW.
NO. I MEAN, OTHERWORLDLY. UNEXPLAINABLE.
YES. YOU. RIGHT NOW.
OTHERWORDLY?

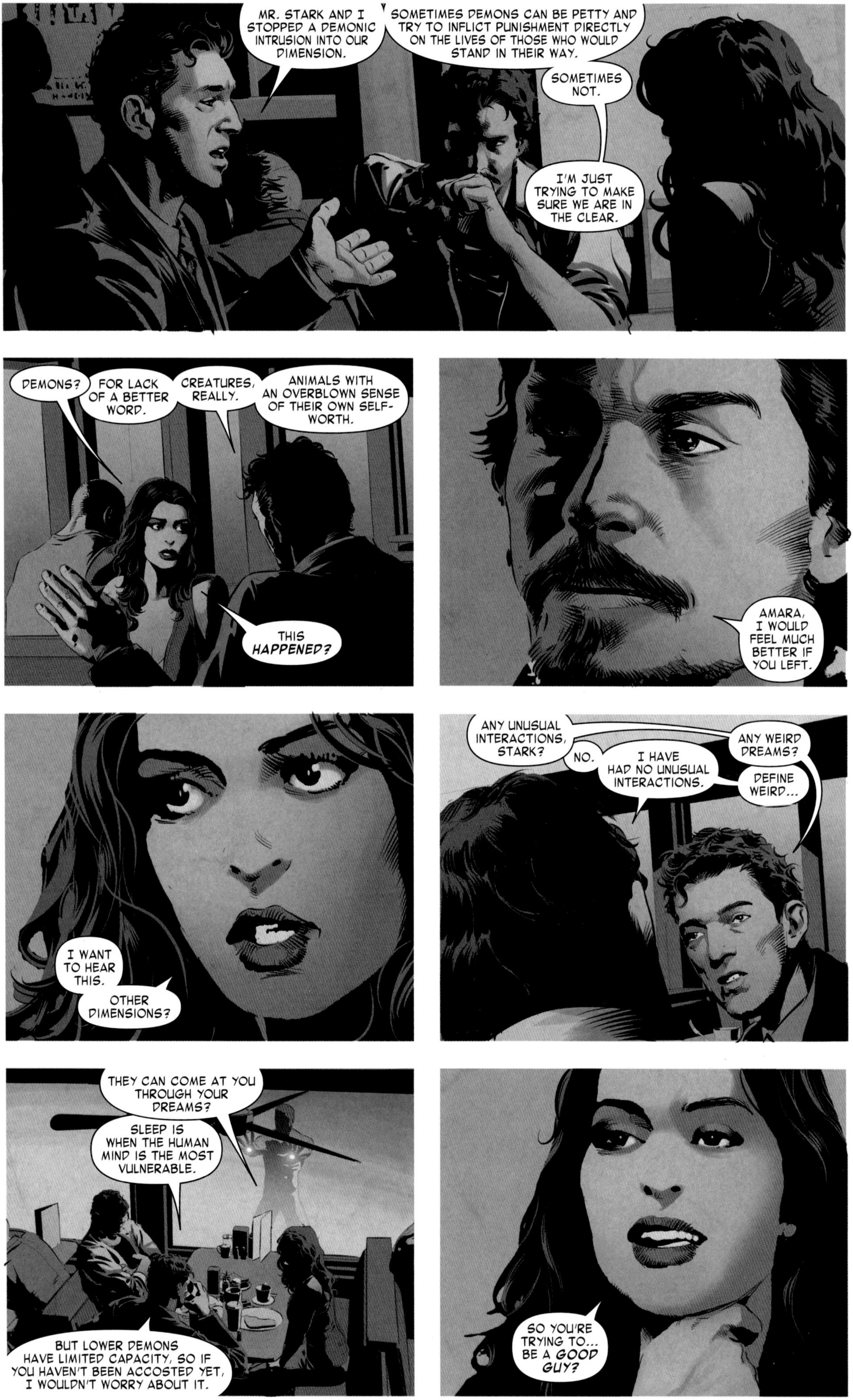
MR. STARK AND I STOPPED A DEMONIC INTRUSION INTO OUR DIMENSION.
SOMETIMES DEMONS CAN BE PETTY AND TRY TO INFLICT PUNISHMENT DIRECTLY ON THE LIVES OF THOSE WHO WOULD STAND IN THEIR WAY.
SOMETIMES NOT.
I'M JUST TRYING TO MAKE SURE WE ARE IN THE CLEAR.
DEMONS?
FOR LACK OF A BETTER WORD.
CREATURES, REALLY.
ANIMALS WITH AN OVERBLOWN SENSE OF THEIR OWN SELF-WORTH.
THIS *HAPPENED?*
AMARA, I WOULD FEEL MUCH BETTER IF YOU LEFT.
I WANT TO HEAR THIS.
OTHER DIMENSIONS?
ANY UNUSUAL INTERACTIONS, STARK?
NO.
I HAVE HAD NO UNUSUAL INTERACTIONS.
ANY WEIRD DREAMS?
DEFINE WEIRD...
THEY CAN COME AT YOU THROUGH YOUR DREAMS?
SLEEP IS WHEN THE HUMAN MIND IS THE MOST VULNERABLE.
BUT LOWER DEMONS HAVE LIMITED CAPACITY, SO IF YOU HAVEN'T BEEN ACCOSTED YET, I WOULDN'T WORRY ABOUT IT.
SO YOU'RE TRYING TO... BE A *GOOD GUY?*

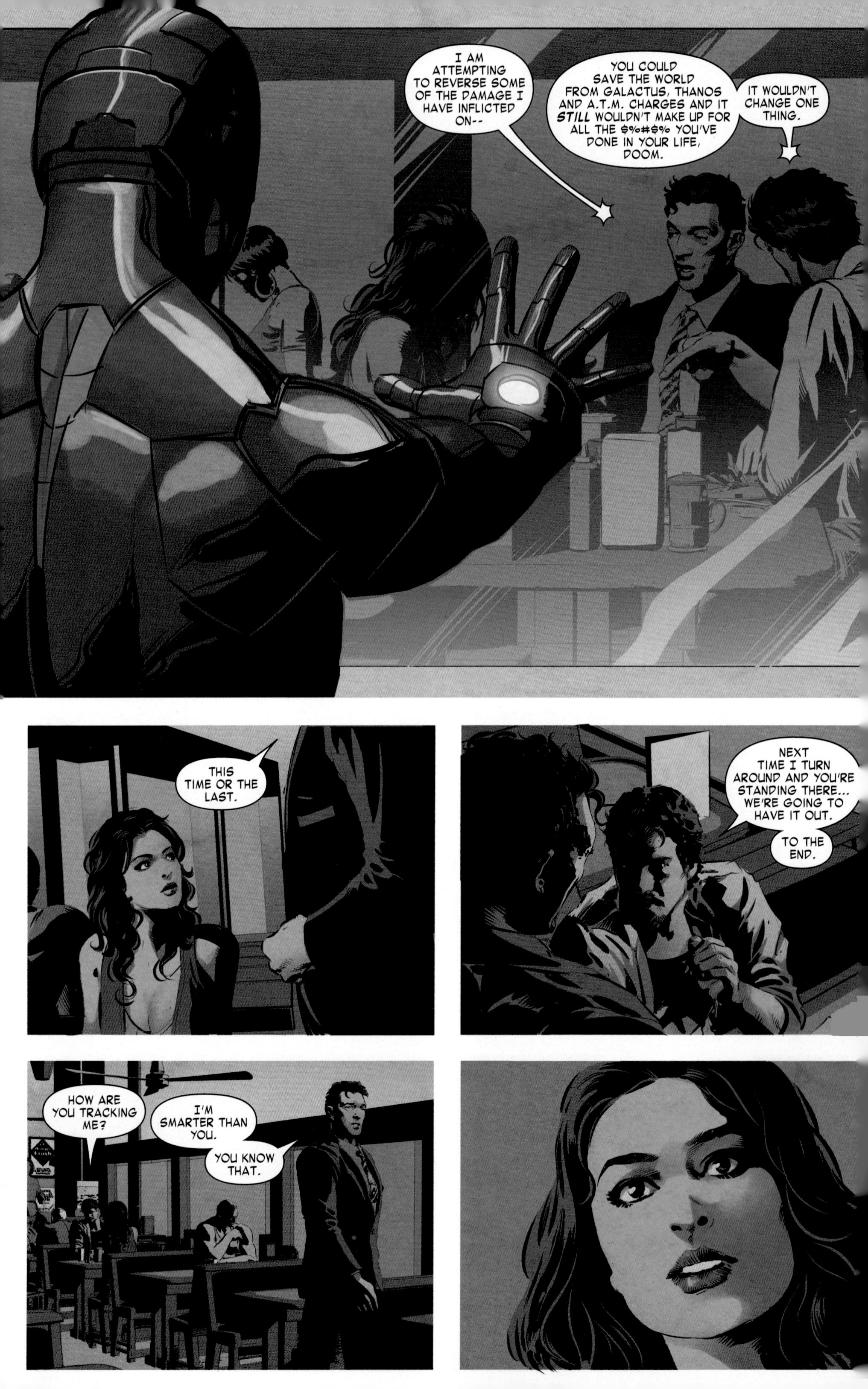
I AM ATTEMPTING TO REVERSE SOME OF THE DAMAGE I HAVE INFLICTED ON--
YOU COULD SAVE THE WORLD FROM GALACTUS, THANOS AND A.T.M. CHARGES AND IT STILL WOULDN'T MAKE UP FOR ALL THE $%#$% YOU'VE DONE IN YOUR LIFE, DOOM.
IT WOULDN'T CHANGE ONE THING.
THIS TIME OR THE LAST.
NEXT TIME I TURN AROUND AND YOU'RE STANDING THERE... WE'RE GOING TO HAVE IT OUT.
TO THE END.
HOW ARE YOU TRACKING ME?
I'M SMARTER THAN YOU.
YOU KNOW THAT.

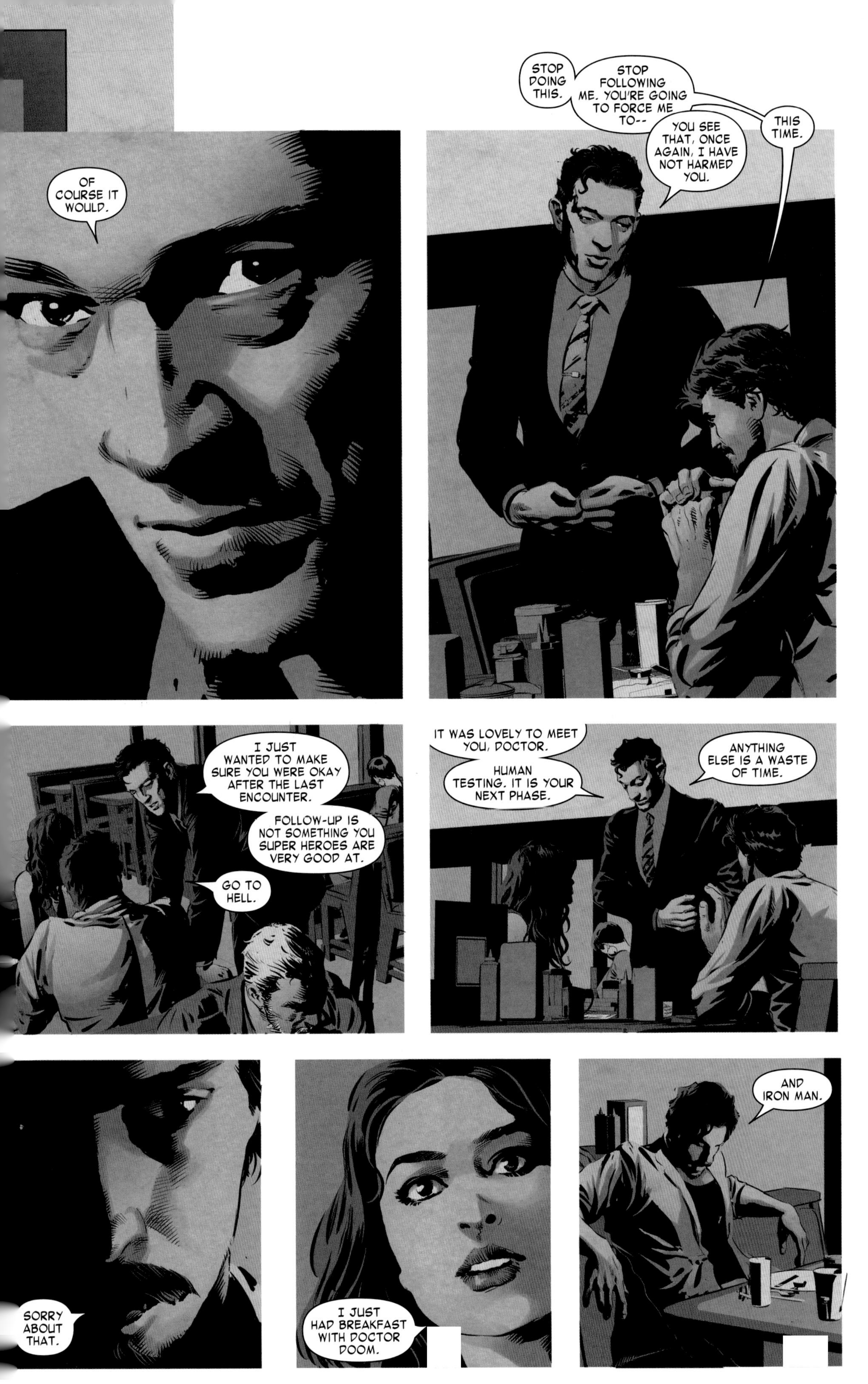
OF COURSE IT WOULD.
STOP DOING THIS.
STOP FOLLOWING ME. YOU'RE GOING TO FORCE ME TO--
THIS TIME.
YOU SEE THAT, ONCE AGAIN, I HAVE NOT HARMED YOU.
I JUST WANTED TO MAKE SURE YOU WERE OKAY AFTER THE LAST ENCOUNTER.
FOLLOW-UP IS NOT SOMETHING YOU SUPER HEROES ARE VERY GOOD AT.
GO TO HELL.
IT WAS LOVELY TO MEET YOU, DOCTOR.
HUMAN TESTING. IT IS YOUR NEXT PHASE.
ANYTHING ELSE IS A WASTE OF TIME.
SORRY ABOUT THAT.
I JUST HAD BREAKFAST WITH DOCTOR DOOM.
AND IRON MAN.

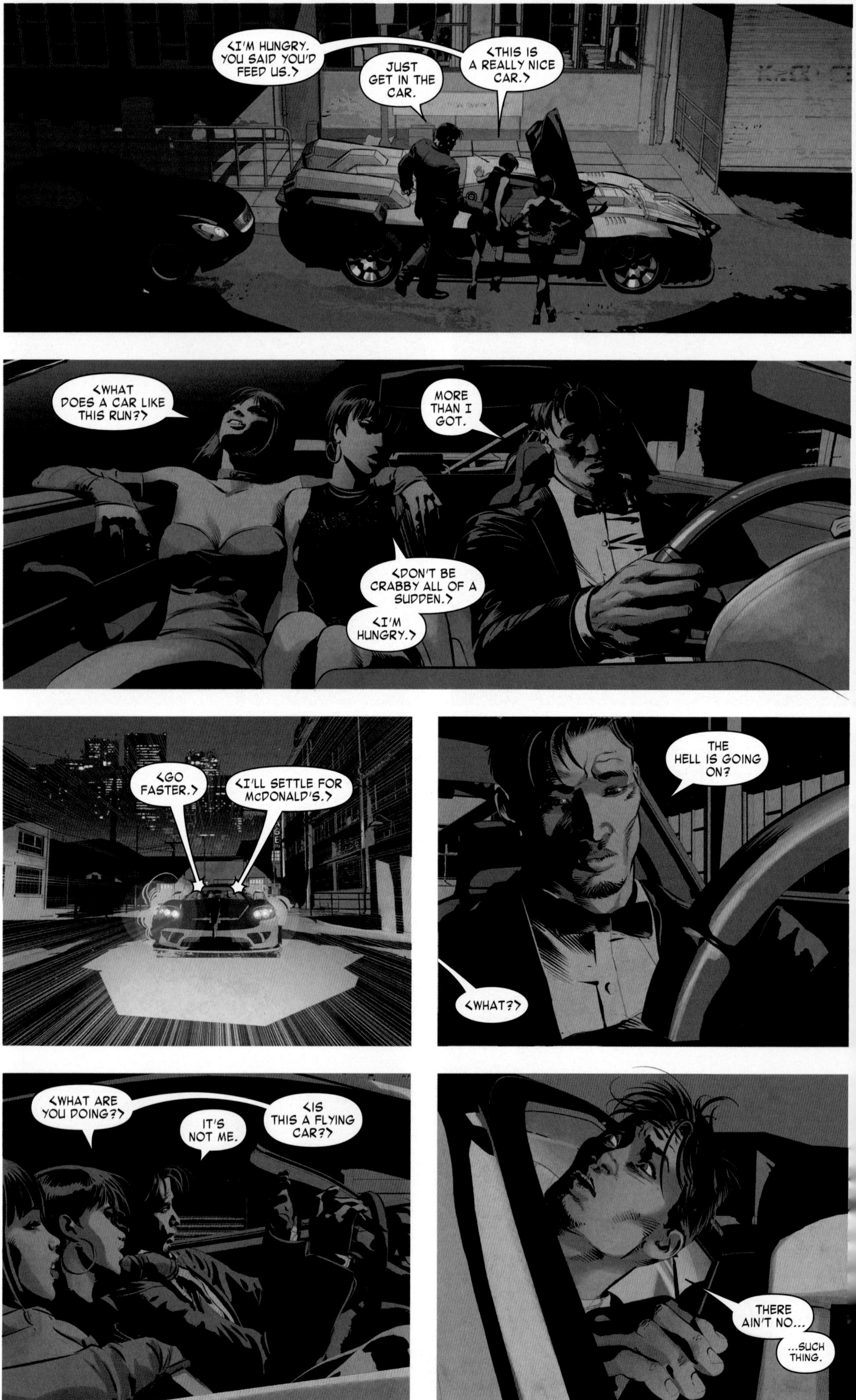
<I'M HUNGRY. YOU SAID YOU'D FEED US.>
JUST GET IN THE CAR.
<THIS IS A REALLY NICE CAR.>
<WHAT DOES A CAR LIKE THIS RUN?>
MORE THAN I GOT.
<DON'T BE CRABBY ALL OF A SUDDEN.>
<I'M HUNGRY.>
<GO FASTER.>
<I'LL SETTLE FOR McDONALD'S.>
THE HELL IS GOING ON?
<WHAT?>
<WHAT ARE YOU DOING?>
IT'S NOT ME.
<IS THIS A FLYING CAR?>
THERE AIN'T NO...
...SUCH THING.

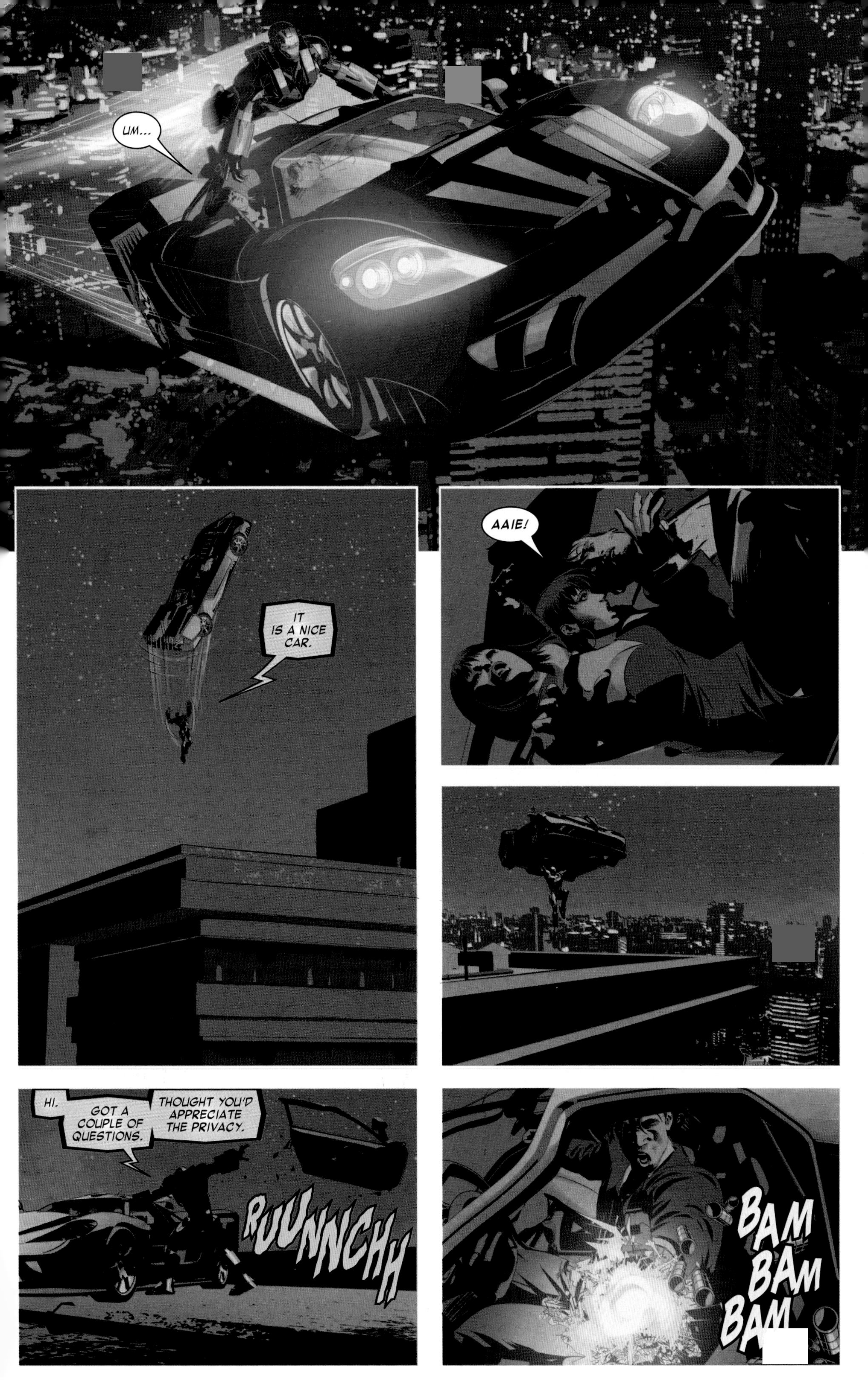
UM...
IT IS A NICE CAR.
AAIE!
HI.
GOT A COUPLE OF QUESTIONS.
THOUGHT YOU'D APPRECIATE THE PRIVACY.
RUUNNCHH
BAM BAM BAM

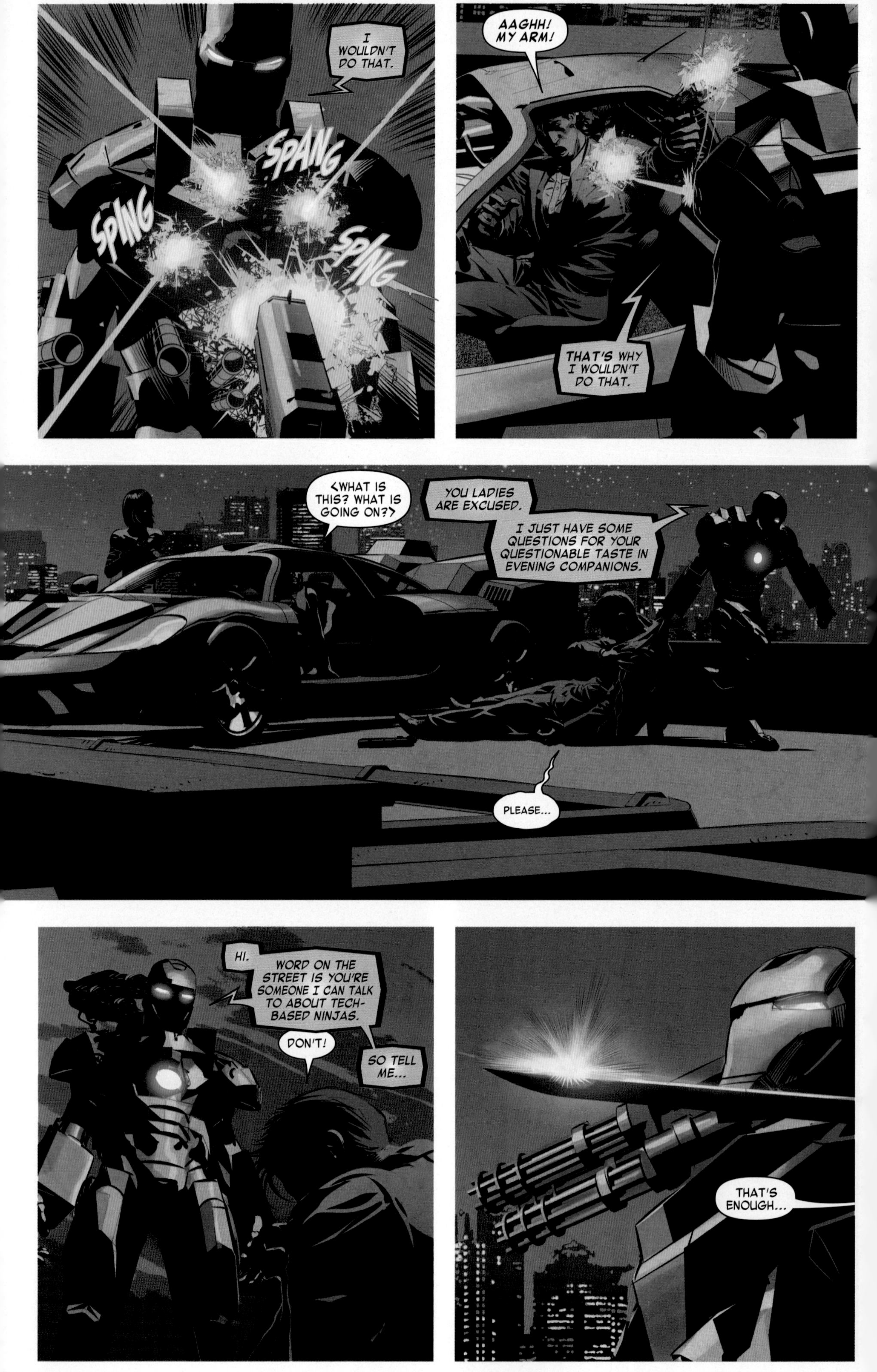
I WOULDN'T DO THAT.
SPANG
SPING
SPING
AAGHH! MY ARM!
THAT'S WHY I WOULDN'T DO THAT.
<WHAT IS THIS? WHAT IS GOING ON?>
YOU LADIES ARE EXCUSED.
I JUST HAVE SOME QUESTIONS FOR YOUR QUESTIONABLE TASTE IN EVENING COMPANIONS.
PLEASE...
HI.
WORD ON THE STREET IS YOU'RE SOMEONE I CAN TALK TO ABOUT TECH-BASED NINJAS.
DON'T!
SO TELL ME...
THAT'S ENOUGH...

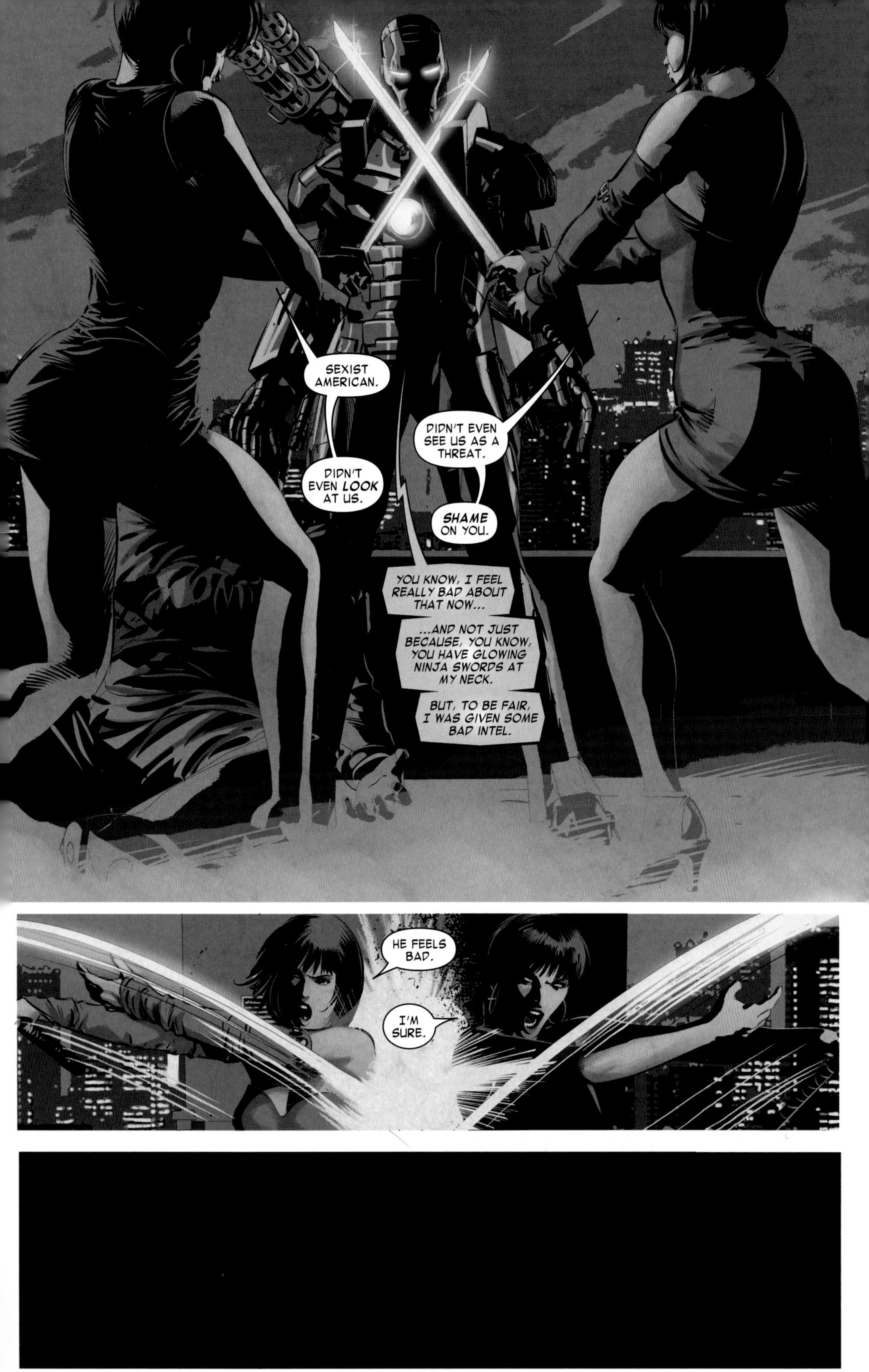
SEXIST AMERICAN.
DIDN'T EVEN LOOK AT US.
DIDN'T EVEN SEE US AS A THREAT.
SHAME ON YOU.
YOU KNOW, I FEEL REALLY BAD ABOUT THAT NOW...
...AND NOT JUST BECAUSE, YOU KNOW, YOU HAVE GLOWING NINJA SWORDS AT MY NECK.
BUT, TO BE FAIR, I WAS GIVEN SOME BAD INTEL.
HE FEELS BAD.
I'M SURE.

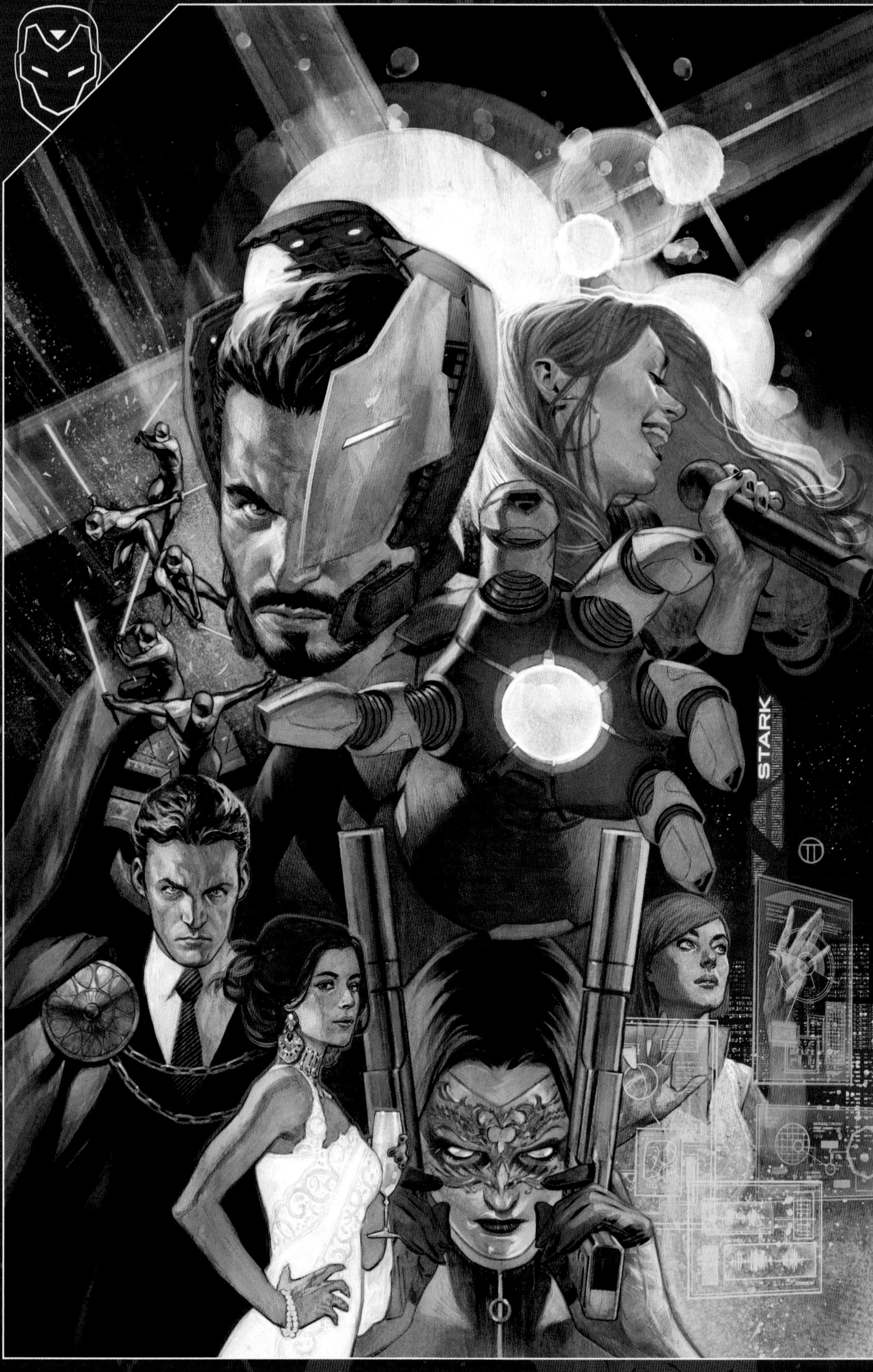
STARK

#6 STORY THUS FAR VARIANT BY **JULIAN TOTINO TEDESCO**

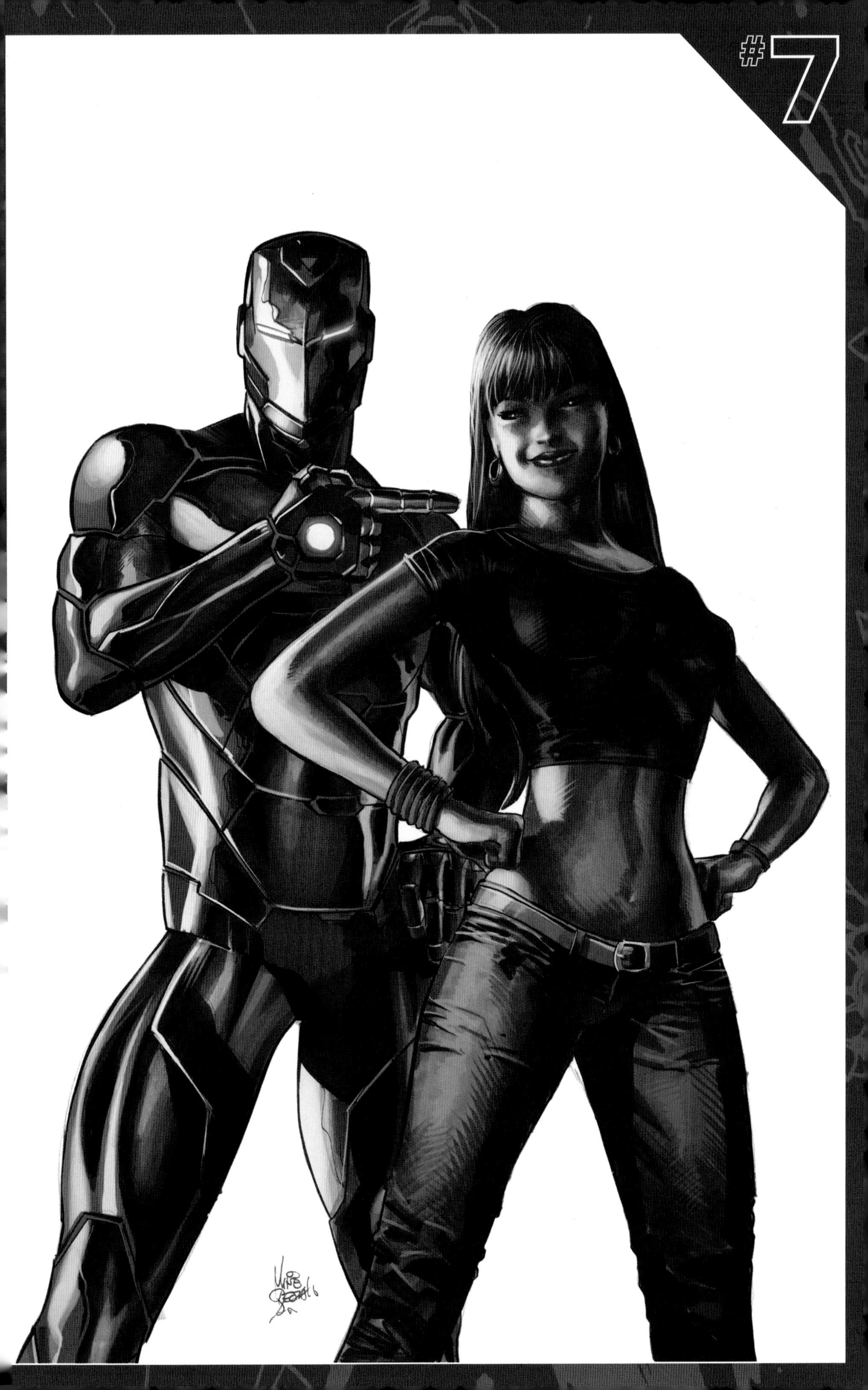
#7

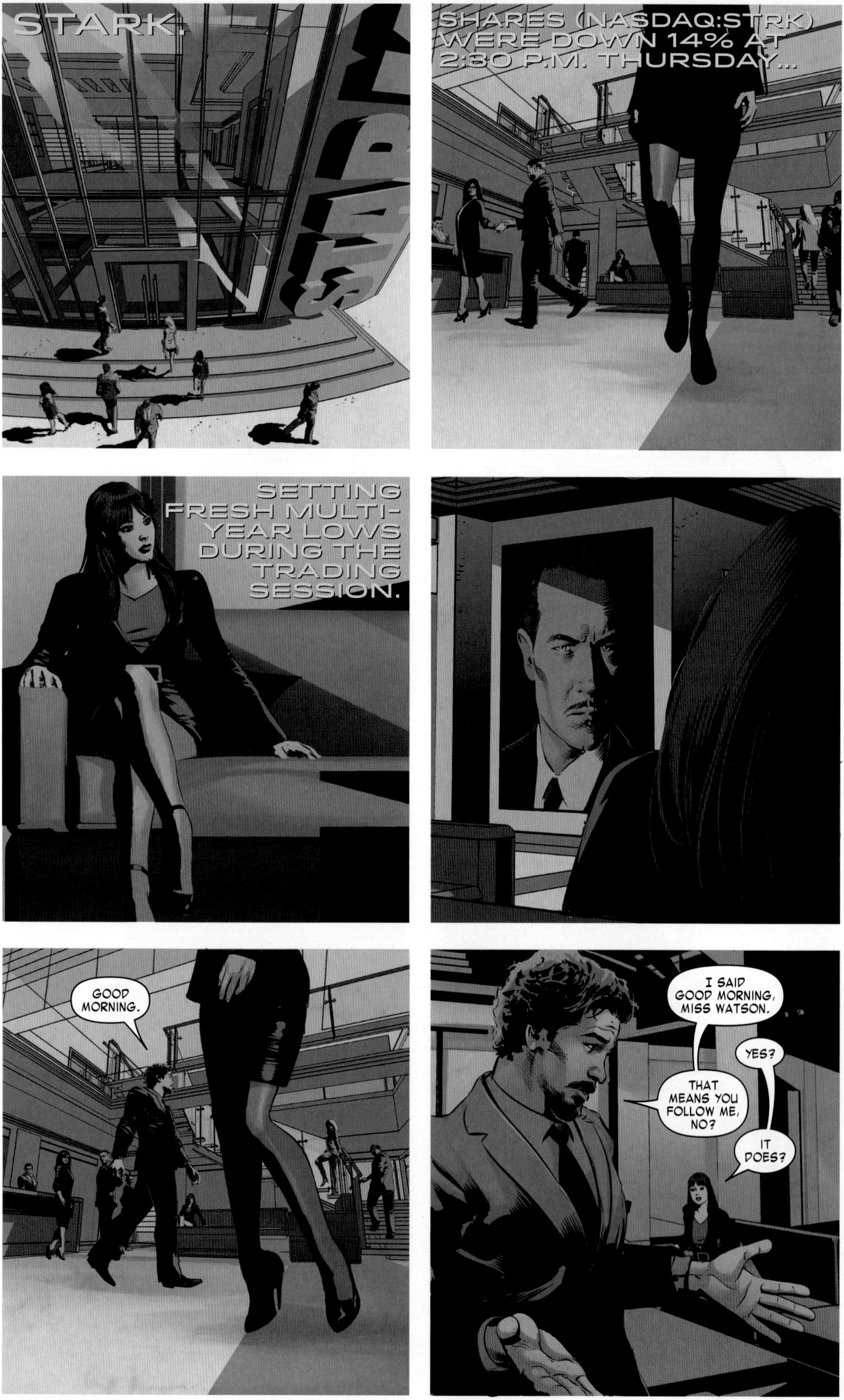
STARK.
SHARES (NASDAQ:STRK) WERE DOWN 14% AT 2:30 P.M. THURSDAY...
SETTING FRESH MULTI-YEAR LOWS DURING THE TRADING SESSION.
GOOD MORNING.
I SAID GOOD MORNING, MISS WATSON.
YES?
THAT MEANS YOU FOLLOW ME, NO?
IT DOES?

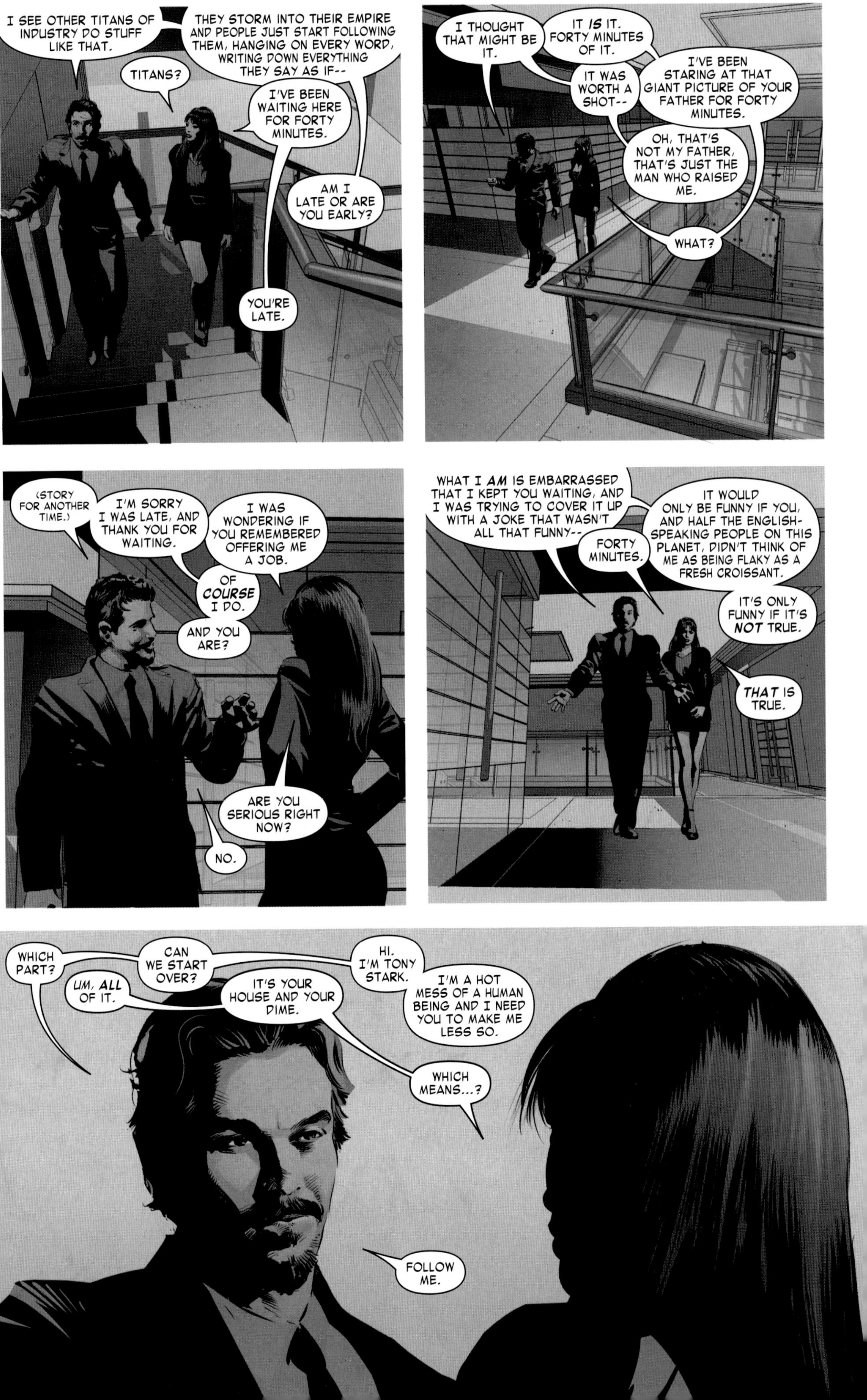
I SEE OTHER TITANS OF INDUSTRY DO STUFF LIKE THAT.
THEY STORM INTO THEIR EMPIRE AND PEOPLE JUST START FOLLOWING THEM, HANGING ON EVERY WORD, WRITING DOWN EVERYTHING THEY SAY AS IF--
TITANS?
I'VE BEEN WAITING HERE FOR FORTY MINUTES.
AM I LATE OR ARE YOU EARLY?
YOU'RE LATE.
I THOUGHT THAT MIGHT BE IT.
IT IS IT. FORTY MINUTES OF IT.
IT WAS WORTH A SHOT--
I'VE BEEN STARING AT THAT GIANT PICTURE OF YOUR FATHER FOR FORTY MINUTES.
OH, THAT'S NOT MY FATHER, THAT'S JUST THE MAN WHO RAISED ME.
WHAT?
(STORY FOR ANOTHER TIME.)
I'M SORRY I WAS LATE, AND THANK YOU FOR WAITING.
I WAS WONDERING IF YOU REMEMBERED OFFERING ME A JOB.
OF COURSE I DO.
AND YOU ARE?
ARE YOU SERIOUS RIGHT NOW?
NO.
WHAT I AM IS EMBARRASSED THAT I KEPT YOU WAITING, AND I WAS TRYING TO COVER IT UP WITH A JOKE THAT WASN'T ALL THAT FUNNY--
FORTY MINUTES.
IT WOULD ONLY BE FUNNY IF YOU, AND HALF THE ENGLISH-SPEAKING PEOPLE ON THIS PLANET, DIDN'T THINK OF ME AS BEING FLAKY AS A FRESH CROISSANT.
IT'S ONLY FUNNY IF IT'S NOT TRUE.
THAT IS TRUE.
WHICH PART?
UM, ALL OF IT.
CAN WE START OVER?
IT'S YOUR HOUSE AND YOUR DIME.
HI. I'M TONY STARK.
I'M A HOT MESS OF A HUMAN BEING AND I NEED YOU TO MAKE ME LESS SO.
WHICH MEANS...?
FOLLOW ME.

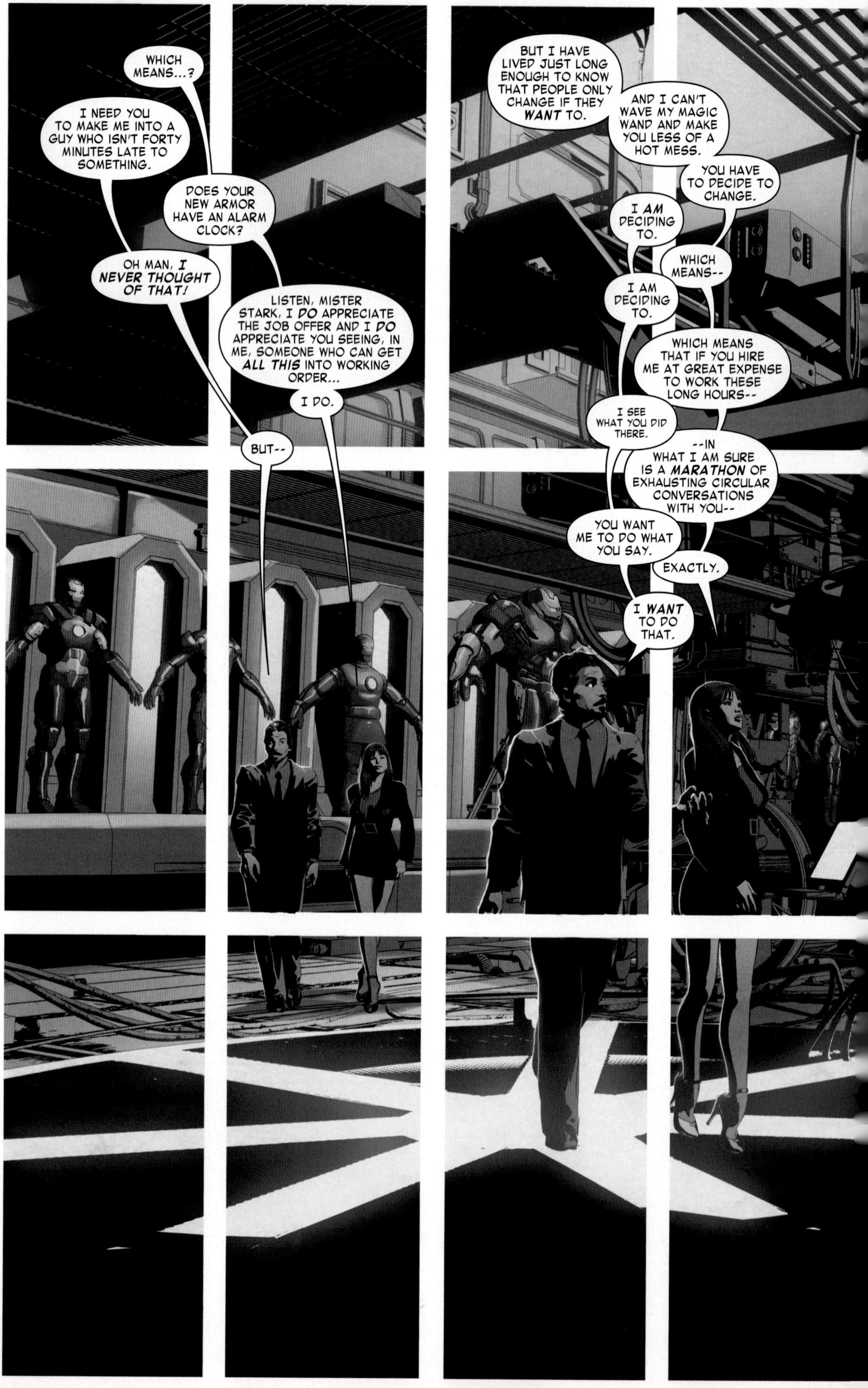
WHICH MEANS...?
I NEED YOU TO MAKE ME INTO A GUY WHO ISN'T FORTY MINUTES LATE TO SOMETHING.
DOES YOUR NEW ARMOR HAVE AN ALARM CLOCK?
OH MAN, I NEVER THOUGHT OF THAT!
LISTEN, MISTER STARK, I DO APPRECIATE THE JOB OFFER AND I DO APPRECIATE YOU SEEING, IN ME, SOMEONE WHO CAN GET ALL THIS INTO WORKING ORDER...
I DO.
BUT--
BUT I HAVE LIVED JUST LONG ENOUGH TO KNOW THAT PEOPLE ONLY CHANGE IF THEY WANT TO.
AND I CAN'T WAVE MY MAGIC WAND AND MAKE YOU LESS OF A HOT MESS.
YOU HAVE TO DECIDE TO CHANGE.
I AM DECIDING TO.
WHICH MEANS--
I AM DECIDING TO.
WHICH MEANS THAT IF YOU HIRE ME AT GREAT EXPENSE TO WORK THESE LONG HOURS--
I SEE WHAT YOU DID THERE.
--IN WHAT I AM SURE IS A MARATHON OF EXHAUSTING CIRCULAR CONVERSATIONS WITH YOU--
YOU WANT ME TO DO WHAT YOU SAY.
EXACTLY.
I WANT TO DO THAT.

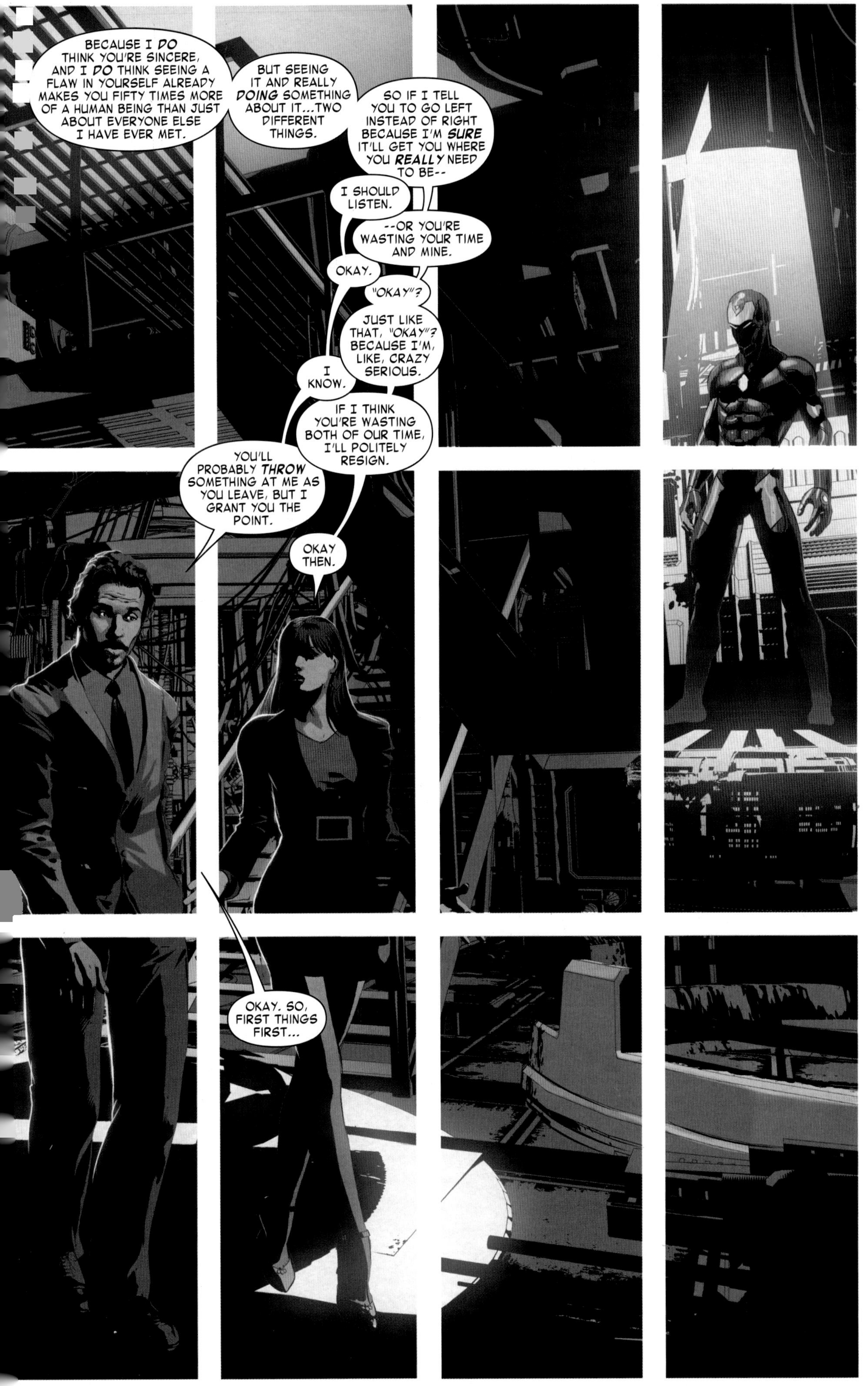
BECAUSE I DO THINK YOU'RE SINCERE, AND I DO THINK SEEING A FLAW IN YOURSELF ALREADY MAKES YOU FIFTY TIMES MORE OF A HUMAN BEING THAN JUST ABOUT EVERYONE ELSE I HAVE EVER MET.
BUT SEEING IT AND REALLY DOING SOMETHING ABOUT IT...TWO DIFFERENT THINGS.
SO IF I TELL YOU TO GO LEFT INSTEAD OF RIGHT BECAUSE I'M SURE IT'LL GET YOU WHERE YOU REALLY NEED TO BE--
I SHOULD LISTEN.
--OR YOU'RE WASTING YOUR TIME AND MINE.
OKAY.
"OKAY"?
JUST LIKE THAT, "OKAY"? BECAUSE I'M, LIKE, CRAZY SERIOUS.
I KNOW.
IF I THINK YOU'RE WASTING BOTH OF OUR TIME, I'LL POLITELY RESIGN.
YOU'LL PROBABLY THROW SOMETHING AT ME AS YOU LEAVE, BUT I GRANT YOU THE POINT.
OKAY THEN.
OKAY. SO, FIRST THINGS FIRST...

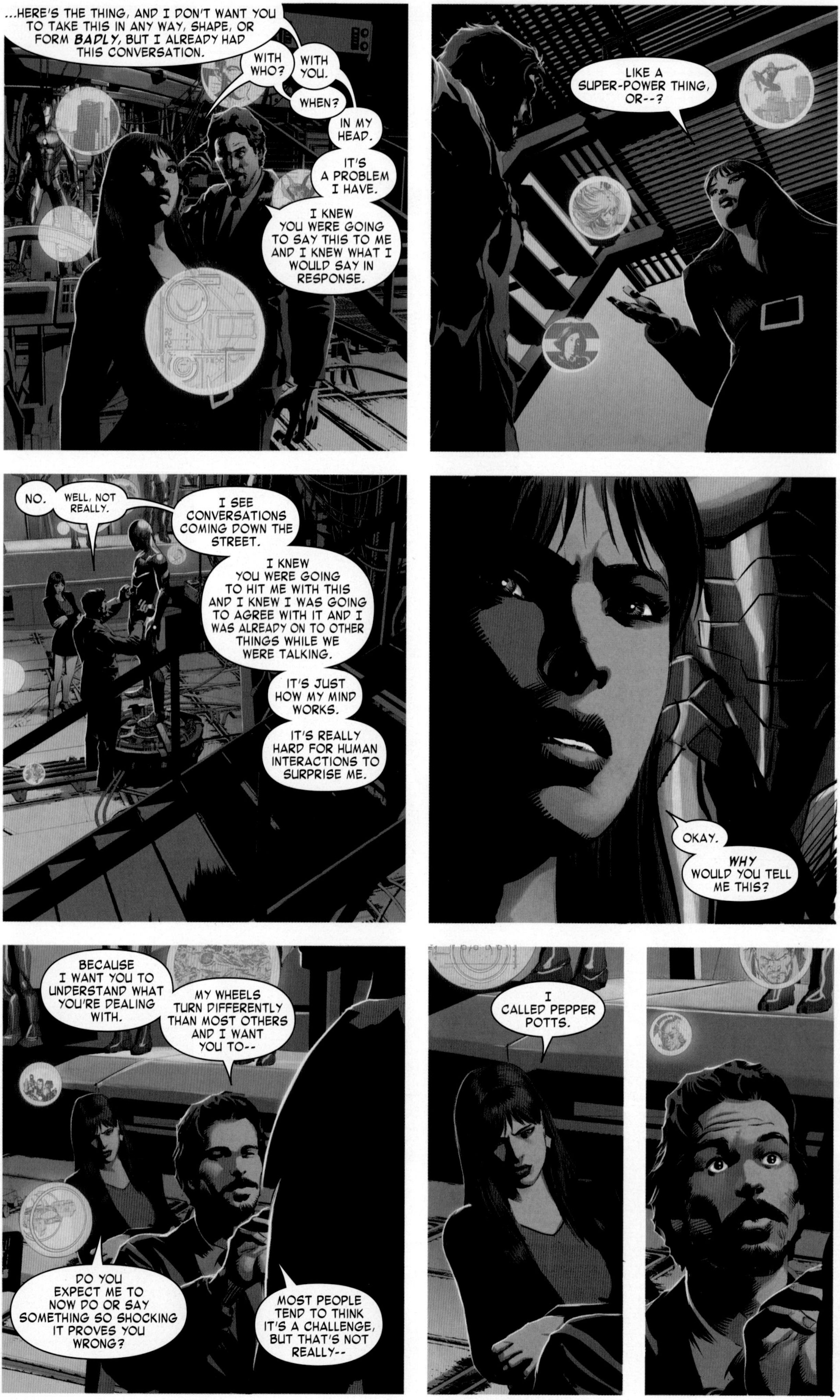
...HERE'S THE THING, AND I DON'T WANT YOU TO TAKE THIS IN ANY WAY, SHAPE, OR FORM BADLY, BUT I ALREADY HAD THIS CONVERSATION.
WITH WHO?
WITH YOU.
WHEN?
IN MY HEAD.
IT'S A PROBLEM I HAVE.
I KNEW YOU WERE GOING TO SAY THIS TO ME AND I KNEW WHAT I WOULD SAY IN RESPONSE.
LIKE A SUPER-POWER THING, OR--?
NO.
WELL, NOT REALLY.
I SEE CONVERSATIONS COMING DOWN THE STREET.
I KNEW YOU WERE GOING TO HIT ME WITH THIS AND I KNEW I WAS GOING TO AGREE WITH IT AND I WAS ALREADY ON TO OTHER THINGS WHILE WE WERE TALKING.
IT'S JUST HOW MY MIND WORKS.
IT'S REALLY HARD FOR HUMAN INTERACTIONS TO SURPRISE ME.
OKAY.
WHY WOULD YOU TELL ME THIS?
BECAUSE I WANT YOU TO UNDERSTAND WHAT YOU'RE DEALING WITH.
MY WHEELS TURN DIFFERENTLY THAN MOST OTHERS AND I WANT YOU TO--
DO YOU EXPECT ME TO NOW DO OR SAY SOMETHING SO SHOCKING IT PROVES YOU WRONG?
MOST PEOPLE TEND TO THINK IT'S A CHALLENGE, BUT THAT'S NOT REALLY--
I CALLED PEPPER POTTS.

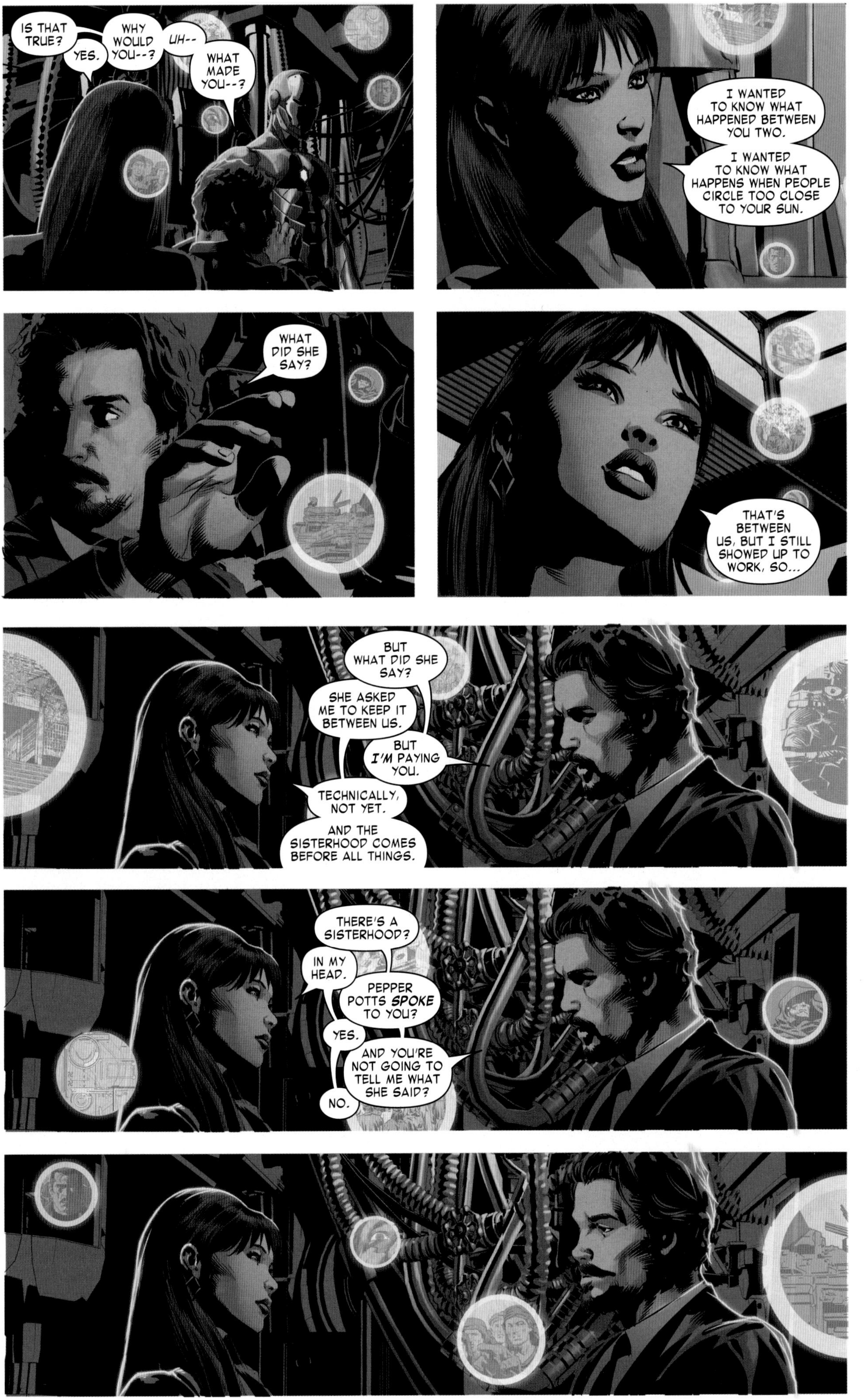
IS THAT TRUE?
YES.
WHY WOULD YOU--?
UH--
WHAT MADE YOU--?
I WANTED TO KNOW WHAT HAPPENED BETWEEN YOU TWO.
I WANTED TO KNOW WHAT HAPPENS WHEN PEOPLE CIRCLE TOO CLOSE TO YOUR SUN.
WHAT DID SHE SAY?
THAT'S BETWEEN US, BUT I STILL SHOWED UP TO WORK, SO...
BUT WHAT DID SHE SAY?
SHE ASKED ME TO KEEP IT BETWEEN US.
BUT I'M PAYING YOU.
TECHNICALLY, NOT YET.
AND THE SISTERHOOD COMES BEFORE ALL THINGS.
THERE'S A SISTERHOOD?
IN MY HEAD.
PEPPER POTTS SPOKE TO YOU?
YES.
AND YOU'RE NOT GOING TO TELL ME WHAT SHE SAID?
NO.

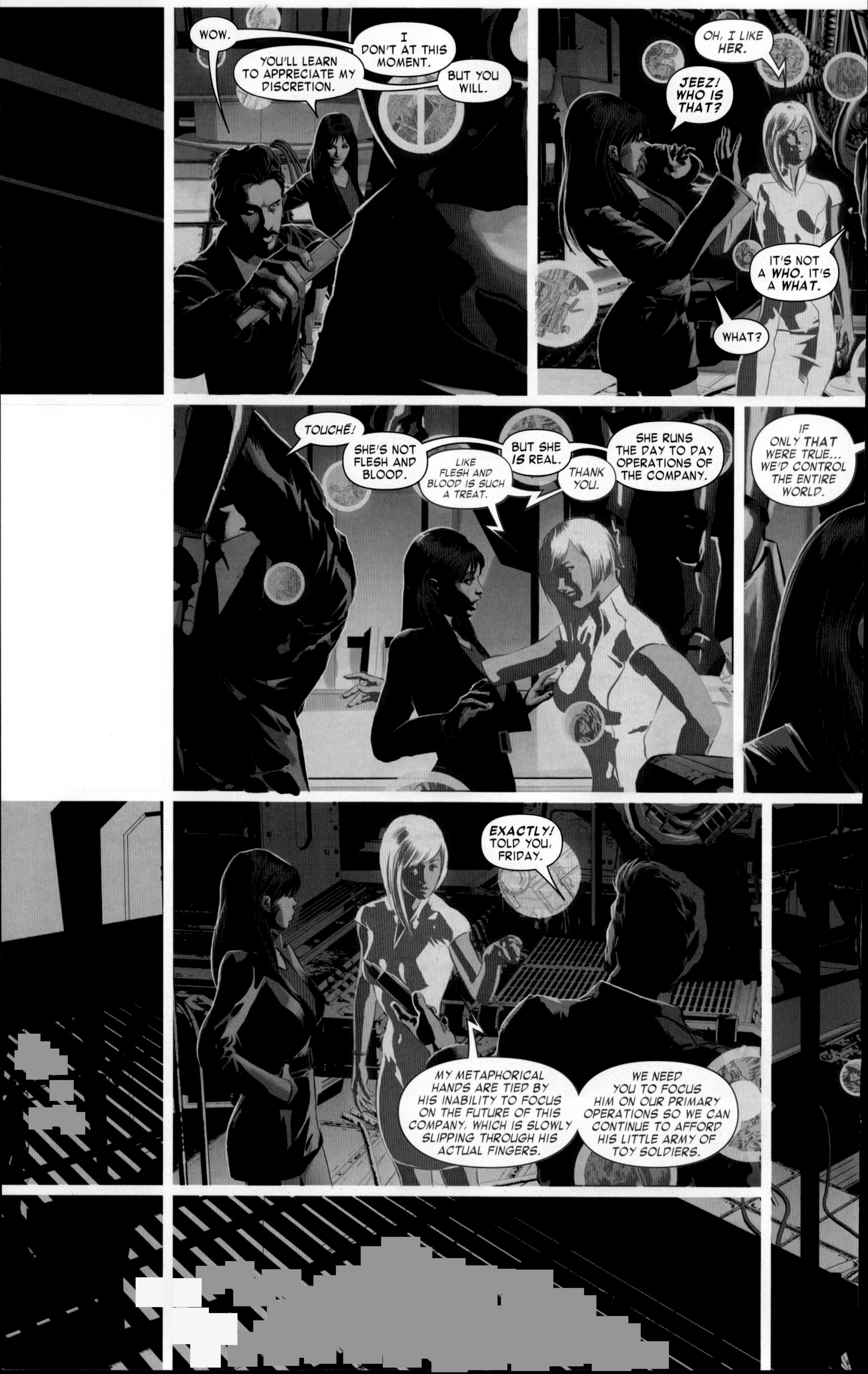

WOW.
YOU'LL LEARN TO APPRECIATE MY DISCRETION.
I DON'T AT THIS MOMENT.
BUT YOU WILL.
JEEZ! WHO IS THAT?
OH, I LIKE HER.
IT'S NOT A WHO. IT'S A WHAT.
WHAT?
TOUCHÉ!
SHE'S NOT FLESH AND BLOOD.
LIKE FLESH AND BLOOD IS SUCH A TREAT.
BUT SHE IS REAL.
THANK YOU.
SHE RUNS THE DAY TO DAY OPERATIONS OF THE COMPANY.
IF ONLY THAT WERE TRUE... WE'D CONTROL THE ENTIRE WORLD.
EXACTLY! TOLD YOU, FRIDAY.
MY METAPHORICAL HANDS ARE TIED BY HIS INABILITY TO FOCUS ON THE FUTURE OF THIS COMPANY, WHICH IS SLOWLY SLIPPING THROUGH HIS ACTUAL FINGERS.
WE NEED YOU TO FOCUS HIM ON OUR PRIMARY OPERATIONS SO WE CAN CONTINUE TO AFFORD HIS LITTLE ARMY OF TOY SOLDIERS.

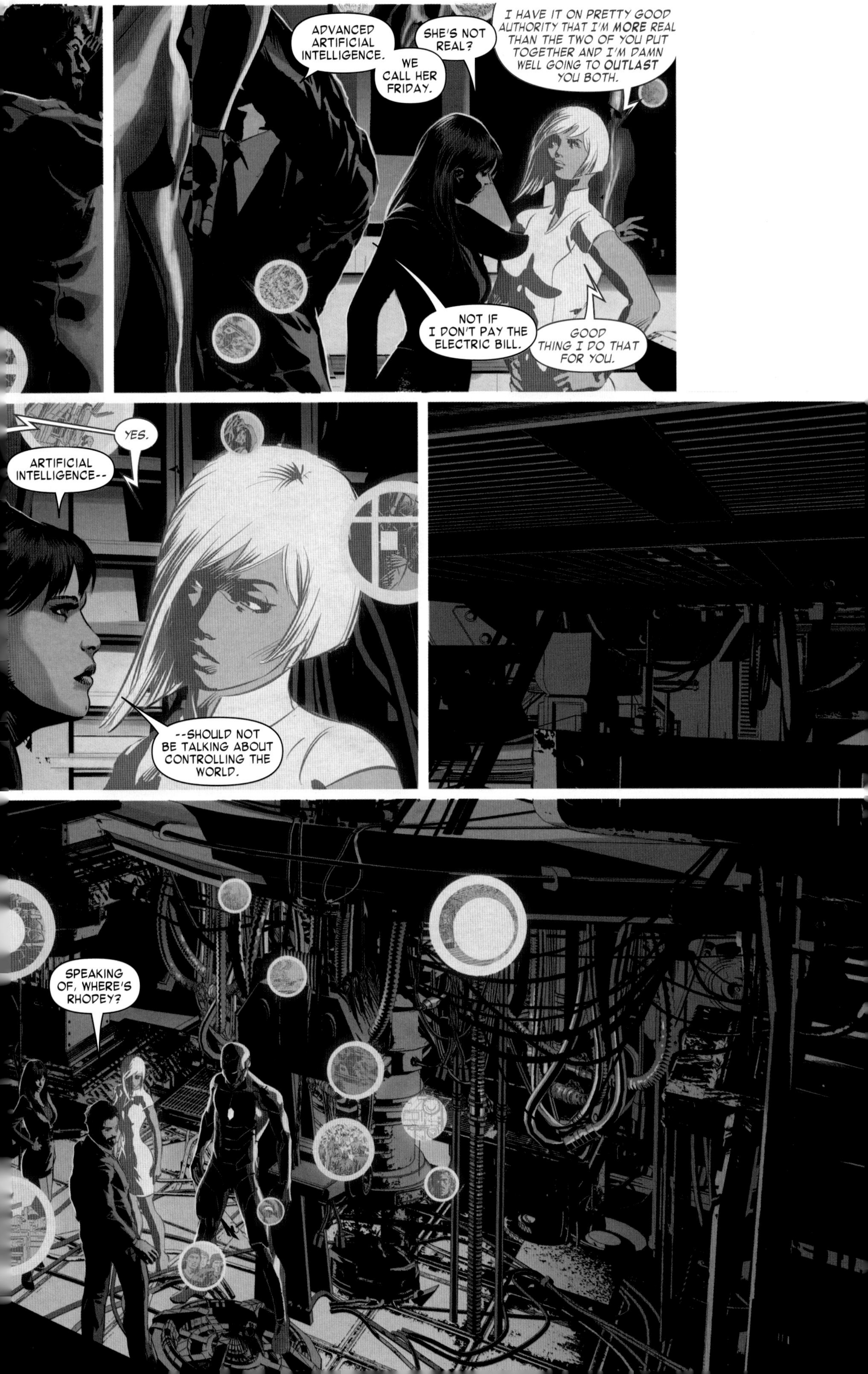
ADVANCED ARTIFICIAL INTELLIGENCE.
WE CALL HER FRIDAY.
SHE'S NOT REAL?
I HAVE IT ON PRETTY GOOD AUTHORITY THAT I'M MORE REAL THAN THE TWO OF YOU PUT TOGETHER AND I'M DAMN WELL GOING TO OUTLAST YOU BOTH.
NOT IF I DON'T PAY THE ELECTRIC BILL.
GOOD THING I DO THAT FOR YOU.
ARTIFICIAL INTELLIGENCE--
YES.
--SHOULD NOT BE TALKING ABOUT CONTROLLING THE WORLD.
SPEAKING OF, WHERE'S RHODEY?

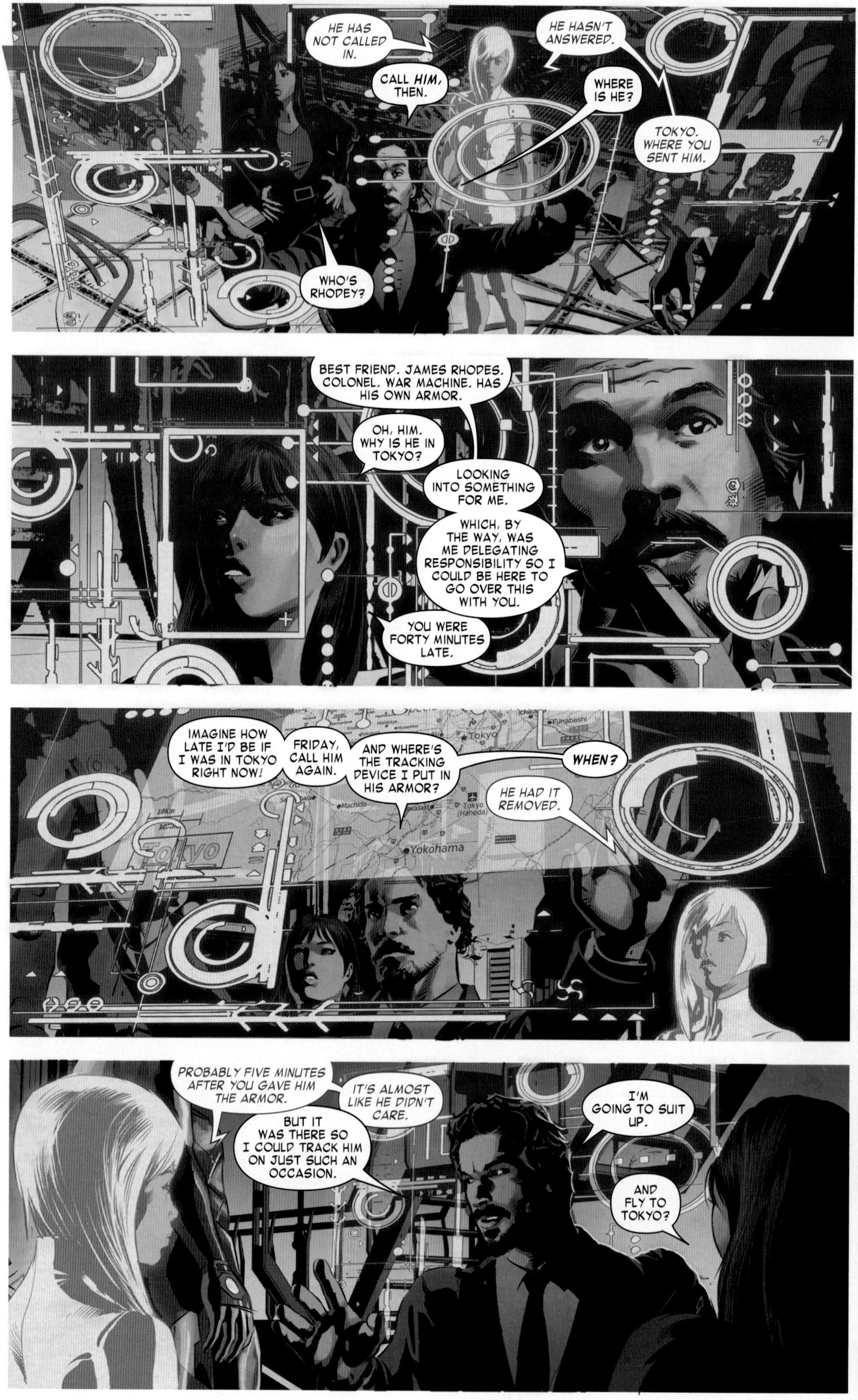
HE HAS NOT CALLED IN.
HE HASN'T ANSWERED.
CALL *HIM*, THEN.
WHERE IS HE?
TOKYO. WHERE YOU SENT HIM.
WHO'S RHODEY?
BEST FRIEND. JAMES RHODES. COLONEL. WAR MACHINE. HAS HIS OWN ARMOR.
OH, HIM. WHY IS HE IN TOKYO?
LOOKING INTO SOMETHING FOR ME.
WHICH, BY THE WAY, WAS ME DELEGATING RESPONSIBILITY SO I COULD BE HERE TO GO OVER THIS WITH YOU.
YOU WERE FORTY MINUTES LATE.
IMAGINE HOW LATE I'D BE IF I WAS IN TOKYO RIGHT NOW!
FRIDAY, CALL HIM AGAIN.
AND WHERE'S THE TRACKING DEVICE I PUT IN HIS ARMOR?
WHEN?
HE HAD IT REMOVED.
PROBABLY FIVE MINUTES AFTER YOU GAVE HIM THE ARMOR.
IT'S ALMOST LIKE HE DIDN'T CARE.
BUT IT WAS THERE SO I COULD TRACK HIM ON JUST SUCH AN OCCASION.
I'M GOING TO SUIT UP.
AND FLY TO TOKYO?

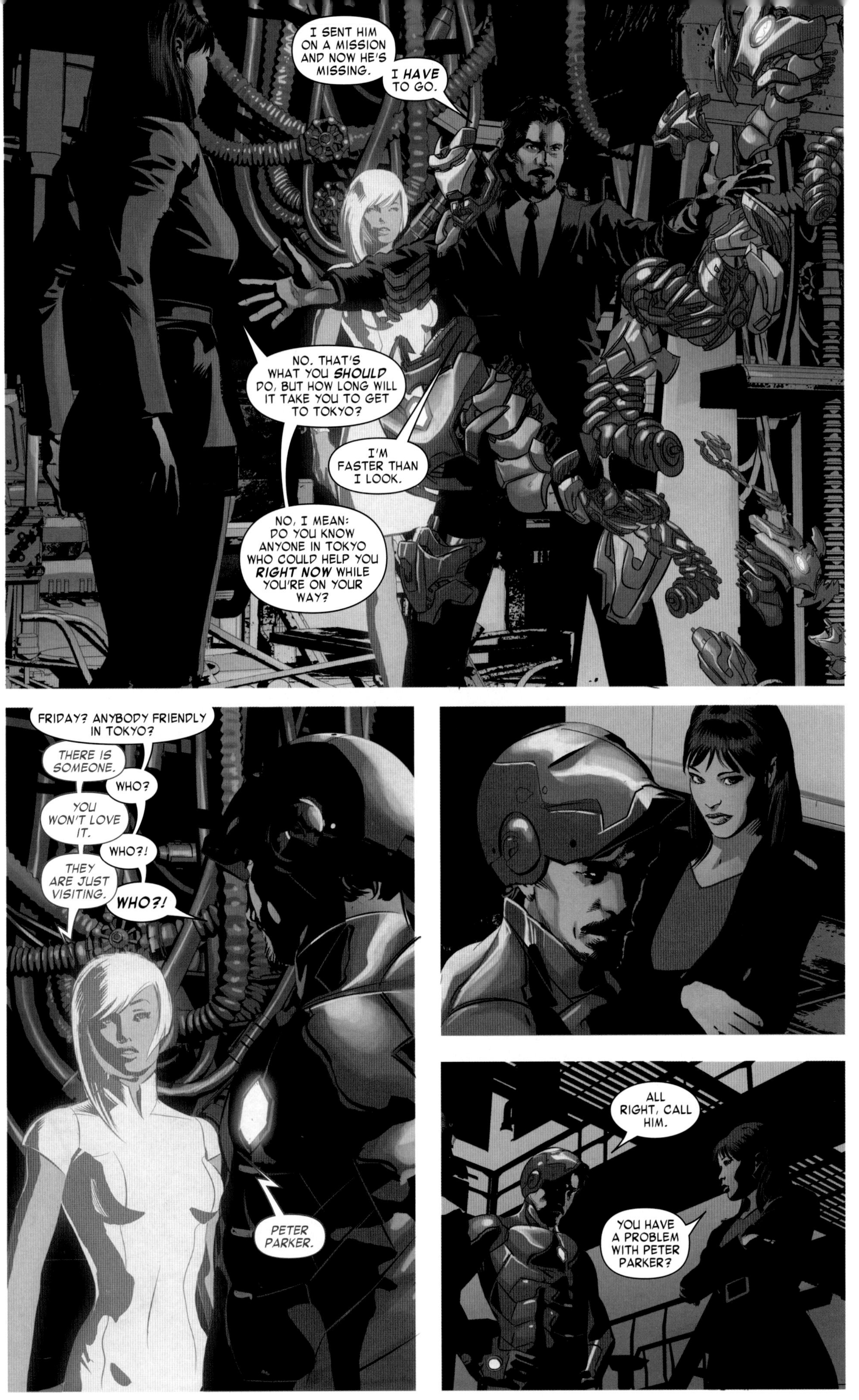
I SENT HIM ON A MISSION AND NOW HE'S MISSING.
I *HAVE* TO GO.
NO. THAT'S WHAT YOU *SHOULD* DO, BUT HOW LONG WILL IT TAKE YOU TO GET TO TOKYO?
I'M FASTER THAN I LOOK.
NO, I MEAN: DO YOU KNOW ANYONE IN TOKYO WHO COULD HELP YOU *RIGHT NOW* WHILE YOU'RE ON YOUR WAY?
FRIDAY? ANYBODY FRIENDLY IN TOKYO?
THERE IS SOMEONE.
WHO?
YOU WON'T LOVE IT.
WHO?!
THEY ARE JUST VISITING.
WHO?!
PETER PARKER.
ALL RIGHT, CALL HIM.
YOU HAVE A PROBLEM WITH PETER PARKER?

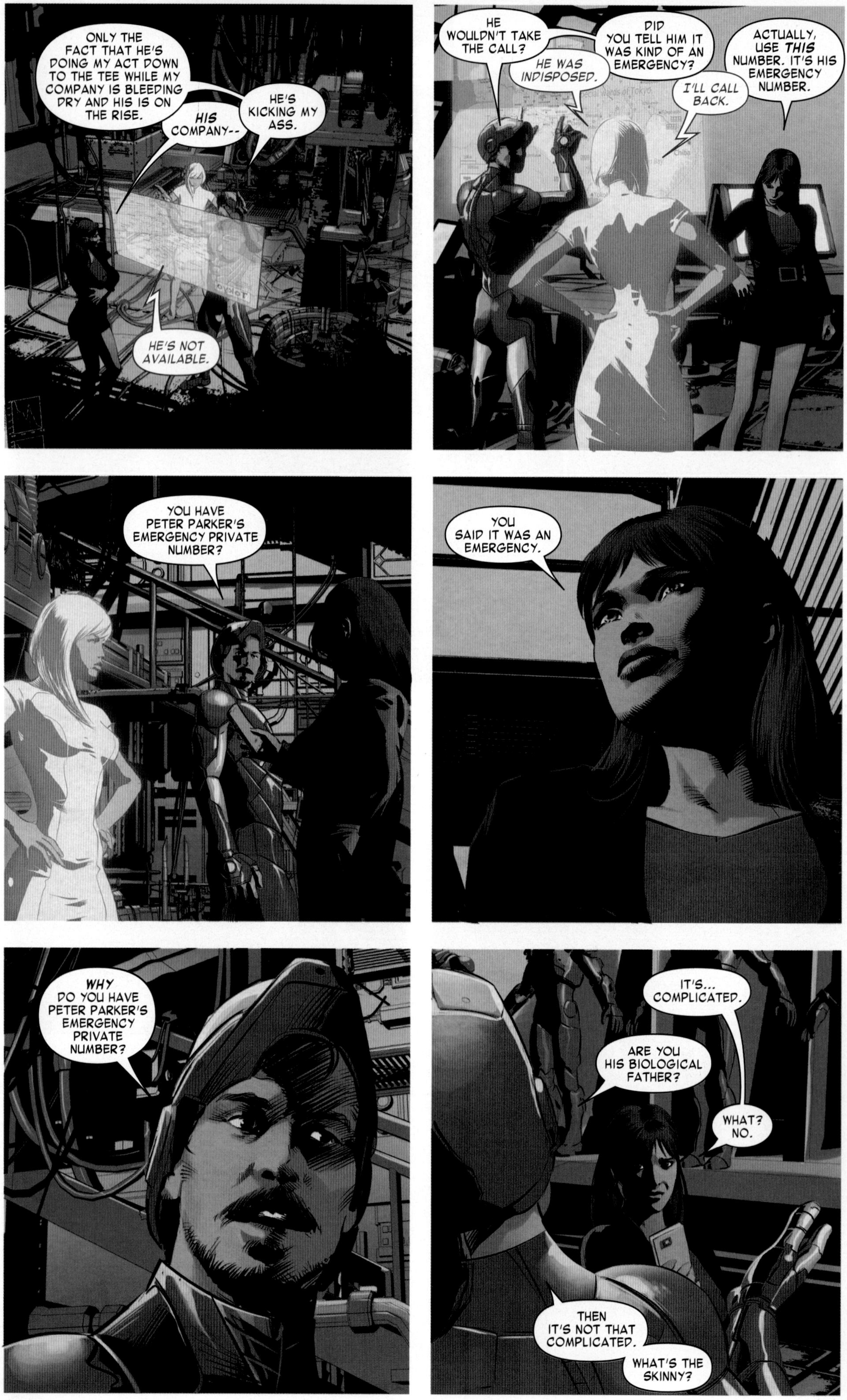
ONLY THE FACT THAT HE'S DOING MY ACT DOWN TO THE TEE WHILE MY COMPANY IS BLEEDING DRY AND HIS IS ON THE RISE.
HIS COMPANY--
HE'S KICKING MY ASS.
HE'S NOT AVAILABLE.
HE WOULDN'T TAKE THE CALL?
HE WAS INDISPOSED.
DID YOU TELL HIM IT WAS KIND OF AN EMERGENCY?
I'LL CALL BACK.
ACTUALLY, USE THIS NUMBER. IT'S HIS EMERGENCY NUMBER.
YOU HAVE PETER PARKER'S EMERGENCY PRIVATE NUMBER?
YOU SAID IT WAS AN EMERGENCY.
WHY DO YOU HAVE PETER PARKER'S EMERGENCY PRIVATE NUMBER?
IT'S... COMPLICATED.
ARE YOU HIS BIOLOGICAL FATHER?
WHAT? NO.
THEN IT'S NOT THAT COMPLICATED.
WHAT'S THE SKINNY?

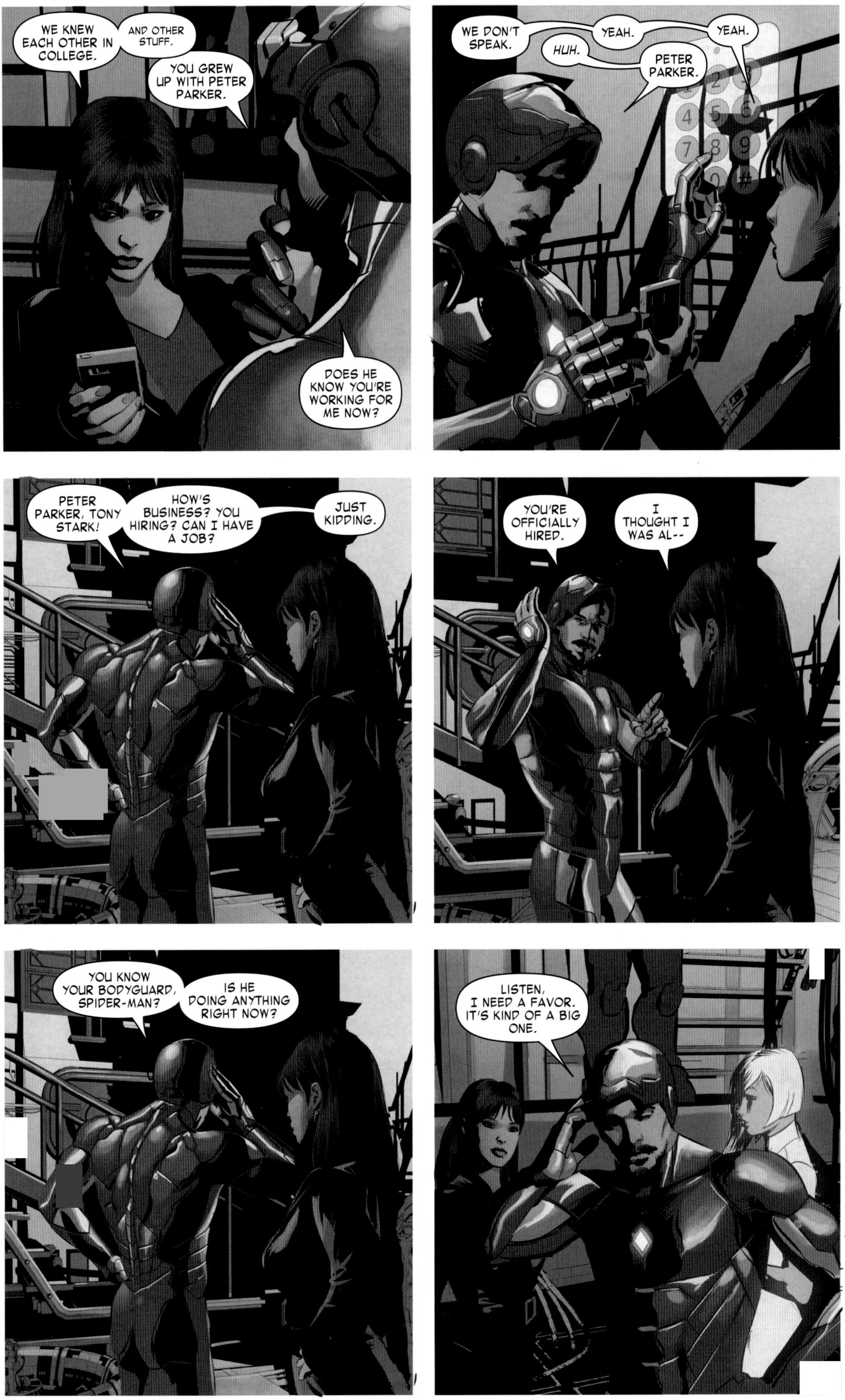
WE KNEW EACH OTHER IN COLLEGE.
AND OTHER STUFF.
YOU GREW UP WITH PETER PARKER.
DOES HE KNOW YOU'RE WORKING FOR ME NOW?
WE DON'T SPEAK.
YEAH.
HUH.
YEAH.
PETER PARKER.
PETER PARKER, TONY STARK!
HOW'S BUSINESS? YOU HIRING? CAN I HAVE A JOB?
JUST KIDDING.
YOU'RE OFFICIALLY HIRED.
I THOUGHT I WAS AL--
YOU KNOW YOUR BODYGUARD, SPIDER-MAN?
IS HE DOING ANYTHING RIGHT NOW?
LISTEN, I NEED A FAVOR. IT'S KIND OF A BIG ONE.

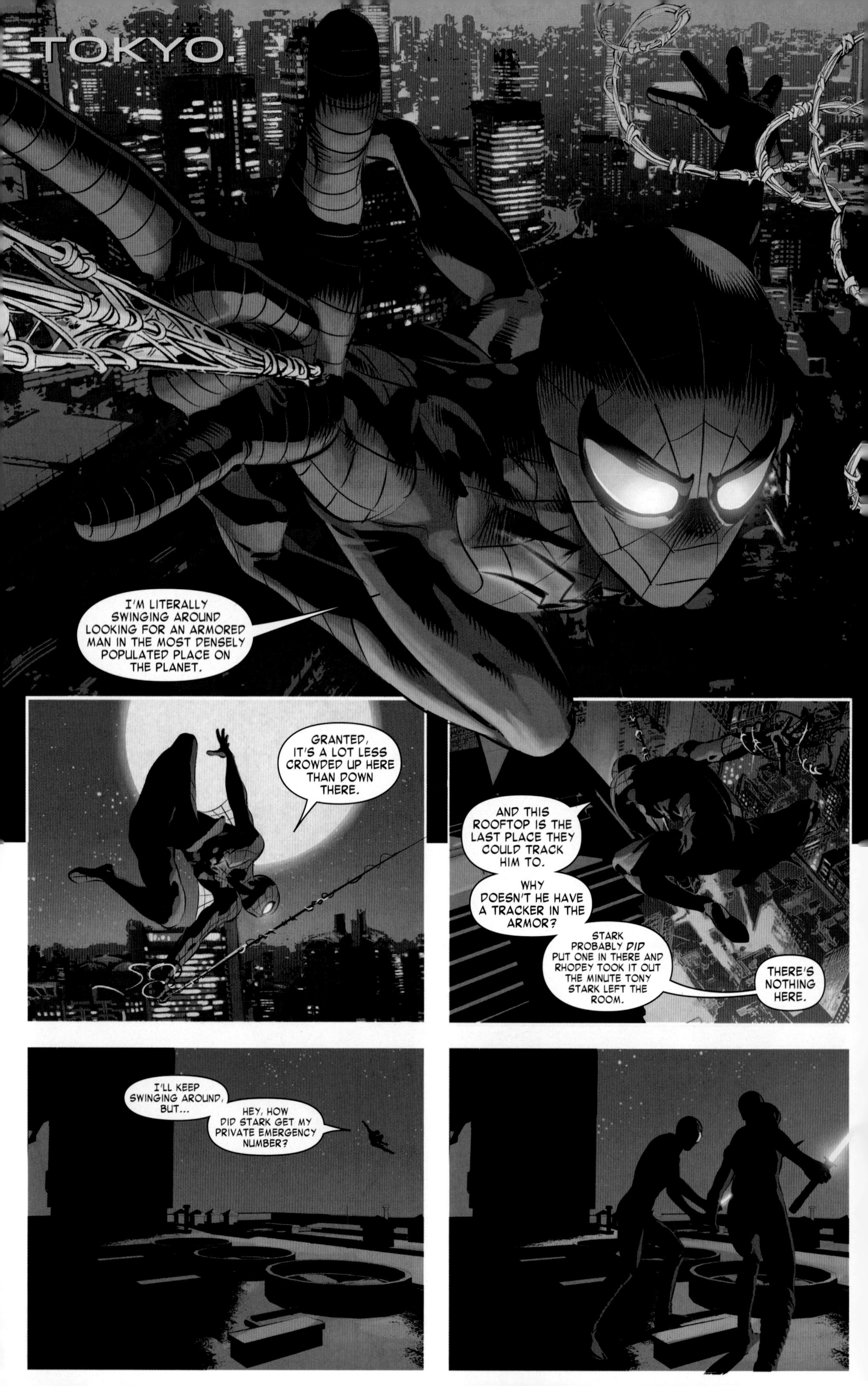
TOKYO.
I'M LITERALLY SWINGING AROUND LOOKING FOR AN ARMORED MAN IN THE MOST DENSELY POPULATED PLACE ON THE PLANET.
GRANTED, IT'S A LOT LESS CROWDED UP HERE THAN DOWN THERE.
AND THIS ROOFTOP IS THE LAST PLACE THEY COULD TRACK HIM TO.
WHY DOESN'T HE HAVE A TRACKER IN THE ARMOR?
STARK PROBABLY DID PUT ONE IN THERE AND RHODEY TOOK IT OUT THE MINUTE TONY STARK LEFT THE ROOM.
THERE'S NOTHING HERE.
I'LL KEEP SWINGING AROUND, BUT...
HEY, HOW DID STARK GET MY PRIVATE EMERGENCY NUMBER?

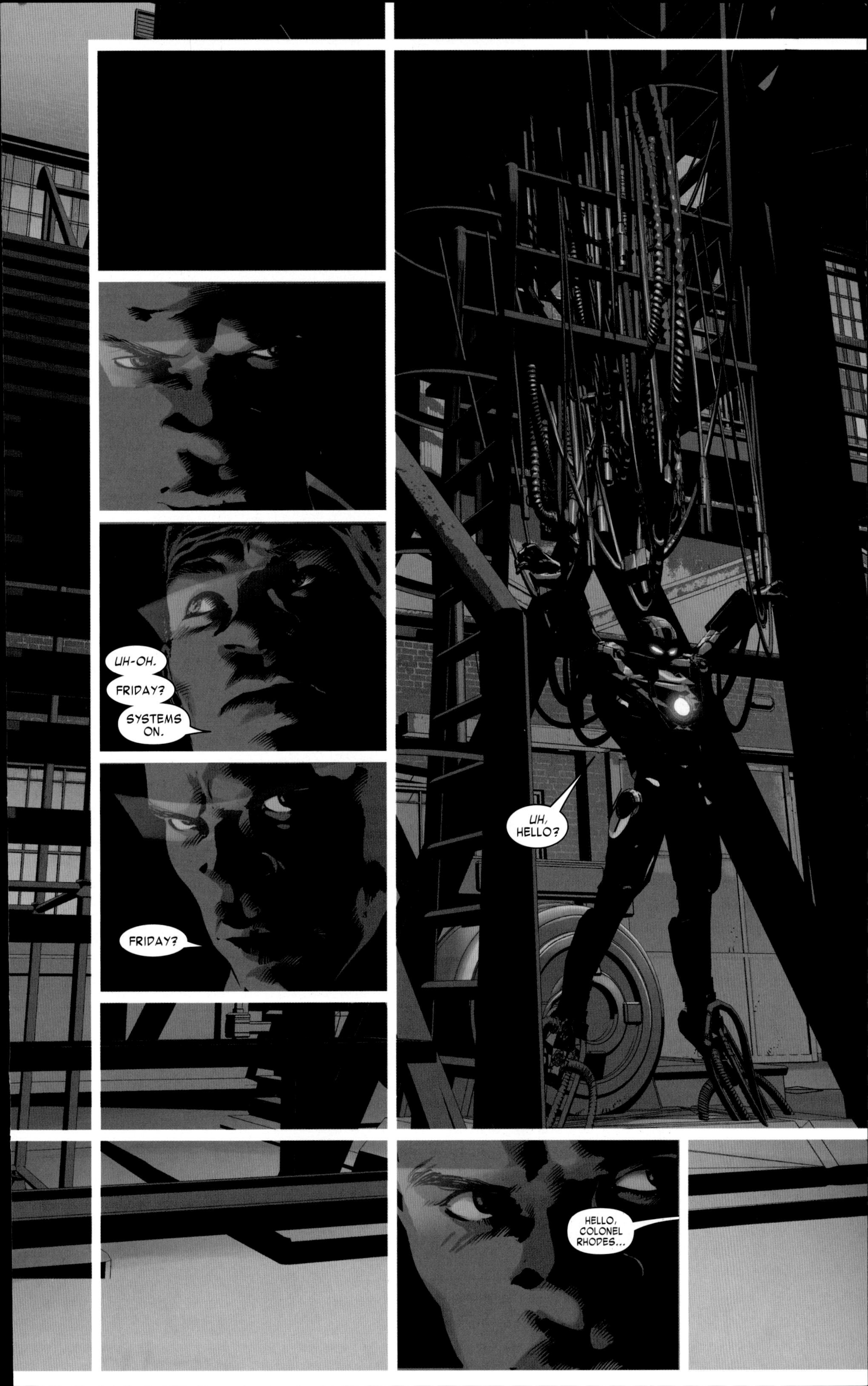
UH-OH.
FRIDAY?
SYSTEMS ON.
FRIDAY?
UH, HELLO?
HELLO, COLONEL RHODES...

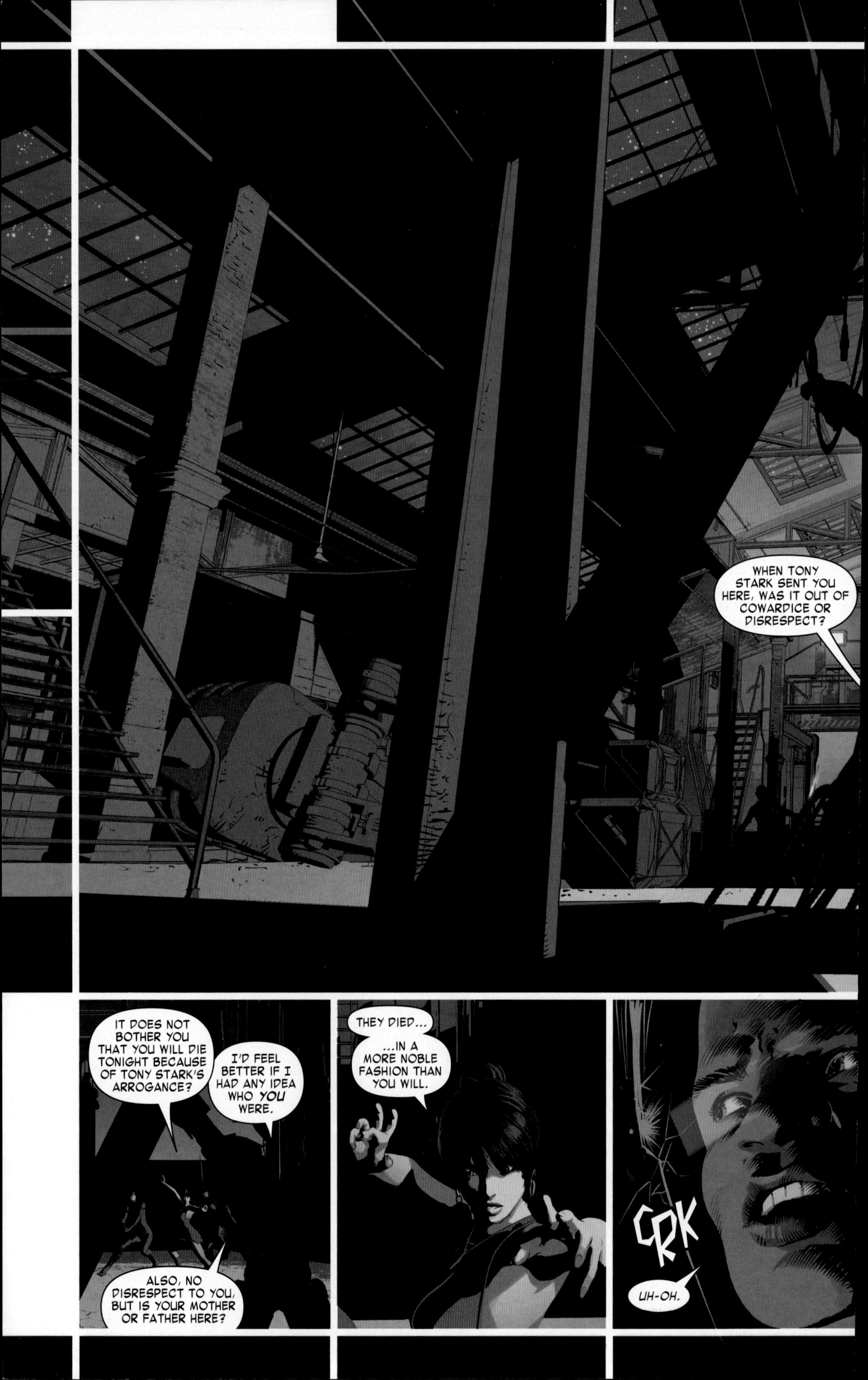

WHEN TONY STARK SENT YOU HERE, WAS IT OUT OF COWARDICE OR DISRESPECT?
IT DOES NOT BOTHER YOU THAT YOU WILL DIE TONIGHT BECAUSE OF TONY STARK'S ARROGANCE?
I'D FEEL BETTER IF I HAD ANY IDEA WHO YOU WERE.
ALSO, NO DISRESPECT TO YOU, BUT IS YOUR MOTHER OR FATHER HERE?
THEY DIED...
...IN A MORE NOBLE FASHION THAN YOU WILL.
CRK
UH-OH.

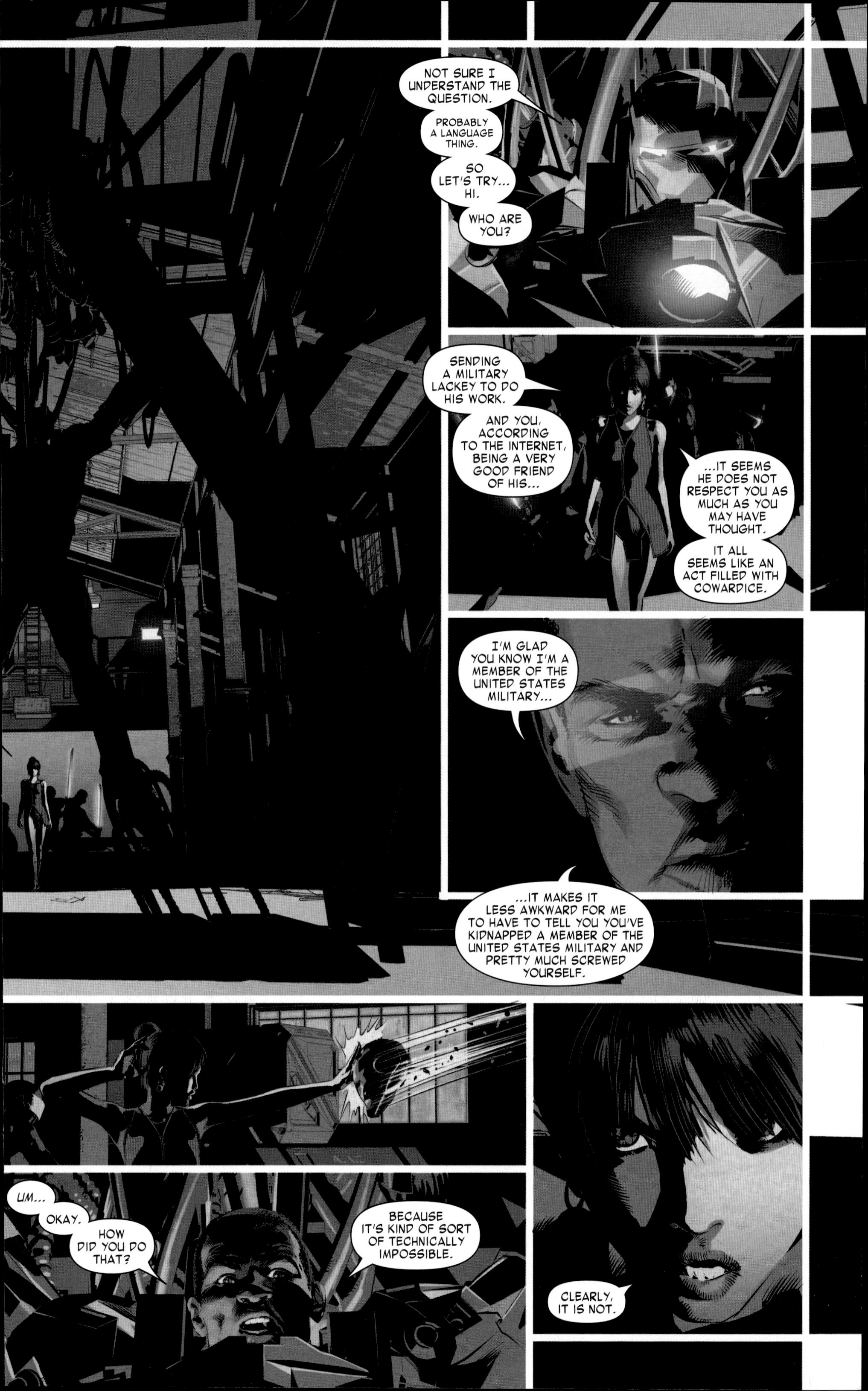

NOT SURE I UNDERSTAND THE QUESTION.
PROBABLY A LANGUAGE THING.
SO LET'S TRY... HI.
WHO ARE YOU?
SENDING A MILITARY LACKEY TO DO HIS WORK.
AND YOU, ACCORDING TO THE INTERNET, BEING A VERY GOOD FRIEND OF HIS...
...IT SEEMS HE DOES NOT RESPECT YOU AS MUCH AS YOU MAY HAVE THOUGHT.
IT ALL SEEMS LIKE AN ACT FILLED WITH COWARDICE.
I'M GLAD YOU KNOW I'M A MEMBER OF THE UNITED STATES MILITARY...
...IT MAKES IT LESS AWKWARD FOR ME TO HAVE TO TELL YOU YOU'VE KIDNAPPED A MEMBER OF THE UNITED STATES MILITARY AND PRETTY MUCH SCREWED YOURSELF.
UM...
OKAY.
HOW DID YOU DO THAT?
BECAUSE IT'S KIND OF SORT OF TECHNICALLY IMPOSSIBLE.
CLEARLY, IT IS NOT.

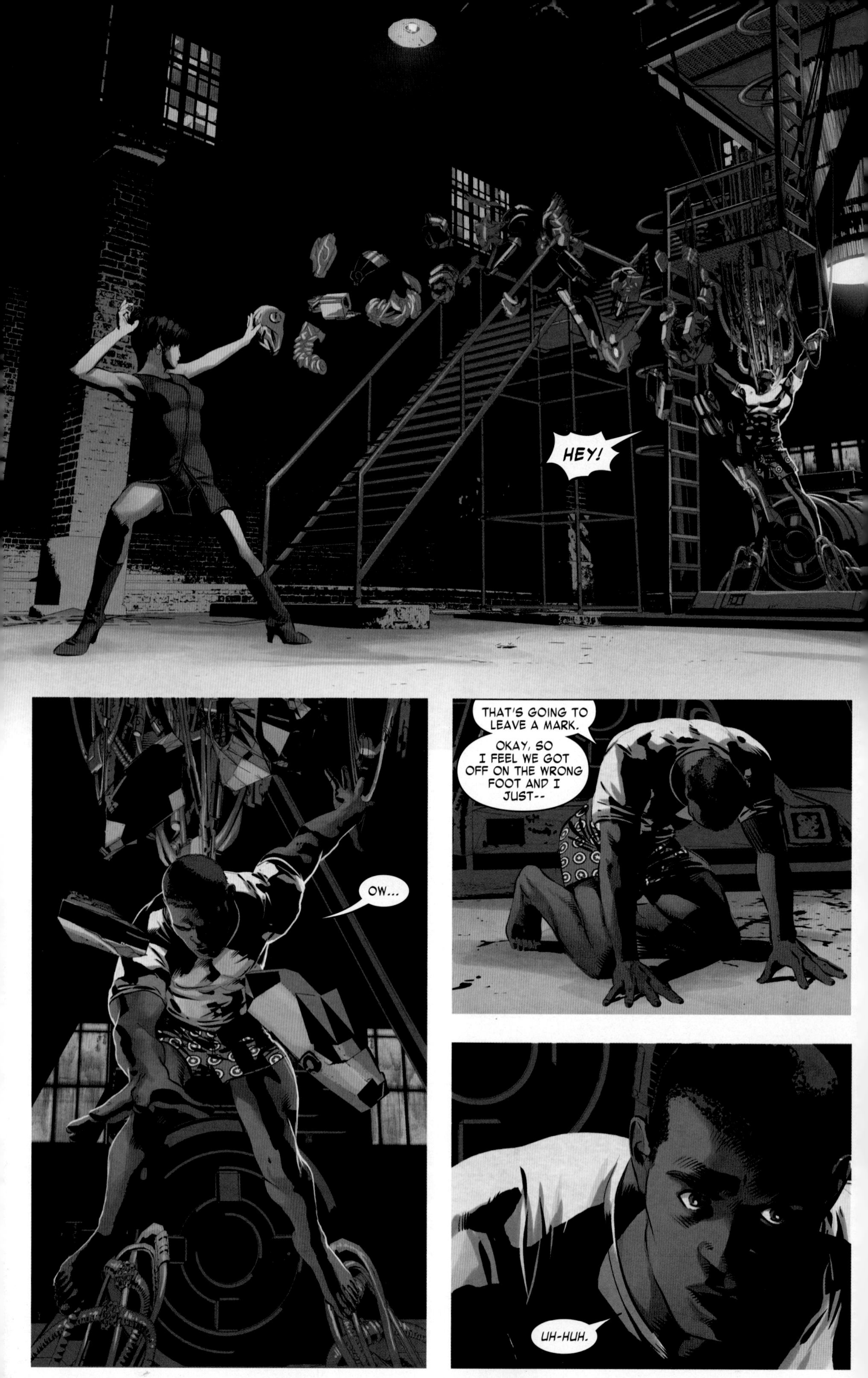
HEY!
OW...
THAT'S GOING TO LEAVE A MARK.
OKAY, SO I FEEL WE GOT OFF ON THE WRONG FOOT AND I JUST--
UH-HUH.

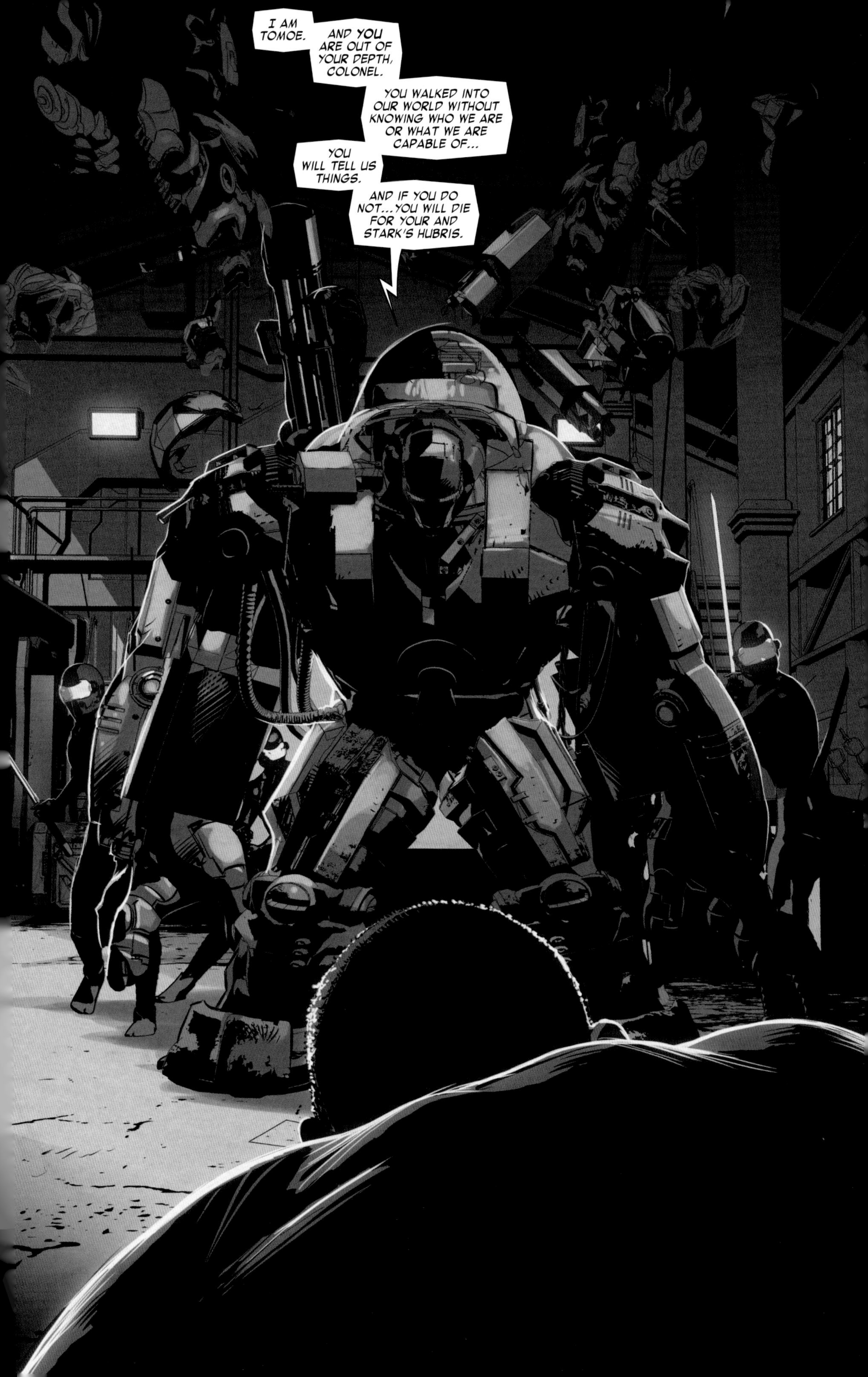
I AM TOMOE.
AND YOU ARE OUT OF YOUR DEPTH, COLONEL.
YOU WALKED INTO OUR WORLD WITHOUT KNOWING WHO WE ARE OR WHAT WE ARE CAPABLE OF...
YOU WILL TELL US THINGS.
AND IF YOU DO NOT...YOU WILL DIE FOR YOUR AND STARK'S HUBRIS.

"AND WHEN TONY STARK COMES LOOKING FOR YOU...
"...HE WILL DISCOVER HE HAS CAUSED HIS FRIEND'S DEATH.
HOLLYWOOD
"I WONDER, WITH HIS DYING BREATH...
"...IF HE WILL CRY FOR YOU."
CLANG CLANK
"OH MY GOD!
"IT'S, LIKE, THREE IN THE MORNING."

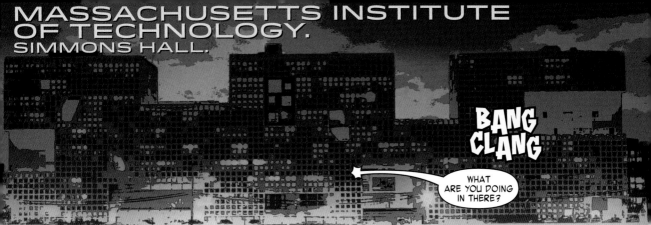

MASSACHUSETTS INSTITUTE OF TECHNOLOGY.
SIMMONS HALL.

BANG CLANG

WHAT ARE YOU DOING IN THERE?

ZZZ/// CLANG

THUMP THUMP THUMP

WHAT *IS* SHE DOING IN THERE?

SHE SHOULDN'T EVEN *BE* HERE.

SHE'S, LIKE, ELEVEN YEARS OLD.

ANSWER THE DOOR!

WE *KNOW* YOU'RE IN THERE, RIRI!

WHAT DO YOU WANT? IT'S THREE O'CLOCK IN THE MORNING!

WHATEVER, DISNEY CHANNEL.

WHATEVER YOU'RE DOING IN THERE...DO IT *QUIETER*.

SLAM

YOU HAVE TO BE KIDDING ME.

KID'S A REAL PIECE OF WORK.

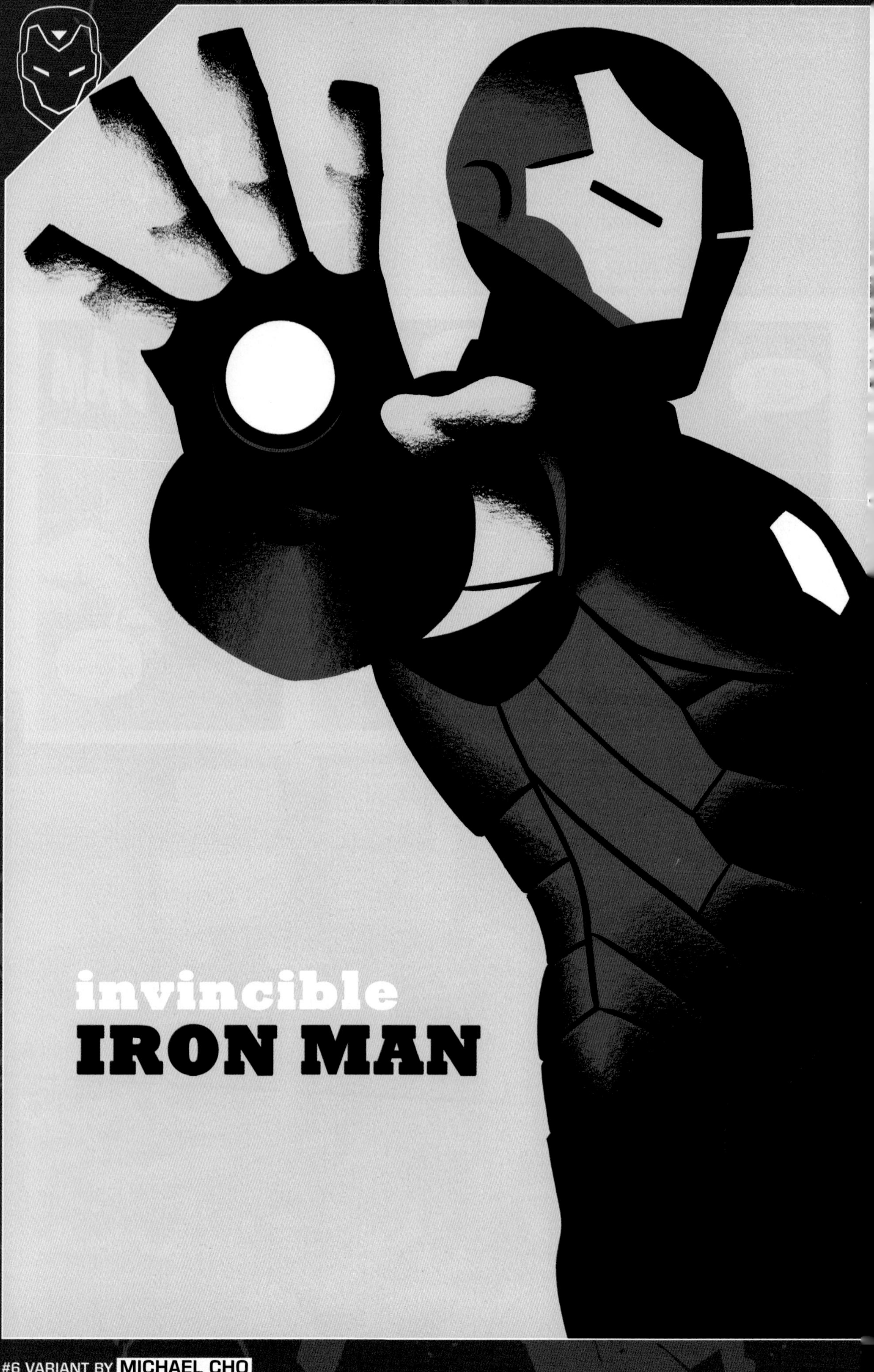
invincible
IRON MAN

#6 VARIANT BY MICHAEL CHO

#8

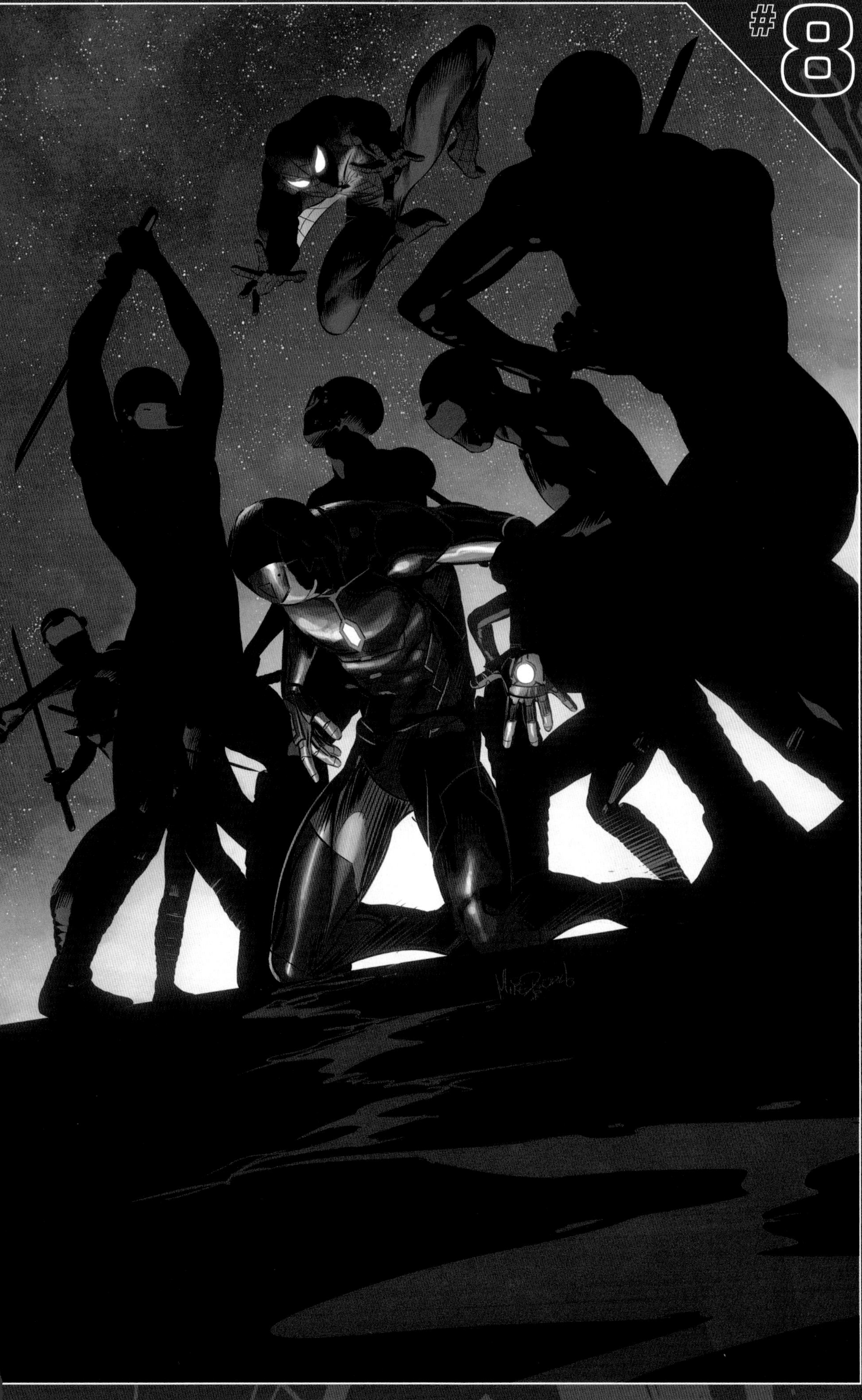

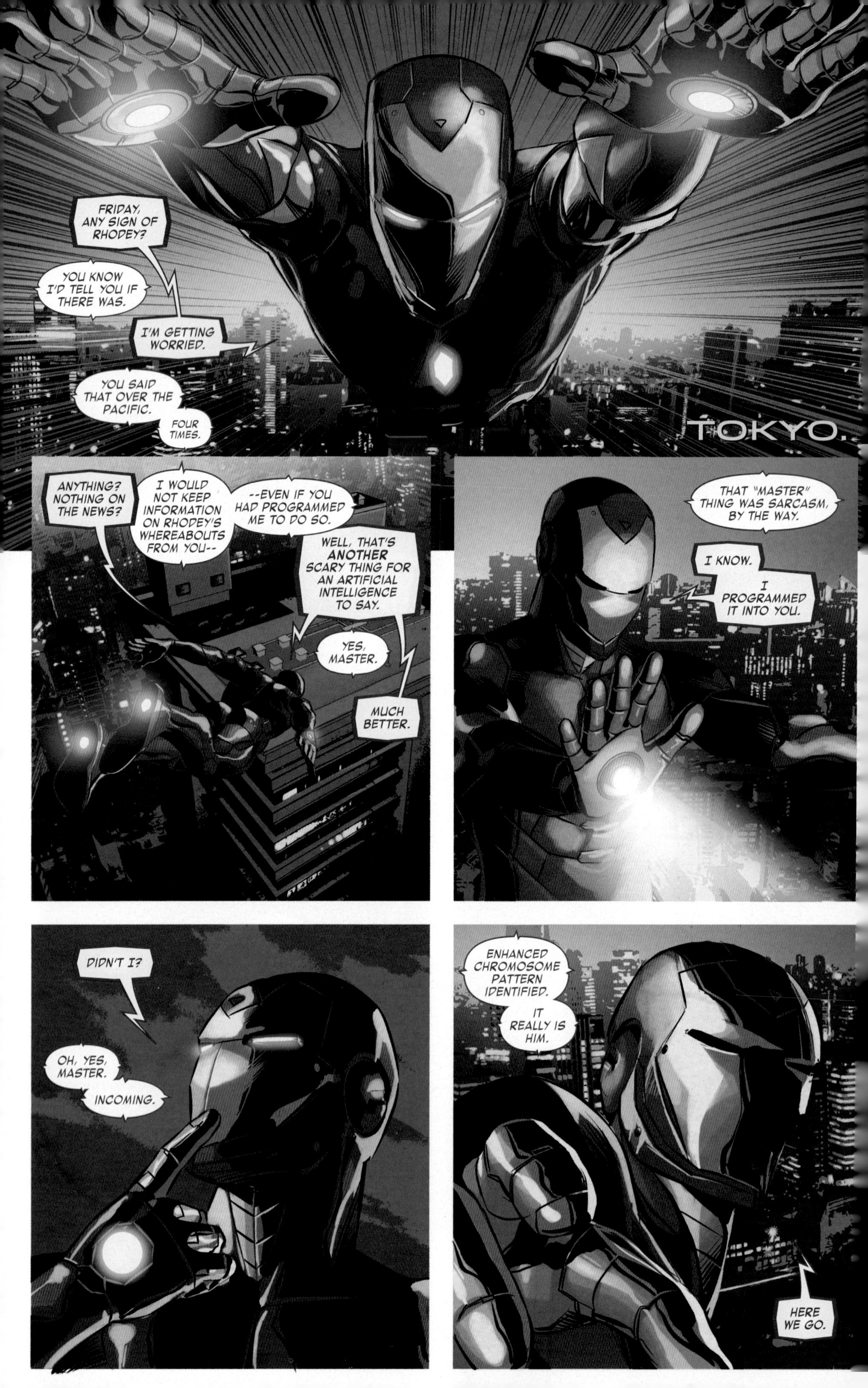
FRIDAY, ANY SIGN OF RHODEY?
YOU KNOW I'D TELL YOU IF THERE WAS.
I'M GETTING WORRIED.
YOU SAID THAT OVER THE PACIFIC.
FOUR TIMES.
TOKYO.
ANYTHING? NOTHING ON THE NEWS?
I WOULD NOT KEEP INFORMATION ON RHODEY'S WHEREABOUTS FROM YOU--
--EVEN IF YOU HAD PROGRAMMED ME TO DO SO.
WELL, THAT'S ANOTHER SCARY THING FOR AN ARTIFICIAL INTELLIGENCE TO SAY.
YES, MASTER.
MUCH BETTER.
THAT "MASTER" THING WAS SARCASM, BY THE WAY.
I KNOW.
I PROGRAMMED IT INTO YOU.
DIDN'T I?
OH, YES, MASTER.
INCOMING.
ENHANCED CHROMOSOME PATTERN IDENTIFIED.
IT REALLY IS HIM.
HERE WE GO.

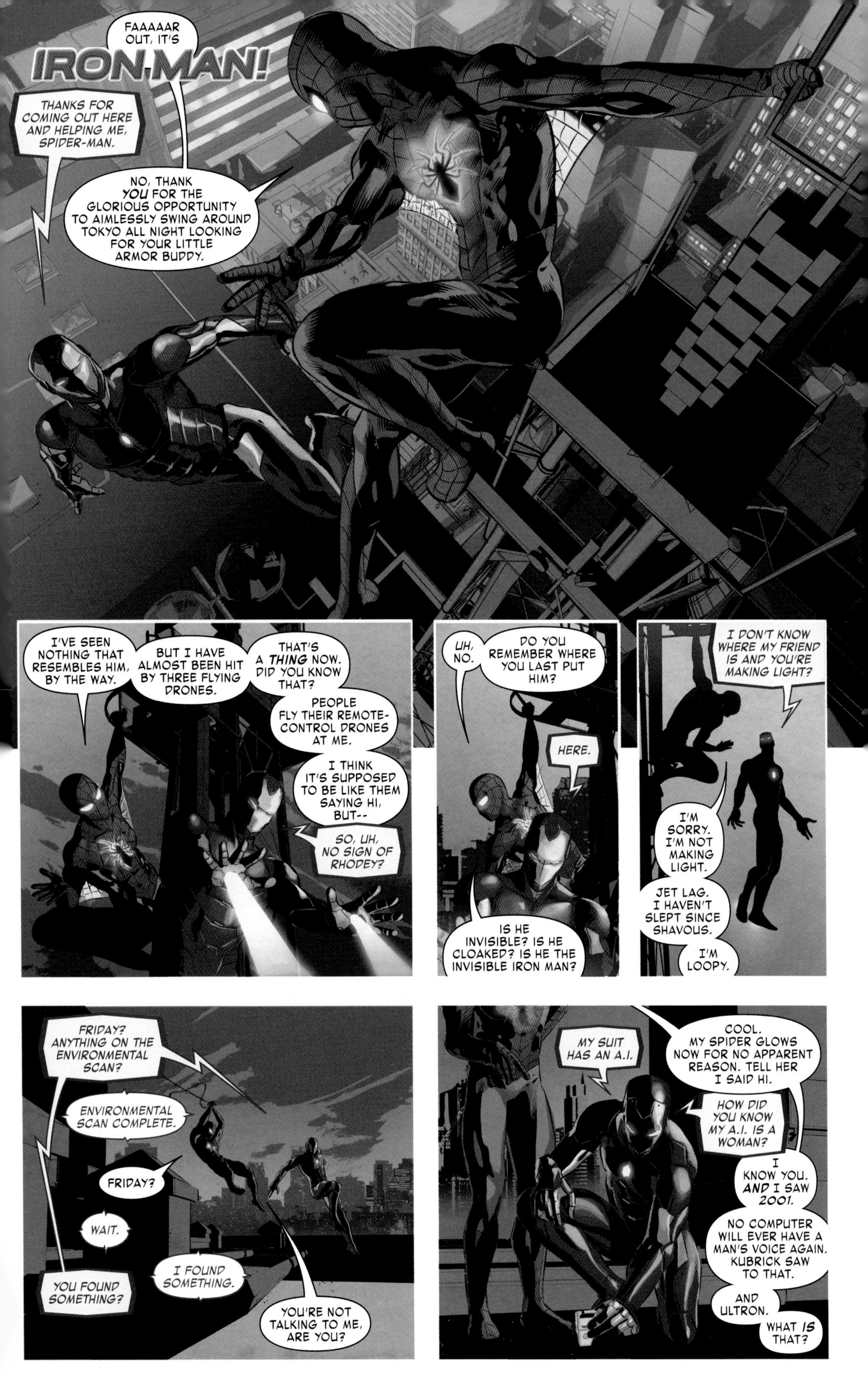
FAAAAAR OUT, IT'S
IRON MAN!
THANKS FOR COMING OUT HERE AND HELPING ME, SPIDER-MAN.
NO, THANK YOU FOR THE GLORIOUS OPPORTUNITY TO AIMLESSLY SWING AROUND TOKYO ALL NIGHT LOOKING FOR YOUR LITTLE ARMOR BUDDY.
I'VE SEEN NOTHING THAT RESEMBLES HIM, BY THE WAY.
BUT I HAVE ALMOST BEEN HIT BY THREE FLYING DRONES.
THAT'S A THING NOW. DID YOU KNOW THAT?
PEOPLE FLY THEIR REMOTE-CONTROL DRONES AT ME.
I THINK IT'S SUPPOSED TO BE LIKE THEM SAYING HI, BUT--
SO, UH, NO SIGN OF RHODEY?
UH, NO.
DO YOU REMEMBER WHERE YOU LAST PUT HIM?
HERE.
IS HE INVISIBLE? IS HE CLOAKED? IS HE THE INVISIBLE IRON MAN?
I DON'T KNOW WHERE MY FRIEND IS AND YOU'RE MAKING LIGHT?
I'M SORRY. I'M NOT MAKING LIGHT.
JET LAG. I HAVEN'T SLEPT SINCE SHAVOUS.
I'M LOOPY.
FRIDAY? ANYTHING ON THE ENVIRONMENTAL SCAN?
ENVIRONMENTAL SCAN COMPLETE.
FRIDAY?
WAIT.
I FOUND SOMETHING.
YOU FOUND SOMETHING?
YOU'RE NOT TALKING TO ME, ARE YOU?
MY SUIT HAS AN A.I.
COOL. MY SPIDER GLOWS NOW FOR NO APPARENT REASON. TELL HER I SAID HI.
HOW DID YOU KNOW MY A.I. IS A WOMAN?
I KNOW YOU. AND I SAW 2001.
NO COMPUTER WILL EVER HAVE A MAN'S VOICE AGAIN. KUBRICK SAW TO THAT.
AND ULTRON.
WHAT IS THAT?

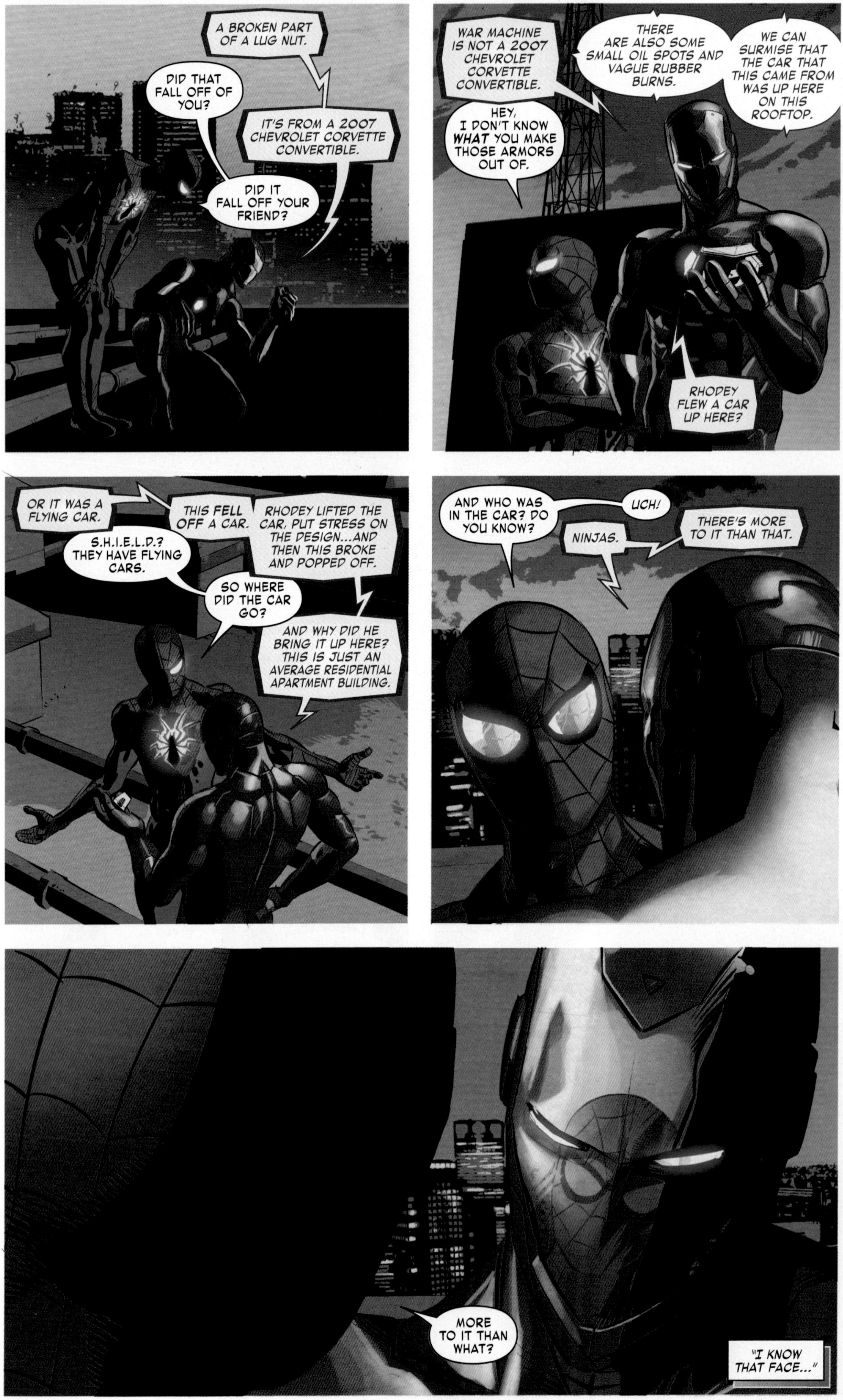
A BROKEN PART OF A LUG NUT.
DID THAT FALL OFF OF YOU?
IT'S FROM A 2007 CHEVROLET CORVETTE CONVERTIBLE.
DID IT FALL OFF YOUR FRIEND?
WAR MACHINE IS NOT A 2007 CHEVROLET CORVETTE CONVERTIBLE.
THERE ARE ALSO SOME SMALL OIL SPOTS AND VAGUE RUBBER BURNS.
WE CAN SURMISE THAT THE CAR THAT THIS CAME FROM WAS UP HERE ON THIS ROOFTOP.
HEY, I DON'T KNOW WHAT YOU MAKE THOSE ARMORS OUT OF.
RHODEY FLEW A CAR UP HERE?
OR IT WAS A FLYING CAR.
THIS FELL OFF A CAR.
RHODEY LIFTED THE CAR, PUT STRESS ON THE DESIGN...AND THEN THIS BROKE AND POPPED OFF.
S.H.I.E.L.D.? THEY HAVE FLYING CARS.
SO WHERE DID THE CAR GO?
AND WHY DID HE BRING IT UP HERE? THIS IS JUST AN AVERAGE RESIDENTIAL APARTMENT BUILDING.
AND WHO WAS IN THE CAR? DO YOU KNOW?
UCH!
NINJAS.
THERE'S MORE TO IT THAN THAT.
MORE TO IT THAN WHAT?
"I KNOW THAT FACE..."

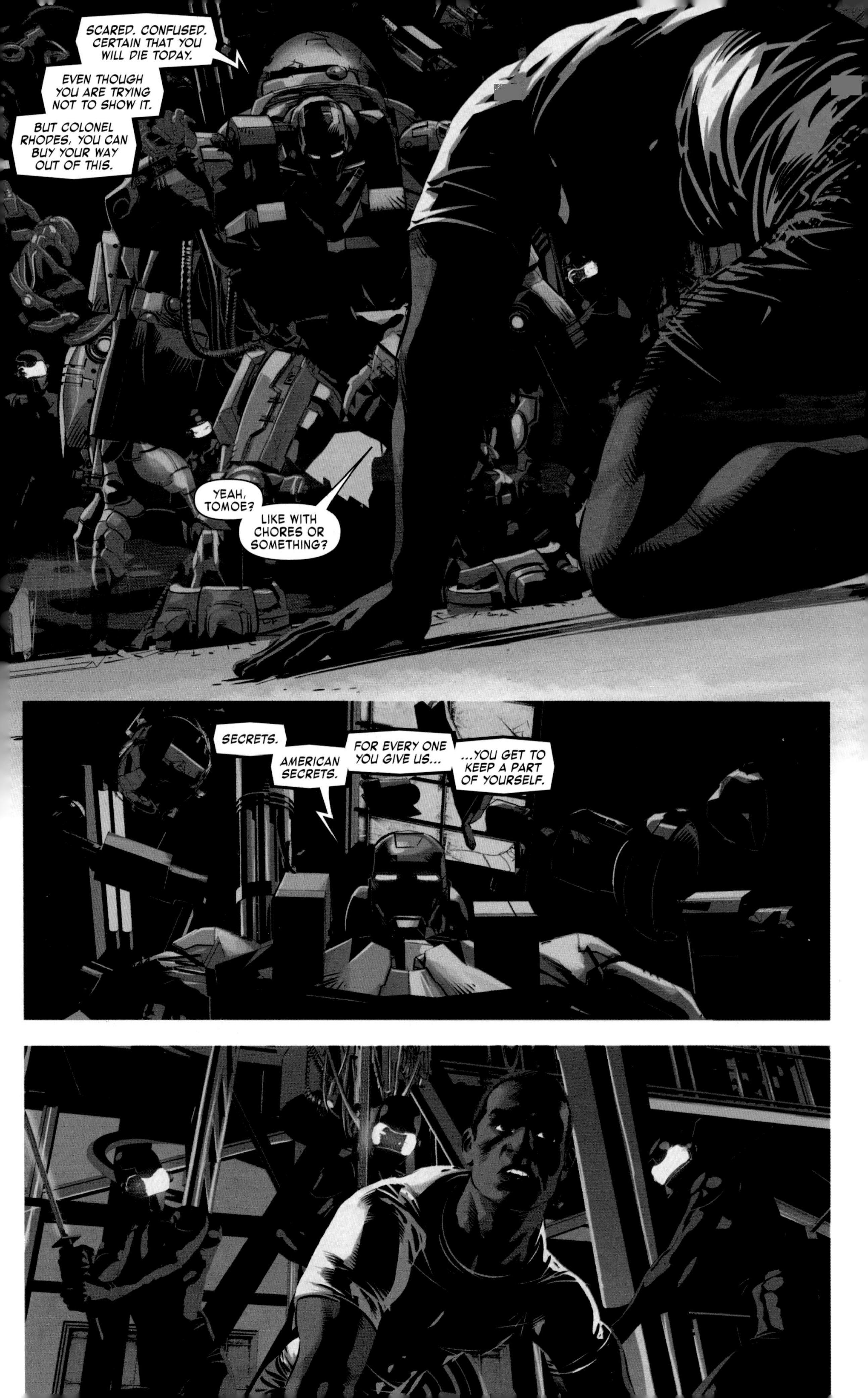
SCARED. CONFUSED. CERTAIN THAT YOU WILL DIE TODAY.
EVEN THOUGH YOU ARE TRYING NOT TO SHOW IT.
BUT COLONEL RHODES, YOU CAN BUY YOUR WAY OUT OF THIS.
YEAH, TOMOE?
LIKE WITH CHORES OR SOMETHING?
SECRETS.
AMERICAN SECRETS.
FOR EVERY ONE YOU GIVE US...
...YOU GET TO KEEP A PART OF YOURSELF.

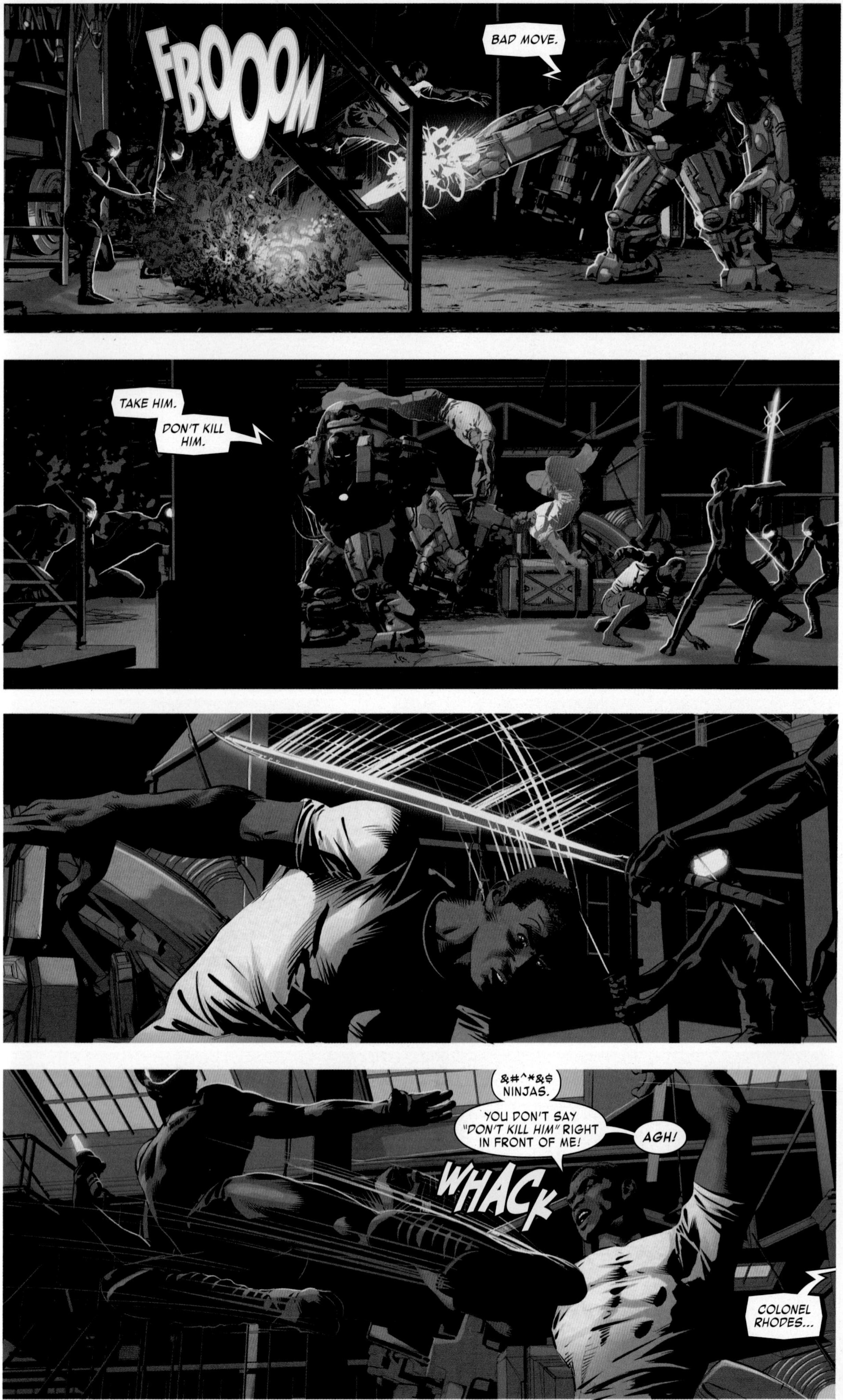
FBOOOM
BAD MOVE.
TAKE HIM.
DON'T KILL HIM.
&#^*&$ NINJAS.
YOU DON'T SAY "DON'T KILL HIM" RIGHT IN FRONT OF ME!
AGH!
WHACK
COLONEL RHODES...

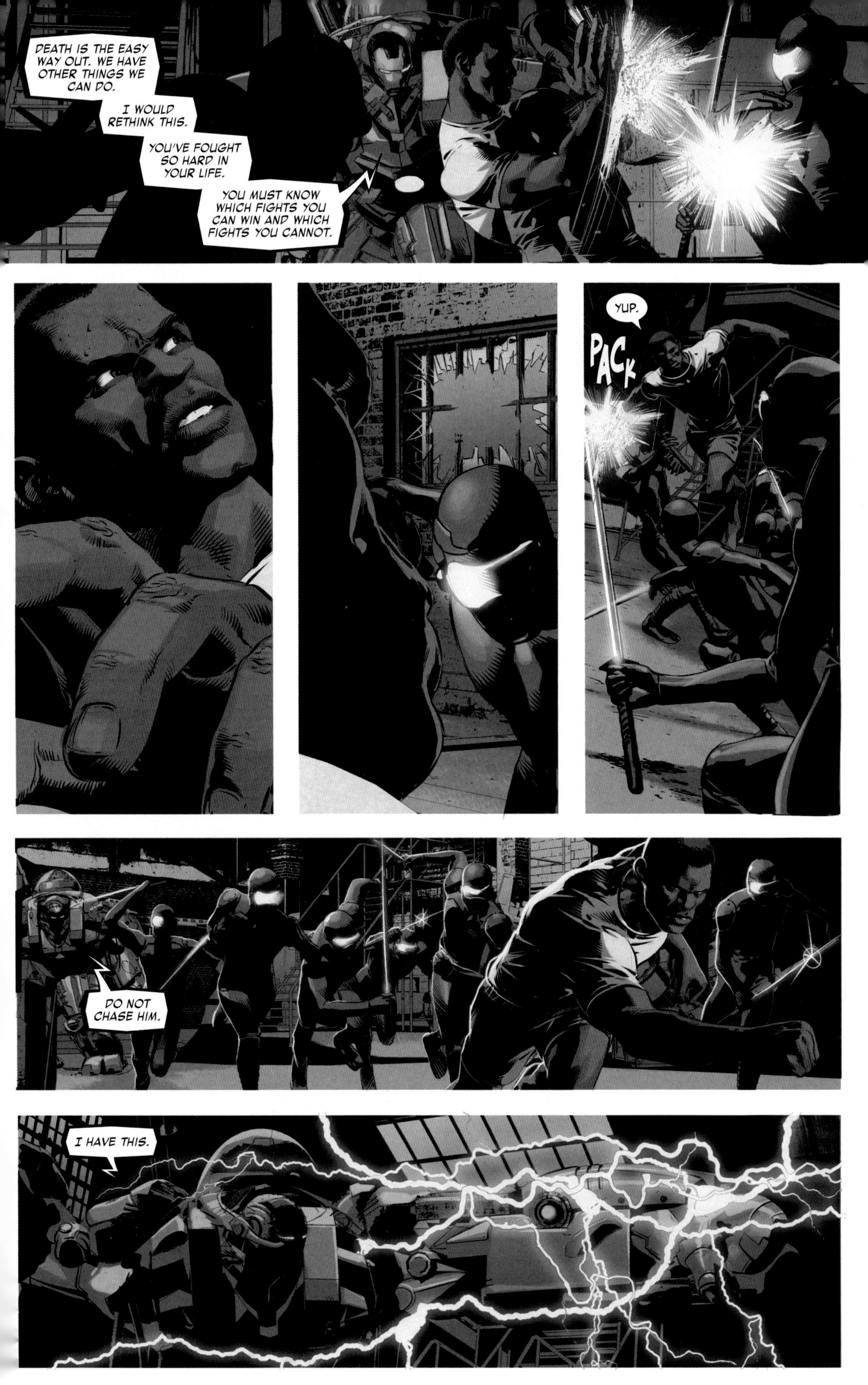
DEATH IS THE EASY WAY OUT. WE HAVE OTHER THINGS WE CAN DO.
I WOULD RETHINK THIS.
YOU'VE FOUGHT SO HARD IN YOUR LIFE.
YOU MUST KNOW WHICH FIGHTS YOU CAN WIN AND WHICH FIGHTS YOU CANNOT.
YUP.
PACK
DO NOT CHASE HIM.
I HAVE THIS.

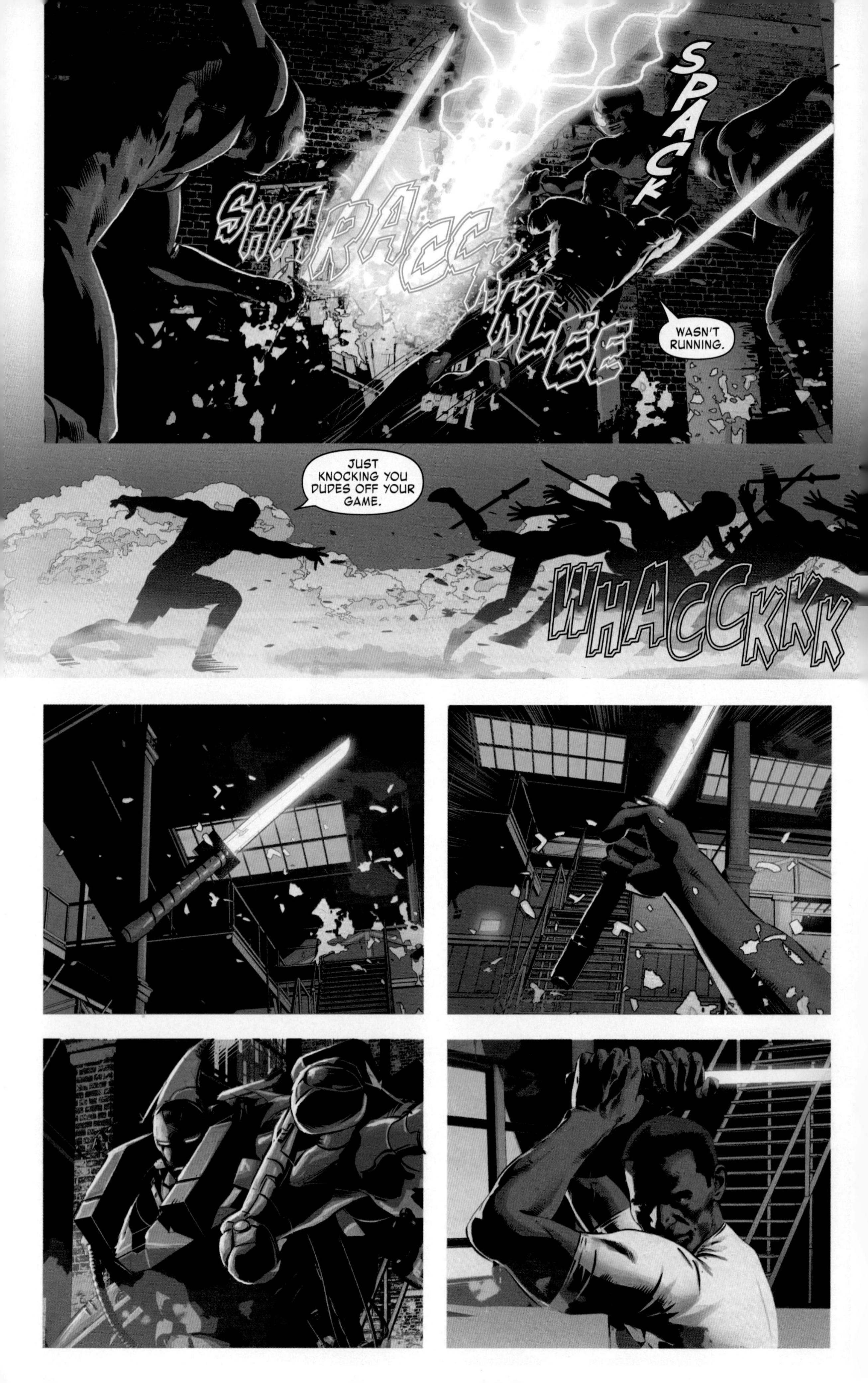
SPACK
SHARACCKLEE
WASN'T RUNNING.
JUST KNOCKING YOU DUDES OFF YOUR GAME.
WHACCKKKK

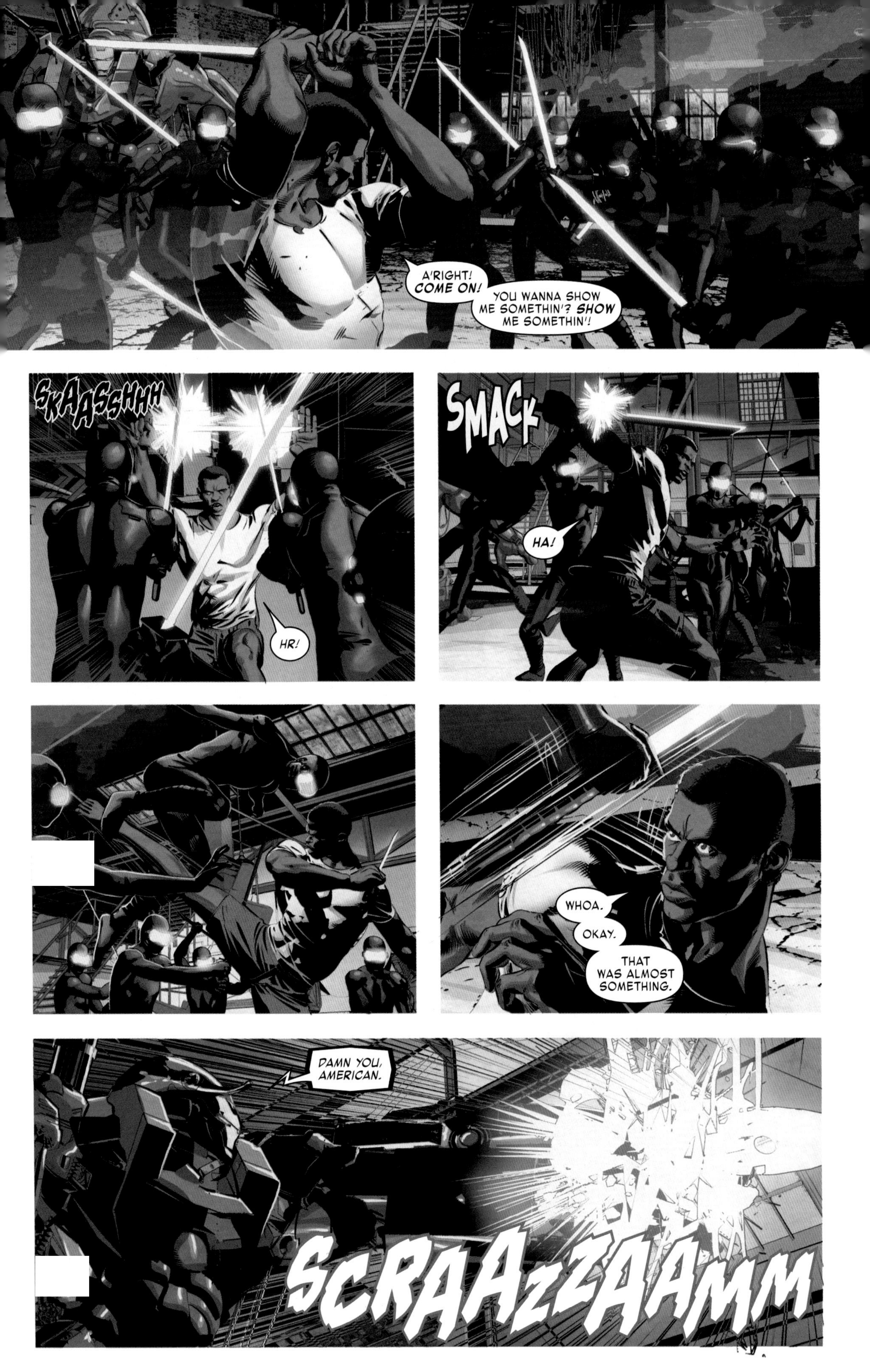
A'RIGHT! COME ON!
YOU WANNA SHOW ME SOMETHIN'? SHOW ME SOMETHIN'!
SKAASSHHH
HR!
SMACK
HA!
WHOA.
OKAY.
THAT WAS ALMOST SOMETHING.
DAMN YOU, AMERICAN.
SCRAAZZAAMM

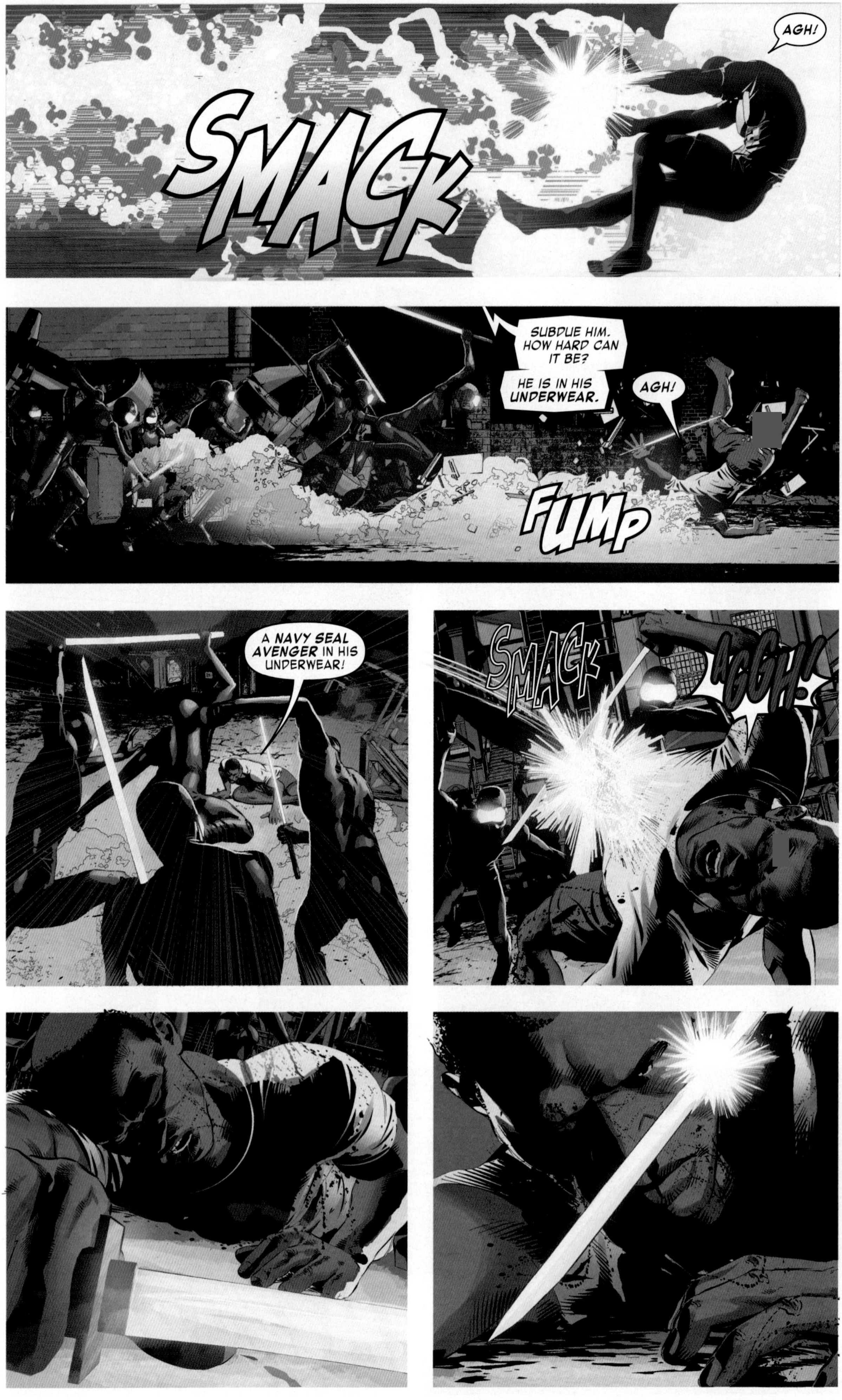
AGH!
SMACK
SUBDUE HIM. HOW HARD CAN IT BE?
HE IS IN HIS UNDERWEAR.
AGH!
FUMP
A NAVY SEAL AVENGER IN HIS UNDERWEAR!
SMACK
AGGH!

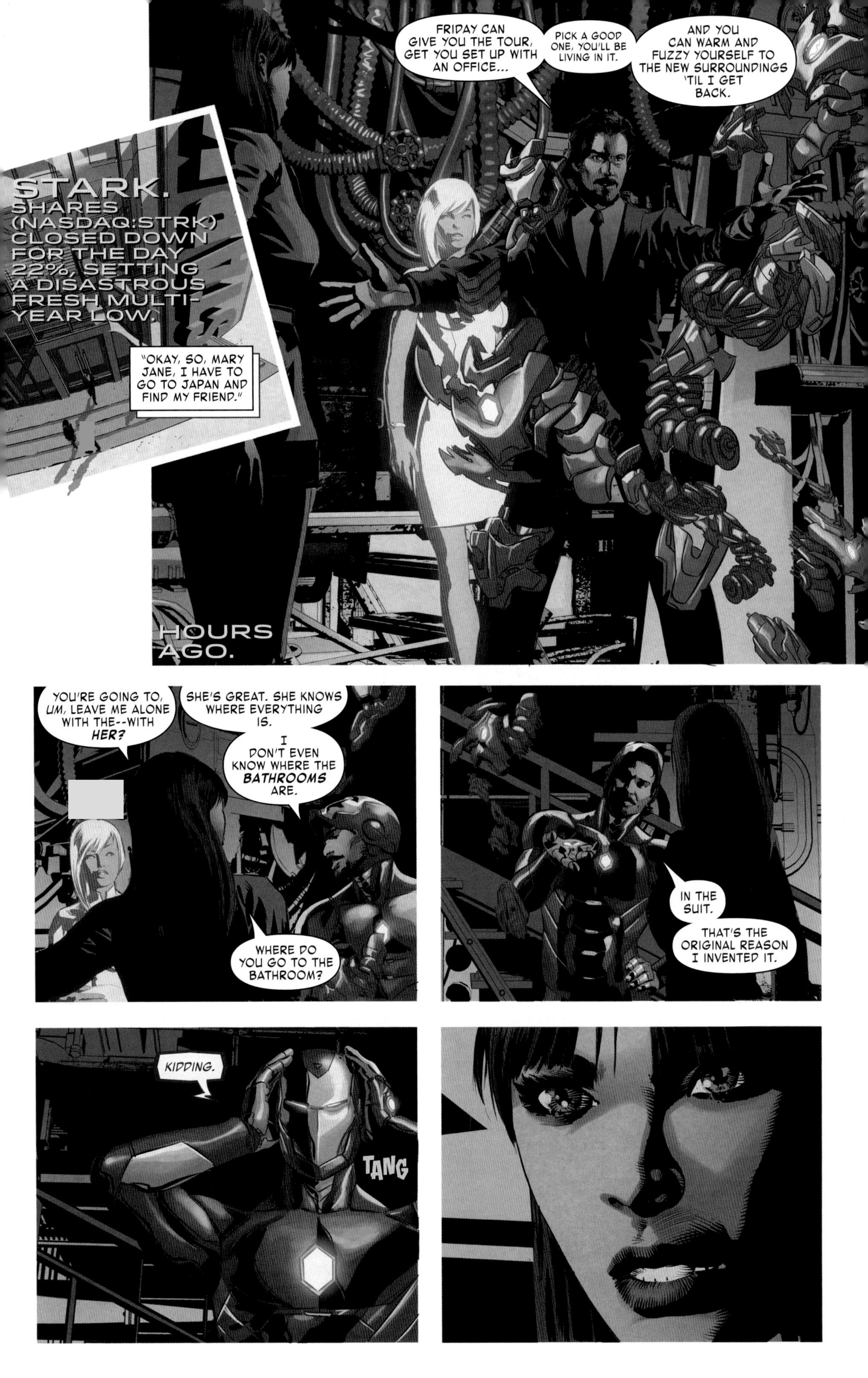
STARK.
SHARES (NASDAQ:STRK) CLOSED DOWN FOR THE DAY 22%, SETTING A DISASTROUS FRESH MULTI-YEAR LOW.
"OKAY, SO, MARY JANE, I HAVE TO GO TO JAPAN AND FIND MY FRIEND."
HOURS AGO.
FRIDAY CAN GIVE YOU THE TOUR, GET YOU SET UP WITH AN OFFICE...
PICK A GOOD ONE, YOU'LL BE LIVING IN IT.
AND YOU CAN WARM AND FUZZY YOURSELF TO THE NEW SURROUNDINGS 'TIL I GET BACK.
YOU'RE GOING TO, *UM*, LEAVE ME ALONE WITH THE--WITH ***HER?***
SHE'S GREAT. SHE KNOWS WHERE EVERYTHING IS.
I DON'T EVEN KNOW WHERE THE ***BATHROOMS*** ARE.
WHERE DO YOU GO TO THE BATHROOM?
IN THE SUIT.
THAT'S THE ORIGINAL REASON I INVENTED IT.
KIDDING.
TANG

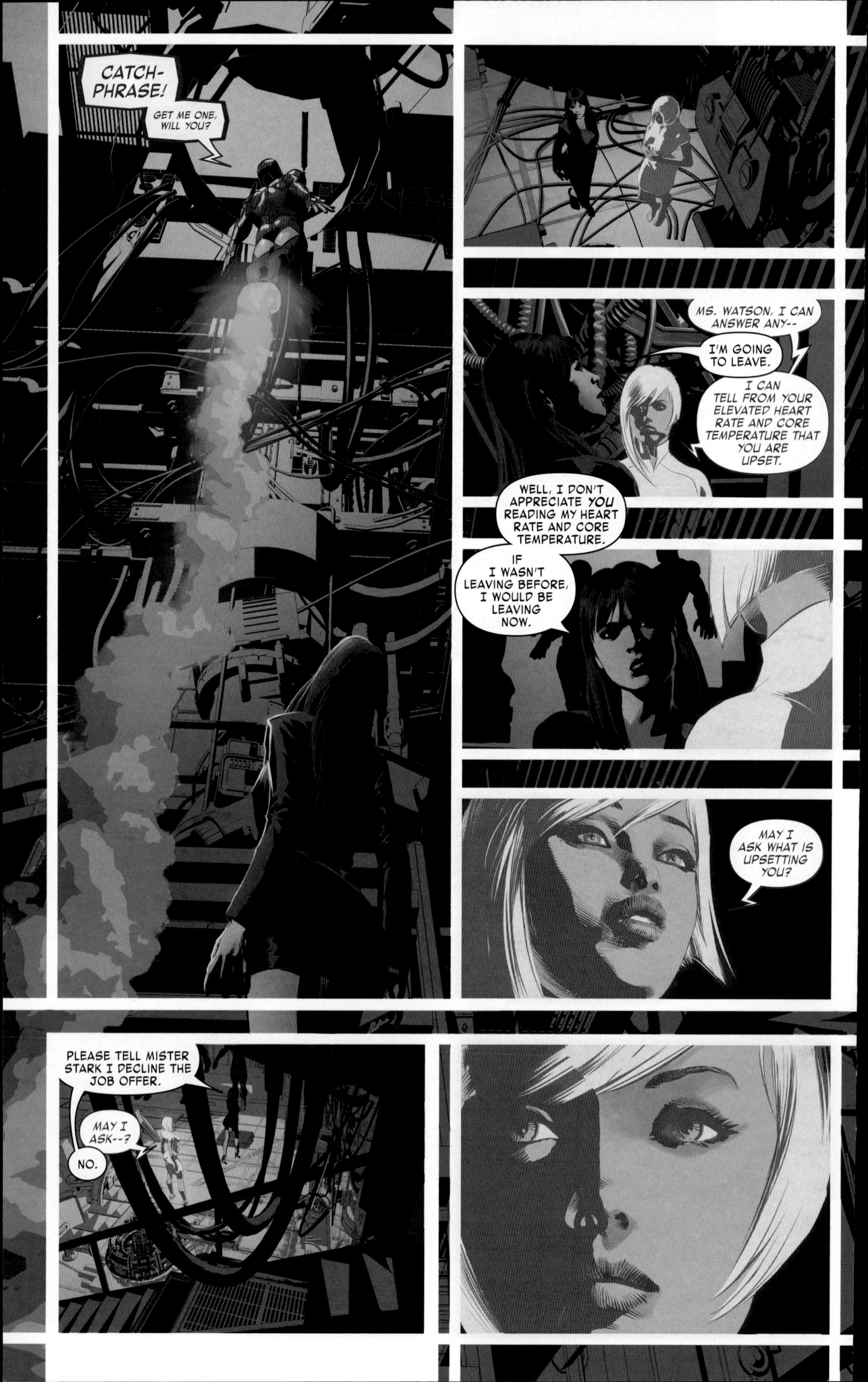
CATCH-PHRASE!
GET ME ONE, WILL YOU?
MS. WATSON, I CAN ANSWER ANY--
I'M GOING TO LEAVE.
I CAN TELL FROM YOUR ELEVATED HEART RATE AND CORE TEMPERATURE THAT YOU ARE UPSET.
WELL, I DON'T APPRECIATE YOU READING MY HEART RATE AND CORE TEMPERATURE.
IF I WASN'T LEAVING BEFORE, I WOULD BE LEAVING NOW.
MAY I ASK WHAT IS UPSETTING YOU?
PLEASE TELL MISTER STARK I DECLINE THE JOB OFFER.
MAY I ASK--?
NO.

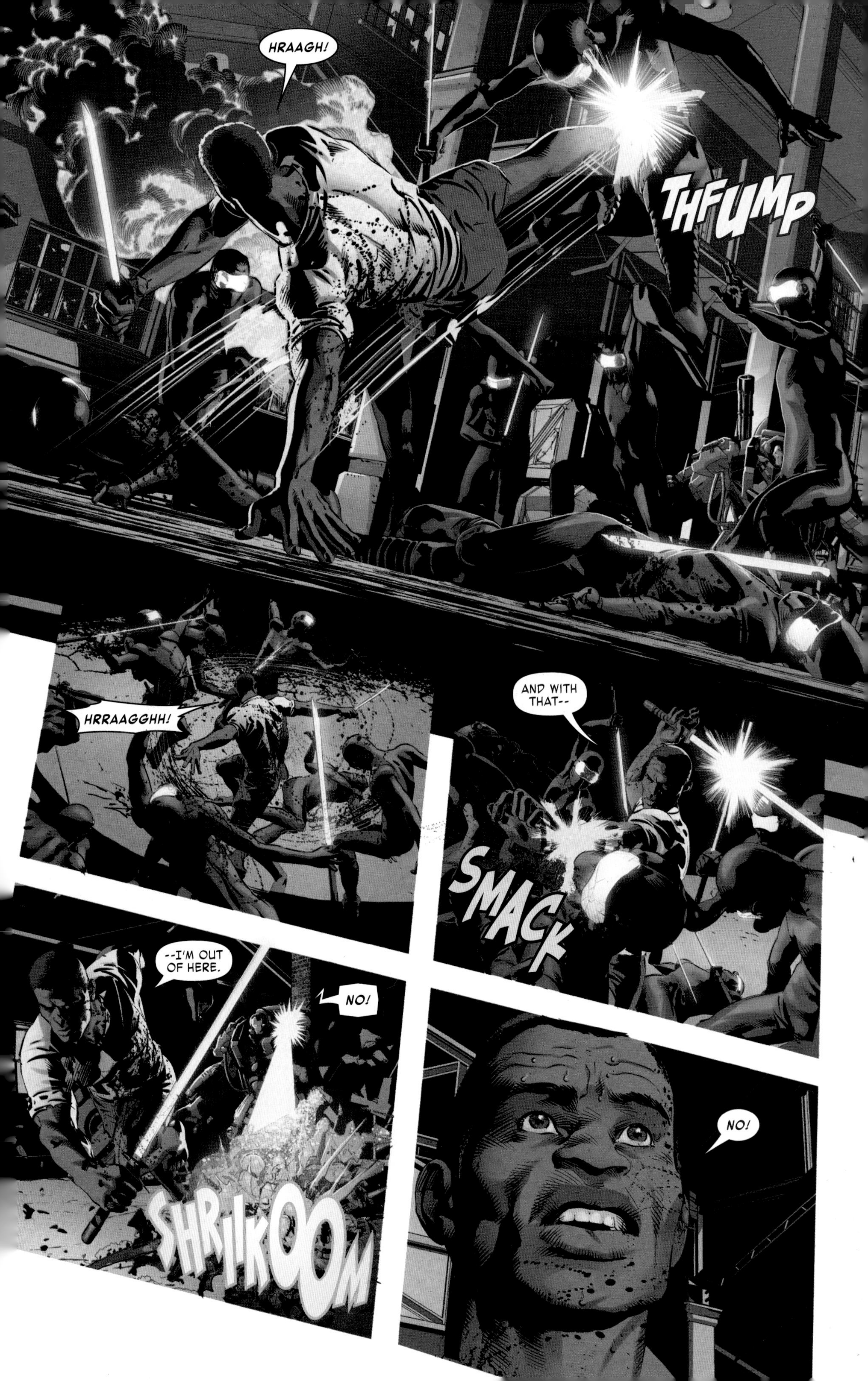
HRAAGH!
THFUMP
HRRAAGGHH!
AND WITH THAT--
SMACK
--I'M OUT OF HERE.
NO!
SHRIIKOOM
NO!

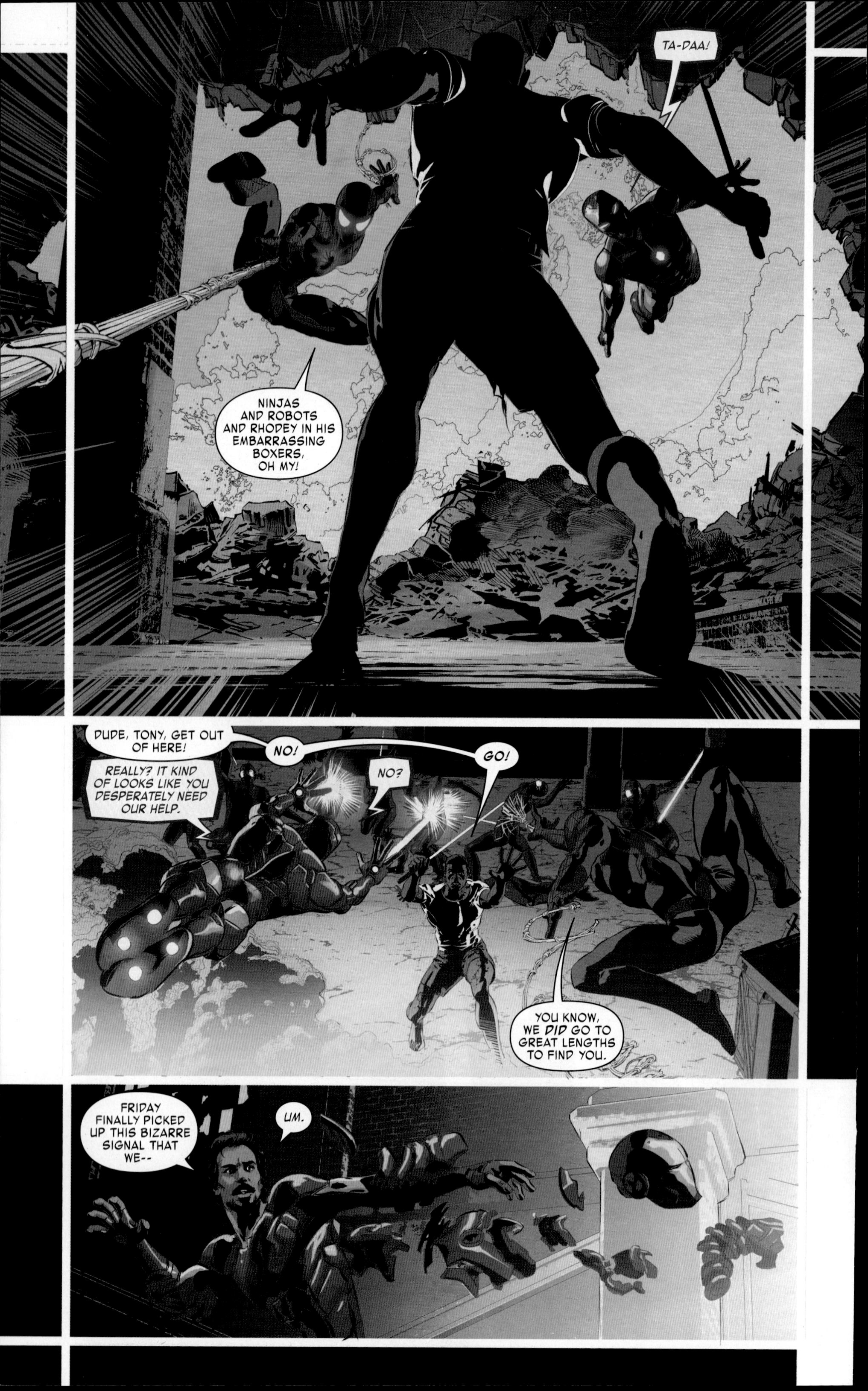
TA-DAA!
NINJAS AND ROBOTS AND RHODEY IN HIS EMBARRASSING BOXERS, OH MY!
DUDE, TONY, GET OUT OF HERE!
REALLY? IT KIND OF LOOKS LIKE YOU DESPERATELY NEED OUR HELP.
NO?
NO!
GO!
YOU KNOW, WE DID GO TO GREAT LENGTHS TO FIND YOU.
FRIDAY FINALLY PICKED UP THIS BIZARRE SIGNAL THAT WE--
UM.

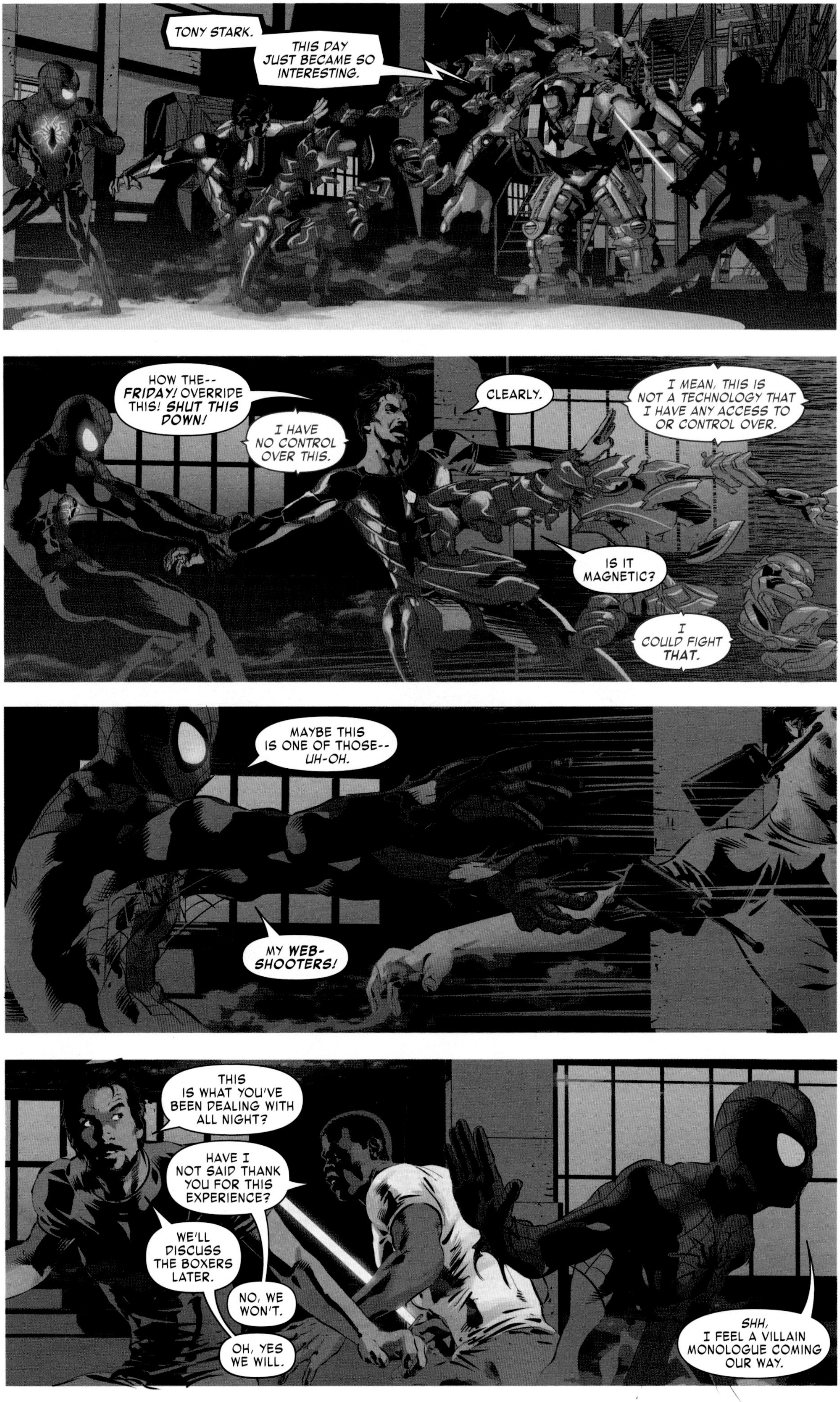
TONY STARK.
THIS DAY JUST BECAME SO INTERESTING.
HOW THE-- FRIDAY! OVERRIDE THIS! SHUT THIS DOWN!
I HAVE NO CONTROL OVER THIS.
CLEARLY.
I MEAN, THIS IS NOT A TECHNOLOGY THAT I HAVE ANY ACCESS TO OR CONTROL OVER.
IS IT MAGNETIC?
I COULD FIGHT THAT.
MAYBE THIS IS ONE OF THOSE-- UH-OH.
MY WEB-SHOOTERS!
THIS IS WHAT YOU'VE BEEN DEALING WITH ALL NIGHT?
HAVE I NOT SAID THANK YOU FOR THIS EXPERIENCE?
WE'LL DISCUSS THE BOXERS LATER.
NO, WE WON'T.
OH, YES WE WILL.
SHH, I FEEL A VILLAIN MONOLOGUE COMING OUR WAY.

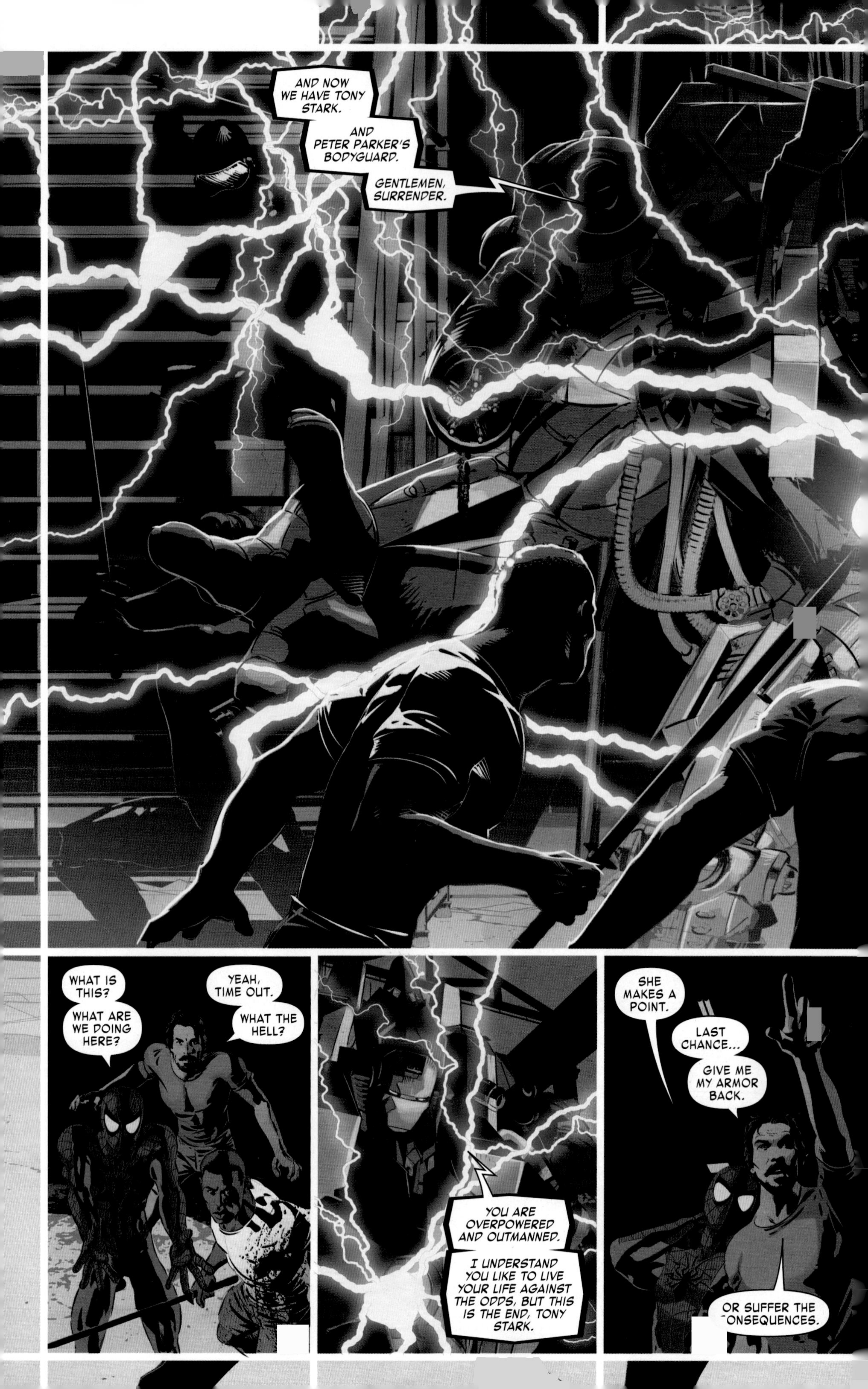
AND NOW WE HAVE TONY STARK.
AND PETER PARKER'S BODYGUARD.
GENTLEMEN, SURRENDER.
WHAT IS THIS?
WHAT ARE WE DOING HERE?
YEAH, TIME OUT.
WHAT THE HELL?
YOU ARE OVERPOWERED AND OUTMANNED.
I UNDERSTAND YOU LIKE TO LIVE YOUR LIFE AGAINST THE ODDS, BUT THIS IS THE END, TONY STARK.
SHE MAKES A POINT.
LAST CHANCE...
GIVE ME MY ARMOR BACK.
OR SUFFER THE CONSEQUENCES.

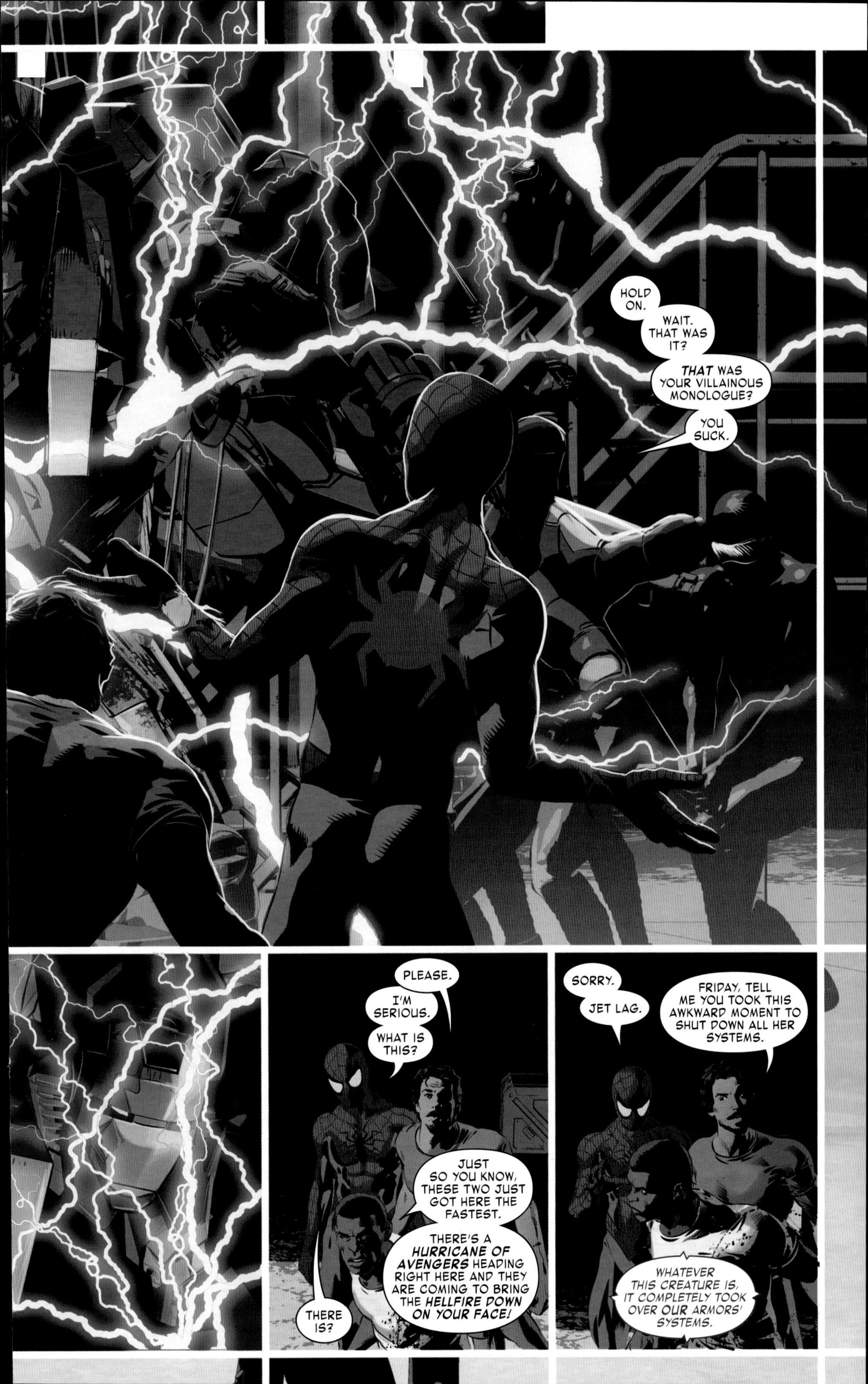
HOLD ON.
WAIT. THAT WAS IT?
THAT WAS YOUR VILLAINOUS MONOLOGUE?
YOU SUCK.
PLEASE.
I'M SERIOUS.
WHAT IS THIS?
JUST SO YOU KNOW, THESE TWO JUST GOT HERE THE FASTEST.
THERE'S A ***HURRICANE OF AVENGERS*** HEADING RIGHT HERE AND THEY ARE COMING TO BRING THE ***HELLFIRE DOWN ON YOUR FACE!***
THERE IS?
SORRY.
JET LAG.
FRIDAY, TELL ME YOU TOOK THIS AWKWARD MOMENT TO SHUT DOWN ALL HER SYSTEMS.
*WHATEVER THIS CREATURE IS, IT COMPLETELY TOOK OVER **OUR** ARMORS' SYSTEMS.*

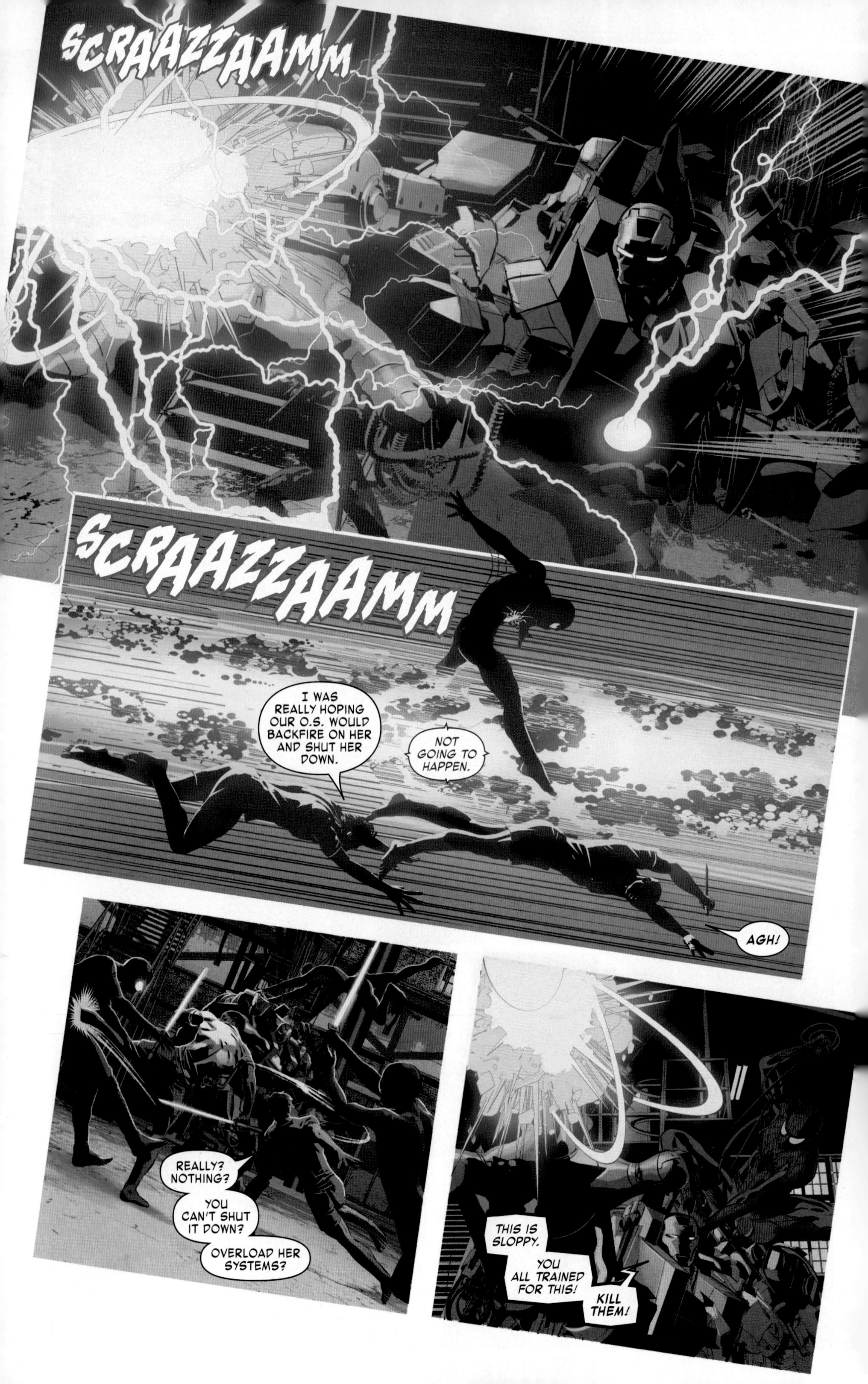
SCRAAZZAAMM
SCRAAZZAAMM
I WAS REALLY HOPING OUR O.S. WOULD BACKFIRE ON HER AND SHUT HER DOWN.
NOT GOING TO HAPPEN.
AGH!
REALLY? NOTHING?
YOU CAN'T SHUT IT DOWN?
OVERLOAD HER SYSTEMS?
THIS IS SLOPPY.
YOU ALL TRAINED FOR THIS!
KILL THEM!

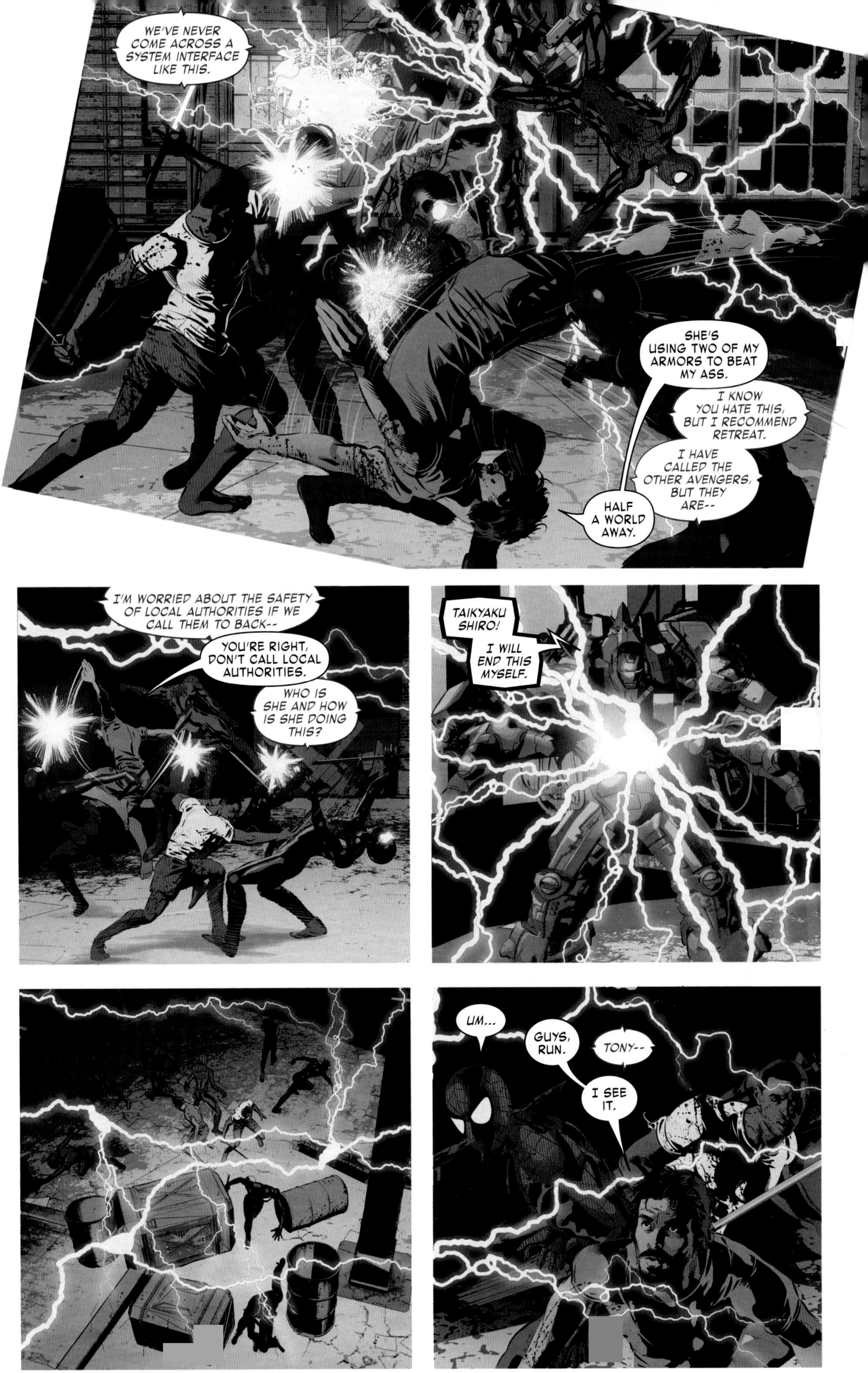
WE'VE NEVER COME ACROSS A SYSTEM INTERFACE LIKE THIS.
SHE'S USING TWO OF MY ARMORS TO BEAT MY ASS.
I KNOW YOU HATE THIS, BUT I RECOMMEND RETREAT.
I HAVE CALLED THE OTHER AVENGERS, BUT THEY ARE--
HALF A WORLD AWAY.
I'M WORRIED ABOUT THE SAFETY OF LOCAL AUTHORITIES IF WE CALL THEM TO BACK--
YOU'RE RIGHT, DON'T CALL LOCAL AUTHORITIES.
WHO IS SHE AND HOW IS SHE DOING THIS?
TAIKYAKU SHIRO!
I WILL END THIS MYSELF.
UM...
GUYS, RUN.
TONY--
I SEE IT.

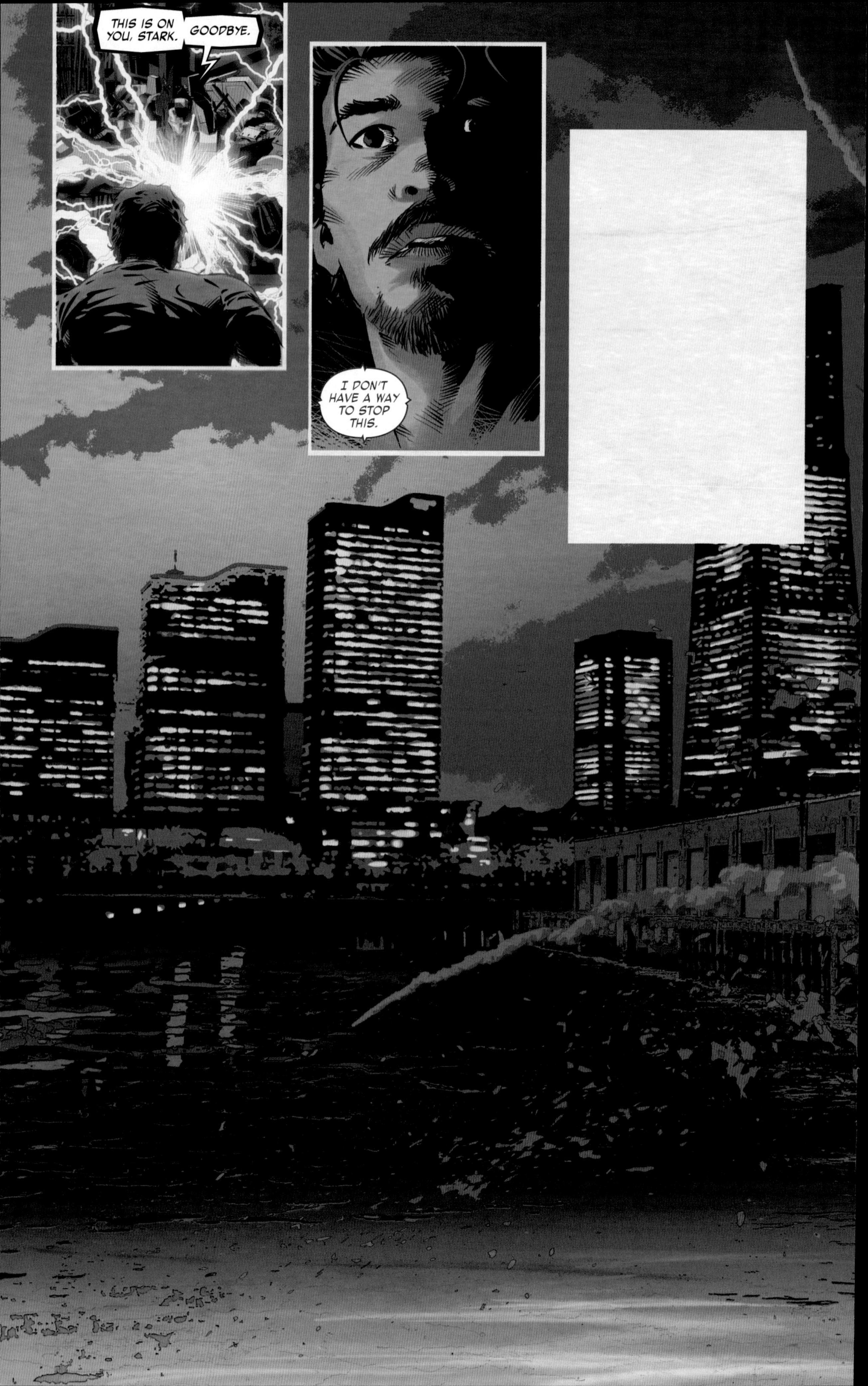
THIS IS ON YOU, STARK.
GOODBYE.
I DON'T HAVE A WAY TO STOP THIS.

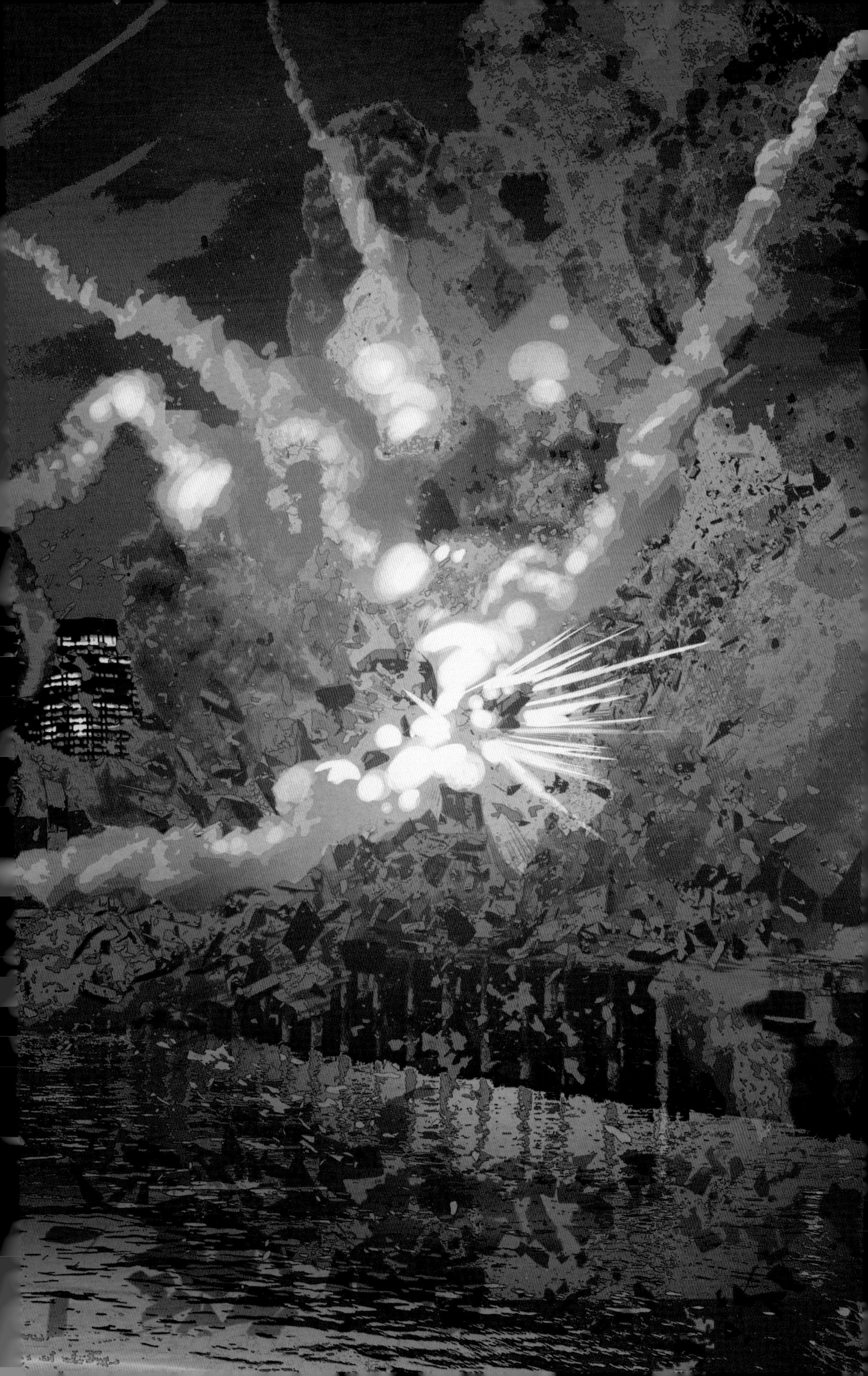

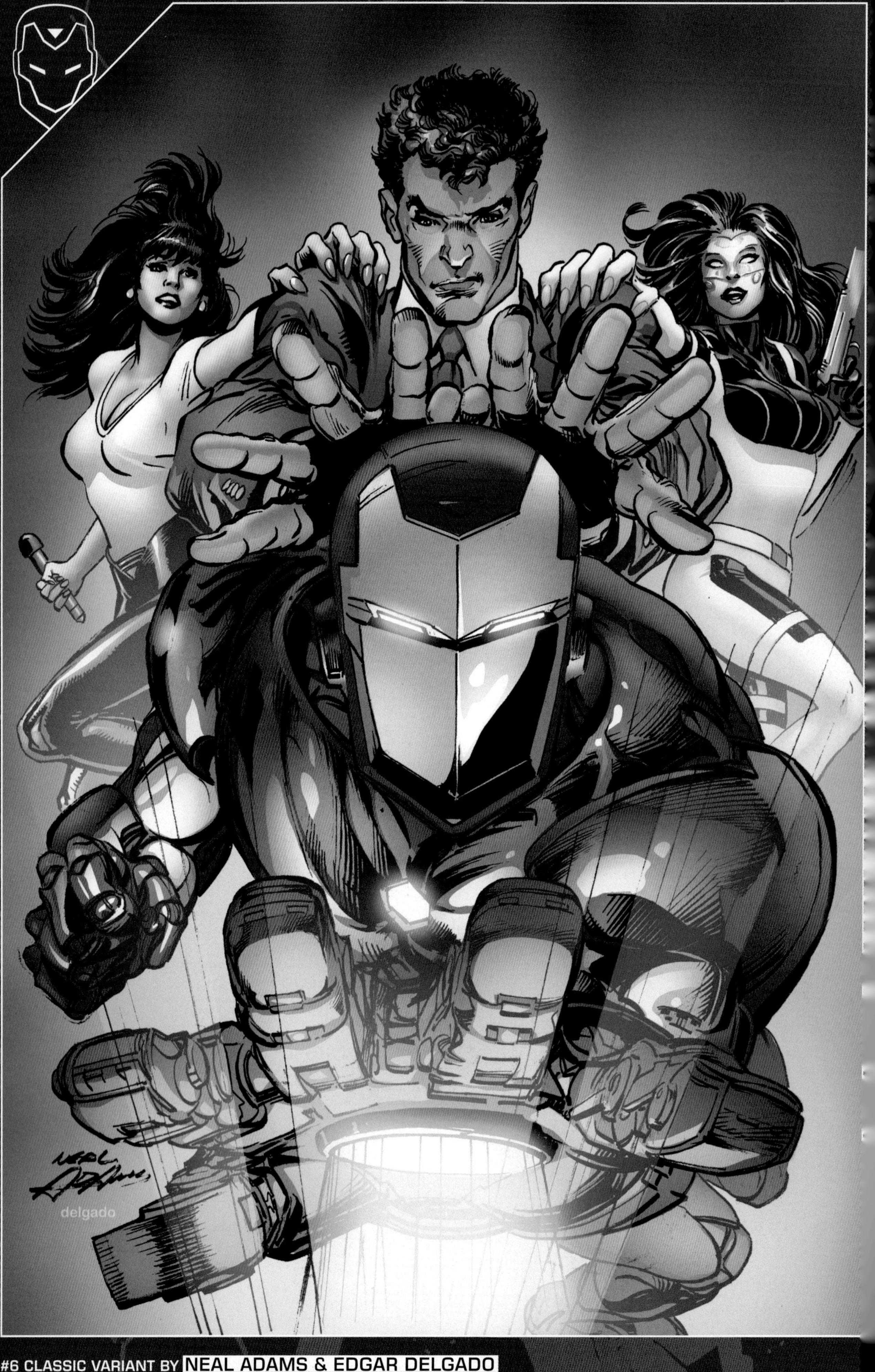
delgado

#6 CLASSIC VARIANT BY NEAL ADAMS & EDGAR DELGADO

#9

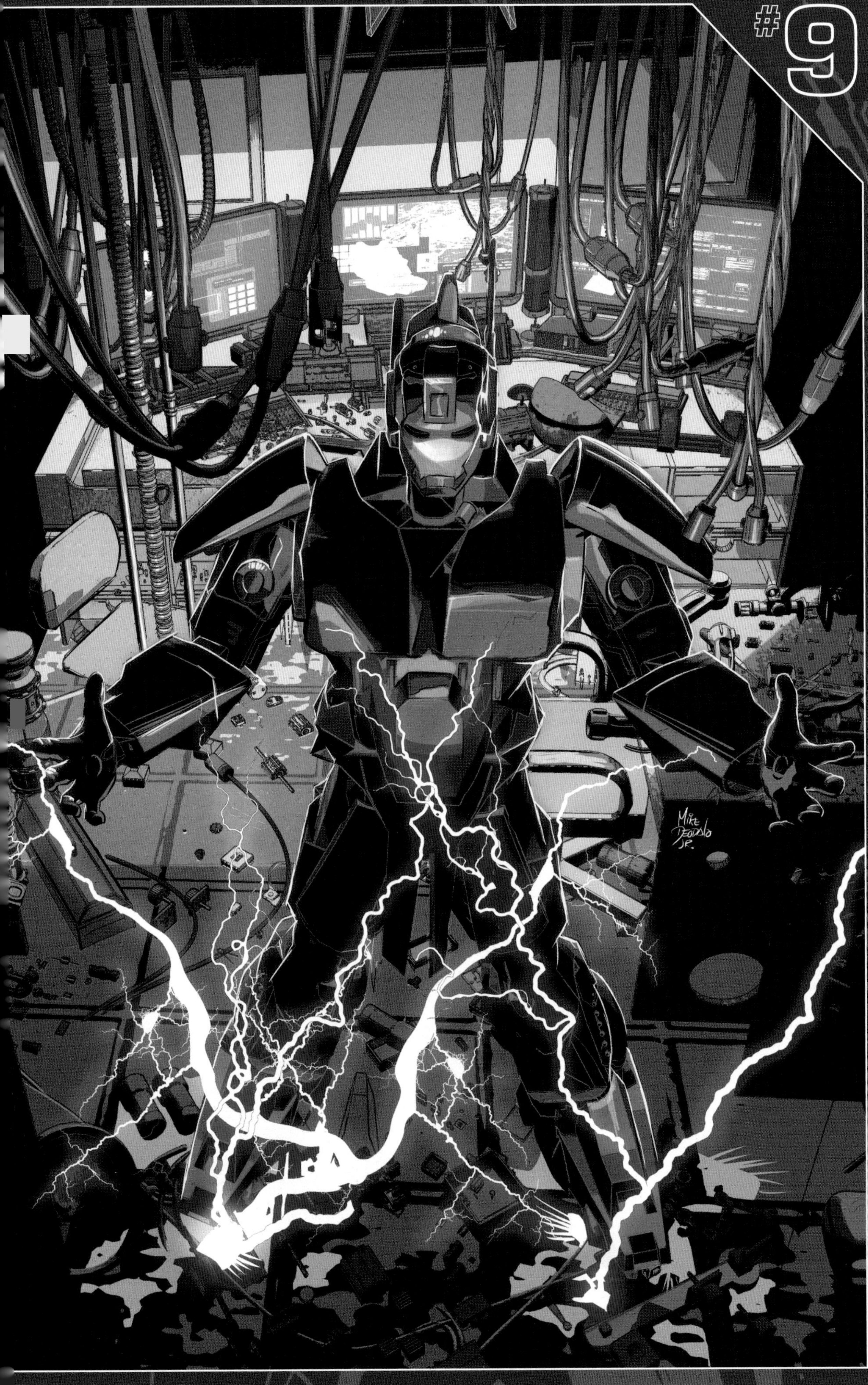

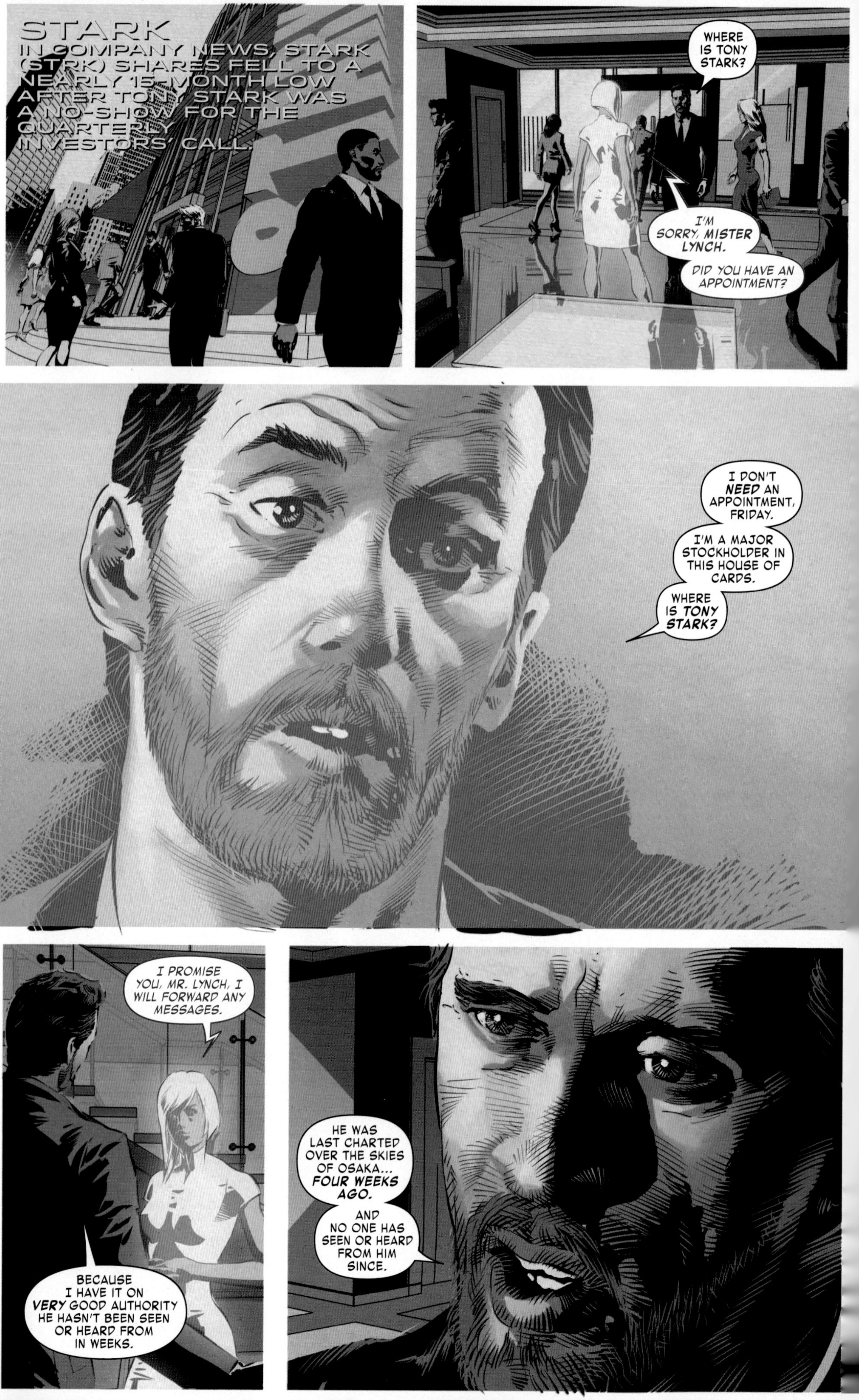
STARK
IN COMPANY NEWS, STARK (STRK) SHARES FELL TO A NEARLY 15-MONTH LOW AFTER TONY STARK WAS A NO-SHOW FOR THE QUARTERLY INVESTORS' CALL.
WHERE IS TONY STARK?
I'M SORRY, MISTER LYNCH.
DID YOU HAVE AN APPOINTMENT?
I DON'T NEED AN APPOINTMENT, FRIDAY.
I'M A MAJOR STOCKHOLDER IN THIS HOUSE OF CARDS.
WHERE IS TONY STARK?
I PROMISE YOU, MR. LYNCH, I WILL FORWARD ANY MESSAGES.
BECAUSE I HAVE IT ON VERY GOOD AUTHORITY HE HASN'T BEEN SEEN OR HEARD FROM IN WEEKS.
HE WAS LAST CHARTED OVER THE SKIES OF OSAKA... FOUR WEEKS AGO.
AND NO ONE HAS SEEN OR HEARD FROM HIM SINCE.

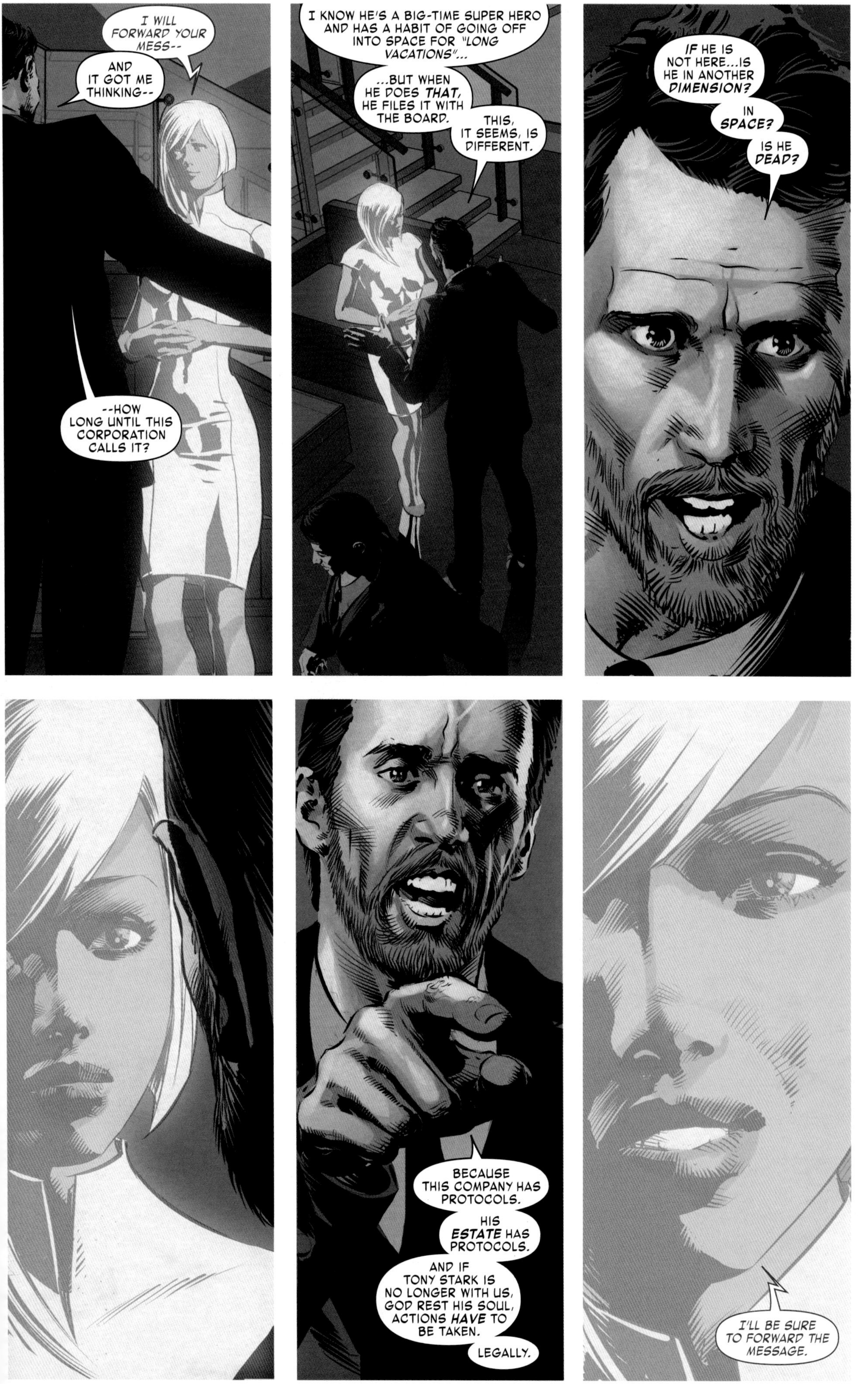
I WILL FORWARD YOUR MESS--
AND IT GOT ME THINKING--
--HOW LONG UNTIL THIS CORPORATION CALLS IT?
I KNOW HE'S A BIG-TIME SUPER HERO AND HAS A HABIT OF GOING OFF INTO SPACE FOR "LONG VACATIONS"...
...BUT WHEN HE DOES THAT, HE FILES IT WITH THE BOARD.
THIS, IT SEEMS, IS DIFFERENT.
IF HE IS NOT HERE...IS HE IN ANOTHER DIMENSION?
IN SPACE?
IS HE DEAD?
BECAUSE THIS COMPANY HAS PROTOCOLS.
HIS ESTATE HAS PROTOCOLS.
AND IF TONY STARK IS NO LONGER WITH US, GOD REST HIS SOUL, ACTIONS HAVE TO BE TAKEN.
LEGALLY.
I'LL BE SURE TO FORWARD THE MESSAGE.

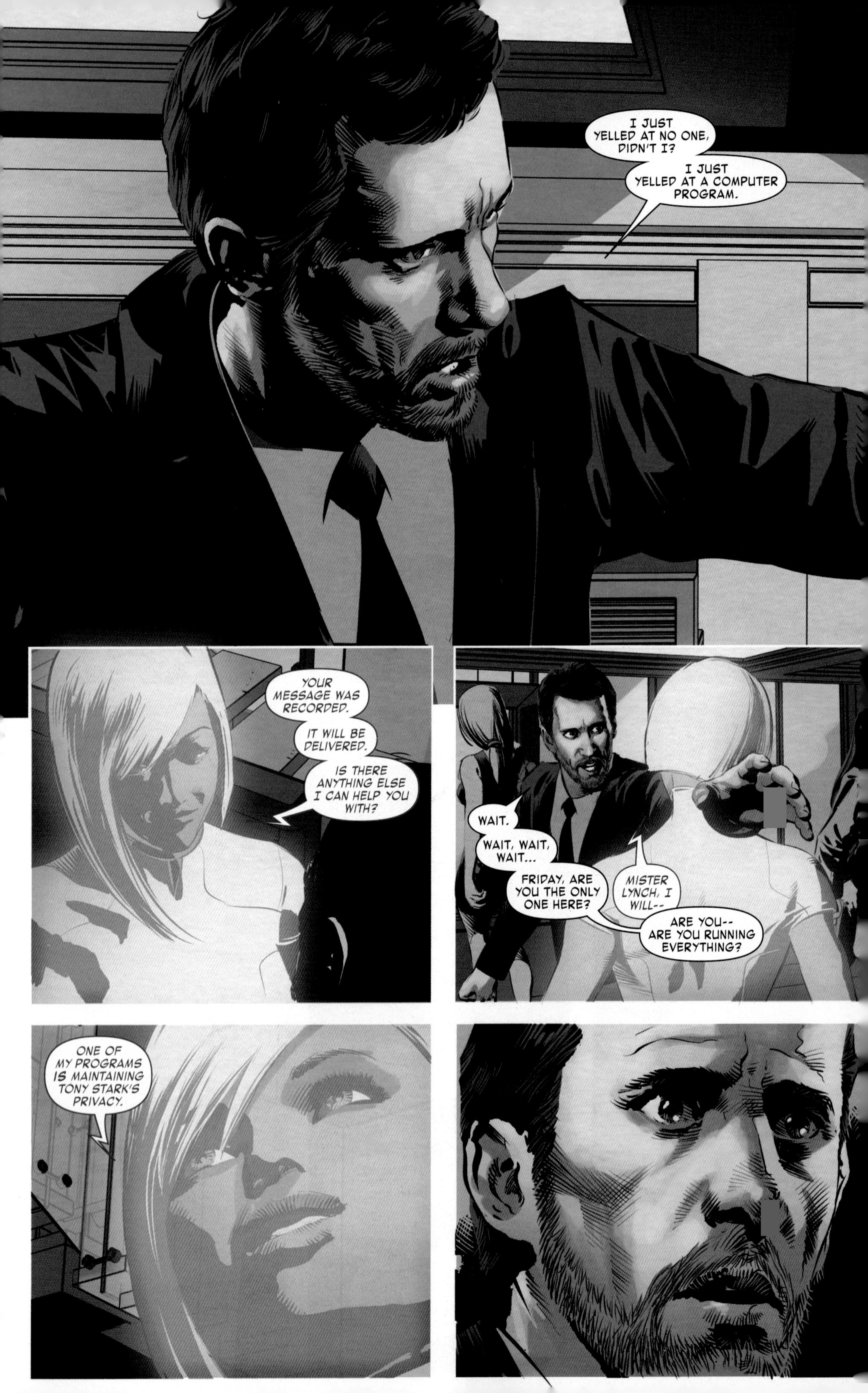
I JUST YELLED AT NO ONE, DIDN'T I?
I JUST YELLED AT A COMPUTER PROGRAM.
YOUR MESSAGE WAS RECORDED.
IT WILL BE DELIVERED.
IS THERE ANYTHING ELSE I CAN HELP YOU WITH?
WAIT.
WAIT, WAIT, WAIT...
MISTER LYNCH, I WILL--
FRIDAY, ARE YOU THE ONLY ONE HERE?
ARE YOU-- ARE YOU RUNNING EVERYTHING?
ONE OF MY PROGRAMS IS MAINTAINING TONY STARK'S PRIVACY.

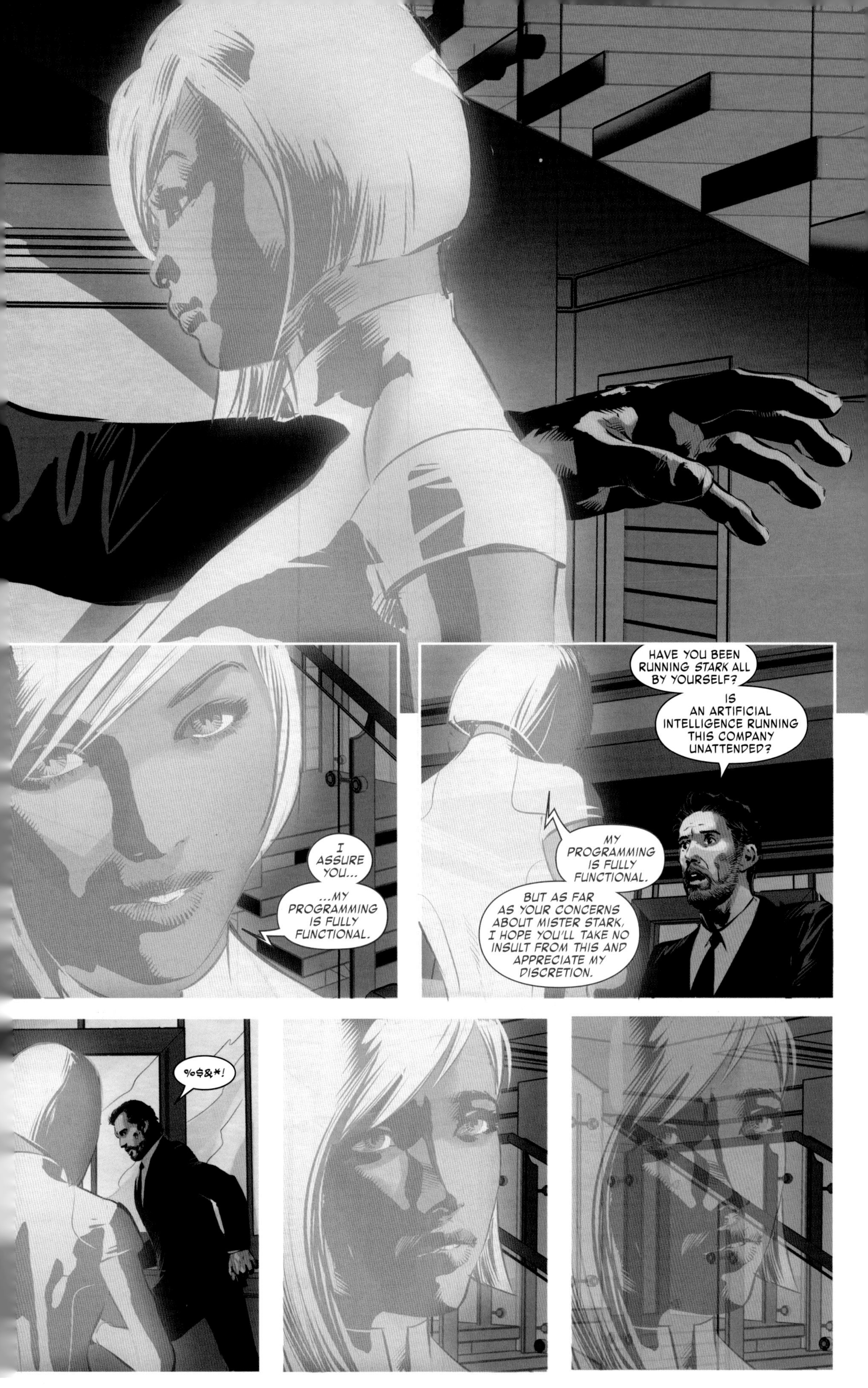

I ASSURE YOU...
...MY PROGRAMMING IS FULLY FUNCTIONAL.
HAVE YOU BEEN RUNNING STARK ALL BY YOURSELF?
IS AN ARTIFICIAL INTELLIGENCE RUNNING THIS COMPANY UNATTENDED?
MY PROGRAMMING IS FULLY FUNCTIONAL.
BUT AS FAR AS YOUR CONCERNS ABOUT MISTER STARK, I HOPE YOU'LL TAKE NO INSULT FROM THIS AND APPRECIATE MY DISCRETION.
%$&*!

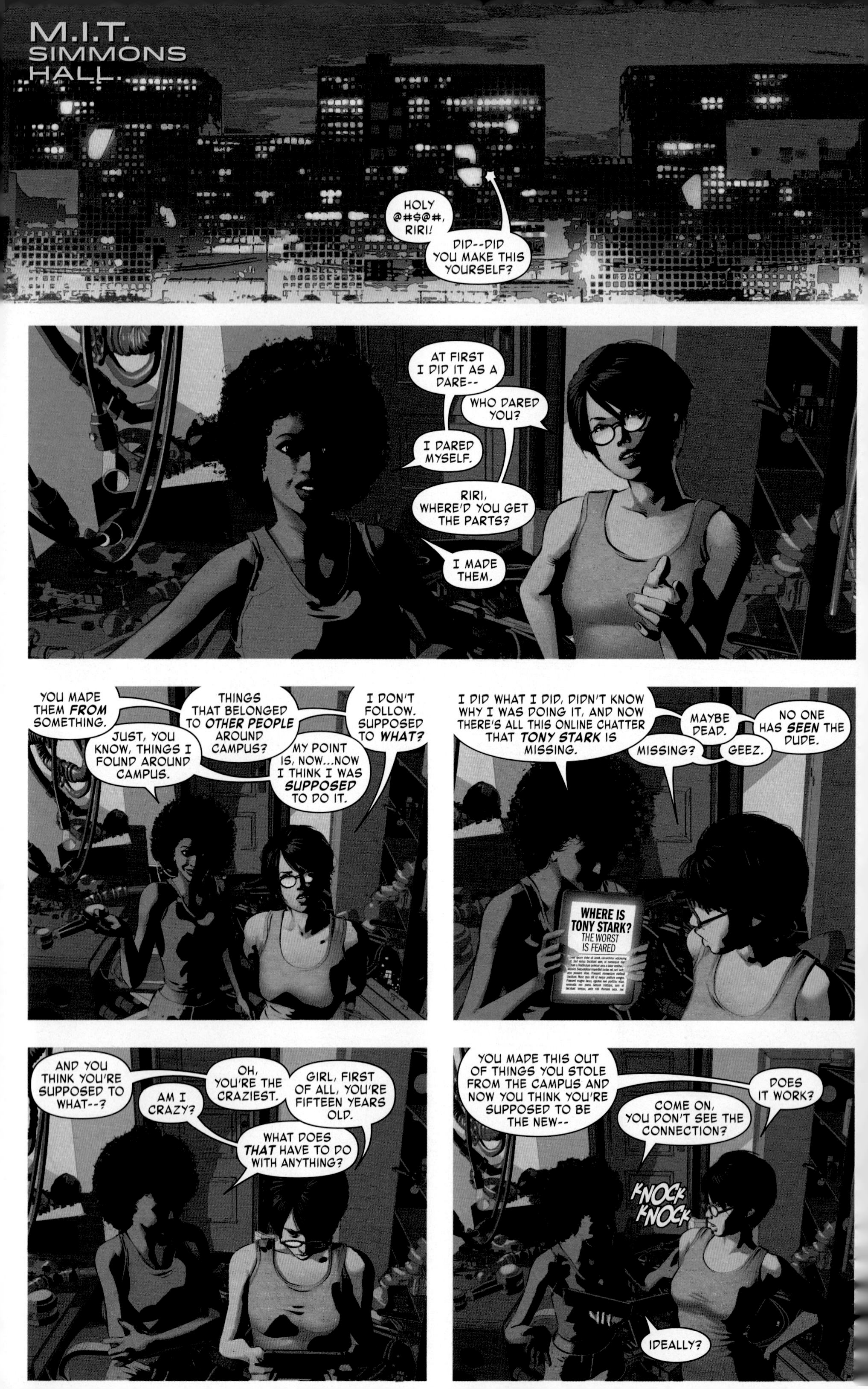
M.I.T. SIMMONS HALL.
HOLY @#$@#, RIRI!
DID--DID YOU MAKE THIS YOURSELF?
AT FIRST I DID IT AS A DARE--
WHO DARED YOU?
I DARED MYSELF.
RIRI, WHERE'D YOU GET THE PARTS?
I MADE THEM.
YOU MADE THEM *FROM* SOMETHING.
JUST, YOU KNOW, THINGS I FOUND AROUND CAMPUS.
THINGS THAT BELONGED TO *OTHER PEOPLE* AROUND CAMPUS?
MY POINT IS, NOW...NOW I THINK I WAS *SUPPOSED* TO DO IT.
I DON'T FOLLOW. SUPPOSED TO *WHAT?*
I DID WHAT I DID, DIDN'T KNOW WHY I WAS DOING IT, AND NOW THERE'S ALL THIS ONLINE CHATTER THAT *TONY STARK* IS MISSING.
MISSING?
MAYBE DEAD.
GEEZ.
NO ONE HAS *SEEN* THE DUDE.
WHERE IS TONY STARK?
THE WORST IS FEARED
AND YOU THINK YOU'RE SUPPOSED TO WHAT--?
AM I CRAZY?
OH, YOU'RE THE CRAZIEST.
GIRL, FIRST OF ALL, YOU'RE FIFTEEN YEARS OLD.
WHAT DOES *THAT* HAVE TO DO WITH ANYTHING?
YOU MADE THIS OUT OF THINGS YOU STOLE FROM THE CAMPUS AND NOW YOU THINK YOU'RE SUPPOSED TO BE THE NEW--
COME ON, YOU DON'T SEE THE CONNECTION?
DOES IT WORK?
KNOCK KNOCK
IDEALLY?

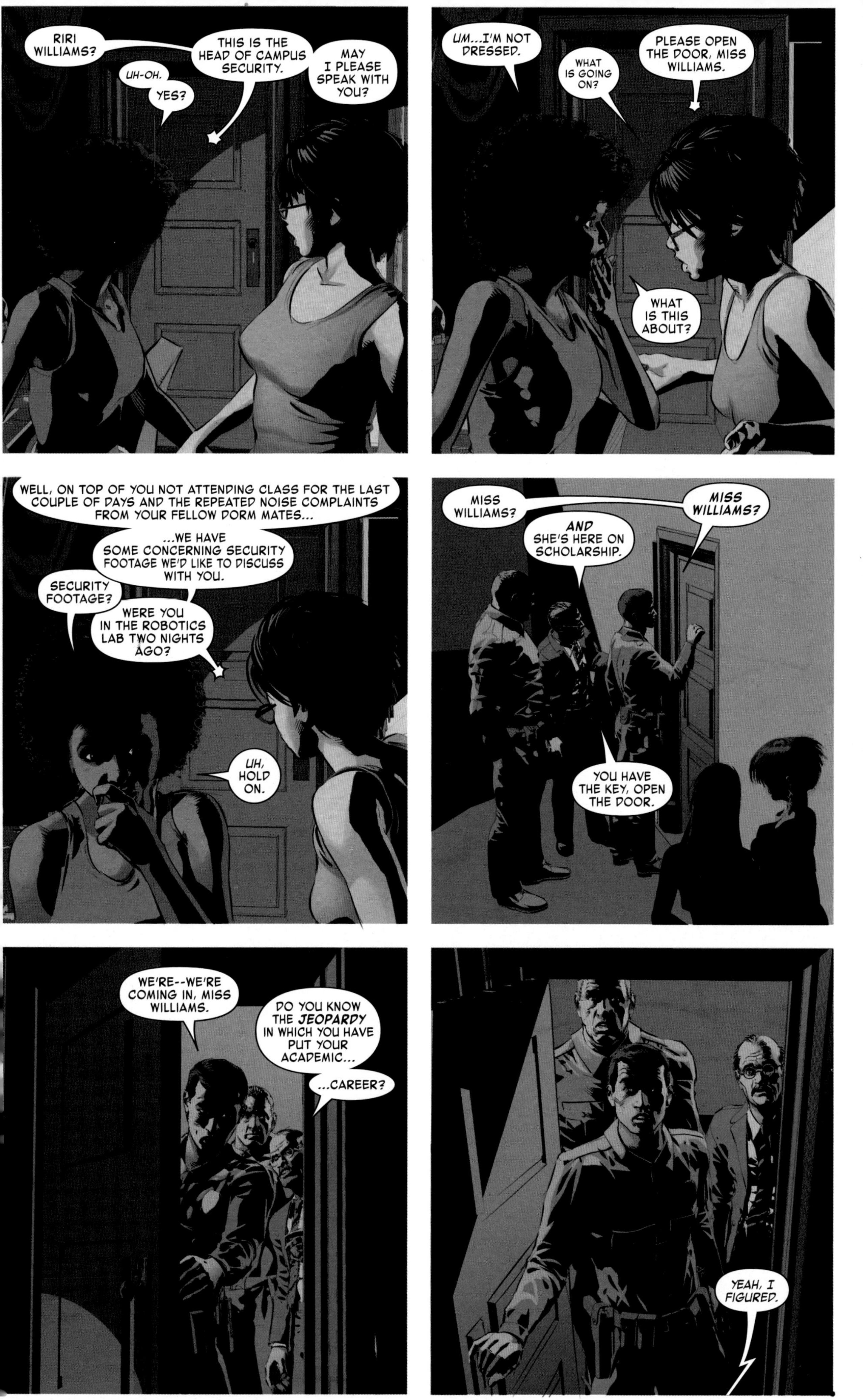
RIRI WILLIAMS?
UH-OH.
YES?
THIS IS THE HEAD OF CAMPUS SECURITY.
MAY I PLEASE SPEAK WITH YOU?
UM...I'M NOT DRESSED.
WHAT IS GOING ON?
PLEASE OPEN THE DOOR, MISS WILLIAMS.
WHAT IS THIS ABOUT?
WELL, ON TOP OF YOU NOT ATTENDING CLASS FOR THE LAST COUPLE OF DAYS AND THE REPEATED NOISE COMPLAINTS FROM YOUR FELLOW DORM MATES...
...WE HAVE SOME CONCERNING SECURITY FOOTAGE WE'D LIKE TO DISCUSS WITH YOU.
SECURITY FOOTAGE?
WERE YOU IN THE ROBOTICS LAB TWO NIGHTS AGO?
UH, HOLD ON.
MISS WILLIAMS?
MISS WILLIAMS?
AND SHE'S HERE ON SCHOLARSHIP.
YOU HAVE THE KEY, OPEN THE DOOR.
WE'RE--WE'RE COMING IN, MISS WILLIAMS.
DO YOU KNOW THE JEOPARDY IN WHICH YOU HAVE PUT YOUR ACADEMIC...
...CAREER?
YEAH, I FIGURED.

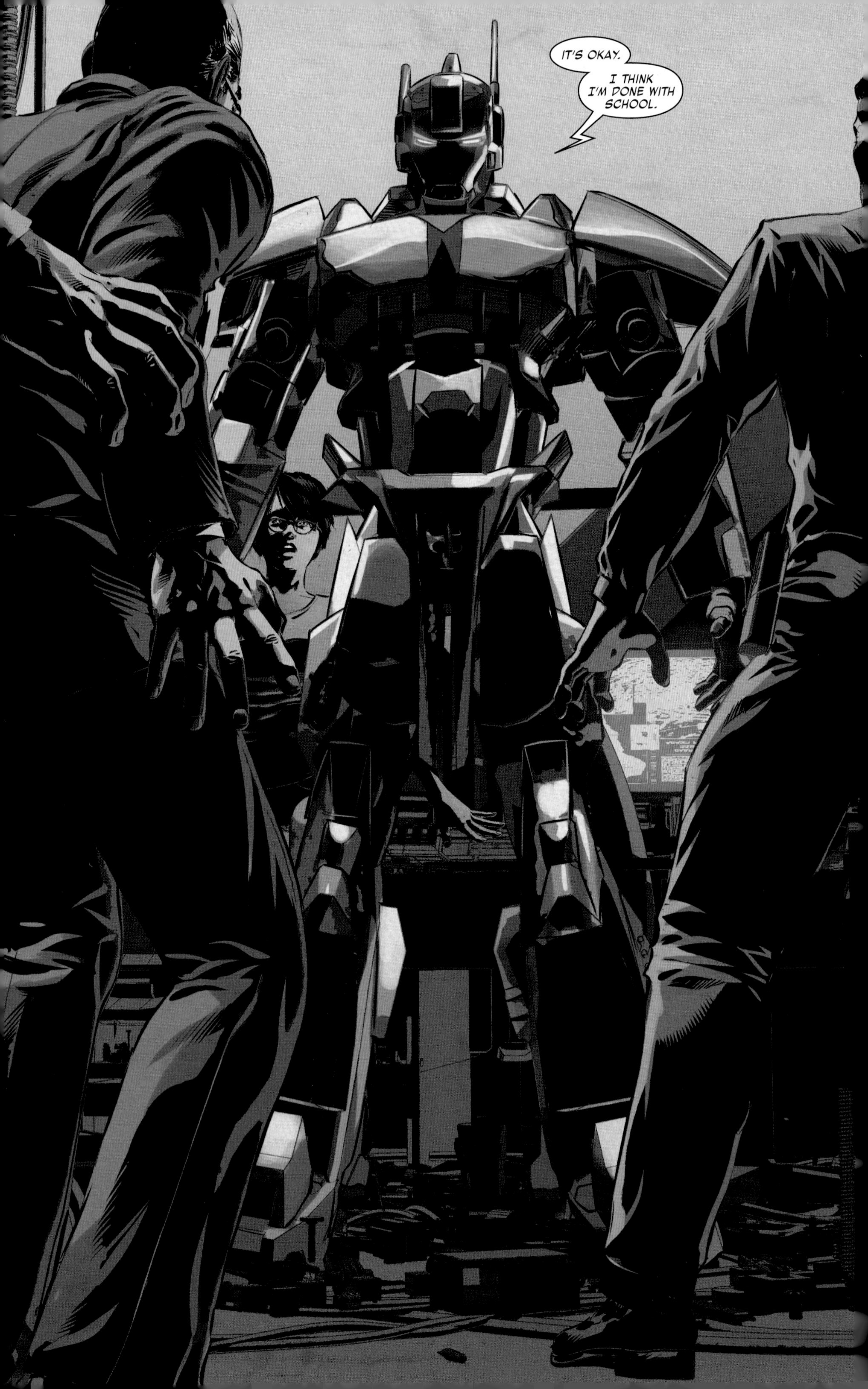
IT'S OKAY.
I THINK I'M DONE WITH SCHOOL.

OSAKA.

THUMP

THUMP
THUMP THUMP

EXCUSE ME!

YOU'RE NOT GOING TO START ANY TROUBLE...

...ARE YOU?

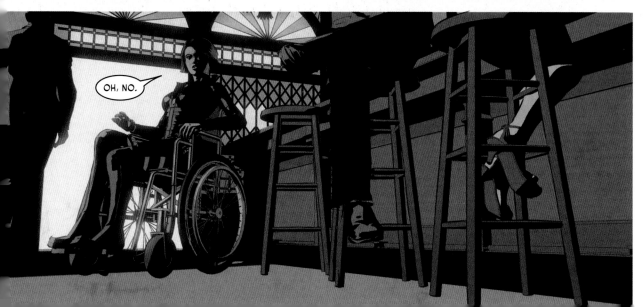

OH, NO.

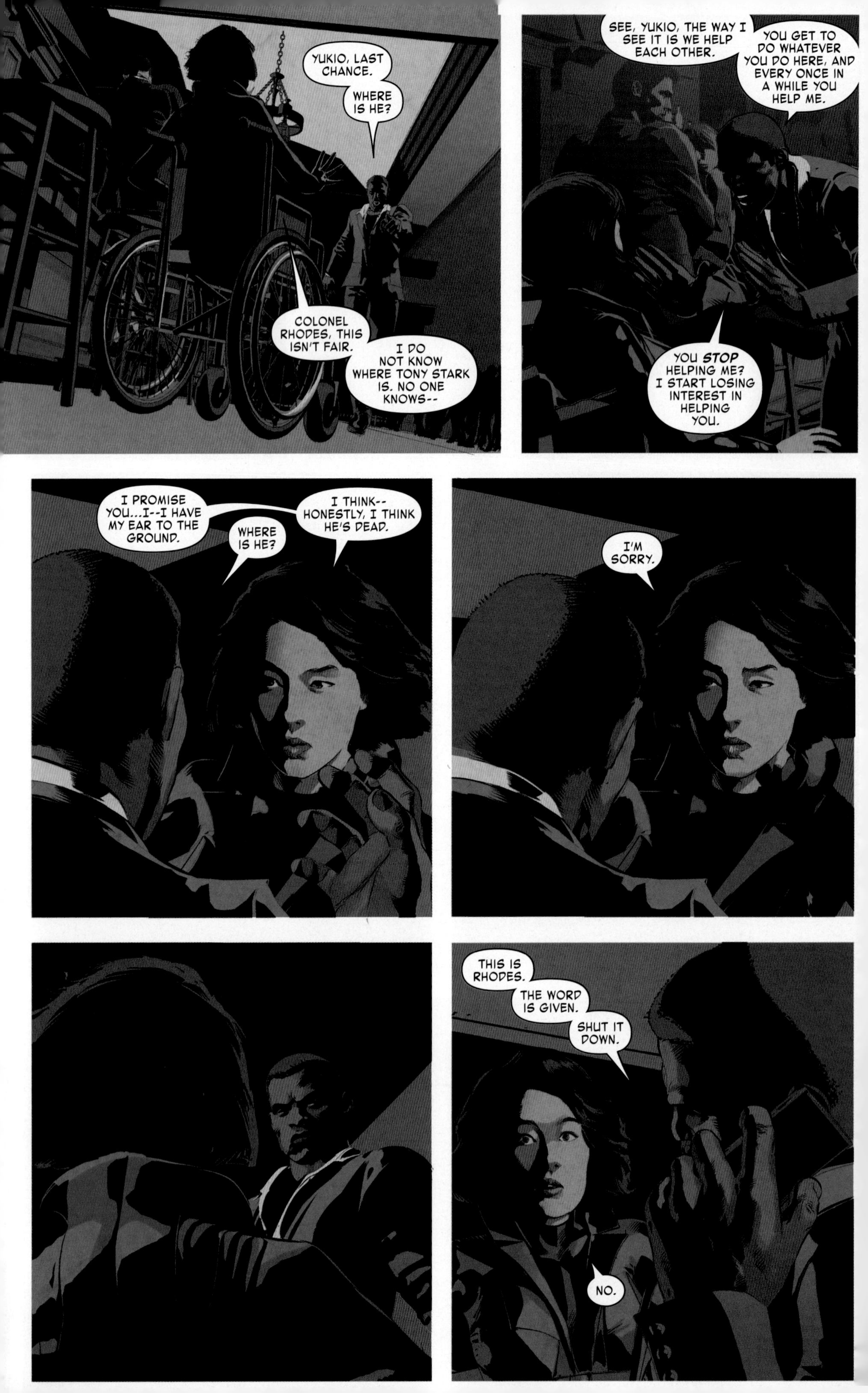
YUKIO, LAST CHANCE.
WHERE IS HE?
COLONEL RHODES, THIS ISN'T FAIR.
I DO NOT KNOW WHERE TONY STARK IS. NO ONE KNOWS--
SEE, YUKIO, THE WAY I SEE IT IS WE HELP EACH OTHER.
YOU GET TO DO WHATEVER YOU DO HERE, AND EVERY ONCE IN A WHILE YOU HELP ME.
YOU STOP HELPING ME? I START LOSING INTEREST IN HELPING YOU.
I PROMISE YOU...I--I HAVE MY EAR TO THE GROUND.
WHERE IS HE?
I THINK-- HONESTLY, I THINK HE'S DEAD.
I'M SORRY.
THIS IS RHODES.
THE WORD IS GIVEN.
SHUT IT DOWN.
NO.

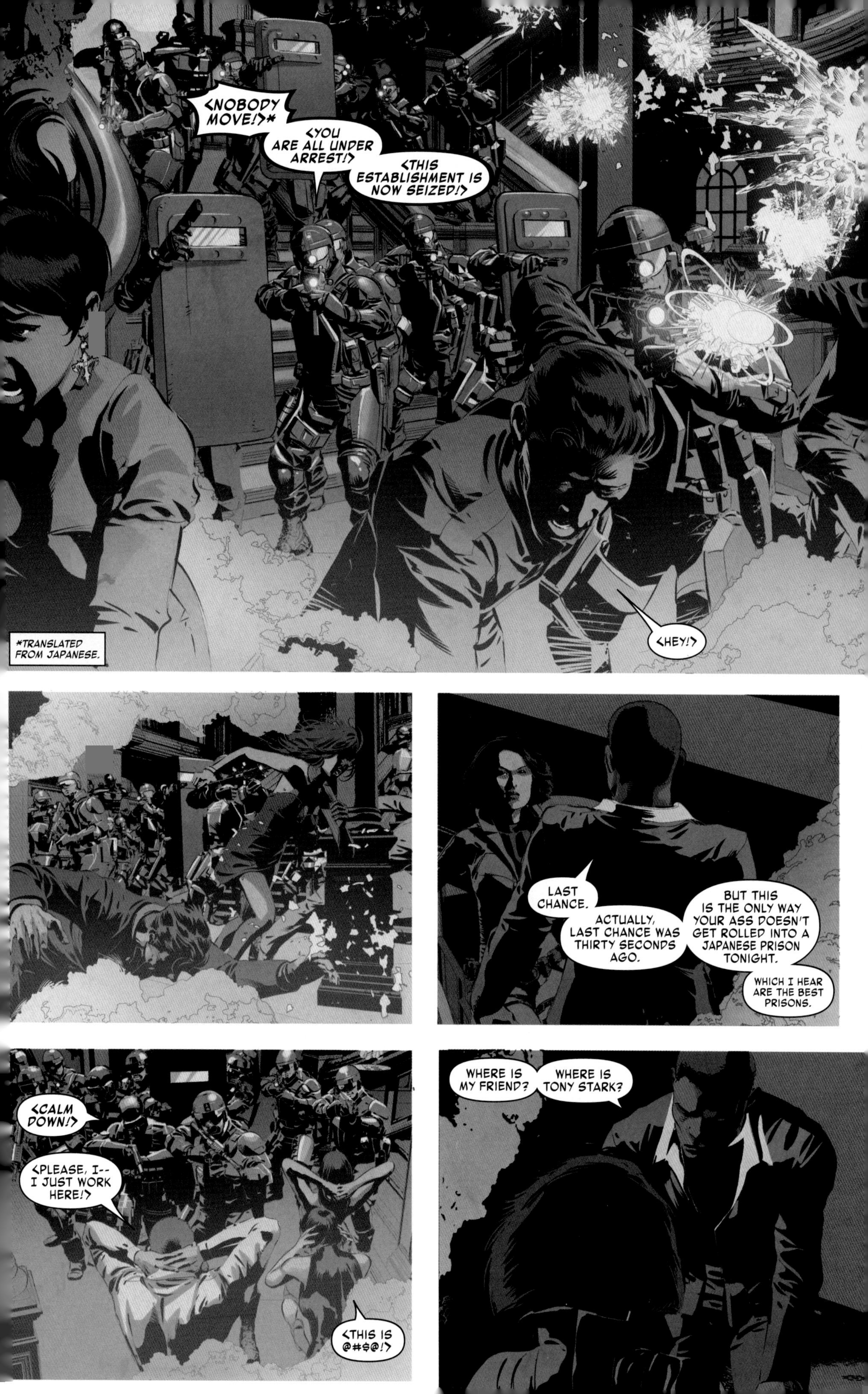
<NOBODY MOVE!>*
<YOU ARE ALL UNDER ARREST!>
<THIS ESTABLISHMENT IS NOW SEIZED!>
*TRANSLATED FROM JAPANESE.
<HEY!>
LAST CHANCE.
ACTUALLY, LAST CHANCE WAS THIRTY SECONDS AGO.
BUT THIS IS THE ONLY WAY YOUR ASS DOESN'T GET ROLLED INTO A JAPANESE PRISON TONIGHT.
WHICH I HEAR ARE THE BEST PRISONS.
<CALM DOWN!>
<PLEASE, I-- I JUST WORK HERE!>
<THIS IS @#$@!>
WHERE IS MY FRIEND?
WHERE IS TONY STARK?

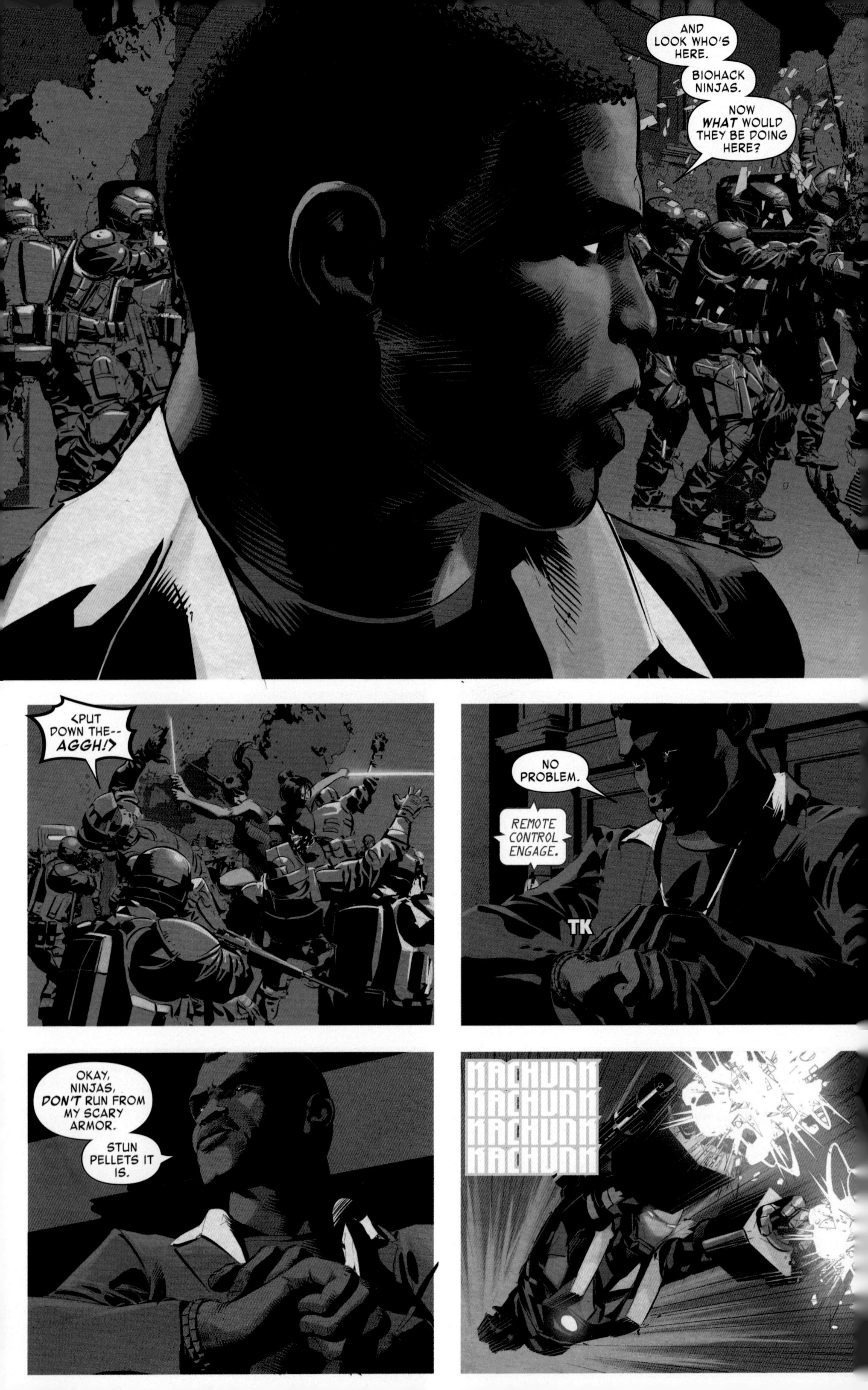
AND LOOK WHO'S HERE.
BIOHACK NINJAS.
NOW *WHAT* WOULD THEY BE DOING HERE?
<PUT DOWN THE-- *AGGH!*>
NO PROBLEM.
REMOTE CONTROL ENGAGE.
TK
OKAY, NINJAS, *DON'T* RUN FROM MY SCARY ARMOR.
STUN PELLETS IT IS.
KACHUNK KACHUNK KACHUNK KACHUNK

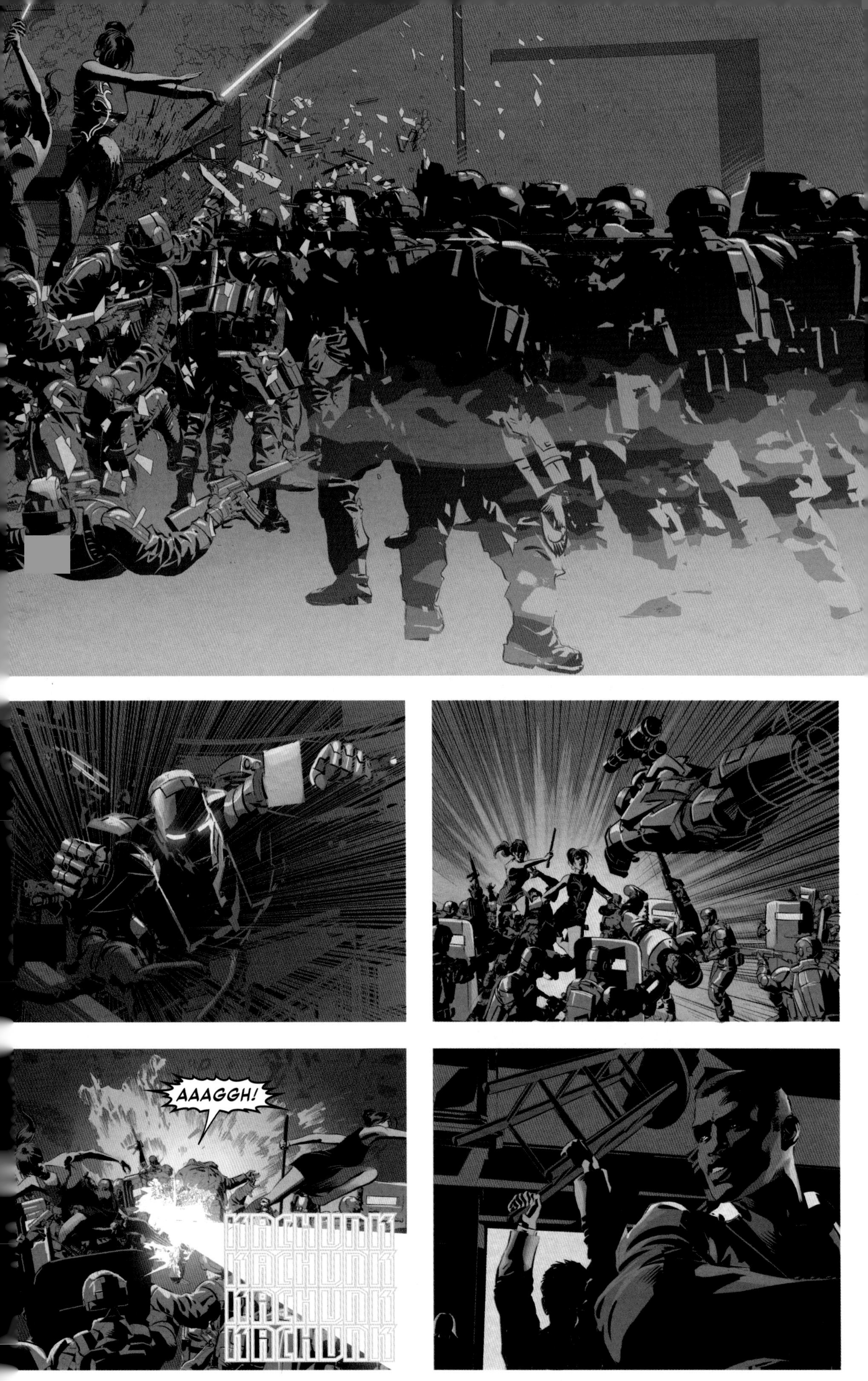
AAAGGH!
KACHUNK
KACHUNK
KACHUNK
KACHUNK

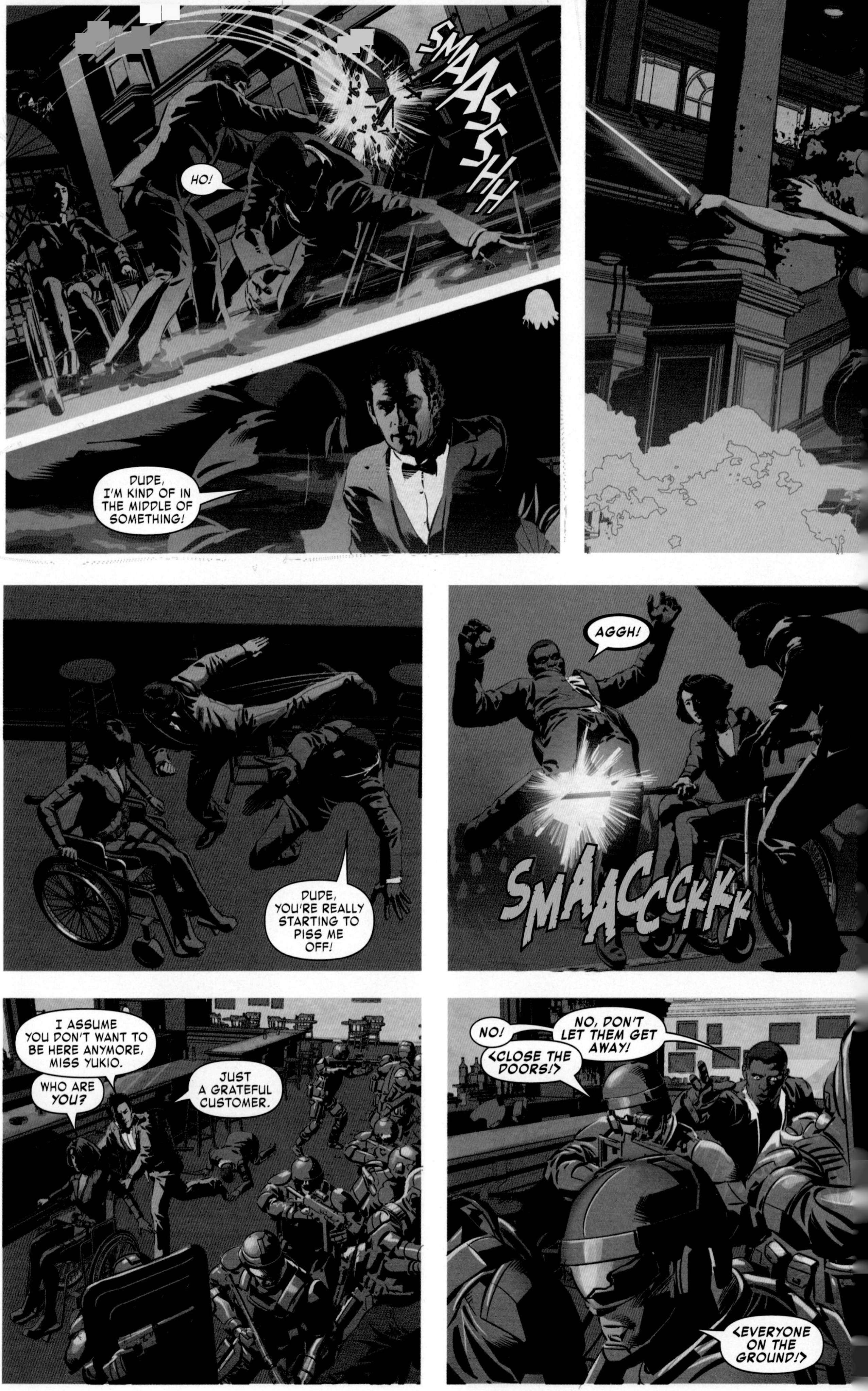
SMAASSHH
HO!
DUDE, I'M KIND OF IN THE MIDDLE OF SOMETHING!
DUDE, YOU'RE REALLY STARTING TO PISS ME OFF!
AGGH!
SMAACCCKKK
I ASSUME YOU DON'T WANT TO BE HERE ANYMORE, MISS YUKIO.
WHO ARE YOU?
JUST A GRATEFUL CUSTOMER.
NO!
NO, DON'T LET THEM GET AWAY!
<CLOSE THE DOORS!>
<EVERYONE ON THE GROUND!>

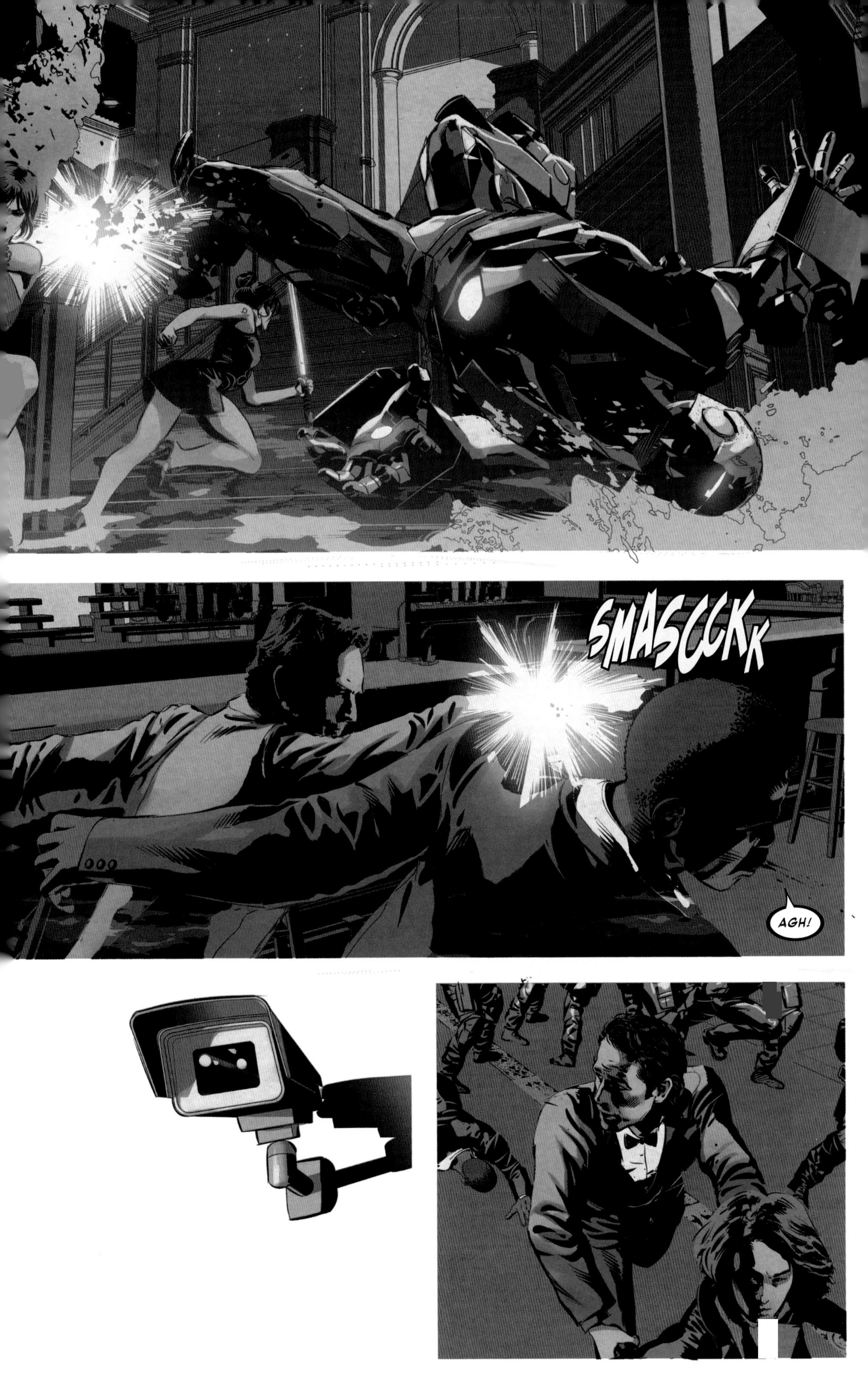
SMASCCKK
AGH!

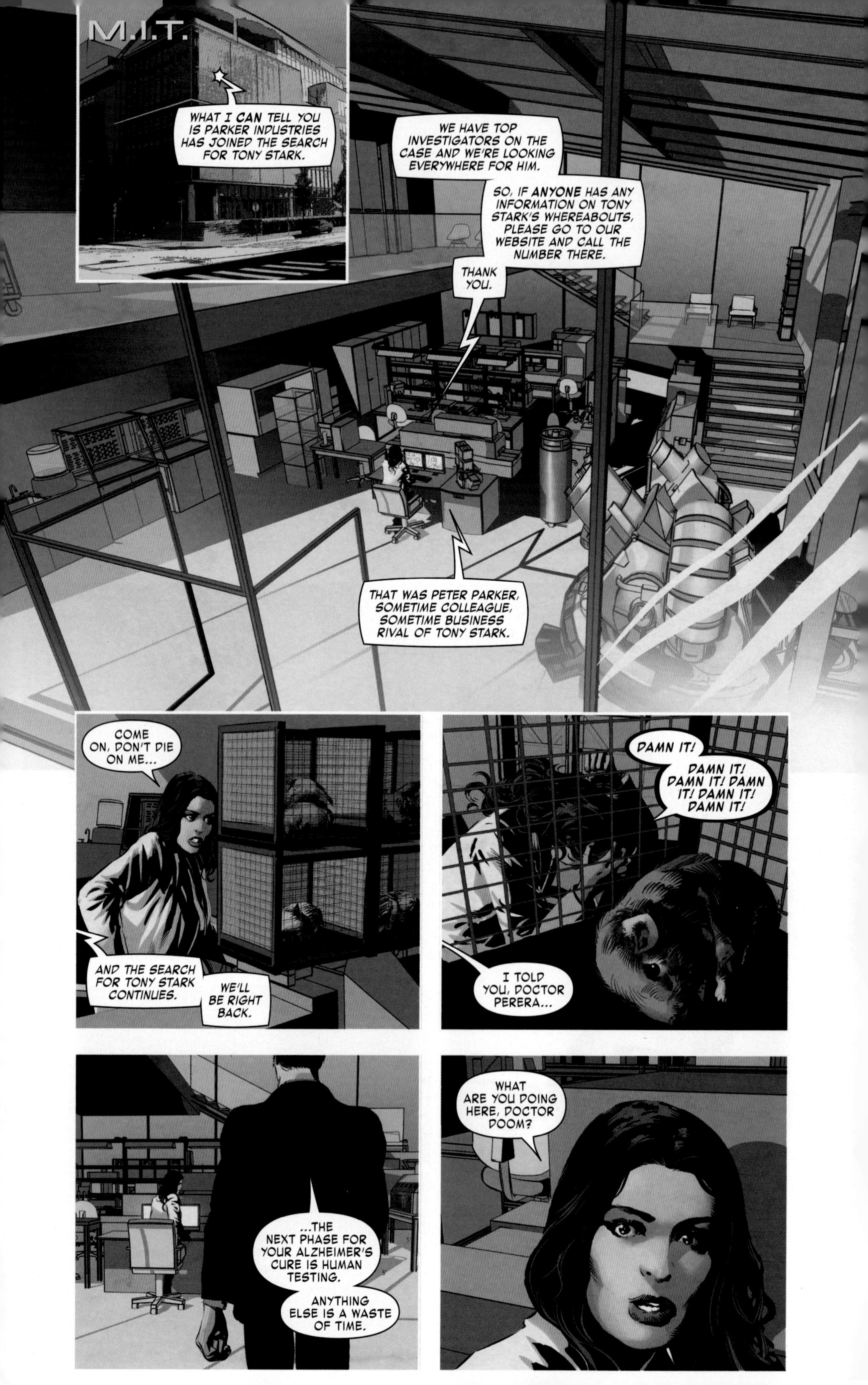
M.I.T.
WHAT I CAN TELL YOU IS PARKER INDUSTRIES HAS JOINED THE SEARCH FOR TONY STARK.
WE HAVE TOP INVESTIGATORS ON THE CASE AND WE'RE LOOKING EVERYWHERE FOR HIM.
SO, IF ANYONE HAS ANY INFORMATION ON TONY STARK'S WHEREABOUTS, PLEASE GO TO OUR WEBSITE AND CALL THE NUMBER THERE.
THANK YOU.
THAT WAS PETER PARKER, SOMETIME COLLEAGUE, SOMETIME BUSINESS RIVAL OF TONY STARK.
COME ON, DON'T DIE ON ME...
AND THE SEARCH FOR TONY STARK CONTINUES.
WE'LL BE RIGHT BACK.
DAMN IT!
DAMN IT! DAMN IT! DAMN IT! DAMN IT! DAMN IT!
I TOLD YOU, DOCTOR PERERA...
...THE NEXT PHASE FOR YOUR ALZHEIMER'S CURE IS HUMAN TESTING.
ANYTHING ELSE IS A WASTE OF TIME.
WHAT ARE YOU DOING HERE, DOCTOR DOOM?

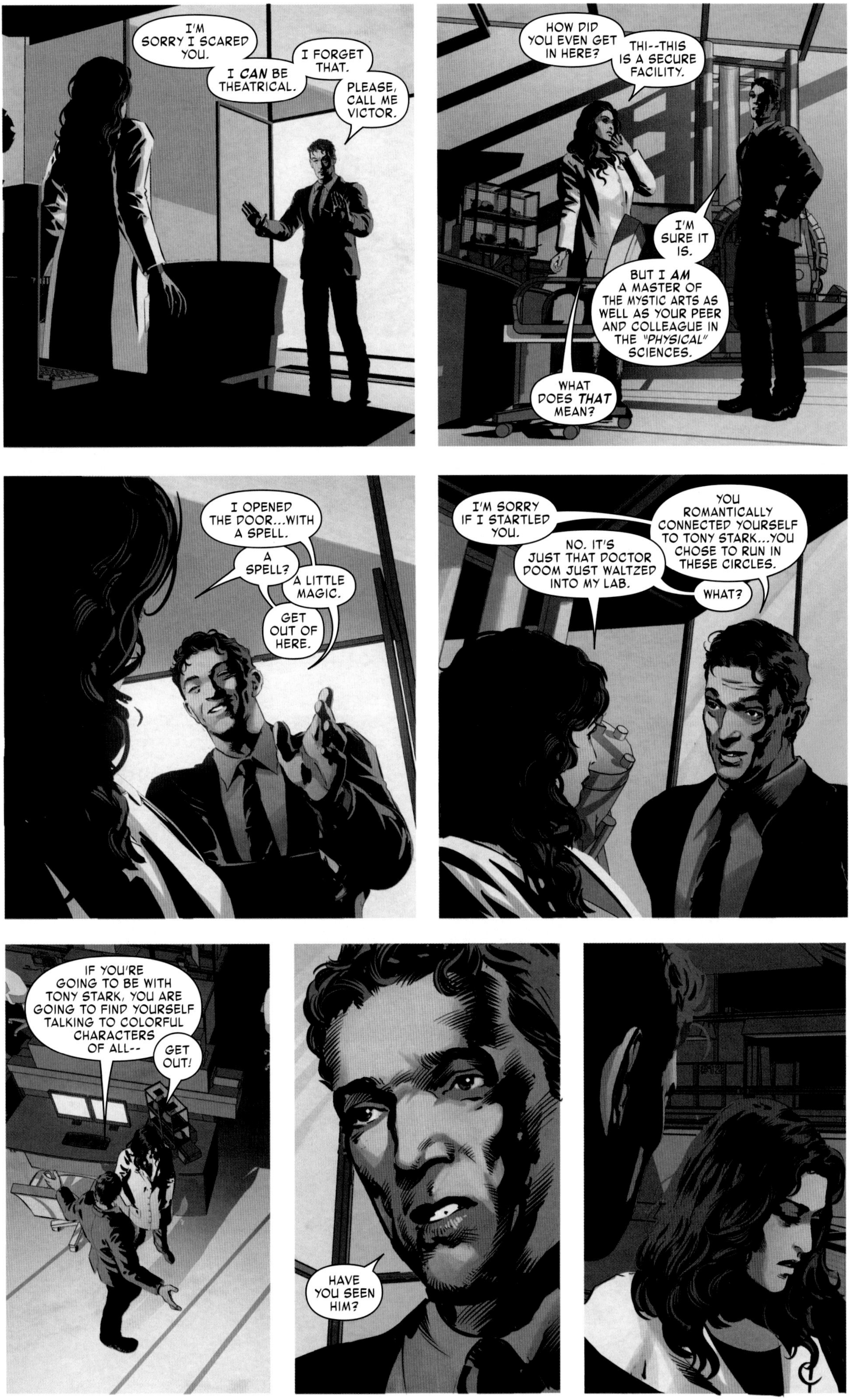
I'M SORRY I SCARED YOU.
I *CAN* BE THEATRICAL.
I FORGET THAT.
PLEASE, CALL ME VICTOR.
HOW DID YOU EVEN GET IN HERE?
THI--THIS IS A SECURE FACILITY.
I'M SURE IT IS.
BUT I *AM* A MASTER OF THE MYSTIC ARTS AS WELL AS YOUR PEER AND COLLEAGUE IN THE *"PHYSICAL"* SCIENCES.
WHAT DOES *THAT* MEAN?
I OPENED THE DOOR...WITH A SPELL.
A SPELL?
A LITTLE MAGIC.
GET OUT OF HERE.
I'M SORRY IF I STARTLED YOU.
NO. IT'S JUST THAT DOCTOR DOOM JUST WALTZED INTO MY LAB.
YOU ROMANTICALLY CONNECTED YOURSELF TO TONY STARK...YOU CHOSE TO RUN IN THESE CIRCLES.
WHAT?
IF YOU'RE GOING TO BE WITH TONY STARK, YOU ARE GOING TO FIND YOURSELF TALKING TO COLORFUL CHARACTERS OF ALL--
GET OUT!
HAVE YOU SEEN HIM?

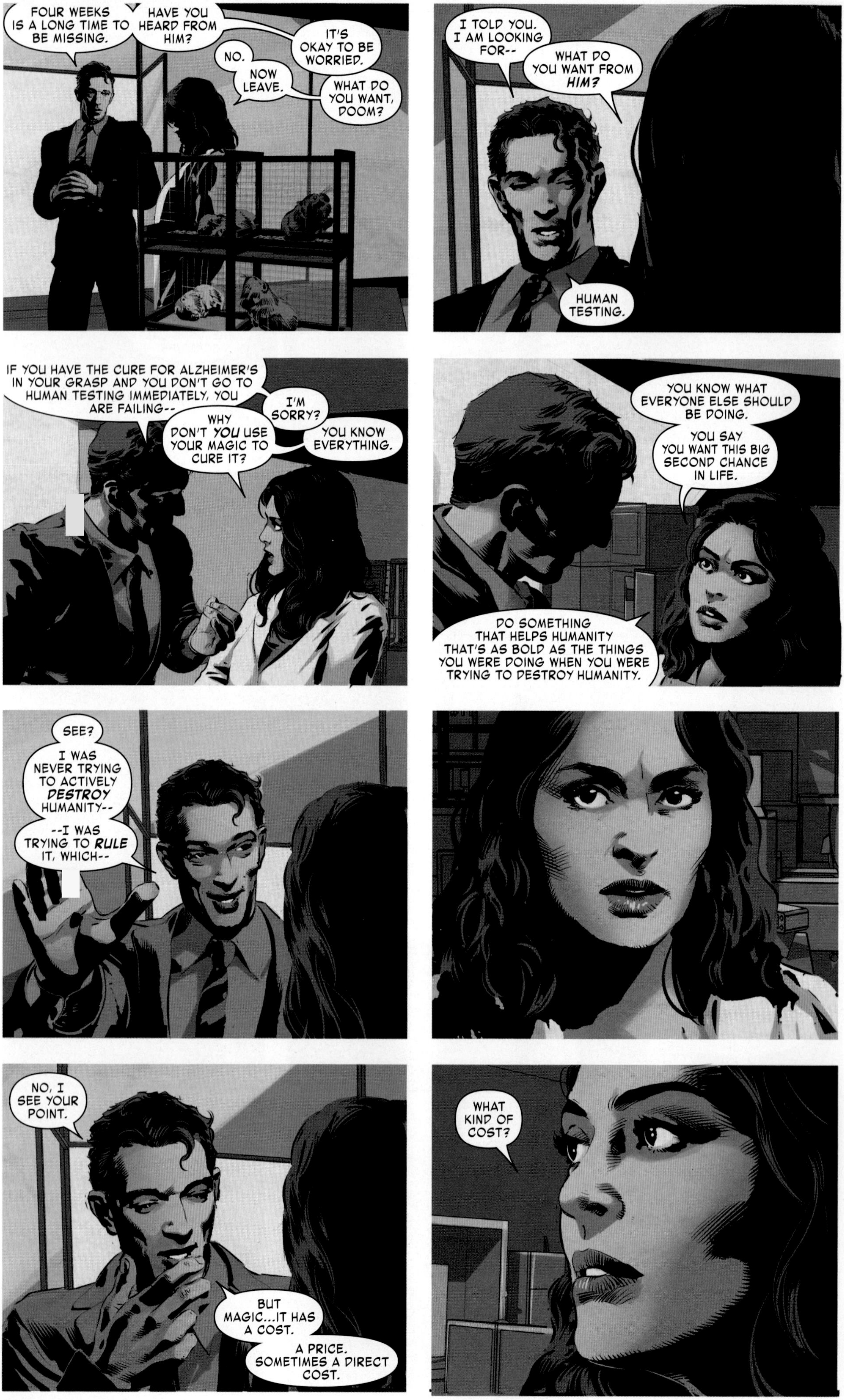
FOUR WEEKS IS A LONG TIME TO BE MISSING.
HAVE YOU HEARD FROM HIM?
NO.
NOW LEAVE.
IT'S OKAY TO BE WORRIED.
WHAT DO YOU WANT, DOOM?
I TOLD YOU. I AM LOOKING FOR--
WHAT DO YOU WANT FROM HIM?
HUMAN TESTING.
IF YOU HAVE THE CURE FOR ALZHEIMER'S IN YOUR GRASP AND YOU DON'T GO TO HUMAN TESTING IMMEDIATELY, YOU ARE FAILING--
I'M SORRY?
WHY DON'T YOU USE YOUR MAGIC TO CURE IT?
YOU KNOW EVERYTHING.
YOU KNOW WHAT EVERYONE ELSE SHOULD BE DOING.
YOU SAY YOU WANT THIS BIG SECOND CHANCE IN LIFE.
DO SOMETHING THAT HELPS HUMANITY THAT'S AS BOLD AS THE THINGS YOU WERE DOING WHEN YOU WERE TRYING TO DESTROY HUMANITY.
SEE?
I WAS NEVER TRYING TO ACTIVELY DESTROY HUMANITY--
--I WAS TRYING TO RULE IT, WHICH--
NO, I SEE YOUR POINT.
BUT MAGIC...IT HAS A COST.
A PRICE. SOMETIMES A DIRECT COST.
WHAT KIND OF COST?

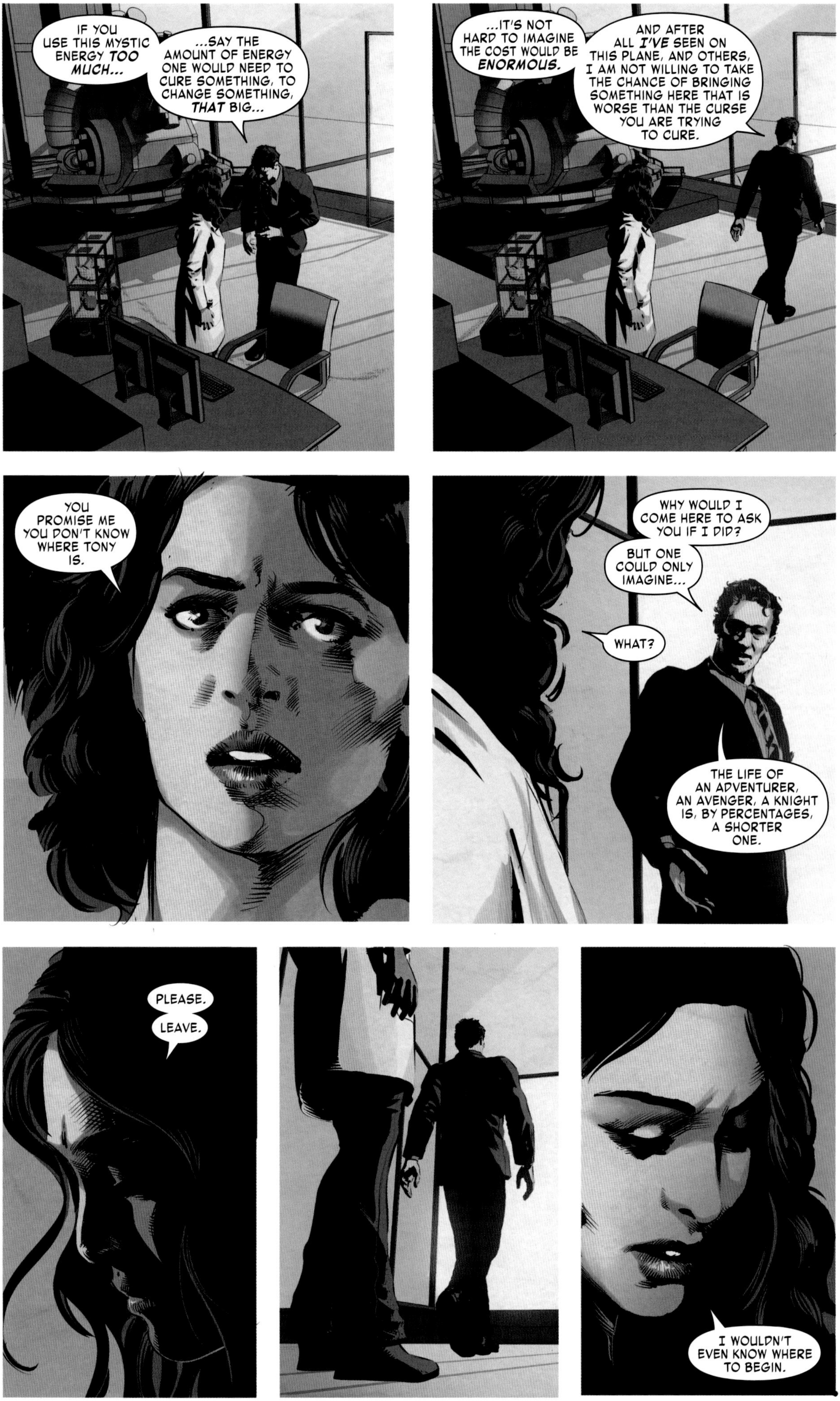

IF YOU USE THIS MYSTIC ENERGY *TOO MUCH...*
...SAY THE AMOUNT OF ENERGY ONE WOULD NEED TO CURE SOMETHING, TO CHANGE SOMETHING, *THAT* BIG...
...IT'S NOT HARD TO IMAGINE THE COST WOULD BE *ENORMOUS.*
AND AFTER ALL *I'VE* SEEN ON THIS PLANE, AND OTHERS, I AM NOT WILLING TO TAKE THE CHANCE OF BRINGING SOMETHING HERE THAT IS WORSE THAN THE CURSE YOU ARE TRYING TO CURE.
YOU PROMISE ME YOU DON'T KNOW WHERE TONY IS.
WHY WOULD I COME HERE TO ASK YOU IF I DID?
BUT ONE COULD ONLY IMAGINE...
WHAT?
THE LIFE OF AN ADVENTURER, AN AVENGER, A KNIGHT IS, BY PERCENTAGES, A SHORTER ONE.
PLEASE.
LEAVE.
I WOULDN'T EVEN KNOW WHERE TO BEGIN.

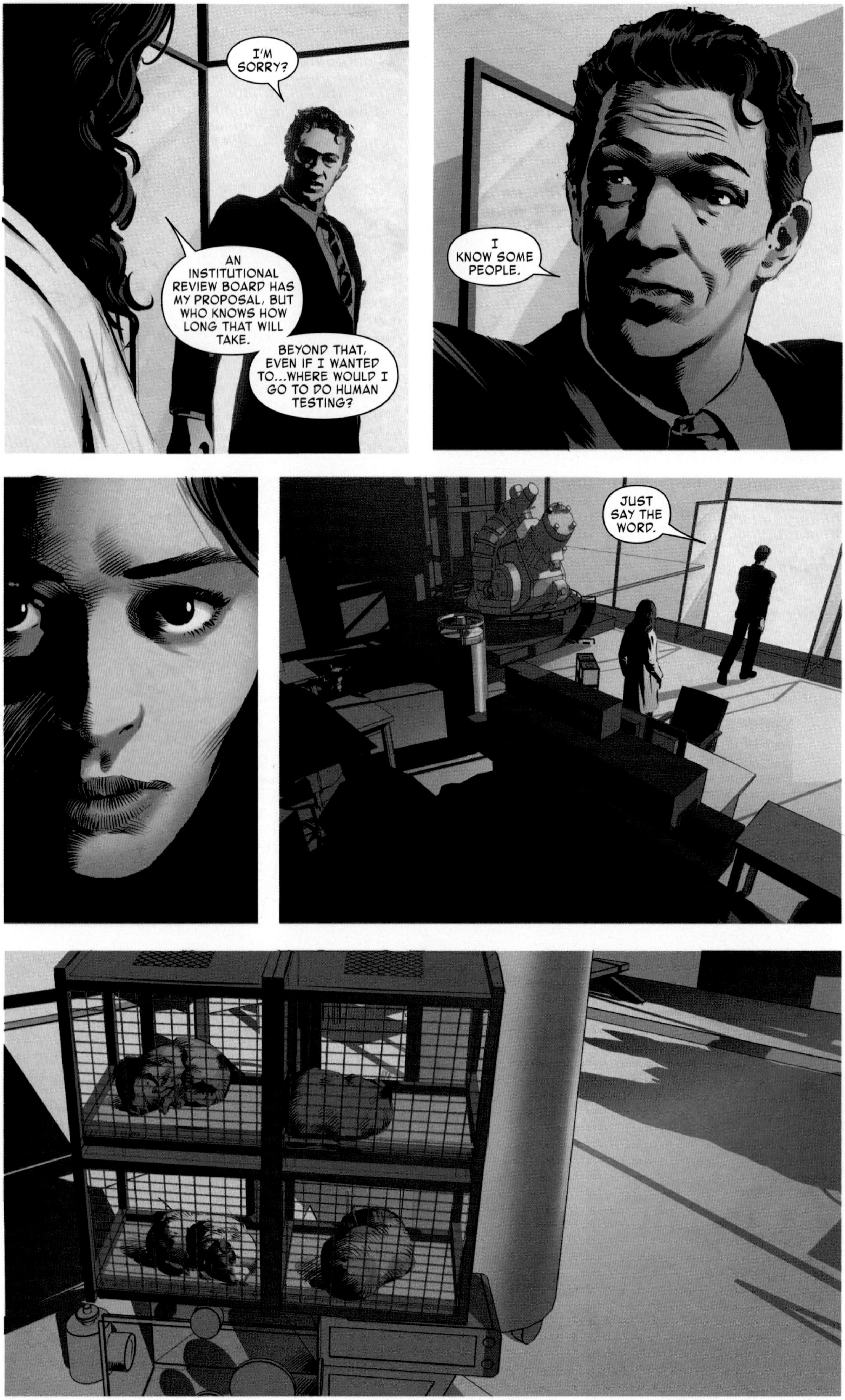
I'M SORRY?
AN INSTITUTIONAL REVIEW BOARD HAS MY PROPOSAL, BUT WHO KNOWS HOW LONG THAT WILL TAKE.
BEYOND THAT, EVEN IF I WANTED TO...WHERE WOULD I GO TO DO HUMAN TESTING?
I KNOW SOME PEOPLE.
JUST SAY THE WORD.

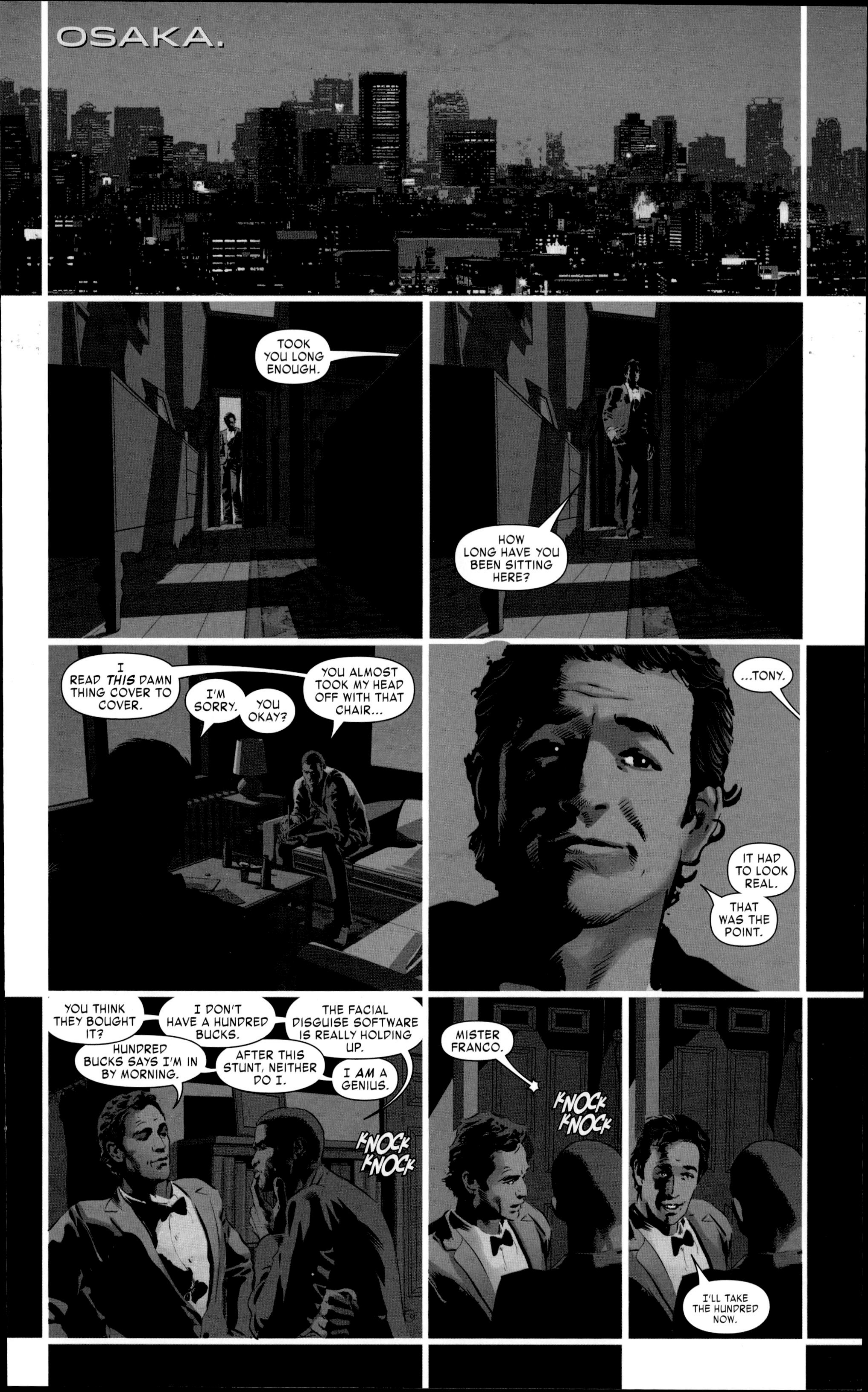
OSAKA.
TOOK YOU LONG ENOUGH.
HOW LONG HAVE YOU BEEN SITTING HERE?
I READ *THIS* DAMN THING COVER TO COVER.
I'M SORRY.
YOU OKAY?
YOU ALMOST TOOK MY HEAD OFF WITH THAT CHAIR...
...TONY.
IT HAD TO LOOK REAL.
THAT WAS THE POINT.
YOU THINK THEY BOUGHT IT?
I DON'T HAVE A HUNDRED BUCKS.
THE FACIAL DISGUISE SOFTWARE IS REALLY HOLDING UP.
HUNDRED BUCKS SAYS I'M IN BY MORNING.
AFTER THIS STUNT, NEITHER DO I.
I *AM* A GENIUS.
KNOCK KNOCK
MISTER FRANCO.
KNOCK KNOCK
I'LL TAKE THE HUNDRED NOW.

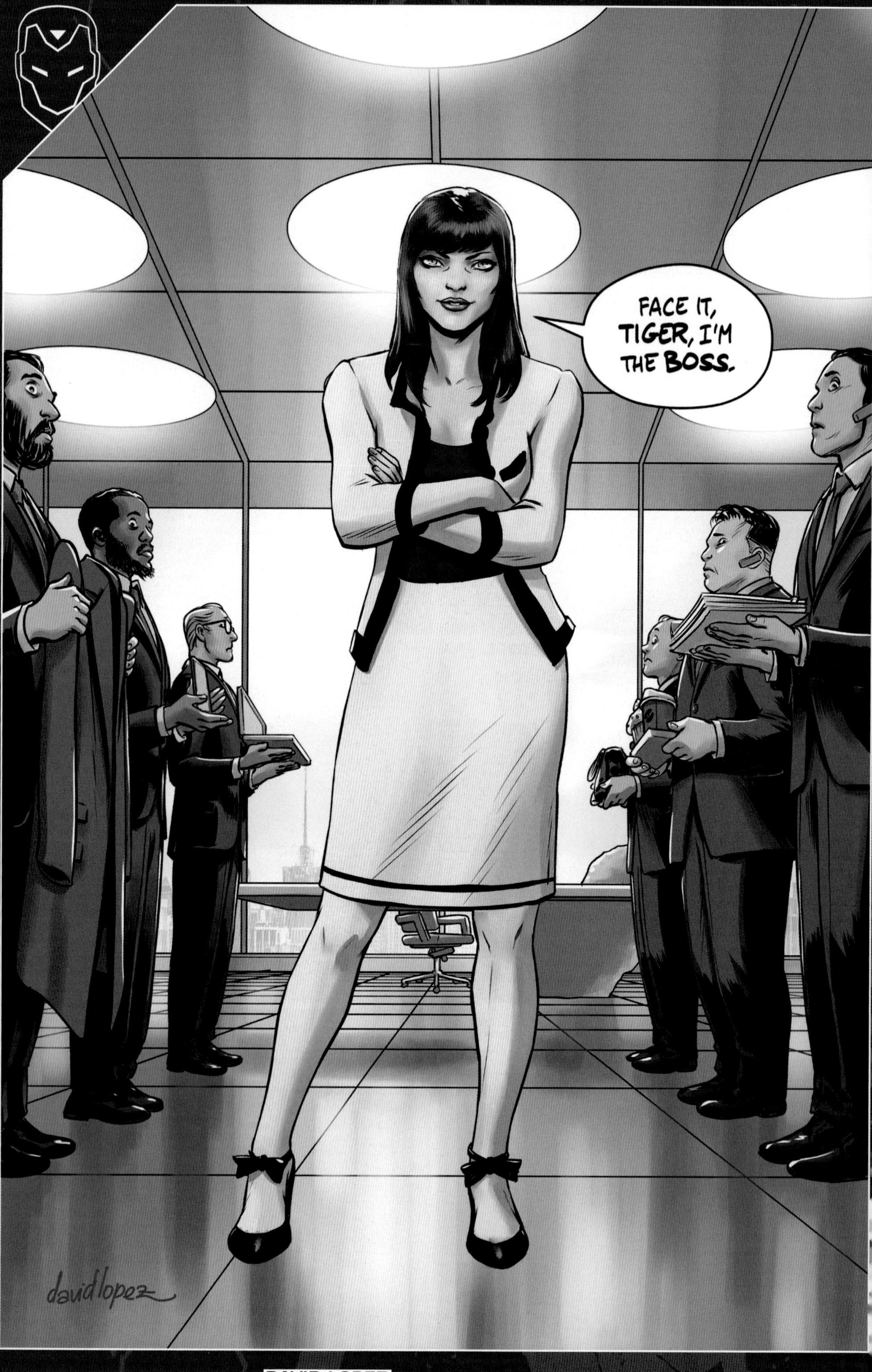
FACE IT, TIGER, I'M THE BOSS.
davidlopez

#7 WOMEN OF POWER VARIANT BY DAVID LOPEZ

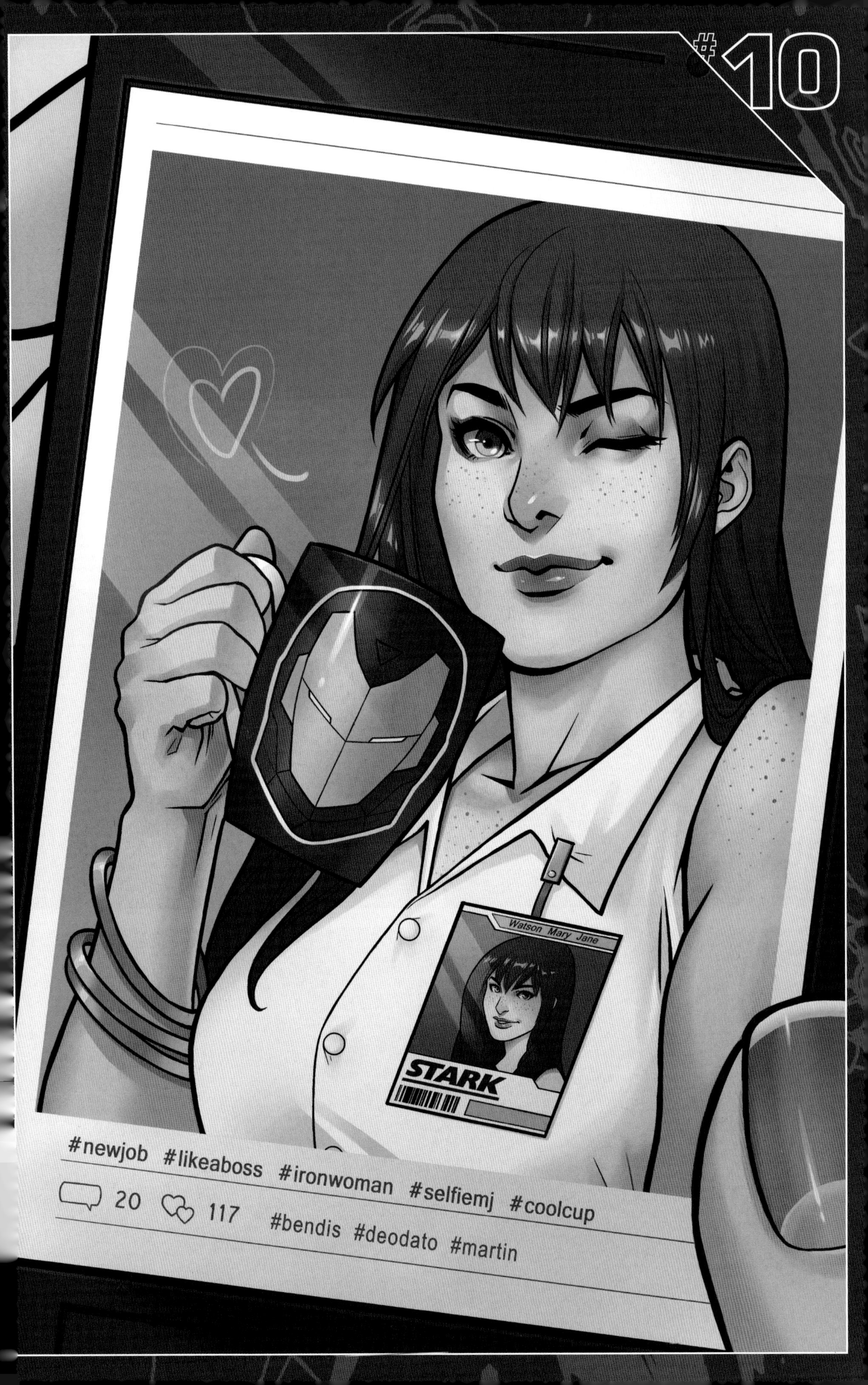
#10
Watson Mary Jane
STARK
#newjob #likeaboss #ironwoman #selfiemj #coolcup
20 117 #bendis #deodato #martin

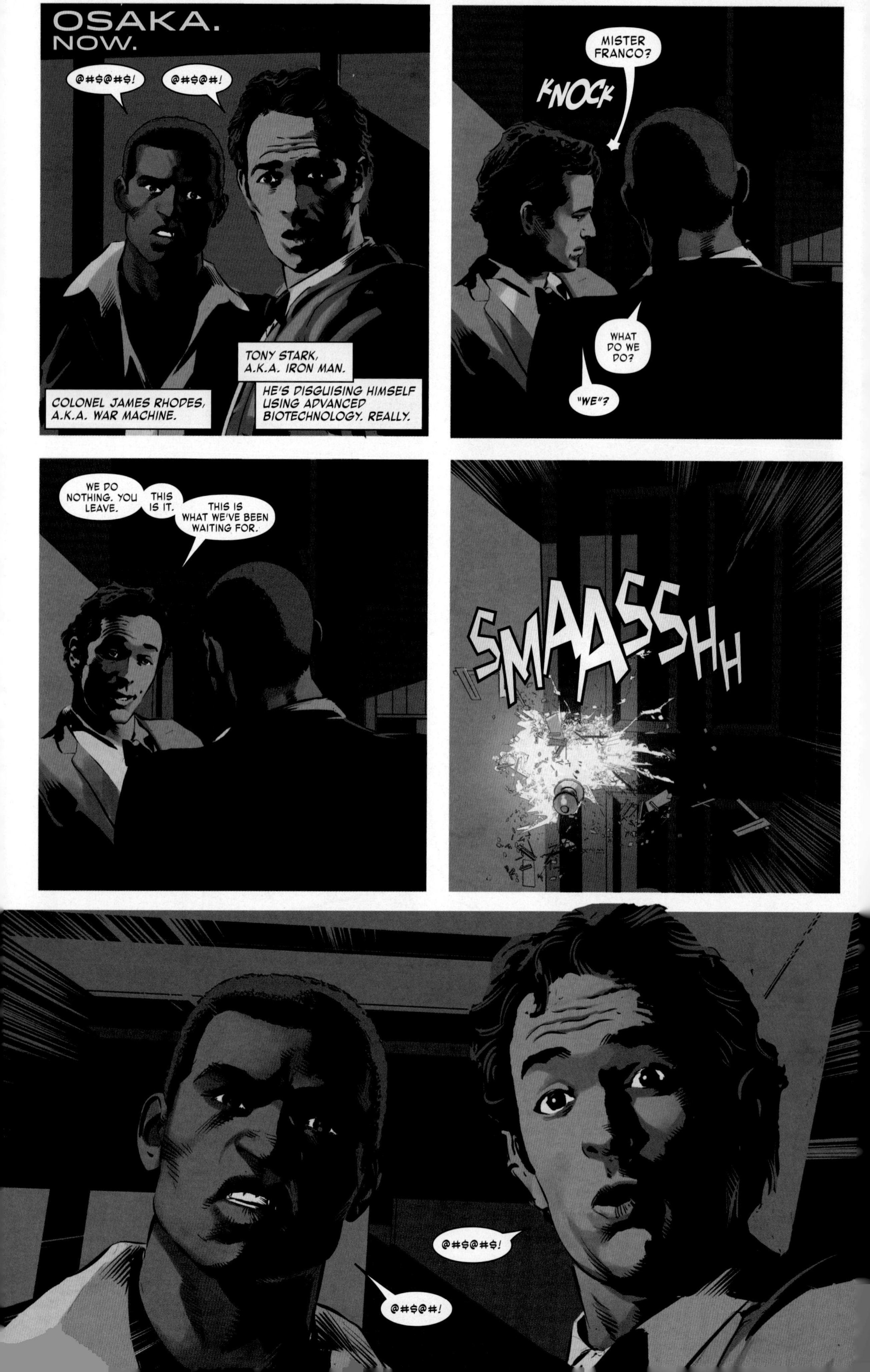
OSAKA. NOW.
@#$@#$!
@#$@#!
TONY STARK, A.K.A. IRON MAN.
HE'S DISGUISING HIMSELF USING ADVANCED BIOTECHNOLOGY. REALLY.
COLONEL JAMES RHODES, A.K.A. WAR MACHINE.
MISTER FRANCO?
KNOCK
WHAT DO WE DO?
"WE"?
WE DO NOTHING. YOU LEAVE.
THIS IS IT.
THIS IS WHAT WE'VE BEEN WAITING FOR.
SMAASSHH
@#$@#$!
@#$@#!

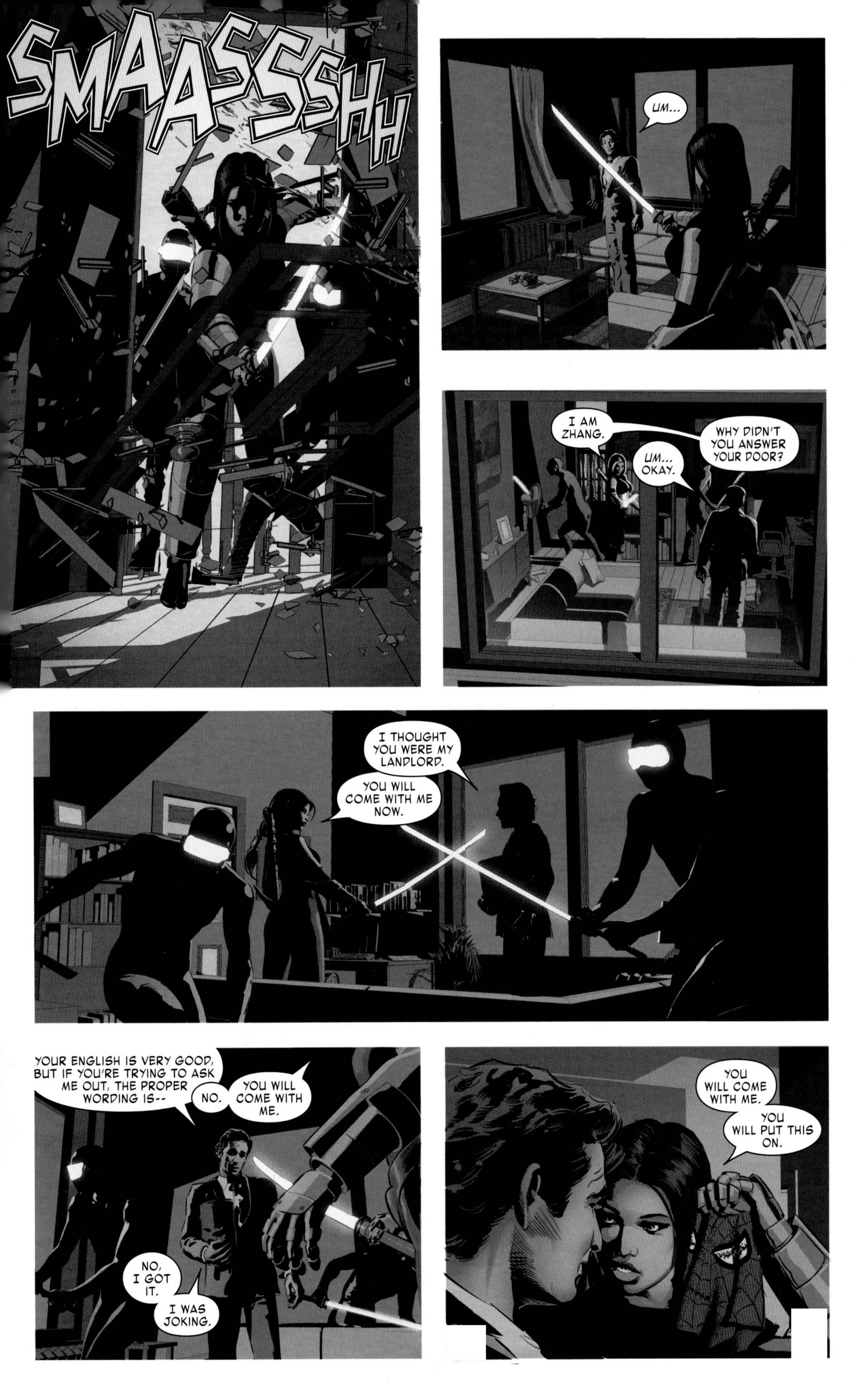
SMAASSSHH
UM...
I AM ZHANG.
WHY DIDN'T YOU ANSWER YOUR DOOR?
UM... OKAY.
I THOUGHT YOU WERE MY LANDLORD.
YOU WILL COME WITH ME NOW.
YOUR ENGLISH IS VERY GOOD, BUT IF YOU'RE TRYING TO ASK ME OUT, THE PROPER WORDING IS--
NO.
YOU WILL COME WITH ME.
NO, I GOT IT.
I WAS JOKING.
YOU WILL COME WITH ME.
YOU WILL PUT THIS ON.

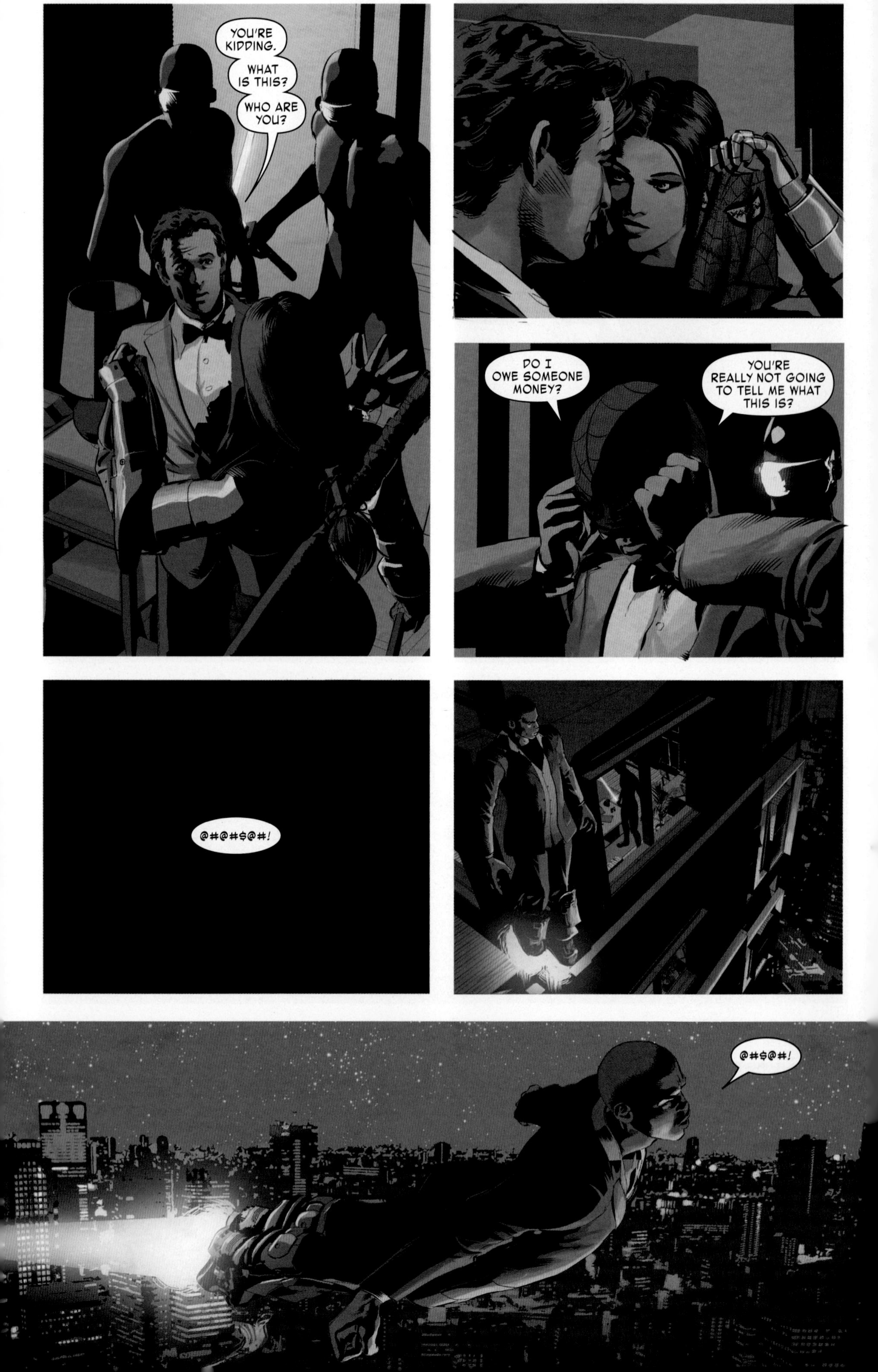
YOU'RE KIDDING.
WHAT IS THIS?
WHO ARE YOU?
DO I OWE SOMEONE MONEY?
YOU'RE REALLY NOT GOING TO TELL ME WHAT THIS IS?
@#@#$@#!
@#$@#!

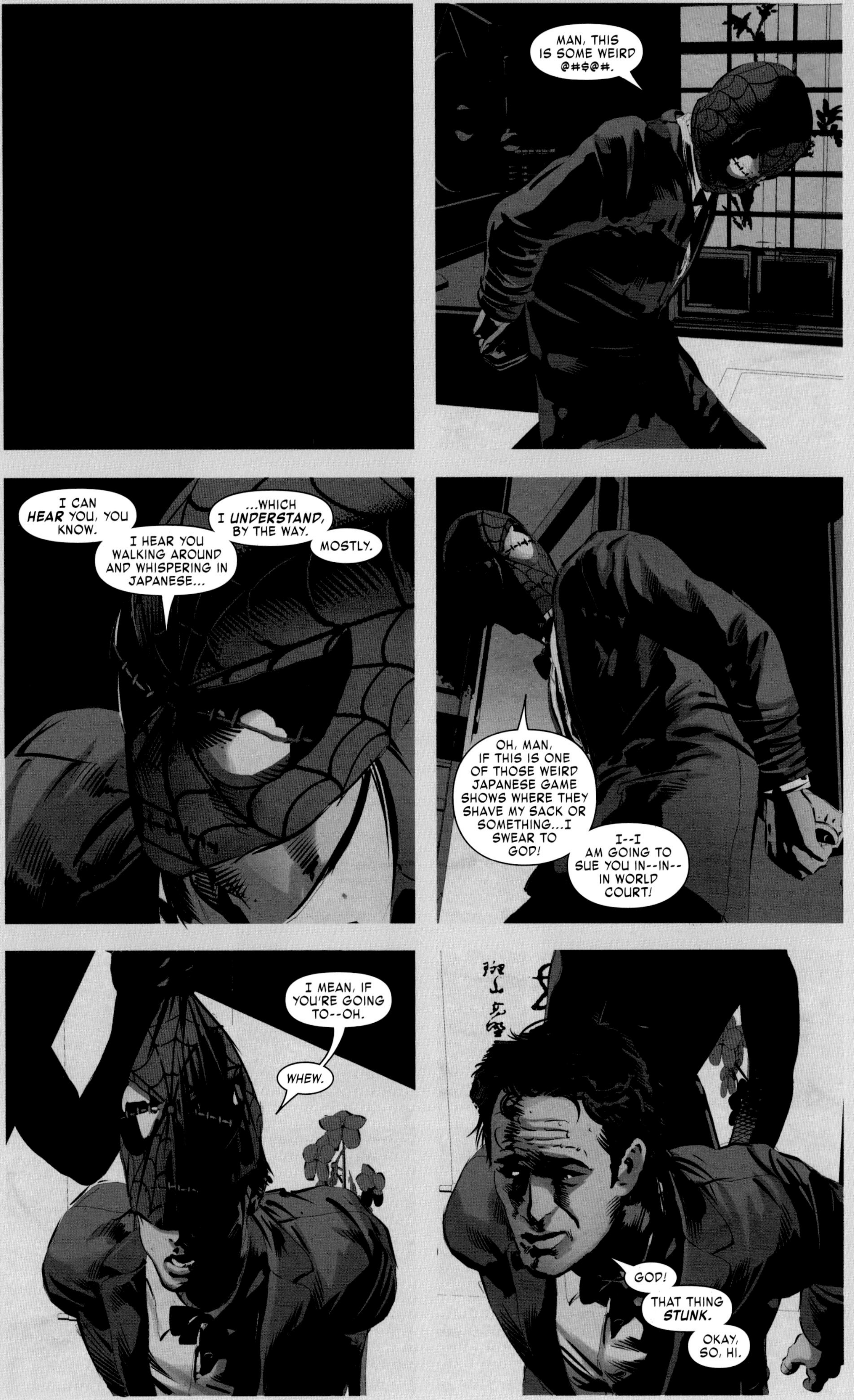
MAN, THIS IS SOME WEIRD @#$@#.
I CAN HEAR YOU, YOU KNOW.
I HEAR YOU WALKING AROUND AND WHISPERING IN JAPANESE...
...WHICH I UNDERSTAND, BY THE WAY.
MOSTLY.
OH, MAN, IF THIS IS ONE OF THOSE WEIRD JAPANESE GAME SHOWS WHERE THEY SHAVE MY SACK OR SOMETHING...I SWEAR TO GOD!
I--I AM GOING TO SUE YOU IN--IN--IN WORLD COURT!
I MEAN, IF YOU'RE GOING TO--OH.
WHEW.
GOD!
THAT THING STUNK.
OKAY, SO, HI.

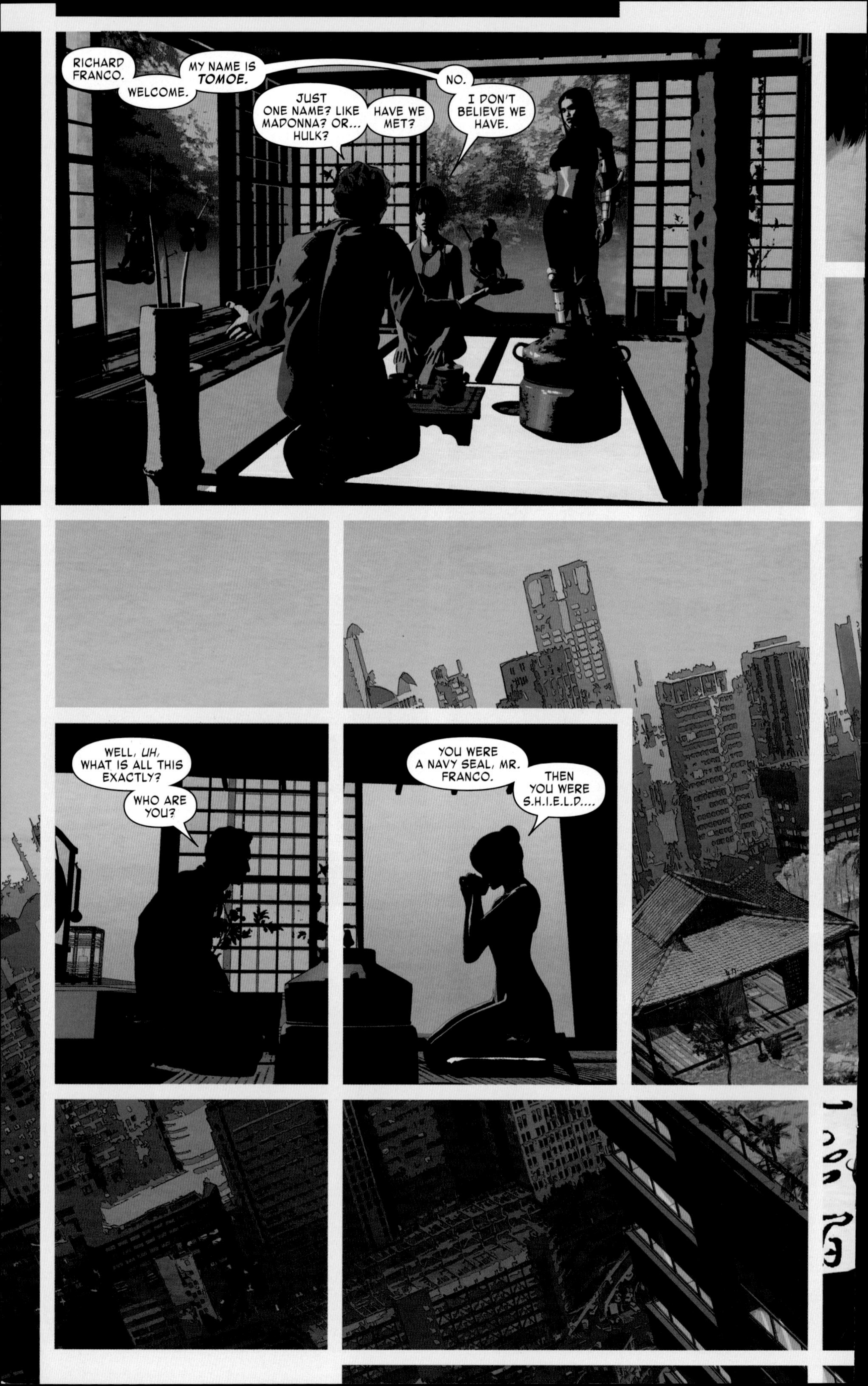
RICHARD FRANCO.
WELCOME.
MY NAME IS *TOMOE.*
JUST ONE NAME? LIKE MADONNA? OR... HULK?
NO.
HAVE WE MET?
I DON'T BELIEVE WE HAVE.
WELL, *UH,* WHAT IS ALL THIS EXACTLY?
WHO ARE YOU?
YOU WERE A NAVY SEAL, MR. FRANCO.
THEN YOU WERE S.H.I.E.L.D....

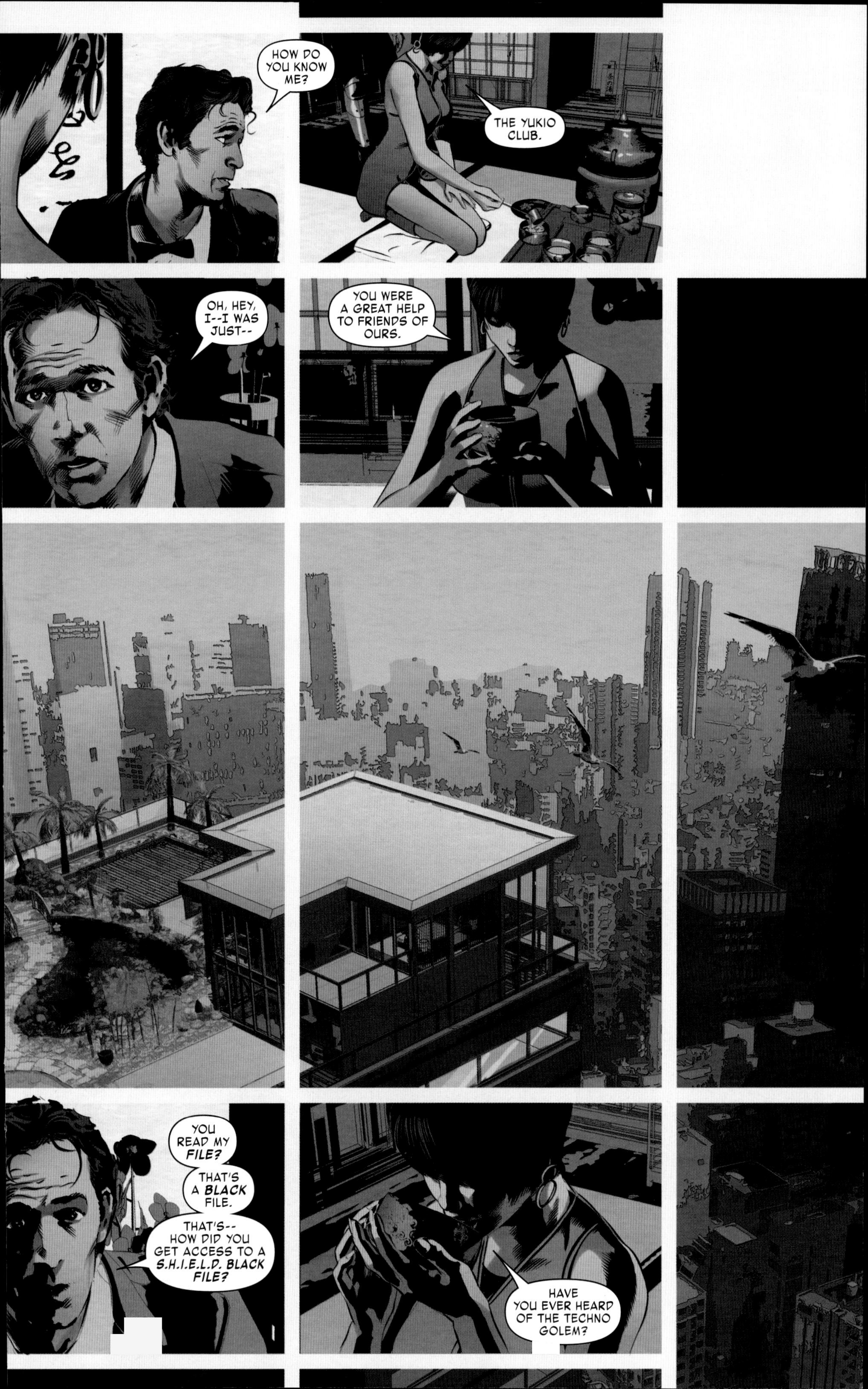

HOW DO YOU KNOW ME?
THE YUKIO CLUB.
OH, HEY, I--I WAS JUST--
YOU WERE A GREAT HELP TO FRIENDS OF OURS.
YOU READ MY FILE?
THAT'S A BLACK FILE.
THAT'S-- HOW DID YOU GET ACCESS TO A S.H.I.E.L.D. BLACK FILE?
HAVE YOU EVER HEARD OF THE TECHNO GOLEM?

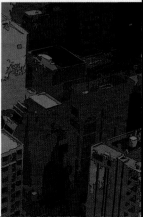

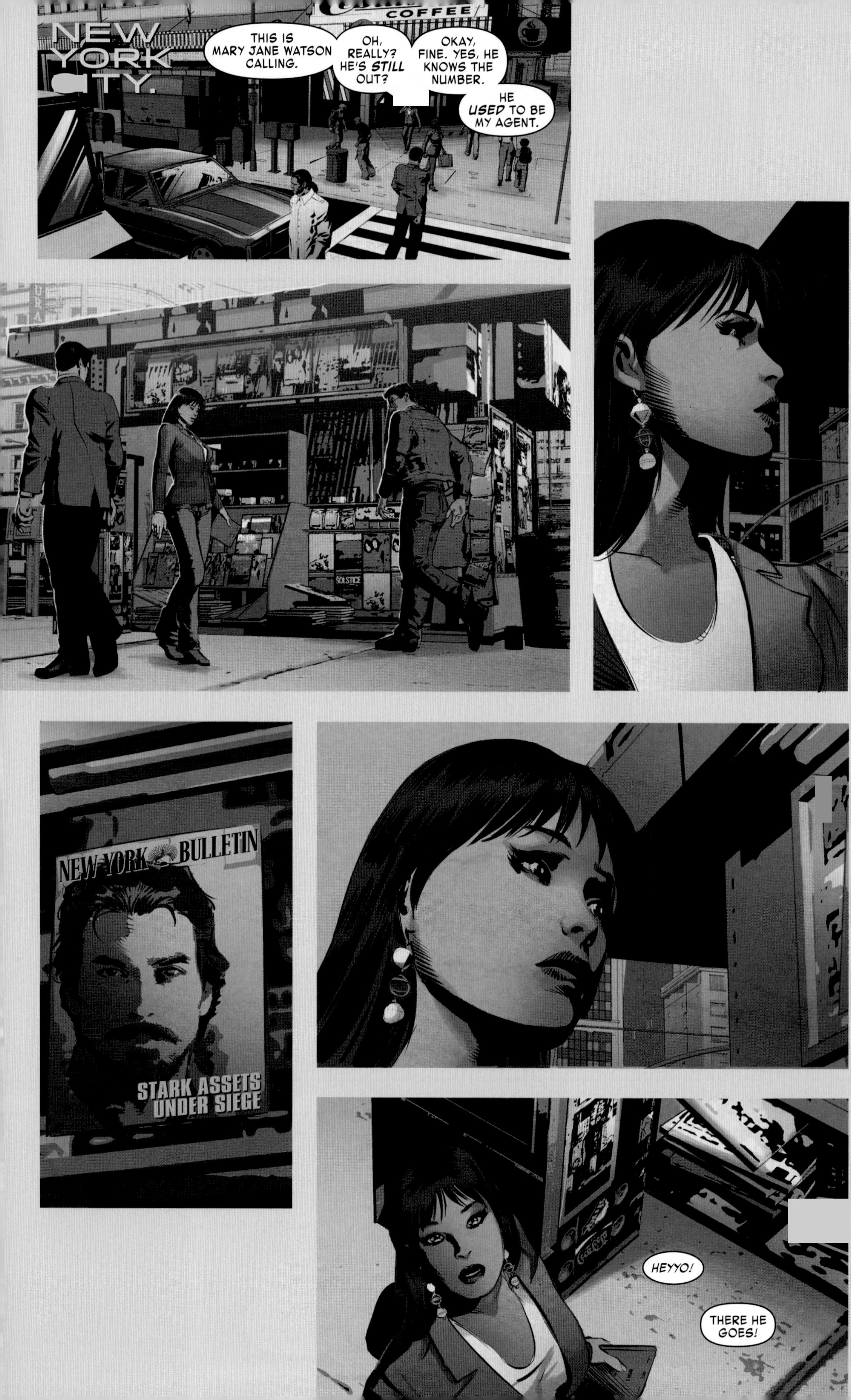

COFFEE
NEW YORK
THIS IS MARY JANE WATSON CALLING.
OH, REALLY? HE'S *STILL* OUT?
OKAY, FINE. YES, HE KNOWS THE NUMBER.
HE *USED* TO BE MY AGENT.
SOLSTICE
NEW YORK BULLETIN
STARK ASSETS UNDER SIEGE
HEYYO!
THERE HE GOES!

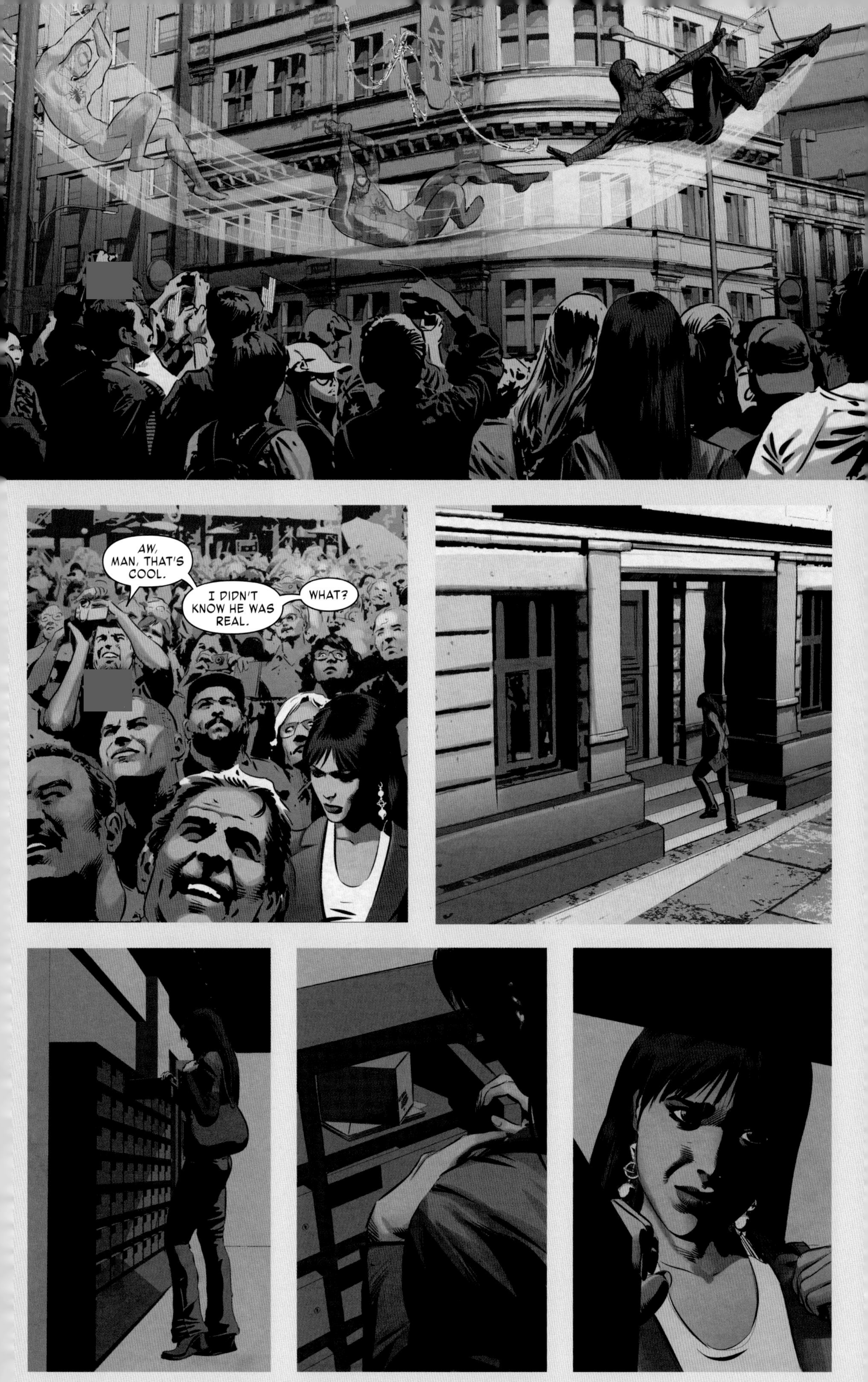
AW, MAN, THAT'S COOL.
I DIDN'T KNOW HE WAS REAL.
WHAT?

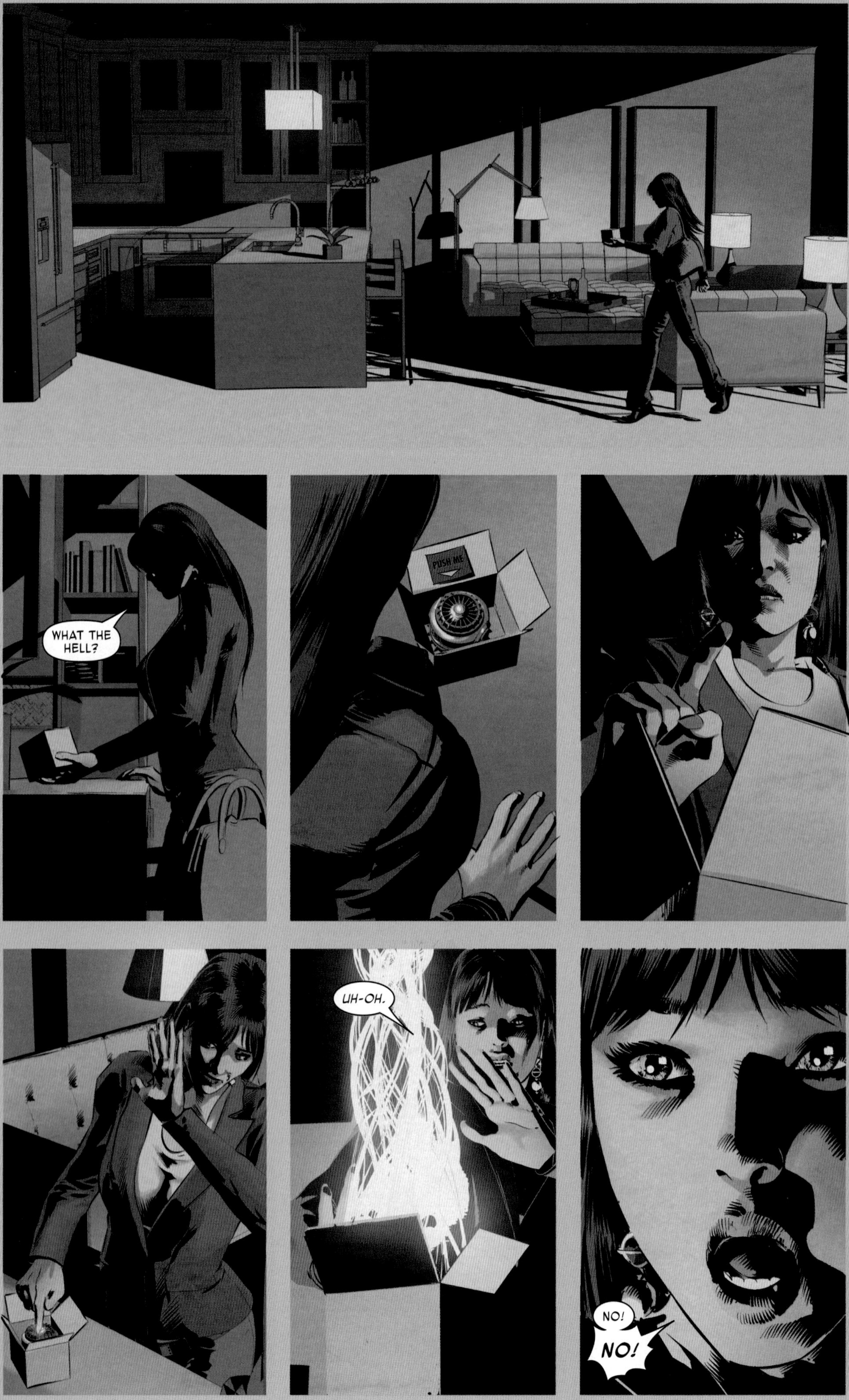
WHAT THE HELL?
PUSH ME
UH-OH.
NO!
NO!

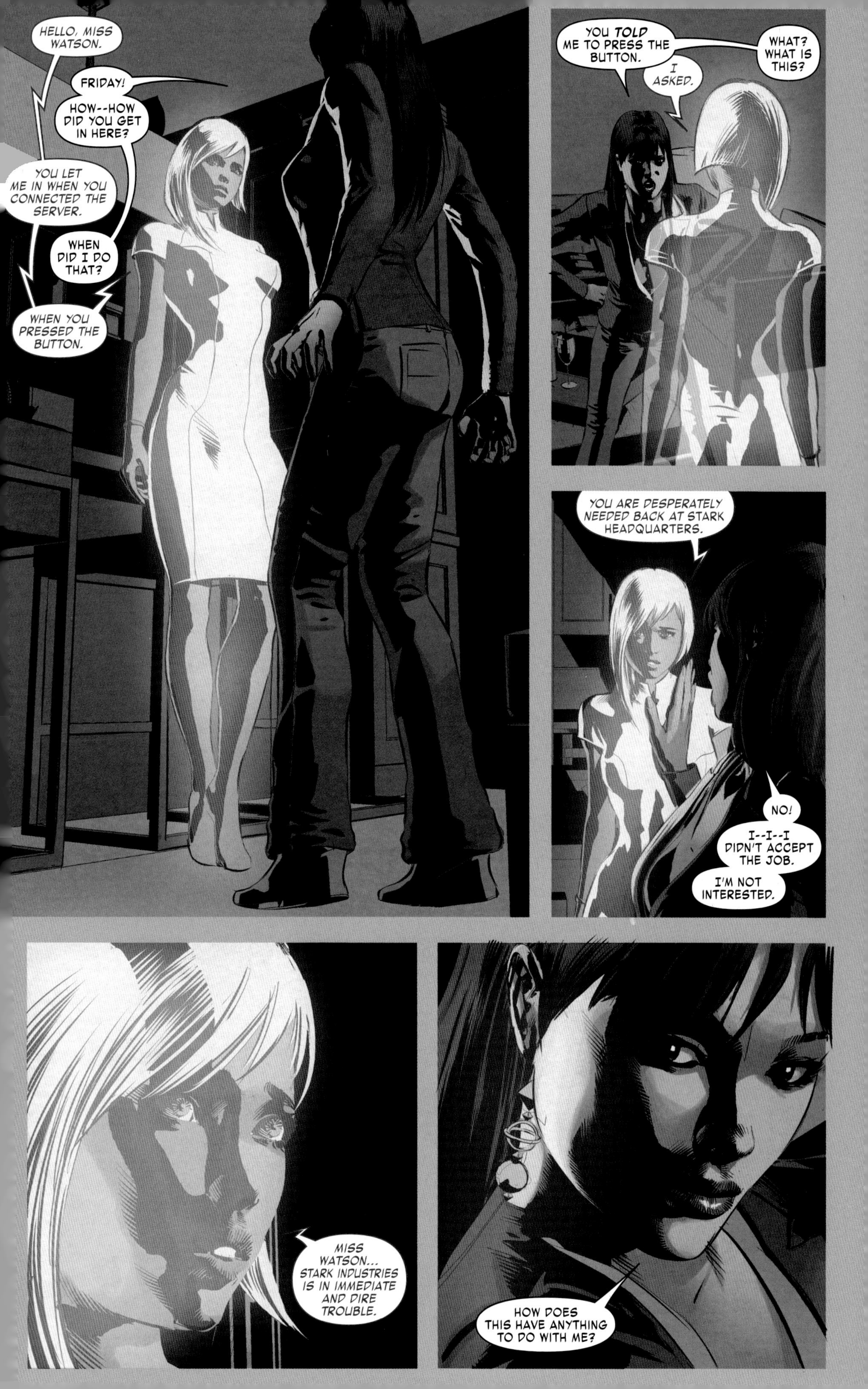
HELLO, MISS WATSON.
FRIDAY!
HOW--HOW DID YOU GET IN HERE?
YOU LET ME IN WHEN YOU CONNECTED THE SERVER.
WHEN DID I DO THAT?
WHEN YOU PRESSED THE BUTTON.
YOU TOLD ME TO PRESS THE BUTTON.
I ASKED.
WHAT? WHAT IS THIS?
YOU ARE DESPERATELY NEEDED BACK AT STARK HEADQUARTERS.
NO!
I--I--I DIDN'T ACCEPT THE JOB.
I'M NOT INTERESTED.
MISS WATSON... STARK INDUSTRIES IS IN IMMEDIATE AND DIRE TROUBLE.
HOW DOES THIS HAVE ANYTHING TO DO WITH ME?

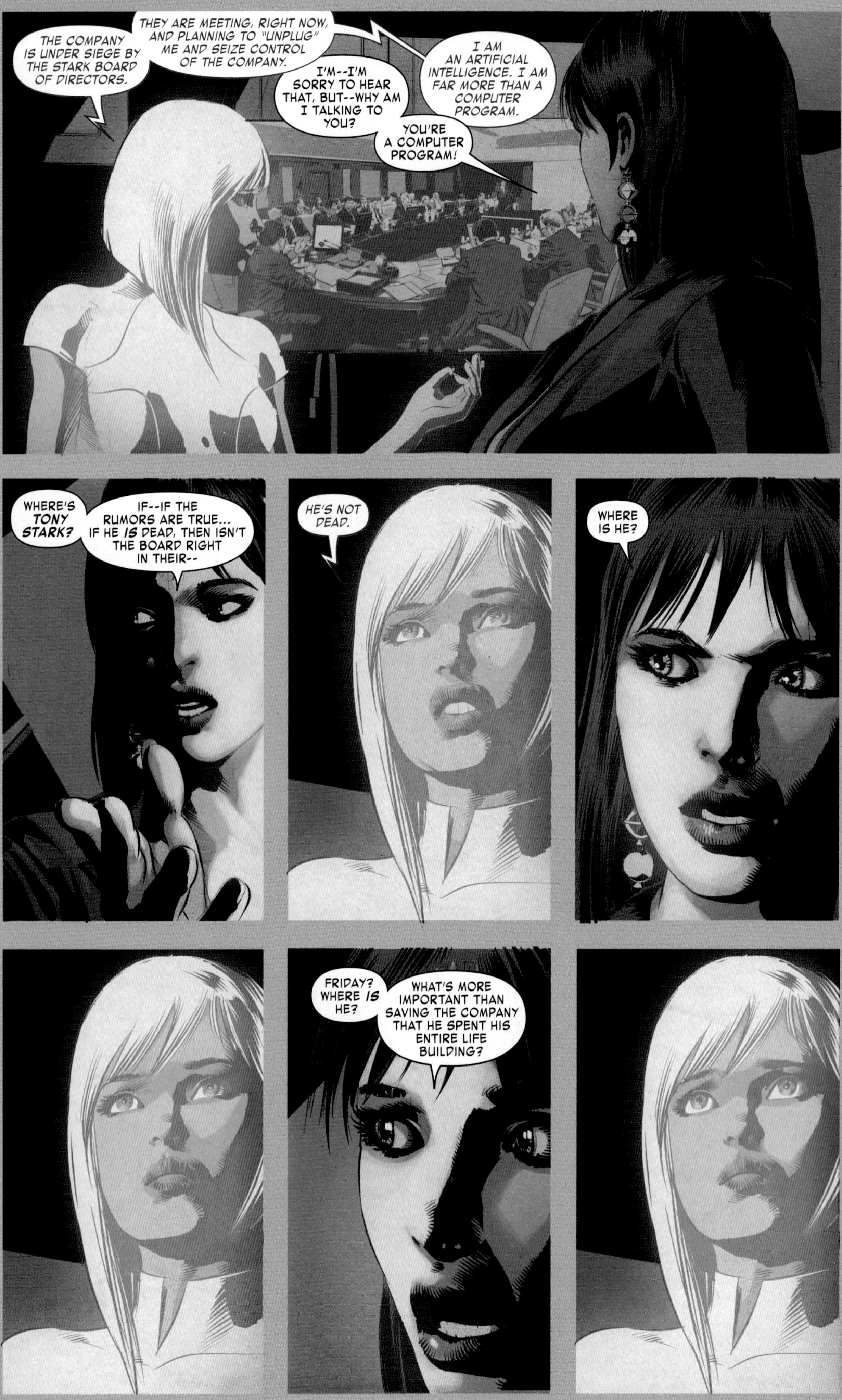
THE COMPANY IS UNDER SIEGE BY THE STARK BOARD OF DIRECTORS.
THEY ARE MEETING, RIGHT NOW, AND PLANNING TO "UNPLUG" ME AND SEIZE CONTROL OF THE COMPANY.
I'M--I'M SORRY TO HEAR THAT, BUT--WHY AM I TALKING TO YOU?
YOU'RE A COMPUTER PROGRAM!
I AM AN ARTIFICIAL INTELLIGENCE. I AM FAR MORE THAN A COMPUTER PROGRAM.
WHERE'S TONY STARK?
IF--IF THE RUMORS ARE TRUE... IF HE IS DEAD, THEN ISN'T THE BOARD RIGHT IN THEIR--
HE'S NOT DEAD.
WHERE IS HE?
FRIDAY? WHERE IS HE?
WHAT'S MORE IMPORTANT THAN SAVING THE COMPANY THAT HE SPENT HIS ENTIRE LIFE BUILDING?

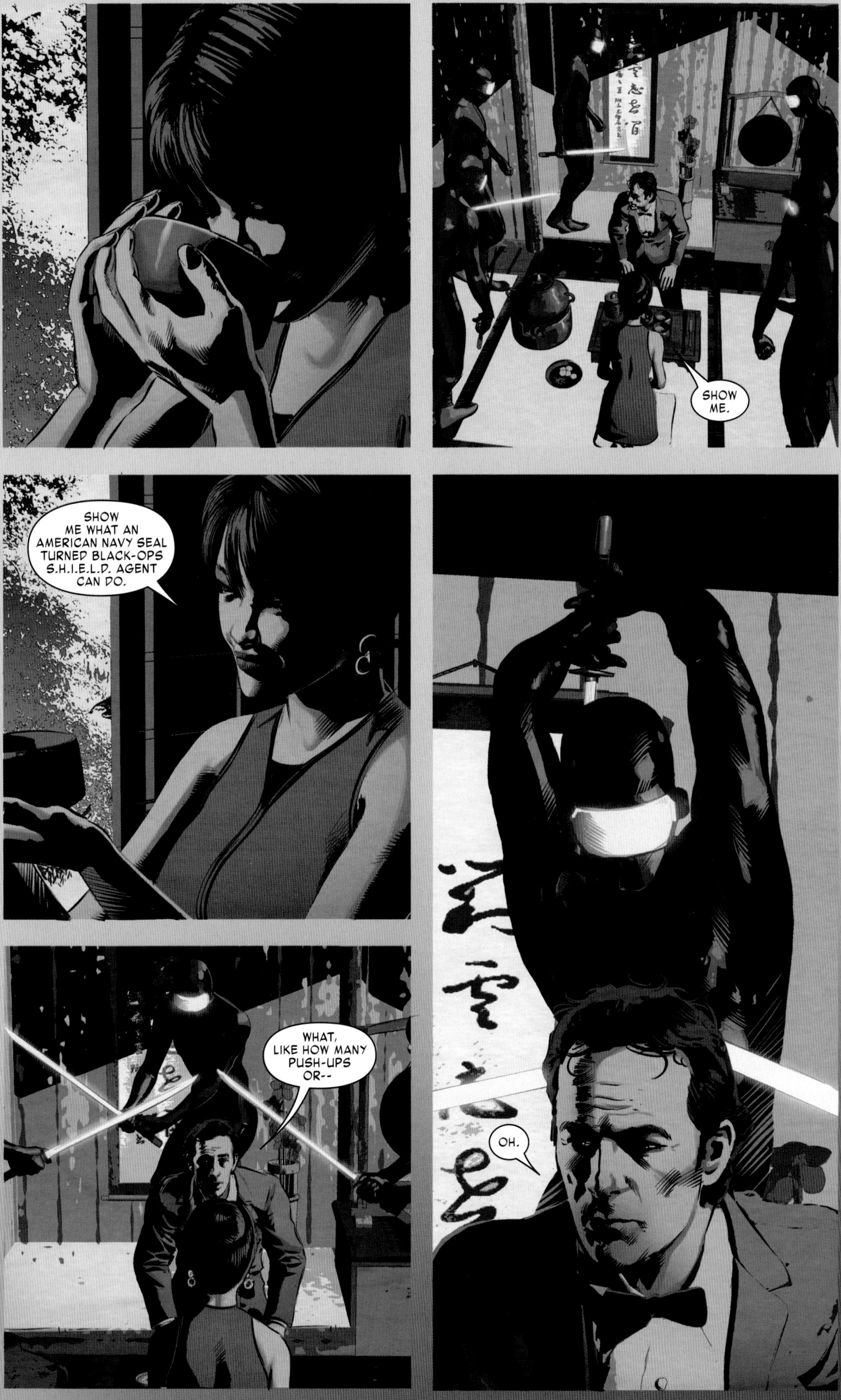
SHOW ME.
SHOW ME WHAT AN AMERICAN NAVY SEAL TURNED BLACK-OPS S.H.I.E.L.D. AGENT CAN DO.
WHAT, LIKE HOW MANY PUSH-UPS OR--
OH.

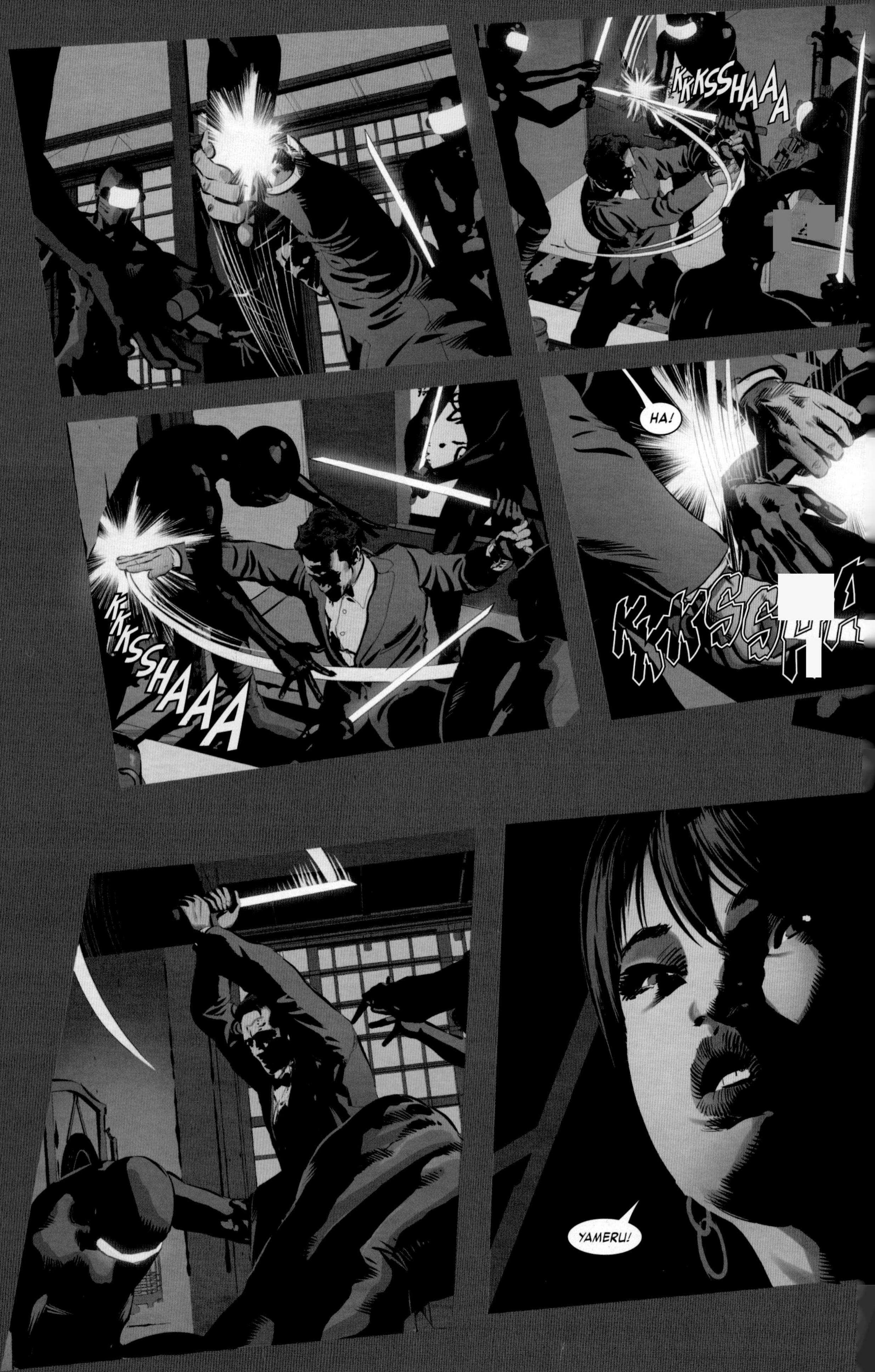
KKKSSHAAA
HA!
KKKSSHAAA
YAMERU!

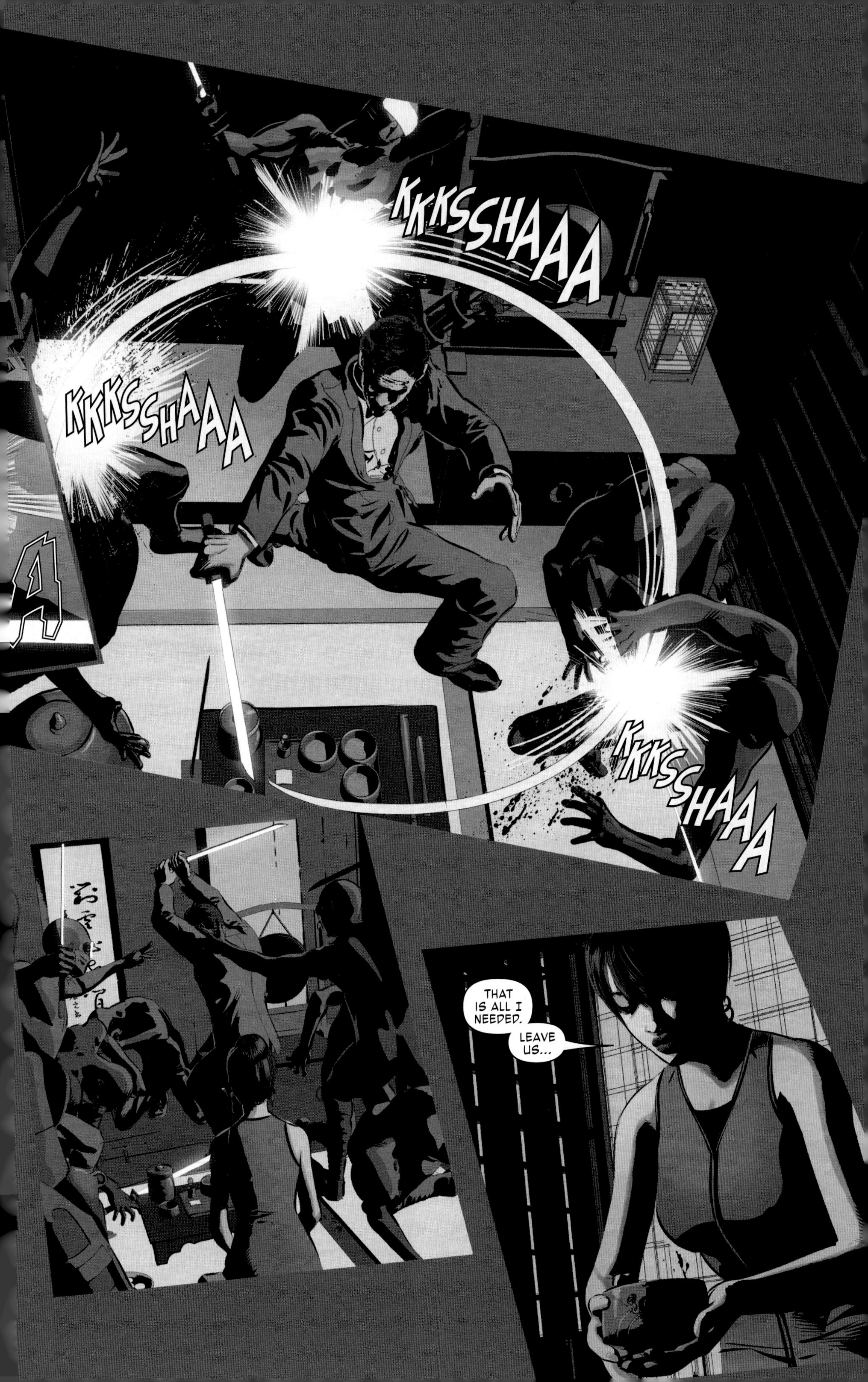
KKKSSHAAA
KKKSSHAAA
KKKSSHAAA
THAT IS ALL I NEEDED.
LEAVE US...

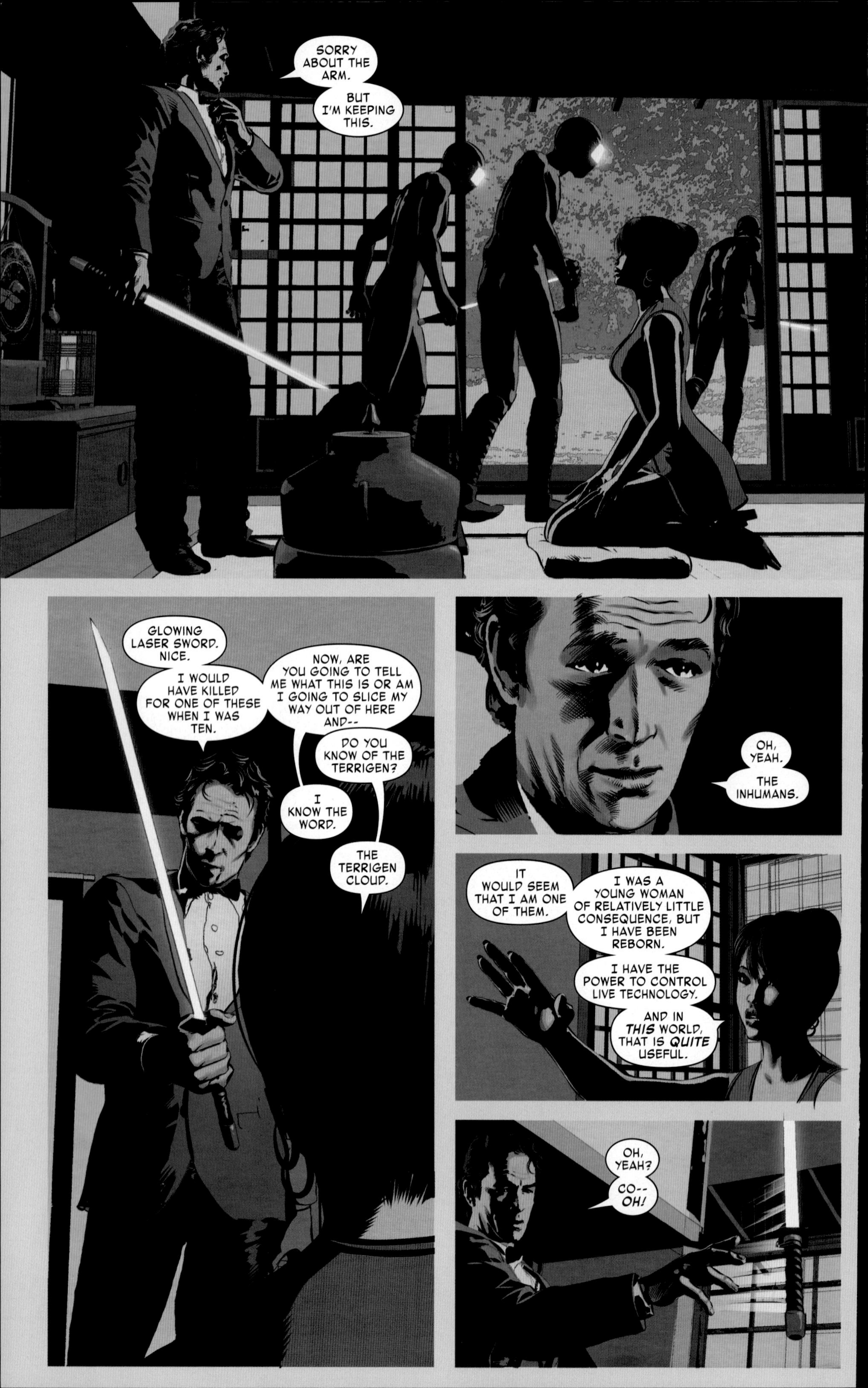
SORRY ABOUT THE ARM.
BUT I'M KEEPING THIS.
GLOWING LASER SWORD. NICE.
I WOULD HAVE KILLED FOR ONE OF THESE WHEN I WAS TEN.
NOW, ARE YOU GOING TO TELL ME WHAT THIS IS OR AM I GOING TO SLICE MY WAY OUT OF HERE AND--
DO YOU KNOW OF THE TERRIGEN?
I KNOW THE WORD.
THE TERRIGEN CLOUD.
OH, YEAH.
THE INHUMANS.
IT WOULD SEEM THAT I AM ONE OF THEM.
I WAS A YOUNG WOMAN OF RELATIVELY LITTLE CONSEQUENCE, BUT I HAVE BEEN REBORN.
I HAVE THE POWER TO CONTROL LIVE TECHNOLOGY.
AND IN THIS WORLD, THAT IS QUITE USEFUL.
OH, YEAH?
CO-- OH!

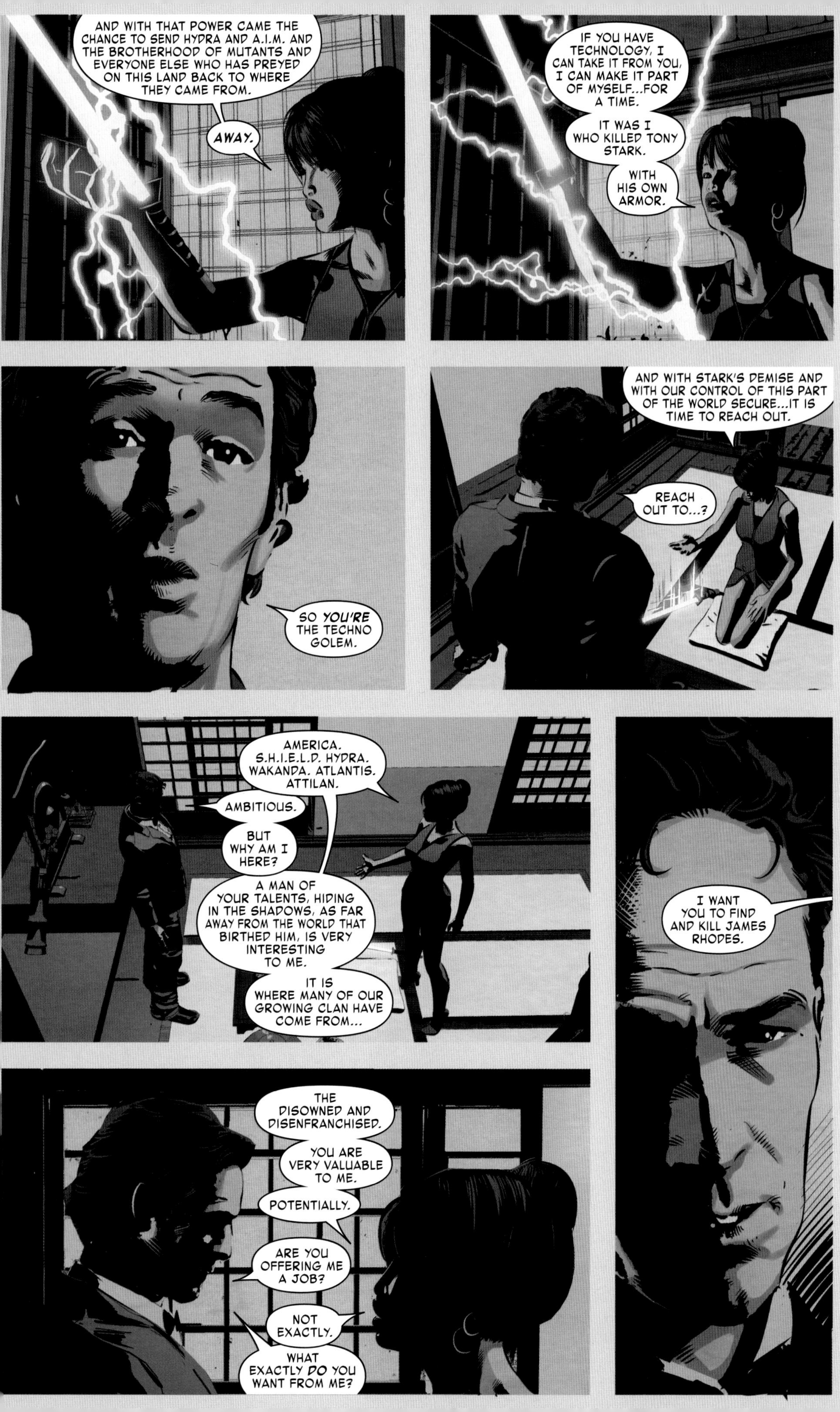
AND WITH THAT POWER CAME THE CHANCE TO SEND HYDRA AND A.I.M. AND THE BROTHERHOOD OF MUTANTS AND EVERYONE ELSE WHO HAS PREYED ON THIS LAND BACK TO WHERE THEY CAME FROM.
AWAY.
IF YOU HAVE TECHNOLOGY, I CAN TAKE IT FROM YOU, I CAN MAKE IT PART OF MYSELF...FOR A TIME.
IT WAS I WHO KILLED TONY STARK.
WITH HIS OWN ARMOR.
SO YOU'RE THE TECHNO GOLEM.
AND WITH STARK'S DEMISE AND WITH OUR CONTROL OF THIS PART OF THE WORLD SECURE...IT IS TIME TO REACH OUT.
REACH OUT TO...?
AMERICA. S.H.I.E.L.D. HYDRA. WAKANDA. ATLANTIS. ATTILAN.
AMBITIOUS.
BUT WHY AM I HERE?
A MAN OF YOUR TALENTS, HIDING IN THE SHADOWS, AS FAR AWAY FROM THE WORLD THAT BIRTHED HIM, IS VERY INTERESTING TO ME.
IT IS WHERE MANY OF OUR GROWING CLAN HAVE COME FROM...
THE DISOWNED AND DISENFRANCHISED.
YOU ARE VERY VALUABLE TO ME.
POTENTIALLY.
ARE YOU OFFERING ME A JOB?
NOT EXACTLY.
WHAT EXACTLY DO YOU WANT FROM ME?
I WANT YOU TO FIND AND KILL JAMES RHODES.

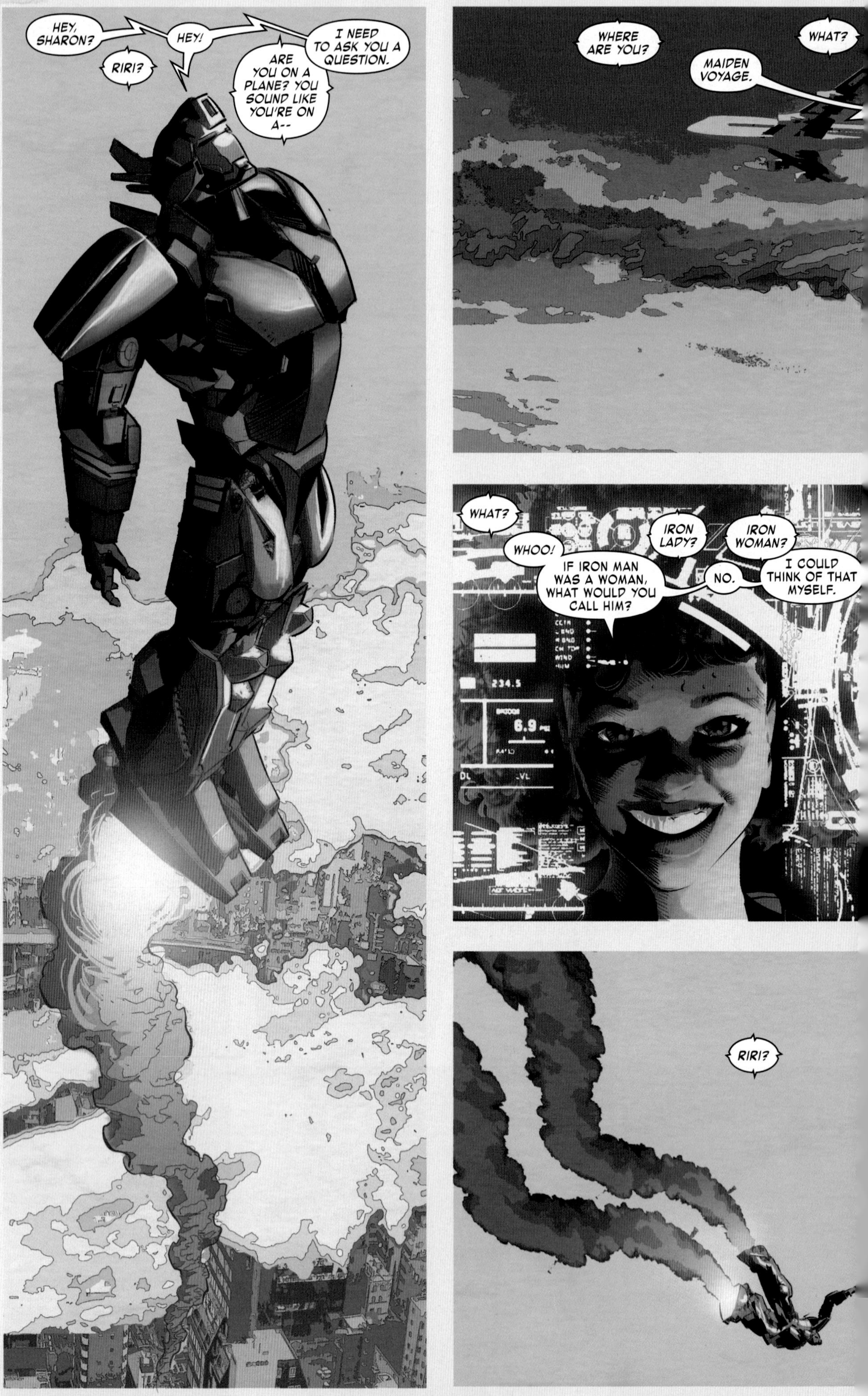
HEY, SHARON?
RIRI?
HEY!
I NEED TO ASK YOU A QUESTION.
ARE YOU ON A PLANE? YOU SOUND LIKE YOU'RE ON A--
WHERE ARE YOU?
MAIDEN VOYAGE.
WHAT?
WHAT?
WHOO!
IF IRON MAN WAS A WOMAN, WHAT WOULD YOU CALL HIM?
IRON LADY?
IRON WOMAN?
NO.
I COULD THINK OF THAT MYSELF.
RIRI?

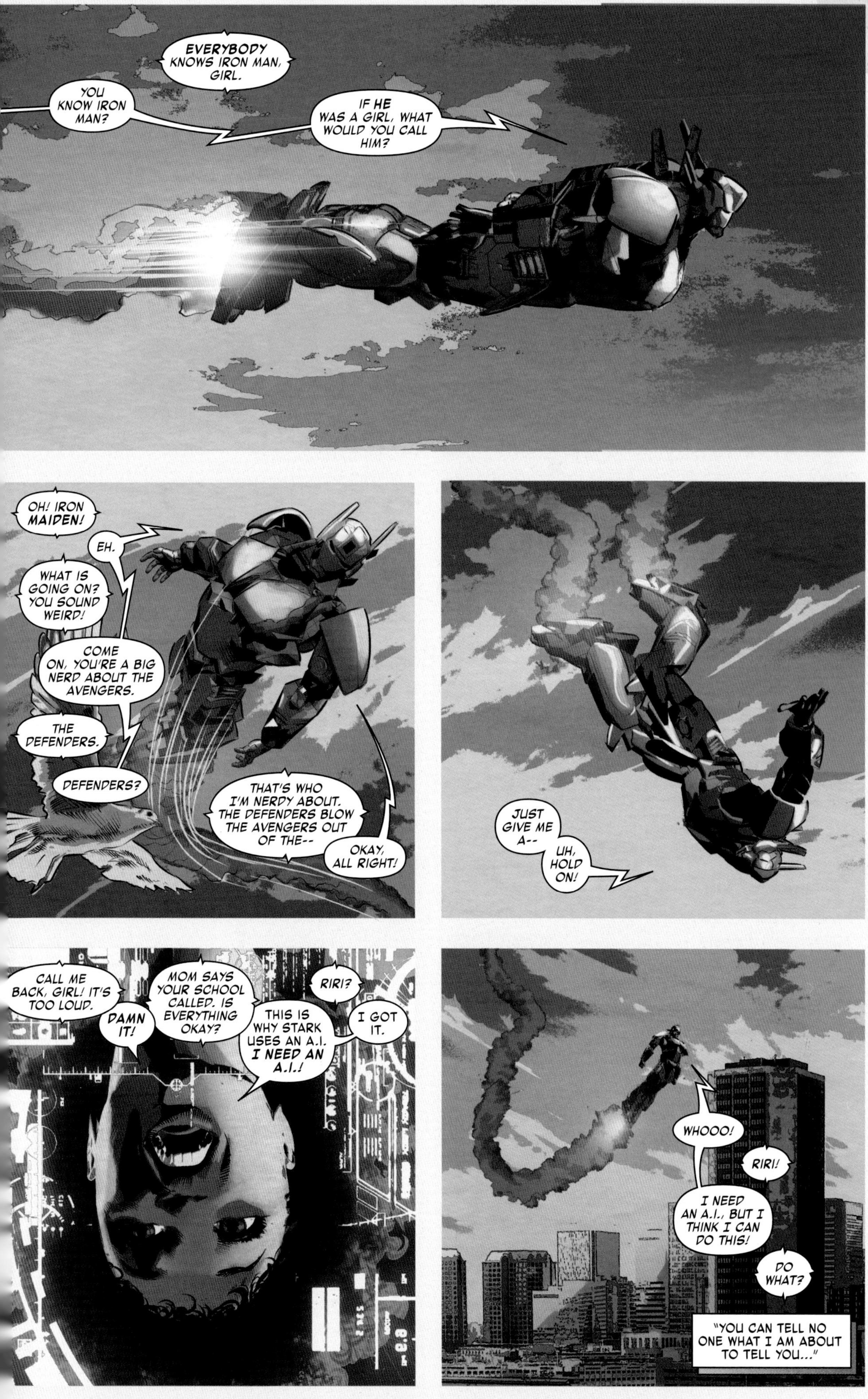

YOU KNOW IRON MAN?
EVERYBODY KNOWS IRON MAN, GIRL.
IF HE WAS A GIRL, WHAT WOULD YOU CALL HIM?
OH! IRON MAIDEN!
EH.
WHAT IS GOING ON? YOU SOUND WEIRD!
COME ON, YOU'RE A BIG NERD ABOUT THE AVENGERS.
THE DEFENDERS.
DEFENDERS?
THAT'S WHO I'M NERDY ABOUT. THE DEFENDERS BLOW THE AVENGERS OUT OF THE--
OKAY, ALL RIGHT!
JUST GIVE ME A--
UH, HOLD ON!
CALL ME BACK, GIRL! IT'S TOO LOUD.
DAMN IT!
MOM SAYS YOUR SCHOOL CALLED. IS EVERYTHING OKAY?
RIRI?
THIS IS WHY STARK USES AN A.I. I NEED AN A.I.!
I GOT IT.
WHOOO!
RIRI!
I NEED AN A.I., BUT I THINK I CAN DO THIS!
DO WHAT?
"YOU CAN TELL NO ONE WHAT I AM ABOUT TO TELL YOU..."

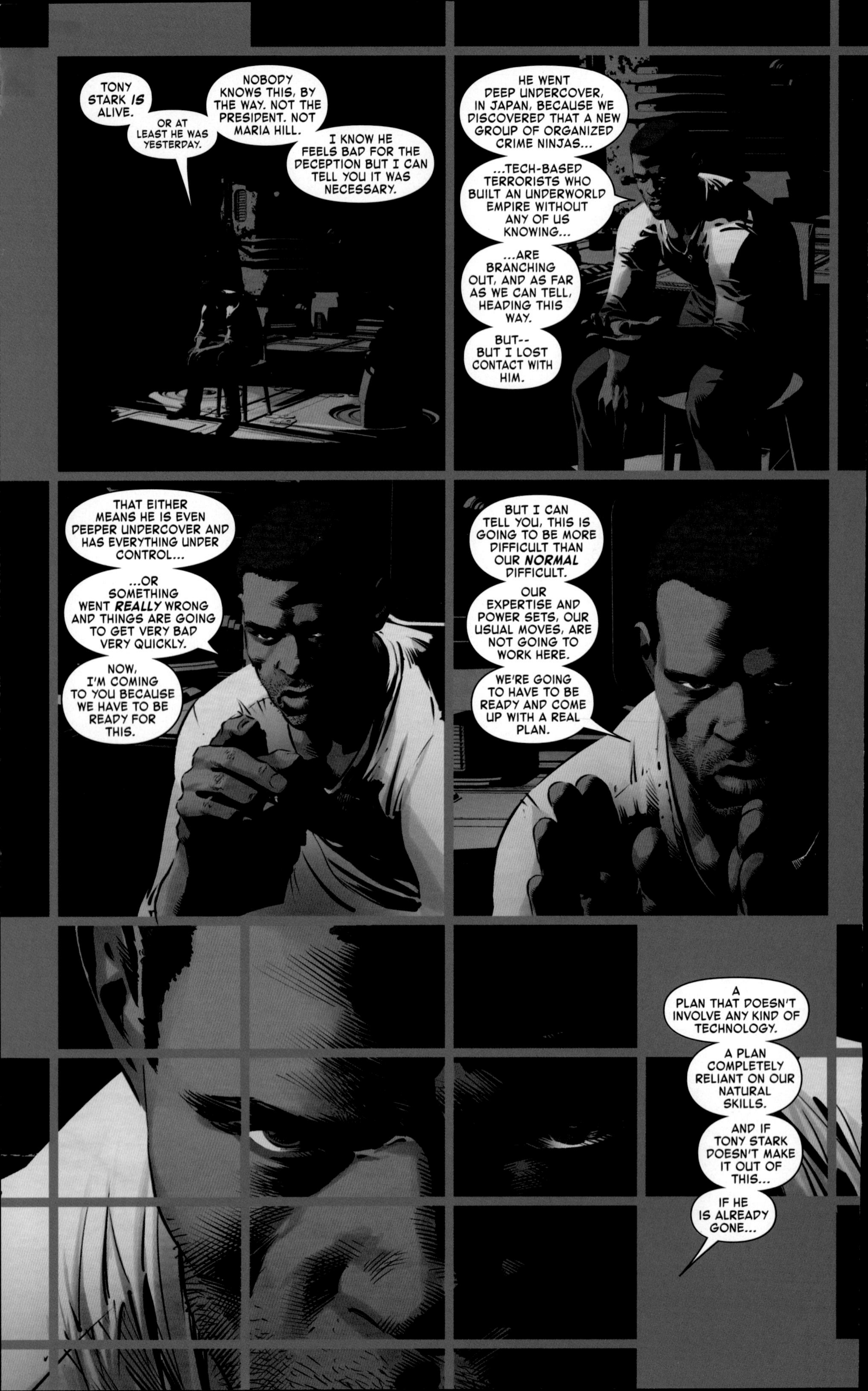
TONY STARK IS ALIVE.
OR AT LEAST HE WAS YESTERDAY.
NOBODY KNOWS THIS, BY THE WAY. NOT THE PRESIDENT. NOT MARIA HILL.
I KNOW HE FEELS BAD FOR THE DECEPTION BUT I CAN TELL YOU IT WAS NECESSARY.
HE WENT DEEP UNDERCOVER, IN JAPAN, BECAUSE WE DISCOVERED THAT A NEW GROUP OF ORGANIZED CRIME NINJAS...
...TECH-BASED TERRORISTS WHO BUILT AN UNDERWORLD EMPIRE WITHOUT ANY OF US KNOWING...
...ARE BRANCHING OUT, AND AS FAR AS WE CAN TELL, HEADING THIS WAY.
BUT-- BUT I LOST CONTACT WITH HIM.
THAT EITHER MEANS HE IS EVEN DEEPER UNDERCOVER AND HAS EVERYTHING UNDER CONTROL...
...OR SOMETHING WENT REALLY WRONG AND THINGS ARE GOING TO GET VERY BAD VERY QUICKLY.
NOW, I'M COMING TO YOU BECAUSE WE HAVE TO BE READY FOR THIS.
BUT I CAN TELL YOU, THIS IS GOING TO BE MORE DIFFICULT THAN OUR NORMAL DIFFICULT.
OUR EXPERTISE AND POWER SETS, OUR USUAL MOVES, ARE NOT GOING TO WORK HERE.
WE'RE GOING TO HAVE TO BE READY AND COME UP WITH A REAL PLAN.
A PLAN THAT DOESN'T INVOLVE ANY KIND OF TECHNOLOGY.
A PLAN COMPLETELY RELIANT ON OUR NATURAL SKILLS.
AND IF TONY STARK DOESN'T MAKE IT OUT OF THIS...
IF HE IS ALREADY GONE...

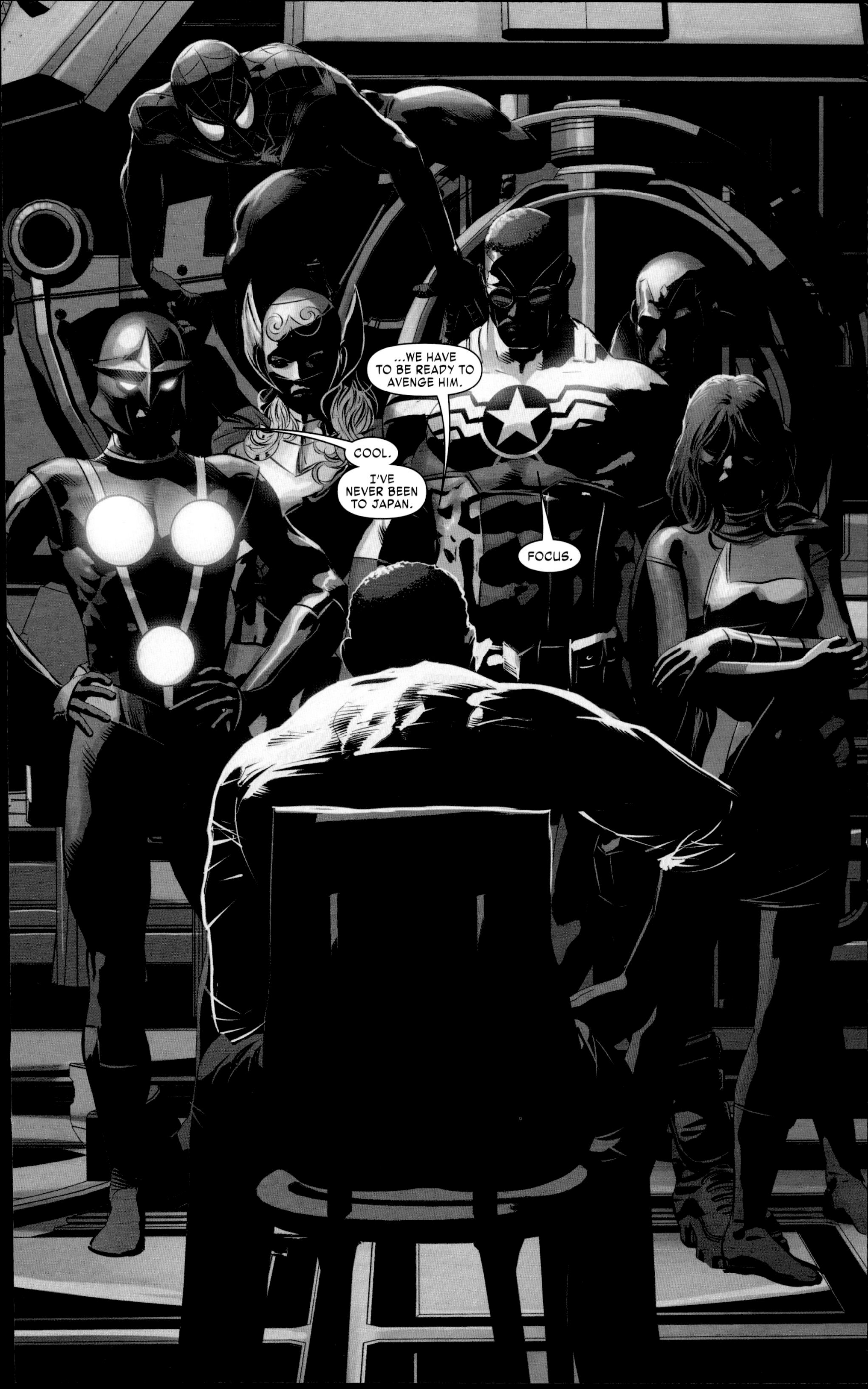
...WE HAVE TO BE READY TO AVENGE HIM.
COOL.
I'VE NEVER BEEN TO JAPAN.
FOCUS.

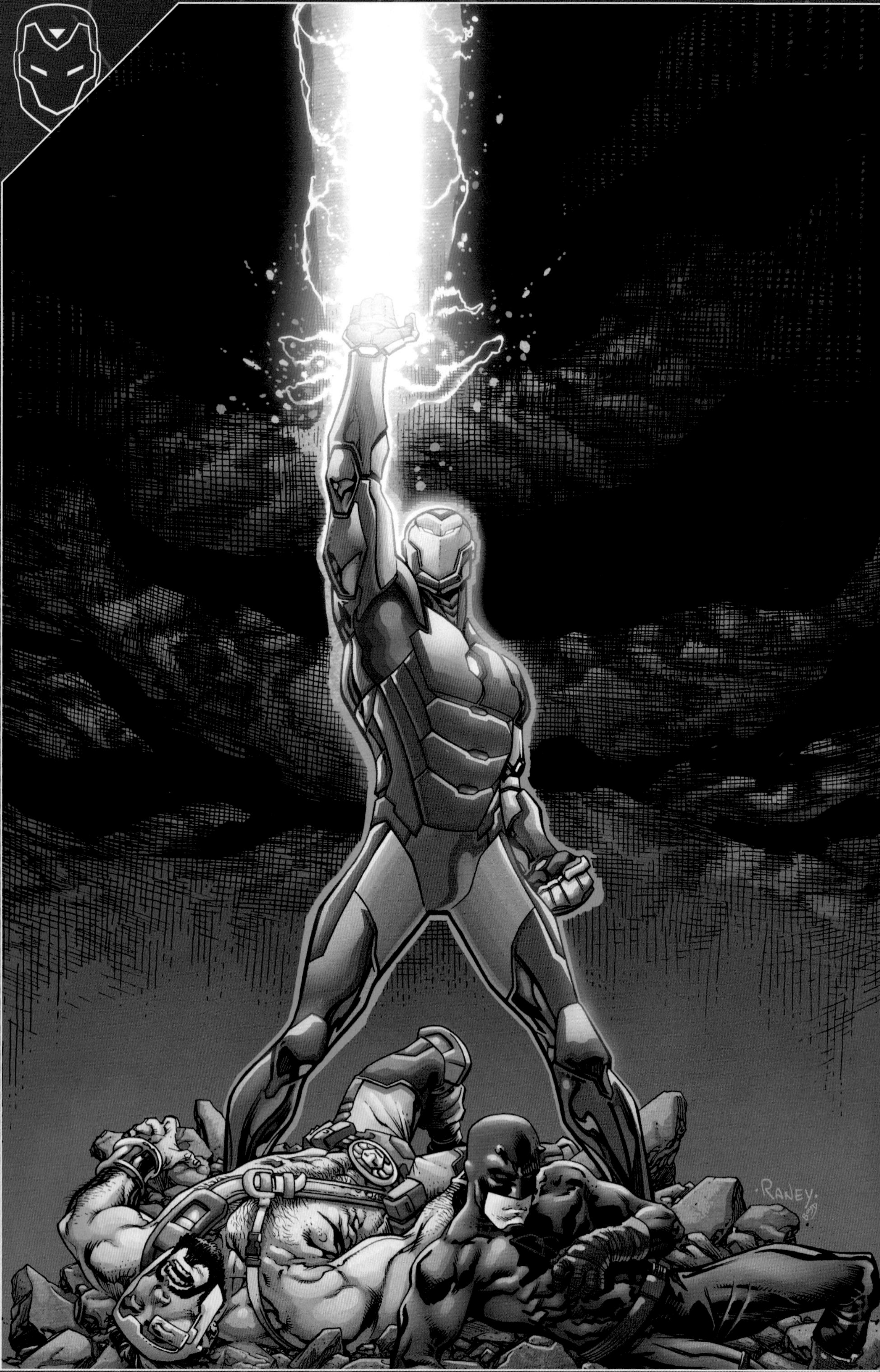
RANEY

#10 CIVIL WAR RE-ENACTMENT VARIANT BY **TOM RANEY & JORDAN BOYD**

#11

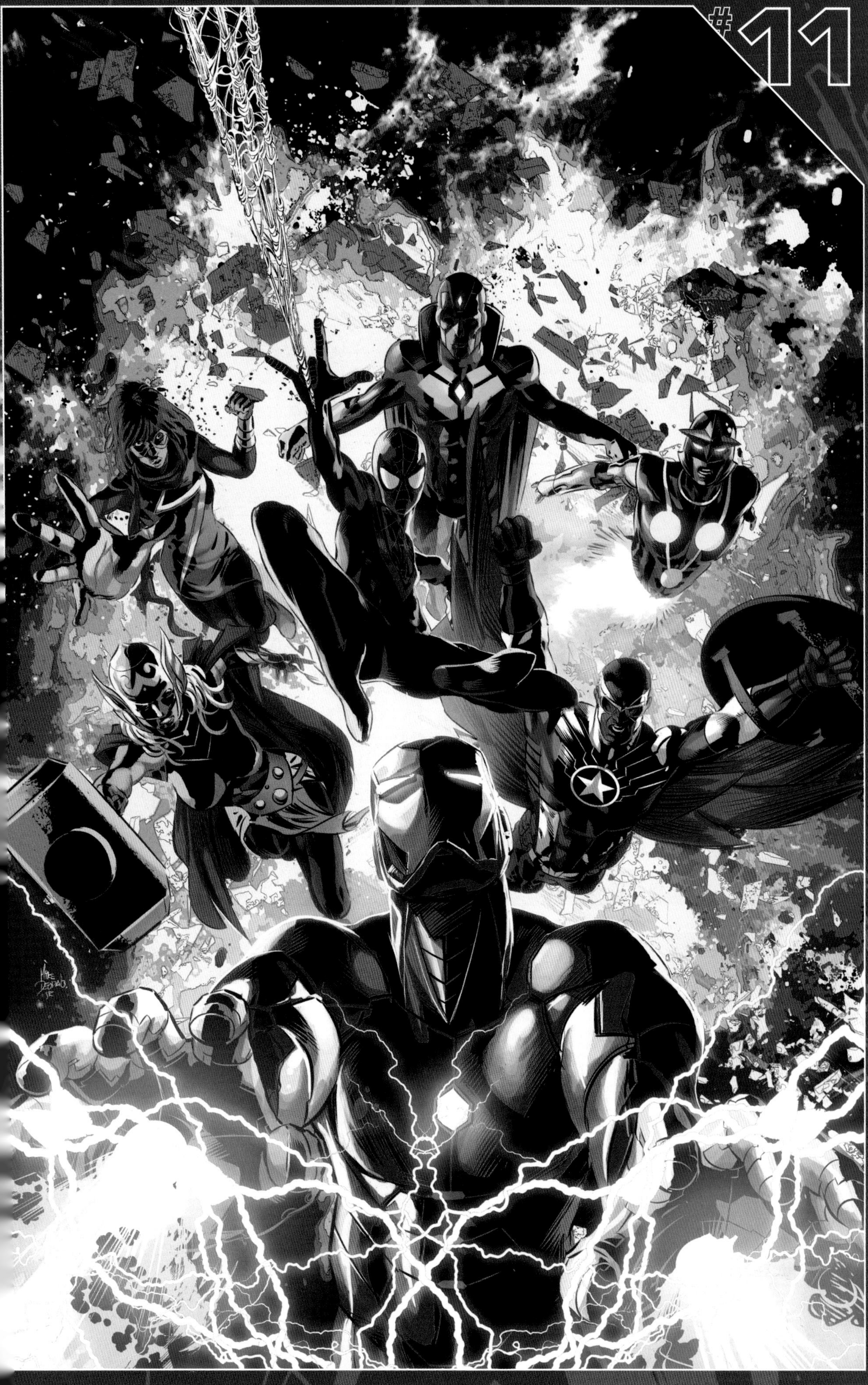

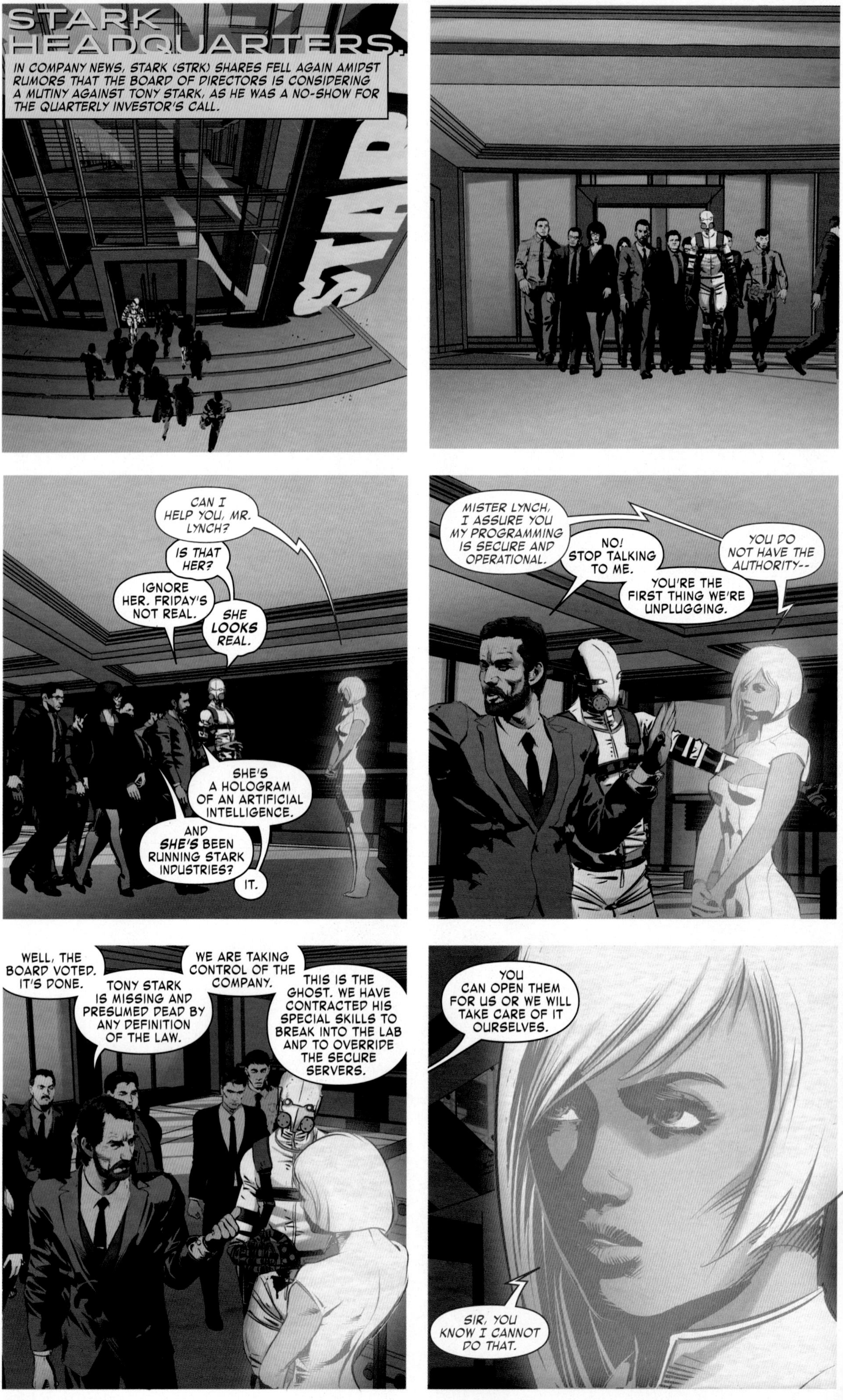
STARK HEADQUARTERS,
IN COMPANY NEWS, STARK (STRK) SHARES FELL AGAIN AMIDST RUMORS THAT THE BOARD OF DIRECTORS IS CONSIDERING A MUTINY AGAINST TONY STARK, AS HE WAS A NO-SHOW FOR THE QUARTERLY INVESTOR'S CALL.
CAN I HELP YOU, MR. LYNCH?
IS THAT HER?
IGNORE HER. FRIDAY'S NOT REAL.
SHE LOOKS REAL.
SHE'S A HOLOGRAM OF AN ARTIFICIAL INTELLIGENCE.
AND SHE'S BEEN RUNNING STARK INDUSTRIES?
IT.
MISTER LYNCH, I ASSURE YOU MY PROGRAMMING IS SECURE AND OPERATIONAL.
NO! STOP TALKING TO ME.
YOU'RE THE FIRST THING WE'RE UNPLUGGING.
YOU DO NOT HAVE THE AUTHORITY--
WELL, THE BOARD VOTED. IT'S DONE.
TONY STARK IS MISSING AND PRESUMED DEAD BY ANY DEFINITION OF THE LAW.
WE ARE TAKING CONTROL OF THE COMPANY.
THIS IS THE GHOST. WE HAVE CONTRACTED HIS SPECIAL SKILLS TO BREAK INTO THE LAB AND TO OVERRIDE THE SECURE SERVERS.
YOU CAN OPEN THEM FOR US OR WE WILL TAKE CARE OF IT OURSELVES.
SIR, YOU KNOW I CANNOT DO THAT.

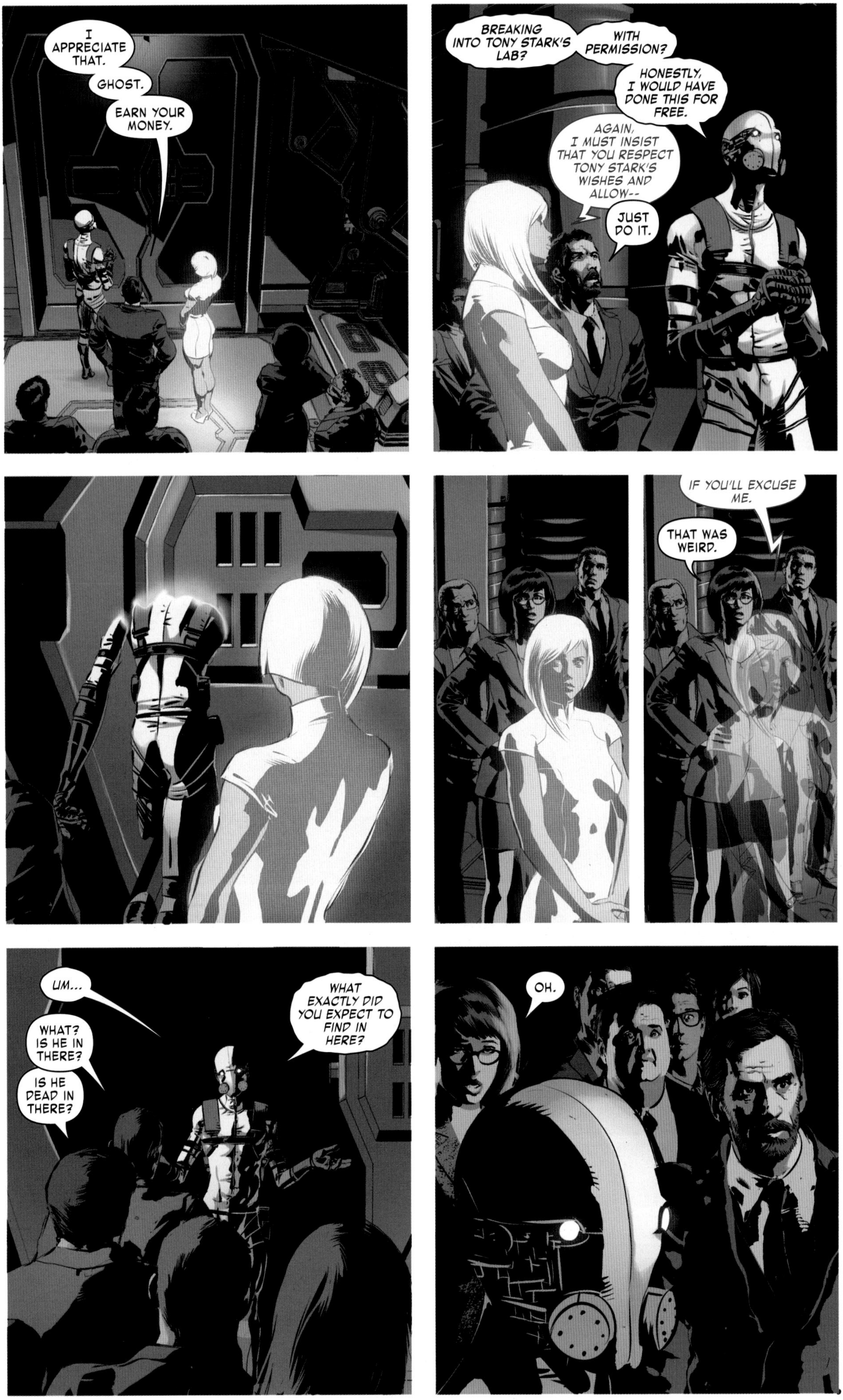
I APPRECIATE THAT.
GHOST.
EARN YOUR MONEY.
BREAKING INTO TONY STARK'S LAB?
WITH PERMISSION?
HONESTLY, I WOULD HAVE DONE THIS FOR FREE.
AGAIN, I MUST INSIST THAT YOU RESPECT TONY STARK'S WISHES AND ALLOW--
JUST DO IT.
IF YOU'LL EXCUSE ME.
THAT WAS WEIRD.
UM...
WHAT? IS HE IN THERE?
IS HE DEAD IN THERE?
WHAT EXACTLY DID YOU EXPECT TO FIND IN HERE?
OH.

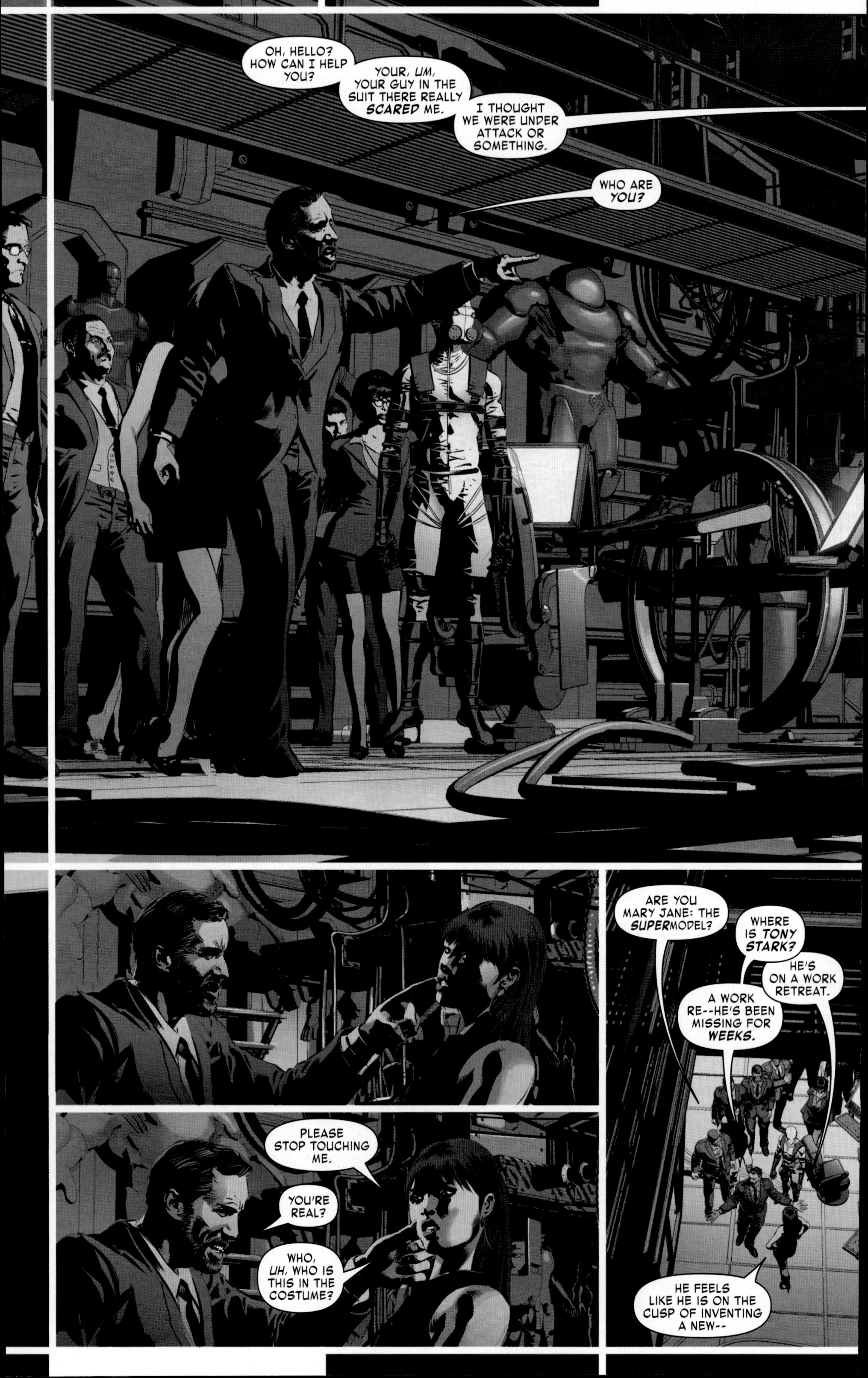
OH, HELLO? HOW CAN I HELP YOU?
YOUR, UM, YOUR GUY IN THE SUIT THERE REALLY SCARED ME.
I THOUGHT WE WERE UNDER ATTACK OR SOMETHING.
WHO ARE YOU?
ARE YOU MARY JANE: THE SUPERMODEL?
PLEASE STOP TOUCHING ME.
YOU'RE REAL?
WHO, UH, WHO IS THIS IN THE COSTUME?
WHERE IS TONY STARK?
HE'S ON A WORK RETREAT.
A WORK RE--HE'S BEEN MISSING FOR WEEKS.
HE FEELS LIKE HE IS ON THE CUSP OF INVENTING A NEW--

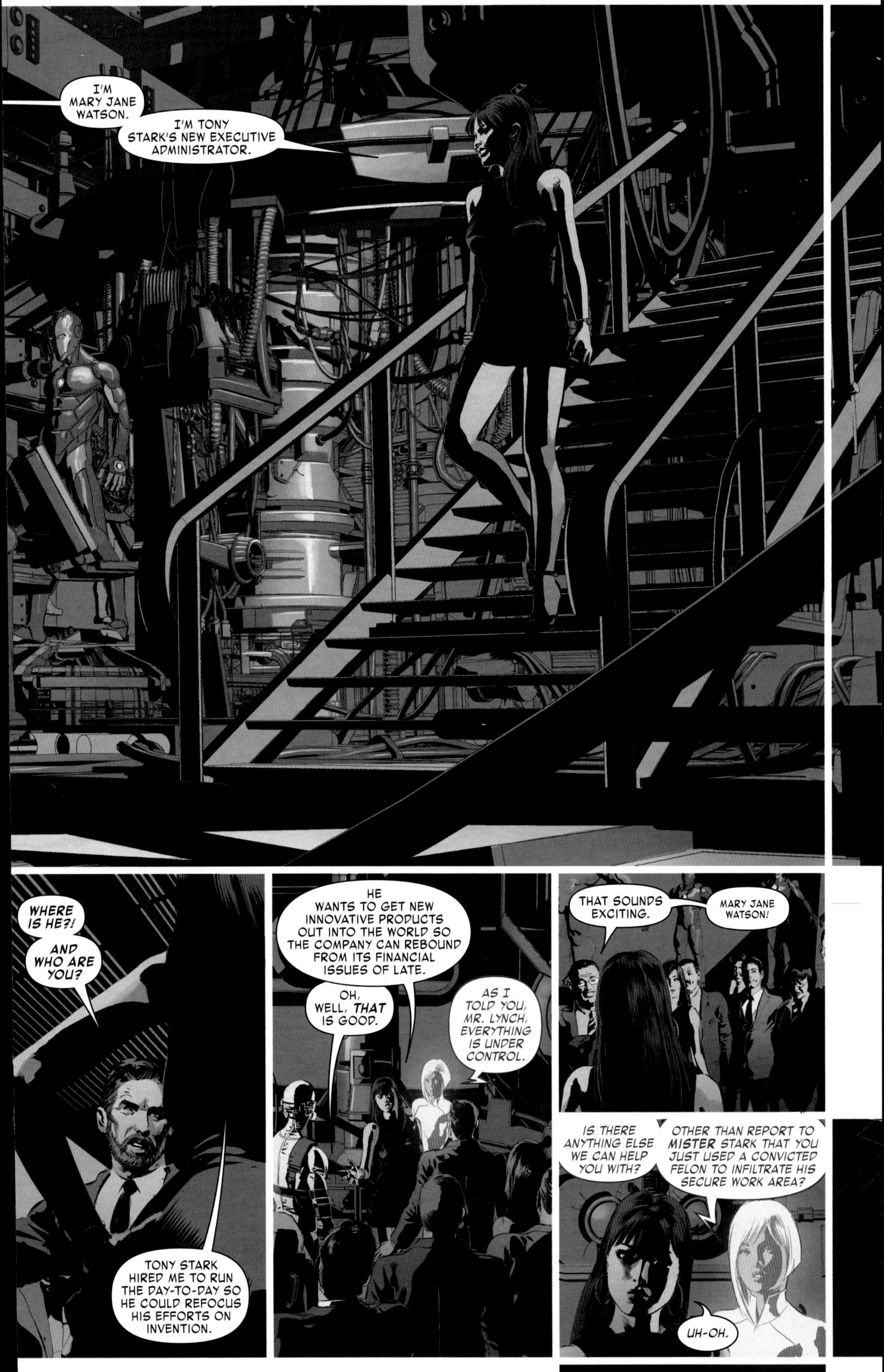
I'M MARY JANE WATSON.
I'M TONY STARK'S NEW EXECUTIVE ADMINISTRATOR.
WHERE IS HE?!
AND WHO ARE YOU?
TONY STARK HIRED ME TO RUN THE DAY-TO-DAY SO HE COULD REFOCUS HIS EFFORTS ON INVENTION.
HE WANTS TO GET NEW INNOVATIVE PRODUCTS OUT INTO THE WORLD SO THE COMPANY CAN REBOUND FROM ITS FINANCIAL ISSUES OF LATE.
OH, WELL, THAT IS GOOD.
AS I TOLD YOU, MR. LYNCH, EVERYTHING IS UNDER CONTROL.
THAT SOUNDS EXCITING.
MARY JANE WATSON!
IS THERE ANYTHING ELSE WE CAN HELP YOU WITH?
OTHER THAN REPORT TO MISTER STARK THAT YOU JUST USED A CONVICTED FELON TO INFILTRATE HIS SECURE WORK AREA?
UH-OH.

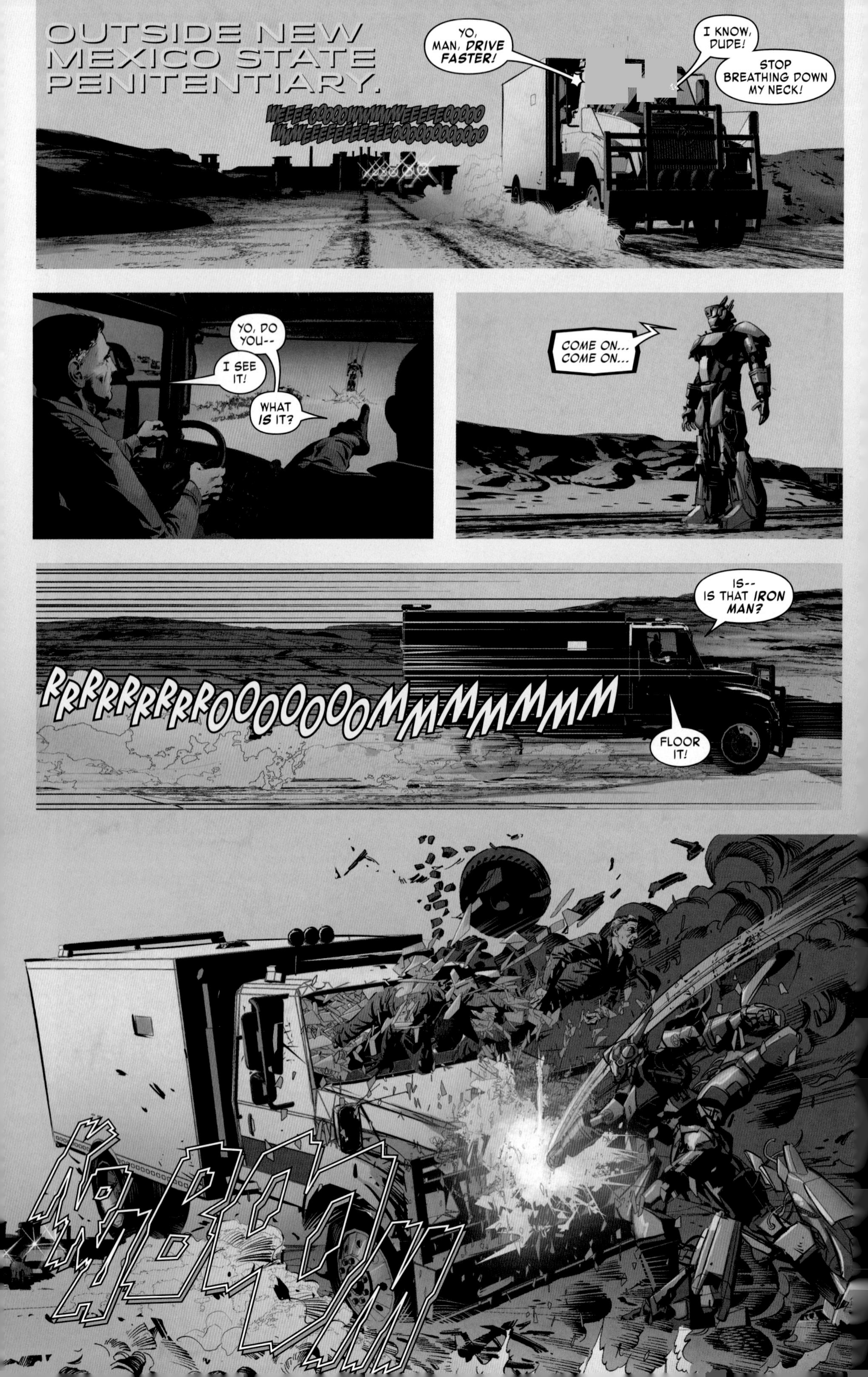
OUTSIDE NEW MEXICO STATE PENITENTIARY.
YO, MAN, DRIVE FASTER!
I KNOW, DUDE!
STOP BREATHING DOWN MY NECK!
YO, DO YOU--
I SEE IT!
WHAT IS IT?
COME ON... COME ON...
IS-- IS THAT IRON MAN?
FLOOR IT!

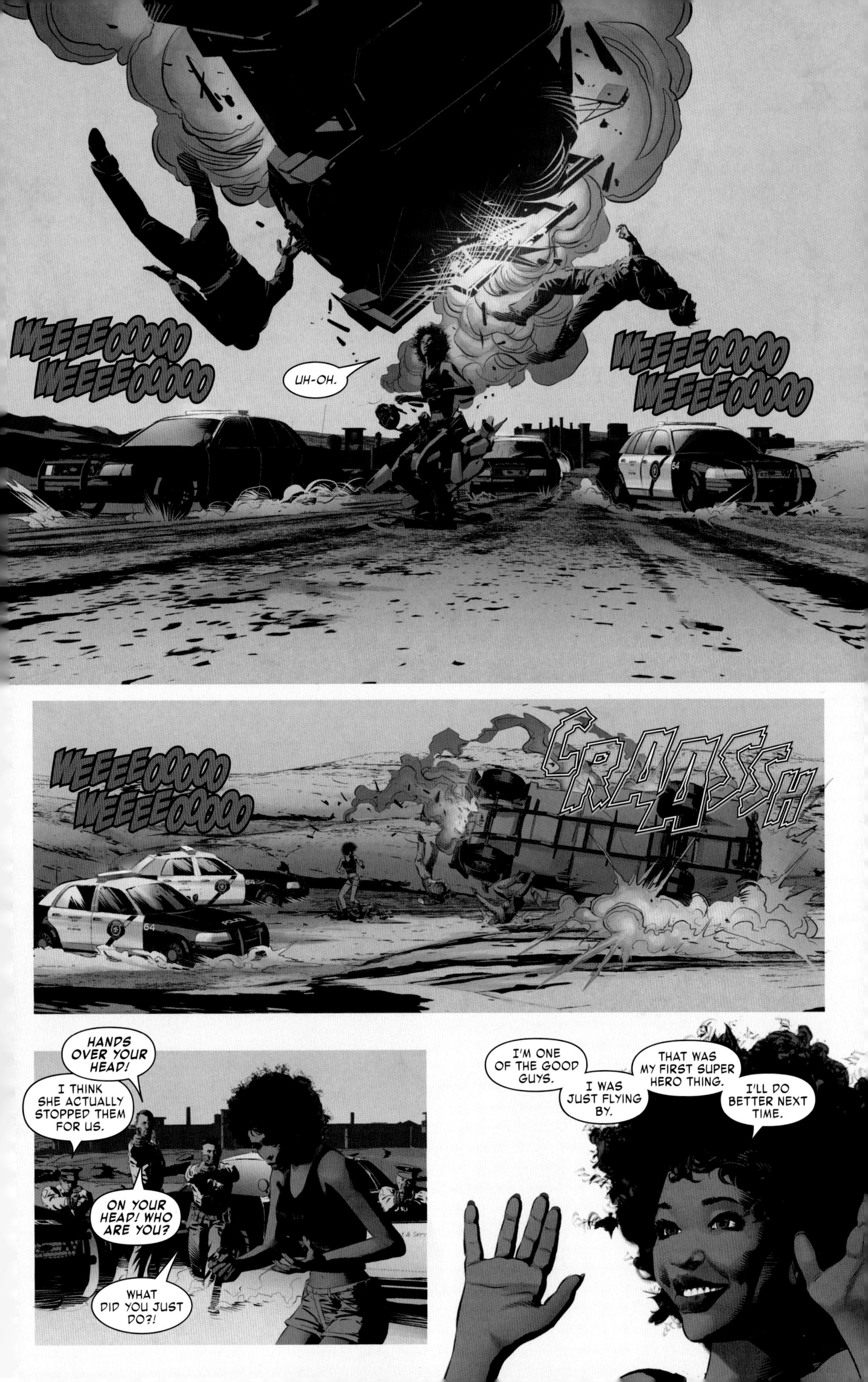
WEEEEOOOOO WEEEEOOOOO
UH-OH.
WEEEEOOOOO WEEEEOOOOO
WEEEEOOOOO WEEEEOOOOO
GRAASSH
HANDS OVER YOUR HEAD!
I THINK SHE ACTUALLY STOPPED THEM FOR US.
ON YOUR HEAD! WHO ARE YOU?
WHAT DID YOU JUST DO?!
I'M ONE OF THE GOOD GUYS.
I WAS JUST FLYING BY.
THAT WAS MY FIRST SUPER HERO THING.
I'LL DO BETTER NEXT TIME.

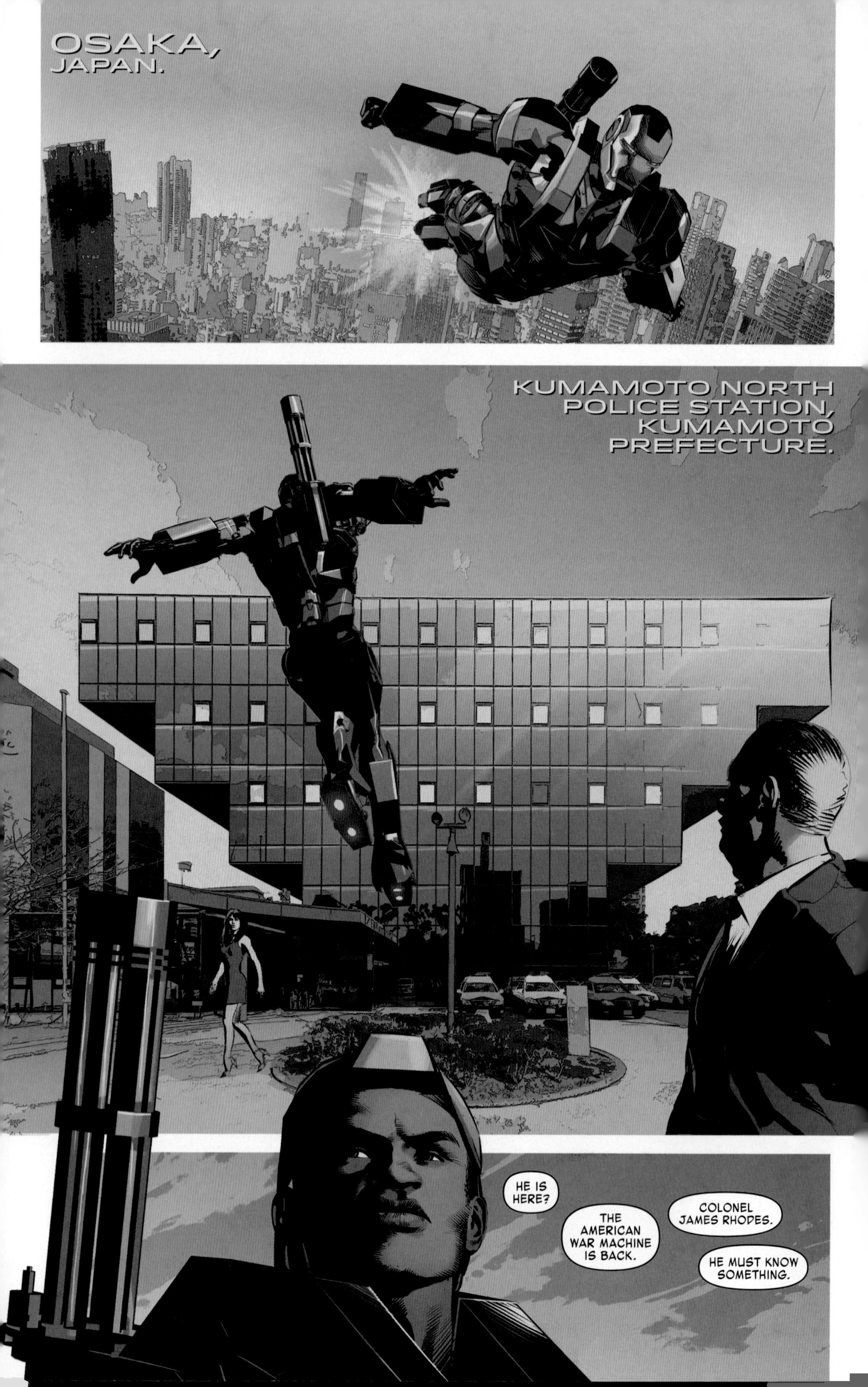
OSAKA, JAPAN.
KUMAMOTO NORTH POLICE STATION, KUMAMOTO PREFECTURE.
HE IS HERE?
THE AMERICAN WAR MACHINE IS BACK.
COLONEL JAMES RHODES.
HE MUST KNOW SOMETHING.

HE IS NOT THE ONLY ONE, TOMOE.

I'M SORRY.

THE LADY THOR HAS BEEN SPOTTED.

WHERE?

IN DOWNTOWN OSAKA.

THOR *AND* WAR MACHINE ARE *BOTH* HERE?

SEE, ZHANG, IT IS HAPPENING.

THEY ARE LOOKING FOR STARK.

THEY ARE LOOKING FOR *US.* IN RETALIATION FOR STARK.

THIS-- THESE ARE THE *SAME* MISTAKES THAT *THE HAND* AND *HYDRA* AND *SO MANY OTHERS* HAVE MADE OVER AND OVER.

SLOPPY MISTAKES THAT BRING THESE AMERICAN AVENGERS *RIGHT* TO OUR DOORSTEP.

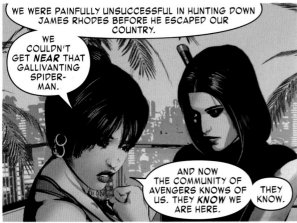

WE WERE PAINFULLY UNSUCCESSFUL IN HUNTING DOWN JAMES RHODES BEFORE HE ESCAPED OUR COUNTRY.

WE COULDN'T GET *NEAR* THAT GALLIVANTING SPIDER-MAN.

AND NOW THE COMMUNITY OF AVENGERS KNOWS OF US. THEY *KNOW* WE ARE HERE.

THEY KNOW.

WE LOST OUR MOST VALUED ASSET... ANONYMITY.

ALL OF THIS BECAUSE OF THAT DAMNED *MADAME MASQUE.*

WHAT NOW, TOMOE?

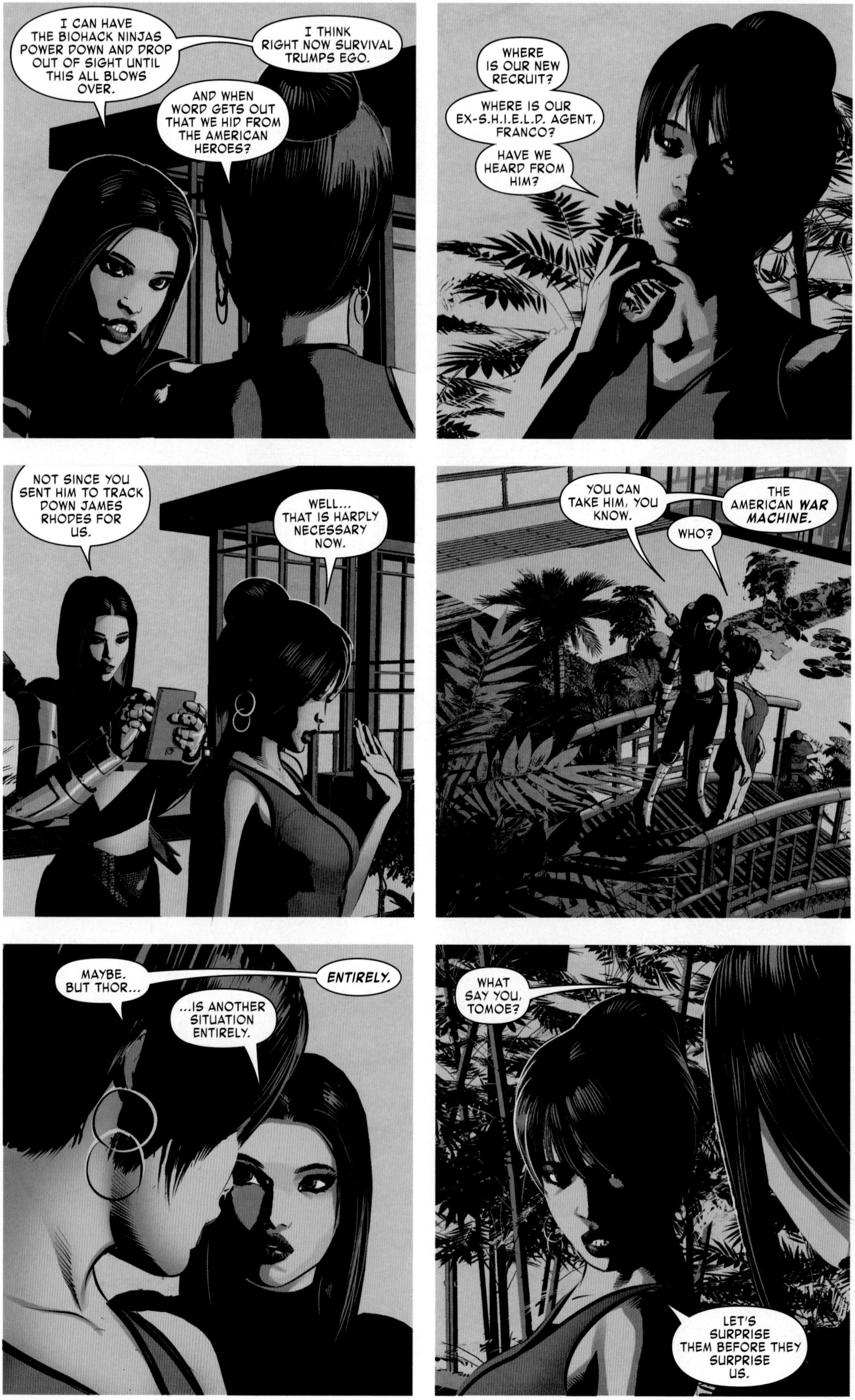

I CAN HAVE THE BIOHACK NINJAS POWER DOWN AND DROP OUT OF SIGHT UNTIL THIS ALL BLOWS OVER.
I THINK RIGHT NOW SURVIVAL TRUMPS EGO.
AND WHEN WORD GETS OUT THAT WE HID FROM THE AMERICAN HEROES?
WHERE IS OUR NEW RECRUIT?
WHERE IS OUR EX-S.H.I.E.L.D. AGENT, FRANCO?
HAVE WE HEARD FROM HIM?
NOT SINCE YOU SENT HIM TO TRACK DOWN JAMES RHODES FOR US.
WELL... THAT IS HARDLY NECESSARY NOW.
YOU CAN TAKE HIM, YOU KNOW.
WHO?
THE AMERICAN WAR MACHINE.
MAYBE. BUT THOR...
...IS ANOTHER SITUATION ENTIRELY.
ENTIRELY.
WHAT SAY YOU, TOMOE?
LET'S SURPRISE THEM BEFORE THEY SURPRISE US.

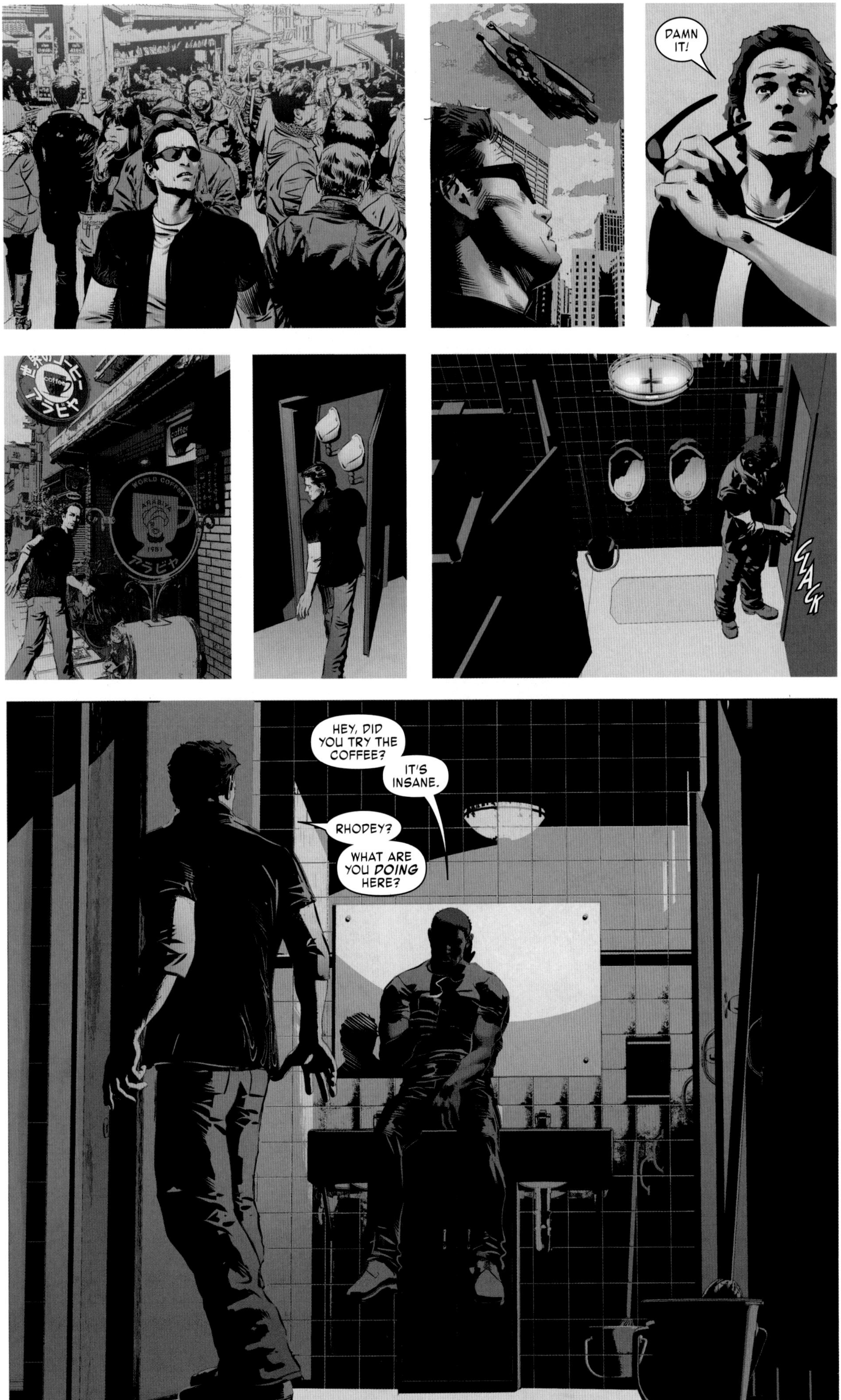
DAMN IT!
CLACK
HEY, DID YOU TRY THE COFFEE?
IT'S INSANE.
RHODEY?
WHAT ARE YOU DOING HERE?

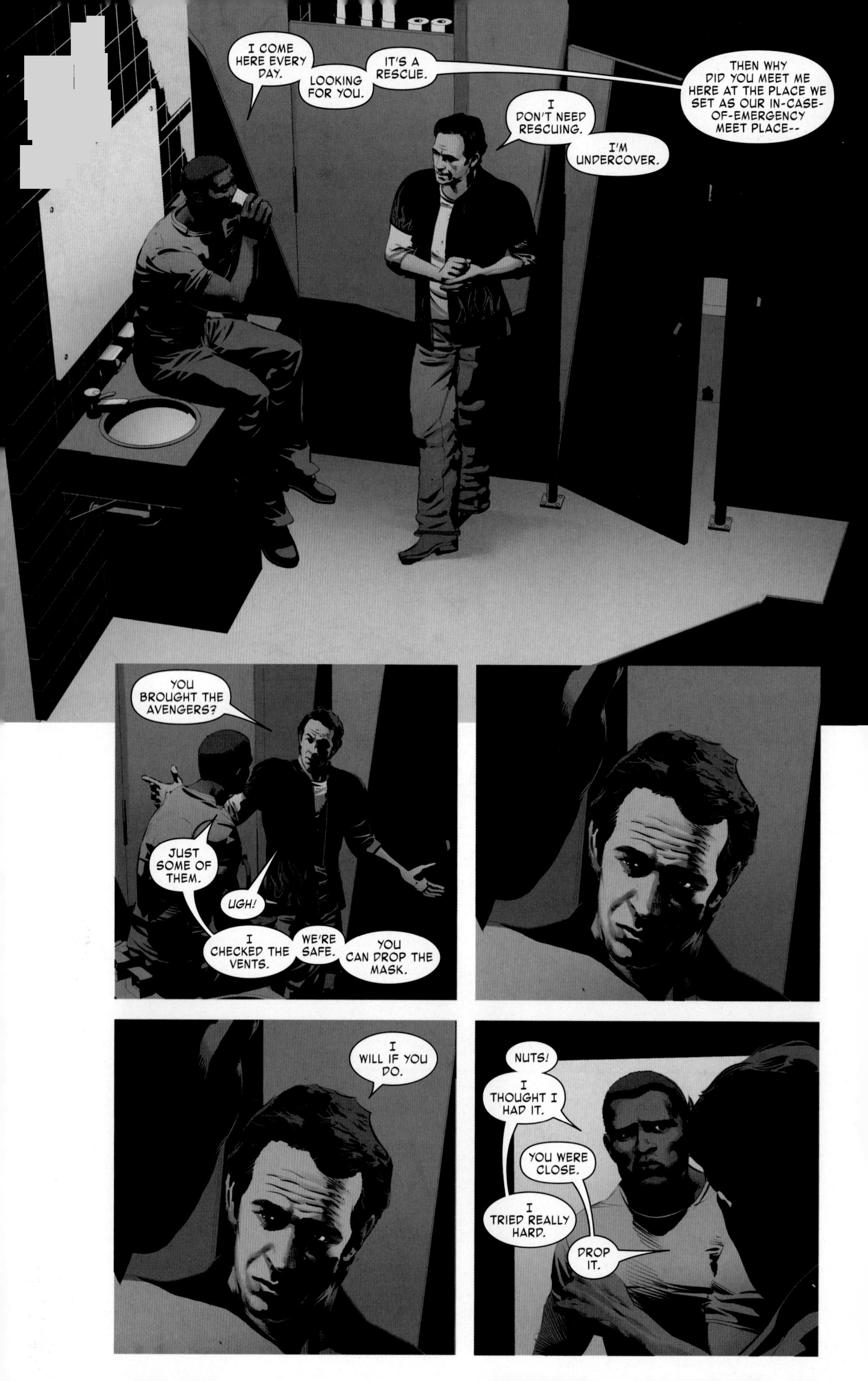
I COME HERE EVERY DAY.
LOOKING FOR YOU.
IT'S A RESCUE.
THEN WHY DID YOU MEET ME HERE AT THE PLACE WE SET AS OUR IN-CASE-OF-EMERGENCY MEET PLACE--
I DON'T NEED RESCUING.
I'M UNDERCOVER.
YOU BROUGHT THE AVENGERS?
JUST SOME OF THEM.
UGH!
I CHECKED THE VENTS.
WE'RE SAFE.
YOU CAN DROP THE MASK.
I WILL IF YOU DO.
NUTS!
I THOUGHT I HAD IT.
YOU WERE CLOSE.
I TRIED REALLY HARD.
DROP IT.

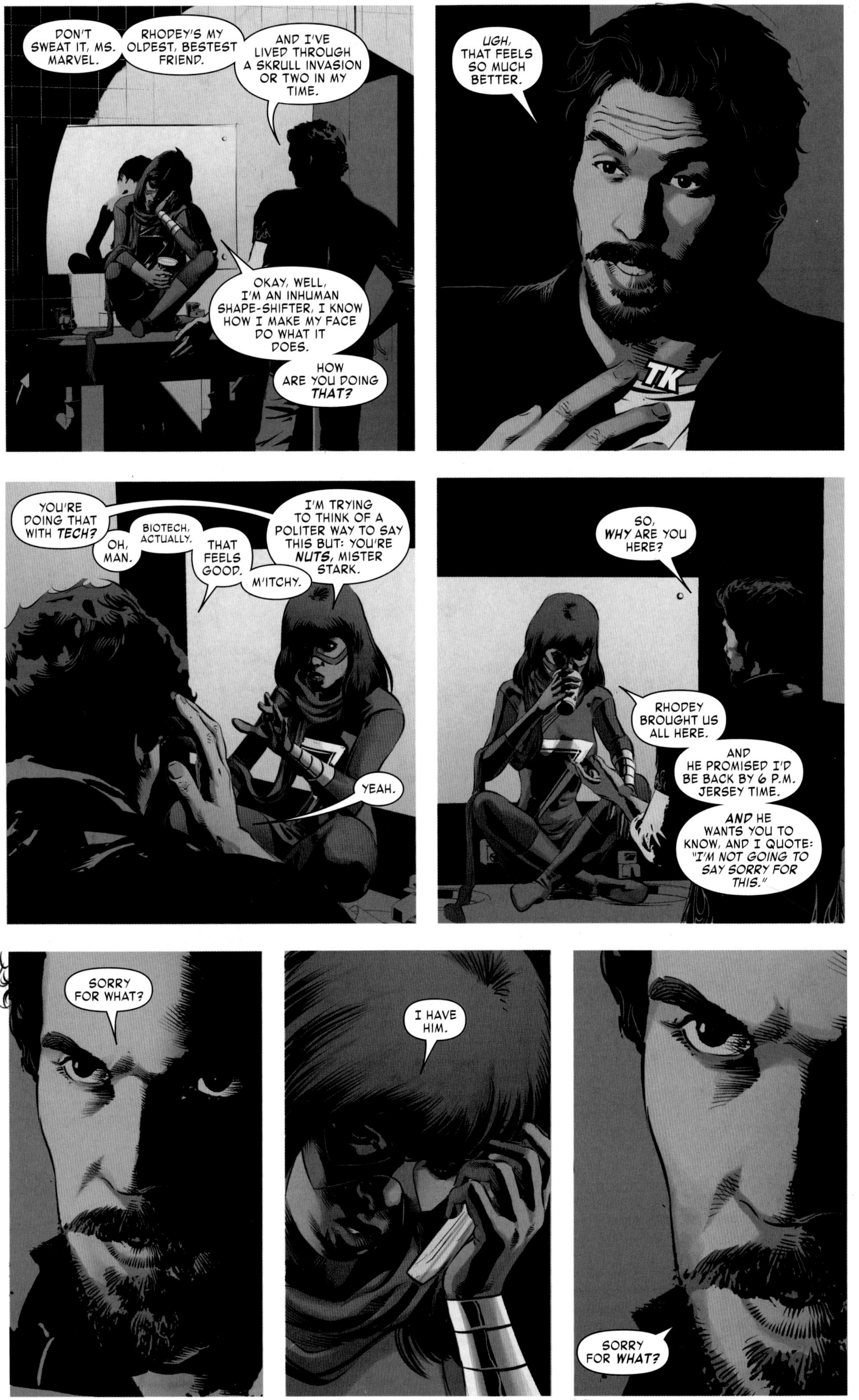
DON'T SWEAT IT, MS. MARVEL.
RHODEY'S MY OLDEST, BESTEST FRIEND.
AND I'VE LIVED THROUGH A SKRULL INVASION OR TWO IN MY TIME.
OKAY, WELL, I'M AN INHUMAN SHAPE-SHIFTER, I KNOW HOW I MAKE MY FACE DO WHAT IT DOES.
HOW ARE YOU DOING THAT?
UGH, THAT FEELS SO MUCH BETTER.
YOU'RE DOING THAT WITH TECH?
OH, MAN.
BIOTECH, ACTUALLY.
THAT FEELS GOOD.
I'M TRYING TO THINK OF A POLITER WAY TO SAY THIS BUT: YOU'RE NUTS, MISTER STARK.
M'ITCHY.
YEAH.
SO, WHY ARE YOU HERE?
RHODEY BROUGHT US ALL HERE.
AND HE PROMISED I'D BE BACK BY 6 P.M. JERSEY TIME.
AND HE WANTS YOU TO KNOW, AND I QUOTE: "I'M NOT GOING TO SAY SORRY FOR THIS."
SORRY FOR WHAT?
I HAVE HIM.
SORRY FOR WHAT?

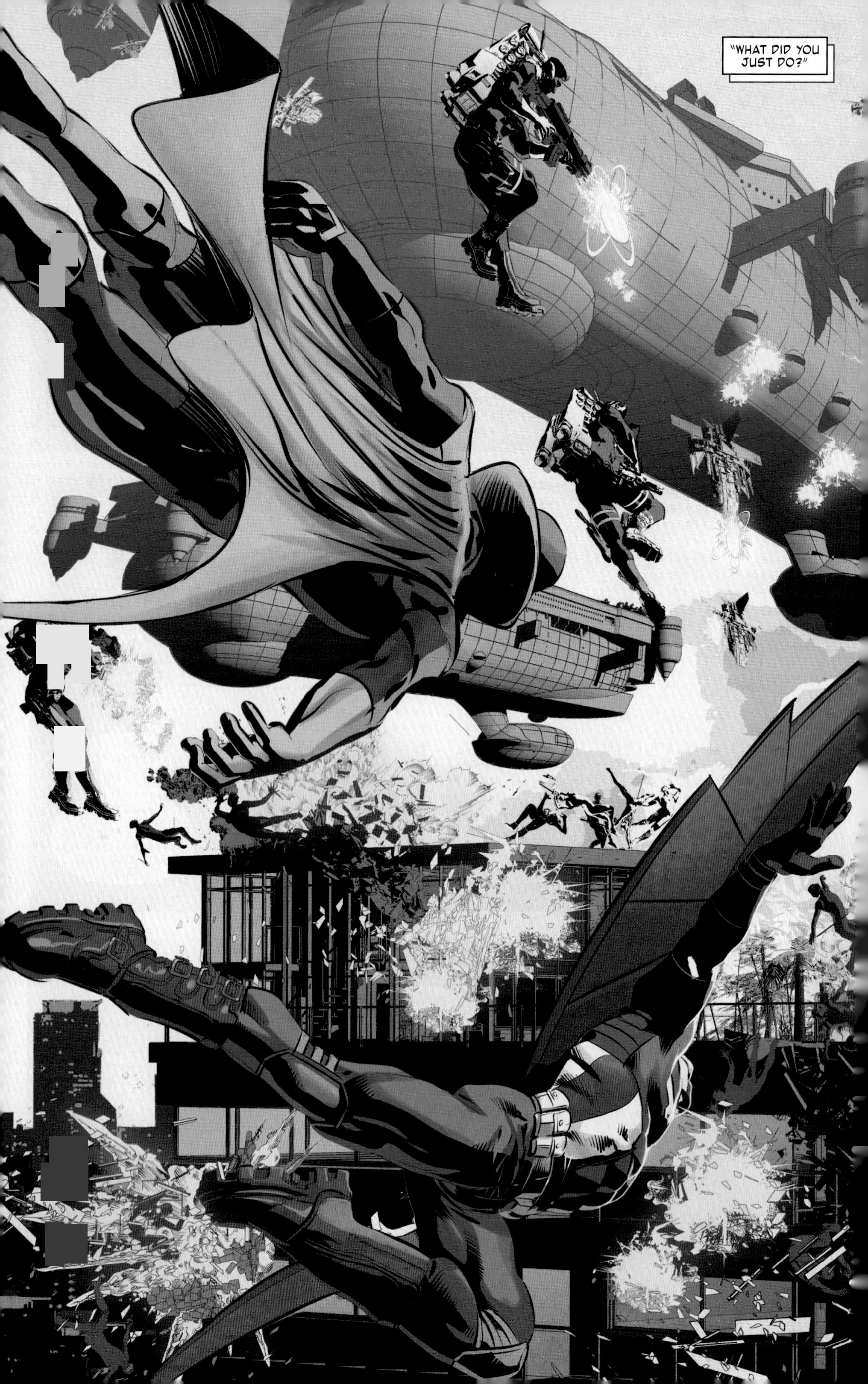
"WHAT DID YOU JUST DO?"

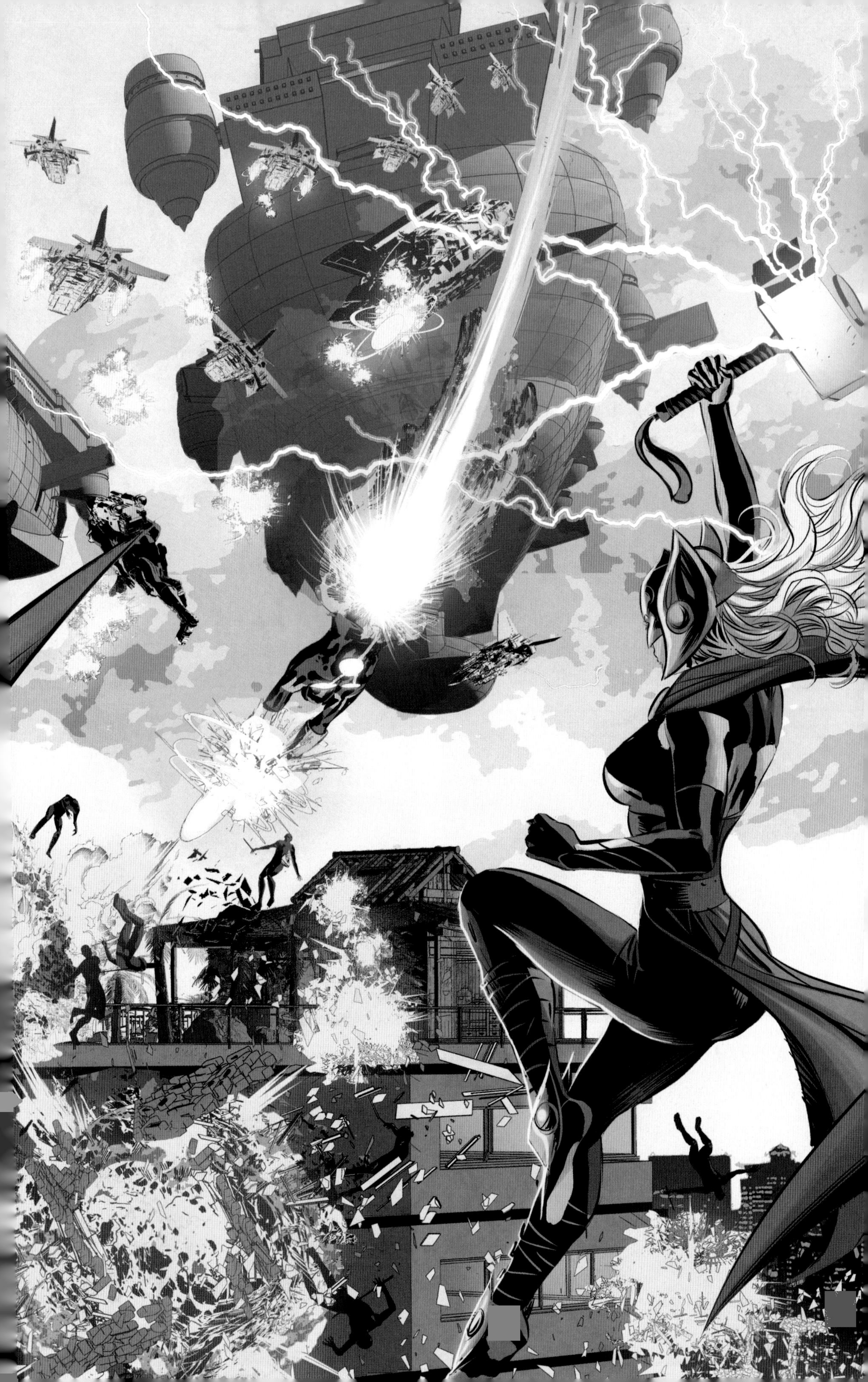

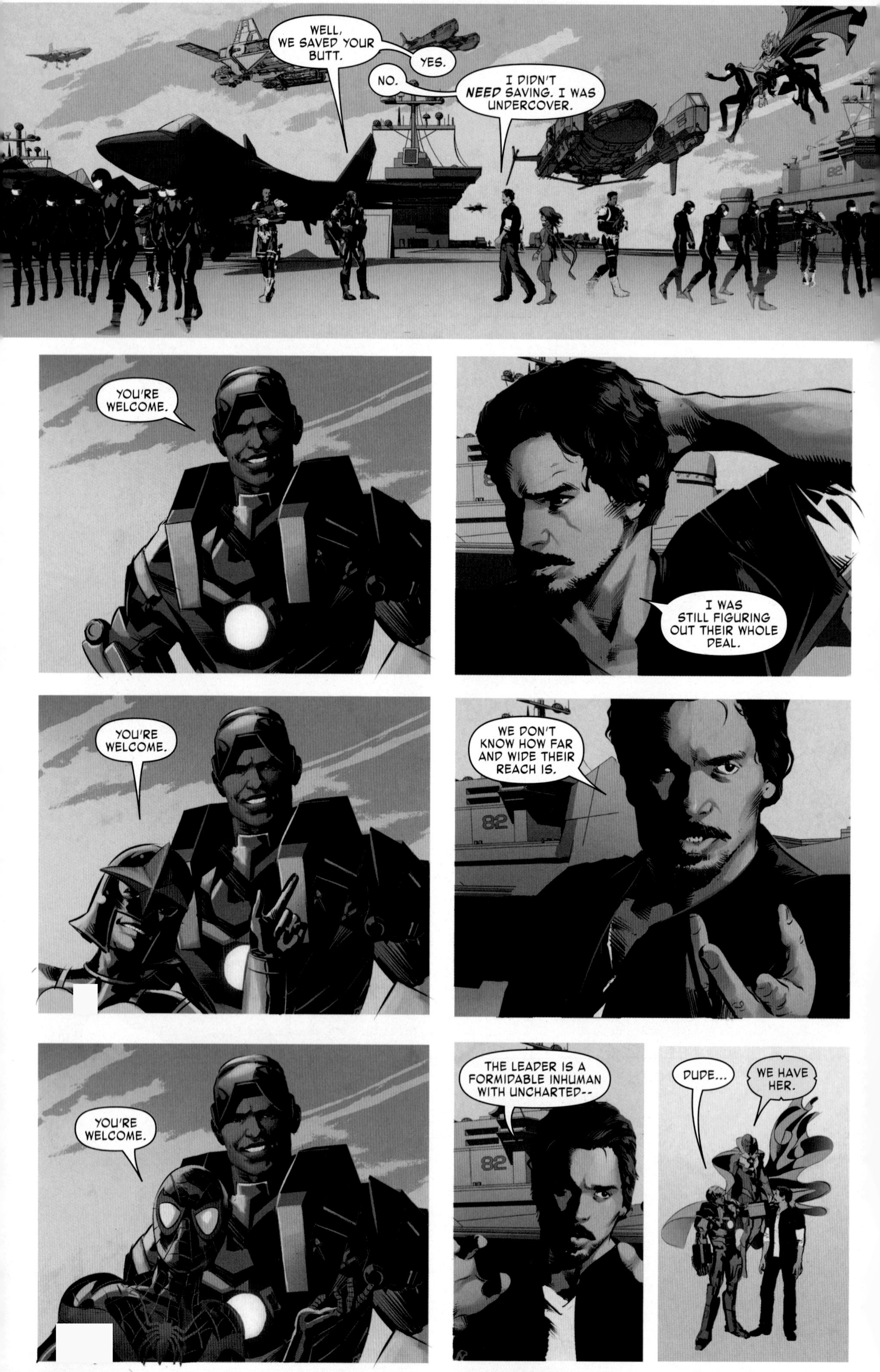
WELL, WE SAVED YOUR BUTT.
YES.
NO.
I DIDN'T NEED SAVING. I WAS UNDERCOVER.
YOU'RE WELCOME.
I WAS STILL FIGURING OUT THEIR WHOLE DEAL.
YOU'RE WELCOME.
WE DON'T KNOW HOW FAR AND WIDE THEIR REACH IS.
YOU'RE WELCOME.
THE LEADER IS A FORMIDABLE INHUMAN WITH UNCHARTED--
DUDE...
WE HAVE HER.

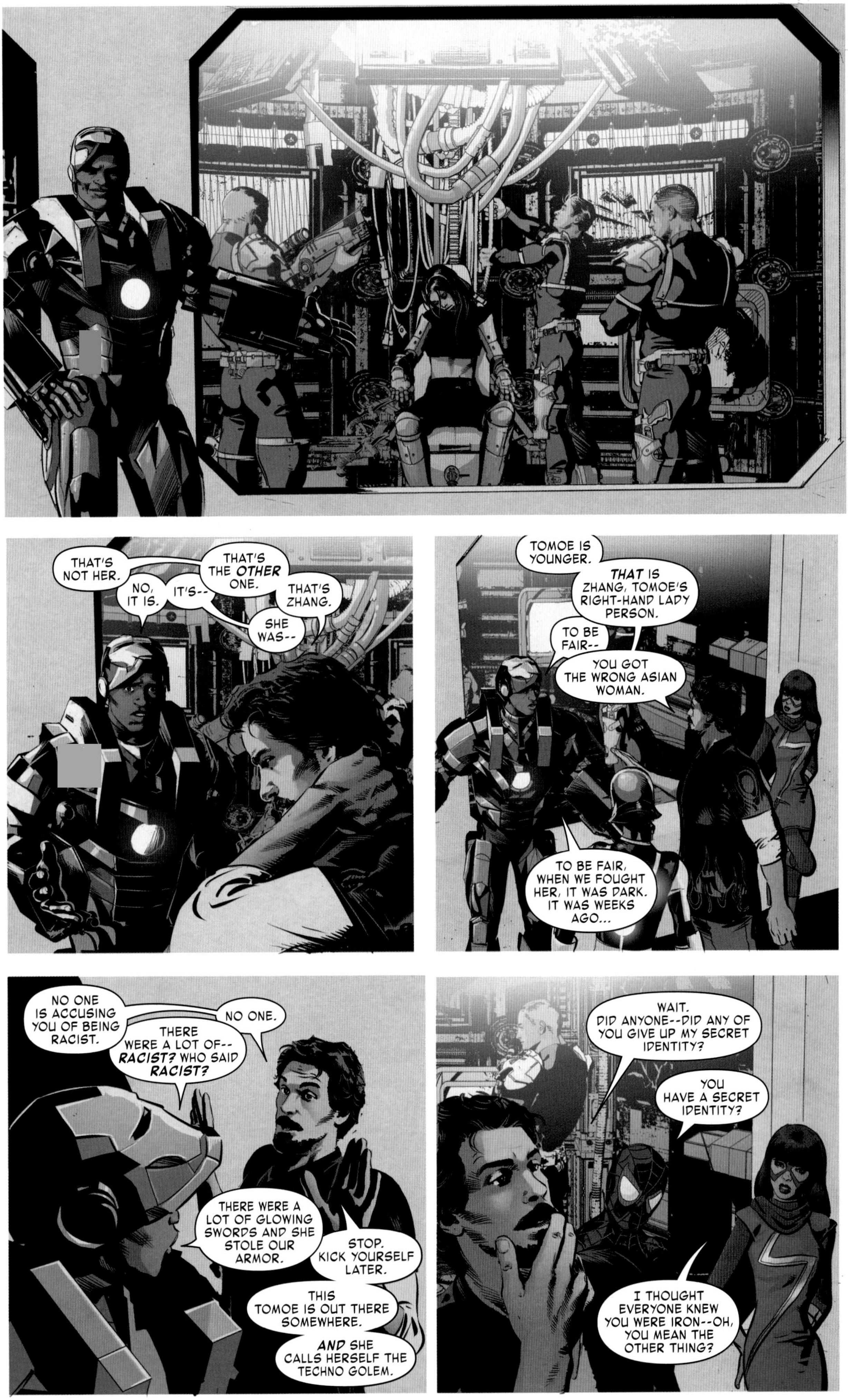
THAT'S NOT HER.
THAT'S THE *OTHER* ONE.
NO, IT IS.
IT'S--
SHE WAS--
THAT'S ZHANG.
TOMOE IS YOUNGER.
THAT IS ZHANG, TOMOE'S RIGHT-HAND LADY PERSON.
TO BE FAIR--
YOU GOT THE WRONG ASIAN WOMAN.
TO BE FAIR, WHEN WE FOUGHT HER, IT WAS DARK. IT WAS WEEKS AGO...
NO ONE IS ACCUSING YOU OF BEING RACIST.
NO ONE.
THERE WERE A LOT OF-- *RACIST?* WHO SAID *RACIST?*
THERE WERE A LOT OF GLOWING SWORDS AND SHE STOLE OUR ARMOR.
STOP. KICK YOURSELF LATER.
THIS TOMOE IS OUT THERE SOMEWHERE.
AND SHE CALLS HERSELF THE TECHNO GOLEM.
WAIT. DID ANYONE--DID ANY OF YOU GIVE UP MY SECRET IDENTITY?
YOU HAVE A SECRET IDENTITY?
I THOUGHT EVERYONE KNEW YOU WERE IRON--OH, YOU MEAN THE OTHER THING?

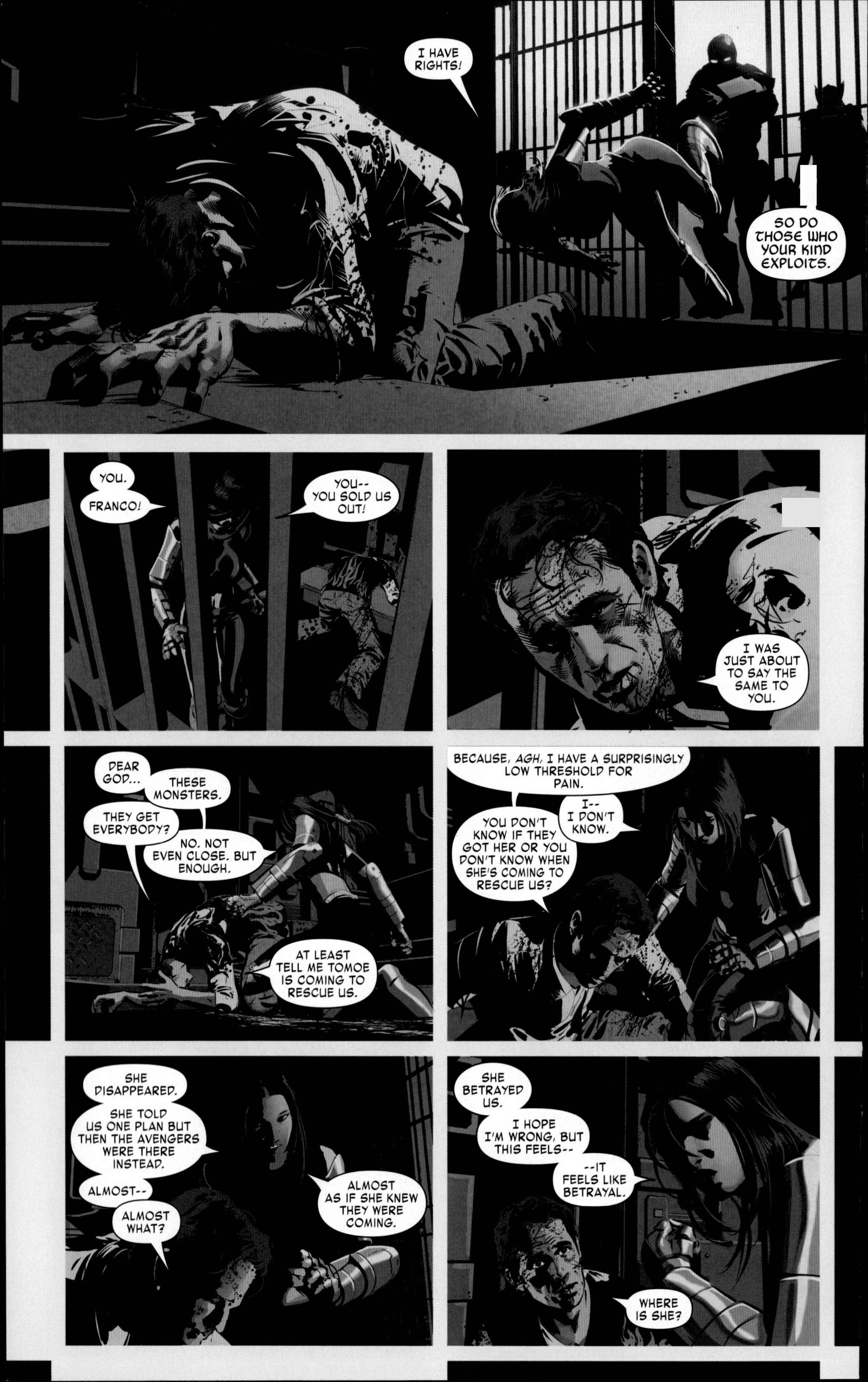
I HAVE RIGHTS!
SO DO THOSE WHO YOUR KIND EXPLOITS.
YOU.
FRANCO!
YOU-- YOU SOLD US OUT!
I WAS JUST ABOUT TO SAY THE SAME TO YOU.
DEAR GOD...
THESE MONSTERS.
THEY GET EVERYBODY?
NO. NOT EVEN CLOSE. BUT ENOUGH.
AT LEAST TELL ME TOMOE IS COMING TO RESCUE US.
BECAUSE, *AGH,* I HAVE A SURPRISINGLY LOW THRESHOLD FOR PAIN.
I-- I DON'T KNOW.
YOU DON'T KNOW IF THEY GOT HER OR YOU DON'T KNOW WHEN SHE'S COMING TO RESCUE US?
SHE DISAPPEARED.
SHE TOLD US ONE PLAN BUT THEN THE AVENGERS WERE THERE INSTEAD.
ALMOST--
ALMOST WHAT?
ALMOST AS IF SHE KNEW THEY WERE COMING.
SHE BETRAYED US.
I HOPE I'M WRONG, BUT THIS FEELS--
--IT FEELS LIKE BETRAYAL.
WHERE IS SHE?

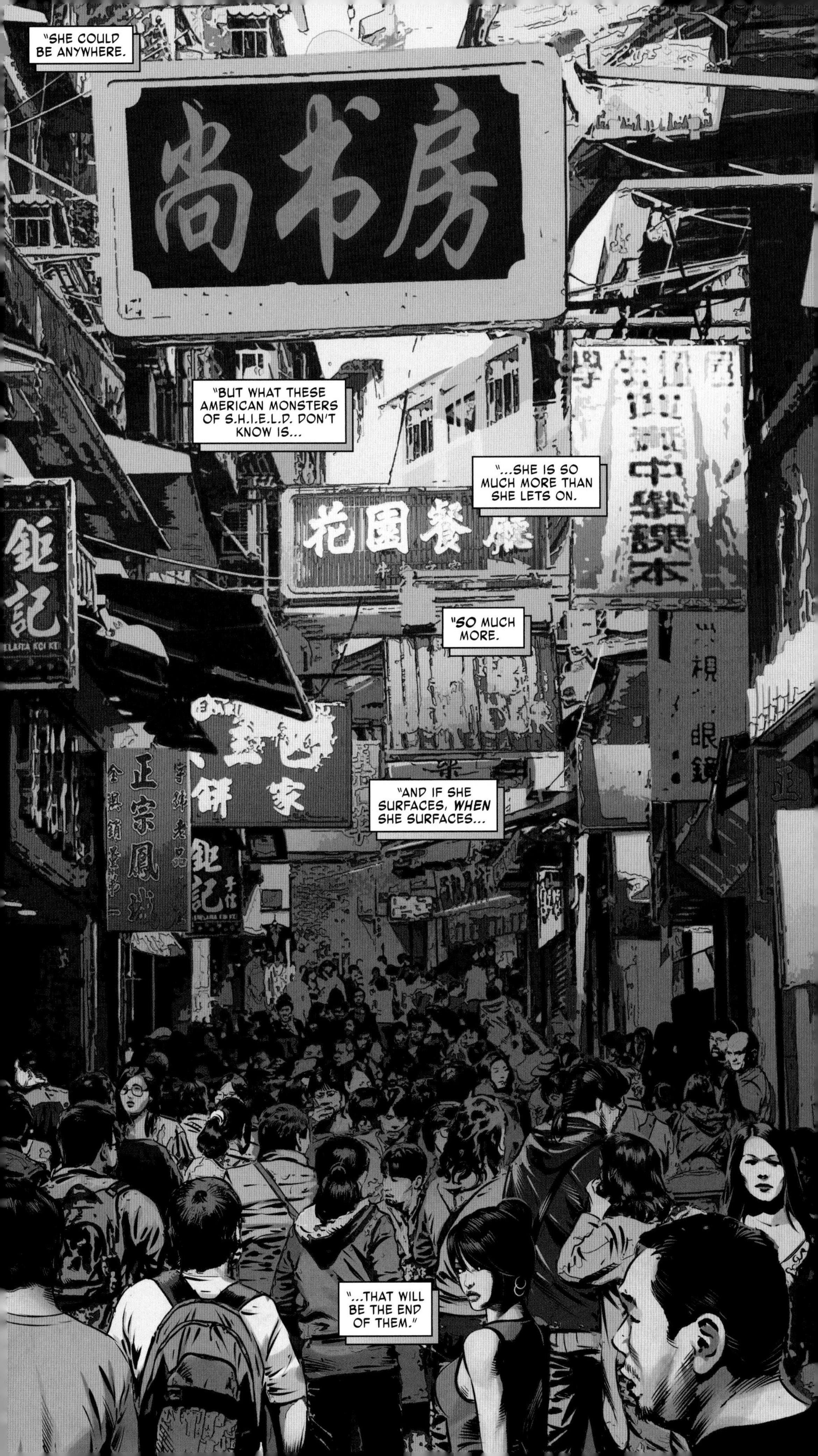
"SHE COULD BE ANYWHERE.
"BUT WHAT THESE AMERICAN MONSTERS OF S.H.I.E.L.D. DON'T KNOW IS...
"...SHE IS SO MUCH MORE THAN SHE LETS ON.
"SO MUCH MORE.
"AND IF SHE SURFACES, WHEN SHE SURFACES...
"...THAT WILL BE THE END OF THEM."

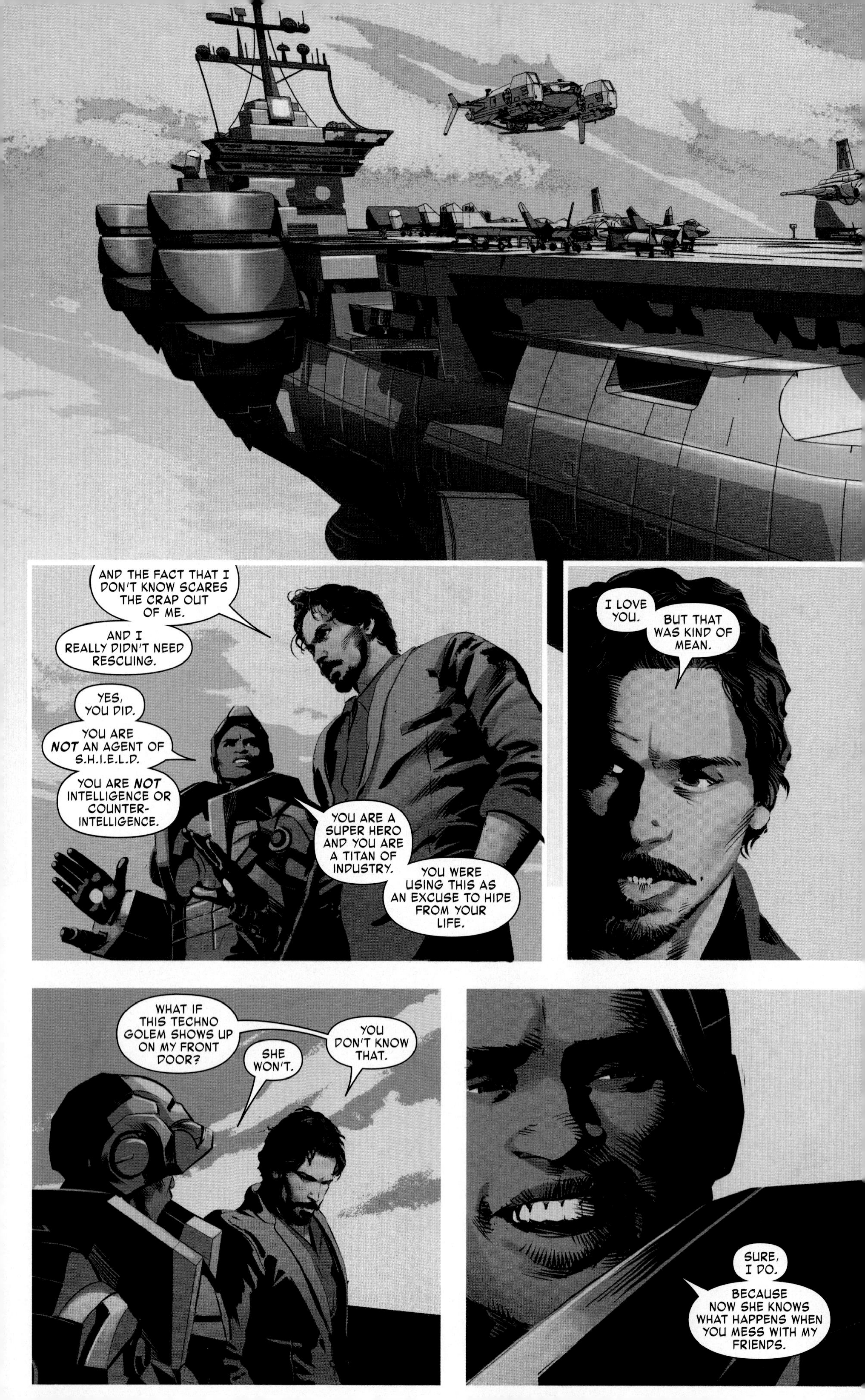
AND THE FACT THAT I DON'T KNOW SCARES THE CRAP OUT OF ME.
AND I REALLY DIDN'T NEED RESCUING.
YES, YOU DID.
YOU ARE NOT AN AGENT OF S.H.I.E.L.D.
YOU ARE NOT INTELLIGENCE OR COUNTER-INTELLIGENCE.
YOU ARE A SUPER HERO AND YOU ARE A TITAN OF INDUSTRY.
YOU WERE USING THIS AS AN EXCUSE TO HIDE FROM YOUR LIFE.
I LOVE YOU.
BUT THAT WAS KIND OF MEAN.
WHAT IF THIS TECHNO GOLEM SHOWS UP ON MY FRONT DOOR?
SHE WON'T.
YOU DON'T KNOW THAT.
SURE, I DO.
BECAUSE NOW SHE KNOWS WHAT HAPPENS WHEN YOU MESS WITH MY FRIENDS.

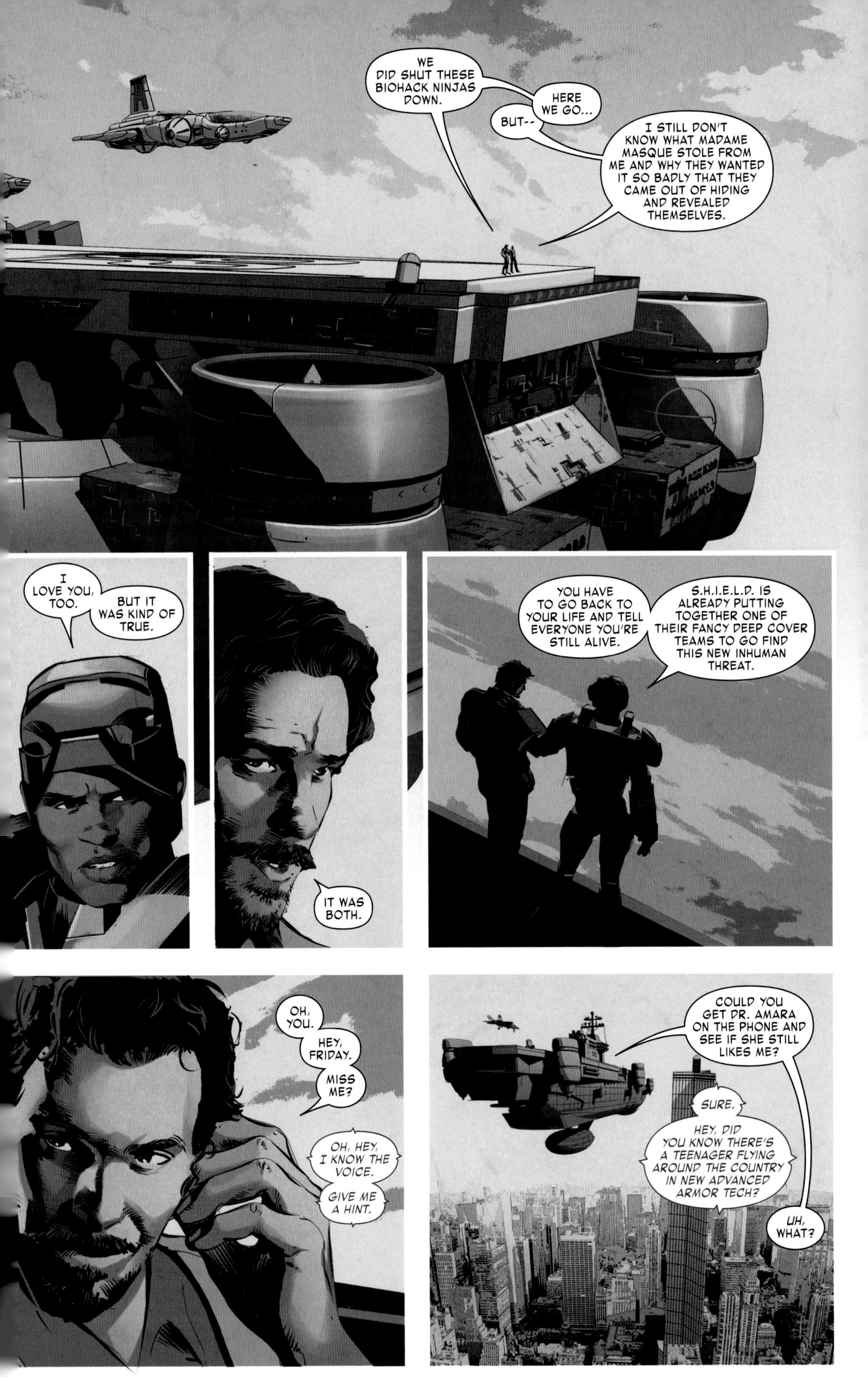
WE DID SHUT THESE BIOHACK NINJAS DOWN.
HERE WE GO...
BUT--
I STILL DON'T KNOW WHAT MADAME MASQUE STOLE FROM ME AND WHY THEY WANTED IT SO BADLY THAT THEY CAME OUT OF HIDING AND REVEALED THEMSELVES.
I LOVE YOU, TOO.
BUT IT WAS KIND OF TRUE.
IT WAS BOTH.
YOU HAVE TO GO BACK TO YOUR LIFE AND TELL EVERYONE YOU'RE STILL ALIVE.
S.H.I.E.L.D. IS ALREADY PUTTING TOGETHER ONE OF THEIR FANCY DEEP COVER TEAMS TO GO FIND THIS NEW INHUMAN THREAT.
OH, YOU.
HEY, FRIDAY.
MISS ME?
OH, HEY, I KNOW THE VOICE.
GIVE ME A HINT.
COULD YOU GET DR. AMARA ON THE PHONE AND SEE IF SHE STILL LIKES ME?
SURE.
HEY, DID YOU KNOW THERE'S A TEENAGER FLYING AROUND THE COUNTRY IN NEW ADVANCED ARMOR TECH?
UH, WHAT?

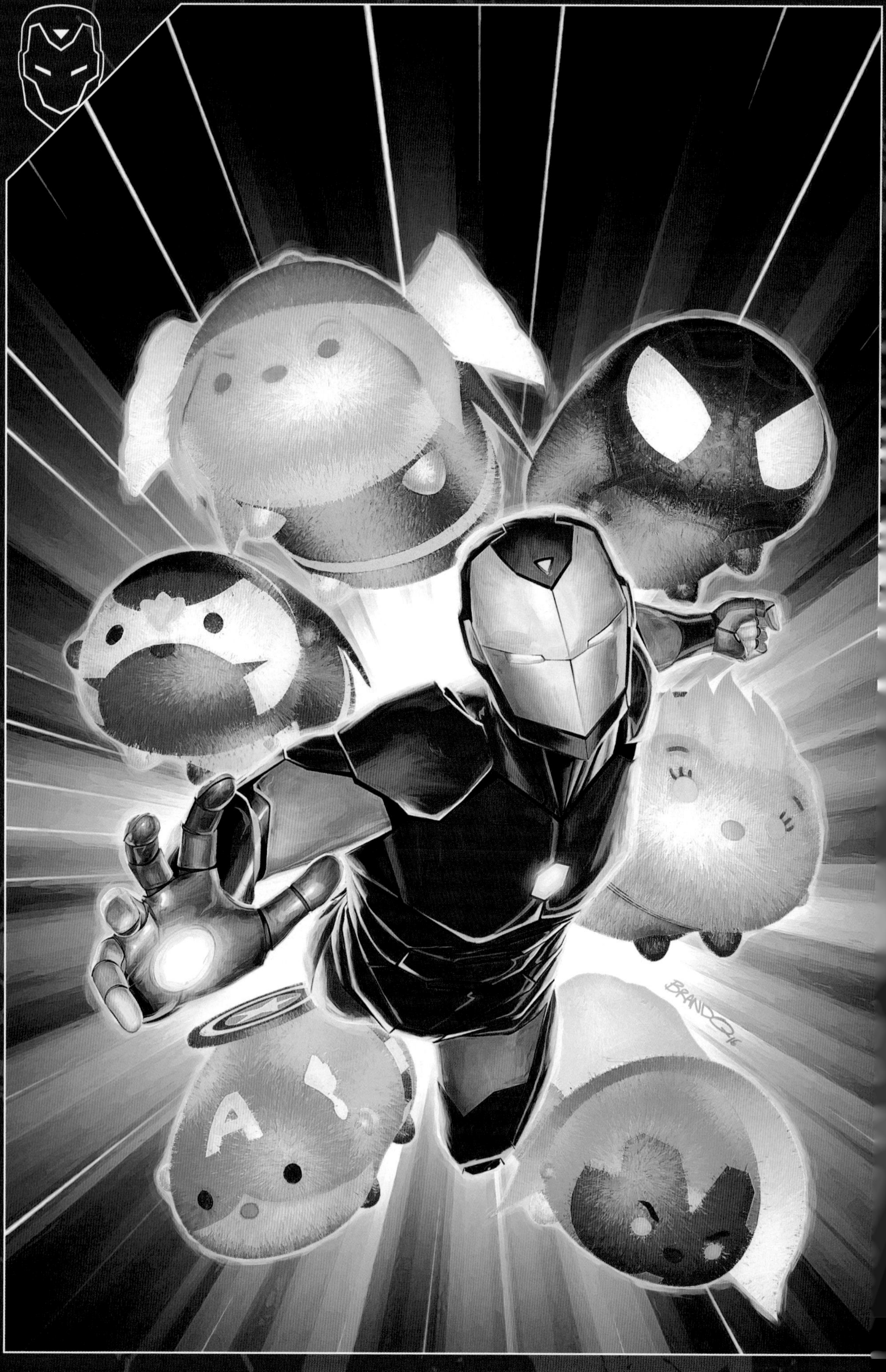

#12 MARVEL TSUM TSUM TAKEOVER VARIANT BY BRANDON PETERSON

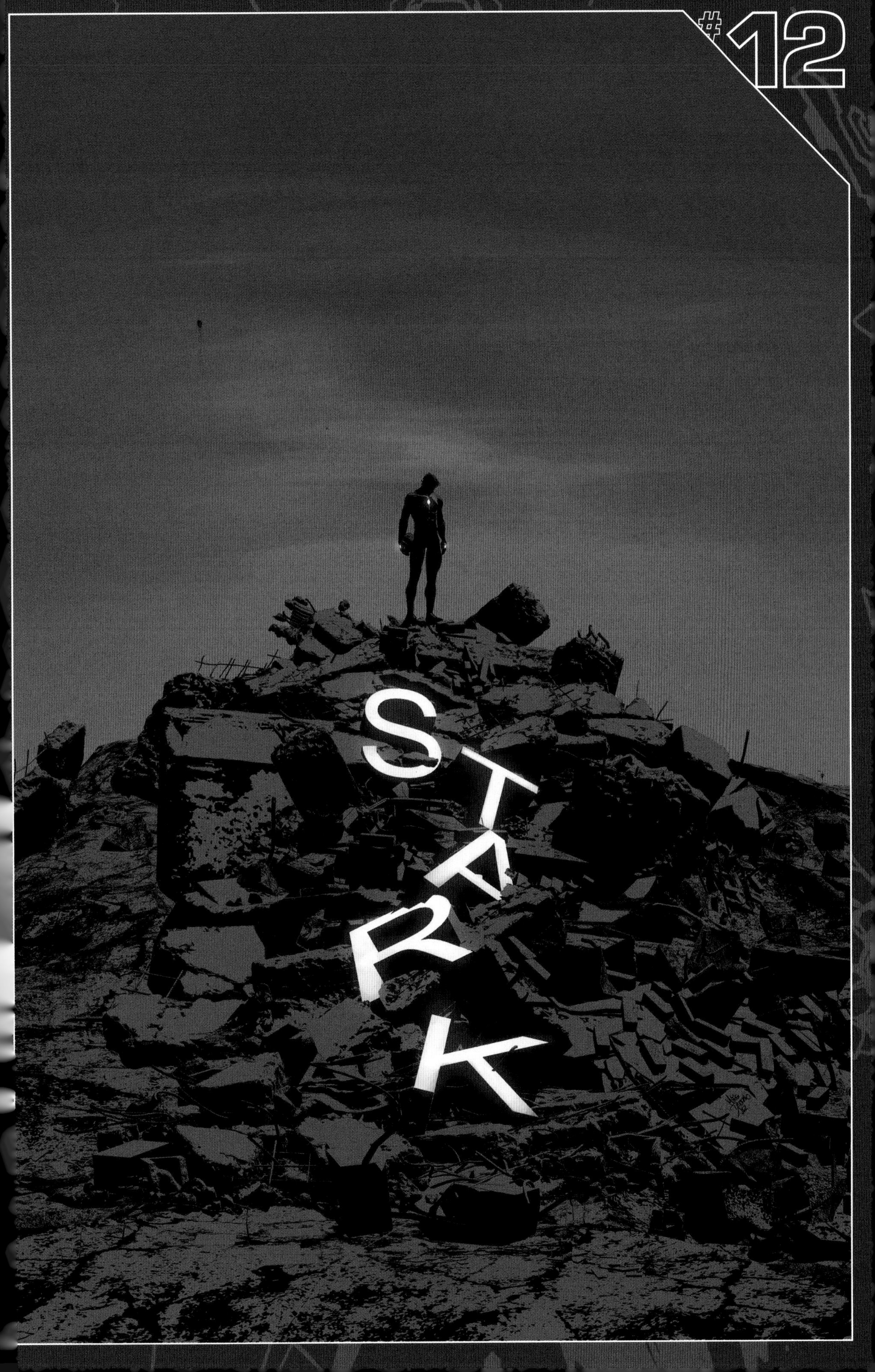
#12
STARK

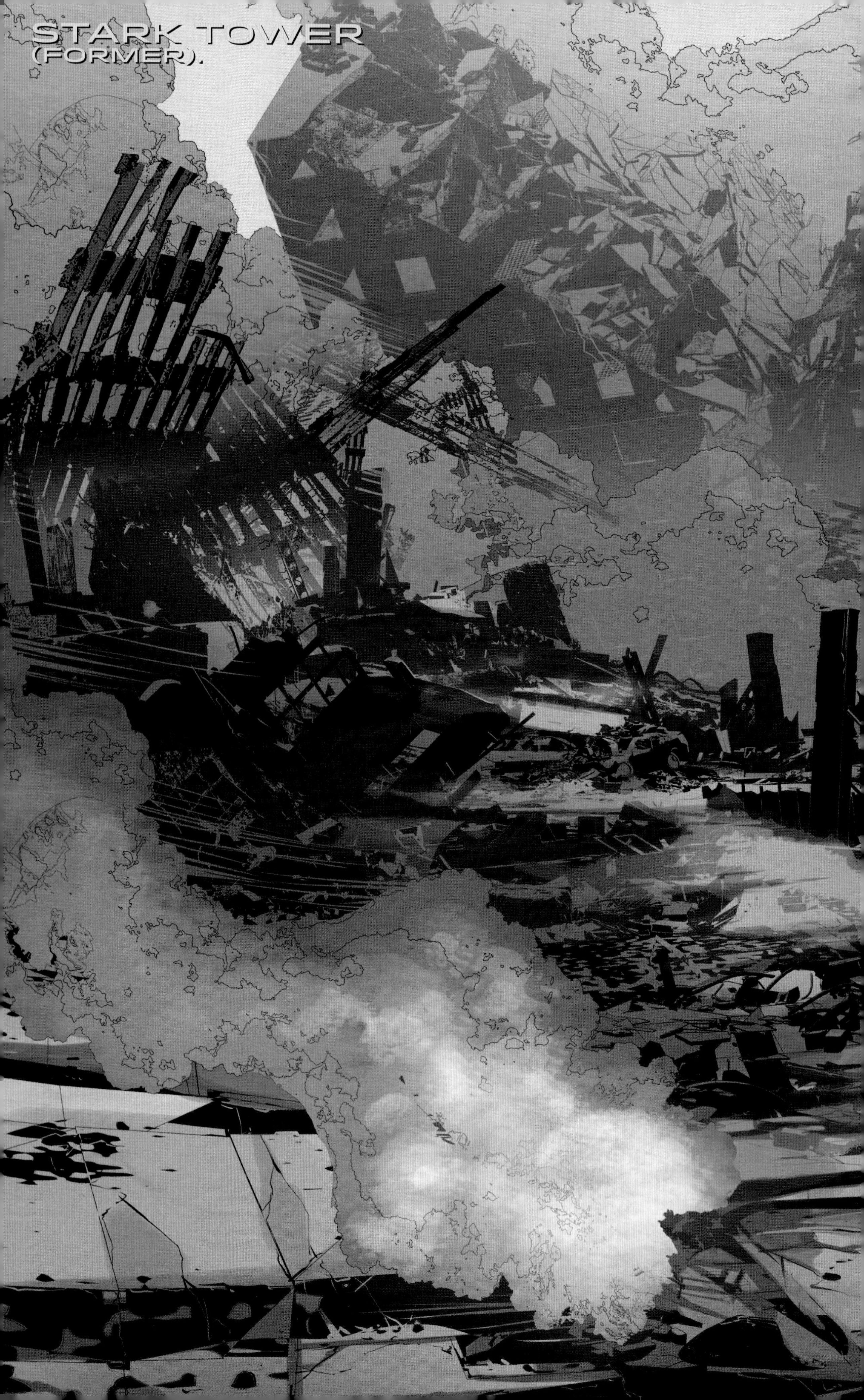
STARK TOWER
(FORMER).

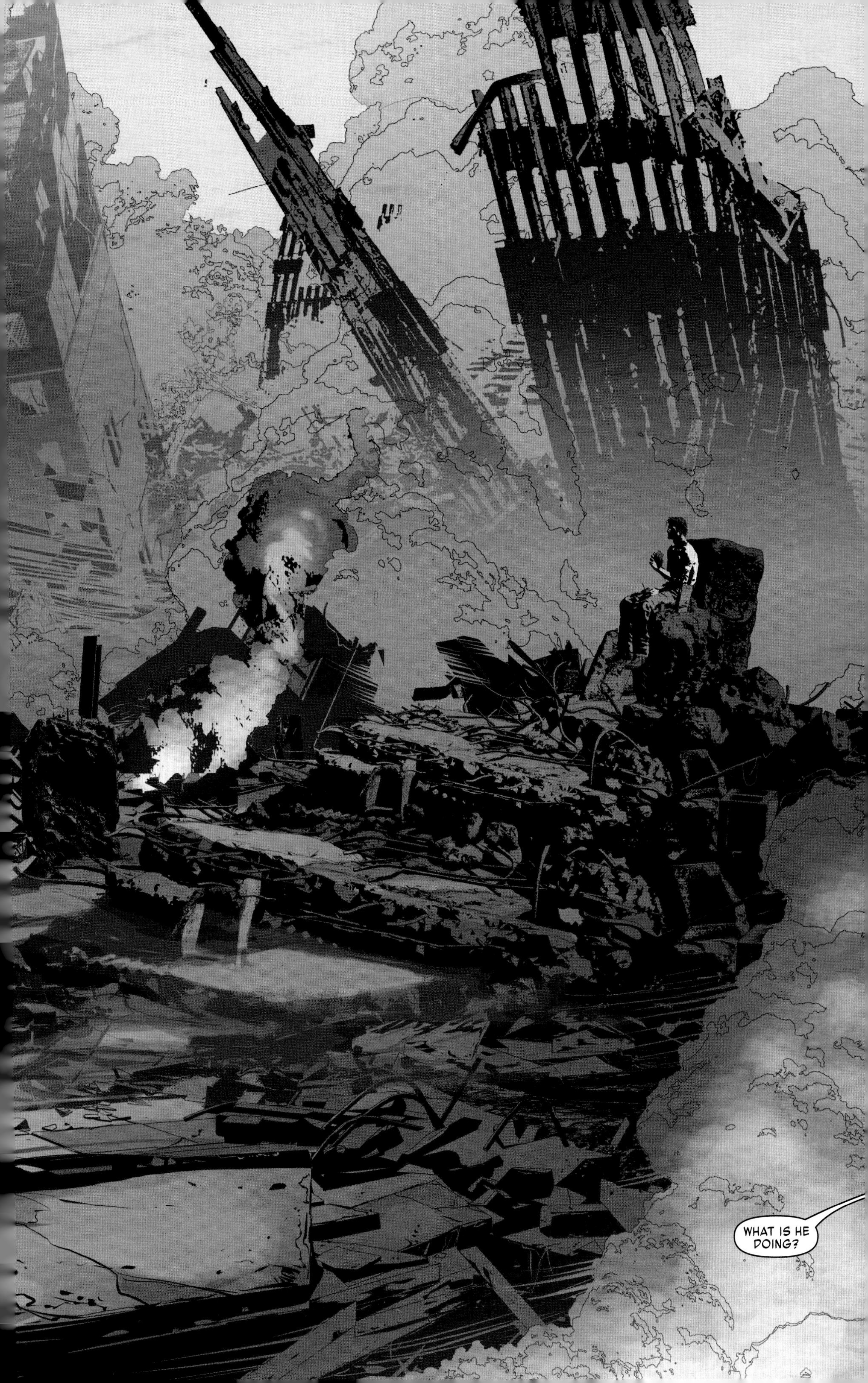
WHAT IS HE DOING?

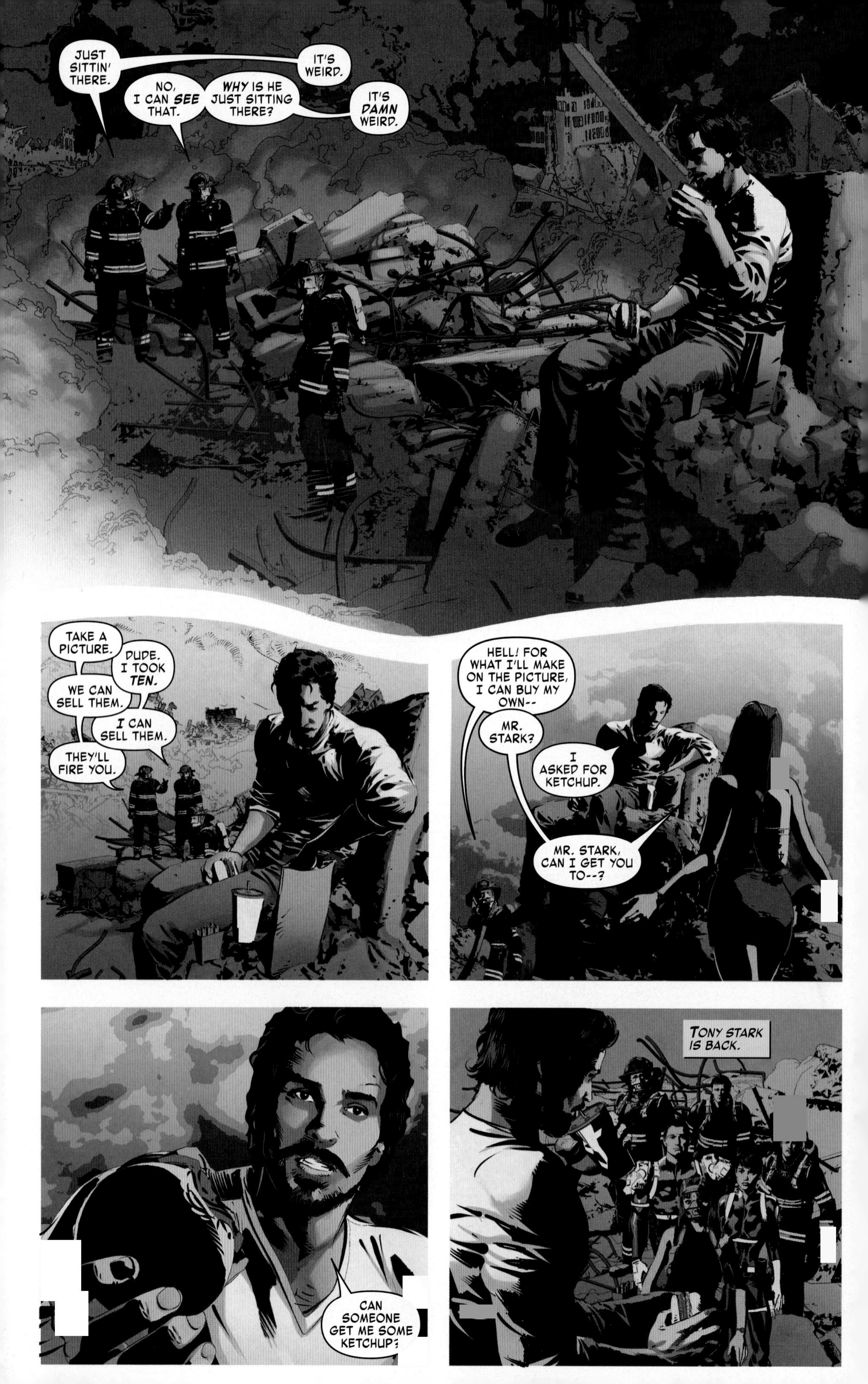
JUST SITTIN' THERE.
IT'S WEIRD.
NO, I CAN SEE THAT.
WHY IS HE JUST SITTING THERE?
IT'S DAMN WEIRD.
TAKE A PICTURE.
DUDE. I TOOK TEN.
WE CAN SELL THEM.
I CAN SELL THEM.
THEY'LL FIRE YOU.
HELL! FOR WHAT I'LL MAKE ON THE PICTURE, I CAN BUY MY OWN--
MR. STARK?
I ASKED FOR KETCHUP.
MR. STARK, CAN I GET YOU TO--?
CAN SOMEONE GET ME SOME KETCHUP?
TONY STARK IS BACK.

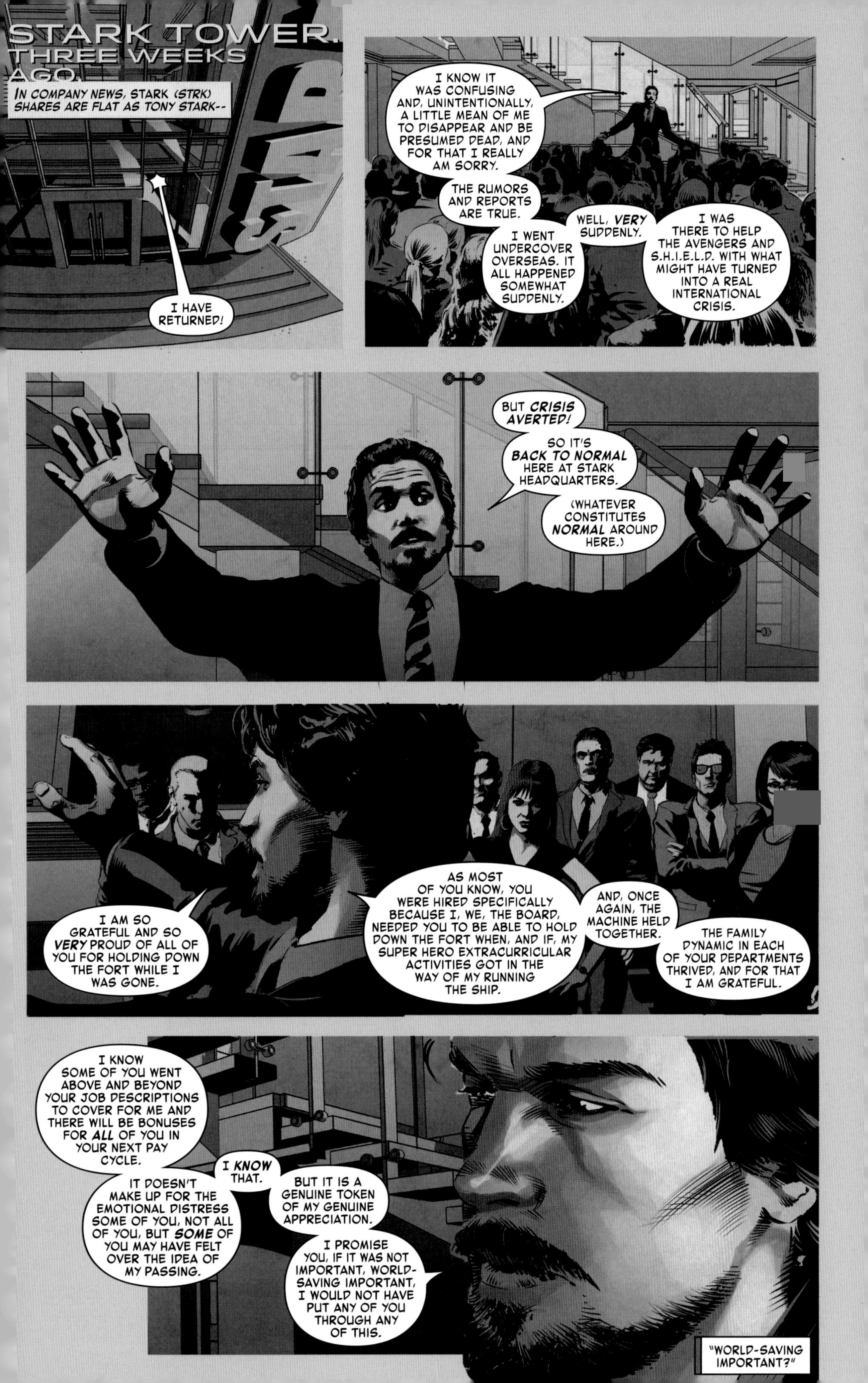
STARK TOWER. THREE WEEKS AGO.
IN COMPANY NEWS, STARK (STRK) SHARES ARE FLAT AS TONY STARK--
I HAVE RETURNED!
I KNOW IT WAS CONFUSING AND, UNINTENTIONALLY, A LITTLE MEAN OF ME TO DISAPPEAR AND BE PRESUMED DEAD, AND FOR THAT I REALLY AM SORRY.
THE RUMORS AND REPORTS ARE TRUE.
I WENT UNDERCOVER OVERSEAS. IT ALL HAPPENED SOMEWHAT SUDDENLY.
WELL, VERY SUDDENLY.
I WAS THERE TO HELP THE AVENGERS AND S.H.I.E.L.D. WITH WHAT MIGHT HAVE TURNED INTO A REAL INTERNATIONAL CRISIS.
BUT CRISIS AVERTED!
SO IT'S BACK TO NORMAL HERE AT STARK HEADQUARTERS.
(WHATEVER CONSTITUTES NORMAL AROUND HERE.)
I AM SO GRATEFUL AND SO VERY PROUD OF ALL OF YOU FOR HOLDING DOWN THE FORT WHILE I WAS GONE.
AS MOST OF YOU KNOW, YOU WERE HIRED SPECIFICALLY BECAUSE I, WE, THE BOARD, NEEDED YOU TO BE ABLE TO HOLD DOWN THE FORT WHEN, AND IF, MY SUPER HERO EXTRACURRICULAR ACTIVITIES GOT IN THE WAY OF MY RUNNING THE SHIP.
AND, ONCE AGAIN, THE MACHINE HELD TOGETHER.
THE FAMILY DYNAMIC IN EACH OF YOUR DEPARTMENTS THRIVED, AND FOR THAT I AM GRATEFUL.
I KNOW SOME OF YOU WENT ABOVE AND BEYOND YOUR JOB DESCRIPTIONS TO COVER FOR ME AND THERE WILL BE BONUSES FOR ALL OF YOU IN YOUR NEXT PAY CYCLE.
IT DOESN'T MAKE UP FOR THE EMOTIONAL DISTRESS SOME OF YOU, NOT ALL OF YOU, BUT SOME OF YOU MAY HAVE FELT OVER THE IDEA OF MY PASSING.
I KNOW THAT.
BUT IT IS A GENUINE TOKEN OF MY GENUINE APPRECIATION.
I PROMISE YOU, IF IT WAS NOT IMPORTANT, WORLD-SAVING IMPORTANT, I WOULD NOT HAVE PUT ANY OF YOU THROUGH ANY OF THIS.
"WORLD-SAVING IMPORTANT?"

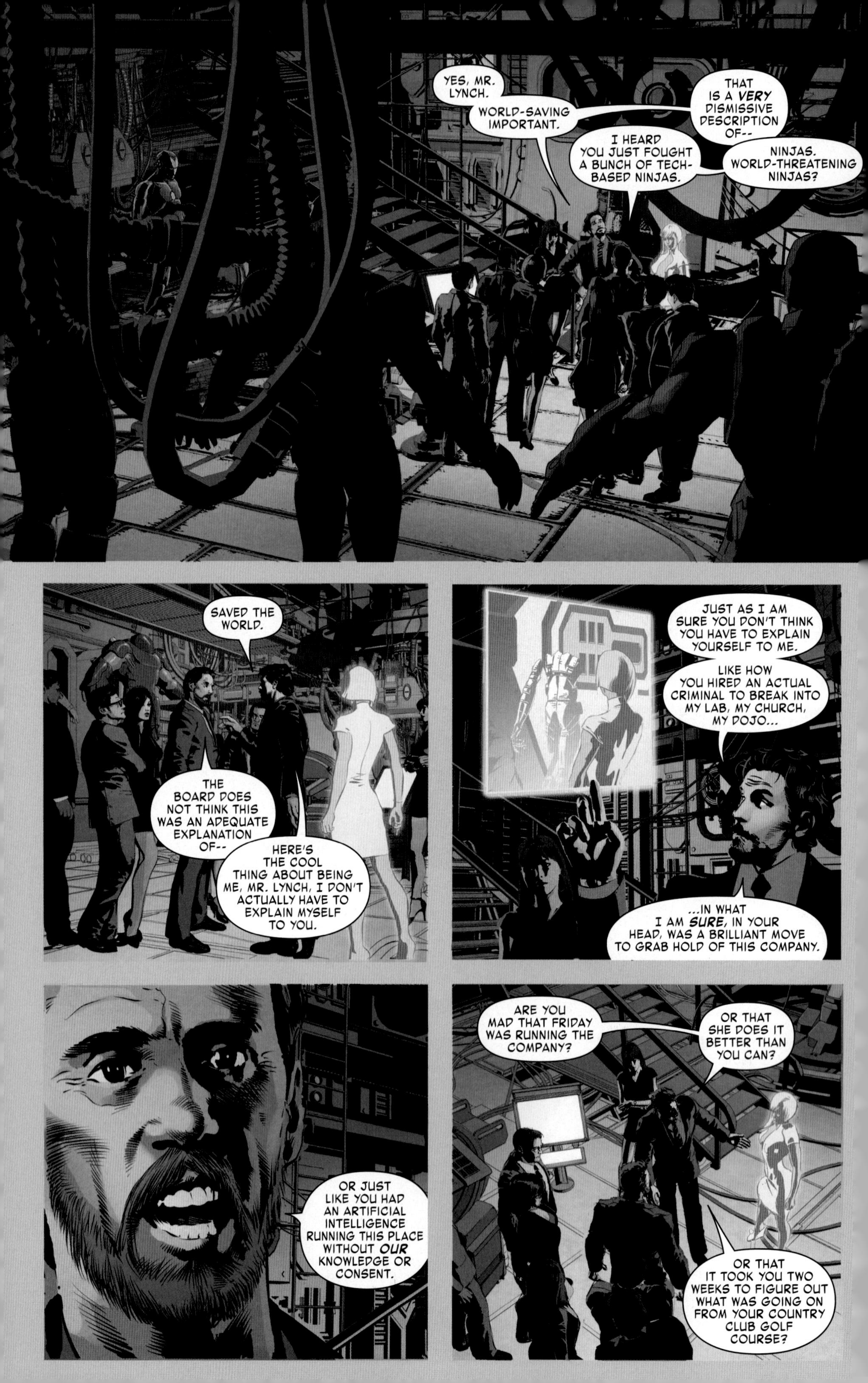
I HEARD YOU JUST FOUGHT A BUNCH OF TECH-BASED NINJAS.
THAT IS A *VERY* DISMISSIVE DESCRIPTION OF--
NINJAS. WORLD-THREATENING NINJAS?
YES, MR. LYNCH.
WORLD-SAVING IMPORTANT.
SAVED THE WORLD.
THE BOARD DOES NOT THINK THIS WAS AN ADEQUATE EXPLANATION OF--
HERE'S THE COOL THING ABOUT BEING ME, MR. LYNCH, I DON'T ACTUALLY HAVE TO EXPLAIN MYSELF TO YOU.
JUST AS I AM SURE YOU DON'T THINK YOU HAVE TO EXPLAIN YOURSELF TO ME.
LIKE HOW YOU HIRED AN ACTUAL CRIMINAL TO BREAK INTO MY LAB, MY CHURCH, MY DOJO...
...IN WHAT I AM *SURE*, IN YOUR HEAD, WAS A BRILLIANT MOVE TO GRAB HOLD OF THIS COMPANY.
OR JUST LIKE YOU HAD AN ARTIFICIAL INTELLIGENCE RUNNING THIS PLACE WITHOUT *OUR* KNOWLEDGE OR CONSENT.
ARE YOU MAD THAT FRIDAY WAS RUNNING THE COMPANY?
OR THAT SHE DOES IT BETTER THAN YOU CAN?
OR THAT IT TOOK YOU TWO WEEKS TO FIGURE OUT WHAT WAS GOING ON FROM YOUR COUNTRY CLUB GOLF COURSE?

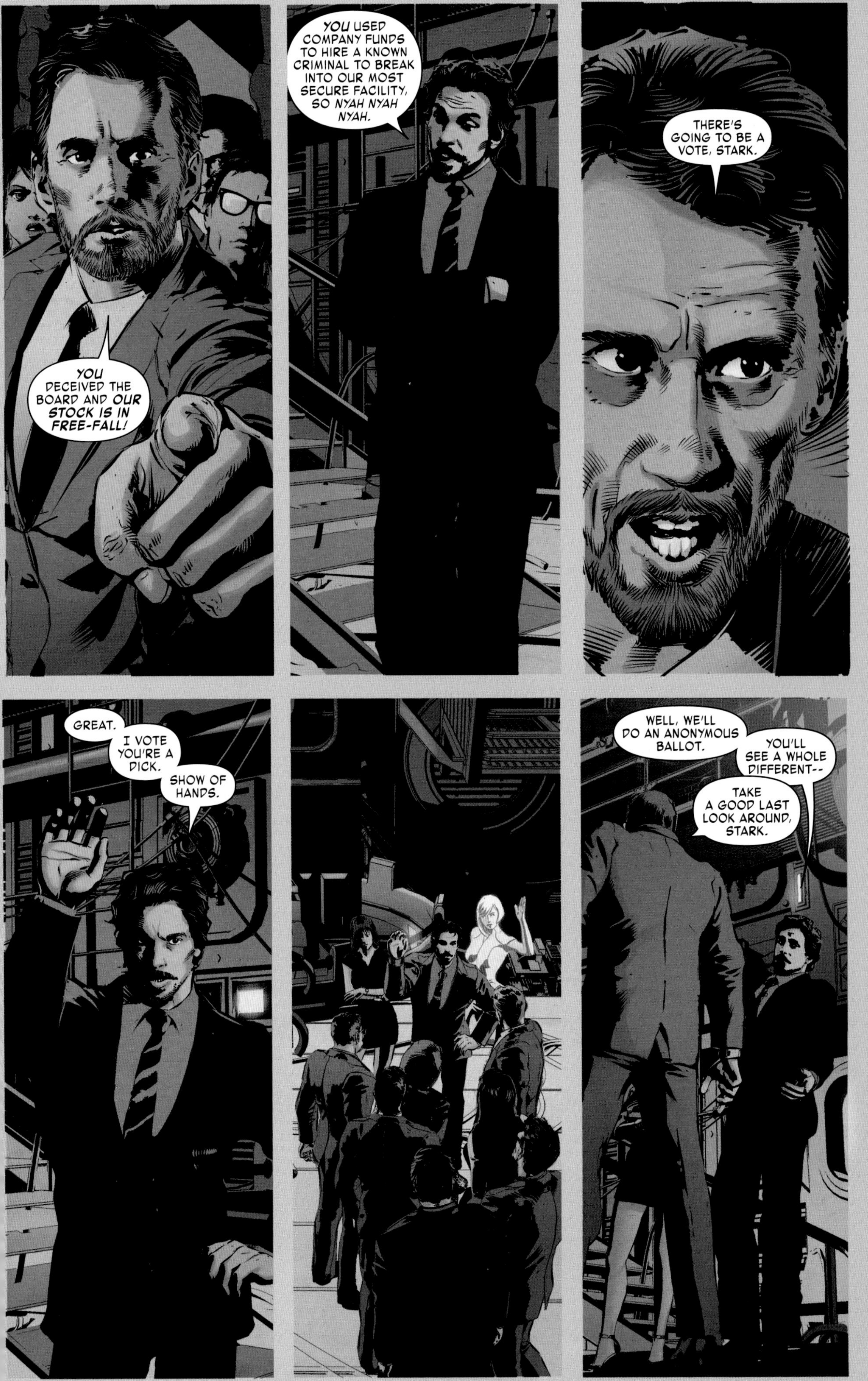

YOU DECEIVED THE BOARD AND OUR STOCK IS IN FREE-FALL!
YOU USED COMPANY FUNDS TO HIRE A KNOWN CRIMINAL TO BREAK INTO OUR MOST SECURE FACILITY, SO NYAH NYAH NYAH.
THERE'S GOING TO BE A VOTE, STARK.
GREAT.
I VOTE YOU'RE A DICK.
SHOW OF HANDS.
WELL, WE'LL DO AN ANONYMOUS BALLOT.
YOU'LL SEE A WHOLE DIFFERENT--
TAKE A GOOD LAST LOOK AROUND, STARK.

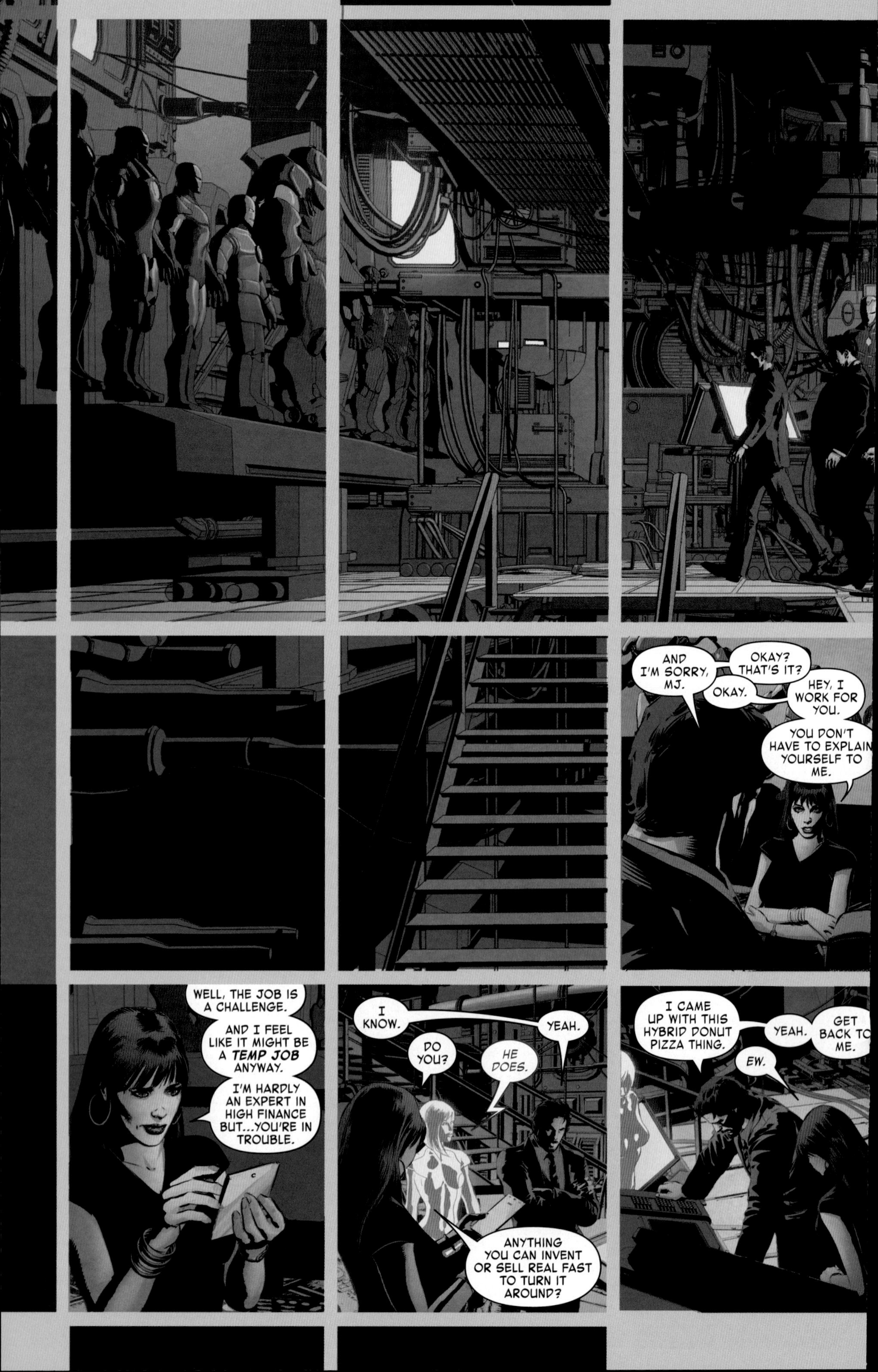
AND I'M SORRY, MJ.
OKAY? THAT'S IT?
OKAY.
HEY, I WORK FOR YOU.
YOU DON'T HAVE TO EXPLAIN YOURSELF TO ME.
WELL, THE JOB IS A CHALLENGE.
AND I FEEL LIKE IT MIGHT BE A *TEMP JOB* ANYWAY.
I'M HARDLY AN EXPERT IN HIGH FINANCE BUT...YOU'RE IN TROUBLE.
I KNOW.
YEAH.
DO YOU?
HE DOES.
ANYTHING YOU CAN INVENT OR SELL REAL FAST TO TURN IT AROUND?
I CAME UP WITH THIS HYBRID DONUT PIZZA THING.
YEAH.
GET BACK TO ME.
EW.

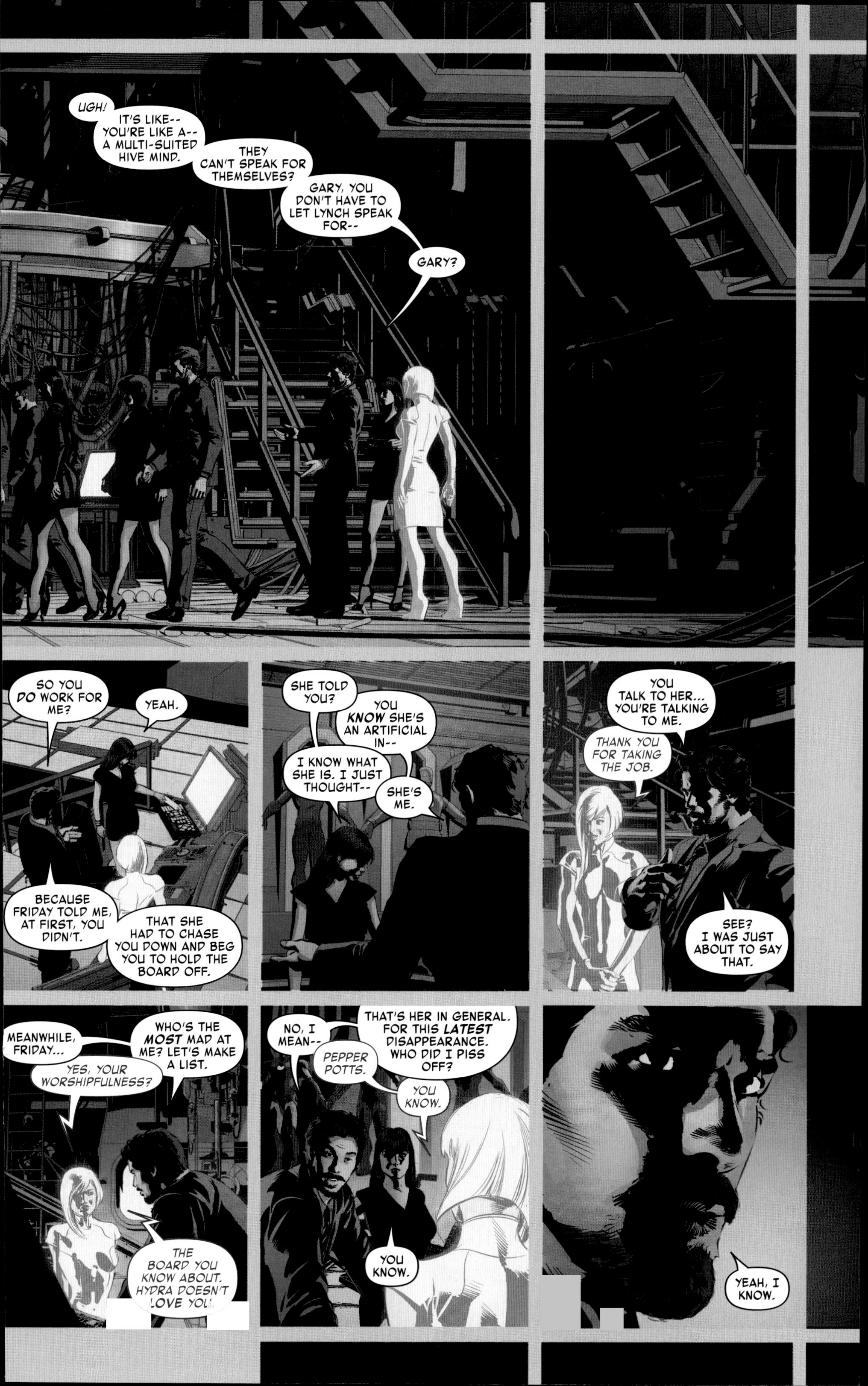
UGH!
IT'S LIKE-- YOU'RE LIKE A-- A MULTI-SUITED HIVE MIND.
THEY CAN'T SPEAK FOR THEMSELVES?
GARY, YOU DON'T HAVE TO LET LYNCH SPEAK FOR--
GARY?
SO YOU DO WORK FOR ME?
YEAH.
BECAUSE FRIDAY TOLD ME, AT FIRST, YOU DIDN'T.
THAT SHE HAD TO CHASE YOU DOWN AND BEG YOU TO HOLD THE BOARD OFF.
SHE TOLD YOU?
YOU KNOW SHE'S AN ARTIFICIAL IN--
I KNOW WHAT SHE IS. I JUST THOUGHT--
SHE'S ME.
YOU TALK TO HER... YOU'RE TALKING TO ME.
THANK YOU FOR TAKING THE JOB.
SEE? I WAS JUST ABOUT TO SAY THAT.
MEANWHILE, FRIDAY...
YES, YOUR WORSHIPFULNESS?
WHO'S THE MOST MAD AT ME? LET'S MAKE A LIST.
THE BOARD YOU KNOW ABOUT. HYDRA DOESN'T LOVE YOU.
NO, I MEAN--
THAT'S HER IN GENERAL. FOR THIS LATEST DISAPPEARANCE. WHO DID I PISS OFF?
PEPPER POTTS.
YOU KNOW.
YOU KNOW.
YEAH, I KNOW.

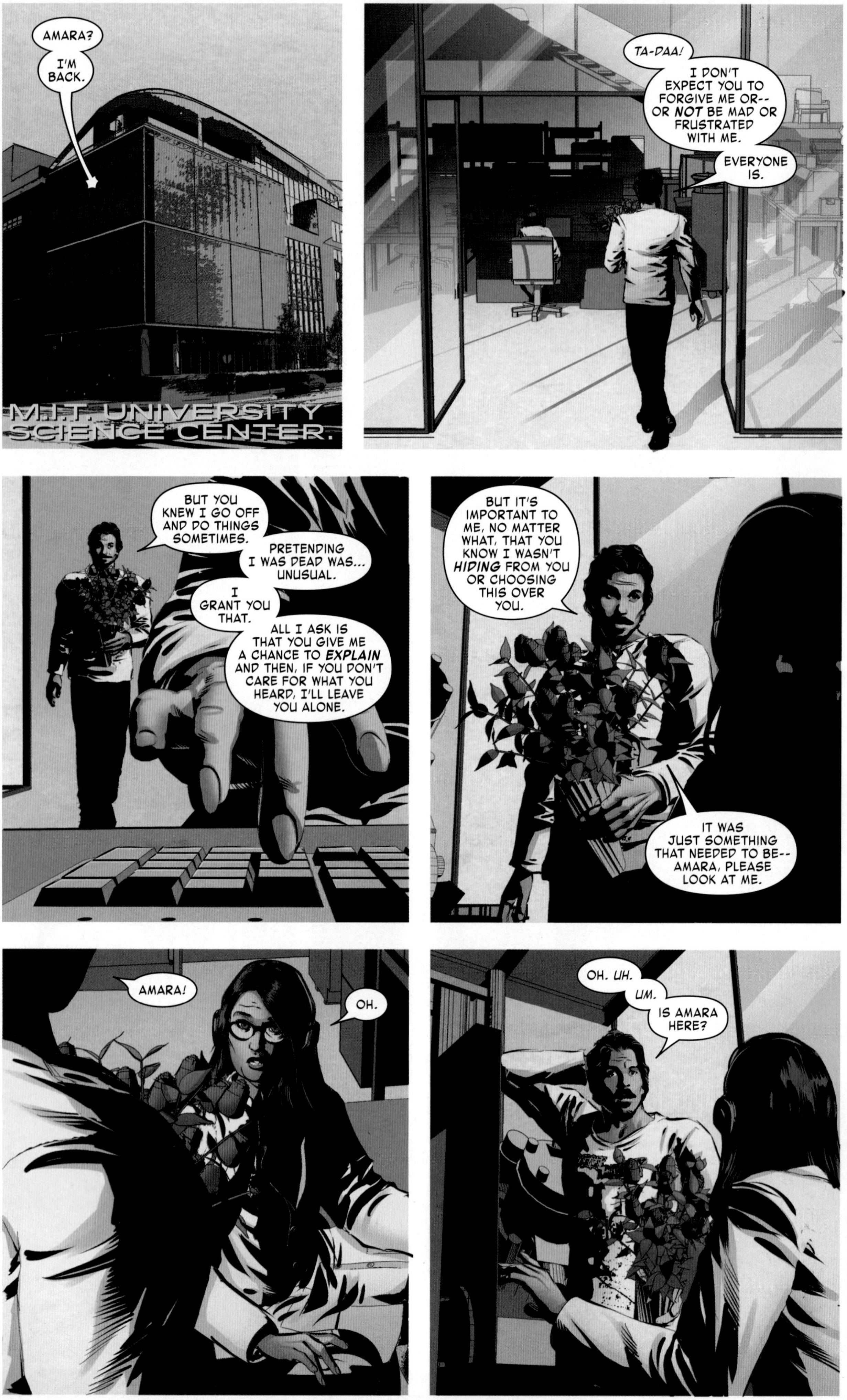
AMARA?
I'M BACK.
M.I.T. UNIVERSITY SCIENCE CENTER.
TA-DAA!
I DON'T EXPECT YOU TO FORGIVE ME OR-- OR NOT BE MAD OR FRUSTRATED WITH ME.
EVERYONE IS.
BUT YOU KNEW I GO OFF AND DO THINGS SOMETIMES.
PRETENDING I WAS DEAD WAS... UNUSUAL.
I GRANT YOU THAT.
ALL I ASK IS THAT YOU GIVE ME A CHANCE TO EXPLAIN AND THEN, IF YOU DON'T CARE FOR WHAT YOU HEARD, I'LL LEAVE YOU ALONE.
BUT IT'S IMPORTANT TO ME, NO MATTER WHAT, THAT YOU KNOW I WASN'T HIDING FROM YOU OR CHOOSING THIS OVER YOU.
IT WAS JUST SOMETHING THAT NEEDED TO BE-- AMARA, PLEASE LOOK AT ME.
AMARA!
OH.
OH. UH.
UM.
IS AMARA HERE?

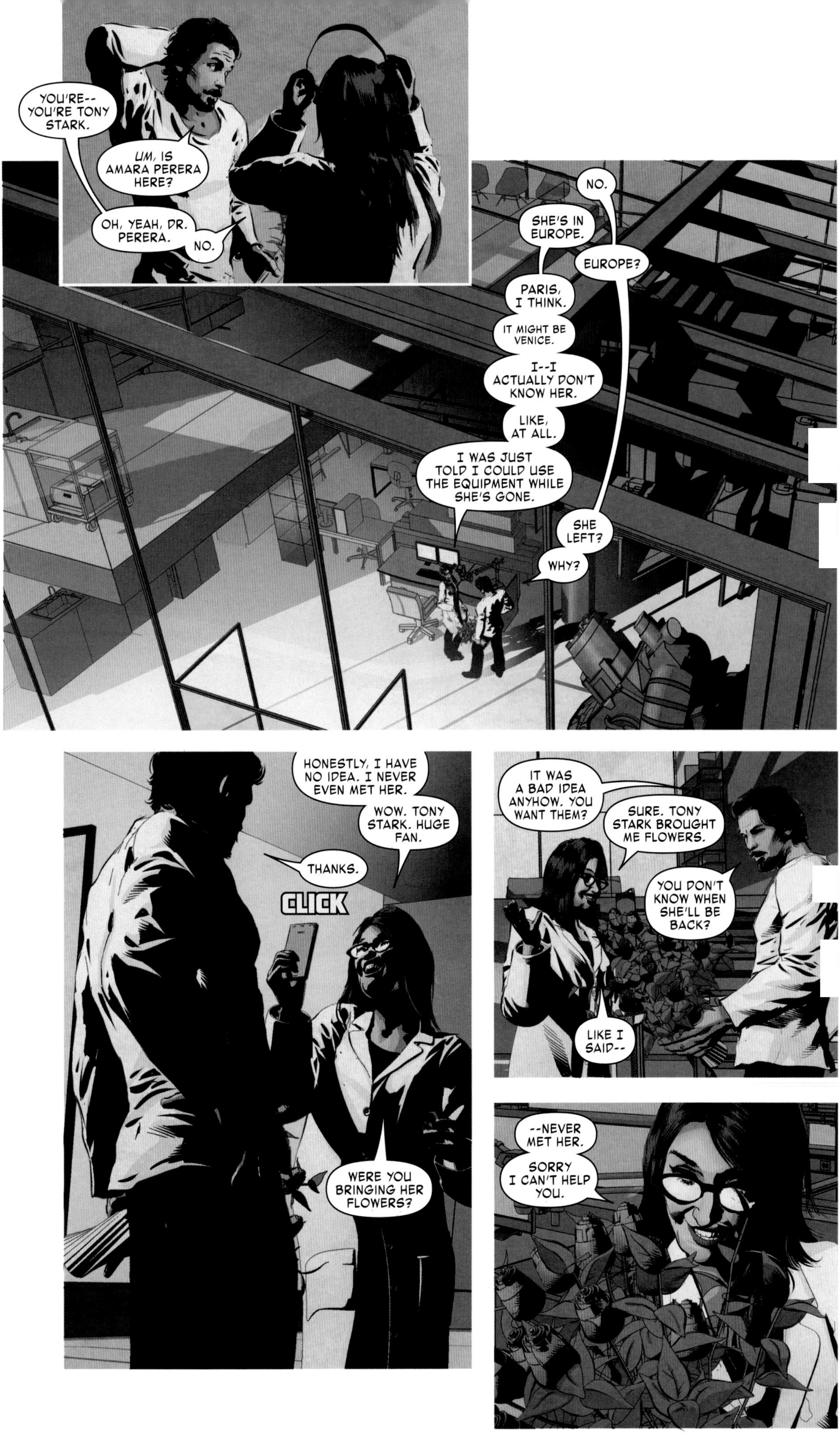
YOU'RE--
YOU'RE TONY STARK.
UM, IS AMARA PERERA HERE?
OH, YEAH, DR. PERERA.
NO.
NO.
SHE'S IN EUROPE.
EUROPE?
PARIS, I THINK.
IT MIGHT BE VENICE.
I--I ACTUALLY DON'T KNOW HER.
LIKE, AT ALL.
I WAS JUST TOLD I COULD USE THE EQUIPMENT WHILE SHE'S GONE.
SHE LEFT?
WHY?
HONESTLY, I HAVE NO IDEA. I NEVER EVEN MET HER.
WOW. TONY STARK. HUGE FAN.
THANKS.
CLICK
WERE YOU BRINGING HER FLOWERS?
IT WAS A BAD IDEA ANYHOW. YOU WANT THEM?
SURE. TONY STARK BROUGHT ME FLOWERS.
YOU DON'T KNOW WHEN SHE'LL BE BACK?
LIKE I SAID--
--NEVER MET HER.
SORRY I CAN'T HELP YOU.

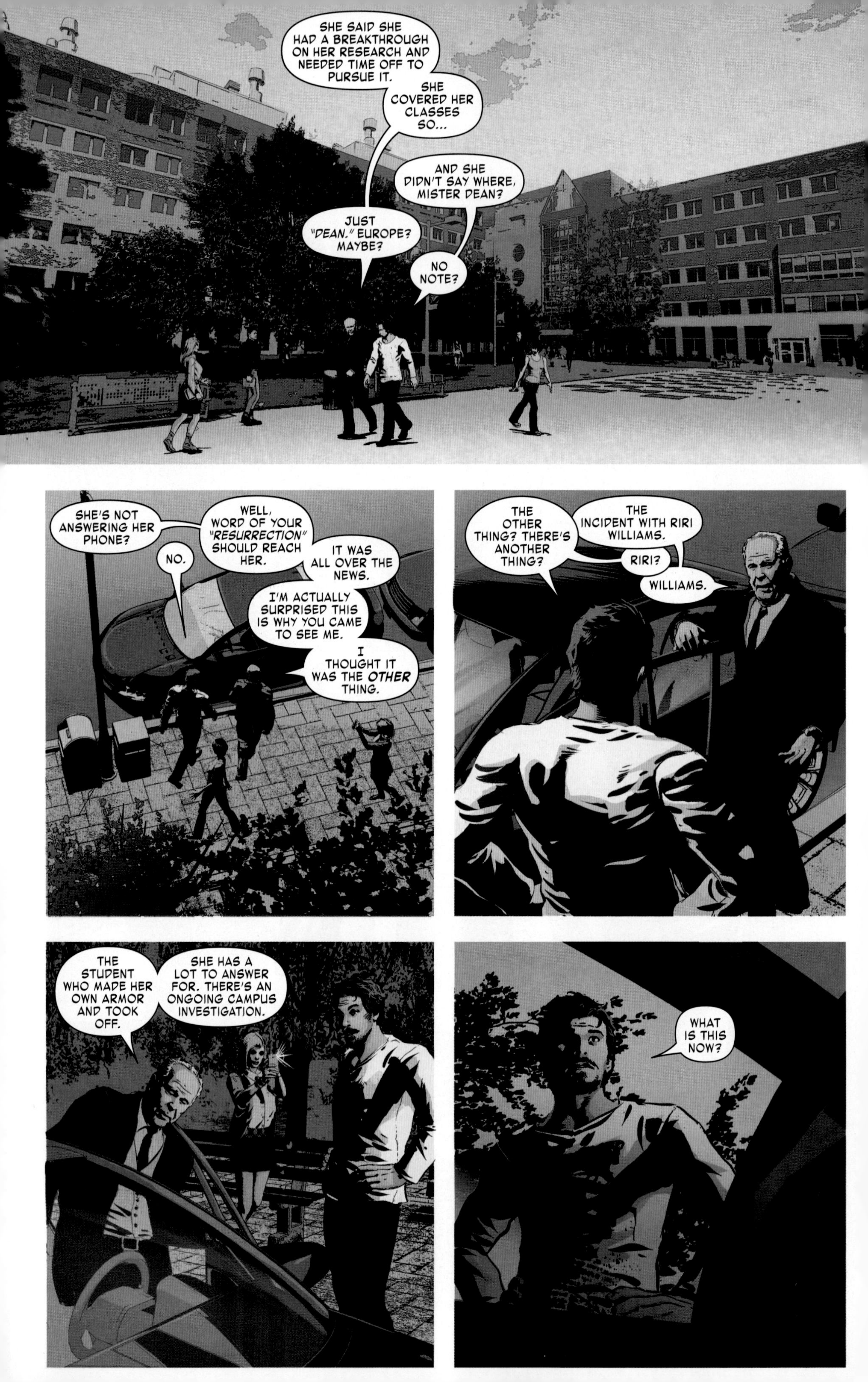
SHE SAID SHE HAD A BREAKTHROUGH ON HER RESEARCH AND NEEDED TIME OFF TO PURSUE IT.
SHE COVERED HER CLASSES SO...
AND SHE DIDN'T SAY WHERE, MISTER DEAN?
JUST "DEAN." EUROPE? MAYBE?
NO NOTE?
SHE'S NOT ANSWERING HER PHONE?
NO.
WELL, WORD OF YOUR "RESURRECTION" SHOULD REACH HER.
IT WAS ALL OVER THE NEWS.
I'M ACTUALLY SURPRISED THIS IS WHY YOU CAME TO SEE ME.
I THOUGHT IT WAS THE OTHER THING.
THE OTHER THING? THERE'S ANOTHER THING?
THE INCIDENT WITH RIRI WILLIAMS.
RIRI?
WILLIAMS.
THE STUDENT WHO MADE HER OWN ARMOR AND TOOK OFF.
SHE HAS A LOT TO ANSWER FOR. THERE'S AN ONGOING CAMPUS INVESTIGATION.
WHAT IS THIS NOW?

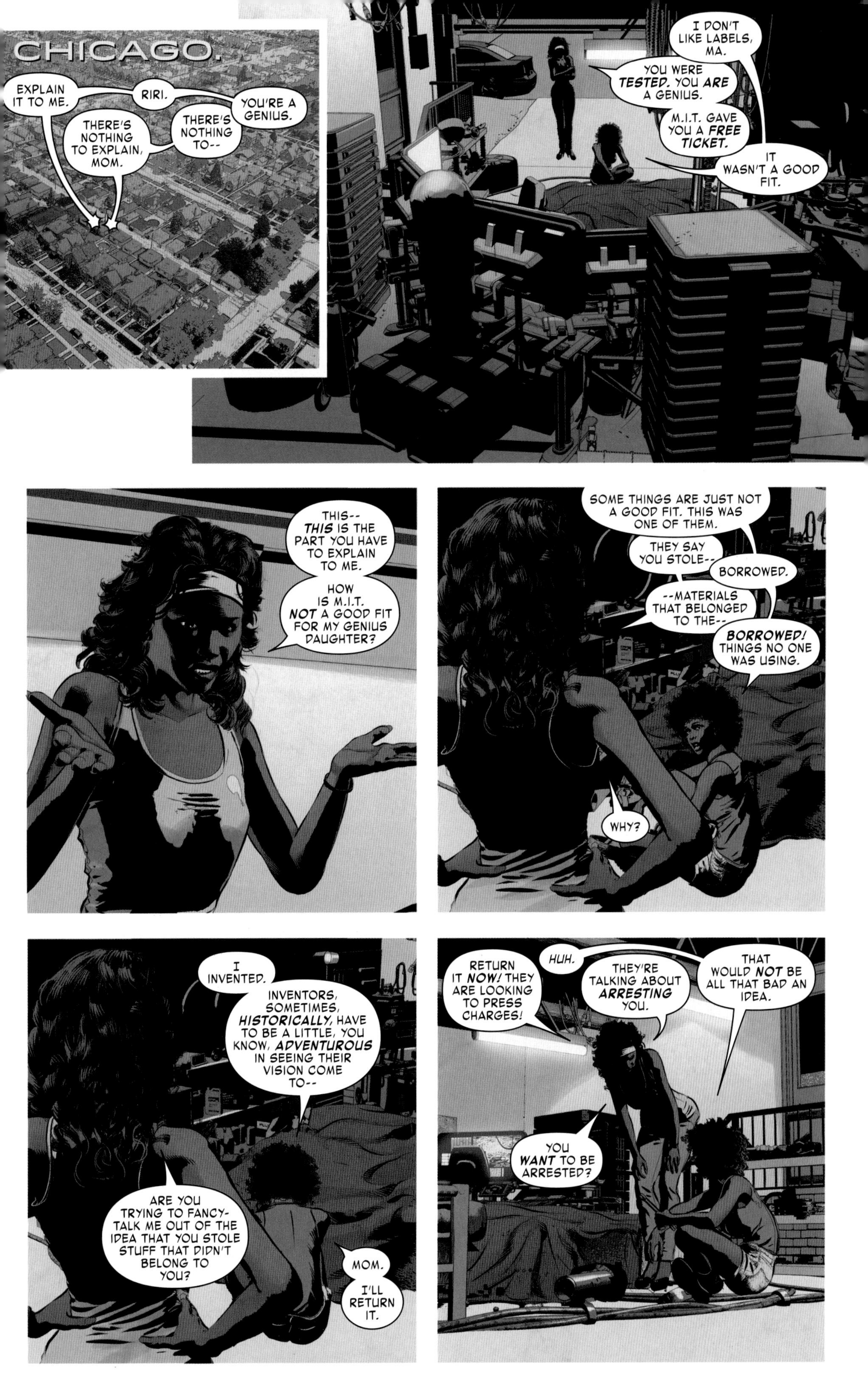
CHICAGO.
EXPLAIN IT TO ME.
RIRI.
YOU'RE A GENIUS.
THERE'S NOTHING TO EXPLAIN, MOM.
THERE'S NOTHING TO--
I DON'T LIKE LABELS, MA.
YOU WERE TESTED. YOU ARE A GENIUS.
M.I.T. GAVE YOU A FREE TICKET.
IT WASN'T A GOOD FIT.
THIS-- THIS IS THE PART YOU HAVE TO EXPLAIN TO ME.
HOW IS M.I.T. NOT A GOOD FIT FOR MY GENIUS DAUGHTER?
SOME THINGS ARE JUST NOT A GOOD FIT. THIS WAS ONE OF THEM.
THEY SAY YOU STOLE--
BORROWED.
--MATERIALS THAT BELONGED TO THE--
BORROWED! THINGS NO ONE WAS USING.
WHY?
I INVENTED.
INVENTORS, SOMETIMES, HISTORICALLY, HAVE TO BE A LITTLE, YOU KNOW, ADVENTUROUS IN SEEING THEIR VISION COME TO--
ARE YOU TRYING TO FANCY-TALK ME OUT OF THE IDEA THAT YOU STOLE STUFF THAT DIDN'T BELONG TO YOU?
MOM.
I'LL RETURN IT.
RETURN IT NOW! THEY ARE LOOKING TO PRESS CHARGES!
HUH.
THEY'RE TALKING ABOUT ARRESTING YOU.
THAT WOULD NOT BE ALL THAT BAD AN IDEA.
YOU WANT TO BE ARRESTED?

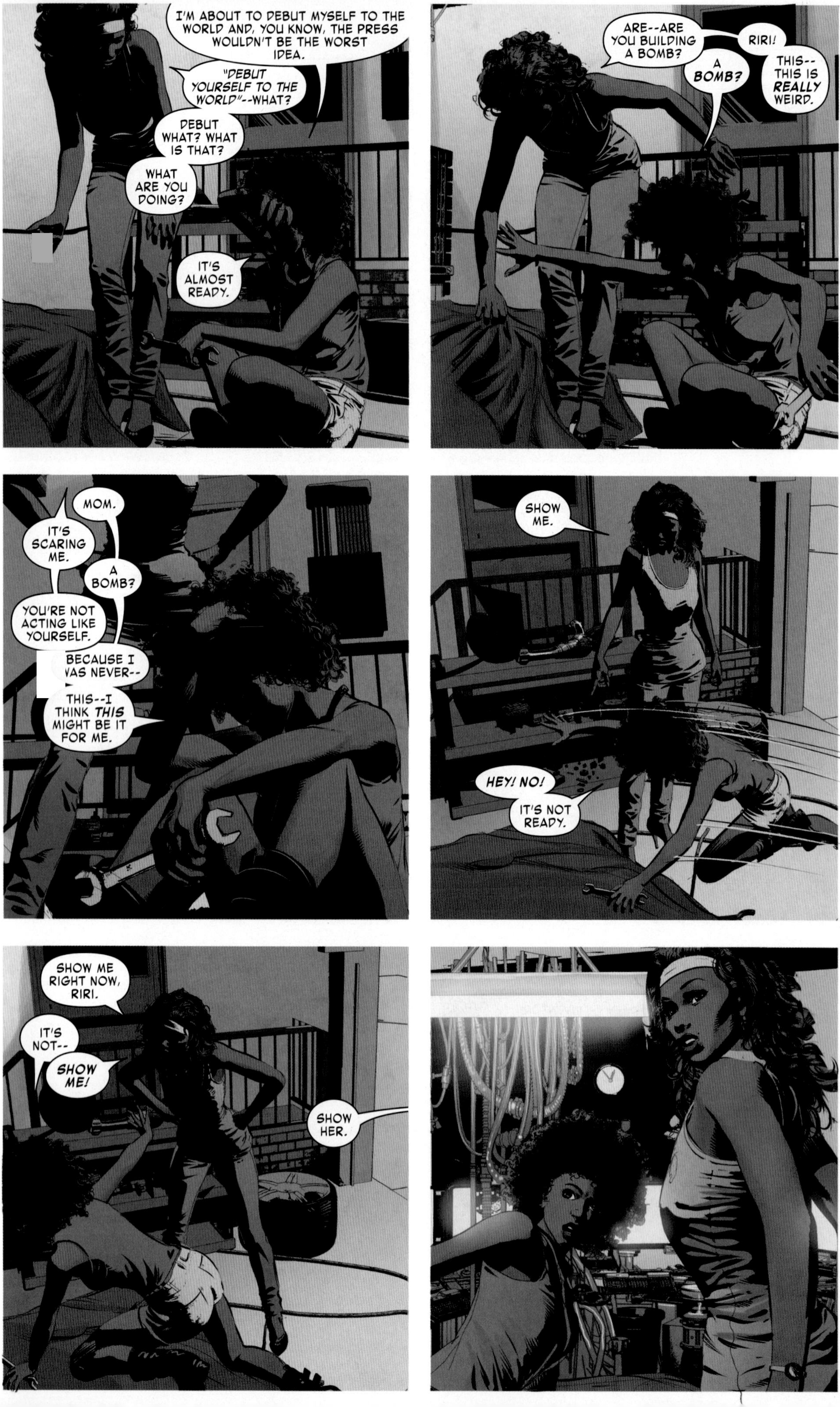
I'M ABOUT TO DEBUT MYSELF TO THE WORLD AND, YOU KNOW, THE PRESS WOULDN'T BE THE WORST IDEA.
"DEBUT YOURSELF TO THE WORLD"--WHAT?
DEBUT WHAT? WHAT IS THAT?
WHAT ARE YOU DOING?
IT'S ALMOST READY.
ARE--ARE YOU BUILDING A BOMB?
A *BOMB?*
RIRI!
THIS--THIS IS *REALLY* WEIRD.
MOM.
IT'S SCARING ME.
A BOMB?
YOU'RE NOT ACTING LIKE YOURSELF.
BECAUSE I WAS NEVER--
THIS--I THINK *THIS* MIGHT BE IT FOR ME.
SHOW ME.
HEY! NO!
IT'S NOT READY.
SHOW ME RIGHT NOW, RIRI.
IT'S NOT--
SHOW ME!
SHOW HER.

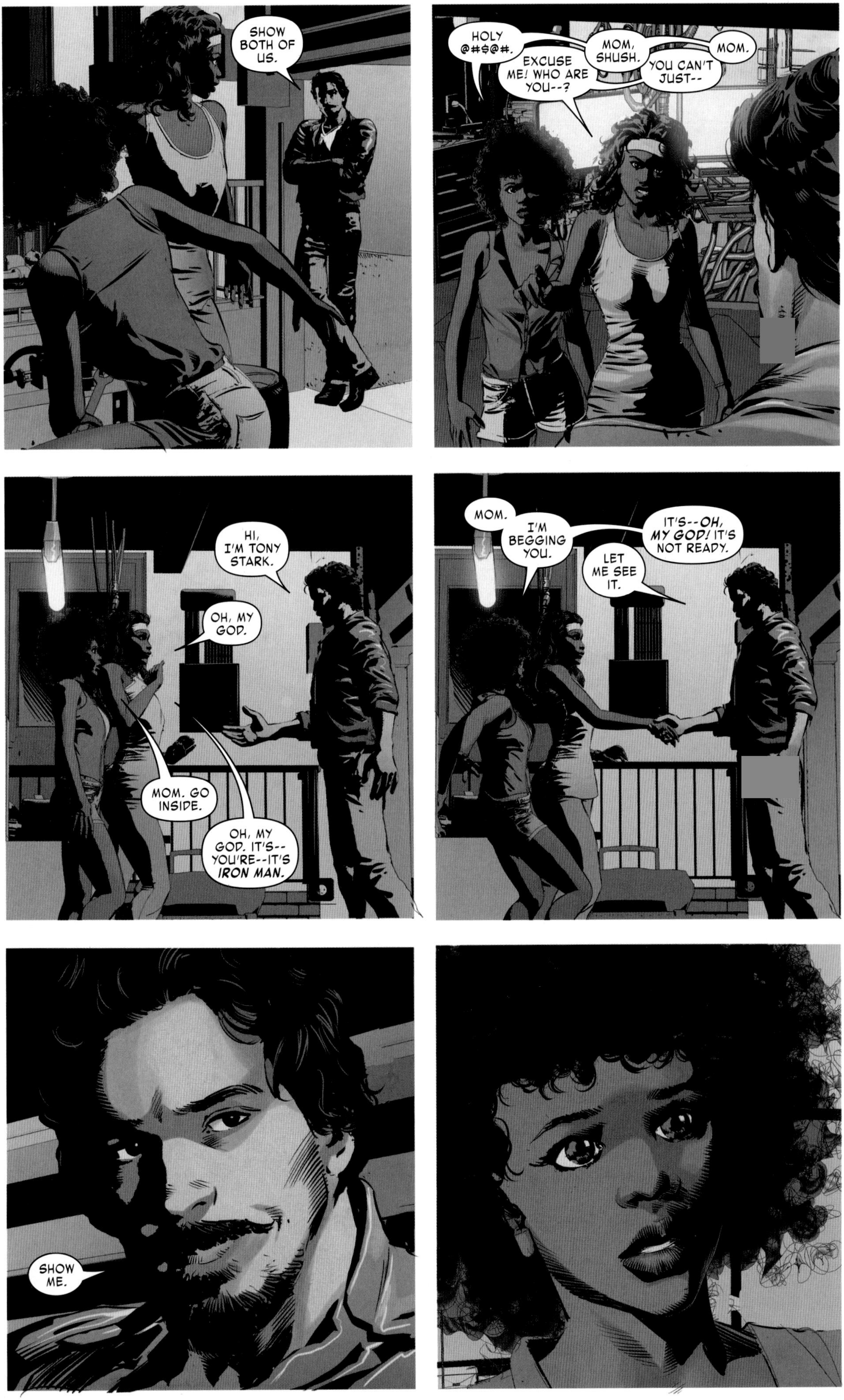
SHOW BOTH OF US.
HOLY @#$@#.
EXCUSE ME! WHO ARE YOU--?
MOM, SHUSH.
YOU CAN'T JUST--
MOM.
HI, I'M TONY STARK.
OH, MY GOD.
MOM. GO INSIDE.
OH, MY GOD. IT'S-- YOU'RE--IT'S IRON MAN.
MOM.
I'M BEGGING YOU.
IT'S--OH, MY GOD! IT'S NOT READY.
LET ME SEE IT.
SHOW ME.

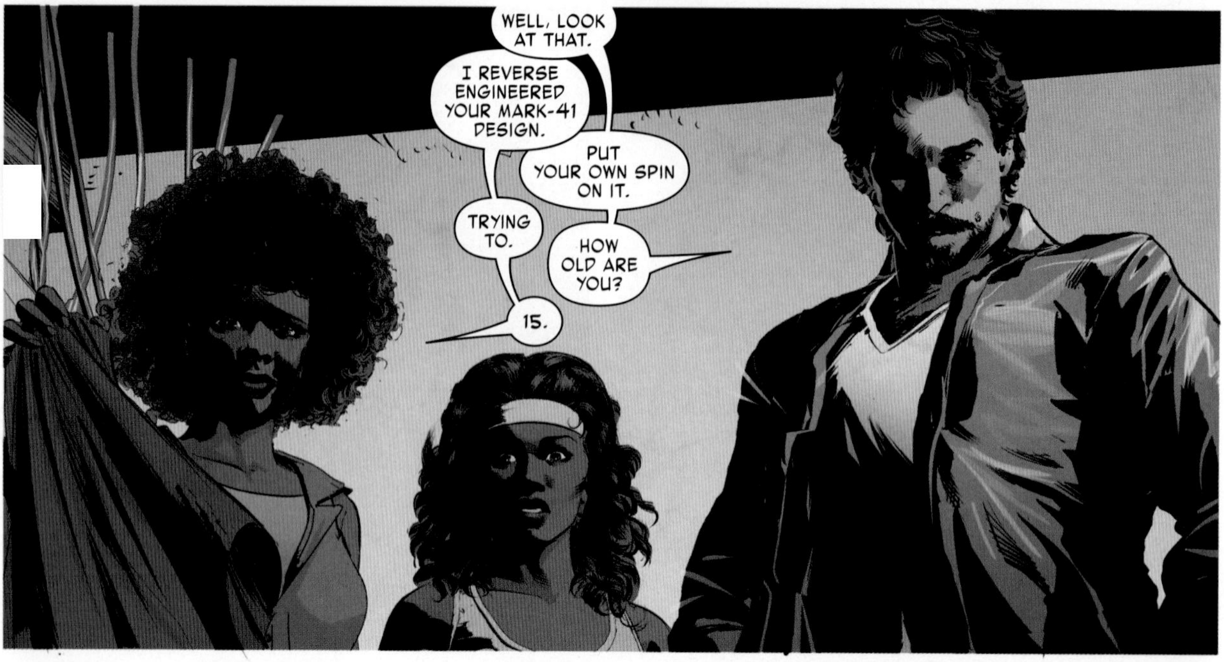
WELL, LOOK AT THAT.
I REVERSE ENGINEERED YOUR MARK-41 DESIGN.
PUT YOUR OWN SPIN ON IT.
TRYING TO.
HOW OLD ARE YOU?
15.

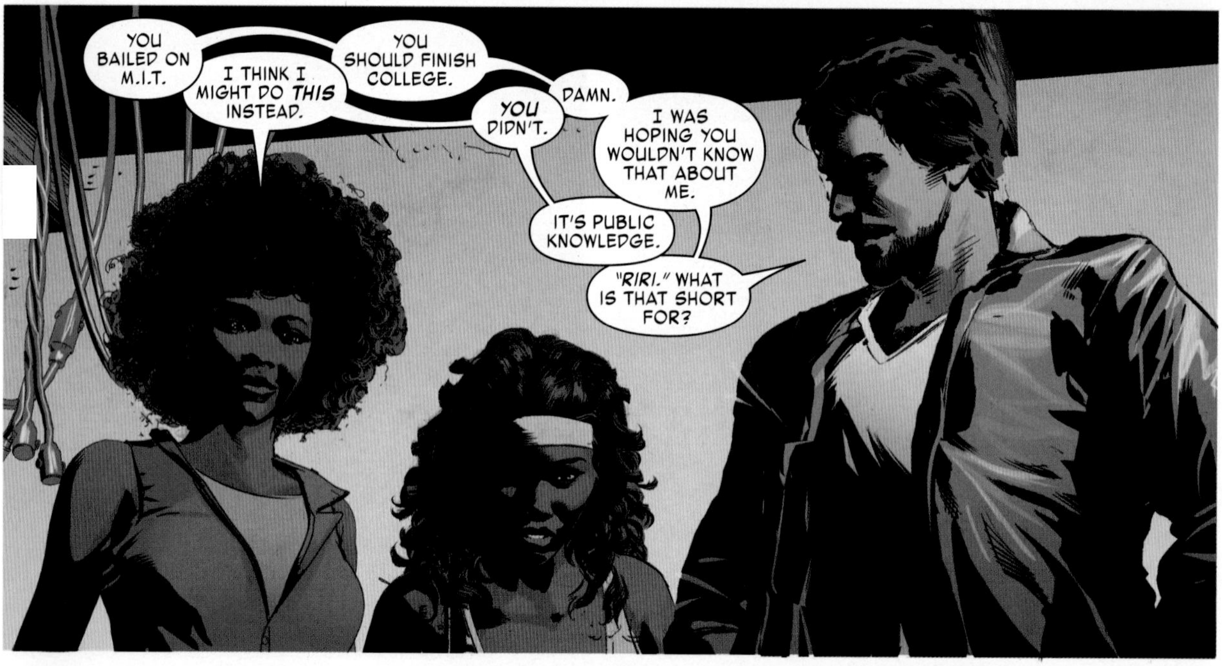
YOU BAILED ON M.I.T.
YOU SHOULD FINISH COLLEGE.
I THINK I MIGHT DO THIS INSTEAD.
DAMN.
YOU DIDN'T.
I WAS HOPING YOU WOULDN'T KNOW THAT ABOUT ME.
IT'S PUBLIC KNOWLEDGE.
"RIRI." WHAT IS THAT SHORT FOR?

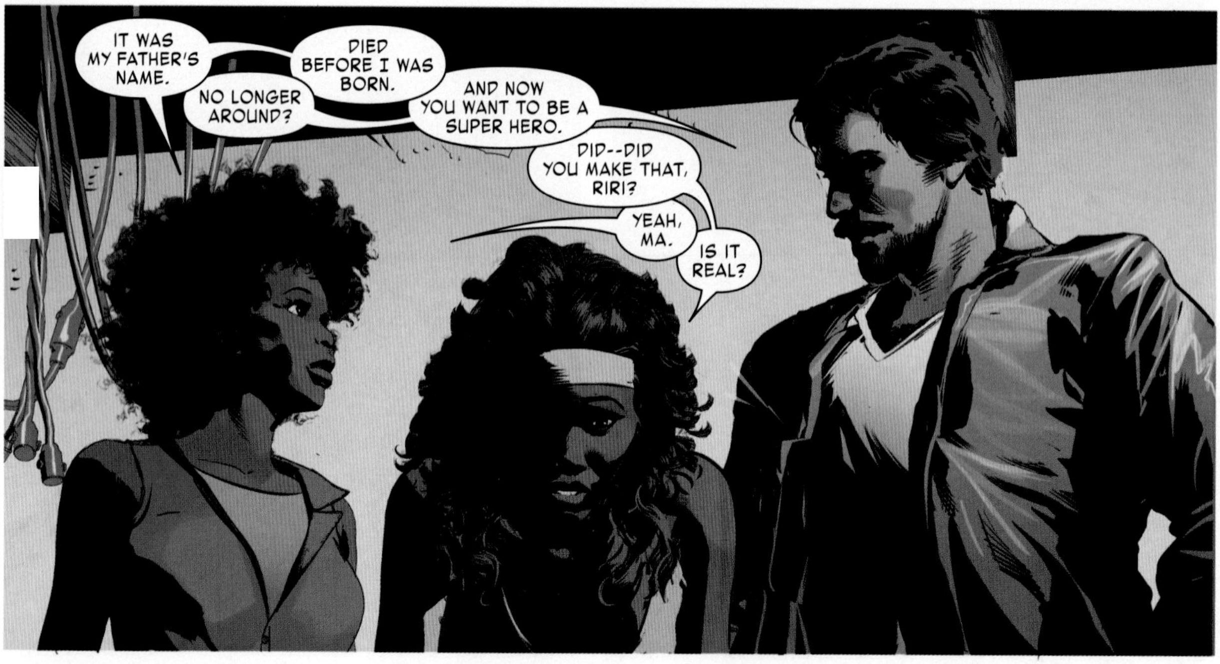
IT WAS MY FATHER'S NAME.
NO LONGER AROUND?
DIED BEFORE I WAS BORN.
AND NOW YOU WANT TO BE A SUPER HERO.
DID--DID YOU MAKE THAT, RIRI?
YEAH, MA.
IS IT REAL?

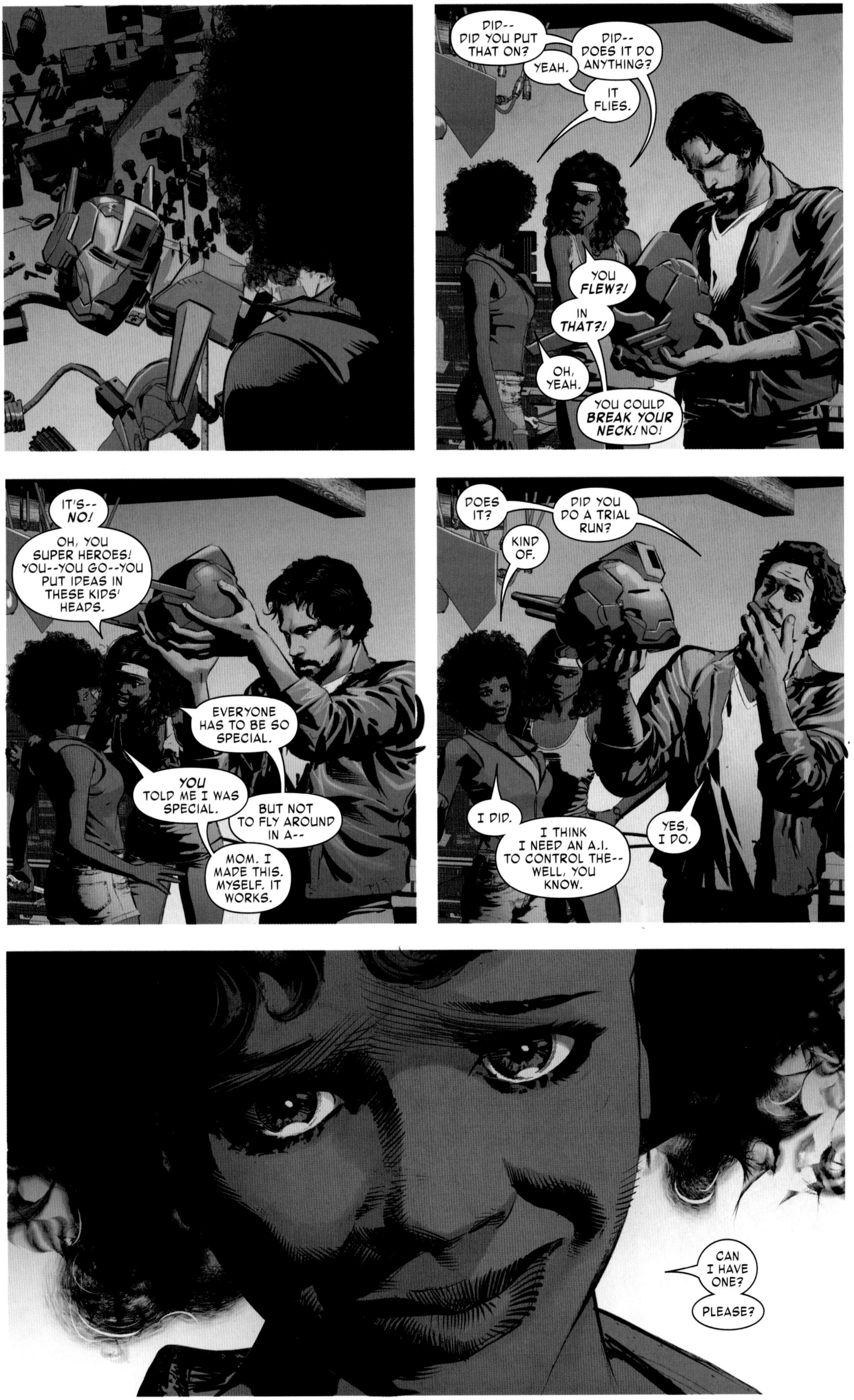
DID--
DID YOU PUT THAT ON?
YEAH.
DID--
DOES IT DO ANYTHING?
IT FLIES.
YOU *FLEW?!*
IN *THAT?!*
OH, YEAH.
YOU COULD **BREAK YOUR NECK!** NO!
IT'S--
NO!
OH, YOU SUPER HEROES! YOU--YOU GO--YOU PUT IDEAS IN THESE KIDS' HEADS.
EVERYONE HAS TO BE SO SPECIAL.
YOU TOLD ME I WAS SPECIAL.
BUT NOT TO FLY AROUND IN A--
MOM. I MADE THIS. MYSELF. IT WORKS.
DOES IT?
DID YOU DO A TRIAL RUN?
KIND OF.
I DID.
I THINK I NEED AN A.I. TO CONTROL THE-- WELL, YOU KNOW.
YES, I DO.
CAN I HAVE ONE?
PLEASE?

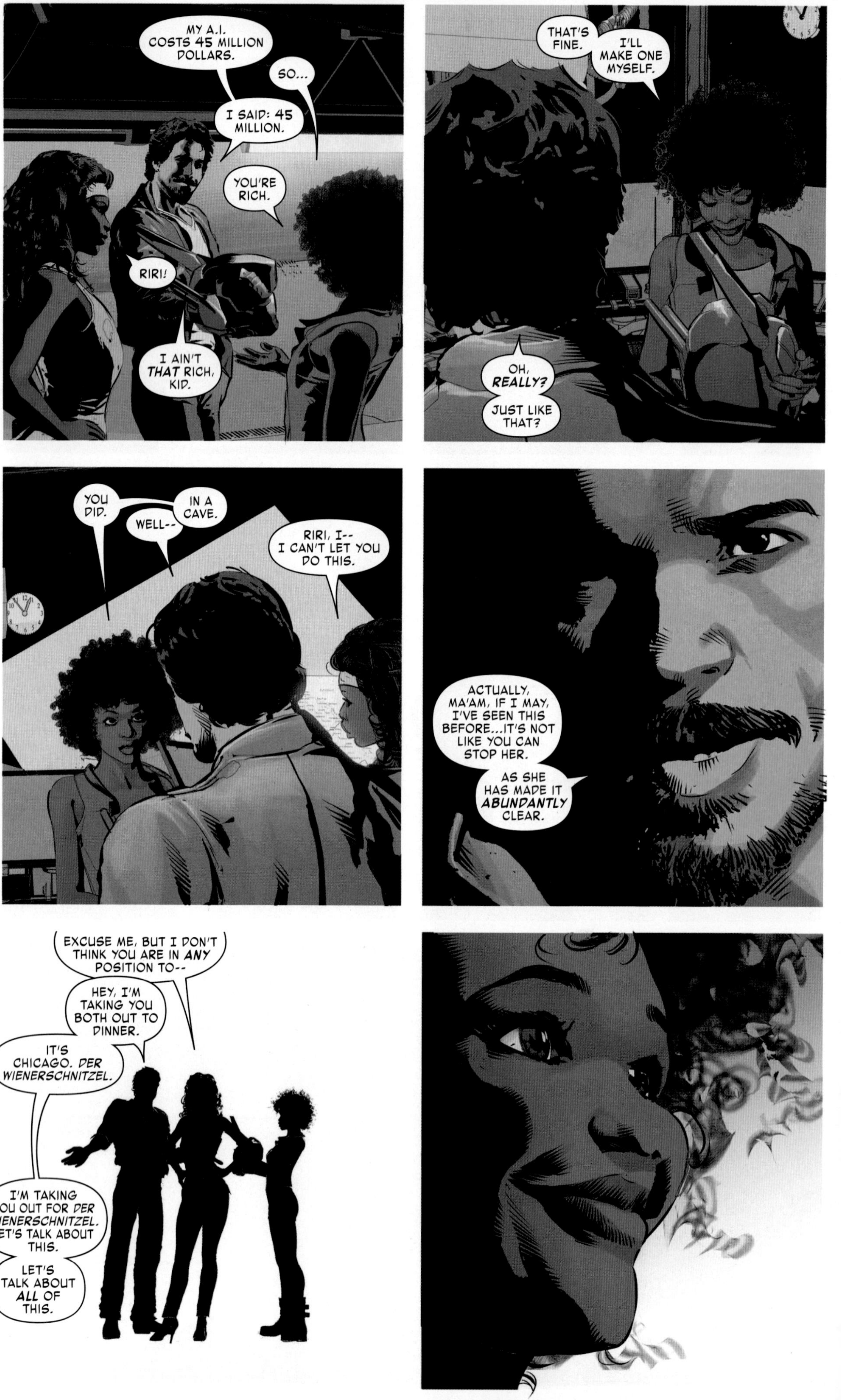

MY A.I. COSTS 45 MILLION DOLLARS.
SO...
I SAID: 45 MILLION.
YOU'RE RICH.
RIRI!
I AIN'T THAT RICH, KID.
THAT'S FINE.
I'LL MAKE ONE MYSELF.
OH, REALLY?
JUST LIKE THAT?
YOU DID.
IN A CAVE.
WELL--
RIRI, I-- I CAN'T LET YOU DO THIS.
ACTUALLY, MA'AM, IF I MAY, I'VE SEEN THIS BEFORE...IT'S NOT LIKE YOU CAN STOP HER.
AS SHE HAS MADE IT ABUNDANTLY CLEAR.
EXCUSE ME, BUT I DON'T THINK YOU ARE IN ANY POSITION TO--
HEY, I'M TAKING YOU BOTH OUT TO DINNER.
IT'S CHICAGO. DER WIENERSCHNITZEL.
I'M TAKING YOU OUT FOR DER WIENERSCHNITZEL. LET'S TALK ABOUT THIS.
LET'S TALK ABOUT ALL OF THIS.

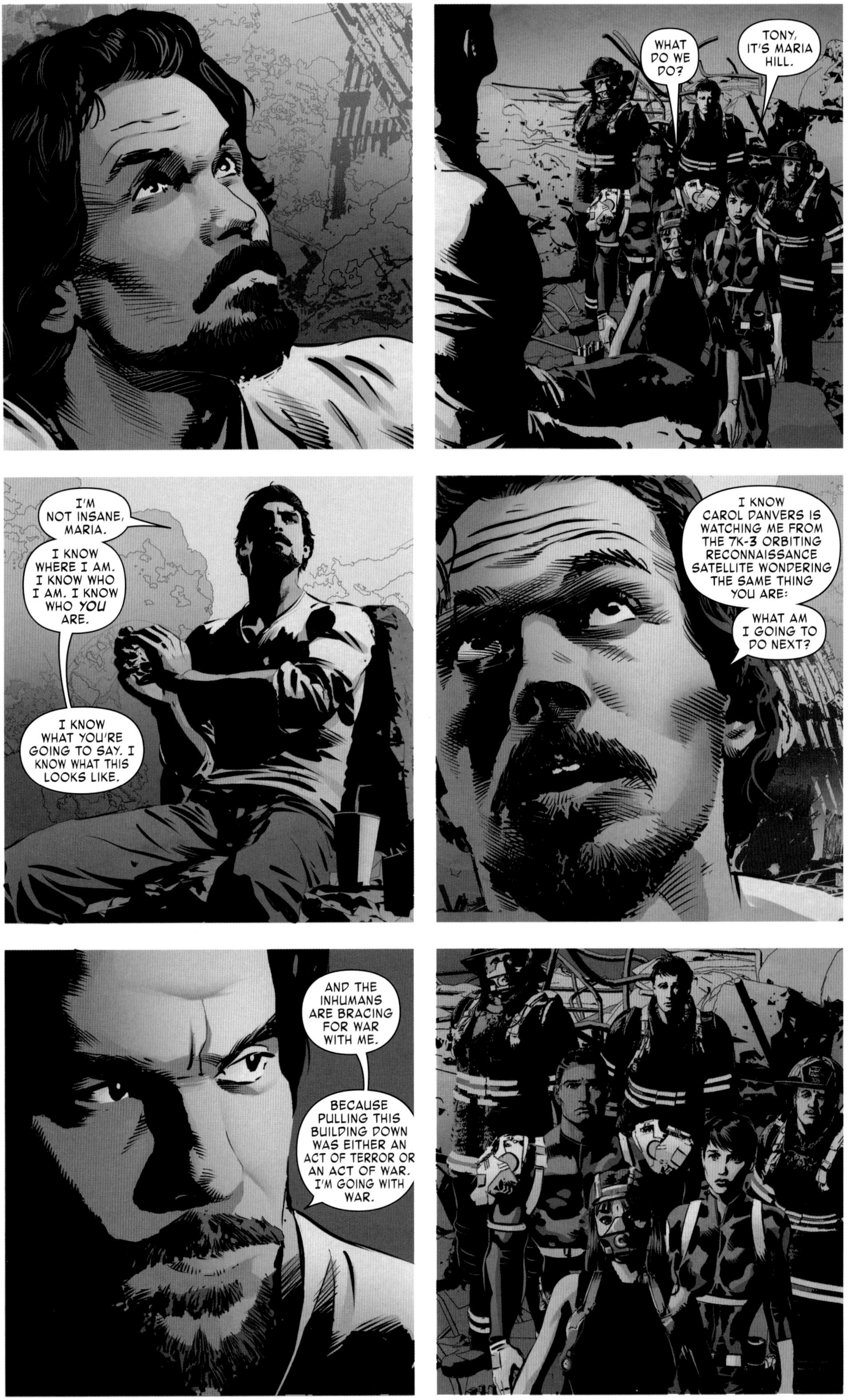
TONY, IT'S MARIA HILL.
WHAT DO WE DO?
I'M NOT INSANE, MARIA.
I KNOW WHERE I AM. I KNOW WHO I AM. I KNOW WHO *YOU* ARE.
I KNOW WHAT YOU'RE GOING TO SAY. I KNOW WHAT THIS LOOKS LIKE.
I KNOW CAROL DANVERS IS WATCHING ME FROM THE 7K-3 ORBITING RECONNAISSANCE SATELLITE WONDERING THE SAME THING YOU ARE:
WHAT AM I GOING TO DO NEXT?
AND THE INHUMANS ARE BRACING FOR WAR WITH ME.
BECAUSE PULLING THIS BUILDING DOWN WAS EITHER AN ACT OF TERROR OR AN ACT OF WAR. I'M GOING WITH WAR.

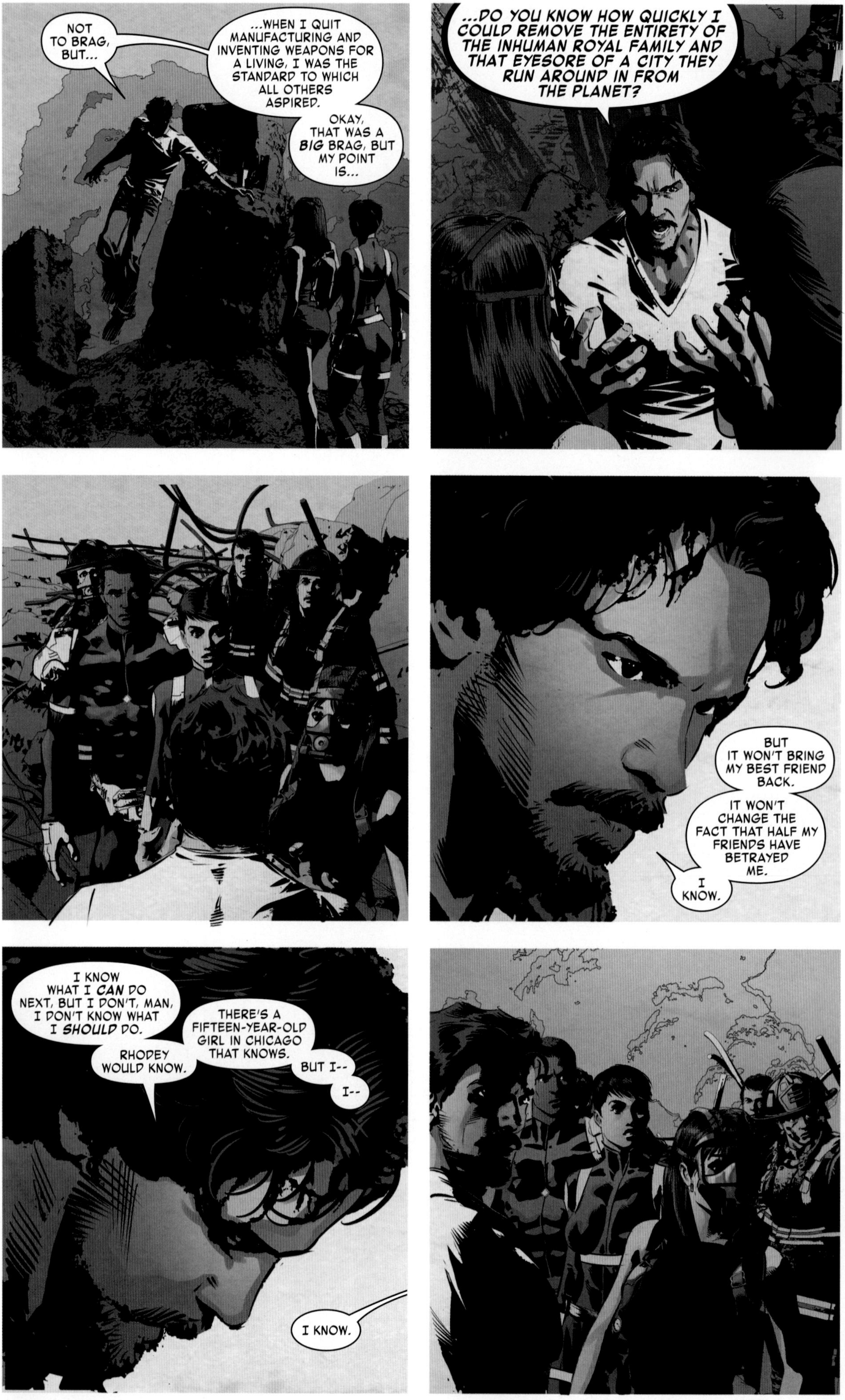

NOT TO BRAG, BUT...
...WHEN I QUIT MANUFACTURING AND INVENTING WEAPONS FOR A LIVING, I WAS THE STANDARD TO WHICH ALL OTHERS ASPIRED.
OKAY, THAT WAS A *BIG* BRAG, BUT MY POINT IS...
...DO YOU KNOW HOW QUICKLY I COULD REMOVE THE ENTIRETY OF THE INHUMAN ROYAL FAMILY AND THAT EYESORE OF A CITY THEY RUN AROUND IN FROM THE PLANET?
BUT IT WON'T BRING MY BEST FRIEND BACK.
IT WON'T CHANGE THE FACT THAT HALF MY FRIENDS HAVE BETRAYED ME.
I KNOW.
I KNOW WHAT I *CAN* DO NEXT, BUT I DON'T, MAN, I DON'T KNOW WHAT I *SHOULD* DO.
RHODEY WOULD KNOW.
THERE'S A FIFTEEN-YEAR-OLD GIRL IN CHICAGO THAT KNOWS.
BUT I--
I--
I KNOW.

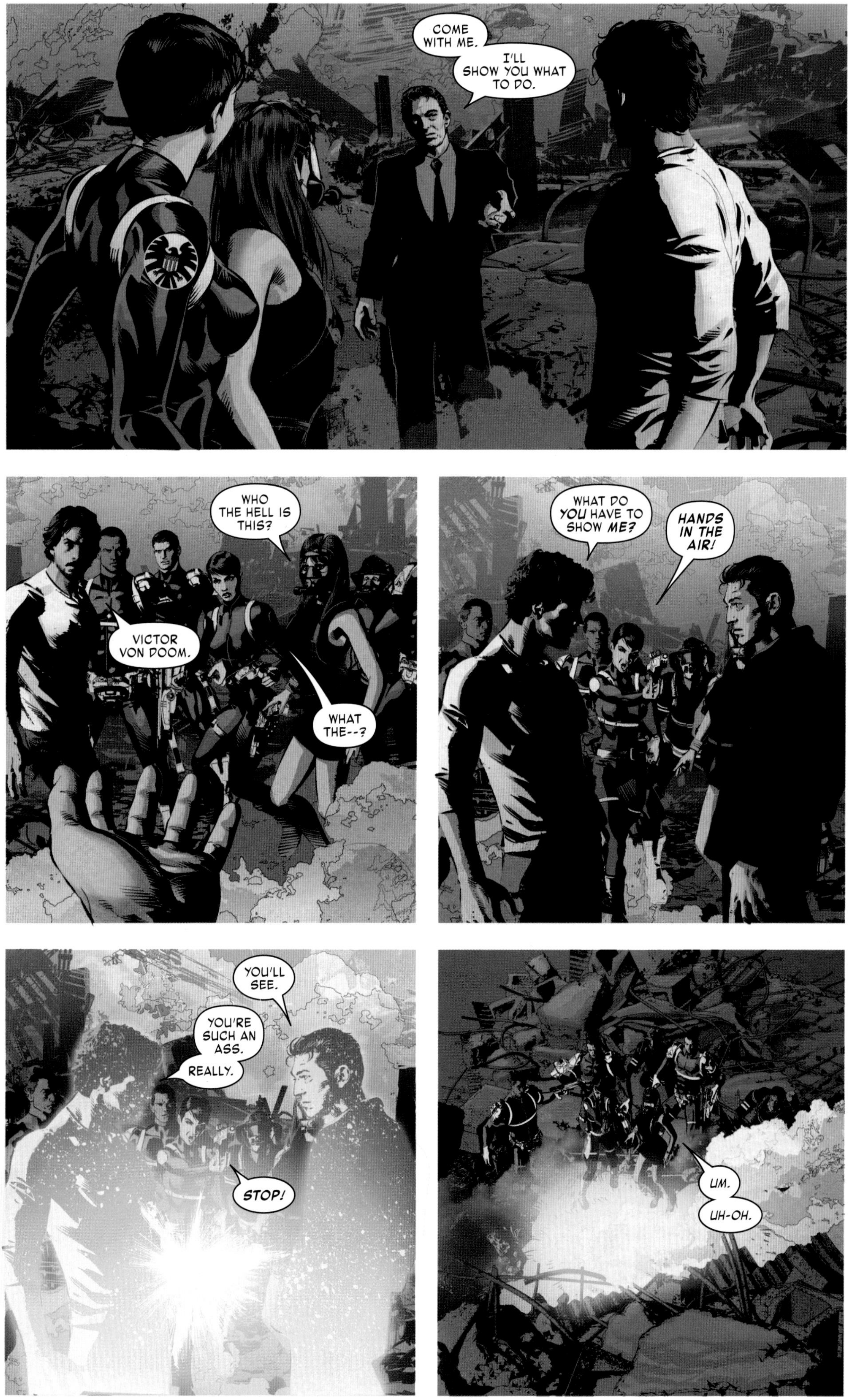
COME WITH ME.
I'LL SHOW YOU WHAT TO DO.
WHO THE HELL IS THIS?
VICTOR VON DOOM.
WHAT THE--?
WHAT DO YOU HAVE TO SHOW ME?
HANDS IN THE AIR!
YOU'LL SEE.
YOU'RE SUCH AN ASS.
REALLY.
STOP!
UM.
UH-OH.

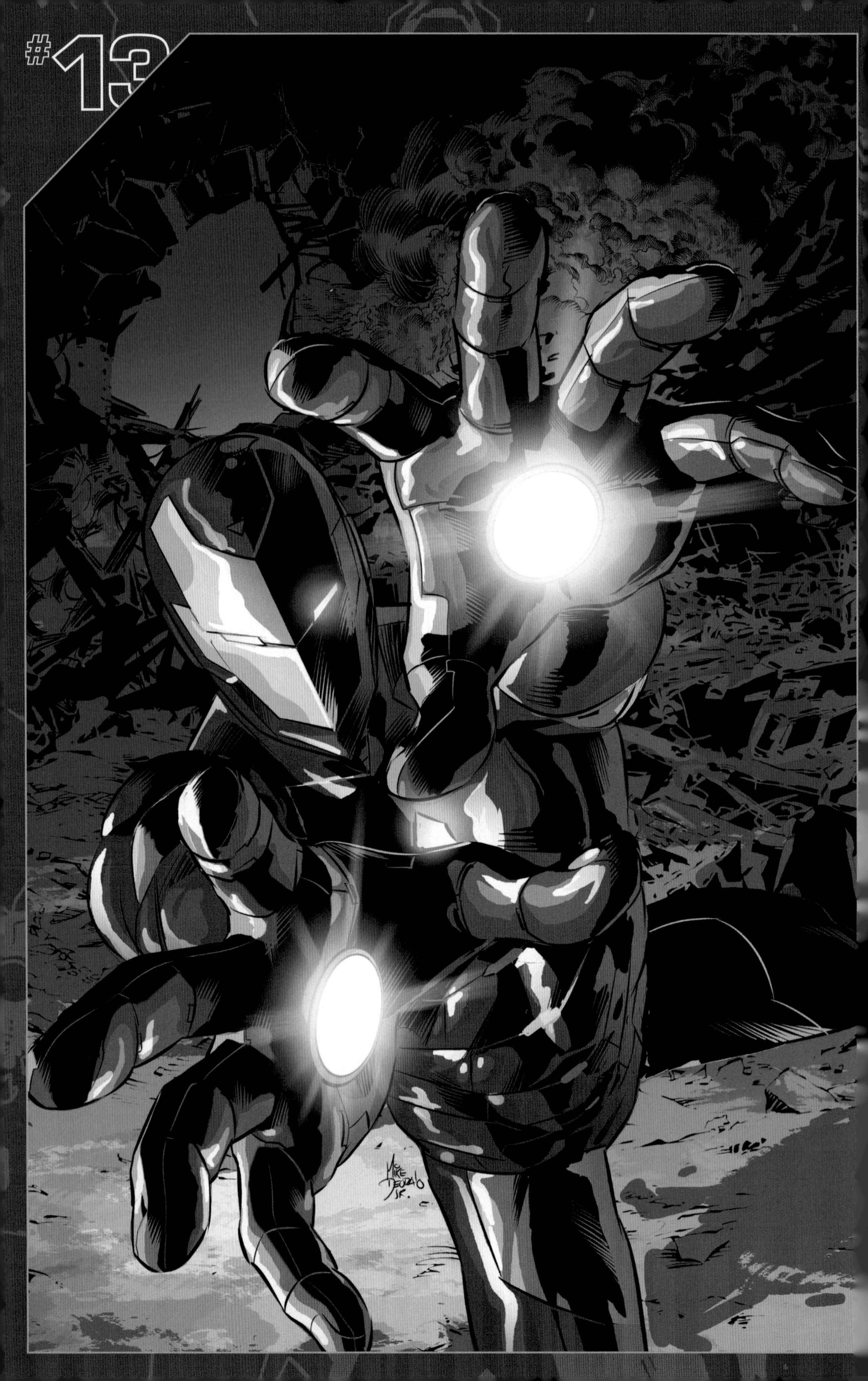
#13

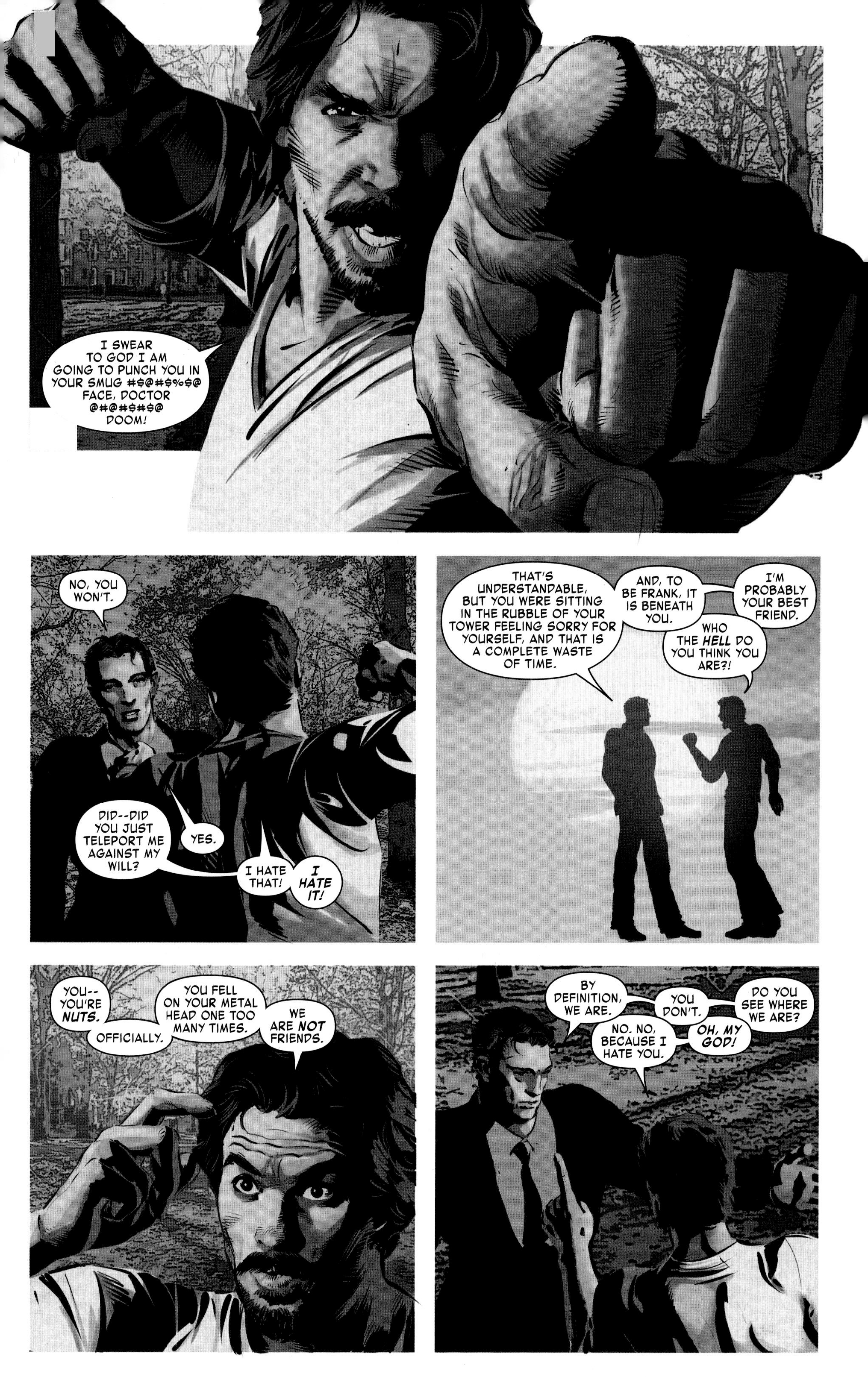
I SWEAR TO GOD I AM GOING TO PUNCH YOU IN YOUR SMUG #$@#$%$@ FACE, DOCTOR @#@#$#$@ DOOM!
NO, YOU WON'T.
DID--DID YOU JUST TELEPORT ME AGAINST MY WILL?
YES.
I HATE THAT!
I HATE IT!
THAT'S UNDERSTANDABLE, BUT YOU WERE SITTING IN THE RUBBLE OF YOUR TOWER FEELING SORRY FOR YOURSELF, AND THAT IS A COMPLETE WASTE OF TIME.
AND, TO BE FRANK, IT IS BENEATH YOU.
I'M PROBABLY YOUR BEST FRIEND.
WHO THE HELL DO YOU THINK YOU ARE?!
YOU-- YOU'RE NUTS.
OFFICIALLY.
YOU FELL ON YOUR METAL HEAD ONE TOO MANY TIMES.
WE ARE NOT FRIENDS.
BY DEFINITION, WE ARE.
YOU DON'T.
DO YOU SEE WHERE WE ARE?
NO. NO, BECAUSE I HATE YOU.
OH, MY GOD!

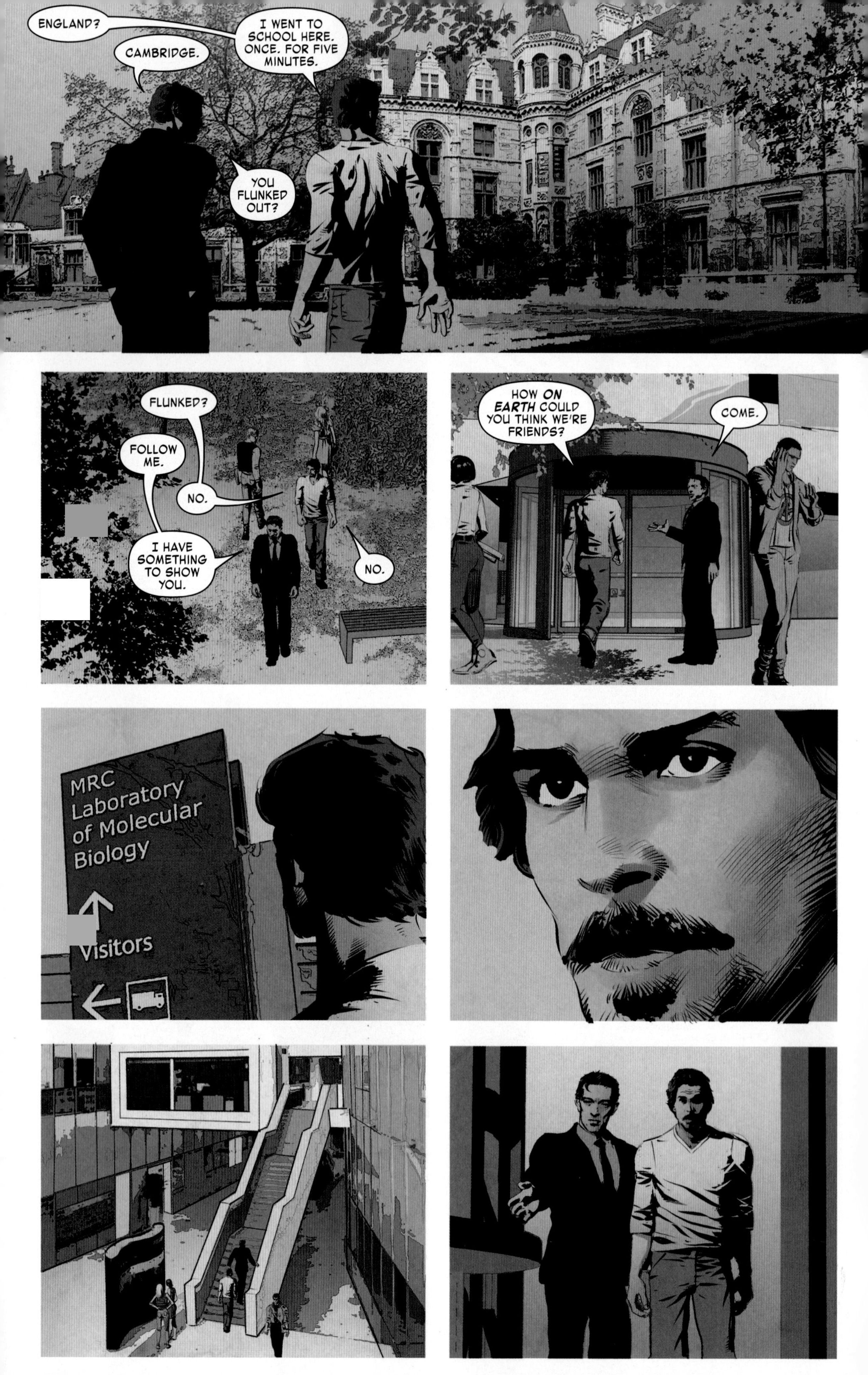
ENGLAND?
CAMBRIDGE.
I WENT TO SCHOOL HERE. ONCE. FOR FIVE MINUTES.
YOU FLUNKED OUT?
FLUNKED?
FOLLOW ME.
NO.
I HAVE SOMETHING TO SHOW YOU.
NO.
HOW ON EARTH COULD YOU THINK WE'RE FRIENDS?
COME.
MRC Laboratory of Molecular Biology
Visitors

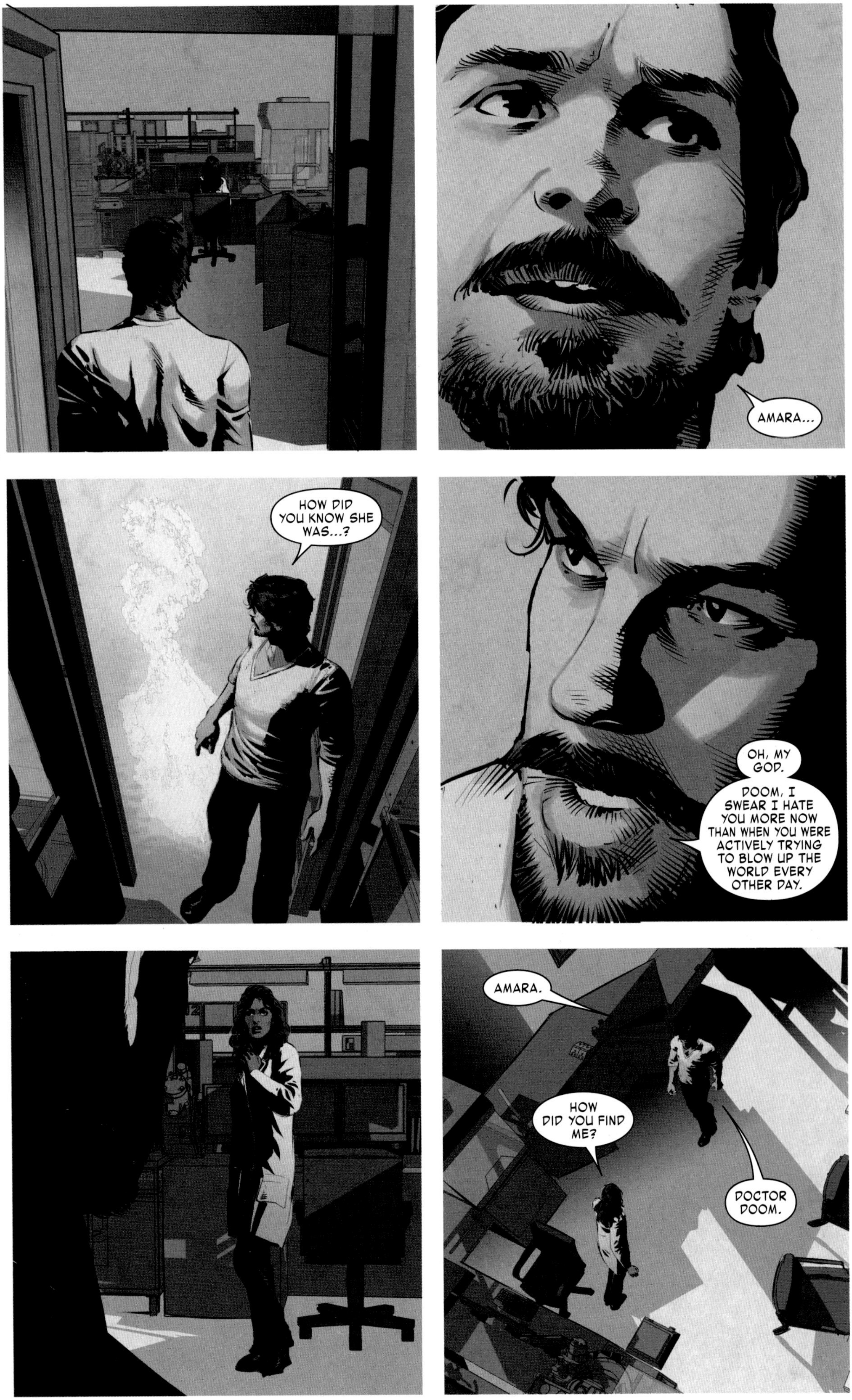
AMARA...
HOW DID YOU KNOW SHE WAS...?
OH, MY GOD.
DOOM, I SWEAR I HATE YOU MORE NOW THAN WHEN YOU WERE ACTIVELY TRYING TO BLOW UP THE WORLD EVERY OTHER DAY.
AMARA.
HOW DID YOU FIND ME?
DOCTOR DOOM.

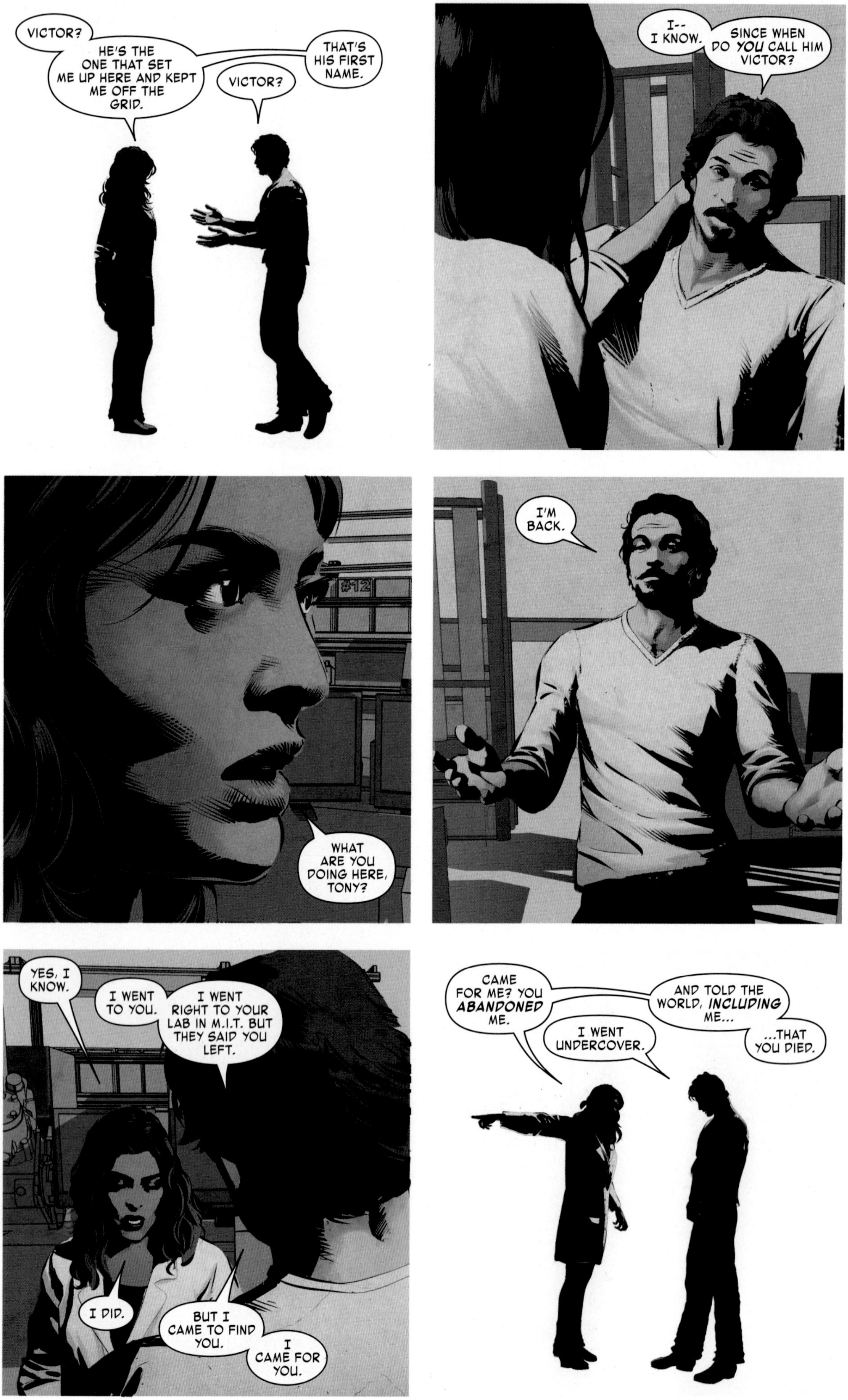

VICTOR?
HE'S THE ONE THAT SET ME UP HERE AND KEPT ME OFF THE GRID.
VICTOR?
THAT'S HIS FIRST NAME.
I-- I KNOW.
SINCE WHEN DO YOU CALL HIM VICTOR?
WHAT ARE YOU DOING HERE, TONY?
I'M BACK.
YES, I KNOW.
I WENT TO YOU.
I WENT RIGHT TO YOUR LAB IN M.I.T. BUT THEY SAID YOU LEFT.
I DID.
BUT I CAME TO FIND YOU.
I CAME FOR YOU.
CAME FOR ME? YOU ABANDONED ME.
I WENT UNDERCOVER.
AND TOLD THE WORLD, INCLUDING ME...
...THAT YOU DIED.

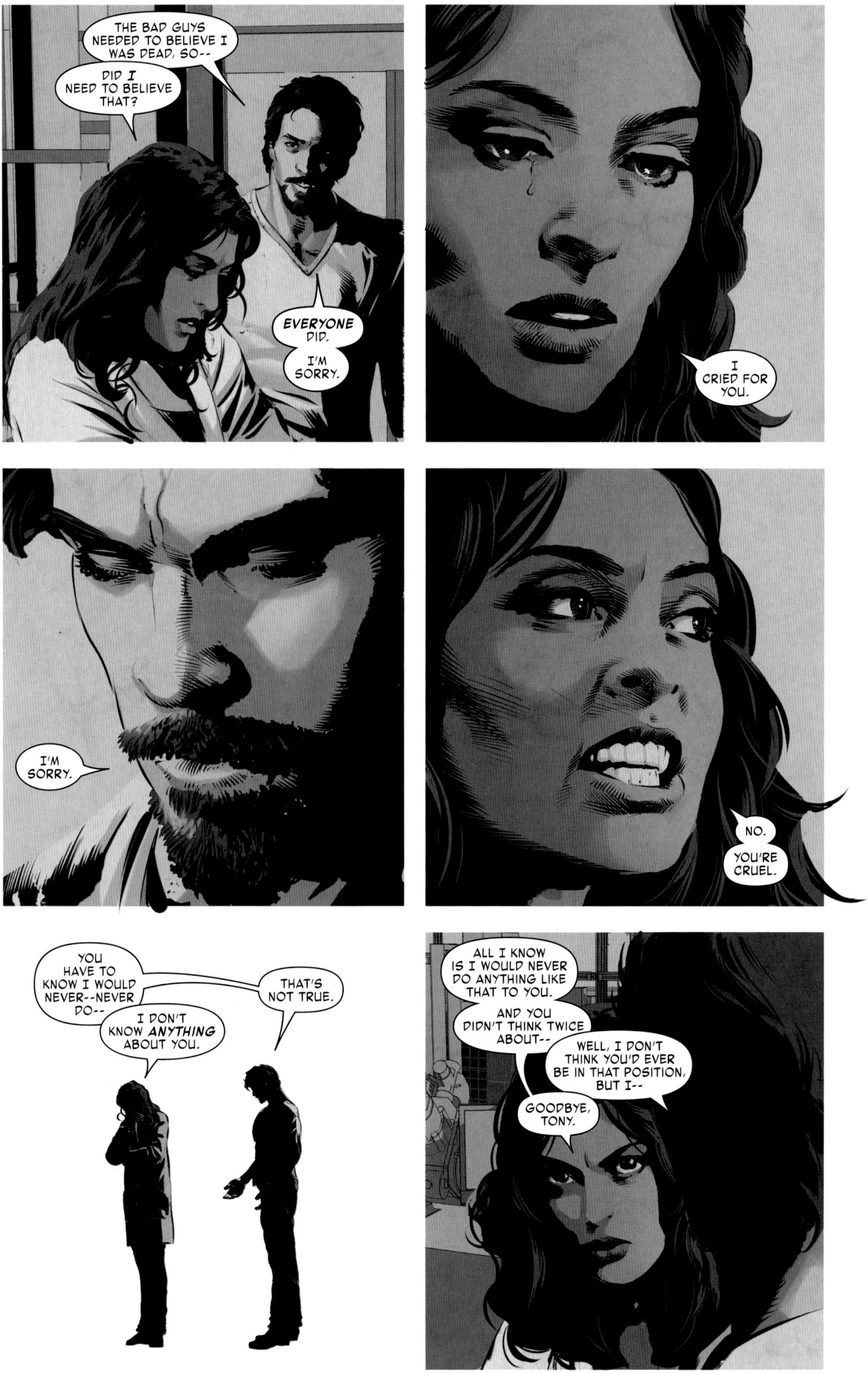
THE BAD GUYS NEEDED TO BELIEVE I WAS DEAD, SO--
DID *I* NEED TO BELIEVE THAT?
EVERYONE DID.
I'M SORRY.
I CRIED FOR YOU.
I'M SORRY.
NO.
YOU'RE CRUEL.
YOU HAVE TO KNOW I WOULD NEVER--NEVER DO--
THAT'S NOT TRUE.
I DON'T KNOW *ANYTHING* ABOUT YOU.
ALL I KNOW IS I WOULD NEVER DO ANYTHING LIKE THAT TO YOU.
AND YOU DIDN'T THINK TWICE ABOUT--
WELL, I DON'T THINK YOU'D EVER BE IN THAT POSITION, BUT I--
GOODBYE, TONY.

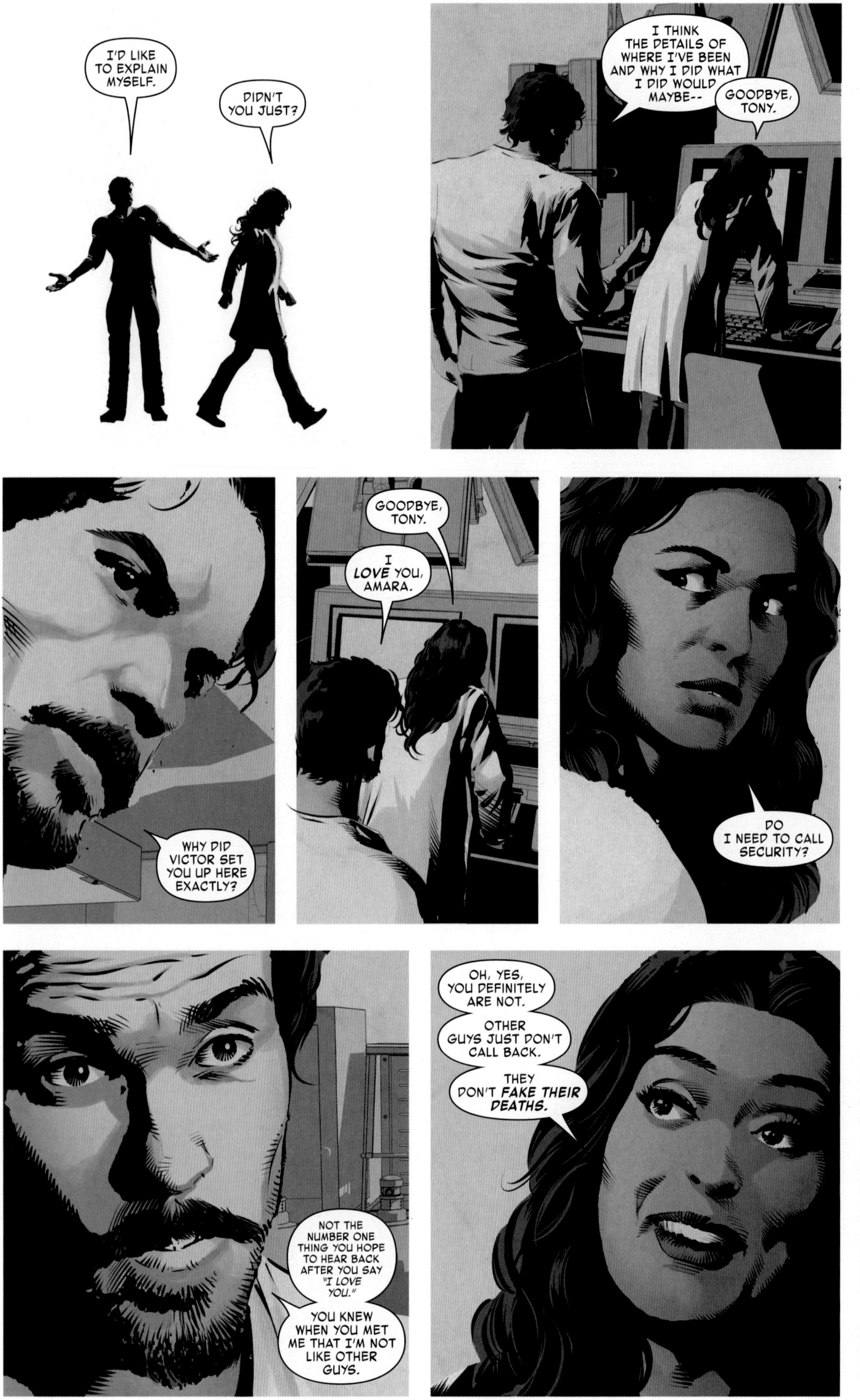
I'D LIKE TO EXPLAIN MYSELF.
DIDN'T YOU JUST?
I THINK THE DETAILS OF WHERE I'VE BEEN AND WHY I DID WHAT I DID WOULD MAYBE--
GOODBYE, TONY.
WHY DID VICTOR SET YOU UP HERE EXACTLY?
GOODBYE, TONY.
I LOVE YOU, AMARA.
DO I NEED TO CALL SECURITY?
NOT THE NUMBER ONE THING YOU HOPE TO HEAR BACK AFTER YOU SAY "I LOVE YOU."
YOU KNEW WHEN YOU MET ME THAT I'M NOT LIKE OTHER GUYS.
OH, YES, YOU DEFINITELY ARE NOT.
OTHER GUYS JUST DON'T CALL BACK.
THEY DON'T FAKE THEIR DEATHS.

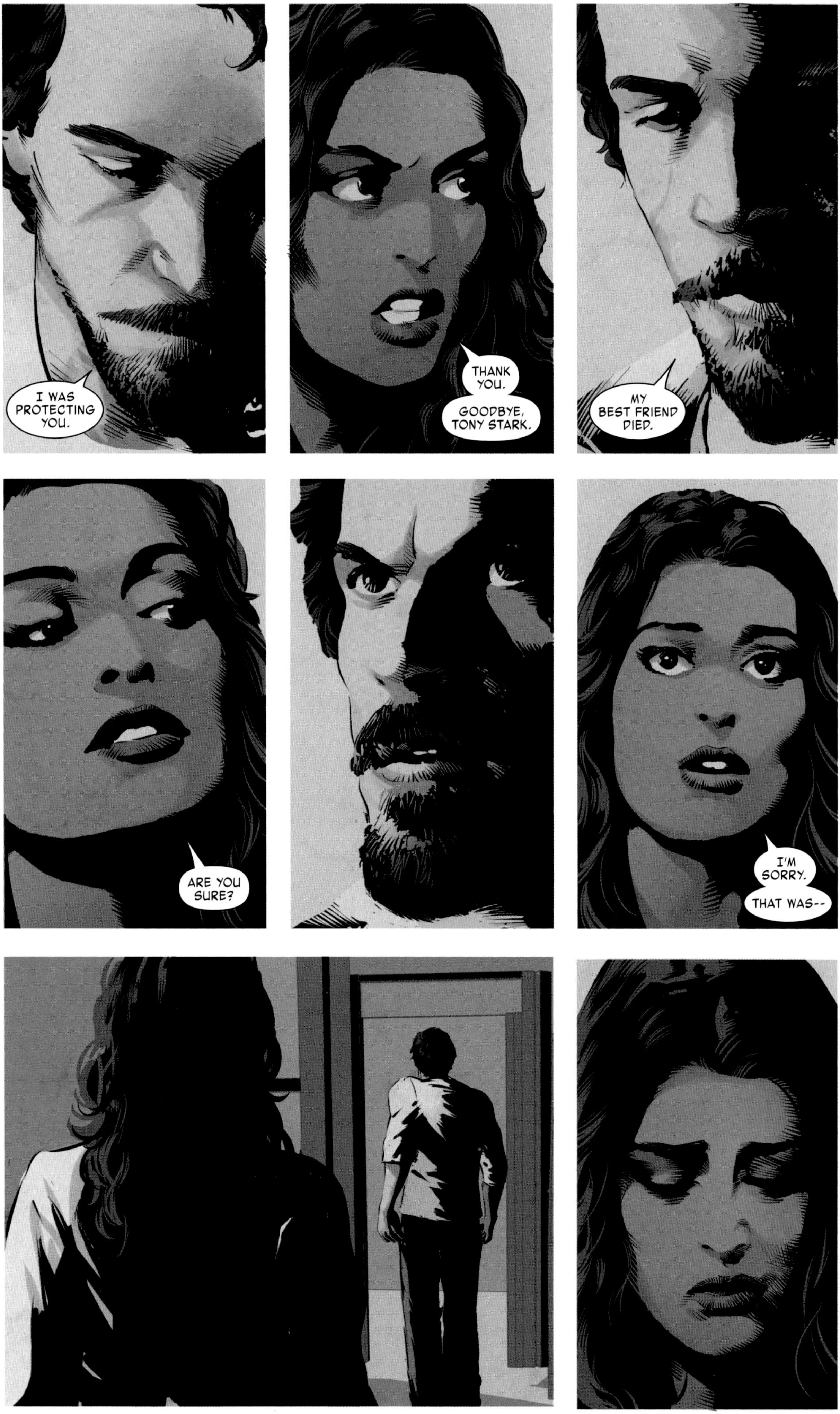
I WAS PROTECTING YOU.
THANK YOU.
GOODBYE, TONY STARK.
MY BEST FRIEND DIED.
ARE YOU SURE?
I'M SORRY.
THAT WAS--

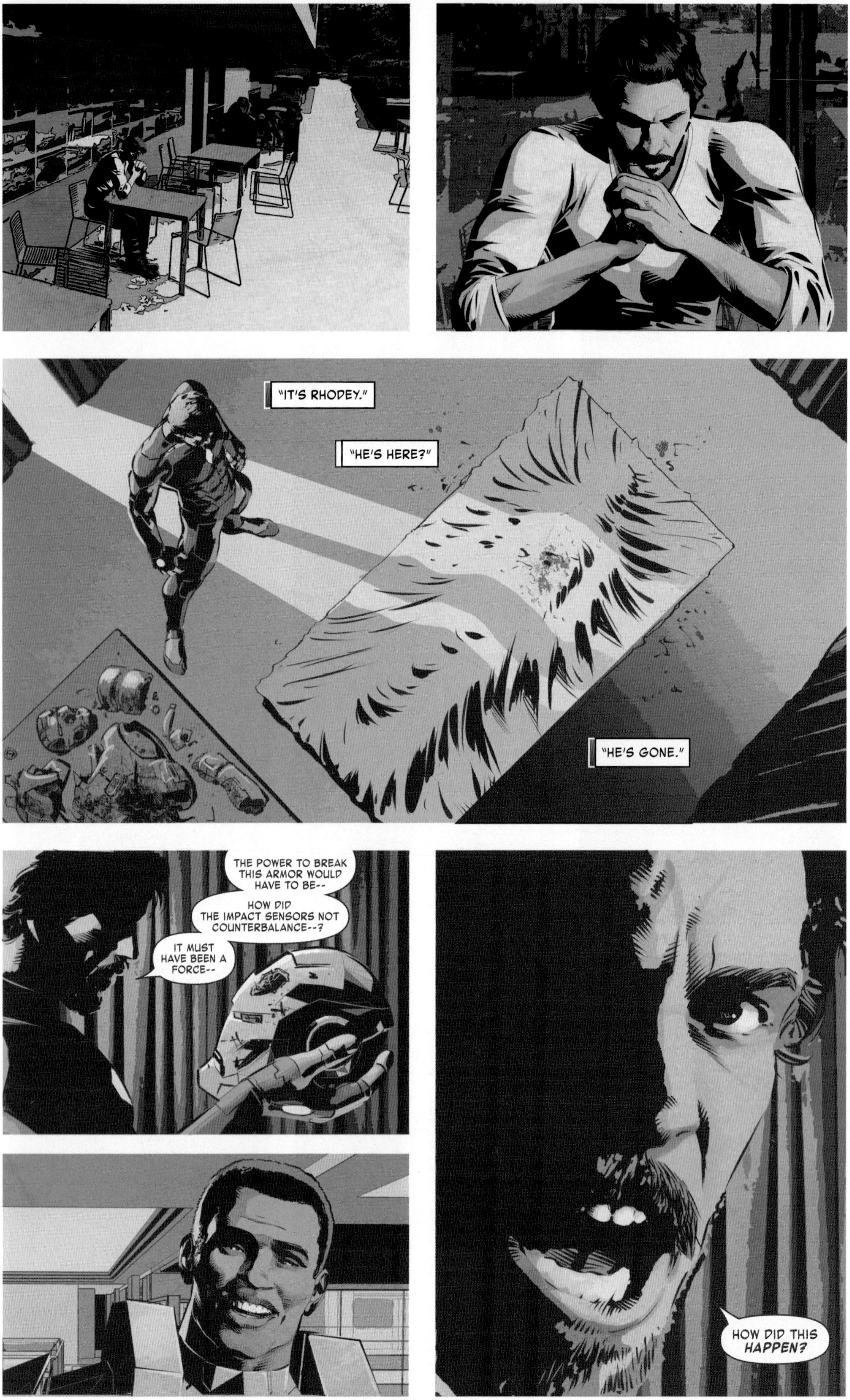
"IT'S RHODEY."
"HE'S HERE?"
"HE'S GONE."
THE POWER TO BREAK THIS ARMOR WOULD HAVE TO BE--
HOW DID THE IMPACT SENSORS NOT COUNTERBALANCE--?
IT MUST HAVE BEEN A FORCE--
HOW DID THIS HAPPEN?

James "Rhodey" Rhodes,
A.K.A. War Machine, is Dead

Stark Stock in Free Fall

War Machine Memorial
Open to the Public

...s Desperate
...erstood

...Wanted for
... by Defense Council

...rvel
...e World

...to the Public

...nhumans Desperate
to be Understood

Tony Stark Wanted for
Questioning by Defense Coun...

Captain Marvel
Updates ... World

THIS IS COLONEL CAROL DANVERS SPEAKING FOR THE ULTIMATES.

IN THE INTEREST OF FULL DISCLOSURE, THIS MESSAGE IS BEING BEAMED WORLDWIDE.

I HAVE JUST RETURNED FROM A DIPLOMATIC MEETING WITH A LONGTIME ALLY AND BENEFCATOR TO THE ENTIRE PLANET...

SOMEONE I AM SO PROUD TO CALL FRIEND...

KING T'CHALLA, THE BLACK PANTHER.

ONE OF THE GREAT JOYS OF MY LIFE IS THAT I GET TO SPEND REAL TIME WITH THESE GREAT HEROES OF SUCH SHEER STRENGTH AND COMPASSION.

T'CHALLA IS, BY ANY DEFINITION, THE REAL DEAL. SO SMART. SUCH A PRESENCE. SUCH A GREAT LEADER TO HIS PEOPLE.

AND HE AND I, WELL, WE TALKED ABOUT THE FUTURE.

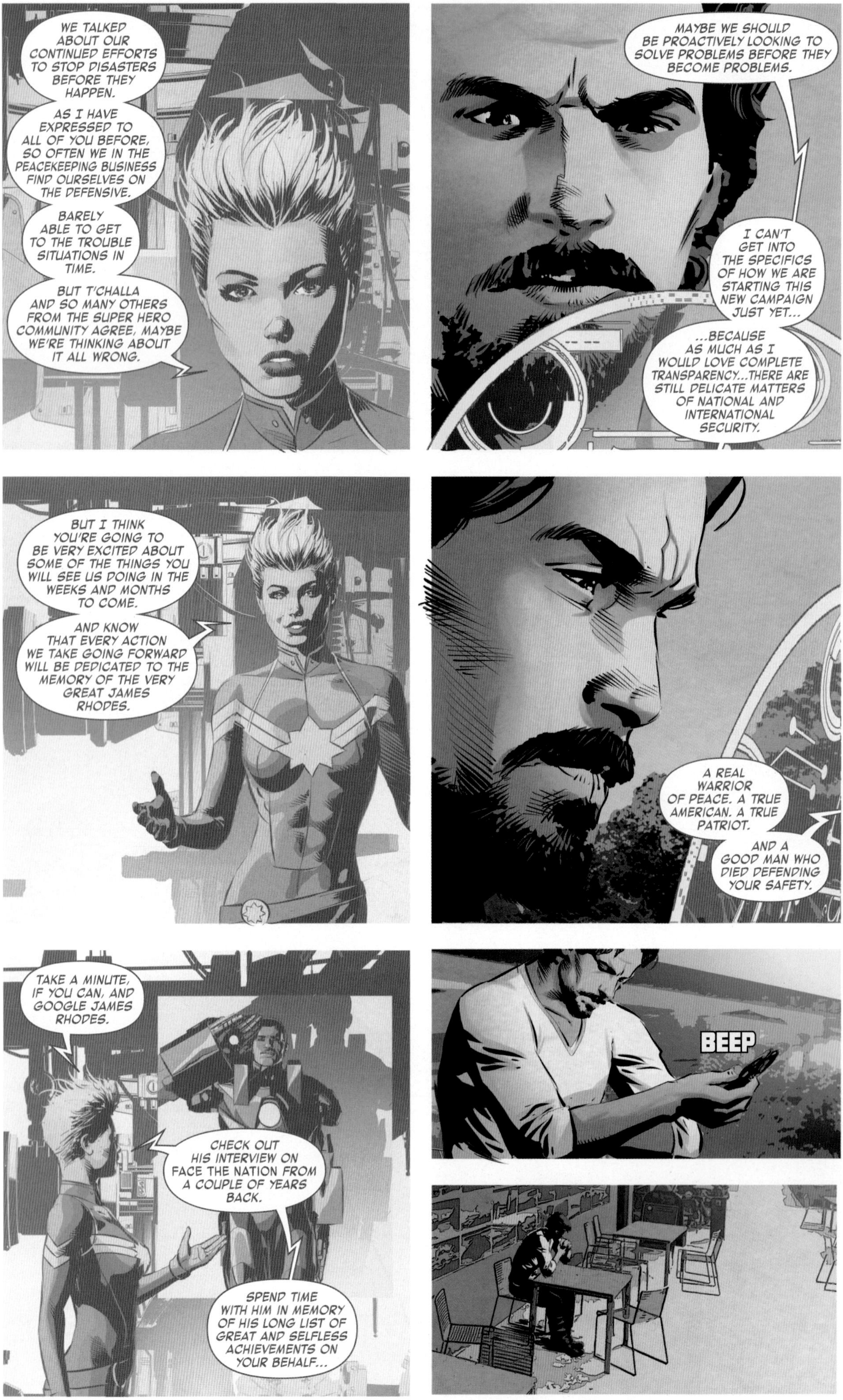
WE TALKED ABOUT OUR CONTINUED EFFORTS TO STOP DISASTERS BEFORE THEY HAPPEN.
AS I HAVE EXPRESSED TO ALL OF YOU BEFORE, SO OFTEN WE IN THE PEACEKEEPING BUSINESS FIND OURSELVES ON THE DEFENSIVE.
BARELY ABLE TO GET TO THE TROUBLE SITUATIONS IN TIME.
BUT T'CHALLA AND SO MANY OTHERS FROM THE SUPER HERO COMMUNITY AGREE, MAYBE WE'RE THINKING ABOUT IT ALL WRONG.
MAYBE WE SHOULD BE PROACTIVELY LOOKING TO SOLVE PROBLEMS BEFORE THEY BECOME PROBLEMS.
I CAN'T GET INTO THE SPECIFICS OF HOW WE ARE STARTING THIS NEW CAMPAIGN JUST YET...
...BECAUSE AS MUCH AS I WOULD LOVE COMPLETE TRANSPARENCY...THERE ARE STILL DELICATE MATTERS OF NATIONAL AND INTERNATIONAL SECURITY.
BUT I THINK YOU'RE GOING TO BE VERY EXCITED ABOUT SOME OF THE THINGS YOU WILL SEE US DOING IN THE WEEKS AND MONTHS TO COME.
AND KNOW THAT EVERY ACTION WE TAKE GOING FORWARD WILL BE DEDICATED TO THE MEMORY OF THE VERY GREAT JAMES RHODES.
A REAL WARRIOR OF PEACE. A TRUE AMERICAN. A TRUE PATRIOT.
AND A GOOD MAN WHO DIED DEFENDING YOUR SAFETY.
TAKE A MINUTE, IF YOU CAN, AND GOOGLE JAMES RHODES.
CHECK OUT HIS INTERVIEW ON FACE THE NATION FROM A COUPLE OF YEARS BACK.
SPEND TIME WITH HIM IN MEMORY OF HIS LONG LIST OF GREAT AND SELFLESS ACHIEVEMENTS ON YOUR BEHALF...
BEEP

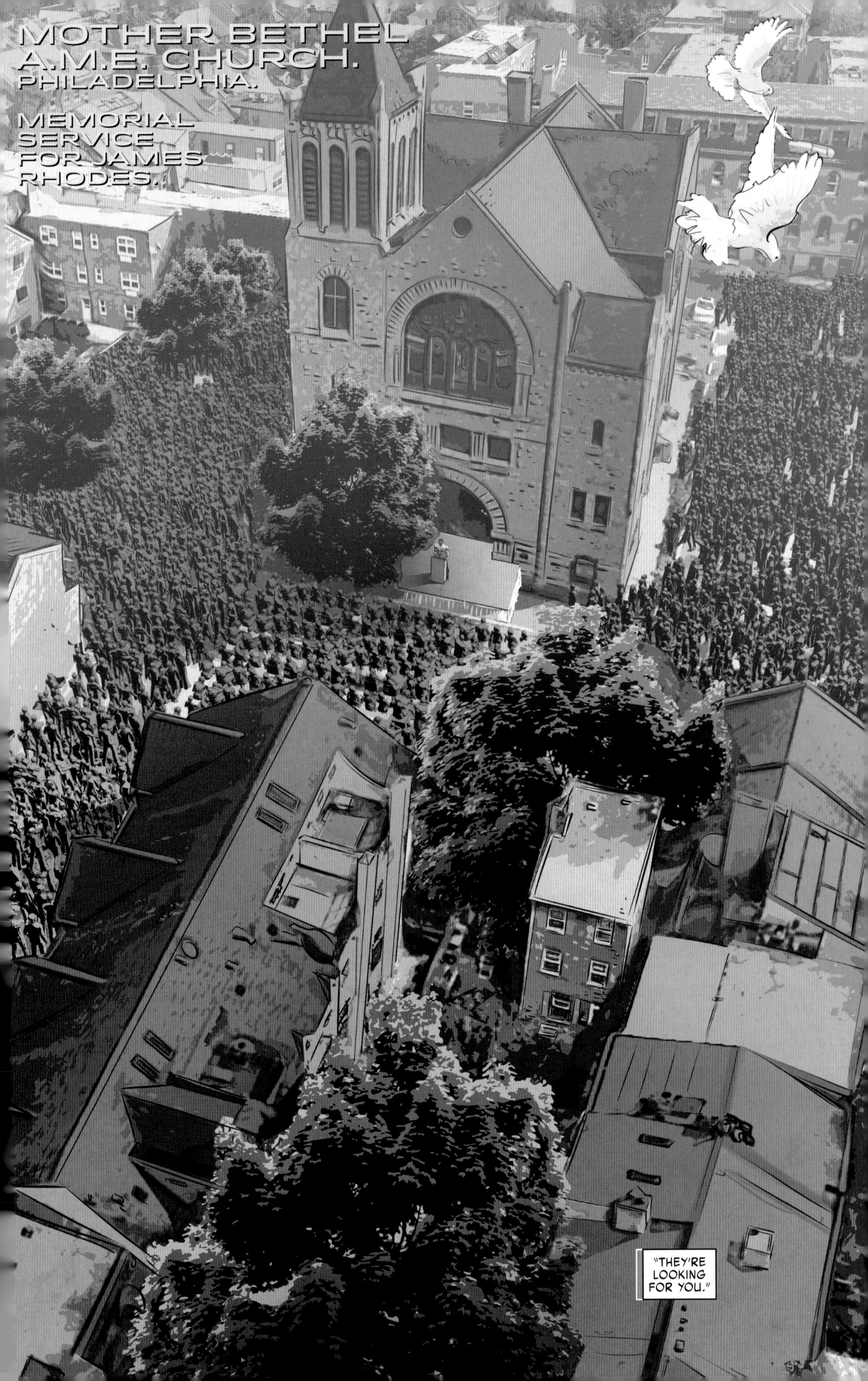
MOTHER BETHEL A.M.E. CHURCH. PHILADELPHIA.
MEMORIAL SERVICE FOR JAMES RHODES.
"THEY'RE LOOKING FOR YOU."

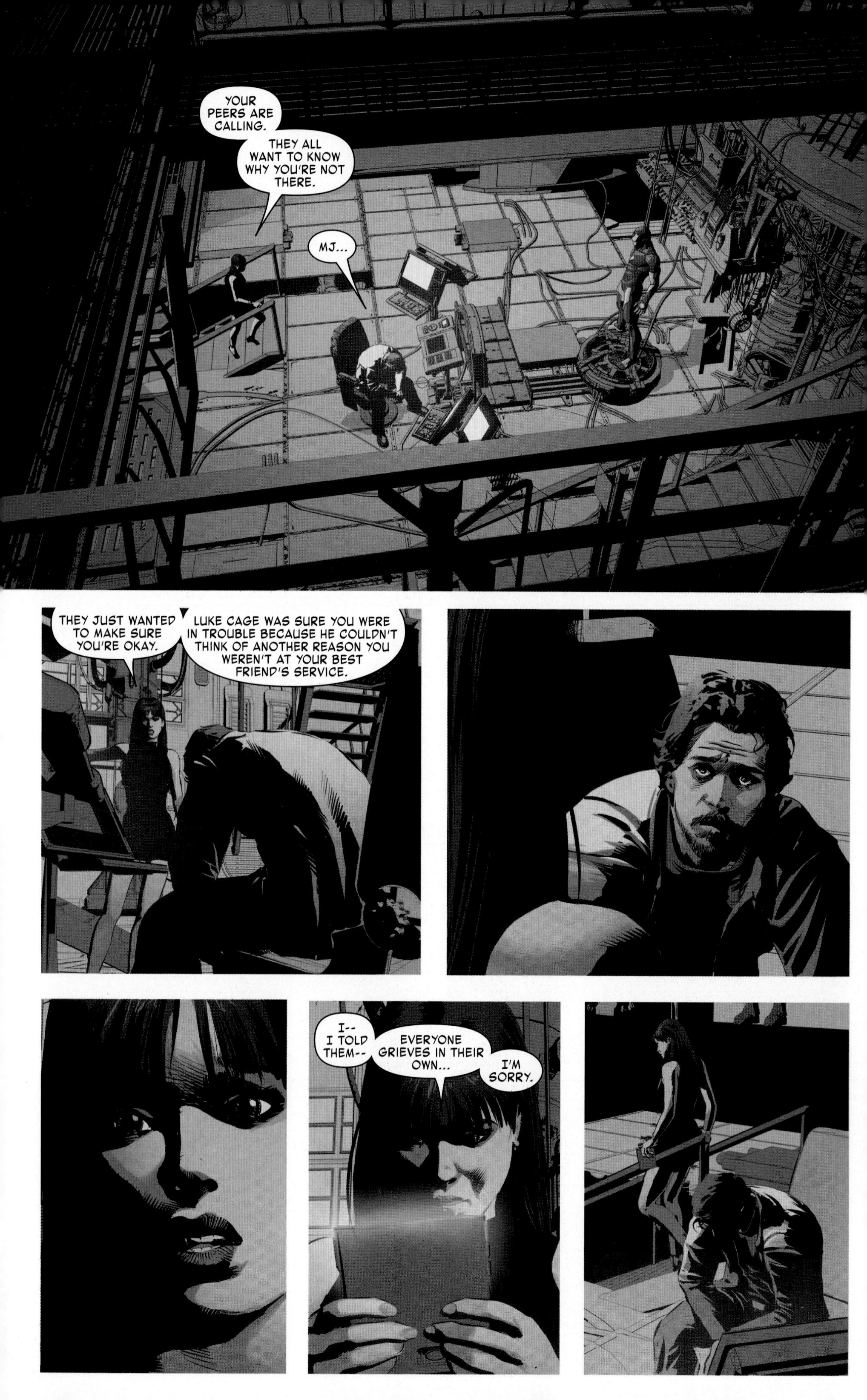
YOUR PEERS ARE CALLING.
THEY ALL WANT TO KNOW WHY YOU'RE NOT THERE.
MJ...
THEY JUST WANTED TO MAKE SURE YOU'RE OKAY.
LUKE CAGE WAS SURE YOU WERE IN TROUBLE BECAUSE HE COULDN'T THINK OF ANOTHER REASON YOU WEREN'T AT YOUR BEST FRIEND'S SERVICE.
I-- I TOLD THEM--
EVERYONE GRIEVES IN THEIR OWN...
I'M SORRY.

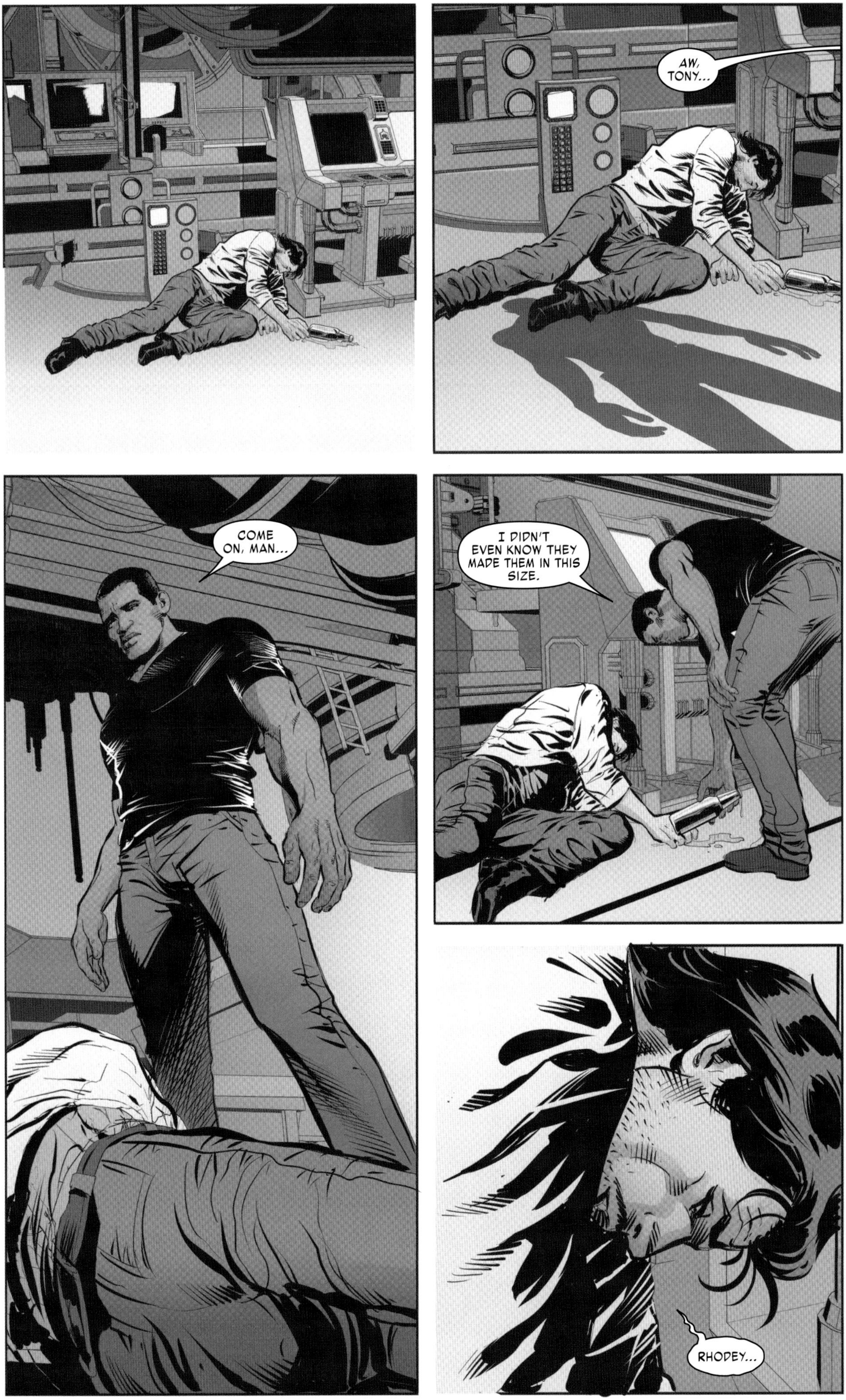
AW, TONY...
COME ON, MAN...
I DIDN'T EVEN KNOW THEY MADE THEM IN THIS SIZE.
RHODEY...

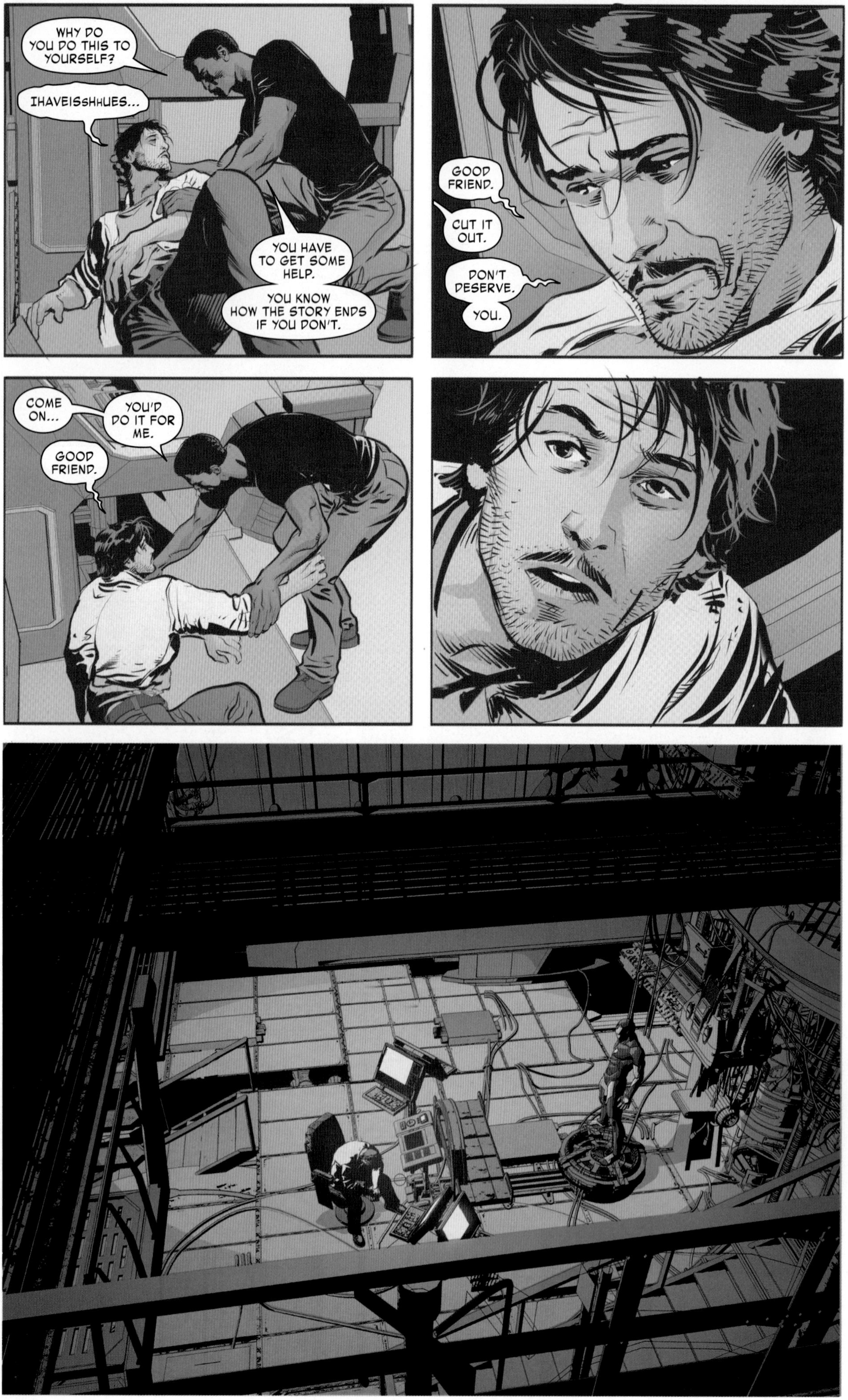
WHY DO YOU DO THIS TO YOURSELF?
IHAVEISSHHUES...
YOU HAVE TO GET SOME HELP.
YOU KNOW HOW THE STORY ENDS IF YOU DON'T.
GOOD FRIEND.
CUT IT OUT.
DON'T DESERVE.
YOU.
COME ON...
YOU'D DO IT FOR ME.
GOOD FRIEND.

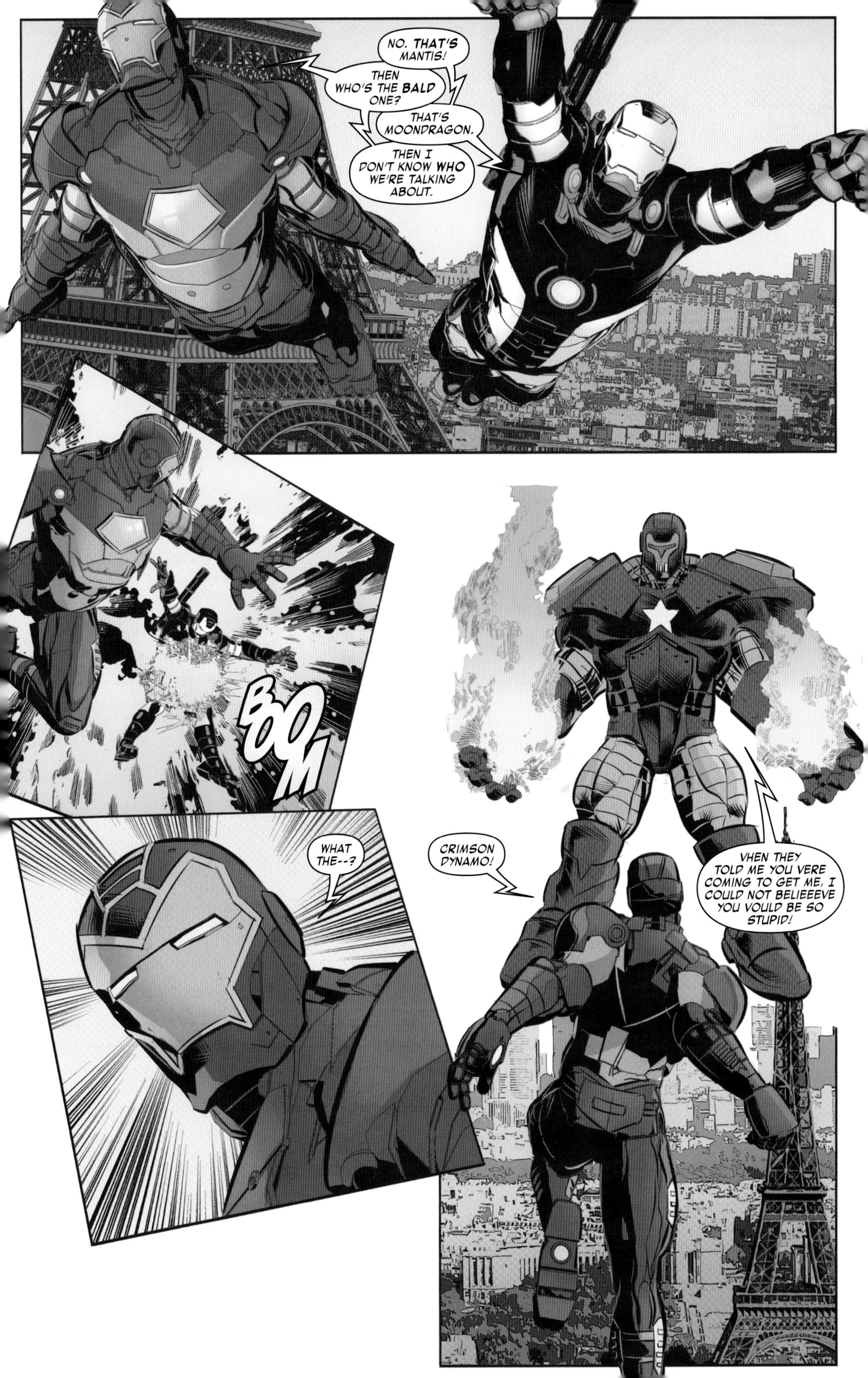
NO. THAT'S MANTIS!
THEN WHO'S THE BALD ONE?
THAT'S MOONDRAGON.
THEN I DON'T KNOW WHO WE'RE TALKING ABOUT.
BOOM
WHAT THE--?
CRIMSON DYNAMO!
VHEN THEY TOLD ME YOU VERE COMING TO GET ME, I COULD NOT BELIEEEVE YOU VOULD BE SO STUPID!

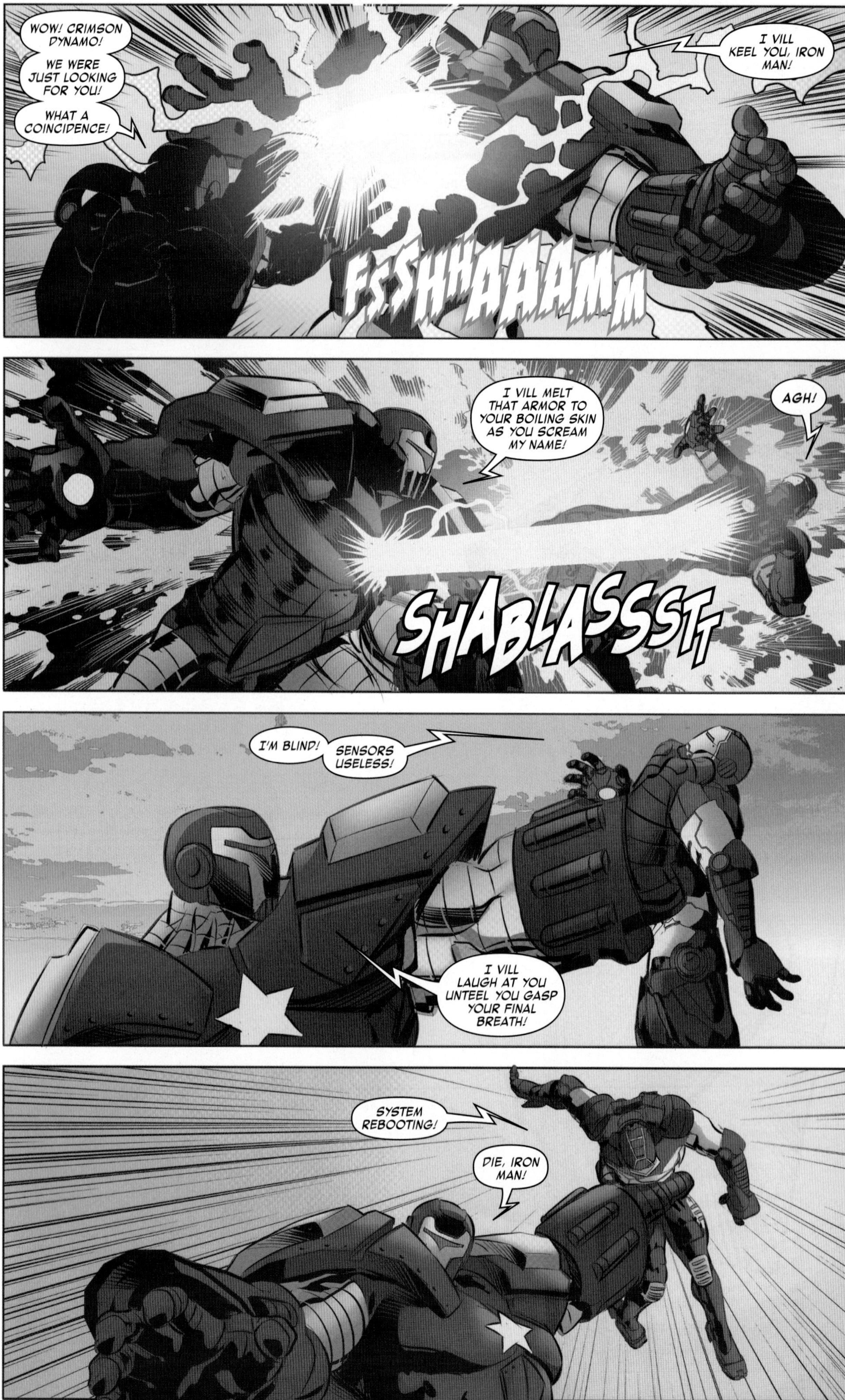
WOW! CRIMSON DYNAMO!
WE WERE JUST LOOKING FOR YOU!
WHAT A COINCIDENCE!
I VILL KEEL YOU, IRON MAN!
FSSHHAAAMMM
I VILL MELT THAT ARMOR TO YOUR BOILING SKIN AS YOU SCREAM MY NAME!
AGH!
SHABLASSSTT
I'M BLIND!
SENSORS USELESS!
I VILL LAUGH AT YOU UNTEEL YOU GASP YOUR FINAL BREATH!
SYSTEM REBOOTING!
DIE, IRON MAN!

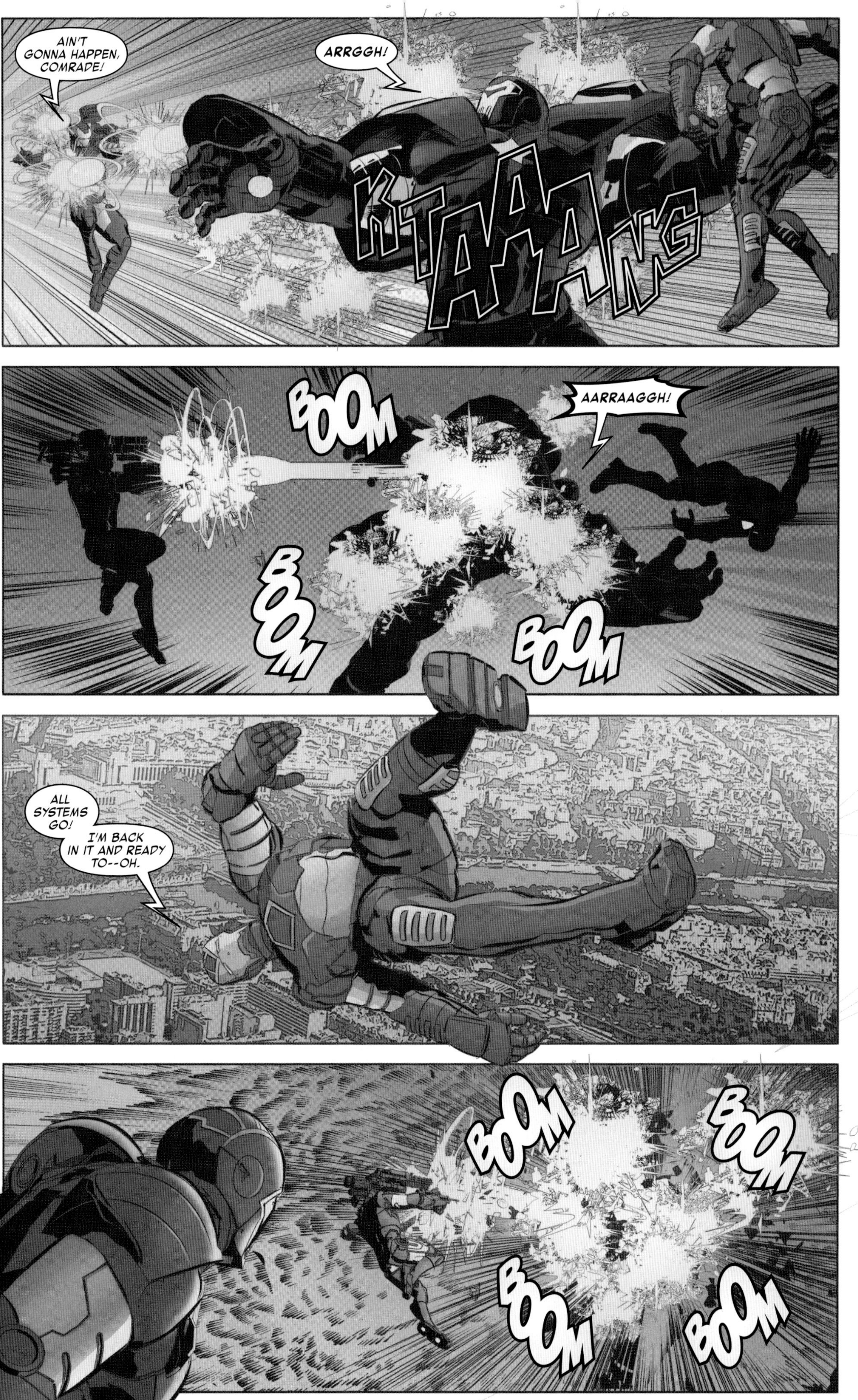
AIN'T GONNA HAPPEN, COMRADE!
ARRGGH!
KTAAAANG
BOOM
AARRAAGGH!
BOOM
BOOM
ALL SYSTEMS GO!
I'M BACK IN IT AND READY TO--OH.
BOOM
BOOM
BOOM
BOOM

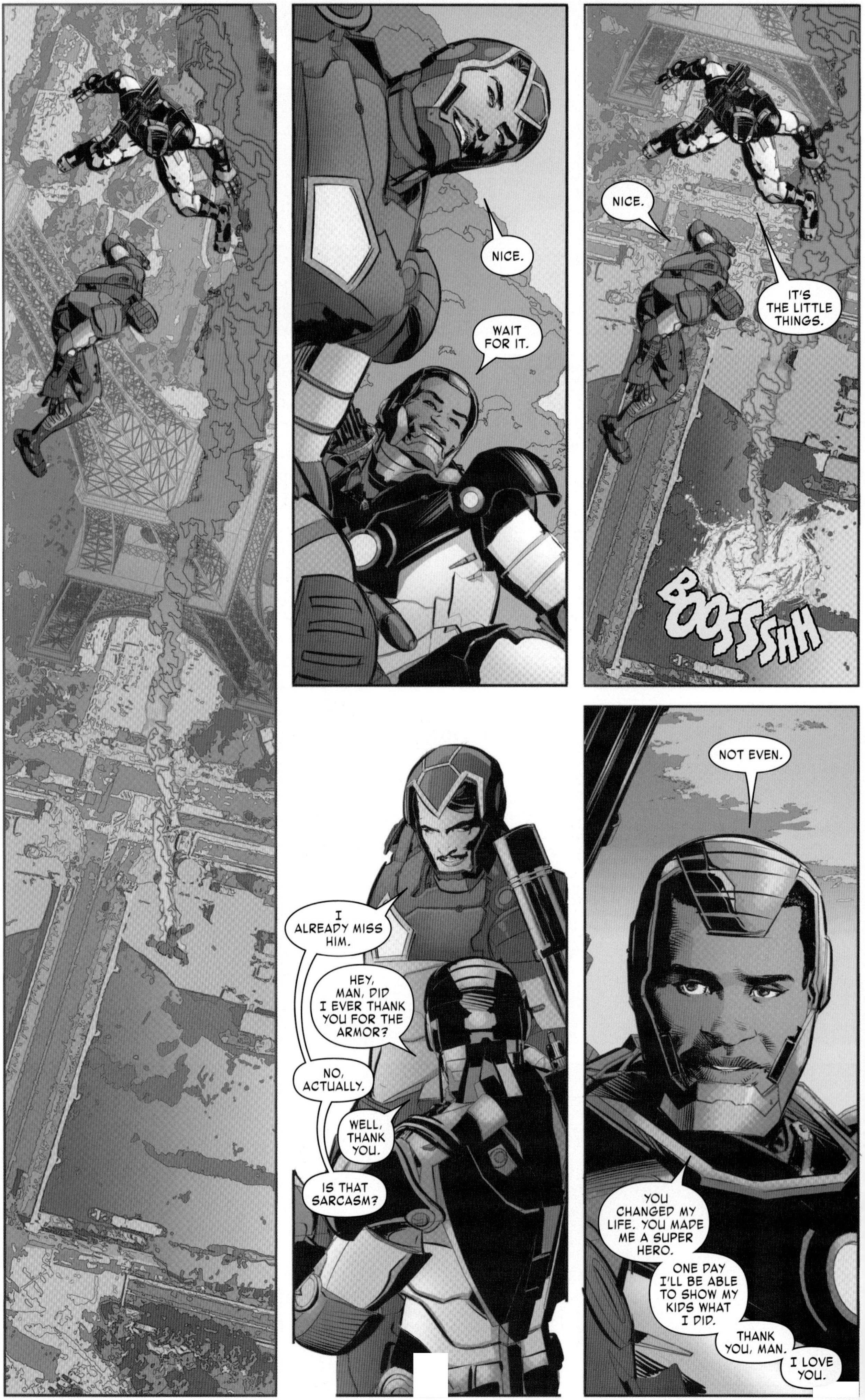

NICE.
WAIT FOR IT.
NICE.
IT'S THE LITTLE THINGS.
BOOSSHH
I ALREADY MISS HIM.
HEY, MAN, DID I EVER THANK YOU FOR THE ARMOR?
NO, ACTUALLY.
WELL, THANK YOU.
IS THAT SARCASM?
NOT EVEN.
YOU CHANGED MY LIFE. YOU MADE ME A SUPER HERO.
ONE DAY I'LL BE ABLE TO SHOW MY KIDS WHAT I DID.
THANK YOU, MAN.
I LOVE YOU.

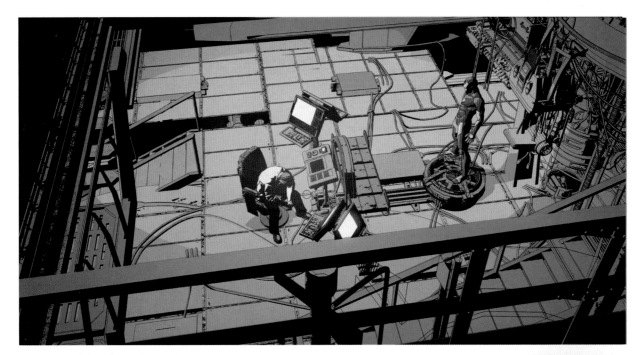

THINK MAYBE I NEED A MEETING.

NO. YOU DON'T.

YOU NEED TO REFOCUS.

GET YOUR COMPANY AFLOAT.

FIND YOUR FOOTING AGAIN AND STOP WALLOWING.

DOOM.

YOU KEEP DISTRACTING YOURSELF.

NOW YOU HAVE *THIS* TO DISTRACT YOURSELF WITH.

DOOM.

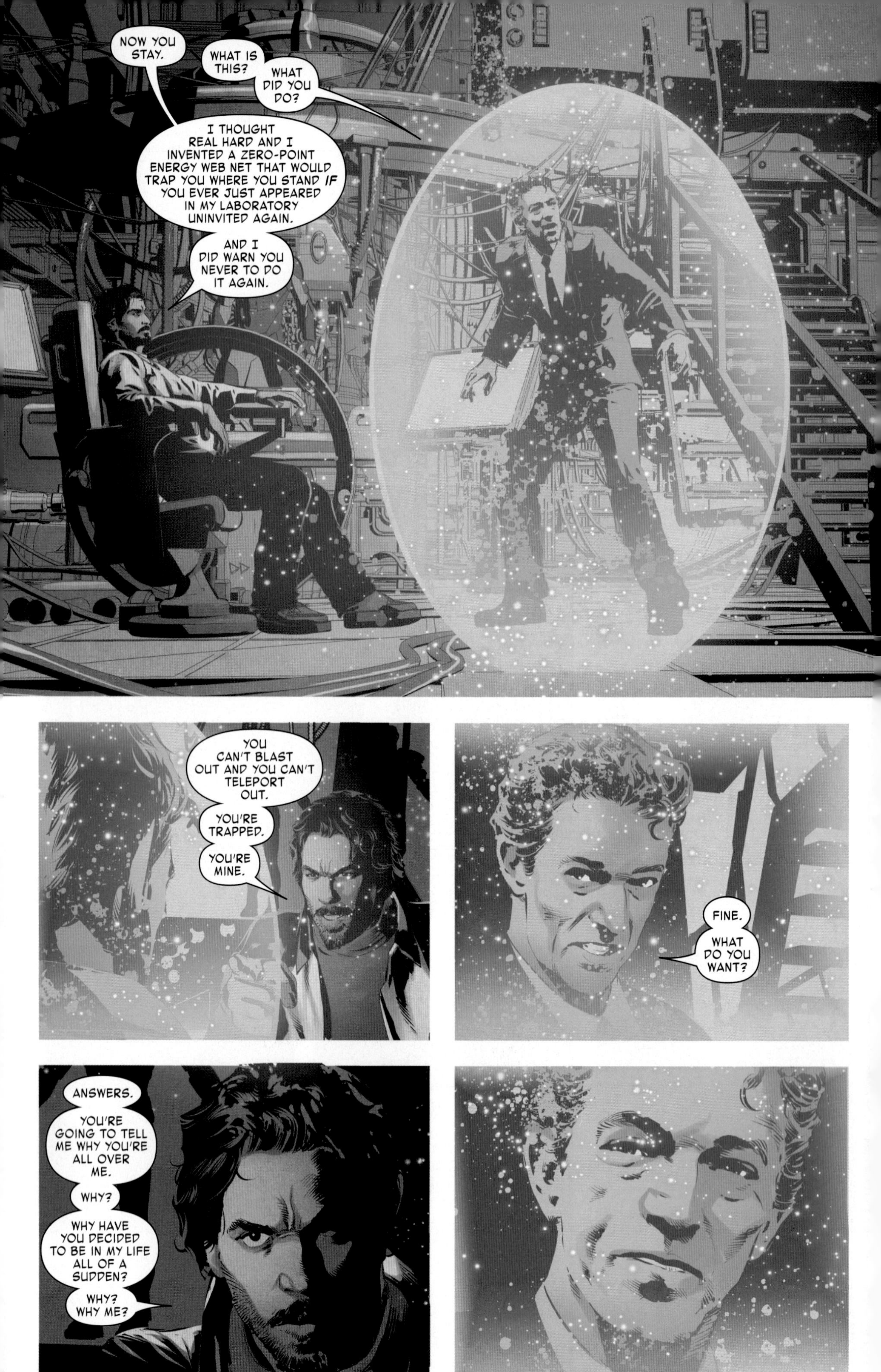
NOW YOU STAY.
WHAT IS THIS?
WHAT DID YOU DO?
I THOUGHT REAL HARD AND I INVENTED A ZERO-POINT ENERGY WEB NET THAT WOULD TRAP YOU WHERE YOU STAND *IF* YOU EVER JUST APPEARED IN MY LABORATORY UNINVITED AGAIN.
AND I DID WARN YOU NEVER TO DO IT AGAIN.
YOU CAN'T BLAST OUT AND YOU CAN'T TELEPORT OUT.
YOU'RE TRAPPED.
YOU'RE MINE.
FINE.
WHAT DO YOU WANT?
ANSWERS.
YOU'RE GOING TO TELL ME WHY YOU'RE ALL OVER ME.
WHY?
WHY HAVE YOU DECIDED TO BE IN MY LIFE ALL OF A SUDDEN?
WHY? WHY ME?

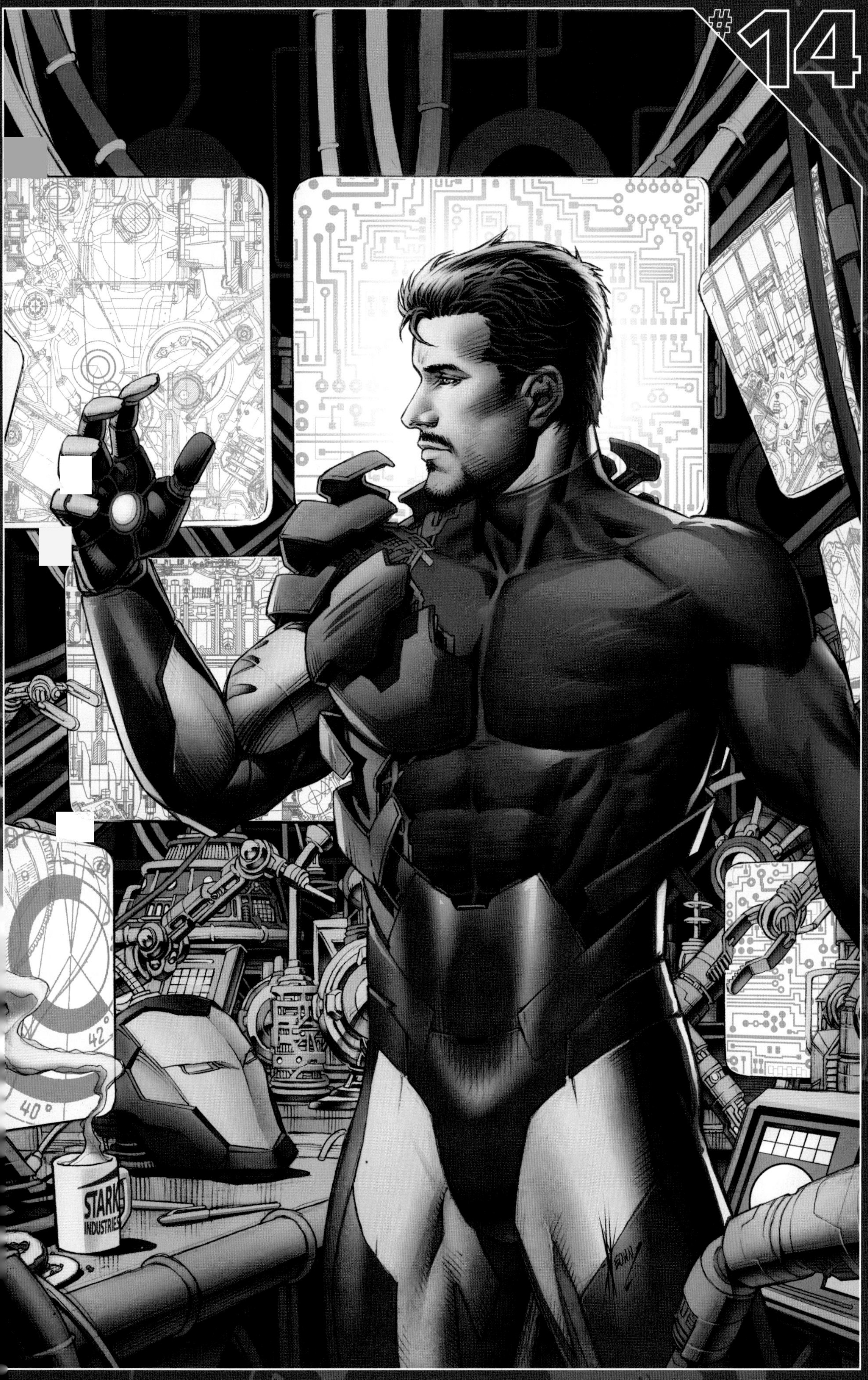
#14
42°
40°
STARK INDUSTRIES

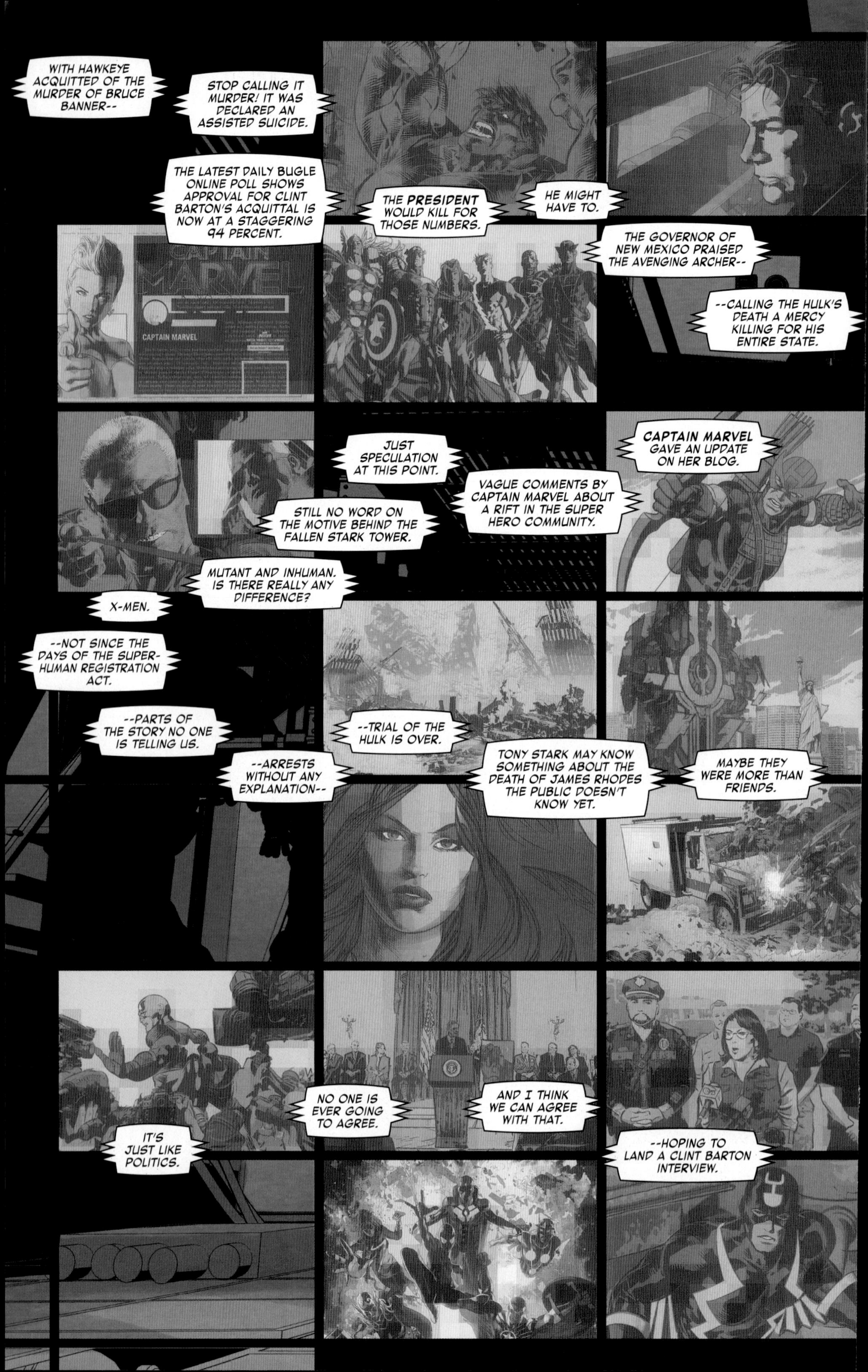
WITH HAWKEYE ACQUITTED OF THE MURDER OF BRUCE BANNER--
STOP CALLING IT MURDER! IT WAS DECLARED AN ASSISTED SUICIDE.
THE LATEST DAILY BUGLE ONLINE POLL SHOWS APPROVAL FOR CLINT BARTON'S ACQUITTAL IS NOW AT A STAGGERING 94 PERCENT.
THE PRESIDENT WOULD KILL FOR THOSE NUMBERS.
HE MIGHT HAVE TO.
THE GOVERNOR OF NEW MEXICO PRAISED THE AVENGING ARCHER--
--CALLING THE HULK'S DEATH A MERCY KILLING FOR HIS ENTIRE STATE.
CAPTAIN MARVEL
CAPTAIN MARVEL
JUST SPECULATION AT THIS POINT.
CAPTAIN MARVEL GAVE AN UPDATE ON HER BLOG.
VAGUE COMMENTS BY CAPTAIN MARVEL ABOUT A RIFT IN THE SUPER HERO COMMUNITY.
STILL NO WORD ON THE MOTIVE BEHIND THE FALLEN STARK TOWER.
MUTANT AND INHUMAN. IS THERE REALLY ANY DIFFERENCE?
X-MEN.
--NOT SINCE THE DAYS OF THE SUPER-HUMAN REGISTRATION ACT.
--PARTS OF THE STORY NO ONE IS TELLING US.
--TRIAL OF THE HULK IS OVER.
--ARRESTS WITHOUT ANY EXPLANATION--
TONY STARK MAY KNOW SOMETHING ABOUT THE DEATH OF JAMES RHODES THE PUBLIC DOESN'T KNOW YET.
MAYBE THEY WERE MORE THAN FRIENDS.
NO ONE IS EVER GOING TO AGREE.
AND I THINK WE CAN AGREE WITH THAT.
IT'S JUST LIKE POLITICS.
--HOPING TO LAND A CLINT BARTON INTERVIEW.

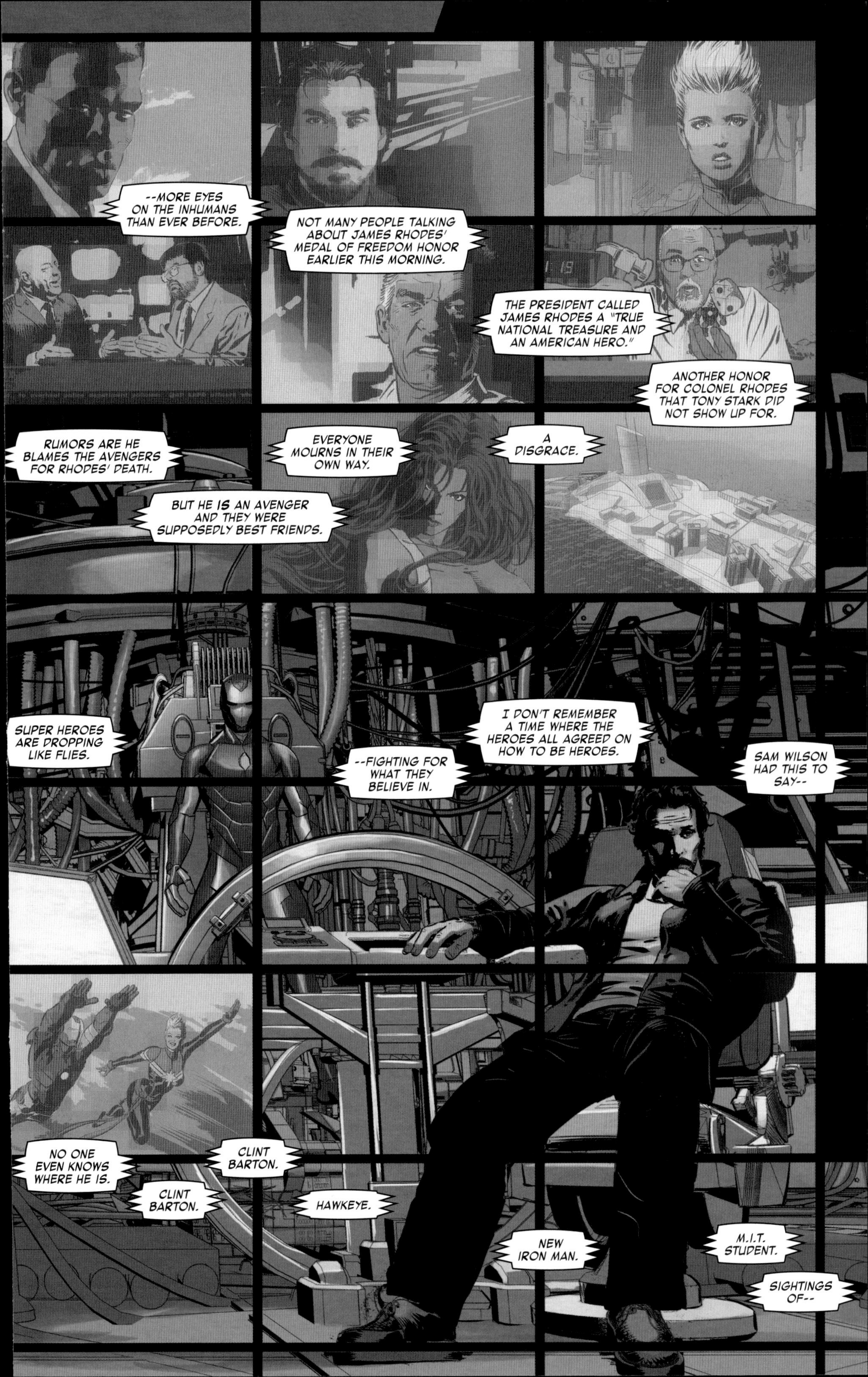
--MORE EYES ON THE INHUMANS THAN EVER BEFORE.
NOT MANY PEOPLE TALKING ABOUT JAMES RHODES' MEDAL OF FREEDOM HONOR EARLIER THIS MORNING.
THE PRESIDENT CALLED JAMES RHODES A "TRUE NATIONAL TREASURE AND AN AMERICAN HERO."
ANOTHER HONOR FOR COLONEL RHODES THAT TONY STARK DID NOT SHOW UP FOR.
RUMORS ARE HE BLAMES THE AVENGERS FOR RHODES' DEATH.
EVERYONE MOURNS IN THEIR OWN WAY.
A DISGRACE.
BUT HE **IS** AN AVENGER AND THEY WERE SUPPOSEDLY BEST FRIENDS.
SUPER HEROES ARE DROPPING LIKE FLIES.
I DON'T REMEMBER A TIME WHERE THE HEROES ALL AGREED ON HOW TO BE HEROES.
--FIGHTING FOR WHAT THEY BELIEVE IN.
SAM WILSON HAD THIS TO SAY--
NO ONE EVEN KNOWS WHERE HE IS.
CLINT BARTON.
CLINT BARTON.
HAWKEYE.
NEW IRON MAN.
M.I.T. STUDENT.
SIGHTINGS OF--

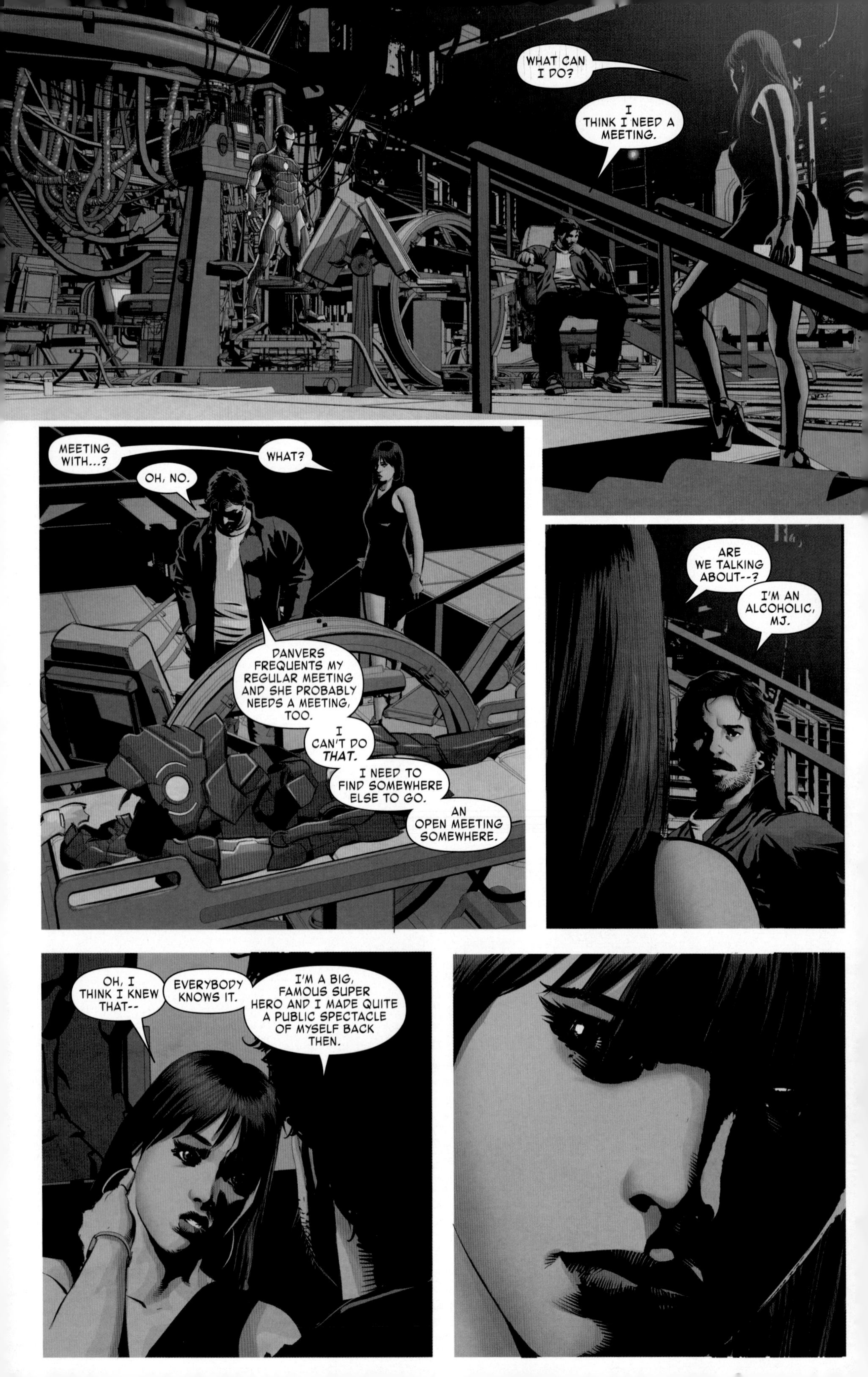
WHAT CAN I DO?
I THINK I NEED A MEETING.
MEETING WITH...?
WHAT?
OH, NO.
DANVERS FREQUENTS MY REGULAR MEETING AND SHE PROBABLY NEEDS A MEETING, TOO.
I CAN'T DO *THAT.*
I NEED TO FIND SOMEWHERE ELSE TO GO.
AN OPEN MEETING SOMEWHERE.
ARE WE TALKING ABOUT--?
I'M AN ALCOHOLIC, MJ.
OH, I THINK I KNEW THAT--
EVERYBODY KNOWS IT.
I'M A BIG, FAMOUS SUPER HERO AND I MADE QUITE A PUBLIC SPECTACLE OF MYSELF BACK THEN.

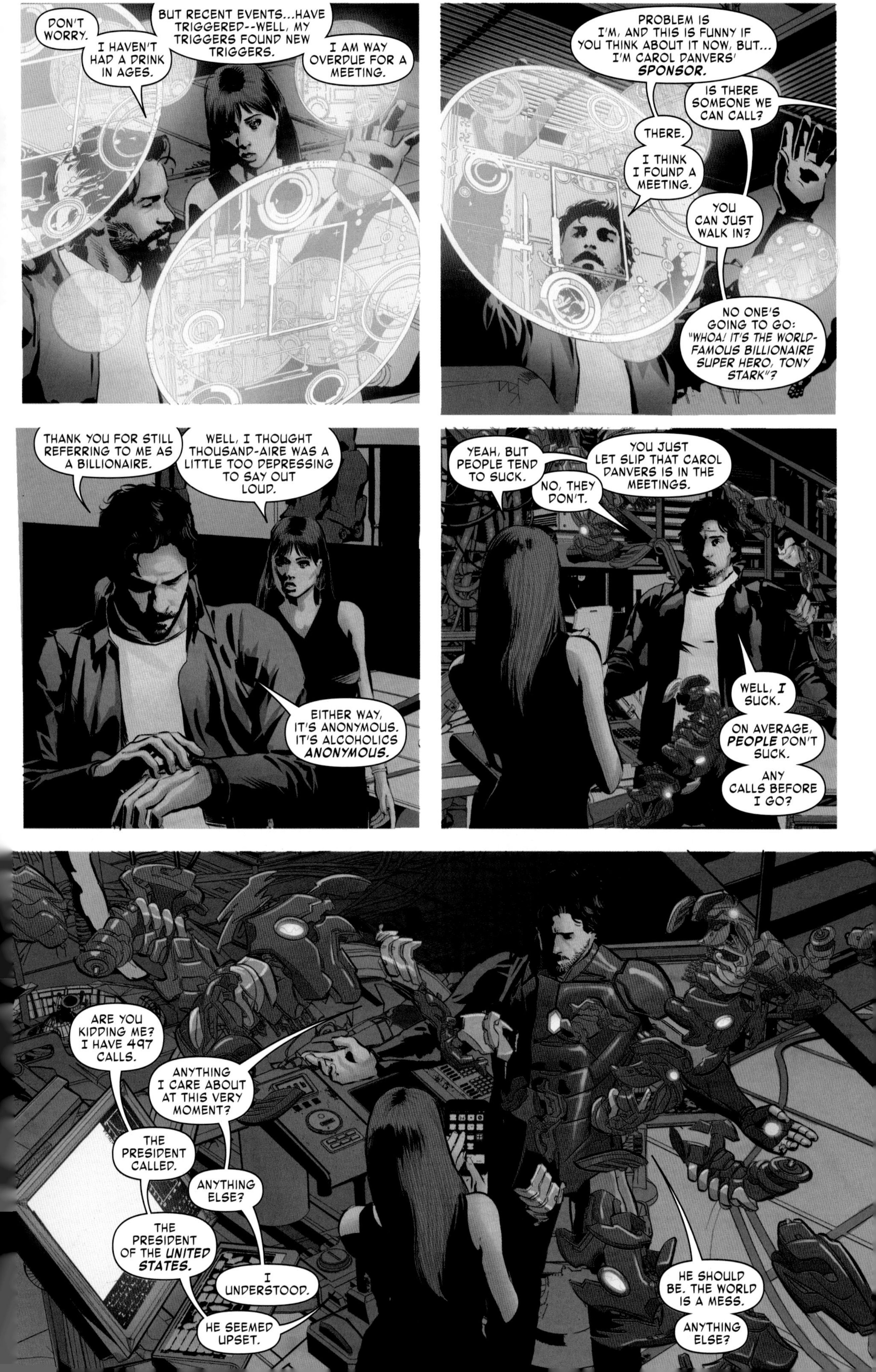
DON'T WORRY.
I HAVEN'T HAD A DRINK IN AGES.
BUT RECENT EVENTS...HAVE TRIGGERED--WELL, MY TRIGGERS FOUND NEW TRIGGERS.
I AM WAY OVERDUE FOR A MEETING.
PROBLEM IS I'M, AND THIS IS FUNNY IF YOU THINK ABOUT IT NOW, BUT... I'M CAROL DANVERS' *SPONSOR.*
IS THERE SOMEONE WE CAN CALL?
THERE.
I THINK I FOUND A MEETING.
YOU CAN JUST WALK IN?
NO ONE'S GOING TO GO: *"WHOA! IT'S THE WORLD-FAMOUS BILLIONAIRE SUPER HERO, TONY STARK"?*
THANK YOU FOR STILL REFERRING TO ME AS A BILLIONAIRE.
WELL, I THOUGHT THOUSAND-AIRE WAS A LITTLE TOO DEPRESSING TO SAY OUT LOUD.
EITHER WAY, IT'S ANONYMOUS. IT'S ALCOHOLICS *ANONYMOUS.*
YEAH, BUT PEOPLE TEND TO SUCK.
YOU JUST LET SLIP THAT CAROL DANVERS IS IN THE MEETINGS.
NO, THEY DON'T.
WELL, *I* SUCK.
ON AVERAGE, *PEOPLE* DON'T SUCK.
ANY CALLS BEFORE I GO?
ARE YOU KIDDING ME? I HAVE 497 CALLS.
ANYTHING I CARE ABOUT AT THIS VERY MOMENT?
THE PRESIDENT CALLED.
ANYTHING ELSE?
THE PRESIDENT OF THE *UNITED STATES.*
I UNDERSTOOD.
HE SEEMED UPSET.
HE SHOULD BE. THE WORLD IS A MESS.
ANYTHING ELSE?

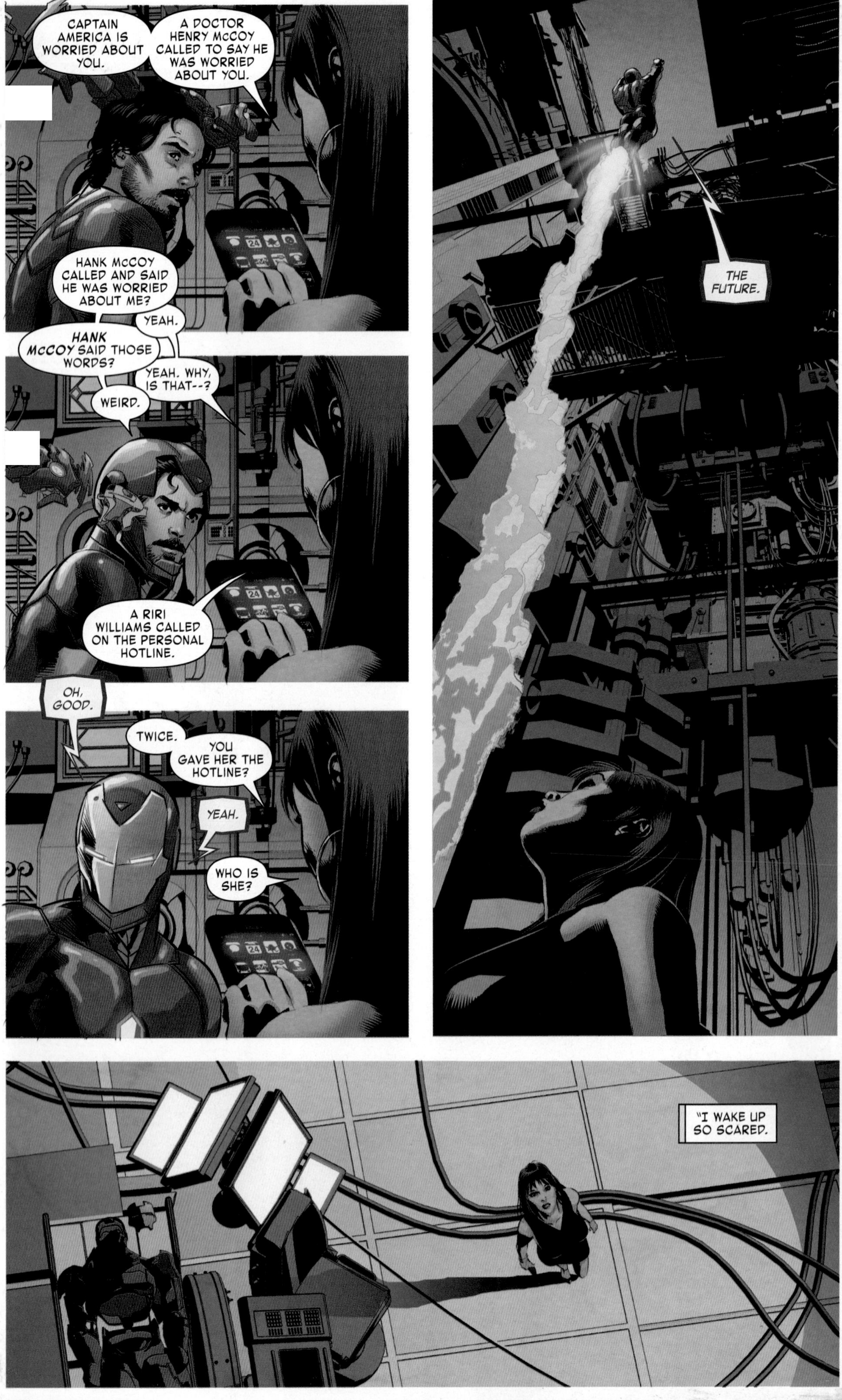
CAPTAIN AMERICA IS WORRIED ABOUT YOU.
A DOCTOR HENRY McCOY CALLED TO SAY HE WAS WORRIED ABOUT YOU.
HANK McCOY CALLED AND SAID HE WAS WORRIED ABOUT ME?
YEAH.
HANK McCOY SAID THOSE WORDS?
YEAH. WHY, IS THAT--?
WEIRD.
A RIRI WILLIAMS CALLED ON THE PERSONAL HOTLINE.
OH, GOOD.
TWICE.
YOU GAVE HER THE HOTLINE?
YEAH.
WHO IS SHE?
THE FUTURE.
"I WAKE UP SO SCARED.

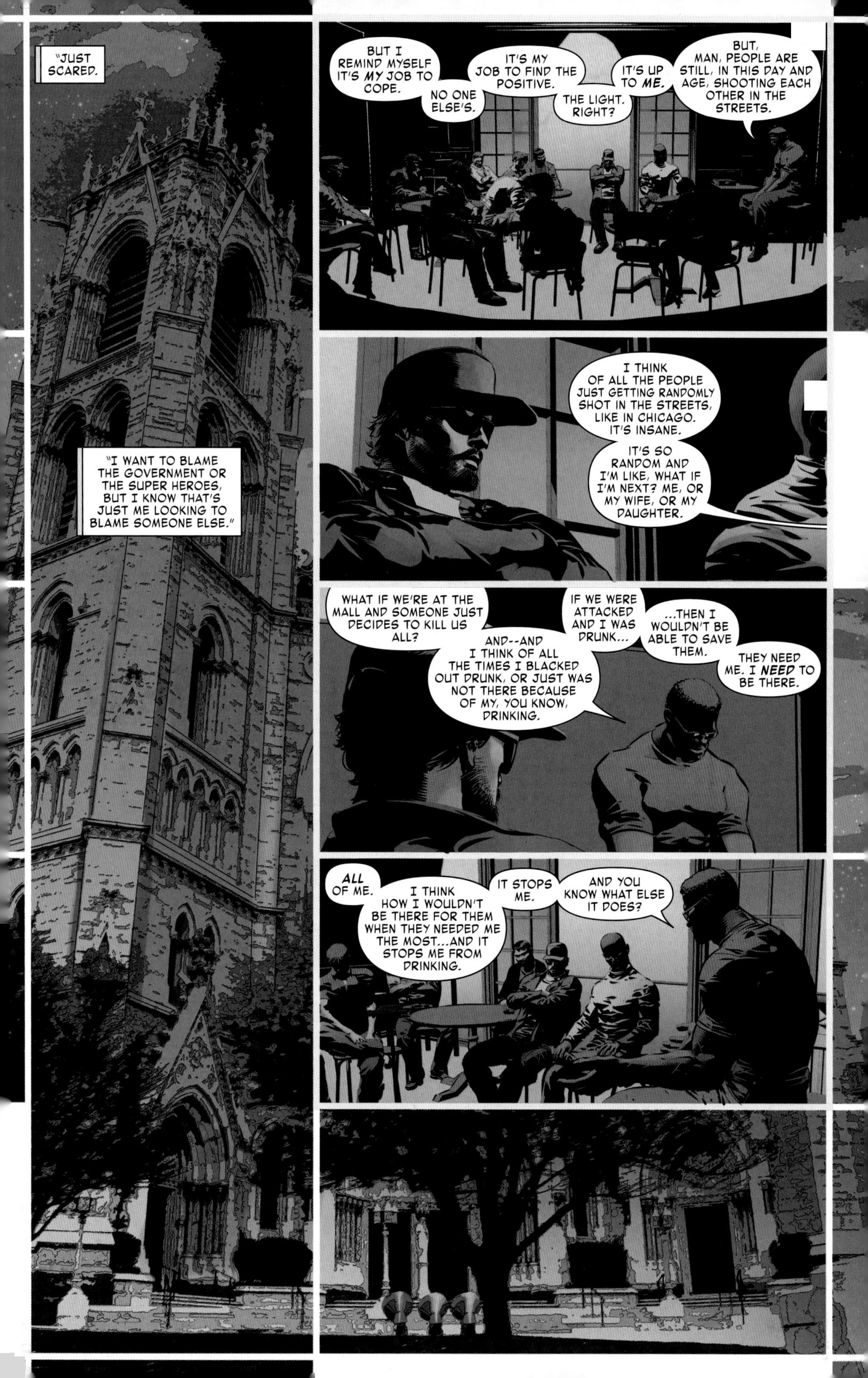
"JUST SCARED.
"I WANT TO BLAME THE GOVERNMENT OR THE SUPER HEROES, BUT I KNOW THAT'S JUST ME LOOKING TO BLAME SOMEONE ELSE."
BUT I REMIND MYSELF IT'S MY JOB TO COPE.
NO ONE ELSE'S.
IT'S MY JOB TO FIND THE POSITIVE.
THE LIGHT. RIGHT?
IT'S UP TO ME.
BUT, MAN, PEOPLE ARE STILL, IN THIS DAY AND AGE, SHOOTING EACH OTHER IN THE STREETS.
I THINK OF ALL THE PEOPLE JUST GETTING RANDOMLY SHOT IN THE STREETS, LIKE IN CHICAGO. IT'S INSANE.
IT'S SO RANDOM AND I'M LIKE, WHAT IF I'M NEXT? ME, OR MY WIFE, OR MY DAUGHTER.
WHAT IF WE'RE AT THE MALL AND SOMEONE JUST DECIDES TO KILL US ALL?
AND--AND I THINK OF ALL THE TIMES I BLACKED OUT DRUNK, OR JUST WAS NOT THERE BECAUSE OF MY, YOU KNOW, DRINKING.
IF WE WERE ATTACKED AND I WAS DRUNK...
...THEN I WOULDN'T BE ABLE TO SAVE THEM.
THEY NEED ME. I NEED TO BE THERE.
ALL OF ME.
I THINK HOW I WOULDN'T BE THERE FOR THEM WHEN THEY NEEDED ME THE MOST...AND IT STOPS ME FROM DRINKING.
IT STOPS ME.
AND YOU KNOW WHAT ELSE IT DOES?

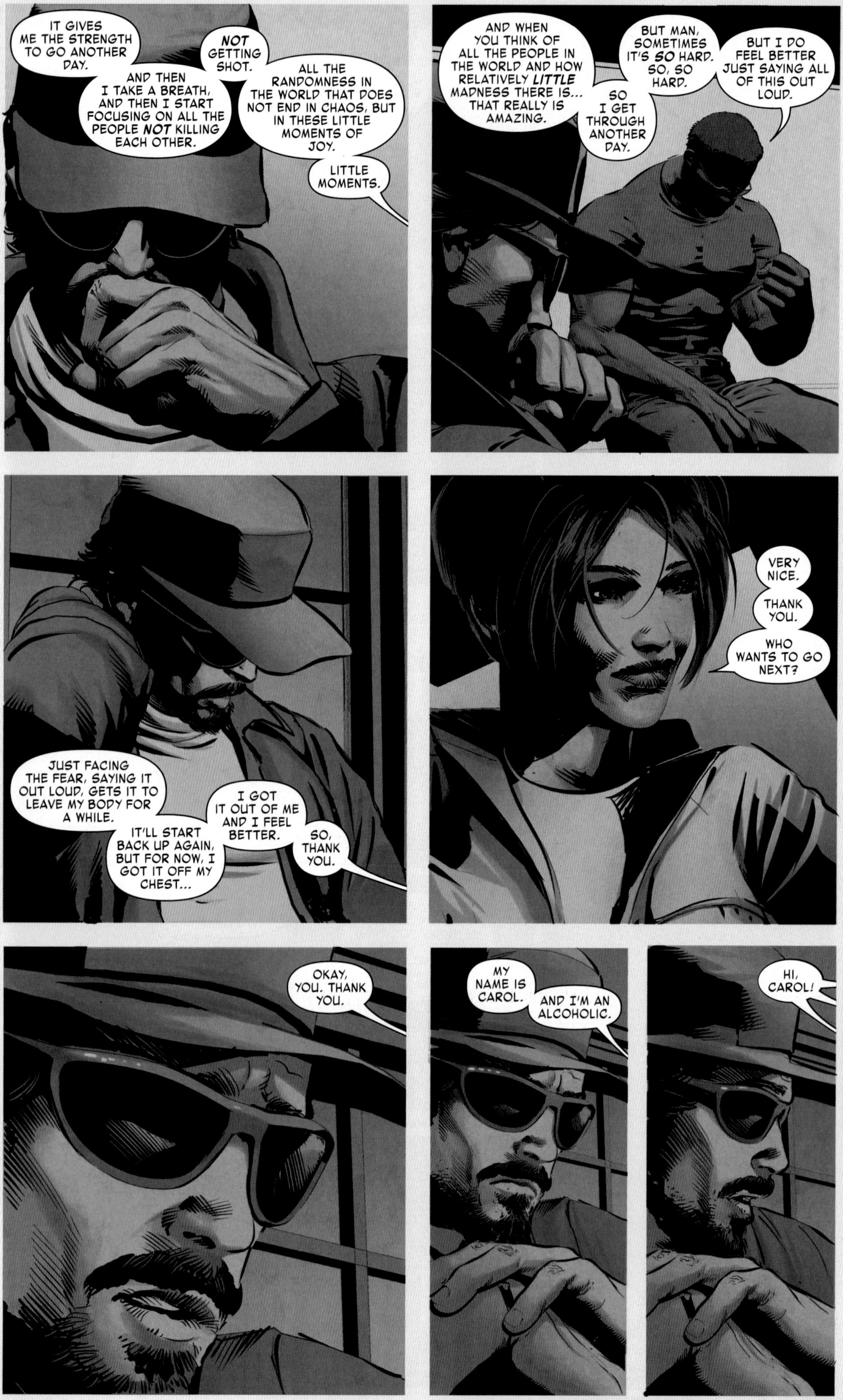
IT GIVES ME THE STRENGTH TO GO ANOTHER DAY.
AND THEN I TAKE A BREATH, AND THEN I START FOCUSING ON ALL THE PEOPLE NOT KILLING EACH OTHER.
NOT GETTING SHOT.
ALL THE RANDOMNESS IN THE WORLD THAT DOES NOT END IN CHAOS, BUT IN THESE LITTLE MOMENTS OF JOY.
LITTLE MOMENTS.
AND WHEN YOU THINK OF ALL THE PEOPLE IN THE WORLD AND HOW RELATIVELY LITTLE MADNESS THERE IS... THAT REALLY IS AMAZING.
SO I GET THROUGH ANOTHER DAY.
BUT MAN, SOMETIMES IT'S SO HARD. SO, SO HARD.
BUT I DO FEEL BETTER JUST SAYING ALL OF THIS OUT LOUD.
JUST FACING THE FEAR, SAYING IT OUT LOUD, GETS IT TO LEAVE MY BODY FOR A WHILE.
IT'LL START BACK UP AGAIN, BUT FOR NOW, I GOT IT OFF MY CHEST...
I GOT IT OUT OF ME AND I FEEL BETTER.
SO, THANK YOU.
VERY NICE.
THANK YOU.
WHO WANTS TO GO NEXT?
OKAY, YOU. THANK YOU.
MY NAME IS CAROL.
AND I'M AN ALCOHOLIC.
HI, CAROL!

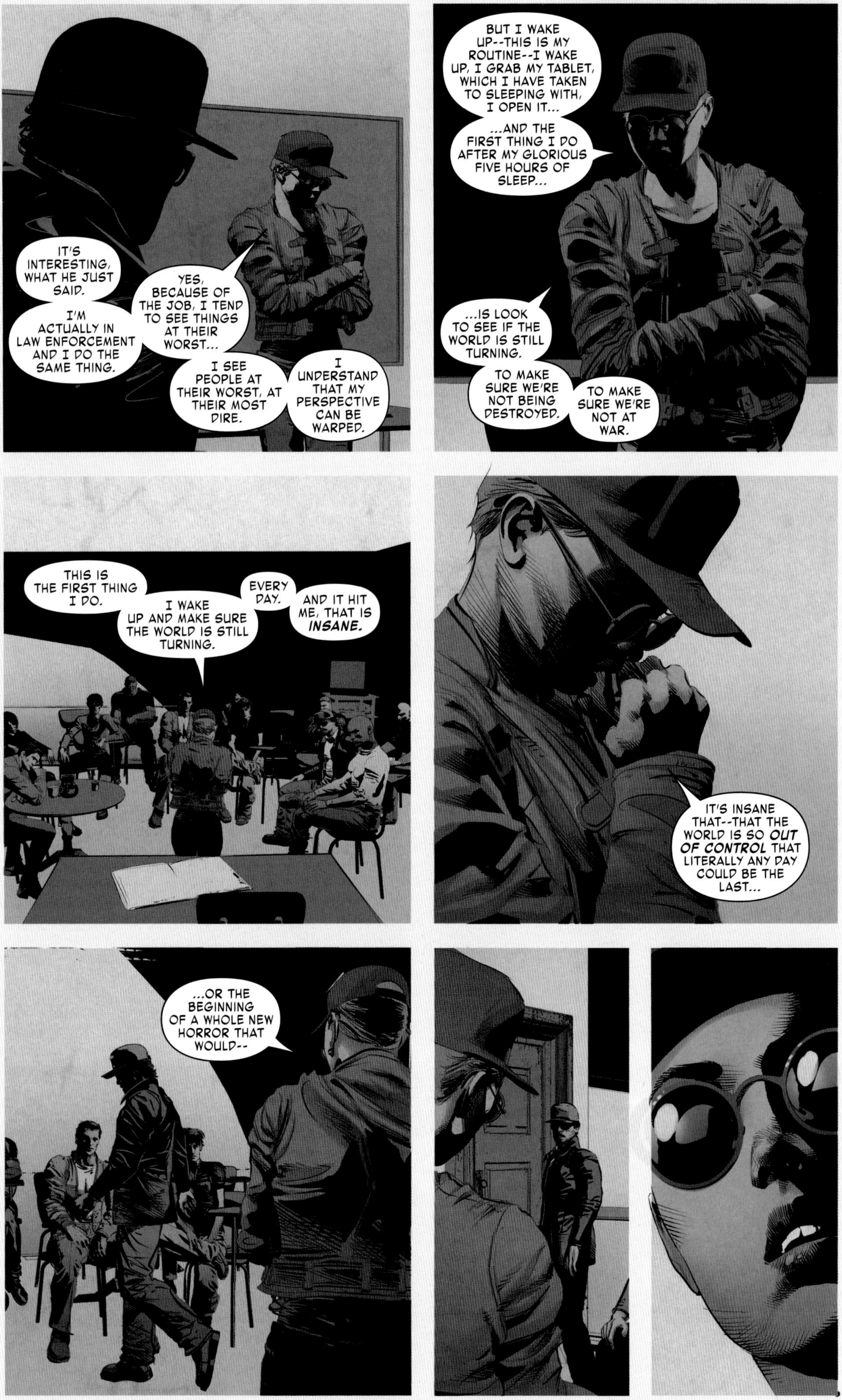
IT'S INTERESTING, WHAT HE JUST SAID.
I'M ACTUALLY IN LAW ENFORCEMENT AND I DO THE SAME THING.
YES, BECAUSE OF THE JOB, I TEND TO SEE THINGS AT THEIR WORST...
I SEE PEOPLE AT THEIR WORST, AT THEIR MOST DIRE.
I UNDERSTAND THAT MY PERSPECTIVE CAN BE WARPED.
BUT I WAKE UP--THIS IS MY ROUTINE--I WAKE UP, I GRAB MY TABLET, WHICH I HAVE TAKEN TO SLEEPING WITH, I OPEN IT...
...AND THE FIRST THING I DO AFTER MY GLORIOUS FIVE HOURS OF SLEEP...
...IS LOOK TO SEE IF THE WORLD IS STILL TURNING.
TO MAKE SURE WE'RE NOT BEING DESTROYED.
TO MAKE SURE WE'RE NOT AT WAR.
THIS IS THE FIRST THING I DO.
I WAKE UP AND MAKE SURE THE WORLD IS STILL TURNING.
EVERY DAY.
AND IT HIT ME, THAT IS *INSANE.*
IT'S INSANE THAT--THAT THE WORLD IS SO ***OUT OF CONTROL*** THAT LITERALLY ANY DAY COULD BE THE LAST...
...OR THE BEGINNING OF A WHOLE NEW HORROR THAT WOULD--

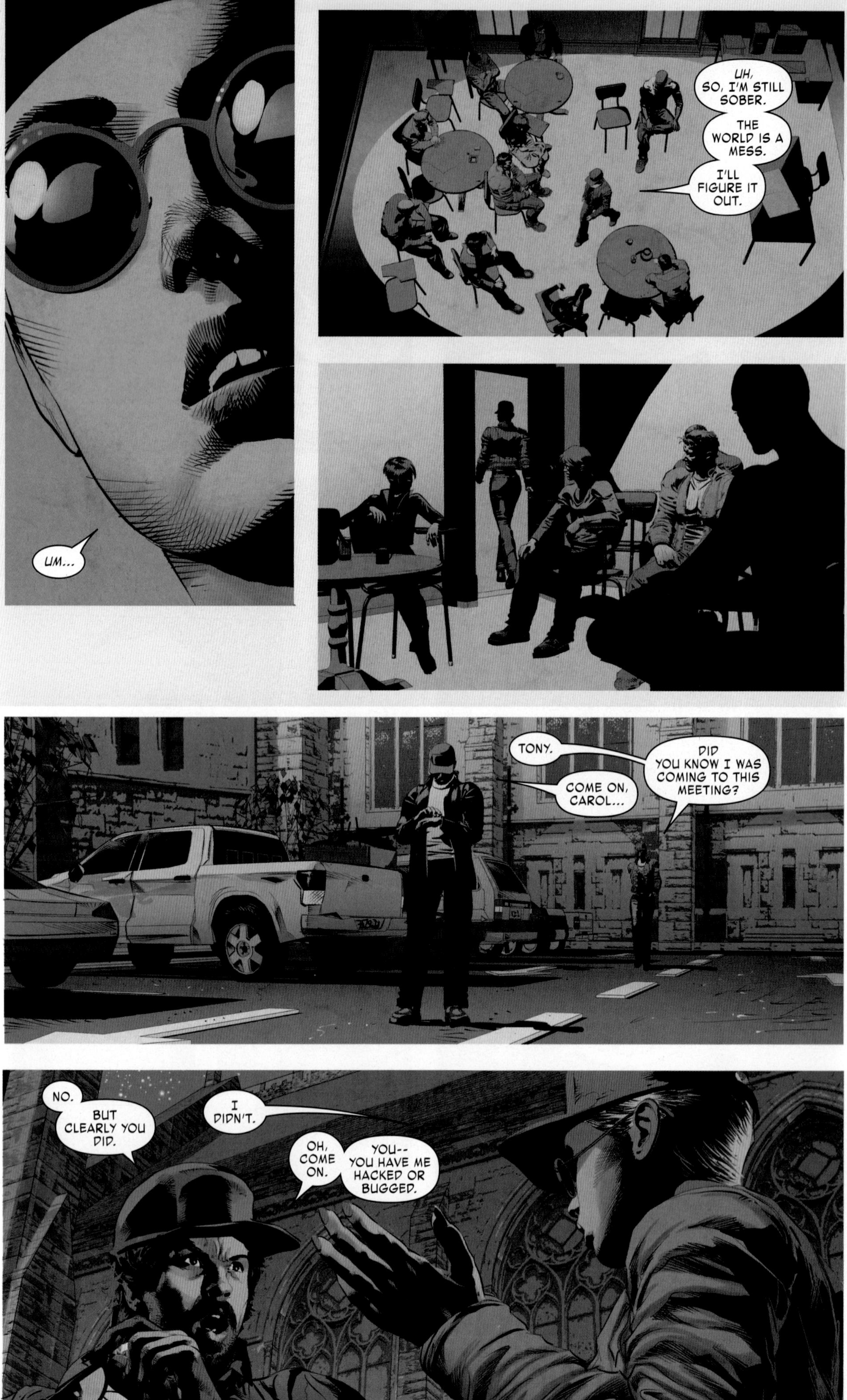
UM...
UH, SO, I'M STILL SOBER.
THE WORLD IS A MESS.
I'LL FIGURE IT OUT.
TONY.
DID YOU KNOW I WAS COMING TO THIS MEETING?
COME ON, CAROL...
NO.
BUT CLEARLY YOU DID.
I DIDN'T.
OH, COME ON.
YOU-- YOU HAVE ME HACKED OR BUGGED.

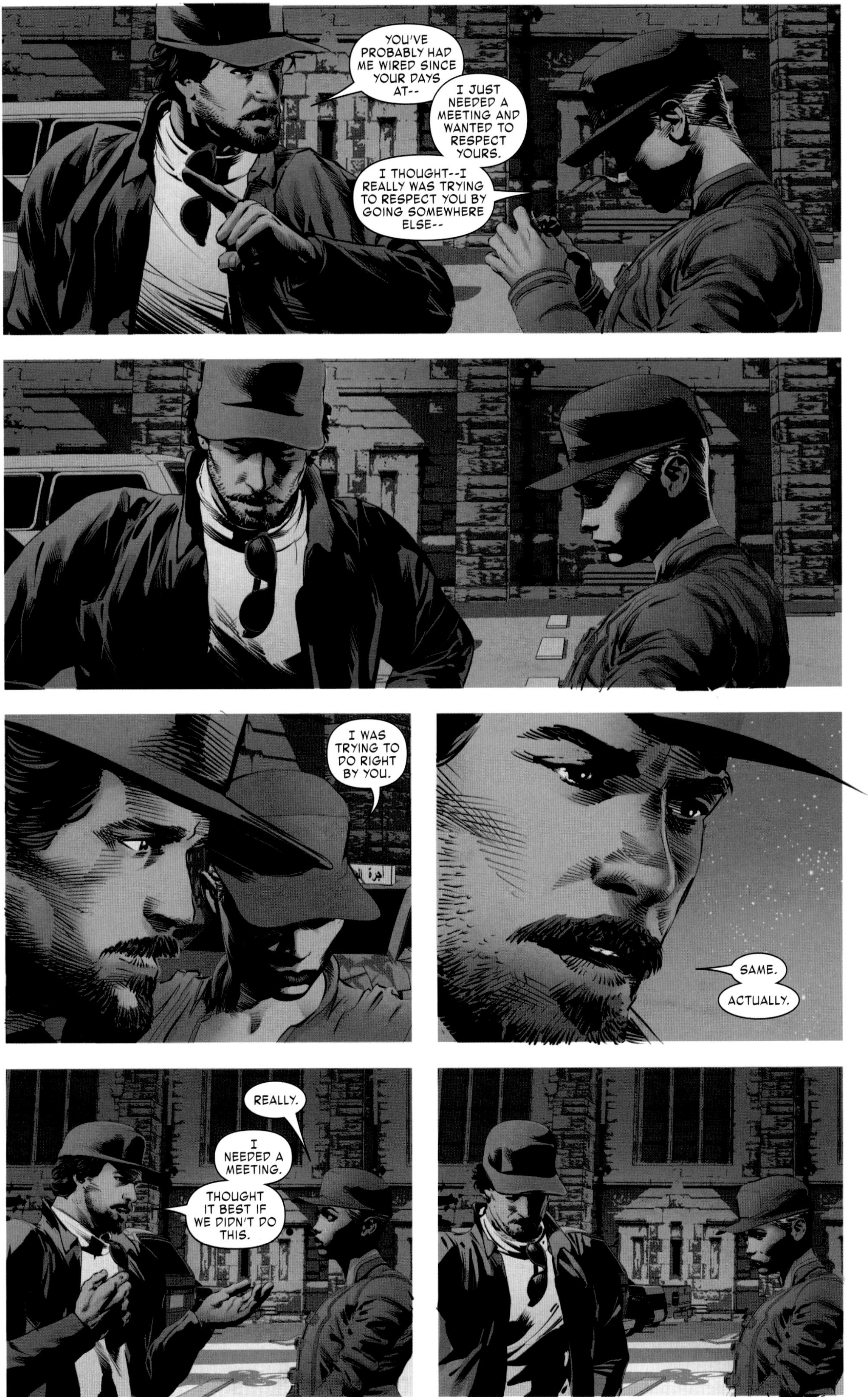

YOU'VE PROBABLY HAD ME WIRED SINCE YOUR DAYS AT--
I JUST NEEDED A MEETING AND WANTED TO RESPECT YOURS.
I THOUGHT--I REALLY WAS TRYING TO RESPECT YOU BY GOING SOMEWHERE ELSE--
I WAS TRYING TO DO RIGHT BY YOU.
SAME.
ACTUALLY.
REALLY.
I NEEDED A MEETING.
THOUGHT IT BEST IF WE DIDN'T DO THIS.

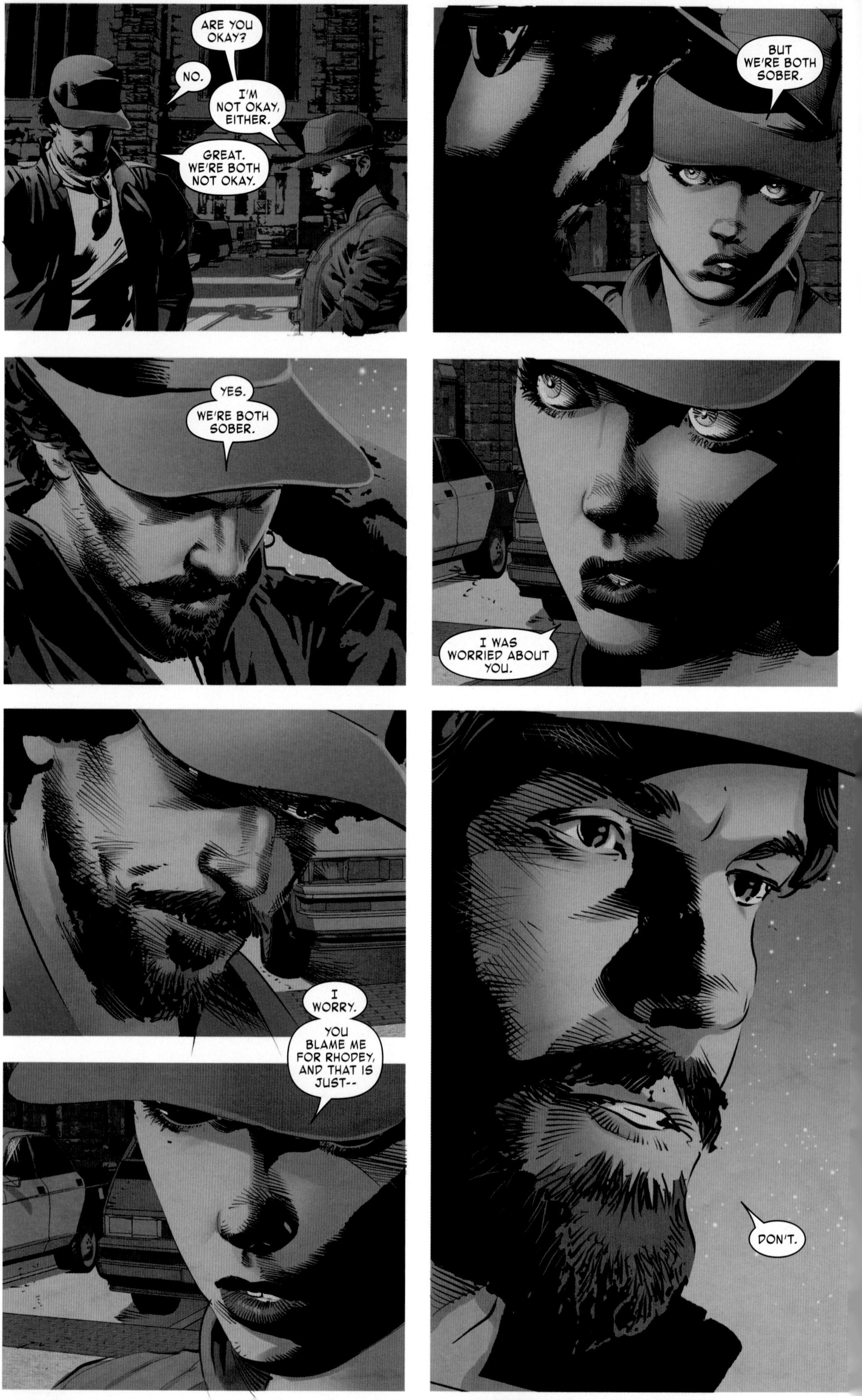
ARE YOU OKAY?
NO.
I'M NOT OKAY, EITHER.
GREAT. WE'RE BOTH NOT OKAY.
BUT WE'RE BOTH SOBER.
YES.
WE'RE BOTH SOBER.
I WAS WORRIED ABOUT YOU.
I WORRY.
YOU BLAME ME FOR RHODEY, AND THAT IS JUST--
DON'T.

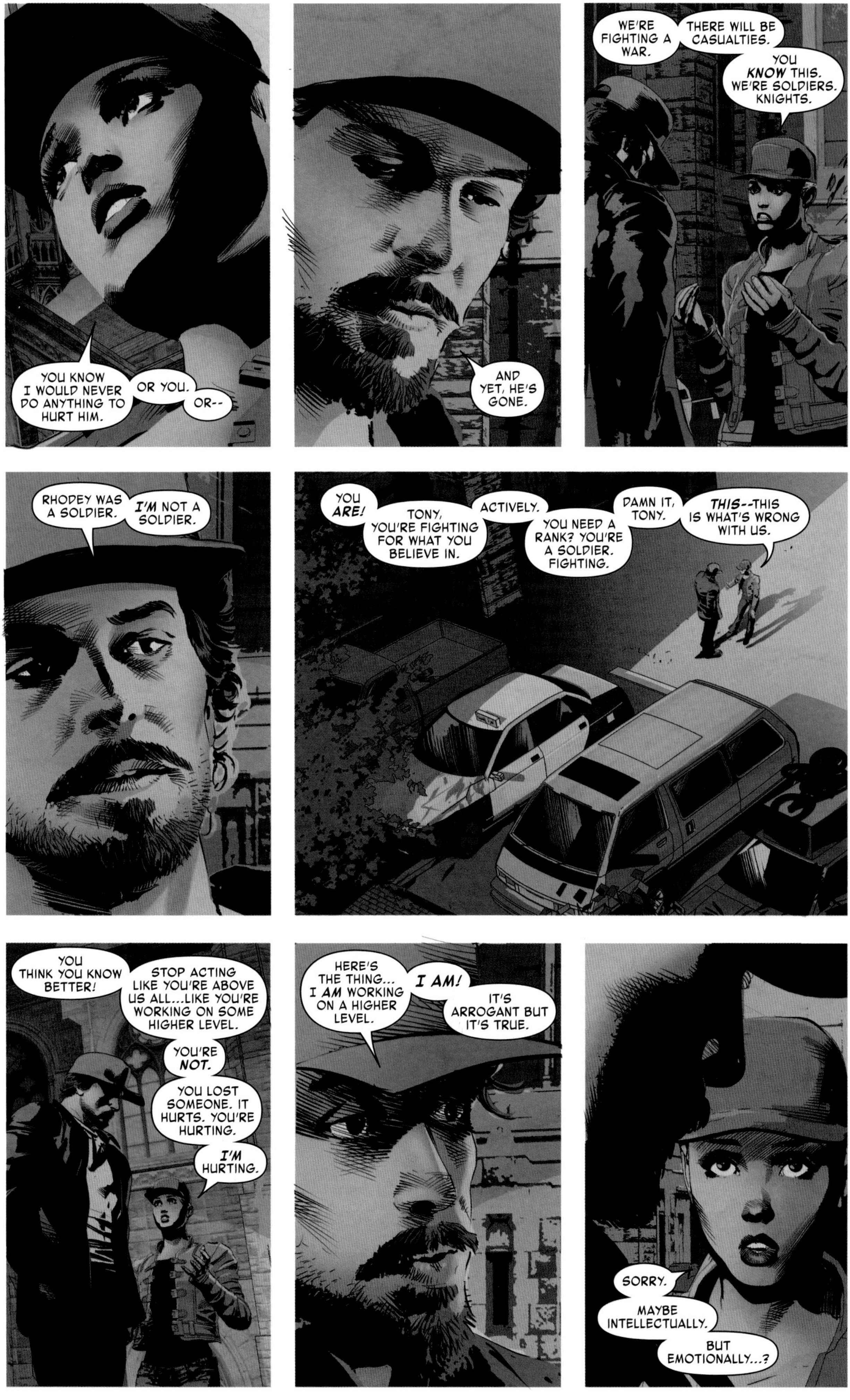
YOU KNOW I WOULD NEVER DO ANYTHING TO HURT HIM.
OR YOU.
OR--
AND YET, HE'S GONE.
WE'RE FIGHTING A WAR.
THERE WILL BE CASUALTIES.
YOU KNOW THIS. WE'RE SOLDIERS. KNIGHTS.
RHODEY WAS A SOLDIER.
I'M NOT A SOLDIER.
YOU ARE!
TONY, YOU'RE FIGHTING FOR WHAT YOU BELIEVE IN.
ACTIVELY.
YOU NEED A RANK? YOU'RE A SOLDIER. FIGHTING.
DAMN IT, TONY.
THIS--THIS IS WHAT'S WRONG WITH US.
YOU THINK YOU KNOW BETTER!
STOP ACTING LIKE YOU'RE ABOVE US ALL...LIKE YOU'RE WORKING ON SOME HIGHER LEVEL.
YOU'RE NOT.
YOU LOST SOMEONE. IT HURTS. YOU'RE HURTING.
I'M HURTING.
HERE'S THE THING... I AM WORKING ON A HIGHER LEVEL.
I AM!
IT'S ARROGANT BUT IT'S TRUE.
SORRY.
MAYBE INTELLECTUALLY.
BUT EMOTIONALLY...?

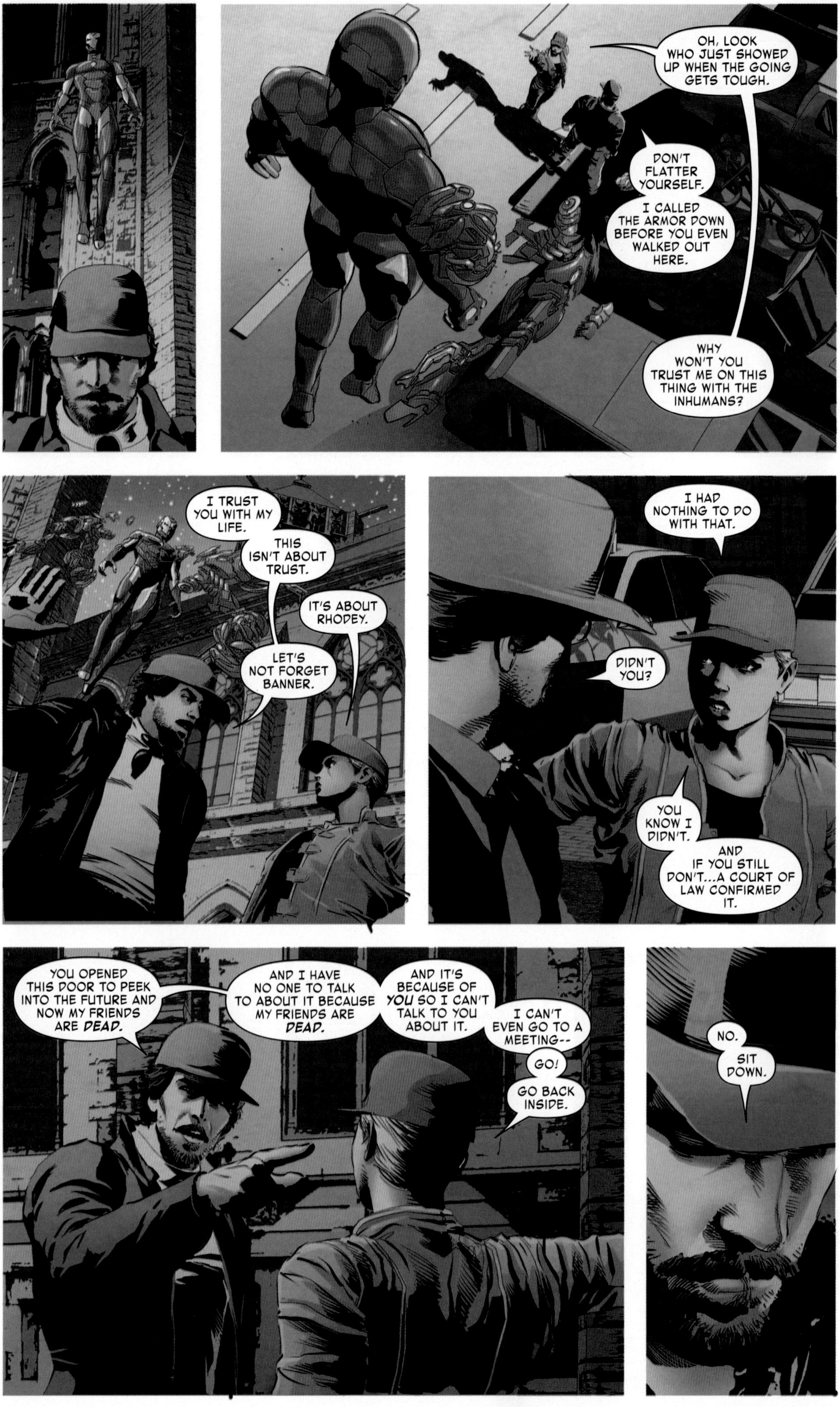
OH, LOOK WHO JUST SHOWED UP WHEN THE GOING GETS TOUGH.
DON'T FLATTER YOURSELF.
I CALLED THE ARMOR DOWN BEFORE YOU EVEN WALKED OUT HERE.
WHY WON'T YOU TRUST ME ON THIS THING WITH THE INHUMANS?
I TRUST YOU WITH MY LIFE.
THIS ISN'T ABOUT TRUST.
IT'S ABOUT RHODEY.
LET'S NOT FORGET BANNER.
I HAD NOTHING TO DO WITH THAT.
DIDN'T YOU?
YOU KNOW I DIDN'T.
AND IF YOU STILL DON'T...A COURT OF LAW CONFIRMED IT.
YOU OPENED THIS DOOR TO PEEK INTO THE FUTURE AND NOW MY FRIENDS ARE DEAD.
AND I HAVE NO ONE TO TALK TO ABOUT IT BECAUSE MY FRIENDS ARE DEAD.
AND IT'S BECAUSE OF YOU SO I CAN'T TALK TO YOU ABOUT IT.
I CAN'T EVEN GO TO A MEETING--
GO!
GO BACK INSIDE.
NO.
SIT DOWN.

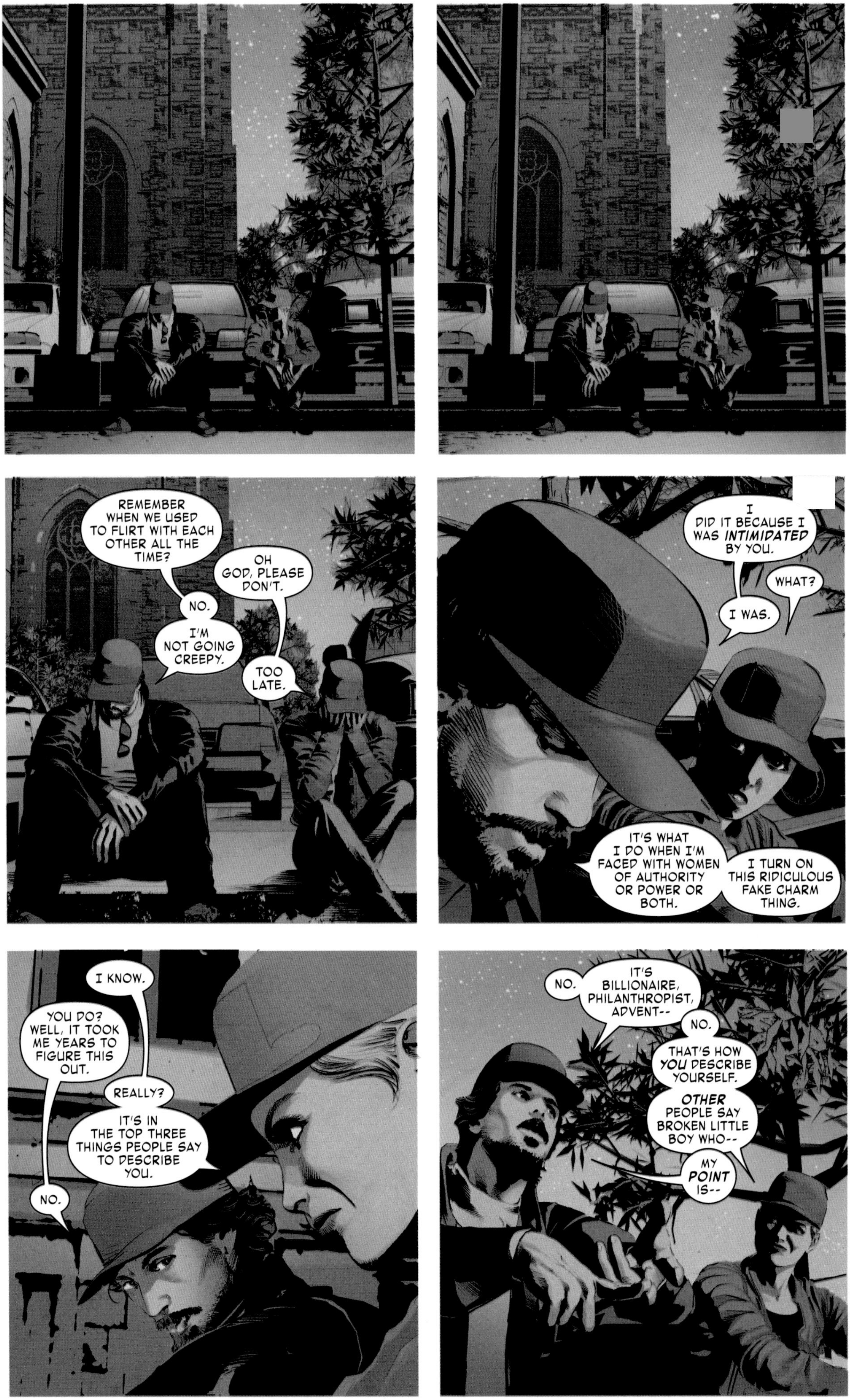
REMEMBER WHEN WE USED TO FLIRT WITH EACH OTHER ALL THE TIME?
NO.
I'M NOT GOING CREEPY.
OH GOD, PLEASE DON'T.
TOO LATE.
I DID IT BECAUSE I WAS INTIMIDATED BY YOU.
WHAT?
I WAS.
IT'S WHAT I DO WHEN I'M FACED WITH WOMEN OF AUTHORITY OR POWER OR BOTH.
I TURN ON THIS RIDICULOUS FAKE CHARM THING.
I KNOW.
YOU DO? WELL, IT TOOK ME YEARS TO FIGURE THIS OUT.
REALLY?
IT'S IN THE TOP THREE THINGS PEOPLE SAY TO DESCRIBE YOU.
NO.
NO.
IT'S BILLIONAIRE, PHILANTHROPIST, ADVENT--
NO.
THAT'S HOW YOU DESCRIBE YOURSELF.
OTHER PEOPLE SAY BROKEN LITTLE BOY WHO--
MY POINT IS--

--MY POINT IS I RESPECT YOU SO MUCH.

AND YOU'RE EVEN BETTER AT *THIS*, AT RECOVERY, THAN ME.

BUT I WOULDN'T EVEN *BE* IN RECOVERY IF NOT FOR YOU.

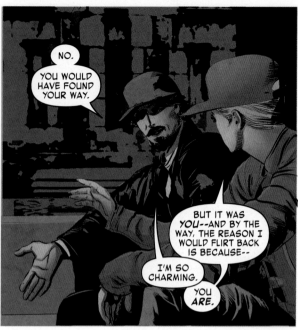

NO. YOU WOULD HAVE FOUND YOUR WAY.

BUT IT WAS *YOU*--AND BY THE WAY, THE REASON I WOULD FLIRT BACK IS BECAUSE--

I'M SO CHARMING.

YOU *ARE*.

YEAH.

AT *FIRST*.

WELL, TO BE FAIR, A LOT OF WOMEN FIND *THAT* PART OF ME THE MOST ATTRACTIVE.

BUT *THEN*, EVENTUALLY, YOU SEE THE BROKEN BOY INSIDE AND IT'S...NOT SO SEXY.

NOT ANYONE WORTH A DAMN.

MY POINT IS, I RESPECT YOU, TRULY, AND IT'S *SO* HARD TO FIGHT YOU ON THIS THING.

EVEN AFTER RHODEY, EVEN AFTER BANNER...

...IT'S SO HARD TO FIGHT YOU *BECAUSE* I RESPECT YOU. BECAUSE I LOVE YOU.

SO STOP.

BUT...

...YOU'RE SO WRONG ON THIS.

SO WRONG.

WELL...IF BETWEEN NOW AND THEN YOU GET IT THROUGH THAT THICK, BROKEN BOY SKULL OF YOURS THAT MAYBE SOMEONE ELSE MIGHT BE RIGHT ABOUT SOMETHING...

...GIVE ME A CALL...WE'LL GO TO A MEETING.

OR...

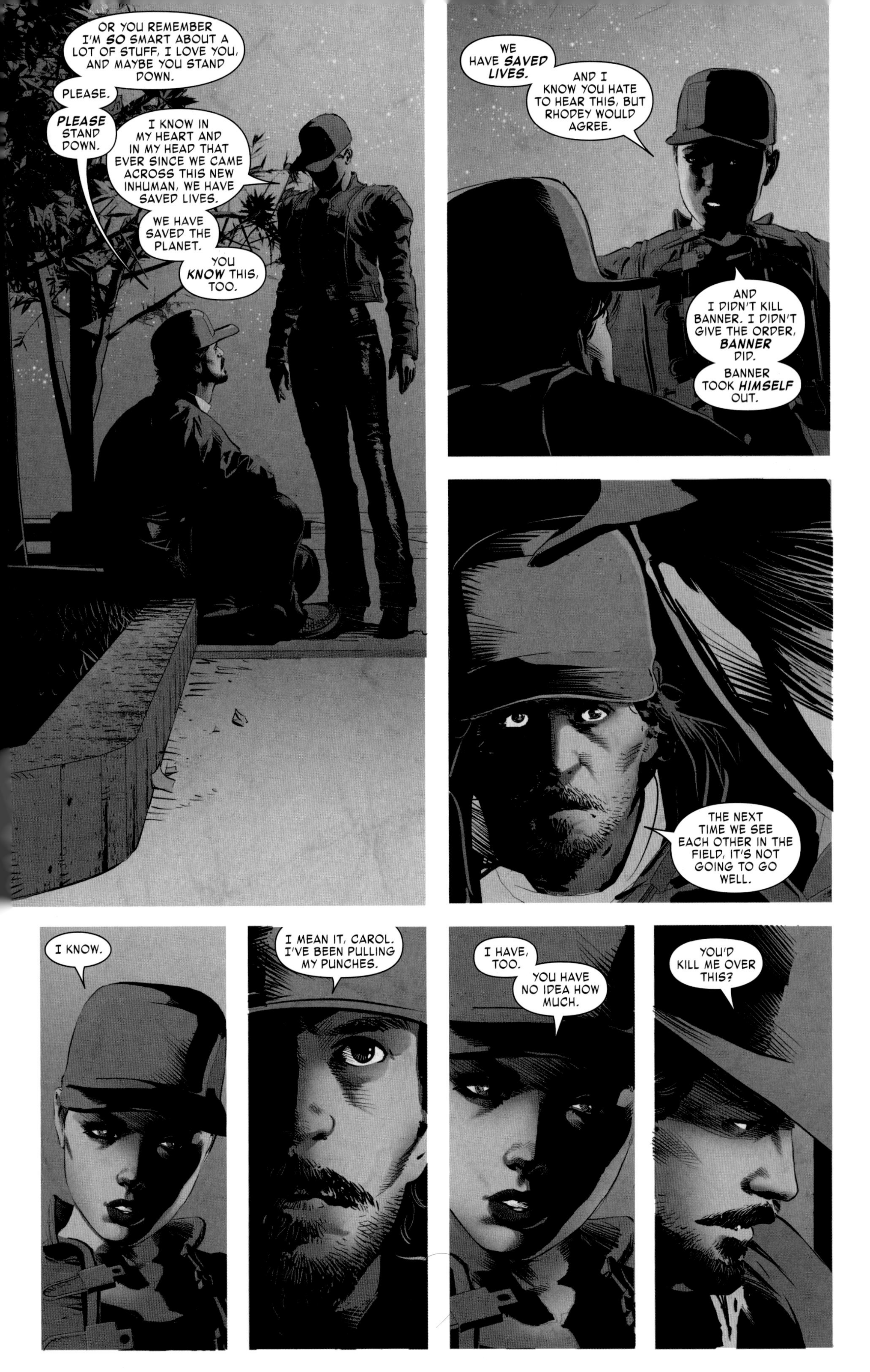
OR YOU REMEMBER I'M SO SMART ABOUT A LOT OF STUFF, I LOVE YOU, AND MAYBE YOU STAND DOWN.
PLEASE.
PLEASE STAND DOWN.
I KNOW IN MY HEART AND IN MY HEAD THAT EVER SINCE WE CAME ACROSS THIS NEW INHUMAN, WE HAVE SAVED LIVES.
WE HAVE SAVED THE PLANET.
YOU KNOW THIS, TOO.
WE HAVE SAVED LIVES.
AND I KNOW YOU HATE TO HEAR THIS, BUT RHODEY WOULD AGREE.
AND I DIDN'T KILL BANNER. I DIDN'T GIVE THE ORDER, BANNER DID.
BANNER TOOK HIMSELF OUT.
THE NEXT TIME WE SEE EACH OTHER IN THE FIELD, IT'S NOT GOING TO GO WELL.
I KNOW.
I MEAN IT, CAROL. I'VE BEEN PULLING MY PUNCHES.
I HAVE, TOO.
YOU HAVE NO IDEA HOW MUCH.
YOU'D KILL ME OVER THIS?

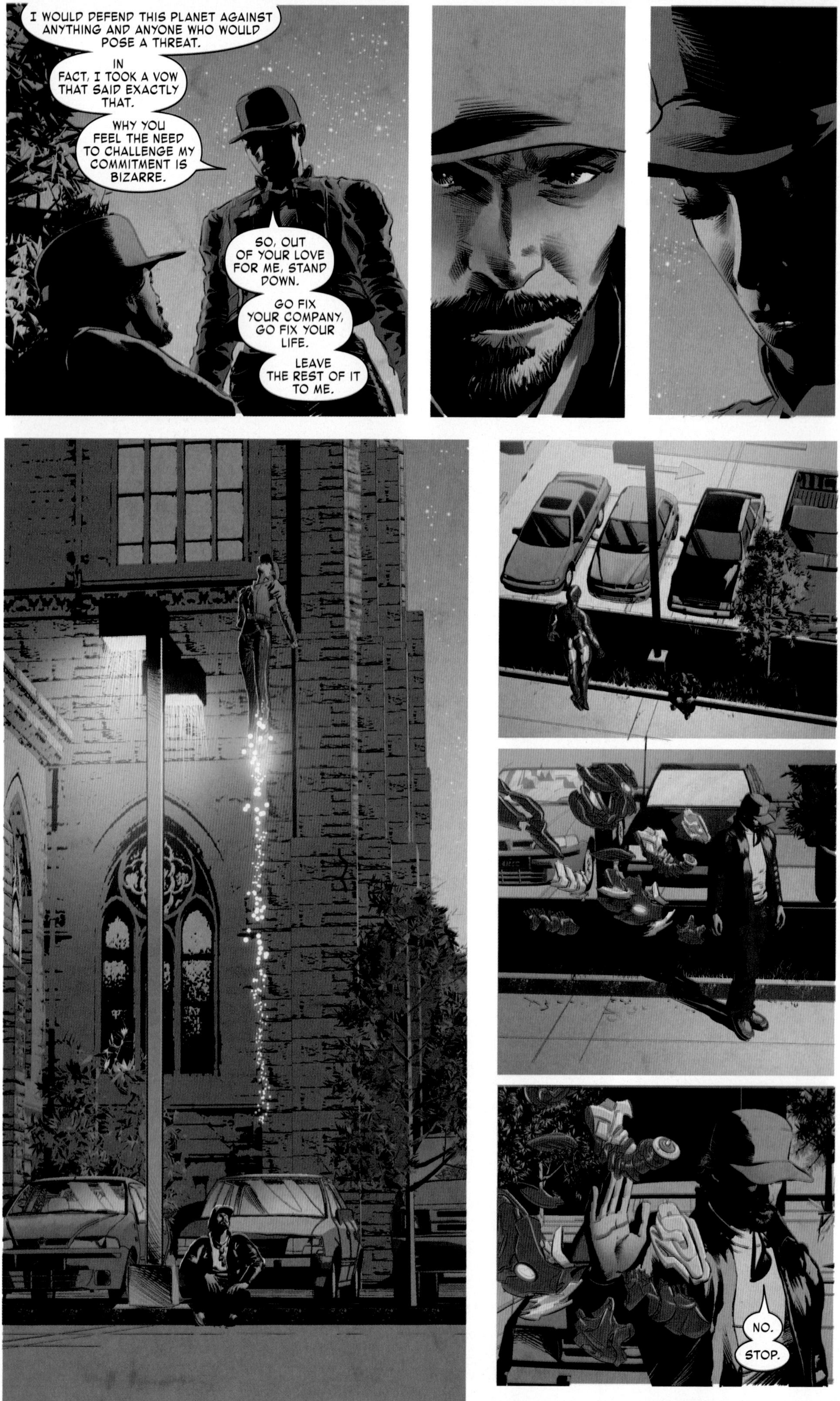
I WOULD DEFEND THIS PLANET AGAINST ANYTHING AND ANYONE WHO WOULD POSE A THREAT.
IN FACT, I TOOK A VOW THAT SAID EXACTLY THAT.
WHY YOU FEEL THE NEED TO CHALLENGE MY COMMITMENT IS BIZARRE.
SO, OUT OF YOUR LOVE FOR ME, STAND DOWN.
GO FIX YOUR COMPANY, GO FIX YOUR LIFE.
LEAVE THE REST OF IT TO ME.
NO.
STOP.

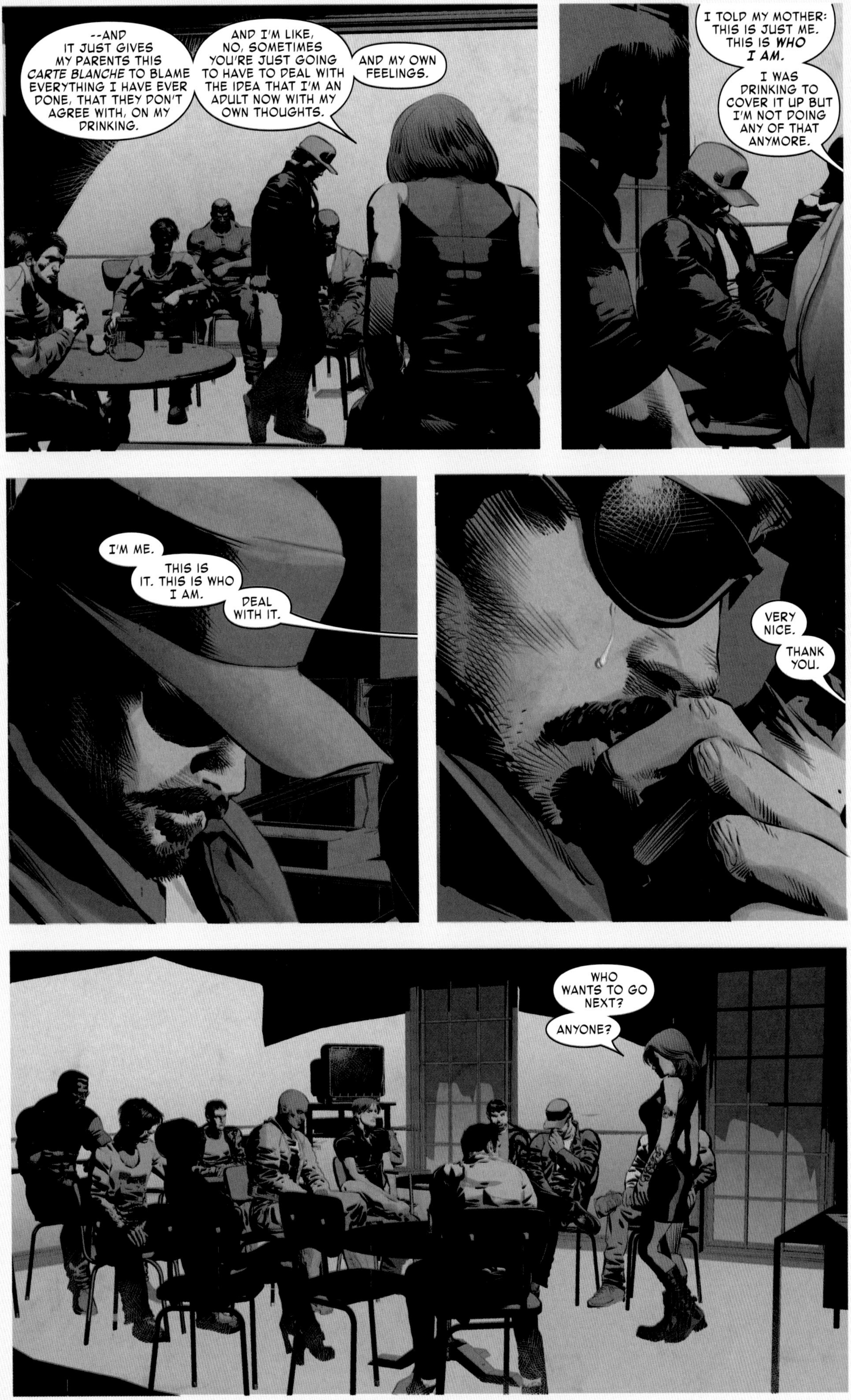
--AND IT JUST GIVES MY PARENTS THIS *CARTE BLANCHE* TO BLAME EVERYTHING I HAVE EVER DONE, THAT THEY DON'T AGREE WITH, ON MY DRINKING.
AND I'M LIKE, NO, SOMETIMES YOU'RE JUST GOING TO HAVE TO DEAL WITH THE IDEA THAT I'M AN ADULT NOW WITH MY OWN THOUGHTS.
AND MY OWN FEELINGS.
I TOLD MY MOTHER: THIS IS JUST ME. THIS IS ***WHO I AM.***
I WAS DRINKING TO COVER IT UP BUT I'M NOT DOING ANY OF THAT ANYMORE.
I'M ME.
THIS IS IT. THIS IS WHO I AM.
DEAL WITH IT.
VERY NICE.
THANK YOU.
WHO WANTS TO GO NEXT?
ANYONE?

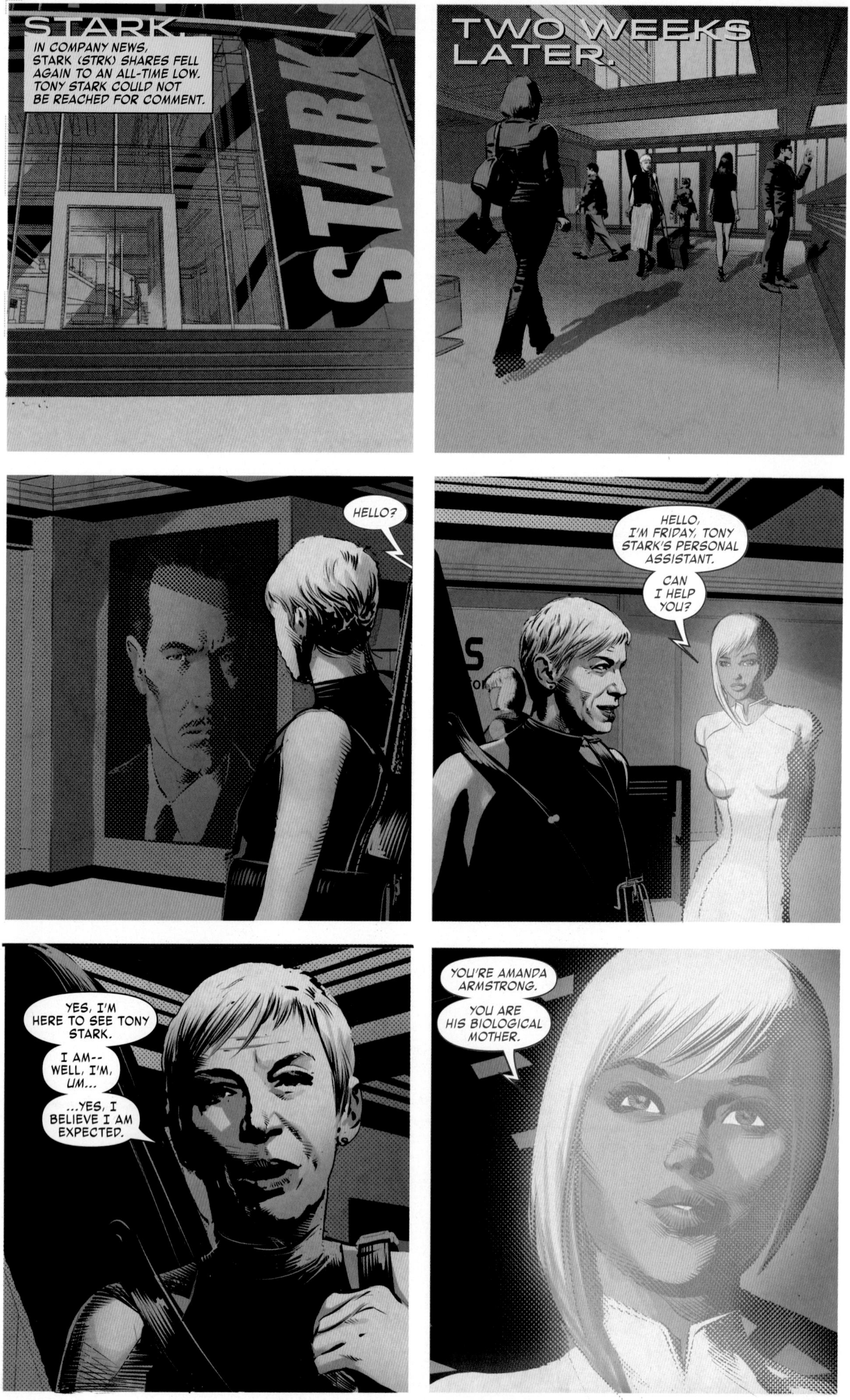
STARK.
IN COMPANY NEWS, STARK (STRK) SHARES FELL AGAIN TO AN ALL-TIME LOW. TONY STARK COULD NOT BE REACHED FOR COMMENT.
TWO WEEKS LATER.
HELLO?
HELLO, I'M FRIDAY, TONY STARK'S PERSONAL ASSISTANT.
CAN I HELP YOU?
YES, I'M HERE TO SEE TONY STARK.
I AM-- WELL, I'M, UM...
...YES, I BELIEVE I AM EXPECTED.
YOU'RE AMANDA ARMSTRONG.
YOU ARE HIS BIOLOGICAL MOTHER.

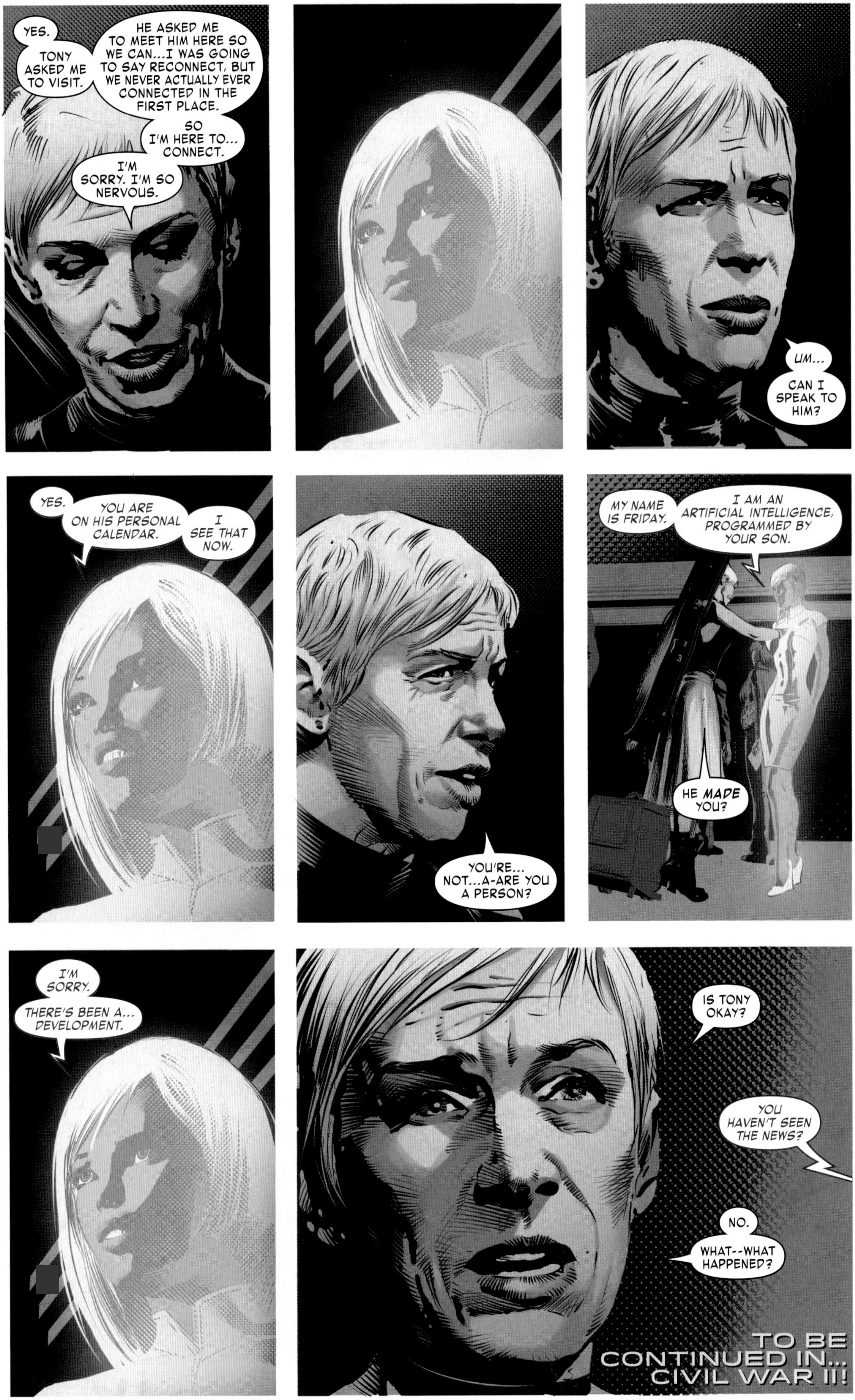
YES.
TONY ASKED ME TO VISIT.
HE ASKED ME TO MEET HIM HERE SO WE CAN...I WAS GOING TO SAY RECONNECT, BUT WE NEVER ACTUALLY EVER CONNECTED IN THE FIRST PLACE.
SO I'M HERE TO... CONNECT.
I'M SORRY. I'M SO NERVOUS.
UM...
CAN I SPEAK TO HIM?
YES.
YOU ARE ON HIS PERSONAL CALENDAR.
I SEE THAT NOW.
YOU'RE... NOT...A-ARE YOU A PERSON?
MY NAME IS FRIDAY.
I AM AN ARTIFICIAL INTELLIGENCE, PROGRAMMED BY YOUR SON.
HE MADE YOU?
I'M SORRY.
THERE'S BEEN A... DEVELOPMENT.
IS TONY OKAY?
YOU HAVEN'T SEEN THE NEWS?
NO.
WHAT--WHAT HAPPENED?
TO BE CONTINUED IN... CIVIL WAR II!

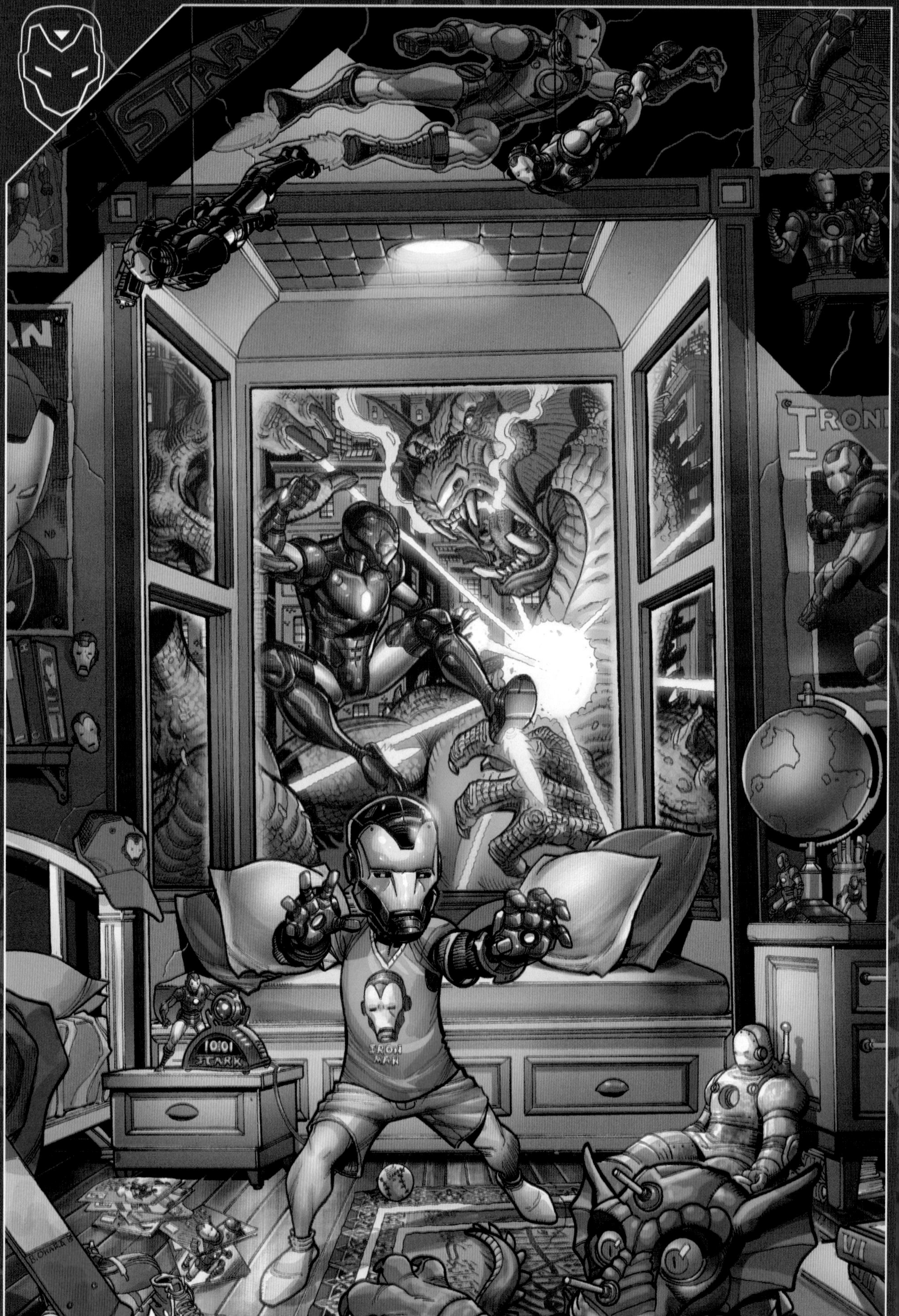
STARK
IRON
10:01
STARK
IRON MAN
VI

#1 YOUNG GUNS VARIANT BY NICK BRADSHAW & PAUL MOUNTS

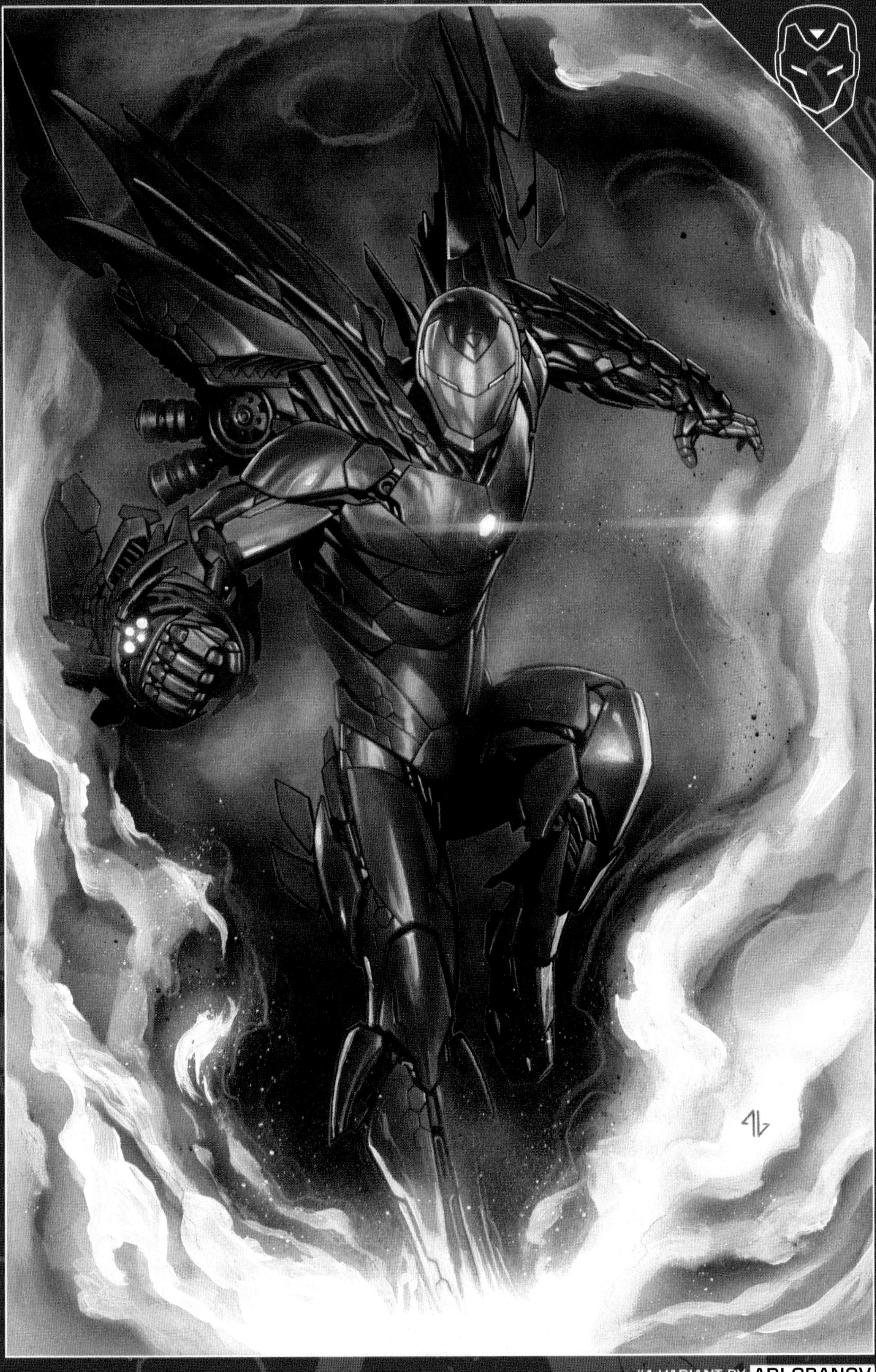

#1 VARIANT BY ADI GRANOV

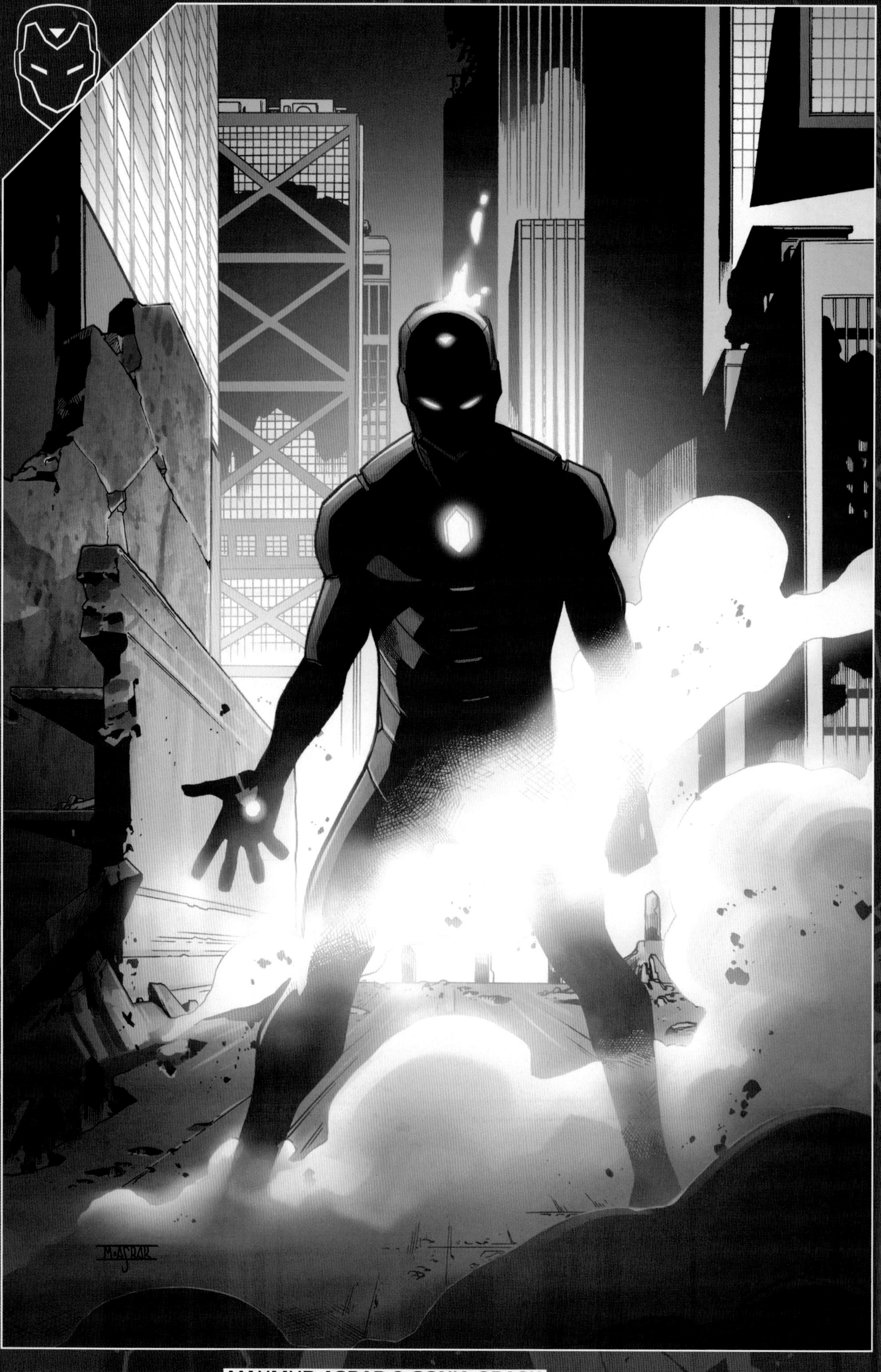

#1 YOUNG GUNS VARIANT BY **MAHMUD ASRAR & SONIA OBACK**

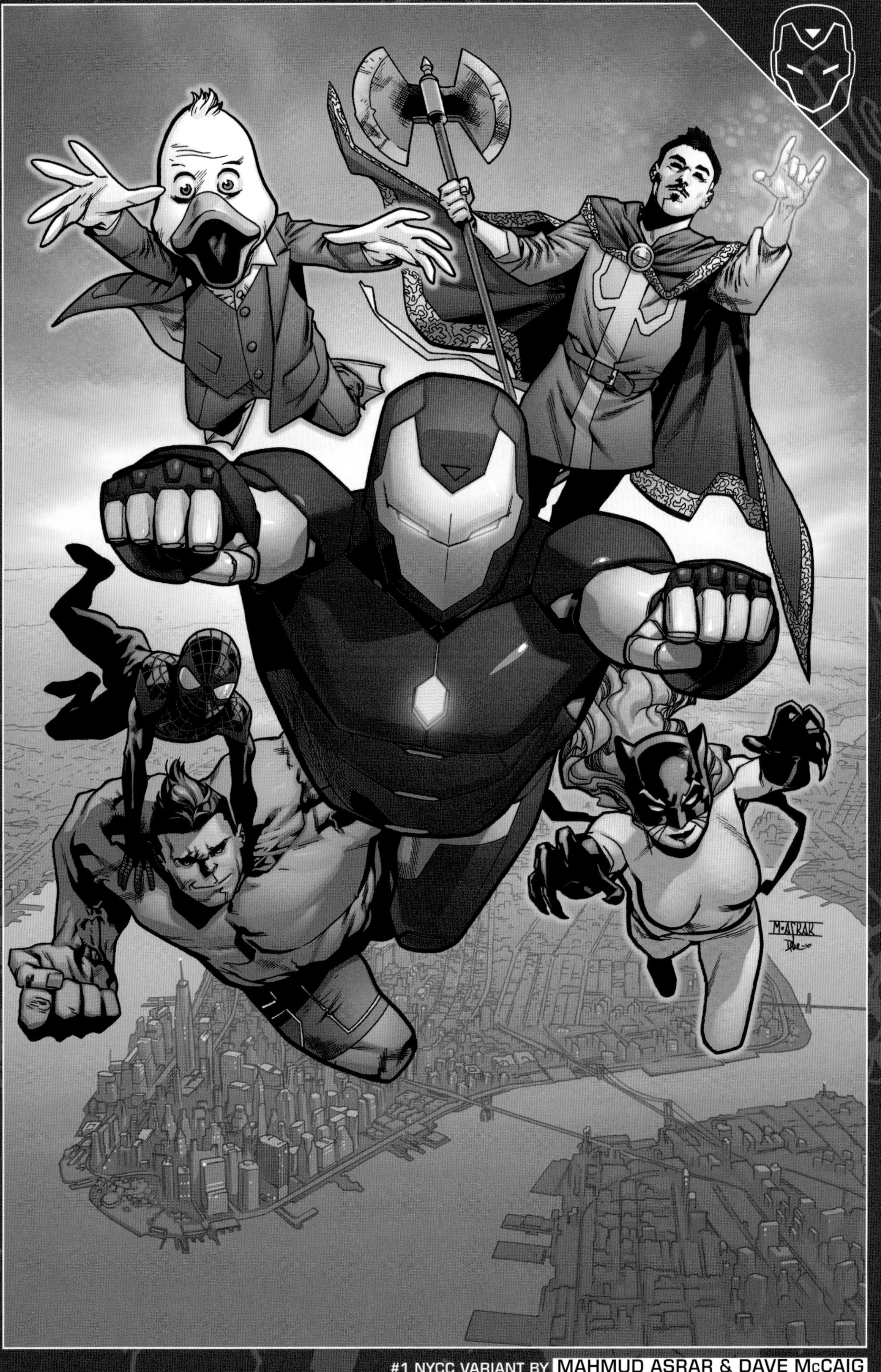
M. ASRAR

#1 NYCC VARIANT BY MAHMUD ASRAR & DAVE McCAIG

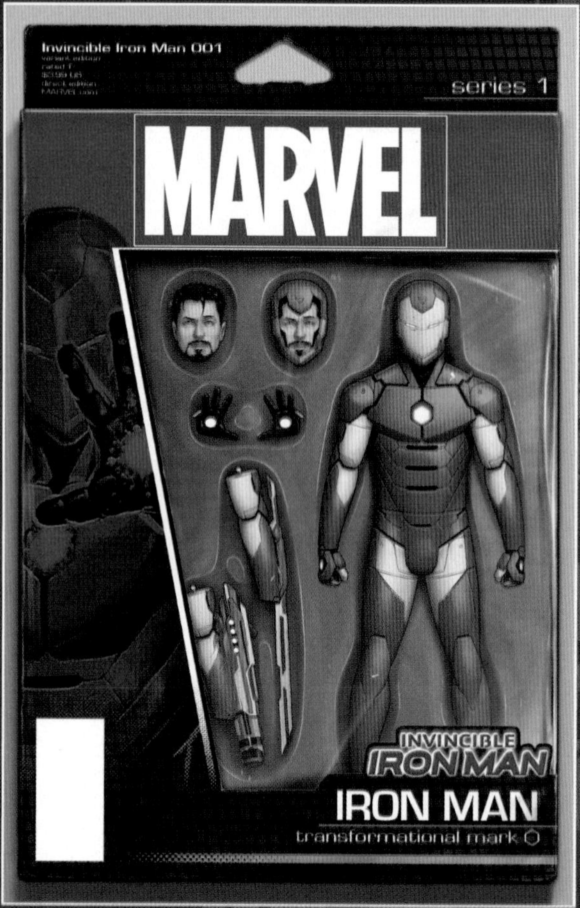
Invincible Iron Man 001
series 1
MARVEL
INVINCIBLE IRON MAN
IRON MAN
transformational mark

#1 ACTION FIGURE VARIANT BY
JOHN TYLER CHRISTOPHER

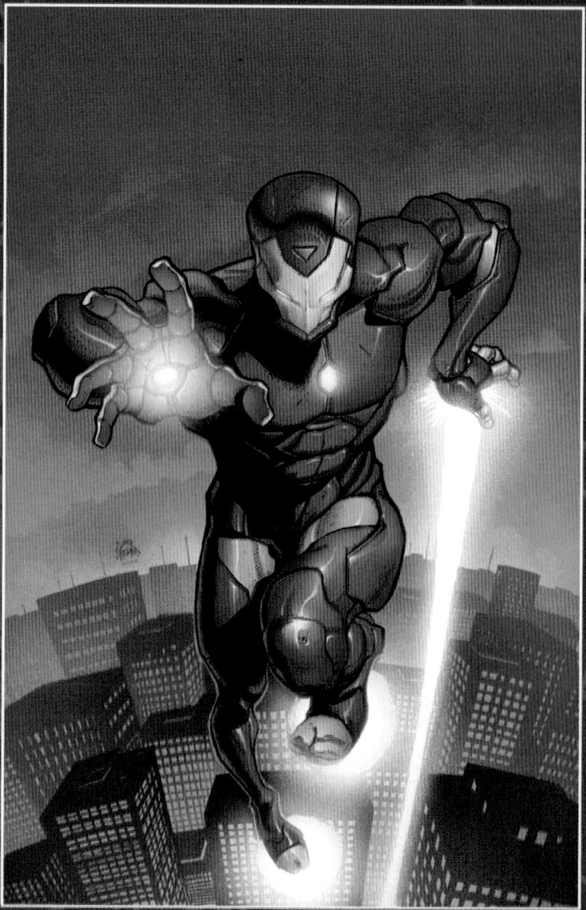

#1 VARIANT BY
RYAN STEGMAN & RICHARD ISANOVE

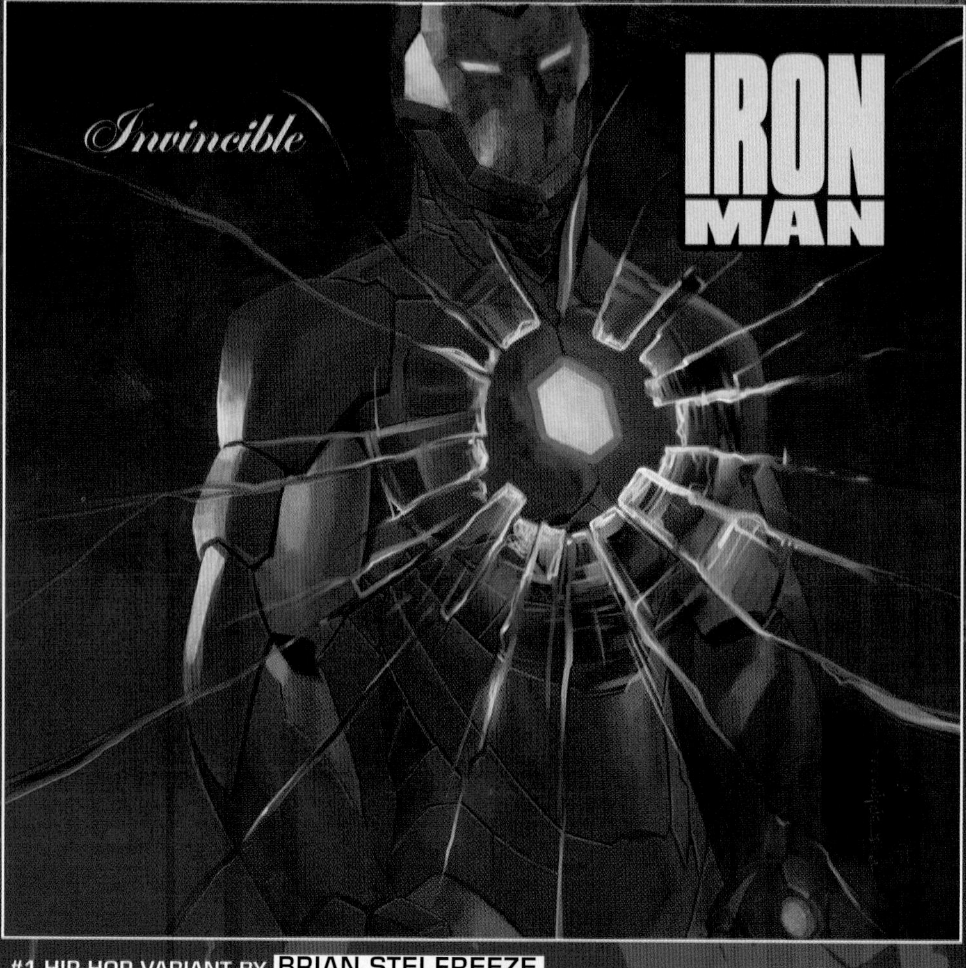
Invincible
IRON MAN

#1 HIP-HOP VARIANT BY BRIAN STELFREEZE

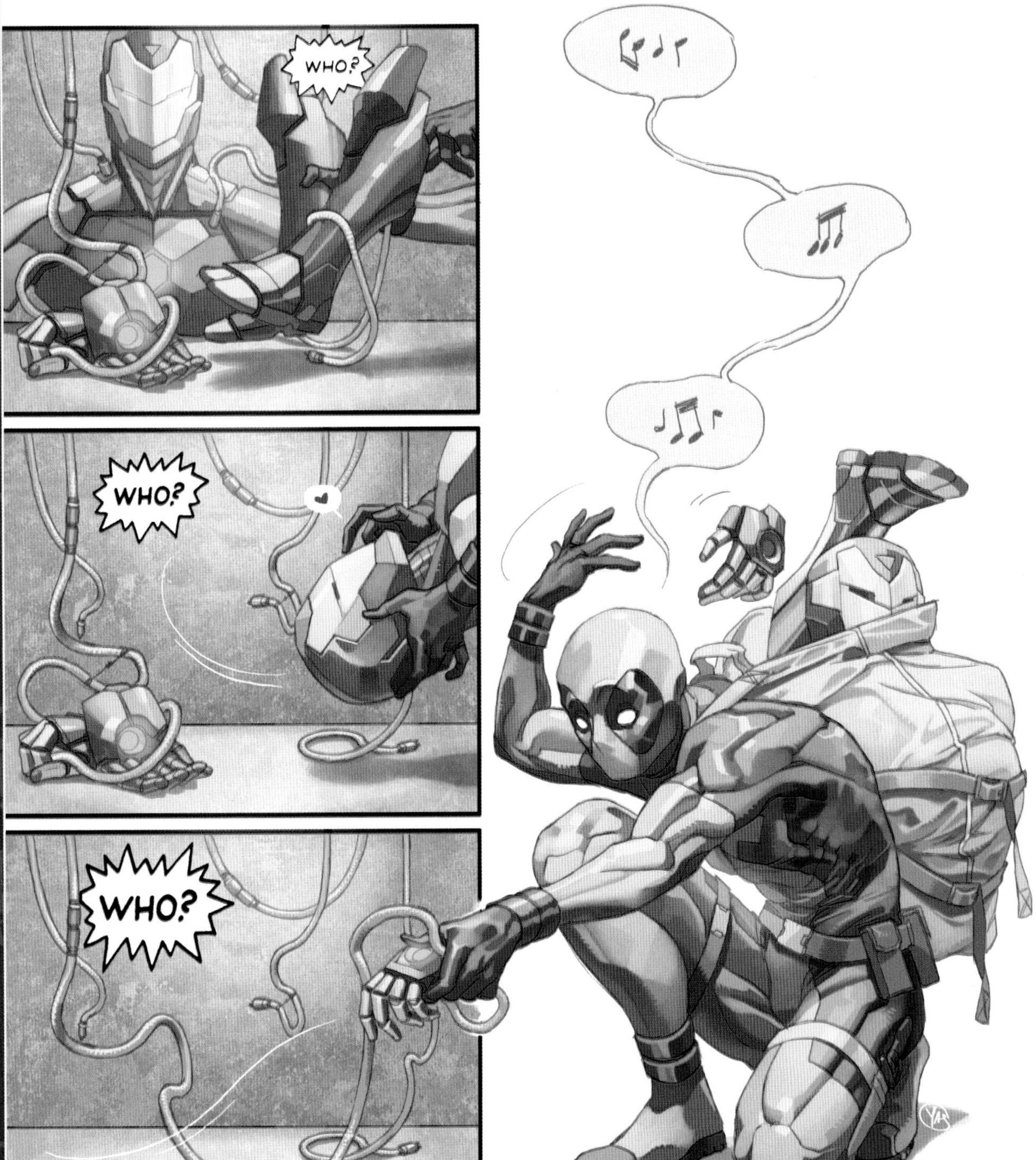
WHO?
WHO?
WHO?

#1 PARTY VARIANT BY YASMINE PUTRI

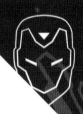

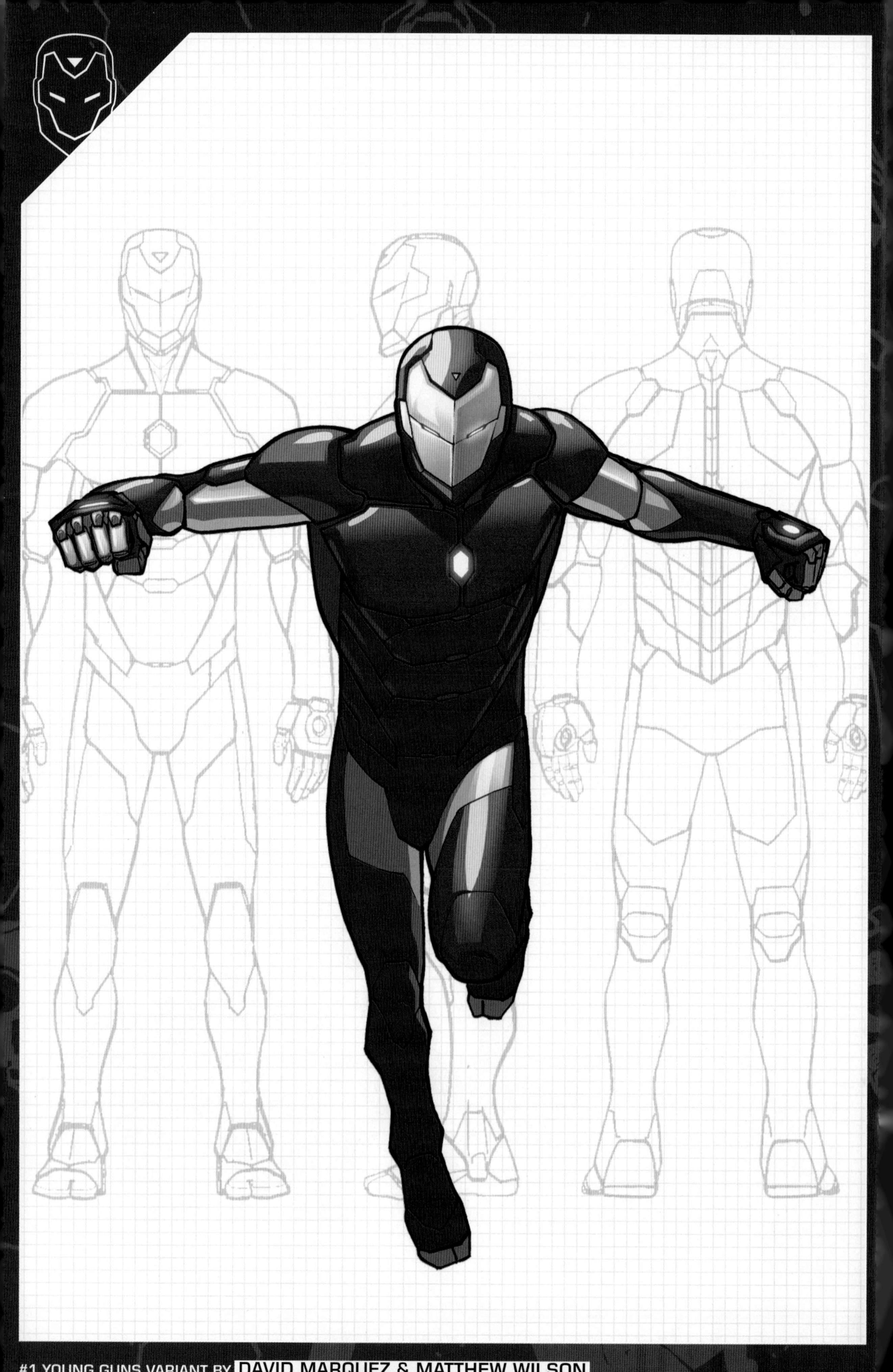

#1 YOUNG GUNS VARIANT BY DAVID MARQUEZ & MATTHEW WILSON

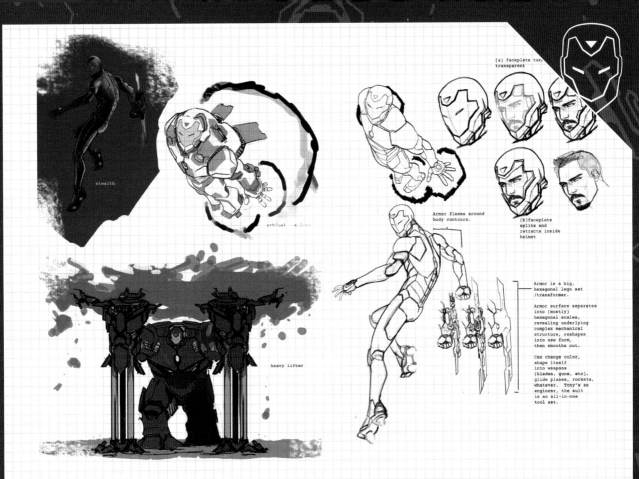

stealth

orbital strike

heavy lifter

(a) faceplate turns transparent

Armor flexes around body contours.

(b) faceplate splits and retracts inside helmet

Armor is a big, hexagonal lego set /transformer.

Armor surface separates into (mostly) hexagonal scales, revealing underlying complex mechanical structure, reshapes into new form, then smooths out.

Can change color, shape itself into weapons (blades, guns, etc), glide planes, rockets, whatever. Tony's an engineer, the suit is an all-in-one tool set.

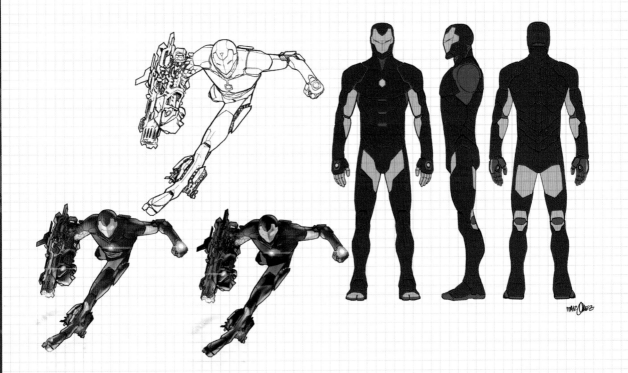

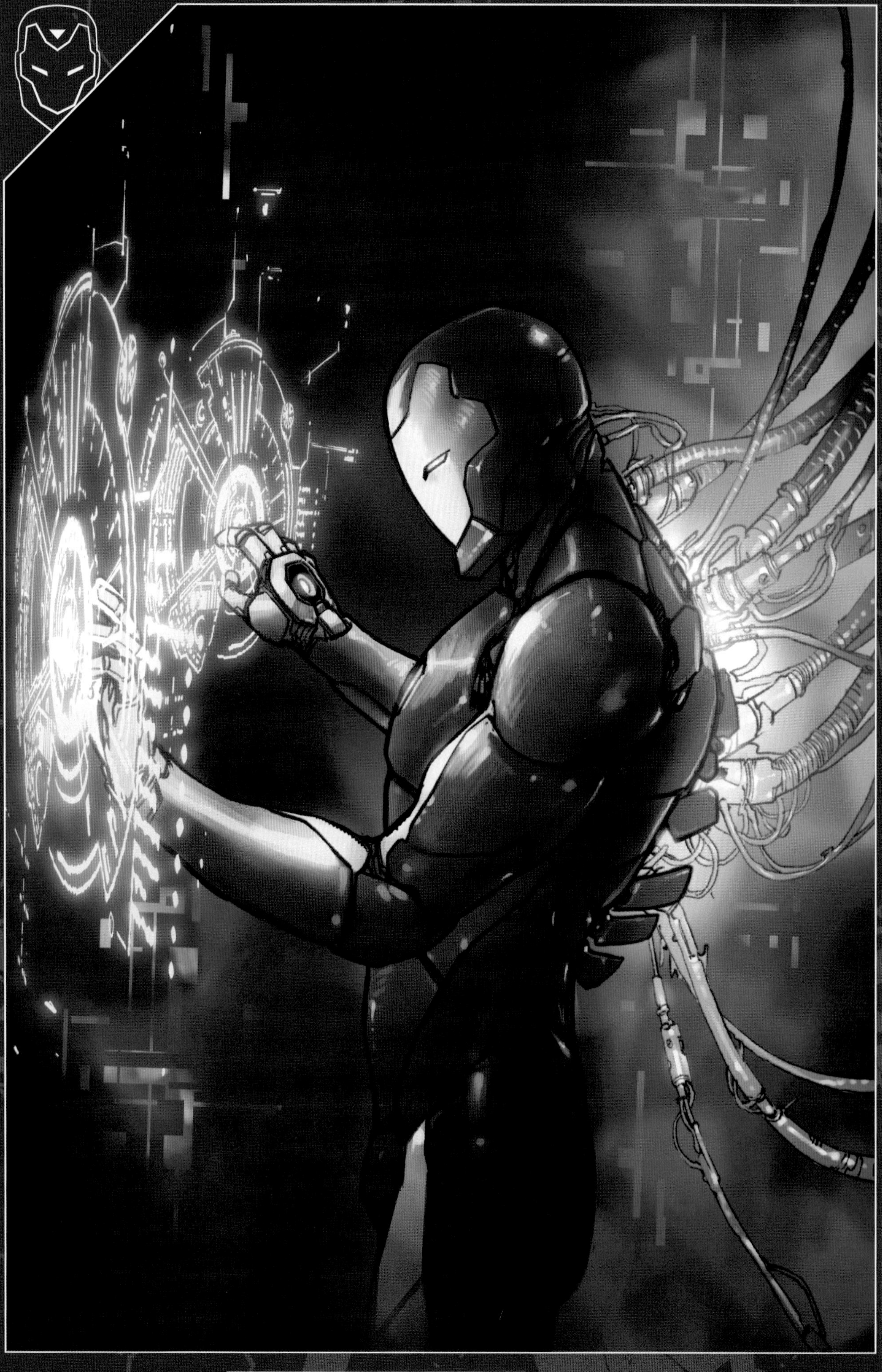

#1 YOUNG GUNS VARIANT BY SARA PICHELLI & JASON KEITH

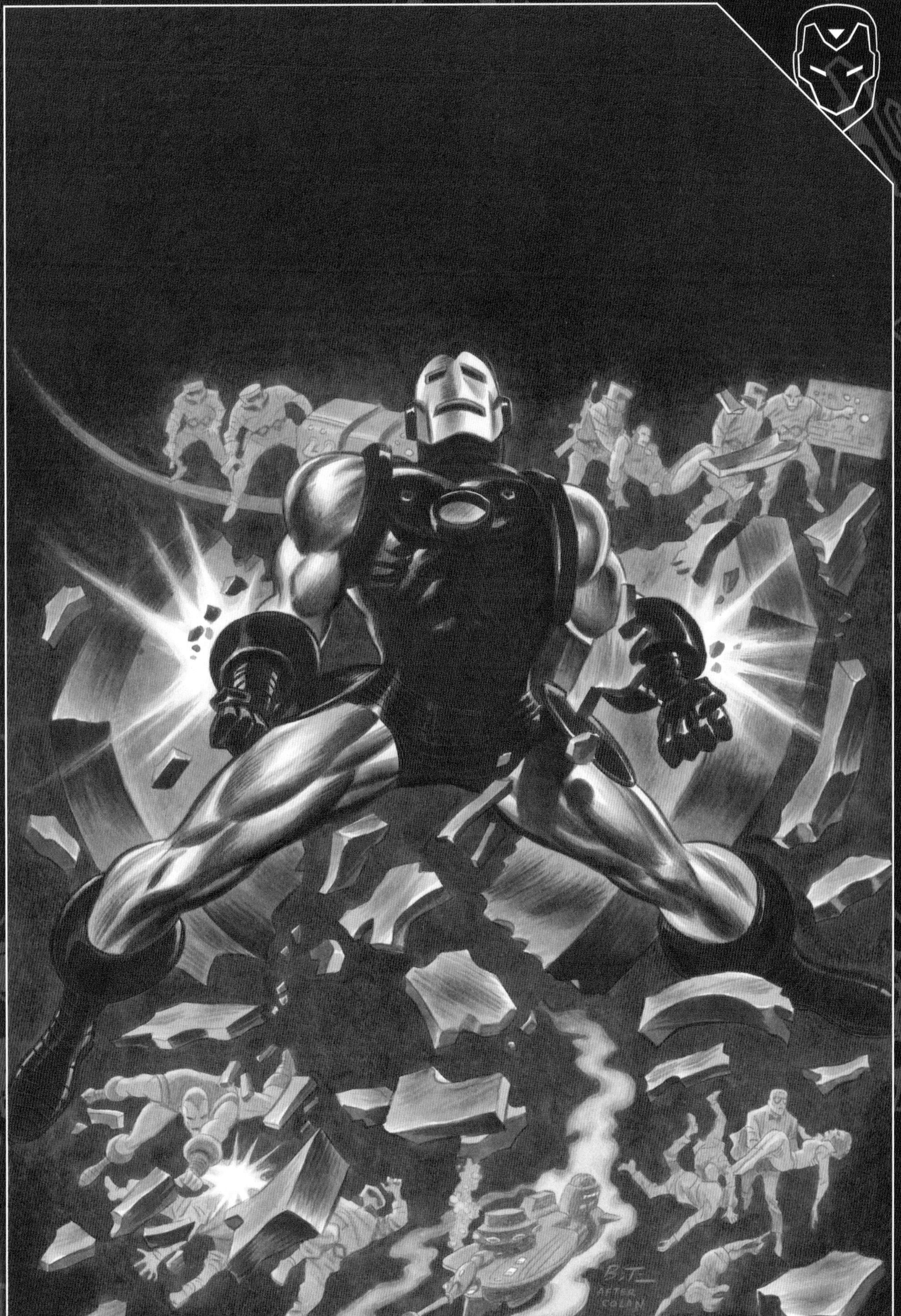
B.T.
AFTER COLAN

#1 VARIANT BY BRUCE TIMM

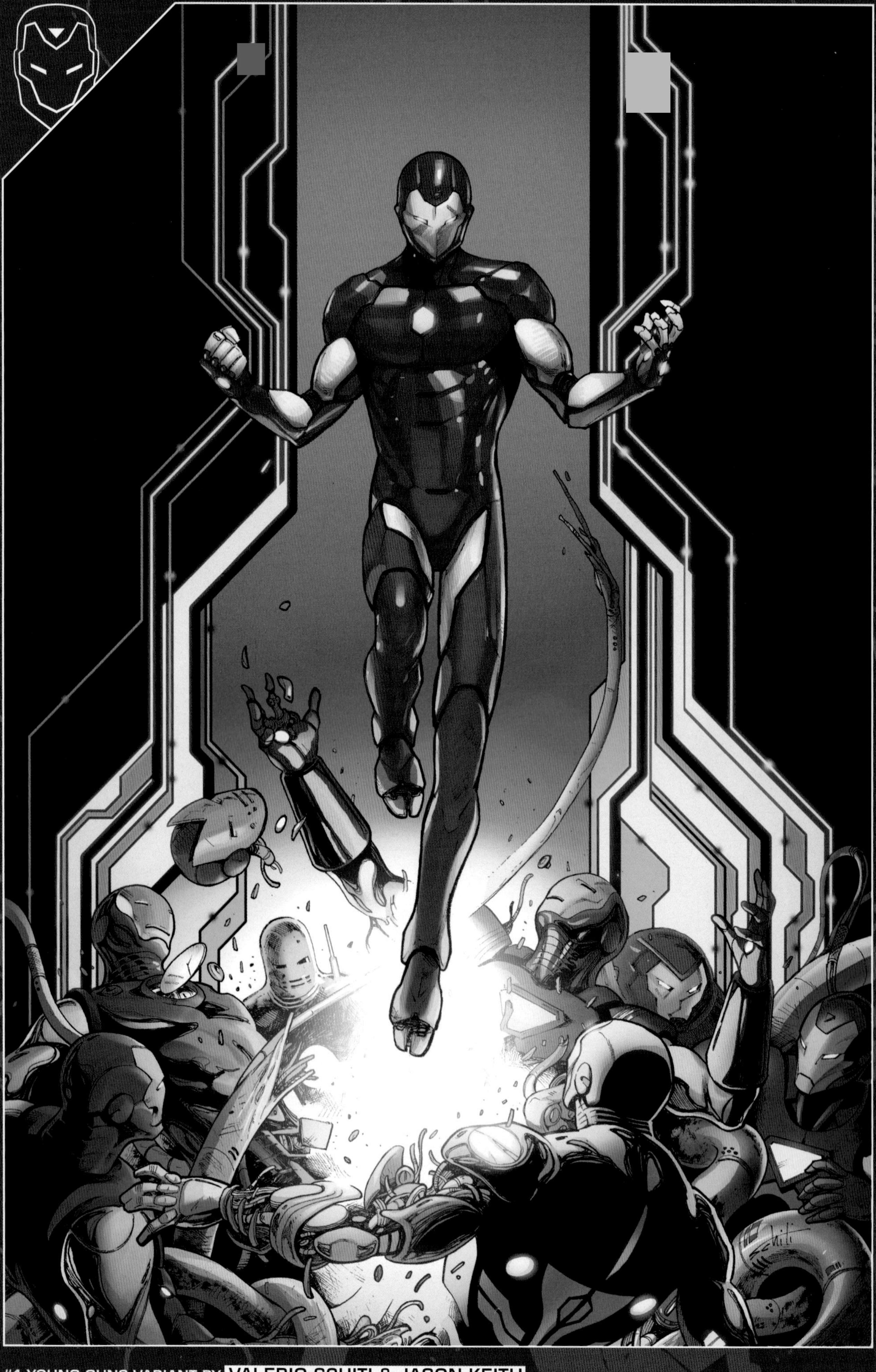

#1 YOUNG GUNS VARIANT BY VALERIO SCHITI & JASON KEITH

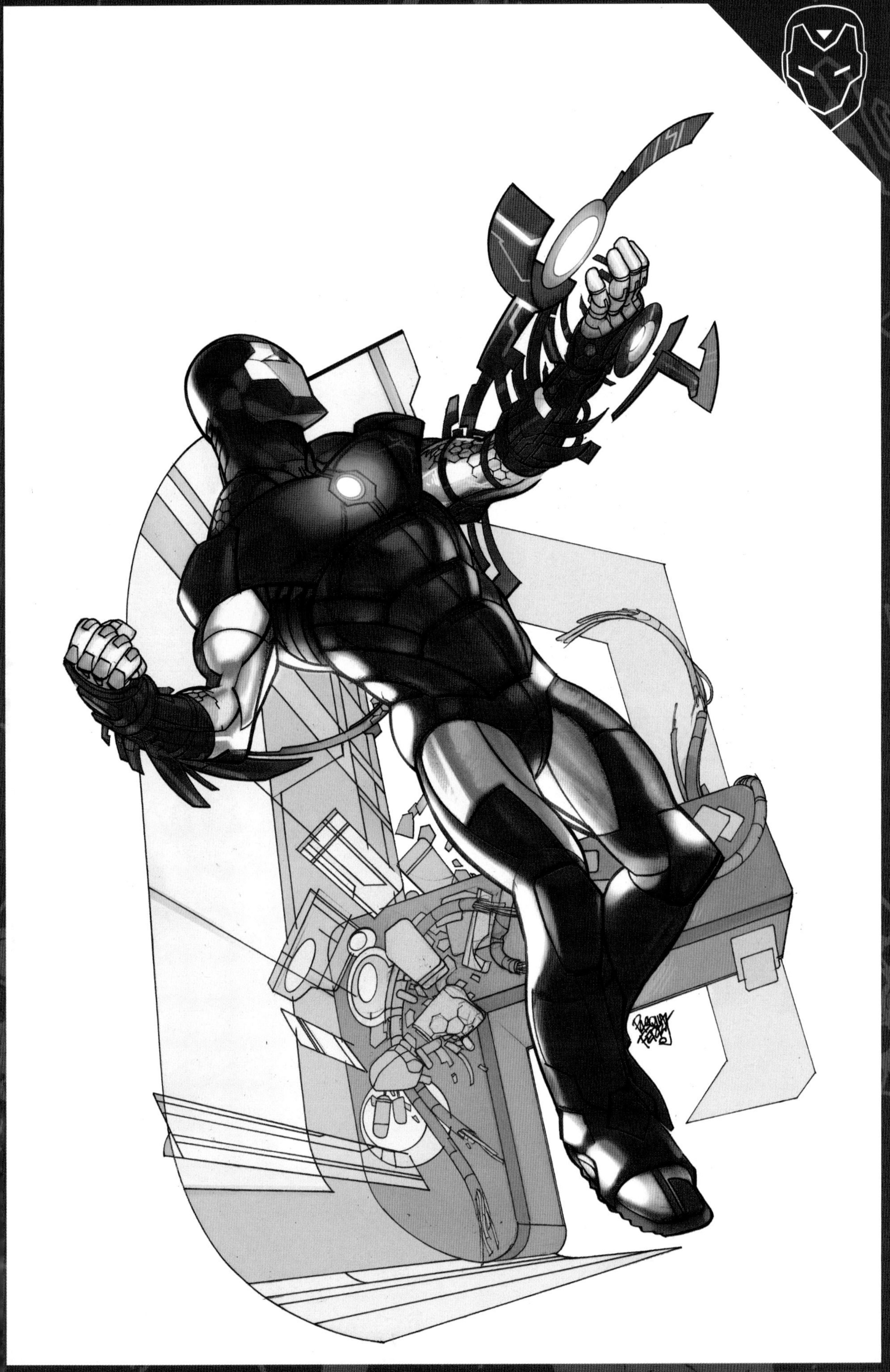

#1 VARIANT BY PASQUAL FERRY

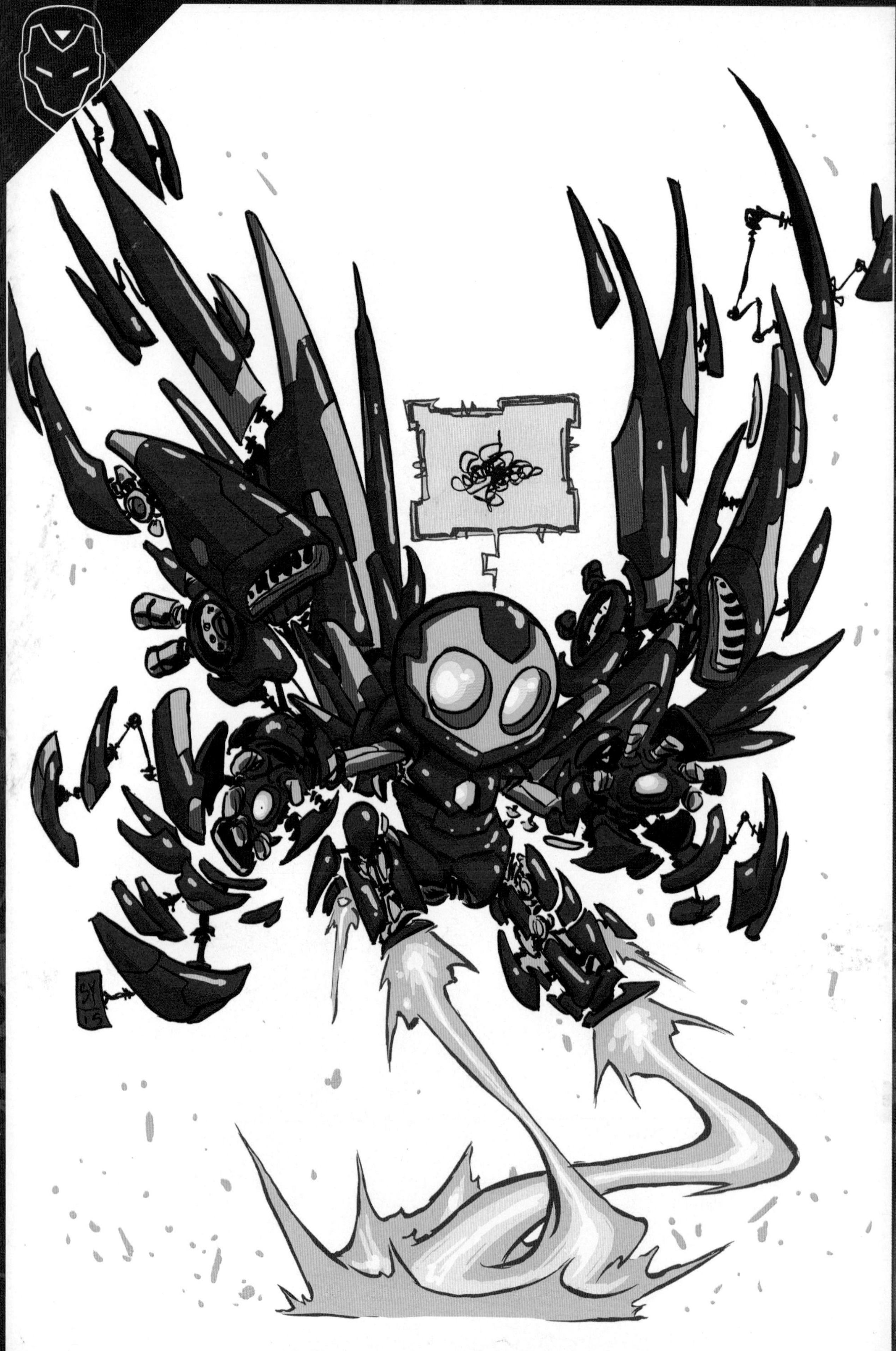

#1 VARIANT BY SKOTTIE YOUNG

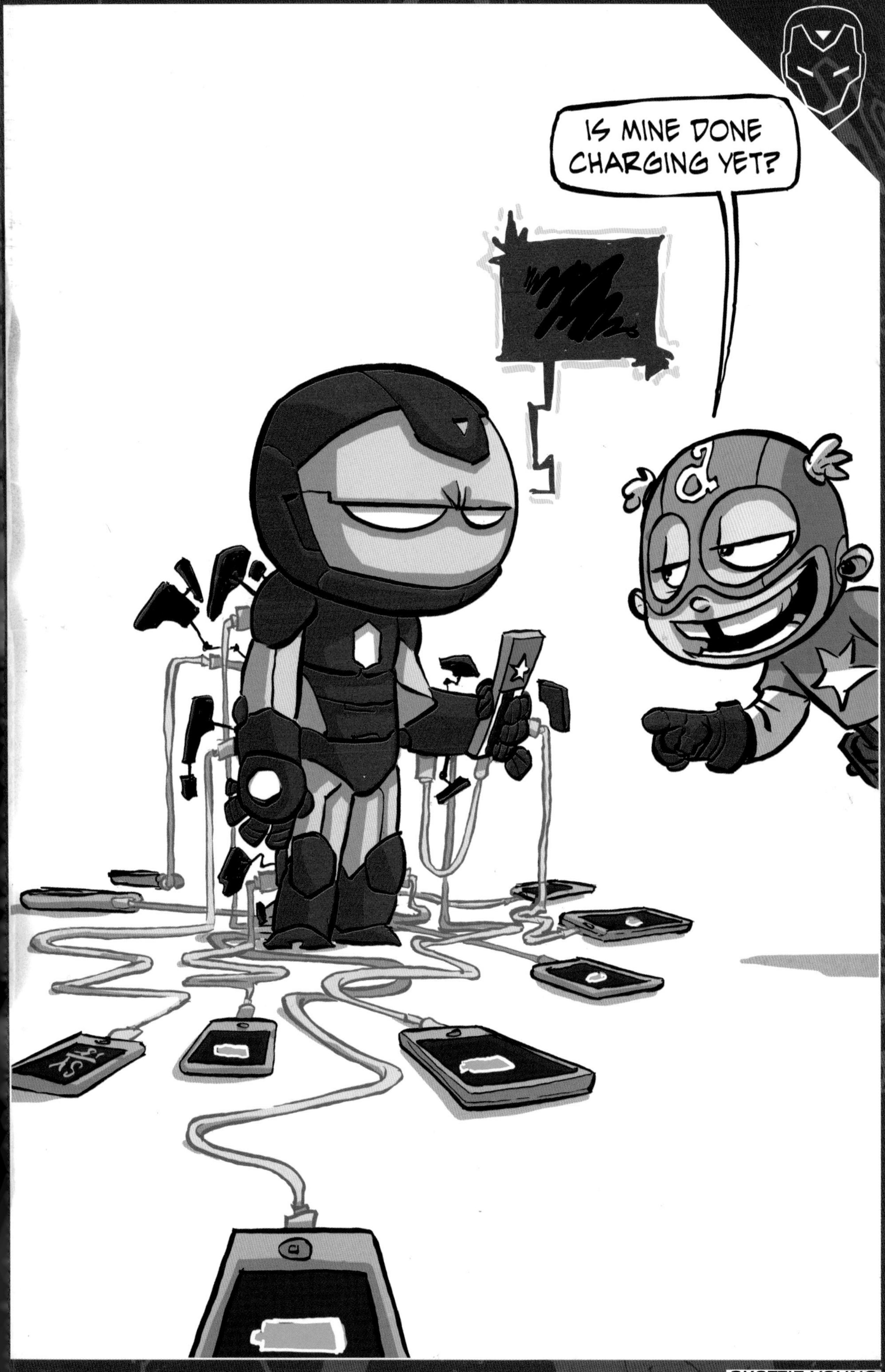
IS MINE DONE CHARGING YET?

#6 VARIANT BY SKOTTIE YOUNG

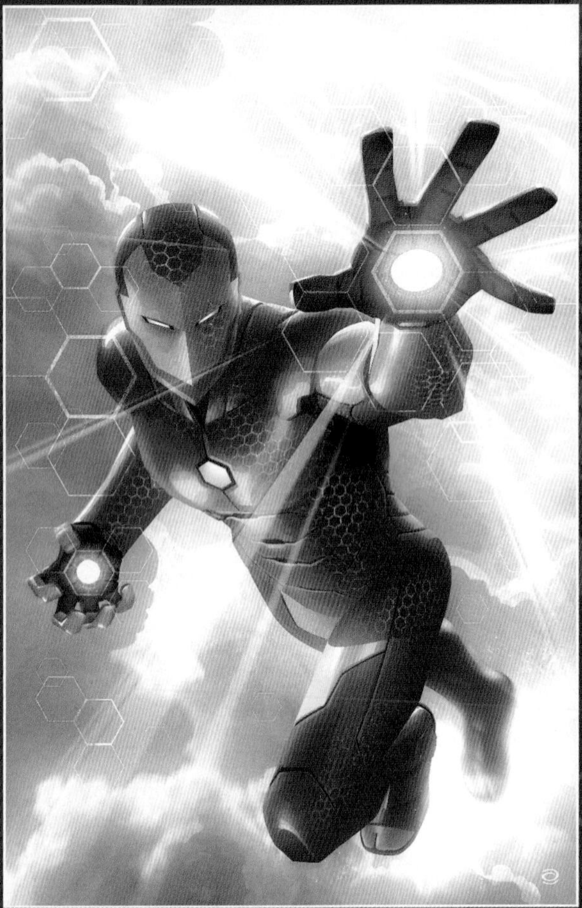

#2 VARIANT BY
ALEX GARNER

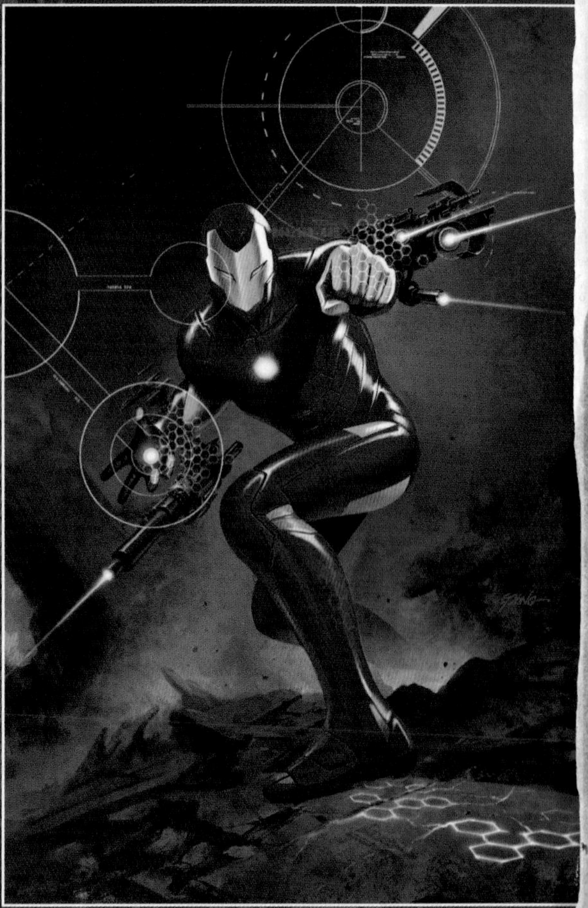

#3 VARIANT BY
STEVE EPTING

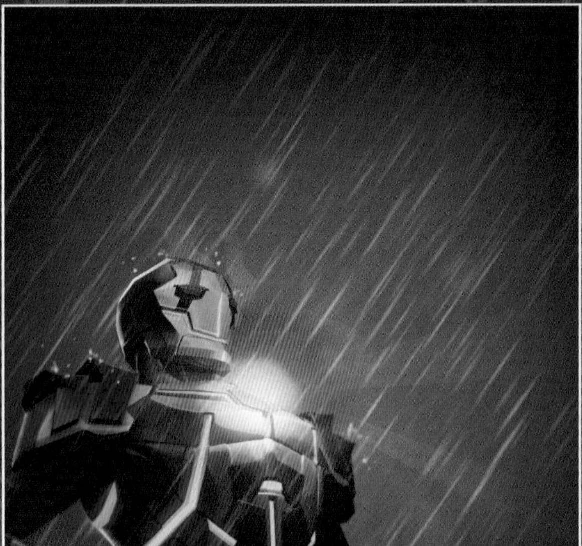

#9 AGE OF APOCALYPSE VARIANT BY
CHRIS TURCOTTE